"David Allen and Steve Lemke have assembled a diverse and impressive team of contributors to provide a thoughtful engagement with major aspects of Calvinism. Rejecting Pelagianism, semi-Pelagianism, hyper-Calvinism, and consistent Calvinism, the various chapters, which include a combination of Arminian, Wesleyan, Calminian, and Amyraldian perspectives, wade through what have been minefields of controversy for centuries. While not all readers will have their questions answered nor will all Calvinists be persuaded, this significant volume is to be commended for offering substantive responses worthy of serious consideration. The book will be beneficial for people representing various theological traditions, whatever one's view may be about Calvinism and how it should be understood. It is my prayer that readers will want to echo the irenic spirit represented in the concluding chapter calling for Calvinists and non-Calvinists to join together for the advancement of the gospel."

—**David S. Dockery**, president, International Alliance for Christian Education, and
distinguished professor of theology, Southwestern Baptist Theological Seminary

"In this volume, an outstanding team of contributors, representing a range of denominational affiliations and theological perspectives, unite to offer a critique of Calvinism. A remarkably wide range of issues is addressed: from key biblical texts and historical considerations to the traditional five points themselves; from the nature of divine election and human freedom to the character of God and the problem of evil. Throughout the volume, critique is conducted without diatribe, and a spirit of generosity and dialogue—even rapprochement—pervades. Highly recommended!"

—**Paul Rhodes Eddy**, professor of biblical and
theological studies, Bethel University

"Over the past two decades, the 'Young, Restless, and Reformed' movement has enthusiastically promoted the set of doctrines popularly called 'Calvinism.' Large conferences, well-organized networks, an aggressive and very effective online presence, and a massive flood of publications have fueled the movement—and sometimes leave the impression that there is no room for informed and thoughtful criticism or alternative views that remain faithful to biblical teaching. This book offers serious and sustained pushback, and it will be helpful to all (including those who, like me, are not fully persuaded by every argument advanced) who want to think better and more biblically about these important matters."

—**Thomas H. McCall**, Timothy C. and Julie M. Tennent
Chair of Theology, Asbury Theological Seminary

"For anyone interested in the historic debate between Calvinists and non-Calvinists, I highly recommend this work. I will want to keep a copy handy in the future, so that I can use it for reference and to read again some of the chapters that give me more to think about. The reader will be impressed by at least two things. First, there really is a brand of non-Calvinism that is grounded in faithfulness to the Scriptures and is truly Reformed (in being true to the three solas). Second, there is within the ranks of those who hold this view (whether they self-identify as 'Arminian' or not) an interesting variety of viewpoints about some of the details. Thanks to editors Lemke and Allen and to B&H Academic for making this available."

—**Robert E. Picirilli**, professor emeritus of New
Testament and philosophy, Welch College

"A Dutch Reformed student of mine once wisely commented that Reformed theology is a field, not just a flower. Yet it's the flower—the (in)famous 'tulip' of five-point Calvinism—that has blossomed over the past several years among younger generations of free-church evangelicals. This volume raises a variety of serious concerns about the growth of popular Calvinism. Read it carefully and judge for yourself!"

—**Jerome Van Kuiken**, dean and professor of ministry and
Christian thought, Oklahoma Wesleyan University

"Anyone paying attention knows that Calvinism has been resurgent the past several years. This volume is a multidisciplinary critique of this formidable theological movement, and how it profoundly misrepresents the wonderful, good news of the gospel. Sharply critical, yet irenic, the essays in this volume are a model of forthright, substantive theological debate."

—**Jerry L. Walls**, professor of philosophy and scholar
in residence, Houston Baptist University

CALVINISM

CALVINISM

A BIBLICAL AND THEOLOGICAL CRITIQUE

EDITED BY

DAVID L. ALLEN &
STEVE W. LEMKE

ACADEMIC
NASHVILLE, TENNESSEE

CONTENTS

ACKNOWLEDGMENTS

We did not complete the production of this volume by ourselves; we were aided at every point by a team of helpers. This book originated with former B&H Academic director Jim Baird, who cast the original vision for this project. We received invaluable help through its development from B&H Academic project manager Audrey Greeson and B&H publisher Madison Trammel. Tony Byrne did an incredible job assisting us in editing the articles. Not only did he help edit the articles for style and check documentation; as a Calvinist, he made us aware of possible misrepresentations or overstatements. We are incredibly indebted to our team of well-qualified contributors for their articles, as we remain thankful to those who contributed to *Whosoever Will*. We also express appreciation to our wives for their patience as we worked many months on this project. Most of all, we acknowledge the Lord whom we serve, whom we pray we have represented accurately.

ABBREVIATIONS

Reference Works

ANF	*The Ante-Nicene Fathers: Translations of the Writings of the Fathers Down to AD 325.* Edited by Alexander Roberts and James Donaldson. 10 vols. 1885–87. Repr., Peabody, MA: Hendrickson, 2004.
BDAG	Walter Bauer, Frederick W. Danker, and William Arndt. *A Greek-English Lexicon of the New Testament and Other Early Christian Literature.* 3rd ed. Chicago: University of Chicago Press, 2000.
BECNT	Baker Exegetical Commentary on the New Testament
BFM	Baptist Faith and Message
EDNT	*Exegetical Dictionary of the New Testament.* Edited by Horst Robert Balz and Gerhard Schneider. 3 vols. Grand Rapids: Eerdmans, 1990–93.
ICC	International Critical Commentary
JETS	*Journal of the Evangelical Theological Society*
JSNTSup/LNTS	*Journal for the Study of the New Testament* Supplement Series/ Library of New Testament Studies
L&N	Johannes P. Louw, and Eugene Albert Nida. *Greek-English Lexicon of the New Testament: Based on Semantic Domains.* 2 vols. New York: United Bible Societies, 1996.
LCC	Library of Christian Classics. 26 vols. Philadelphia: Westminster, 1953–60.

LSJ	Henry George Liddell, Robert Scott, Henry Stuart Jones, and Roderick McKenzie. *A Greek-English Lexicon.* Oxford: Clarendon Press, 1996.
NAC	New American Commentary
NICNT	New International Commentary on the New Testament
NIGTC	New International Greek Testament Commentary
NIDNTTE	*New International Dictionary of New Testament Theology and Exegesis.* Edited by Moisés Silva. 5 vols. Grand Rapids: Zondervan, 2014.
NPNF	A Select Library of Nicene and Post-Nicene Fathers of the Christian Church. Edited by Philip Schaff and Henry Wace. 28 vols. in 2 series. Peabody, MA: Hendrickson, 2004. First published 1886–89. NPNF[1] refers to the first series; NPNF[2] refers to the second.
PG	*Patrologiae Graeca*, ed. J. P. Migne. 161 vols. Paris: Garnier Frères, 1857–66.
PNTC	Pillar New Testament Commentary
TDNT	*Theological Dictionary of the New Testament.* Edited by G. Kittel and G. Friedrich. Translated by Geoffrey W. Bromiley. 10 vols. Grand Rapids: Eerdmans, 1964–76. *TDNTa* refers to the one-volume abridged edition. Eerdmans, 1985.
TLOT	*Theological Lexicon of the Old Testament.* Edited by Ernst Jenni and Claus Westermann. Translated by Mark E. Biddle. 3 vols. Peabody, MA: Hendrickson, 1997.
WSA	The Works of Saint Augustine: A Translation for the 21st Century (series). 44 vols. Brooklyn: New City Press, 1990–.

Bible Translations

CEB	Common English Bible
CPDV	Catholic Public Domain Version
CSB	Christian Standard Bible
ESV	English Standard Version
HCSB	Holman Christian Standard Bible
KJV	King James Version (1611) = AV

LEB	Lexham English Bible
LXX	Septuagint
NAB	New American Bible
NABRE	New American Bible Revised Edition
NASB	New American Standard Bible
NCV	New Century Version
NET	New English Translation
NIV	New International Version (2011)
NJB	New Jerusalem Bible
NKJV	New King James Version
NLT	New Living Translation
NRSV	New Revised Standard Version
REB	Revised English Bible

Works by Augustine of Hippo

Ad Simpl.	*Diversis quaestionibus ad Simplicianum*
Adim.	*Contra Adimantum*
An. et or.	*De anima et eius origine*
Civ.	*De civitate dei*
Conf.	*Confessiones*
C. du. ep. Pel.	*Contra duas epistulas Pelagianorum*
C. Jul.	*Contra Iulianum*
C. Jul. imp.	*Contra secundam Iuliani responsionem opus imperfectum*
C. litt. Petil.	*Contra litteras Petiliani*
Corrept.	*De correptione et gratia*
Div. quaest.	*De diversis quaestionibus octoginta tribus*
Doctr. chr.	*De doctrina christiana*
Enchir.	*Enchiridion ad Laurentium de fide spe et caritate*
Ep.	*Epistulae*
ex. Gal.	*Epistulae ad Galatas expositio*
Ex. quaest. prop. Rm.	*Expositio quarumdam quaestionum in epistula ad Romanos*
Exp. Rom. inch.	*Epistulae ad Romanos inchoata expositio*
Faust.	*Contra Faustum*
Fel.	*Contra Felicem Manichaeum*
Fort.	*Contra Fortunatum Manichaeum*
Gen. litt.	*De Genesi ad litteram*
Gen. Man.	*De Genesi adversus Manichaeos*
Grat. Chr.	*De gratia Christi et de peccato originali*

Grat.	*De gratia et libero arbitrio*
Immort. an.	*De immortalitate animae*
Lib. arb.	*De libero arbitrio voluntatis*
Mus.	*De musica*
Nat. orig.	*De natura et origine anima*
Nupt. et conc.	*De nuptiis et concupiscentia ad Valerium comitem*
Ord.	*De ordine*
Pecc. merit.	*De peccatorum meritis et remissione et de baptismo parvulorum*
Persev.	*De dono perseverantiae*
Praed.	*De praedestinatione sanctorum*
Quant.	*De animae quantitate*
Retract.	*Retractationes*
Serm.	*Sermones*
S. Dom. m.	*De sermone Domini in monte secundum Matthaeum*
Spir. et litt.	*De spiritu et littera*
Symb. cat.	*De symbolo ad catechumenos*
Trin.	*De trinitate*
Util. cred.	*De utilitate credenda*
Ver. rel.	*De vera religione*

Other Ancient Sources

Adv. haer.	*Adversus haeresis*, Irenaeus
Cels.	*Contra Celsum*, Origen
Comm. Eph.	*Commentariorum in Epistulam ad Ephesios*, Jerome
Comm. Ev. Joan.	*Commentarii in evangelium Iohannis*, Origen
Comm. Rom.	*Commentarii Romanos*, Origen
De bapt.	*De baptismo*, Tertullian
Dial.	*Dialogue with Trypho*, Justin Martyr
Div.	*De Divinatione*, Cicero
Enn.	*Enneads*, Plotinus
Ep. P. Eph.	*In Epistulam Pauli ad Ephesios*, Victorinus
Exc. Theod.	*Excerpta ex Theodoto*, Clement
Exp. fid.	*Expositio fidei*, John of Damascus
Fat.	*De Fato*, Cicero
1 Apol.	*Apology 1*, Justin Martyr
P. Arch.	*Peri Archon*, Origen
Philoc.	*Philocalia*, Origen
Quis div. Salv.	*Quis dives salvetur*, Clement
Strom.	*Stromata*, Clement

CONTRIBUTORS

Brian Abasciano (PhD, University of Aberdeen) serves as adjunct professor in New Testament at Gordon-Conwell Theological Seminary; pastor of Faith Community Church in Hampton, New Hampshire; and founder and president of Society for Evangelical Arminians.

David L. Allen (PhD, University of Texas at Arlington) serves as Distinguished Professor of Preaching, occupying the George W. Truett Chair of Ministry, and director of the Center for Text-Driven Preaching at Southwestern Baptist Theological Seminary.

Leighton Flowers (DMin, New Orleans Baptist Theological Seminary) serves as director of evangelism and apologetics at Baptist General Convention of Texas and professor of theology at Trinity College of the Bible and Theological Seminary.

Adam Harwood (PhD, Southwestern Baptist Theological Seminary) serves as professor of theology, occupying the McFarland Chair of Theology, and director of the Baptist Center for Theology and Ministry at New Orleans Baptist Theological Seminary.

Ken Keathley (PhD, Southeastern Baptist Theological Seminary) serves as senior professor of theology, occupying the Jesse Hendley Chair of Theology, and director of the L. Russ Bush Center for Faith and Culture at Southeastern Baptist Theological Seminary.

William W. Klein (PhD, University of Aberdeen) serves as professor of New Testament at Denver Seminary.

John D. Laing (PhD, The Southern Baptist Theological Seminary) serves as chaplain (colonel), United States Army; senior chaplain, Texas Military Department; former professor of systematic theology and philosophy at Southwestern Baptist Theological Seminary; and adjunct teacher at Beeson Divinity School.

Steve Lemke (PhD, Southwestern Baptist Theological Seminary) serves as professor of philosophy and ethics, provost emeritus, and vice president for institutional assessment at New Orleans Baptist Theological Seminary.

Bruce Little (PhD, Southeastern Baptist Theological Seminary) serves as professor emeritus of philosophy, and director of the Francis A. Schaeffer Collection at Southeastern Baptist Theological Seminary.

Roger E. Olson (PhD, Rice University) serves as professor of Christian theology, occupying the Foy Valentine Chair in Christian Ethics at George W. Truett Theological Seminary of Baylor University.

J. Matthew Pinson (EdD, Vanderbilt University) serves as president and professor of theology at Welch College.

Mark Tolbert (DMin, Southwestern Baptist Theological Seminary) serves as professor of preaching and pastoral ministry, occupying the Caskey Chair of Church Excellence, and director of the Caskey Center for Church Excellence at New Orleans Baptist Theological Seminary.

Trevin Wax (PhD, Southeastern Baptist Theological Seminary) serves as vice president of research and resource development at the North American Mission Board and visiting professor at Wheaton College.

Ken Wilson (DPhil, University of Oxford) serves as professor of systematic theology and church history at Grace School of Theology.

Ben Witherington III (PhD, University of Durham) serves as Jean R. Amos Professor of New Testament Interpretation at Asbury Theological Seminary.

INTRODUCTION

—— David L. Allen and Steve W. Lemke, editors ——

The Debate over Calvinism

The issue of Calvinism has garnered significant interest in recent years. Collin Hansen tracked the Calvinistic turn of many young ministers in *Young, Restless, Reformed: A Journalist's Journey with the New Calvinists*.[1] National and regional conferences sponsored by Together for the Gospel, 9Marks, and Sovereign Grace Ministries have highlighted and supported Calvinism. The new attention given to Calvinism has led to many young ministers becoming "new Calvinists."[2] There are also seasoned scholars who fervently believe in and teach Calvinism. Groups for and against Calvinism have waxed and waned throughout church history, but Calvinism appears to be on the rise at this time. We see many young Calvinists in our seminary classes and in our churches.

---

[1] Collin Hansen, *Young, Restless, Reformed: A Journalist's Journey with the New Calvinists* (Wheaton, IL: Crossway, 2008); see also Hansen's "Young, Restless, and Reformed: Calvinism Is Making a Comeback—and Shaking Up the Church," *Christianity Today* 50, no. 9 (September 22, 2006).

[2] Michael Horton, *For Calvinism* (Grand Rapids: Zondervan, 2011), 3, 194. Sometimes "new Calvinists" have the reputation of being somewhat argumentative, even obnoxious. Michael Horton, himself a Calvinist, described many new Calvinists as being in what he labels "the cage phase"; that is, it might be better if they were left in cages until they mature more as Christians. Horton acknowledged that he became "pretty hard to live with" and "imprisoned by my own pride."

The debate about Calvinism is not new. Although the issue of human depravity, important to Calvinism, has incurred debate at least since Augustine, the Dutch Reformed Synod of Dort (1618–19) most famously addressed the issue in response to concerns voiced by the Remonstrants, who were themselves Dutch Reformed Calvinists. Theologian Jacob Arminius best articulated their views, although he did not live to attend the Synod of Dort. Other Calvinists strongly disagreed with the Arminian Remonstrants. In preparation for the synod to discuss these issues, some of these Calvinists wrote down their views on human depravity:

> That man has not saving grace of himself, nor of the energy of his free will, inasmuch as he, in the state of apostasy and sin, can of and by himself neither think, will, nor do any thing that is truly good (such as saving Faith eminently is); but that it is needful that he be born again of God in Christ, through his Holy Spirit, and renewed in understanding, inclination, or will, and all his powers, in order that he may rightly understand, think, will, and effect what is truly good, according to the Word of Christ, John 15:5, "Without me ye can do nothing."
>
> That this grace of God is the beginning, continuance, and accomplishment of all good even to this extent, that the regenerate man himself, without [the grace of God], can neither think, will, nor do good, nor withstand any temptations to evil; so that all good deeds or movements that can be conceived must be ascribed to the grace of God in Christ.[3]

What a strong Calvinist statement of human depravity and our absolute helplessness apart from God to provide for our salvation! It affirms that human beings are so depraved they cannot think, will, or do anything that is truly good. Furthermore, humans cannot save themselves by their own efforts, faith, or free will because they live "in the state of apostasy and sin." It describes their utter helplessness to think, will, or do good, or to withstand temptations. The only hope for salvation is from God—to be born again and renewed by the Holy Spirit of God. The statement affirms that only God can renew human understanding, thinking, and willing so that humans can do good, for Jesus said that without him humans can do nothing. Indeed, it affirms that any good deed "that can be conceived" must be ascribed only "to the grace of God in Christ."[4]

---

[3] Schaff, "Five Arminian Articles," 3:546–47 (Arts. III and V), in *The Creeds of Christendom*, 3 vols., ed. P. Schaff, rev. D. S. Schaff, 6th ed. (Grand Rapids: Baker, 1993).

[4] Schaff, 3:547.

One might infer that such a strong Calvinist statement voiced the opinions of the Calvinists who formed the majority at the Synod of Dort (the Remonstrants were systematically excluded from the synod, so their views had no real representation). In fact, this statement is a quote from articles 3 and 4 of the issues raised by the Remonstrants. Such a strong affirmation of human depravity and the complete inability of humans to save themselves means the Remonstrants cannot responsibly be called Pelagians or even semi-Pelagians. Nothing could be more foreign to the beliefs of these Arminian Remonstrants than the notion that sinful humans could initiate, much less earn, their own salvation.

Are All Non-Calvinists Accurately Described as Pelagians or Semi-Pelagians?

Just as there are different kinds of Calvinists (and many Calvinists rightly bristle at being called hyper-Calvinists), it is likewise totally inappropriate for theologians to describe these Arminian Remonstrants as Pelagian or semi-Pelagian in doctrine. The Synod of Dort unfortunately mislabeled the Arminian Remonstrants as "entirely Pelagian."[5] Some later Arminians do go to that extreme, and they are wrong in doing so. Likewise, some Calvinists became so extreme that they became hyper-Calvinists. But let us abstain from calling them what they are not. The Arminians at Dort were Calvinists—members of Dutch Reformed congregations—who had concerns about the extremes to which some Calvinist theologians had taken Calvinism, at points probably further than Calvin himself. Caricaturing the Remonstrants (or us) as Pelagians or semi-Pelagians is, therefore, historically inaccurate and inappropriate— a *reductio ad Pelagian* caricature.[6] (See appendix on semi-Pelagianism).

---

[5] Rebecca H. Weaver, *Divine Grace and Human Agency: A Study of the Semi-Pelagian Controversy*, Patristic Monograph Series 15 (Macon, GA: Mercer University Press, 1996), ix–x, 1–14. Lest Dr. Weaver's objectivity on this issue be doubted, she is a professor emerita at Union Presbyterian Seminary, a school in the Calvinist tradition.

[6] Jaroslav Pelikan and Valerie Hotchkiss, eds., "The Canons of the Synod of Dort, 1618–19," in *Creeds and Confessions of Faith in the Christian Tradition*, 4 vols. (New Haven, CT: Yale University Press, 2003), 2:590 (Rejection of Errors for Heads 3 and 4, sect. 7). For the Latin, see Schaff, "Five Arminian Articles," 3:570. The Synod further accused the Remonstrants of teaching "that grace and free choice are concurrent partial causes which cooperate to initiate conversion, and that grace does not precede—in the order of causality—the effective influence of the will; that is to say, that God does not effectively help man's will to come to conversion before man's will itself motivates and determines itself. For the early church already condemned this

God's prior initiative in salvation does not have to include Calvinism's paradigm of total inability of the human will, nor does it have to preclude libertarian freedom. Denial of total inability is not denial of total depravity, nor is it semi-Pelagianism. As Arminius rightly made clear in his refutation of the charge of Pelagianism,[7] the sinfulness of humanity is so complete that only by grace, and grace alone, is human freedom even a possibility.[8]

While both Remonstrants and Dortians agreed that all humans are depraved and totally helpless to save themselves apart from the grace of God, why did the leaders of the Synod of Dort oppose the Remonstrants so bitterly and violently that they persecuted them, forced them out of their churches, arrested and imprisoned them, banished and exiled them, and even beheaded one of them? In what way did the Remonstrants and the Dortian Calvinists significantly differ?

Which Calvinism?

Difficulty in addressing the doctrines of Calvinism accurately stems, in part, from having many Calvinisms rather than one monolithic "Calvinism." Various types of Calvinists differ significantly on a number of issues. For example, saying that any Baptist fully endorses Calvinist or Reformed theology is imprecise. A distinction can be drawn between one who is Calvinist or Reformed (that is, someone who embraces all or most of the doctrines of Calvinism) and one who is Calvinistic (that is, someone who embraces some doctrines of Calvinism). Some Baptists are Calvinistic in their soteriology but not Calvinist in the Reformed sense of the term.

Though imprecise, the famous acronym TULIP has provided the distillation of the doctrinal differences between the two theological positions: Total depravity, Unconditional election, Limited atonement, Irresistible grace, and Perseverance of

---

doctrine long ago in the Pelagians, on the basis of the words of the apostle: It does not depend on man's willing or running but on God's mercy (Rom. 9:16)." Pelikan and Hotchkiss, "Synod of Dort, 1618–19," 2:591; see also Schaff, "Five Arminian Articles," 3:588. The Remonstrants explicitly denied any human role in initiating salvation, and they affirmed that salvation is initiated by God's grace rather than any kind of human response.

[7] Pelagianism, as defined by *Encyclopedia Britannica*, is a "5th-century Christian heresy taught by Pelagius and his followers that stressed the essential goodness of human nature and the freedom of the human will." The Editors of Encyclopaedia Britannica, Britannica.com, s.v. "Pelagianism," accessed September 28, 2021, https://www.britannica.com/topic/Pelagianism.

[8] W. Stephen Gunter, *Arminius and His Declaration of Sentiments: An Annotated Translation with Introduction and Theological Commentary* (Waco, TX: Baylor University Press, 2012), 189.

the saints.[9] One reason for the imprecision of the acronym is that some Dortian Calvinists affirmed unlimited atonement.[10]

Since the authors in this volume quote from and respond to so many varieties of Calvinism, other Calvinists may object that these arguments do not address the beliefs of their particular stripe of Calvinism. The articles address Calvinism broadly, as opposed to any particular Calvinist thinker, so quoting Calvinists with whom other Calvinists disagree is unavoidable.

Evangelicalism has always had its Calvinist and Arminian wings, mirroring the positions at the Synod of Dort. In Baptist life there were also two theological trajectories—"General Baptists" leaned toward the Remonstrant position, and "Particular Baptists" basically endorsed the Synod's position (although, being Baptists, neither could fully affirm all the language of the Synod of Dort or the Westminster Confession,[11] and as David L. Allen and David Wenkel have demonstrated, some Particular Baptists held to unlimited atonement).[12]

Richard A. Muller, who has indisputable Calvinist credentials, debunked the notion that evangelicals such as Baptists who think of themselves as Calvinists can appropriately claim to be Calvinists simply because they believe in the five points of Calvinist soteriology:

> I once met a minister who introduced himself to me as a "five-point Calvinist." I later learned that, in addition to being a self-confessed five-point Calvinist, he was also an anti-paedobaptist who assumed that the church was

---

[9] See the more detailed articulation of the five points and their subpoints in the Canons of Dort in Steve W. Lemke, "A More Detailed Analysis of the Five Points of Calvinism," in the papers of the Baptist Center for Theology and Ministry, available online at https://www.nobts .edu/baptist-center-theology/papers-files/Lemke_Five_Points_Methodology.pdf. The TULIP acronym is a twentieth-century development. See Ken Stewart, *Ten Myths about Calvinism* (Downers Grove, IL: InterVarsity, 2011), 78.

[10] See David L. Allen, *The Extent of the Atonement: A Historical and Critical Review* (Nashville: B&H Academic, 2016), 149–62.

[11] For a detailed discussion of the points at which the Particular Baptist Second London Confession diverged from the Westminster Confession, see Steve Lemke, "What Is a Baptist? Nine Marks that Separate Baptists from Presbyterians," in *Journal for Baptist Theology and Ministry* 5.2 (Fall 2008): 10–39, available online at https://www.nobts.edu/baptist-center -theology/journals/journals/JBTM_5-2_Fall_2008.pdf#page=11.

[12] Allen, *Extent of the Atonement*, 463–506; David Wenkel, "The Doctrine of the Extent of the Atonement among the Early English Particular Baptists," *Harvard Theological Review* 112, no. 3 (2019): 358–75.

a voluntary association of adult believers, that the sacraments were not means of grace but were merely "ordinances" of the church, that there was more than one covenant offering salvation in the time between the Fall and the eschaton, and that the church could expect a thousand-year reign on earth after Christ's Second Coming but before the end of the world. He recognized no creeds or confessions of the church as binding in any way. I also found out that he regularly preached on the "five points" in such a way as to indicate the difficulty in finding assurance of salvation: He often taught his congregation that they had to examine their repentance continually in order to determine whether they had exerted themselves enough in renouncing the world and in "accepting" Christ. This view of Christian life was totally in accord with his conception of the church as a visible, voluntary association of "born again" adults who had "a personal relationship with Jesus."

In retrospect, I recognize that I should not have been terribly surprised at the doctrinal context or at the practical application of the famous five points by this minister—although at the time I was astonished. After all, here was a person, proud to be a five-point Calvinist, whose doctrines would have been repudiated by Calvin. In fact, his doctrines would have gotten him tossed out of Geneva had he arrived there with his brand of "Calvinism" at any time during the late sixteenth or the seventeenth century. Perhaps, more to the point, his beliefs stood outside of the theological limits presented by the great confessions of the Reformed churches—whether the Second Helvetic Confession of the Swiss Reformed church or the Belgic Confession and the Heidelberg Catechism of the Dutch Reformed churches or the Westminster standards of the Presbyterian churches. He was, in short, an American evangelical.[13]

Muller disdained Particular Baptists such as John Gill because Gill did not embrace the rest of the Calvinist doctrines.[14] To be fully Calvinistic (Reformed) requires much more than the five points often associated with the Synod of Dort.

---

[13] Richard A. Muller, "How Many Points?," *Calvin Theological Journal* 28, no. 2 (November 1993): 425–26. At the time of his writing this article, Muller's credentials as a Calvinist were evidenced by the fact that he was a professor at Calvin Theological Seminary and wrote this article in *Calvin Theological Journal*.

[14] Muller, 428. "Particular" Baptists were so named because they believed in the "particular" or limited atonement; i.e., they were Calvinistic Baptists.

For Muller, to be truly a Calvinist requires the affirmation of other beliefs such as the baptism of infants, the identification of sacraments as means of grace, and an amillennial eschatology.[15] When these additional Calvinist doctrines "are stripped away or forgotten," Muller lamented, "the remaining famous five make very little sense."[16]

Presuppositions and Presumptions

Calvinists presume that concepts like total inability, irresistible grace, and regeneration preceding faith are matters of fact. These are all disputed by those of us who are not Calvinists (the latter is disputed by some Calvinists as well).

Presuppositions like "original sin entails original guilt" are taken as fact, and any denial of such is considered evidence of semi-Pelagianism. This was the mistaken approach of Herman Bavinck and appears to be followed by some Calvinists. Not even Reformed theologians are in agreement on whether original sin includes original guilt. Henri Blocher in his book *Original Sin* noted the different views among the Reformed.[17]

Calvinists and Arminians err when they claim that theologically one must be either a Calvinist or an Arminian. This approach does not do justice to the varieties of orthodox Christian traditions. Augustinianism is not identical to Calvinism. Nor can Lutheranism be identified as Calvinism. Michael Horton rightly noted that Confessional Lutherans "cannot be pressed into Calvinist-Arminian categories" because they affirm unconditional election and monergism, but deny double predestination, limited atonement, irresistible grace, and perseverance of believers.[18] Douglas A. Sweeney (dean of Beeson Divinity School) informs us that Lutheranism is . . . Lutherans. They are neither "hesitant Calvinists" nor "two-and-a-half-point Calvinists."[19] The same is true for Baptists and for all who are non-Calvinists—they are a varied bunch.

---

[15] Of course, many non-Calvinists also embrace amillennialism.

[16] Muller, "How Many Points?," 428.

[17] Henri Blocher, *Original Sin*, New Studies in Biblical Theology, vol. 5 (Grand Rapids: Eerdmans, 1999).

[18] Michael Horton, *The Christian Faith: A Systematic Theology for Pilgrims on the Way* (Grand Rapids: Zondervan, 2011), 314n11.

[19] See Douglas Sweeney, "Was Luther a Calvinist?," *The Gospel Coalition*, July 15, 2014, https://www.thegospelcoalition.org/article/was-luther-a-calvinist/.

Why This Volume?

A decade ago, we coedited and contributed chapters to another volume concerning Calvinism, *Whosoever Will: A Biblical-Theological Critique of Five-Point Calvinism*.[20] The book was well received beyond our expectations, selling over fifteen thousand copies, including being published in Spanish.[21] We even had a response to it published by some Calvinist friends.[22] The book went through several printings and sold enough copies that the publisher approached the coauthors about writing another such volume. However, this volume is quite different from *Whosoever Will*. In this new volume the focus is not on Southern Baptists specifically, as was *Whosoever Will*, but on the broader evangelical world. This new work includes authors from the Baptist, Methodist, and Arminian traditions. Of the original articles in *Whosoever Will*, only four have been retained in this volume, and each has been revised and updated.[23] Eleven articles are entirely new contributions.

We as contributors do not agree on all theological beliefs. We come from a number of denominational and theological perspectives. Some are "Calminian" Southern Baptists;[24] others hail from various denominations in the Arminian or

---

[20] David L. Allen and Steve Lemke, eds., *Whosoever Will: A Biblical-Theological Critique of Five-Point Calvinism* (Nashville: B&H Academic, 2010). Both of us have addressed Calvinism in other works as well, including David L. Allen, *The Atonement: A Biblical, Theological, and Historical Study of the Cross of Christ* (Nashville: B&H Academic, 2019); Allen, *Extent of the Atonement*; David L. Allen, Eric Hankins, and Adam Harwood, eds., *Anyone Can Be Saved: A Defense of "Traditional" Southern Baptist Soteriology* (Eugene, OR: Wipf and Stock, 2016), with the articles "The Sovereignty of God," and "Five Theological Models Relating Determinism, Divine Sovereignty, and Human Freedom," by Steve Lemke, 103–117, 169–176, and "The Current SBC Calvinism Debate: Observations, Clarifications, and Suggestions," and "The Atonement of Christ," by David L. Allen, 1–8, 55–64; Steve Lemke, "Sola Fide, Sola Gratia, and Sola Scriptura," in *The Popular Encyclopedia of Church History: The People, Places, and Events That Shaped Christianity*, ed. E. Hindson and D. Mitchell (Eugene, OR: Harvest House, 2013), 310–13. We also both served on the Calvinism Advisory Committee of the Southern Baptist Convention and have addressed the topic in various church and conference settings and in blog posts.

[21] David L. Allen and Steve Lemke, eds., *Todo aquel que en Él cree: Una crítica bíblica y teológica a los cinco puntos del calvinismo,* trans. Anabella Vides de Valverde (Nashville: B&H Academic, 2016).

[22] Matthew Barrett and Thomas Nettles, eds., *Whomever* He *Wills: A Surprising Display of Sovereign Mercy* (Cape Coral, FL: Founders Press, 2012).

[23] David L. Allen's chapter on limited atonement is an entirely new chapter.

[24] Tim Stewart, ed., *Mixed Blessings: A Dictionary of Religious Blend Words* (Austin: Laurellia, 2021), s.v. "Calminian."

Wesleyan tradition. The contributors do not all agree on the security of the believer. The editors—both Southern Baptists—affirm the eternal security of the believer, as do other authors, including Ken Keathley, who wrote the article on perseverance of the saints. However, as Keathley's article makes clear, we do not agree with some Puritan views that have no real assurance of salvation. For non-Calvinists to disagree over the issue of perseverance of the saints is nothing new. Even Arminius and the early Remonstrants did not overtly affirm that believers could lose their salvation. What they affirmed is that since the Scriptures pointed both ways, they were non-committal on this issue.[25]

None of the authors in this project is a Pelagian, a semi-Pelagian, or a five-point Calvinist. All these authors join the long history of the church in affirming that Pelagianism is a heresy that overly exaggerates human potential, overly minimizes human sinfulness, and overly minimizes the necessity of salvation solely through the grace of God. All these contributors oppose the "openness of God" perspective that places such a high value on human free will that it affirms God does not have exhaustive foreknowledge of the future. What we do hold in common is that we all share concerns about some doctrines of Calvinism, particularly those related to soteriology. Articulating these concerns is what unifies the contributors to this volume. We address these concerns to the evangelical world to affirm our deep belief in the doctrines of God and salvation that we understand Scripture to support. We believe that God so loved the world (by implication every living human being) that he gave his only Son, Jesus Christ, to be sacrificed on the cross for our sin. Therefore, he has decreed that everyone who believes on Jesus Christ as Savior and Lord will be saved and experience eternal life (John 3:16).

Since reaching the lost is at the heart of God (Matt 18:14; 1 Tim 2:3–4; 2 Pet 3:9), evangelism and missions are at the heart of the concerns of the authors of these chapters, who gladly join hands with all Christians to discover what it means to accomplish the Great Commission in this new millennium. The primary focus of Christians should be to carry out the Great Commission under the lordship of Jesus Christ according to the guidelines found in the inerrant Word of God.

This book includes a variety of perspectives on Calvinism, in four sections that critique Calvinism in four different areas. The contributors address Calvinism from a variety of theological and denominational perspectives.

---

[25] See Art. V in Schaff, "Five Arminian Articles," 3:547–48.

Section 1 includes articles that address each of the classic five points of Calvinist soteriology in the TULIP. Adam Harwood of New Orleans Baptist Theological Seminary addresses total depravity; Leighton Flowers of the Baptist General Convention of Texas and the *Soteriology 101* podcast addresses unconditional election; David L. Allen from Southwestern Baptist Theological Seminary critiques limited atonement; Steve Lemke from New Orleans Baptist Theological Seminary critiques irresistible grace; and Ken Keathley from Southeastern Baptist Theological Seminary addresses perseverance of the saints.

Section 2 addresses Calvinism from a historical perspective. Ken Wilson of Grace Theological Seminary writes on Augustinianism and Calvinism; J. Matthew Pinson of Welch College surveys various Baptist opponents of Calvinism; and Ben Witherington III of Asbury Theological Seminary provides a Wesleyan critique of Calvinism.

Section 3 addresses a variety of crucial issues from theological, biblical, and ecclesiological perspectives. Brian Abasciano of Faith Community Church in Hampton, New Hampshire, addresses Romans 9 and Calvinism; William Klein from Denver Seminary writes on corporate and personal election; Roger Olson of George W. Truett Theological Seminary addresses the character of God in Calvinism; John Laing, senior chaplain for the Army National Guard and staff member at Meadow Brook Baptist Church in Birmingham, Alabama, addresses the interaction of determinism and human freedom; Bruce Little, professor emeritus of philosophy and director of the Francis A. Schaeffer Collection at Southeastern Baptist Theological Seminary, addresses Calvinism and the problem of evil; and Mark Tolbert from New Orleans Baptist Theological Seminary addresses the public invitation and altar call. The book concludes with an epilogue by Trevin Wax of the North American Mission Board about how Calvinists and non-Calvinists can work together for the gospel of Christ.

Differing Views, Unified Spirit

Addressing a controversial issue such as Calvinism without inflaming emotions is difficult. Therefore, the authors enter into this discussion with some reluctance and yet also with determination. Our reluctance to approach these issues stems from our desire for unity among evangelical Christians. The goal of unity is pleasing to God and presents the most positive witness to those who do not know Jesus Christ as their Savior. Arminius himself said, "May God grant that we all may fully agree, in those things which are necessary to His glory, and to the salvation of the church; and that, in other things, if there can not be harmony of opinions, there may at least be harmony of feelings, and that we may 'keep the unity of the Spirit in the bond of peace.'"[26]

So why does this book deal with such a controversial issue? Because it involves the authors' deep convictions concerning what they believe the Bible teaches about who God is and how he works in the world. Clearly, others have different convictions, flowing from their biblical interpretations and views of who God is and how he works in the world. These beliefs matter and they deserve to be heard. They lie at the heart of what Christianity is and what the gospel proclaims. The contributors are not "anti-Calvinist" and therefore are interested in dialogue, not diatribe. As Nathan Finn has said, "If we are to move toward a more cooperative future, we must all be committed to defending and commending our particular convictions but not at the expense of either our cooperation with one another or our personal sanctification."[27]

This book is offered in that spirit and toward that end. We claim Calvinistic believers as fellow believers and work hand in hand with them as we serve the Lord together. However, we honestly disagree with some points of their theology. Our hope is that disagreement can occur in an irenic Christian spirit, without disagreeableness or harshness. We humbly ask forgiveness when we fail to do so, or when we misunderstand what others have intended. We take our stand on God's Word and challenge our readers to search the Scriptures to discover what the Bible says about these key issues.

David L. Allen and Steve W. Lemke
1 Tim 2:4

---

[26] Jacobus Arminius, "An Examination of the Treatise of William Perkins Concerning the Order and Mode of Predestination," in *The Works of James Arminius*, 3 vols., trans. J. Nichols (Buffalo, NY: Derby, Orton, and Mulligan, 1853), 3:282.

[27] Nathan A. Finn, "Southern Baptist Calvinism: Setting the Record Straight," in *Calvinism: A Southern Baptist Dialogue*, ed. E. Ray Clendenen and Brad J. Waggoner (Nashville: B&H, 2008), 192.

SECTION ONE

A Biblical and Theological Critique of the Soteriology of Five-Point Calvinism

1

A Critique of Total Depravity

—— Adam Harwood ——

The Bible uses several words to communicate the concept of sin, such as the Hebrew words *hata* ("to do wrong"), *awon* ("iniquity"), *pasha* ("to rebel"), and the Greek words *adikia* ("unrighteous"), *parabasis* ("transgression"), and *hamartia* ("to miss the mark"). Sin is any deviation from God's revealed will. People sin by either failing to conform to God's standards or explicitly opposing them.[1] People sin by their thoughts, attitudes, speech, or actions—either by acting wrongly or failing to act rightly. Sin is against God and nature.[2] Sin is a reminder that the world is not the way it should be.[3]

God's good creation has been defiled by sin. Presently, neither this world nor humans are the way God created them in the beginning. Since the first couple, Adam

---

[1] David J. Sigrist, "Sin," in *Lexham Theological Wordbook*, ed. Douglas Mangum et al., Lexham Bible Reference Series (Bellingham, WA: Lexham Press, 2014).

[2] Thomas H. McCall, *Against God and Nature: The Doctrine of Sin*, Foundations of Evangelical Theology, ed. John S. Feinberg (Wheaton, IL: Crossway, 2019).

[3] Cornelius Plantinga Jr., *Not the Way It's Supposed to Be: A Breviary of Sin* (Grand Rapids: Eerdmans, 1995).

and Eve, chose to disobey their Creator (Genesis 3), humans have been broken and live in a fallen world. The effects of their rebellion against God can be traced through the book of Genesis in the escalation of violence and death, and the consequences of sin can be seen today. Why does a hurricane drown the coast and cancer ravage a body? The root cause is that we live in a fallen world. Why do some people make sinful choices that result in the abuse or murder of innocent victims? Humans are broken and sinful, which does not excuse sinful deeds. People should be held accountable for their actions. The point is, the Bible accounts for the situation. The first couple's disobedience in the garden introduced these occasions of moral evil (events caused by a person's will) and natural evil (events not caused by a person's will, such as weather and illness) that damage God's "very good" creation (Gen 1:31).[4] Thankfully, God did not leave people in this hopeless and helpless condition. Instead, he came to the rescue by sending his Son to earth to live a perfect life and then die as the perfect sacrifice for the sins of the world (John 1:29). God will redeem and restore his creation in Christ. At that time, the people of God will live with him in a new heaven and new earth, where there will be no sin, death, or dying (Revelation 21–22). However, until God's plan of restoration and salvation is complete at the future return of Christ, we live in bodies and in a creation that longs for restoration (Romans 8). We inhabit a body of death (Rom 7:24) in a beautiful-but-broken world. Three things are true about sin and sinners.

First, *sin is universal*. Every person has been impacted by sin. This impact is unavoidable. Even Jesus, who was sinless and committed no sin (Heb 4:15; 9:14; 1 Pet 2:22), was impacted by sin. Jesus was crucified by sinful people (Acts 2:23), took on the sin of the world (John 1:29), and became sin for us so that we might become the righteousness of God (2 Cor 5:21). The impact of sin is indeed universal. In Romans 1–2, Paul indicted every person as an idolater and lawbreaker, both Jew and non-Jew. "All have sinned," he wrote, "and fall short of the glory of God" (Rom 3:23).

Second, sin is not *a* human problem; sin is *the* human problem. It was the sin of the first couple that ruptured their relationship with their Creator and introduced shame, alienation, and death into the created order. Human sin prompted the sacrificial system, which resulted in God's judgment on sin being deferred (Rom 3:25–26) until its culmination in Jesus's sacrifice on the cross—which Paul calls a demonstration of God's love (Rom 5:8). Jesus "did not come to be served, but to serve, and to

---

[4] Unless otherwise noted, Scripture quotations in this chapter are from the NIV.

give his life as a ransom for many" (Mark 10:45). Jesus came to give his life for sinners. Sin is *the* human problem, and God solved that problem at the cross of Christ.

Third, *sinners cannot save themselves*. Paul reminds believers they are saved by grace through faith, "and this is not from yourselves, it is the gift of God" (Eph 2:8). Salvation is "not by works, so that no one can boast" (v. 9). Any boasting about salvation will be in God because only God saves sinners. Paul clarified to Titus that God saves people because of his kindness, love, and mercy—not because of their righteous actions (Titus 3:4–5).

God created a good world; humans fell, and all of creation and every person is wounded by sin, for which God provides the only remedy in the cross and resurrection of Christ. Christians are broadly unified on these statements about the problem of and solution for sin.

However, rather than maintain this broad and unified understanding of sin, theologians have attempted to explain further the details of the doctrine of sin. Multiple views developed and Christians divided as they attempted to answer these precise doctrinal questions. One of those topics over which Christians differ concerns the doctrine of *original sin*, which refers to the nature and effects of the first couple's sin on all people. Christians agree that sin is the universal human problem, and sinners cannot save themselves; however, Christians differ over the issues of human guilt and salvation. This chapter addresses these areas of difference:

1. What do people inherit from Adam's sin in the garden?
2. When can sinners repent of their sin and confess Jesus as Lord to be saved?

What Do People Inherit from Adam's Sin in the Garden?

Two Christian Views of Original Sin

The first question to be addressed in this chapter is what do people inherit because of Adam's sin in the garden? Though the views can be categorized further and nuanced more precisely, Christians affirm two main positions on original sin. *Inherited guilt* is the view that all people inherit from Adam sinful inclinations, mortality, and the guilt of Adam's sin. *Inherited consequences* is the view that all people inherit from Adam sinful inclinations and mortality, not the guilt of his sin. Theologians who write about original sin assign various terms, but they generally distinguish between those two main positions.

In *The Transmission of Sin: Augustine and the Pre-Augustinian Sources*, Pier Franco Beatrice distinguished between what Joseph Turmel originally called hereditary sin and hereditary decline.[5] *Hereditary sin* is the view that all people suffer the consequences of Adam's sin, primarily physical death, and his descendants are guilty of sin transmitted from him. *Hereditary decline* is the view that all people suffer the consequences of Adam's sin, primarily physical death, but this view denies that sin is passed to Adam's descendants. Hereditary sin corresponds to inherited guilt, and hereditary decline corresponds to inherited consequences.

Donald Macleod, in "Original Sin in Reformed Theology," detailed the debates among Reformed theologians about what was received from Adam. Macleod referred to the two views as immediate imputation and mediate imputation. *Immediate imputation* is the view that Adam's descendants receive an immediate imputation of both corruption and guilt due to Adam's sin. *Mediate imputation* is the view that Adam's descendants inherit corruption from him, but guilt is mediated through their own sinful acts.[6] Immediate imputation corresponds to inherited guilt, and mediate imputation corresponds to inherited consequences.

Thomas H. McCall provided a comprehensive presentation and analysis of the historic Christian theories of original sin. He detailed six major options, definitions, and representatives:

1. *Symbolic and existential interpretations*—deny the existence or importance of Adam and Eve (F. R. Tennant, Paul Tillich)
2. *Corruption-only doctrines*—corruption without corresponding guilt due to Adam's sin (Christian theology before Augustine, the Orthodox Church, Ulrich Zwingli, Richard Swinburne, Stanley Grenz)
3. *Corruption and guilt: federalism*—all people are guilty of Adam's sin because he represented humanity in the garden (Francis Turretin)
4. *Corruption and guilt: realism*—all people are guilty of Adam's sin because they were present with him in the garden (Augustine, Jonathan Edwards)

---

[5] Pier Franco Beatrice, *The Transmission of Sin: Augustine and the Pre-Augustinian Sources*, trans. Adam Kamesar, AAR Religion in Translation (Oxford: Oxford University Press, 2013), 5–8.

[6] Donald Macleod, "Original Sin in Reformed Theology," in *Adam, the Fall, and Original Sin: Theological, Biblical, and Scientific Perspectives*, ed. Hans Maudeme and Michael Reeves (Grand Rapids: Baker Academic, 2014), 139–44.

5. *Corruption and guilt: mediate views*—all people are guilty due to the corruption from original sin, not for the sins of Adam and Eve (Anselm, John Calvin, Henri Blocher)
6. *Conditional imputation of guilt*—all people ratify the guilt of Adam when they knowingly commit their first act of sin (Millard Erickson)[7]

The first view is not considered in the present study because it denies the historicity of the first couple and their sin in the garden. View 2 corresponds to inherited consequences, and views 3–6 correspond to inherited guilt.

Beatrice (who wrote from Italy), Macleod (from Scotland), and McCall (from the United States) used different terms to identify the same theological distinctions. This chart illustrates the relationship between their terms and the terms used in this chapter.

Terms used in this chapter	*Inherited guilt*—all people inherit a fallen world, sinful inclinations, mortality, and the guilt of Adam's sin	*Inherited consequences*—all people inherit a fallen world, sinful inclinations, and mortality
Pier Franco Beatrice, *The Transmission of Sin: Augustine and the Pre-Augustinian Sources*	*Hereditary sin*—all people suffer the effects of Adam's sinful act, and his sin is transmitted to his descendants, resulting in their guilt	*Hereditary decline*—all humanity suffers the consequences of Adam's sin, primarily physical death, with no transmission of sin and guilt
Donald Macleod, "Original Sin in Reformed Theology"	*Immediate imputation*—all people receive an immediate imputation of Adam's guilt	*Mediate imputation*—all people inherit corruption from Adam, but guilt is mediated through their own sinful acts
Thomas H. McCall, *Against God and Nature*	*Corruption and guilt* (federalism, realism, and mediate views); *Conditional imputation of guilt*	*Corruption-only doctrines*

---

[7] McCall, *Against God and Nature*, 149–76.

Both perspectives acknowledge that sin has impacted God's creation, including all of Adam's descendants. Both views also acknowledge all people will inherit corruption (which some refer to as a sinful nature), and both views depend on the person and work of Christ alone for salvation. The inherited guilt view, however, adds that all people are guilty of Adam's sin. In this chapter, I affirm both views as orthodox but argue for the inherited-consequences view.

Early Church Fathers Who Affirmed Inherited Consequences

Historical theologians generally agree that the concept of original sin as people inheriting the guilt of Adam's sin was virtually unknown in the entire Christian tradition until the later writings of Augustine.[8] Instead, the early church—in both the East and the West—affirmed views consistent with inherited consequences.[9] Clement of Alexandria, Athanasius, Cyril of Alexandria, Mark the Hermit, Diodore of Tarsus, John Chrysostom, Theodore of Mopsuestia, and Theodoret of Cyrrhus all rejected inherited guilt.[10] For these and other pastor-theologians, Adam's sin did not result in total human depravity but a weakened will, physical death, and other non-condemnatory results consistent with inherited consequences. J. N. D. Kelly explained, "There is hardly a hint in the Greek fathers that mankind as a whole shares in Adam's guilt." The same was true of the Latin fathers. Though they viewed sin as a "corrupting force," the guilt of Adam's sin "attaches to Adam himself, not to us."[11] Many in the early church rejected Augustine's later views of predestination and the loss of human free will, though they were labeled (many inappropriately) as Pelagians or semi-Pelagians. Most who opposed Augustine were orthodox theologically, affirm-

---

[8] "It is virtually an axiom of historical theology that the doctrine of original sin, as we recognize it today, cannot be traced back beyond Augustine." Gerald Bray, "Original Sin in Patristic Thought," *Churchman* 108, no. 1 (1994): 37.

[9] McCall identified "the affirmation of *corruption* in original sin *without a corresponding affirmation of guilt* [McCall's italics]" as "the view of early (pre-Augustinian) Christian theology." McCall, *Against God and Nature*, 156.

[10] Beatrice, *Transmission of Sin*, 259. See pp. 172–256 for his support for this claim from the primary sources. See also Kurt Jaros, "The Relationship of the So-Called Semi-Pelagians and Eastern Greek Theology on the Doctrine of Original Sin: An Historical-Systematic Analysis and Its Relevance for 21st Century Protestantism" (PhD diss., University of Aberdeen, 2020), for primary and secondary sources on the views of Clement of Alexandria (pp. 120–22), Athanasius (pp. 126–30), and Theodore of Mopsuestia (pp. 141–44).

[11] J. N. D. Kelly, *Early Christian Doctrines*, rev. ed. (New York: HarperCollins, 1978), 350, 354.

ing the necessity of God's grace for salvation and denying that sinners initiate their own salvation.[12]

John Chrysostom (AD 349–407) wrote, "We do baptize infants, although they are not guilty of any sins."[13] He also commented on Rom 5:19 that a person is not a sinner due to Adam's sin but only after an individual transgresses the law.[14] In *On Infants' Early Deaths*, **Gregory of Nyssa** (ca. AD 335–394) addressed the spiritual condition of infants. He considered them to be neither good nor bad. Infants who died would be with God because their souls had never been corrupted by their own sinful actions.[15] **Tertullian** (ca. AD 160–225) mentioned that infant souls are unclean in Adam, which is consistent with the inherited-consequences view. He also questioned why there was a rush to baptize them. Those who later taught inherited guilt insisted on the practice of infant baptism and wrongly assumed that water baptism cleansed the infants of Adam's guilt. Tertullian referred to the souls of infants as "innocent," and he differentiated between infants and children based upon their capability to commit sin.[16] This view of original sin as inherited consequences was affirmed in the early church and continues to be affirmed by other Christians today, including the Orthodox Church.[17]

---

[12] For more on the historical background and writings of the Pelagians and those who were later called semi-Pelagians, see Rebecca Harden Weaver, *Divine Grace and Human Agency: A Study of the Semi-Pelagian Controversy*, Patristic Monograph Series 15 (Macon, GA: Mercer University Press, 1998); Adam Harwood, "Is the Traditional Statement Semi-Pelagian?," in Allen, Hankins, and Harwood, *Anyone Can Be Saved*, 157–68 (see intro., n. 20); Ali Bonner, *The Myth of Pelagianism* (Oxford: Oxford University Press, 2018); and Jaros, "Doctrine of Original Sin." For extensive documentation of Augustine's debates on Pelagianism and his corresponding change of view on free will, see Kenneth M. Wilson, *Augustine's Conversion from Traditional Free Choice to 'Nonfree Free Will': A Comprehensive Methodology*, Studien und Texte zu Antike und Christentum 111 (Tübingen: Mohr Siebeck, 2018).

[13] John Chrysostom, "On Infants," in *The Later Christian Fathers*, ed. and trans. Henry Bettenson (New York: Oxford University Press, 1971), 69.

[14] John Chrysostom, "Homily 10," in NPNF[1], 11:403.

[15] Gregory of Nyssa, "On Infants' Early Deaths," in NPNF[2], 5:372–81.

[16] See Tertullian, *A Treatise on the Soul* 39–41, 56, in *ANF*, 3:219–21, 232; and Tertullian, *On Baptism* 18, in *ANF*, 3:678.

[17] "Most Orthodox theologians reject the idea of 'original guilt.'" Rather, explains Timothy Ware, "Humans (Orthodox usually teach) automatically inherit Adam's corruption and mortality, but not his guilt; they are only guilty in so far as by their own free choice they imitate Adam." Timothy Ware, *The Orthodox Church*, rev. ed. (1963; New York: Penguin, 1993), 224.

Augustine's Views on Inherited Guilt

Historians and theologians are in broad agreement that Augustine, a fifth-century African bishop, shaped the Western world's view of original sin.[18] His theology profoundly influenced both the Roman Catholic and Protestant traditions. Whether or not one is aware of Augustine's influence, all Christians who think about human sin are influenced by his views. This section provides a summary and critique of some of his views on inherited guilt.

Augustine taught that humans were created from sin-infected material. He interprets the lump of clay in Romans 9 to refer to a *massa peccati* (mass of sin), a lump of sin-infected dough from which God subsequently created every human. The single mass of dough fermented and was infected with *originalis reatus* (hereditary guilt) as a result of Adam's sin. Augustine referred to this concept of "mass" frequently in his writings, and it forms the basis of his view that God predestined a certain number of people to salvation to replace the fallen angels.[19]

Augustine taught strange views on sexual union and Christian marriage, rather than affirming the goodness of sexuality within a Christian marriage. For example, Augustine taught that in the garden Adam existed in a spiritual body and therefore did not experience concupiscence—the battle between the flesh and spirit.[20] Instead, Adam and Eve were joined spiritually, and their offspring were spiritual and nonflesh.[21] After their disobedience against God, their bodies became mortal and fleshly, and their union resulted in sinful, mortal offspring.[22]

Augustine taught that hereditary sin—including guilt—is passed from parents to their children through human semen. In the garden, all humanity was

---

[18] Stan Norman wrote, "The Augustinian doctrine of original sin has exerted profound influence upon the theology of the church. Since his time, theologians have affirmed, rejected, or modified the Augustinian position. One cannot construct a Christian understanding of sin without engaging in some way Augustine's doctrine of original sin." R. Stanton Norman, "Human Sinfulness," in *A Theology for the Church*, rev. ed., ed. Daniel L. Akin (Nashville: B&H Academic, 2014), 366.

[19] See Augustine, *To Simplician—On Various Questions* 1.2.16, 19–20, in LCC 6:397–98, 401–4; Letter 186, in The Fathers of the Church: A New Translation, 46 vols. (New York: Fathers of the Church, 1955), 30:191–221; Sermon 294.15, in WSA 3/8:190. See also Paula Fredriksen, "Massa," in *Augustine Through the Ages: An Encyclopedia*, ed. Allan D. Fitzgerald (Grand Rapids: Eerdmans, 1999), 545–47.

[20] Augustine, *On Genesis: A Refutation of the Manichees* 2.8.10, in WSA 1/13:77–78.

[21] Augustine, *On Genesis* 1.19.30, in WSA 1/13:58.

[22] Augustine, *On Genesis* 2.21.32, in WSA 1/13:92–93.

contained in the body of Adam.[23] After Adam freely sinned against God, his human seed was defective, which resulted in the corruption of his progeny.[24] So, all humanity sinned because all were *in illo* (within him), comprising an *omnes unus* (single person).[25] For Augustine, new birth in Christ via baptism answers this corrupt physical birth facilitated by sinful sexual desires and defective human semen.[26]

Augustine taught that infant baptism washed away the guilt of original sin. Augustine supported his view with three arguments. First, humans are produced through sinful desire from corrupt human seed through which parents transmit original sin to their children. Thus, infants are corrupt due to the transmission of sin from their parents. Second, the distress and ills to which infants are subject is explained by punishment due to their guilt.[27] Third, Augustine cited the liturgical practices of exorcism and exsufflation, in which the devil and his demons are cast out and renounced. Thus, baptismal practices confirm infants are under the devil's power.[28] Augustine concluded that humans, at the time of their birth, are destined for damnation unless redeemed by God's grace via water baptism.[29] In his study of original sin, Norman P. Williams observed, "There is no clearer instance of the control exercised by liturgical or devotional practice over the growth of dogma than that provided by

---

[23] Augustine, *On the Merits and Remission of Sins, and On the Baptism of Infants* 3.7, in NPNF[1] 5:71.

[24] Augustine, *Against Julian: Unfinished Work* 4.104, in WSA 1/25:465–67; 2.123, in WSA 1/25:217–18.

[25] "In our own persons we did not yet exist, but we were present in Adam, and therefore whatever befell Adam was our fate too." Augustine, *Expositions of the Psalms* 84.7, in WSA 3/18:208.

[26] Augustine distinguished between other people and Jesus: "God fashioned all of us, you see, from the stock of sin. He, though, was even made man differently, he was born of a virgin, a woman conceived him not by sexual desire, but by faith, he did not derive the stock of sin from Adam." Augustine, Sermon 246.5, in WSA 3/7:106.

[27] See Augustine, *Against Julian: Unfinished Work* 1.22, 5.64, 6.23, in WSA 1/25:63–65, 595–99, 661–64. "I do not say: The newborn are wretched because they are proved guilty. Rather, I say: They are proved to be guilty because they are wretched." Augustine, *Against Julian: Unfinished Work* 6.27.22, in WSA 1/25:682.

[28] "The Church would neither exorcise the children of the faithful nor subject them to the rite of exsufflation, if it did not rescue them from the power of darkness and from the prince of death." Augustine, *Against Julian* 6.5.11, in WSA 1/24:484. Kelly explained that for Augustine, "The practice of baptizing infants with exorcisms and a solemn renunciation of the Devil was in his eyes proof positive that even they were infected with sin." Kelly, *Early Christian Doctrines*, 363.

[29] Augustine, Sermon 294.16–17, in WSA 3/8, 191–92.

the study of the relations between the custom of infant baptism and the doctrine of original sin."[30] In other words, the practice of baptizing infants fostered the doctrine of original sin (understood to include guilt).

Augustine considered unbaptized infants to be condemned. In AD 412, Augustine wrote a letter to Marcellinus in which he addressed the topics of original sin and the baptism of infants. Augustine made the case that infants are incorporated into Christ and his church only via baptism. Without baptism, they are guaranteed damnation. "Damned, however, they could not be if they really had no sin."[31] Augustine concluded that since infants could not have committed a sinful act during their young life, we must believe—even if we cannot understand it—infants inherit original sin. Augustine argued that infants are either saved by union with Christ through water baptism or they will be condemned. Infants could not be damned by their own sinful acts because they have not committed any sinful acts; thus, one must affirm that infants inherit sin.

A Reply to Augustine's Views on Inherited Guilt

Augustine's views on inherited guilt deserve a reply. The idea that the lump of clay in Romans 9 is a mass of sin out of which God creates humans cannot be justified from the biblical text. That interpretation, coupled with his belief that Adam and Eve existed in spiritual bodies to create a child with a body only after the fall, is rooted in gnostic dualism, not a Christian view of creation. Augustine's negative view of sexuality—even within marriage—resulted in his view that human semen was defective, which resulted in the corruption of all humans who supposedly existed in Adam seminally. Augustine's views contradict the Christian view of the goodness of marriage as well as sexual relations between a husband and wife, celebrated in Song of Solomon as well as Proverbs, 1 Corinthians, and Ephesians. Augustine's view that humans are created by defective seed in Adam is contradicted by the psalmist: "For you created my inmost being; you knit me together in my mother's womb. I praise you because I am fearfully and wonderfully made; your works are wonderful, I know that full well" (Ps 139:13–14).

---

[30] Norman P. Williams, *The Ideas of the Fall and of Original Sin: A Historical and Critical Study* (London: Longmans, Green, 1927), 223.

[31] Augustine, *Baptism of Infants* 3.7, in NPNF[1] 5:71.

Against Augustine's views that humans were created from a mass of sin or defective semen since marital sex is bad, Christians should affirm the goodness of God's creation—especially of people, all of whom are made in his image (Gen 1:27)—as well as the goodness of sexual relations in a Christian marriage.

Most Protestant Christian groups do not teach that infants must be baptized to be united with Christ in the event of their physical death. Baptists, for example, argue that the New Testament example is that some people who hear the message of the gospel respond in repentance of sin and faith in Christ; many of the relevant texts indicate those individuals were baptized. There is no explicit example of an infant being baptized. Jesus never called infants and young children to repent of sin—neither their own sin nor Adam's sin. Rather, Jesus welcomed and blessed them, and he pointed to them as examples of citizens of the kingdom of heaven. God can, by his mercy and through the atonement provided by Christ's work on the cross, welcome those who die as infants into heaven—apart from water baptism.

Augustine's Biblical Support for Inherited Guilt with Replies

Augustine found biblical support for his view of inherited guilt in two Old Testament and three New Testament texts. Following is his interpretation of those texts and my critique of his explication.

Job 14:4

Augustine defended infant guilt by citing an idea introduced by the Greek translation of Job 14:4.[32] The Hebrew text of Job 14:4 reads, "Who can bring what is pure from the impure? No one!" However, the Greek translation introduced a concept not found in the Hebrew text, "Who shall be pure of filth? No one, not even if his life on

---

[32] In a letter to Jerome, Augustine referred to infant guilt derived from Adam and quoted approvingly Jerome's citation of the Job 14 passage as evidence of original sin: "In thy sight no one is clean, not even the infant, whose time of life on earth is a single day." Augustine, Letter 166.3.6, in NPNF¹, 1:525. In his *City of God*, Augustine quoted Job 14:4: "There is none clean from stain, not even the babe whose life has been but for a day upon the earth." Augustine, *The City of God* 20.26.1, in NPNF¹, 2:446.

earth is one day!"[33] While the Hebrew text asserts only that no one is able to bring purity out of impurity, the Greek variant adds the idea that a one-day-old person will not avoid the filth. Athanasius referred to "the heretics" who interpret the "filth" mentioned in the Greek translation of Job 14:4 to refer to sin—as did Augustine. Instead, Athanasius interpreted filth as those things that coated an infant at birth, such as vernix, amniotic fluid, and the mother's blood.[34] Athanasius asked a series of rhetorical questions, "What sin can a child that is one day old commit? Adultery? Not at all, because it has not reached the age to have pleasure. Fornication? Not that either, because it does not yet have desire. Murder? But it is unable even to carry a murder weapon. Perjury? No, for it cannot yet make an articulate sound. Greed? It does not yet have awareness of the money of another, or even its own." Athanasius concluded, "Since newborns are completely without a share in these misdeeds, what sin can a one day old baby have, save only, as we said, bodily filth? Scripture does not say, 'No one is pure from sin,' but 'from filth.'"[35] Augustine's appeals to Job 14:4 to support infant guilt rested on a faulty foundation because his interpretation depended on a concept added in the Greek translation that does not appear in the Hebrew text.

Psalm 51:5

Augustine quoted Ps 51:5 in *Confessions* when he asked, "But if 'I was shapen in iniquity, and in sin did my mother conceive me,' where, I pray thee, O my God, where, Lord, or when was I, Thy servant, innocent?"[36] In a sermon, Augustine quoted from the verse, "Lo, I was conceived in iniquity," then asked about the kind of sin to which David would have been referring. He answered with this question,

---

[33] The Greek is *tis gar katharos estai apo rhupou; all'outheis*. Randall K. Tan, David A. deSilva, and Isaiah Hoogendyk, *The Lexham Greek-English Interlinear Septuagint: H.B. Swete Edition* (Bellingham, WA: Lexham Press, 2012), Job 14:4.

[34] Beatrice, *Transmission of Sin*, 197–98.

[35] Athanasius, *Fragments of Matthew* 9, in PG 27:1368–69. As Beatrice explained, "Athanasius rejects the interpretation as heretical, because for him as for all of the Greek Fathers, even if it is true that the sin of Adam passed to his descendants (see *Or. c. Arian.* 1.51 in PG 26.117C: *eis pantas anthrōpous ephthasen hē hamartia*), this is to be understood in the sense that death has reigned over all men, even the just, since all are subject to corruption and to the passions of their nature; see *Or. c. Arian.* 3.33 (PG 26.393b)." Beatrice, *Transmission of Sin*, 198n35.

[36] Augustine, *Confessions* 1.7.12, in NPNF[1], 1:48–49.

"How then can he say he was conceived in iniquity, unless iniquity is derived from Adam?"[37] Augustine continued his exposition of Ps 51:5:

> In another place a prophet declares, "No one is pure in your sight, not even an infant whose life on earth has been but one day" (Jb 14:4–5, LXX). We know that sins are canceled by baptism in Christ; Christ's baptism has power to forgive sins. Well, then, if infants are completely innocent, why do mothers come running to church when their babies are ill? What does that baptism effect, what is there to be forgiven? What I see is an innocent crying, not someone getting angry! What has baptism washed away? What is destroyed by it? The inheritance of sin is destroyed. If the baby could speak, if he had David's reasoning power, he would answer your question, "Why do you regard me simply as an infant? Admittedly you cannot see the load of sin I carry, but I was conceived in iniquity, 'and in sins did my mother nourish me in the womb.'"[38]

In his comments on Ps 51:5, Augustine quoted the Greek translation of Job 14:4 to argue that a one-day-old infant is unclean, and he added that the only remedy for his sin is water baptism. He also speculated that if one were to ask a one-day-old infant about his condition, the infant would declare his iniquity. Augustine explained that people conceived by the flesh are subject to judgment, which is why Jesus was conceived by the Holy Spirit rather than the flesh. Augustine concluded, "The verdict has been solemnly given: in Adam all have sinned. The only new-born baby who could be born innocent is one not born from the work of Adam."[39] For Augustine, fleshly conception transmits Adam's sin.[40]

Unlike Augustine, most Bible interpreters do not read infant guilt into their exegesis of Ps 51:5. Rather, they clarify that David was pointing to the pervasiveness of his sin, which reached to the earliest moments of his life, and he was condemning neither his mother nor sexual union as sinful.[41]

---

[37] In this source, Scripture quotations appear in italics rather than quotation marks. Psalm 51:5 is Ps 50:7 in the Septuagint; thus, Augustine's sermon is on Psalm 50. Augustine, *Exposition of Psalm 50*, in WSA 3/16:418.

[38] Augustine, in WSA 3/16:418.

[39] Augustine, in WSA 3/16:419.

[40] Beatrice, *Transmission of Sin*, 98.

[41] As Allen P. Ross explains, "David then acknowledged that he was morally impotent. He was born *a sinner*, that is, at no time in his life was he without sin" (italics in the original).

Though Ps 51:5 is frequently cited to support the Augustinian view of infant guilt, most English Bibles translate the verse as David saying he was conceived in sin or was sinful, rather than saying he was born guilty.[42] To cite the verse to support infant guilt is to affirm more than the author stated in the verse.

Ephesians 2:3

Augustine supported his view of original sin as hereditary sin with three New Testament texts. The first of those texts, Eph 2:3, includes the Greek phrase *ēmetha tekna physei orgēs* ("we were by nature deserving of wrath"). In context, this passage suggests that people are "dead" in their "transgressions and sins" (v. 1) and walk according to the world and to Satan (v. 2). Because they are not believers in Christ, they are by nature subject to God's wrath. Augustine saw in the Latin translation, however, support for his interpretation that *all* people (not just unbelievers) deserve God's wrath because they were born physically. The Latin text was translated, "by nature, sons of wrath."[43] The Latin word behind "nature" is *natura*, which carries the idea of physical birth and is the way Augustine used the term. In *On the Trinity*, Augustine referred to "the sin of the first man passing over originally into all of both sexes in their birth through conjugal union, and the debt of our first parents binding their whole posterity." In the same passage he quoted Eph 2:1–3 and explained that "by nature" means "as it has been depraved by sin."[44] When discussing the man born blind (John 9), Augustine quoted Eph 2:3 and explained that because of Adam's sin, evil had taken root in every person as a nature and every person is born mentally

---

Allen P. Ross, "Psalms," in *The Bible Knowledge Commentary: An Exposition of the Scriptures*, ed. J. F. Walvoord and R. B. Zuck, 2 vols. (Wheaton, IL: Victor, 1985), 1:832. See also: "David was not saying that his birth was illegitimate, or that his parents sinned when they performed the sexual act at his conception. He was acknowledging that there never was a time when he was without sin. He was born in the state of sin, or rebellion against God, which is common to all humanity until reconciliation with God occurs. David's statement is a poetic expression of the biblical teaching about this pervasive, inborn or 'original' sin (see Rm 3:23)." Allen P. Ross, "Introduction and Notes: Psalms," in *The Apologetics Study Bible: Real Questions, Straight Answers, Stronger Faith*, ed. Ted Cabal et al. (Nashville: Holman Bible, 2007).

[42] The CSB is a notable exception that provides this problematic translation, "Indeed, I was guilty when I was born; I was sinful when my mother conceived me."

[43] The Latin reads *natura filii irœ* (the Latin Vulgate and English translation are from the CPDV).

[44] Augustine, *On the Trinity* 13.12, in NPNF¹, 3:175.

blind.[45] Augustine condemned the fleshly conception of humans, claiming that "carnal generation is from the transgression of original sin."[46] All people are children of wrath by nature, because they originated from the human foreskin, which signifies original sin.[47]

Augustine misinterpreted Eph 2:3 to mean that all people are under God's wrath due to their physical birth because sin is passed on by the fleshly act of conception.[48] The biblical text, however, indicates that *unbelievers* are subject to God's wrath due to their sinful acts rather than due to their physical birth.[49]

Hebrews 7:4–10

Augustine concluded that just as Levi was in the loins of Abraham to pay the tithe to Melchizedek (Heb 7:4–10), all humanity was in the loins of Adam when he sinned in the garden, which makes humanity subject to judgment.[50] In reply, verse 9 says the tithe Levi receives now, he already paid, "so to speak" (NASB; "in a sense," CSB) because he was in Abraham's loins. The phrase indicates some type of analogy is in play, and it is the extent of the analogy that is discussed. The difference between the tithing event and the disobedience in the garden is that Levi was not counted as having paid the tithe simply because he was in his grandfather's loins. To compare the analogies, the consequences of Abraham's actions were not simply imputed to Levi. Rather, upon Levi receiving the tithe, it could be considered that Levi had already paid the tithe. Thus, Heb 7:4–10 does not concern original sin.

---

[45] Augustine, *Tractates on the Gospel of John* 44.9, in NPNF[1], 7:245.

[46] Augustine, *On the Merits and Remission of Sins, and On the Baptism of Infants* 2.15, in NPNF[1], 5:50.

[47] Augustine, *Against Julian* 6.7.20, in WSA 1/24:490.

[48] See also Augustine, *Questions on the Gospels* 2.38, in WSA 1/15–16:401; and Augustine, *Expositions of the Psalms* 57.20, in WSA 3/17:144.

[49] "All Christians, Jew or Gentile, once lived according to the desires of 'our flesh,' by which he means carrying out in actions one's sinful inclinations." Witherington added, "This verse, despite the protest of Barth, does deal with the idea of having a fallen human nature, though it does not say how 'we' obtained it." Ben Witherington III, *The Letters to Philemon, the Colossians, and the Ephesians: A Socio-Rhetorical Commentary on the Captivity Epistles* (Grand Rapids: Eerdmans, 2007), 253

[50] Augustine, *Against Julian: Unfinished Work* 6.22, in WSA 1/25:656–61.

Romans 5:12

Augustine found support for inherited guilt in a misinterpretation of the Latin version of Rom 5:12. At the end of the verse, Paul wrote that all die *eph hō pantes hemartōn* ("because all sinned"). Reading from a Latin text, however, Augustine saw the phrase *in quo omnes peccaverunt* and wrongly interpreted it to mean "in whom all sinned." The resulting interpretation was that all humanity dies because all humanity sinned in Adam. The Greek phrase *eph hō*, however, which corresponds to the Latin *in quo*, means "because." As support for this interpretation, we may simply consult major English Bible translations.[51] Against Augustine's interpretation, Rom 5:12 states all die because all sin. Though Rom 5:12 provides the primary biblical support for an Augustinian view of original sin, the verse became significant for his view only when he began to debate Pelagians on original sin.[52] For Pelagius, Adam's sin brought death into the world, but each person is held responsible for their own sin. Adam's sin was the first and primary example of sinful behavior, but his descendants are indicted as guilty for the same reason as Adam— because of their own acts of rebellion against God.[53] The early church interpreted Romans as well as Adam's relationship to humanity in similar ways. For Augustine, however, the Adam-Christ parallel represented two processes of being born: sinful people are born naturally by the natural man (Adam), but children of God are born spiritually by grace through Christ.[54] This Adam-Christ parallel is seen when Augustine paired the verse with 1 Cor 15:22, which he quoted, "For as in Adam all die, so also in Christ shall all be made alive."[55] For Augustine, Adam passed sin

---

[51] The CSB, ESV, LEB, NASB, NET, NIV, NKJV render the phrase in question as "because all sinned." Other translations use different words to communicate the same idea. For example, the KJV used the phrase "for that all have sinned." Even the NABRE (New American Bible, Revised Edition), the translation used on the website of the US Conference of Catholic Bishops, translated the phrase with a variation of "all sinned."

[52] Augustine quoted Rom 5:12 only three times before his debates with the Pelagians, and none of those occurrences of the verse concerned the transmission of sin. Beatrice, *Transmission of Sin*, 102.

[53] See Pelagius's views in *Pelagius' Commentary on St Paul's Epistle to the Romans*, trans. Theodore de Bruyn, Oxford Early Christian Studies (Oxford: Oxford University Press, 1993), 92–93 (5:12); 94 (5:15); 99 (6:19); 104 (7:17).

[54] Augustine, *On the Merits and Remission of Sins, and On the Baptism of Infants* 1.19, in NPNF[1], 5:22.

[55] Augustine, *Tractates on the Gospel of John* 3.12, in NPNF[1], 7:22.

to his descendants by procreation, resulting in all people being destined for eternal damnation, including unbaptized infants.[56]

Though some interpret Rom 5:12 like Augustine, other Christian scholars reject inherited guilt. James D. G. Dunn wrote on Paul's view of Adam and sin from Rom 5:12–21: "Guilt only enters into the reckoning with the individual's own transgression. Human beings are not held responsible for the state into which they are born. That is the starting point of their personal responsibility, a starting point for which they are not liable."[57] Donald G. Bloesch explained, "The text in Romans to which Augustine often appealed (5:12) does not tell us how Adamic sin is related to general human sin and therefore cannot be used to argue for inherited sin or guilt; it simply informs us that death pervaded the whole human race 'inasmuch as all have sinned' (REB)."[58] Joseph Fitzmyer cautioned readers of Rom 5:12 to distinguish between Paul's writings and the later teachings of the church. This Catholic scholar explains that the doctrine of original sin (the view that all people inherit both a sinful nature and guilt) is a later teaching of the church rather than the explicit teaching of Paul. The doctrine of original sin was developed from later Augustinian writings and solidified through the Sixteenth Council of Carthage, the Second Council of Orange, and the Tridentine Council.[59]

Conclusion on Augustine's View of Inherited Guilt

Augustine's view of inherited guilt was based on his distorted views of humanity, sexual union, and Christian marriage, and his poor interpretations of key biblical texts. Augustine misinterpreted Job 14:4; Ps 51:5; Eph 2:3; Heb 7:4–10; and Rom 5:12. The best-known example is that Augustine quoted Rom 5:12 to affirm that all sinned in Adam, which is not what the apostle Paul wrote. Augustine viewed infant baptism as the solution for the problems of inherited guilt and demonic possession among

---

[56] Augustine, *On the Merits and Remission of Sins, and On the Baptism of Infants* 1.21, in NPNF¹, 5:23: "Such infants as quit the body without being baptized will be involved in the mildest condemnation of all."

[57] James D. G. Dunn, *The Theology of Paul the Apostle* (Grand Rapids: Eerdmans, 1998), 97.

[58] Donald G. Bloesch, *Jesus Christ: Savior & Lord* (Downers Grove, IL: InterVarsity, 1997), 43–44.

[59] Joseph Fitzmyer, *Romans: A New Translation with Introduction and Commentary*, Anchor Bible 33, ed. William F. Albright and David Noel Freedman (Garden City, NY: Doubleday, 1993), 408–9.

infants. The early church affirmed human sinfulness, but Augustine's interpretations of Scripture and views of inherited guilt were innovations that were rejected by many of his contemporaries as well as subsequent generations of Christians.

Reformed Theologians Who Have Rejected Inherited Guilt

This doctrinal dispute is not determined by whether one identifies with the theological ideas of Reformed theology.[60] Macleod identified the "debate that divided Reformed theologians in the middle of the seventeenth century" between advocates of the views of *mediate* and *immediate* imputation.[61] In his monograph on original sin, Henri Blocher acknowledged his debt to Reformed theology but then denied any biblical basis for alien guilt, the view that Adam's sin is imputed to his posterity. Blocher called the view "repugnant."[62] Macleod and Blocher are cited as examples of Reformed theologians who acknowledge different views on inherited guilt among Reformed Christians.

Ulrich Zwingli (1484–1531), a Magisterial Reformer, rejected inherited guilt. Zwingli affirmed Adam's unity with humanity and sin's devastating effects, but he called original sin a "sin that they never had." Though Martin Luther attacked Zwingli's position as Pelagian, Zwingli defended his view of original sin by asking, "For what could be said more briefly and plainly than that original sin is not sin but disease, and that the children of Christians are not condemned to eternal punishment on account of that disease?" Zwingli distinguished between *disease* and *sin*. The word *disease* refers to the "original contamination of man," "defect of humanity," or "the defect of a corrupted nature." Adam's fault brought this to every person (Rom

---

[60] The term "Reformed" here refers to the Arminian-Calvinist tradition.

[61] Macleod, "Original Sin in Reformed Theology," 140.

[62] "With all due respect to the Reformed theology to which I am indebted, I have been led to question the doctrine of alien guilt transferred—that is, the doctrine of the imputation to all of Adam's own trespass, his act of transgression. If Scripture definitely taught such a doctrine, however offensive to modern taste, I should readily bow to its authority. But where does Scripture require it?" Blocher added, "I see no necessity for the idea that alien guilt was transferred (that is, that Adam's particular act was reckoned to the account of all). This idea is repugnant to common moral taste (including that of Christians), and finds no support in Scripture." However, Blocher affirmed a view which entails "guilty depravity." Henri Blocher, *Original Sin: Illuminating the Riddle*, New Studies in Biblical Theology 5, ed. D. A. Carson (Downers Grove, IL: InterVarsity, 1997), 128–30.

5:14). The word *sin*, however, "implies guilt, and guilt comes from a transgression or a trespass on the part of one who designedly perpetrates a deed." Zwingli was unwilling to state that the inheritance from Adam should even be called "sin" because Zwingli denied that the inheritance from Adam involves "guilt," which would imply a sinful deed.[63]

Though some Wesleyan-Arminians affirm inherited guilt, the view of **Jacob Arminius** (1560–1609) was consistent with inherited corruption.[64] Methodist theologian **John Miley** (1813–95) argued for "native depravity without native demerit."[65] Further, he rejected inherited guilt as "openly contradictory to the deepest and most determining principle of the Arminian system."[66] Miley described original sin as "the corruption of the nature of every man . . . whereby man is very far gone from original righteousness, and of his own nature inclined to evil, and that continually."[67]

Alvin Plantinga (b. 1932), a Reformed philosopher who especially identifies with the views of Thomas Aquinas and John Calvin, wrote, "Unlike a sinful act I perform, original sin need not be thought of as something for which I am culpable (original *sin* is not necessarily original *guilt*); insofar as I am born in this predicament, my being in it is not within my control and not up to me."[68] Plantinga distinguished among sinful acts, original sin, and original guilt. He affirmed the first two concepts but not original guilt.

Thomas H. McCall and **Oliver D. Crisp** are, like Plantinga, analytic theologians who reject inherited guilt. McCall, an Arminian, argued for the plausibility of other views but endorsed the "corruption-only" view, which is consistent with inherited consequences.[69] McCall explained, "We are, of course, guilty for sin. But we are guilty for the sins that *we commit*; we are not guilty for something that our

---

[63] Ulrich Zwingli, "On Original Sin," in *On Providence and Other Essays*, trans. S. Jackson (Durham, NC: Labyrinth, 1983), 3–10.

[64] See Keith D. Stanglin and Thomas H. McCall, *Jacob Arminius: Theologian of Grace* (Oxford: Oxford University Press, 2012), 149–50.

[65] John Miley, *Systematic Theology*, 2 vols. (New York: Eaton & Mains, 1892), 1:521.

[66] Miley, 1:522.

[67] Miley, 1:523.

[68] Alvin Plantinga, *Knowledge and Christian Belief* (Grand Rapids: Eerdmans, 2015), 49; italics in the original.

[69] The corruption-only theory "offers consistency with both explicit biblical teaching on sin and death and the broader witness to moral responsibility." McCall, *Against God and Nature*, 203.

first parents did."[70] He argued that original guilt is contrary to Scriptures that teach that the guilt of others is not imputed to us, such as Deut 24:16; Jer 31:29–30; and Ezek 18:20. McCall clarified, "Adam is guilty for his sins. And while we suffer the results of Adam's sin, it is our own sin for which we are guilty."[71] Crisp argued for a "moderate Reformed doctrine of original sin."[72] Crisp notes the "thin" biblical support for original guilt and points out that original guilt is not part of the church's "dogmatic core" of beliefs on original sin; only some Protestants affirm it.[73] He points out that the Anglican *Thirty-nine Articles of Religion* (1562) and Reformed *Belgic Confession* (1561) affirmed the corruption of human nature without any claim of inherited guilt.[74] "Original sin is an inherited corruption of nature," but people do not bear the guilt of Adam's sin. Rather, people are "culpable for their actual sin and condemned for it."[75]

Baptists Who Have Rejected Inherited Guilt

Though some Baptists affirm inherited guilt, many have explicitly rejected the view. English General Baptist **John Smyth** (1570–1612) wrote, "There is no original sin (lit., *no sin of origin or descent*), but all sin is actual and voluntary, viz., a word, a deed, or a design against the law of God; and therefore, infants are without sin."[76] **Edgar Y. Mullins** (1860–1928) rejected the doctrine of inherited guilt.[77] Rather, a man "is guilty when he does wrong." Mullins explained, "Men are not condemned therefore

---

[70] McCall, 161.

[71] McCall, 161.

[72] See Oliver D. Crisp, *Analyzing Doctrine: Toward a Systematic Theology* (Waco, TX: Baylor University Press, 2019), 139–55.

[73] Crisp, 145–46.

[74] Crisp, 147–48.

[75] Crisp, 152–53. Crisp also affirmed, "Possession of original sin leads to death and separation from God irrespective of actual sin" (p. 153). However, God can provide atonement for those who possess original sin yet do not attain moral accountability, such as infants and those with mental impairments (p. 150).

[76] See "A Short Confession of Faith in Twenty Articles by John Smyth," in William L. Lumpkin, *Baptist Confessions of Faith*, 2nd rev. ed., ed. Bill J. Leonard (Valley Forge, PA: Judson, 2011), 94; italics in the original.

[77] Edgar Y. Mullins was a pastor and professor of theology. At various times during the beginning of the previous century, he was president of The Southern Baptist Theological Seminary, the Southern Baptist Convention, and the Baptist World Alliance.

for hereditary or original sin. They are condemned only for their own sins."[78] **Walter T. Conner** (1877–1952) rejected inherited guilt. Conner reasoned that sin implies willful disobedience to God, which requires the knowledge of moral truth. Sin is universal, inevitable, and hereditary due to our relationship with Adam. There are thus "seeds of evil tendency in the child's nature," which will eventually result in the child committing an act of transgression upon reaching an "age of moral responsibility." Before that time, though, the child "does not have personal guilt" because he or she has not yet developed personal responsibility, namely "the powers of self-consciousness and self-determination."[79] Conner emphasized, "The idea that Adam's sin as an act of sin is charged to his descendants and on that account they are guilty and hence condemned, is an idea too preposterous to be seriously entertained."[80] **Stanley Grenz** (1950–2005) wrote, "Romans 5:12–21, like Ephesians 2:3, does not clearly and unequivocally declare that all persons inherit guilt directly because of Adam's sin. The biblical case for original guilt is not strong." Grenz concluded, "Our human nature has been corrupted."[81] He described the development of moral responsibility. "Somewhere in childhood we move from a stage in which our actions are not deemed morally accountable to the responsibility of acting as moral agents. In short, we cross a point which some refer to as the 'age of accountability.'"[82]

James Leo Garrett Jr. (1925–2020) provided historical perspective: "Southern Seminary has had a wide divergence of views on your topic; for example, between Boyce and Dale Moody and between Dale Moody and Al Mohler. Southwestern Seminary, on the other hand, has consistently been on one side: we are not guilty of Adam's sin. Walter T. Conner repeatedly took this stance." It is Garrett's testimony that for more than one century, the theology faculty at Southwestern Baptist Theological Seminary (SWBTS) has affirmed unanimously that people are *not guilty* of Adam's sin. Garrett explained, "Conner was in the theology department at SWBTS from 1910 to 1949. I have known, I believe, every person who has taught theology as a full faculty member since 1949, and I cannot identify any one of these who taught

---

[78] Edgar Y. Mullins, *The Christian Religion in Its Doctrinal Expression* (1917; repr., Valley Forge, PA: Judson Press, 1974), 302.

[79] Walter T. Conner, *Christian Doctrine* (Nashville: Broadman, 1937), 131–43. Conner taught theology at Southwestern Baptist Theological Seminary in Fort Worth, Texas from 1910–49.

[80] Walter T. Conner, *The Gospel of Redemption* (Nashville: Broadman, 1945), 29.

[81] Stanley J. Grenz, *Theology for the Community of God* (Grand Rapids: Eerdmans, 2000), 205.

[82] Grenz, 209.

that we are all guilty of the sin of Adam (and Eve), with one possible exception."[83] According to Garrett, the faculty of Southern Seminary have differed on the view of inherited guilt, but the faculty of Southwestern Seminary have always rejected it.

Billy Graham (1918–2018), a Baptist evangelist who declared the gospel to millions of people, commented on original sin. In Graham's view, Adam and Eve sinned by choice, and subsequent generations inherit "the tendency to sin" and also become "sinners by choice" due to their own sin and rebellion against God upon reaching the age of accountability.[84]

Baptist Confessions That Do Not Affirm Inherited Guilt

The major ecumenical councils of the first five centuries did not address original sin. Those councils addressed topics such as the Trinity and the humanity and divinity of Christ. Though some historic Baptist confessions affirmed inherited guilt,[85] others either did not affirm it or rejected the view. The First London Confession (1644), a Particular Baptist statement of faith, affirmed no theory of imputation.[86] It noted that Adam and Eve fell into disobedience, for which death came upon all. All are conceived in sin and brought forth in iniquity, and all are by nature children of wrath and subjects of death.[87] The statement was consistent with both inherited guilt and inherited consequences. The Faith and Practice of Thirty Congregations, Gathered According to the Primitive Pattern (1651) was the first General Baptist statement representing more than one church. In that statement, "all mankind are liable to

---

[83] The one possible exception was a new faculty member whose view Garrett did not know. James Leo Garrett Jr., correspondence to the author January 22, 2013, used with permission.

[84] Billy Graham, *World Aflame* (New York: Doubleday, 1965), 71.

[85] For a Baptist confession that affirmed inherited guilt, see the Second London Confession (1677, 1689). Chapter 6 portrayed Adam and Eve as representatives of humanity and declared that "the guilt of the *Sin* was imputed, and *corrupted* nature conveyed, to all their posterity." Second London Confession chap. 6, sec. 3, in Lumpkin, *Baptist Confessions of Faith*, 245. Though the Second London Confession followed the 1647 Westminster Confession of Faith (WCF) on many points, James Leo Garrett Jr. noted that the Second London Confession omitted the parent document's first section on guilt, WCF 6.6. James Leo Garrett Jr., *Baptist Theology: A Four-Century Study* (Macon, GA: Mercer University Press, 2009), 75n132.

[86] Garrett, *Baptist Theology*, 54, wrote about the First London Confession: "No specific theory of imputation is defended."

[87] See the First London Confession, art. 4, in Lumpkin, *Baptist Confessions of Faith*, 145.

partake of the same death or punishment" that fell on Adam for his transgression.[88] Jesus Christ suffered for every person, and he will raise all humanity "from that death which fell on them, through or by the first Adam's sin or offence, as surely as they partake of it."[89] In other words, death results from our certain participation in sin—not because Adam's guilt is imputed. The True Gospel Faith (1654) referred to Adam breaking God's law and declared that death was brought on himself and all his posterity—with no mention that his posterity inherits guilt.[90] The New Hampshire Confession (1833) declared "all mankind are now sinners, not by constraint but choice."[91]

The doctrine of inherited guilt is not contained in the Baptist Faith and Message (2000). Article 3 explained that Adam's "posterity inherit a nature and an environment inclined toward sin. Therefore, as soon as they are capable of moral action, they become transgressors and are under condemnation."[92] The article affirmed an inherited human inclination to commit sinful actions but did not affirm inherited guilt. It is reasonable to infer from the BFM that infants and young children have not yet reached an age (or stage) of moral accountability before God.[93] Rather, they will later become capable of moral actions and then will certainly transgress God's laws and fall under just condemnation. The first edition of the BFM, published in 1925, described humans as under condemnation *before* they become transgressors. Article 3 of that edition stated Adam's "posterity inherit a nature corrupt and in bondage to sin, are under condemnation, and as soon as they are capable of moral action, become actual transgressors." That section of the article, among others, was changed in 1963 and remained unchanged in the 2000 revision. **Herschel Hobbs** (1907–95) presided over the BFM 1963 Study Committee. Hobbs described the changes between the 1925 and 1963 editions of the BFM, commenting specifically on article 3.

---

[88] See the Faith and Practice of Thirty Congregations, Gathered According to the Primitive Pattern, statement 16, in Lumpkin, *Baptist Confessions of Faith*, 165.

[89] Thirty Congregations, 165.

[90] See True Gospel Faith, art. 2, in Lumpkin, *Baptist Confessions of Faith*, 176.

[91] New Hampshire Confession, art. 3, in Lumpkin, *Baptist Confessions of Faith*, 379.

[92] See The Baptist Faith and Message: Revised 2000, art. 3, in Lumpkin, *Baptist Confessions of Faith*, 514. Hereafter, the Baptist Faith and Message is BFM.

[93] Chad Brand, "Accountability, Age of," in Chad Brand et al., ed., *Holman Illustrated Bible Dictionary* (Nashville: Holman Bible, 2003), 17: "Age at which God holds children accountable for their sins. When persons come to this point, they face the inevitability of divine judgment if they fail to repent and believe the gospel."

The result of the fall is that men inherit, not "a nature corrupt and in bondage to sin" (1925), but a "nature and an environment inclined toward sin" (1963). In the latter "condemnation" comes upon individuals following transgression "as soon as they are capable of moral action." This, of course, agrees with the position generally held by Baptists concerning God's grace in cases of those under the age of accountability and the mentally incompetent.[94]

Hobbs was clear on the meaning of the revised statement of faith. People do *not* inherit "a nature corrupt and in bondage to sin" (per 1925) but a nature "inclined toward sin." Also, condemnation *follows* transgression, which comes as soon as people are capable of moral action. Although it was *possible* to read inherited guilt into the BFM 1925, the 1963 revision made such a move nearly impossible. Though not all Baptists today agree with Hobbs's interpretation, it is reasonable to suggest that Hobbs, who was the president of the Southern Baptist Convention that convened the study committee that revised the BFM in 1963, was articulating the view of the majority of his constituents.

The Impact of One's View of Original Sin on Other Doctrines

The Doctrines of Humanity and Christ

In previous writings, I argued for an "inherited sinful nature," the view that all people inherit from Adam a sinful nature, not his guilt.[95] Though I am in general agreement with the method and findings of those studies, I no longer refer to inheriting a *sinful nature* and prefer instead to refer to inherited *consequences*. The problem with affirming that people inherit a sinful *nature* is that if human nature is essentially and

---

[94] Herschel H. Hobbs, "Southern Baptists and Confessionalism: A Comparison of the Origins and Contents of the 1925 and 1963 Confessions," *Review and Expositor* 76, no. 1 (1979): 63. Peter Lumpkins first alerted me to this article.

[95] See Adam Harwood, *The Spiritual Condition of Infants: A Biblical-Historical Survey and Systematic Proposal* (Eugene, OR: Wipf & Stock, 2011); Adam Harwood, *Born Guilty?: A Southern Baptist View of Original Sin* (Carrollton, GA: Free Church Press, 2013); Adam Harwood, "Commentary on Article 2: The Sinfulness of Man," in Allen, Hankins, and Harwood, *Anyone Can Be Saved*, 37–53; Adam Harwood, "A Baptist View," in *Infants and Children in the Church: Five Views on Theology and Ministry*, ed. Adam Harwood and Kevin E. Lawson (Nashville: B&H Academic, 2017), 155–85.

inherently sinful, then Jesus (who was truly human and divine) would have been a person whose human nature was sinful. However, Scripture is clear there was no sin in him. Not only did Jesus not sin, but he also was not sinful in any way. If one affirms that human nature is essentially and inherently sinful *and* one denies that Jesus's human nature was sinful, then one would be affirming that Jesus's human nature was not truly human—a conclusion which would fail tests for orthodoxy that have been in place since the early ecumenical councils. Jesus was the perfect sacrifice for human sin because he was both truly divine and truly human.[96] The property of being sinful is common to fallen humanity but not essential to authentic human nature. Though it might be proper to refer to my human nature as corrupted and twisted, this is different than arguing for the existence of a thing called an inherited sinful nature.[97]

The Doctrine of Salvation

An explicit denial of inherited guilt sometimes raises this objection: How can one deny imputed guilt but affirm imputed righteousness? To reply, one must ask what the Bible teaches concerning the conditions required for a person to be counted righteous by God. Romans 3:21–22 states, "But now the righteousness of God has been manifested apart from the law, although the Law and the Prophets bear witness to it—the righteousness of God through faith in Jesus Christ for all who believe" (ESV; see also Rom 3:28 and 4:5). Romans 4:22–25 likewise affirms: "That is why his faith was 'counted to him as righteousness.' But the words 'it was counted to him' were not written for his sake alone, but for ours also. It will be counted to us who believe in him who raised from the dead Jesus our Lord, who was delivered up for our trespasses and raised for our justification" (ESV). Paul's point in Romans 3–4 is that others are made righteous in the same way as Abraham, by faith. In the Bible, being counted by God as righteous does not require one to affirm the imputation of Adam's guilt; one must only believe in Jesus.

---

[96] For the classic argument for this position, see Athanasius, *On the Incarnation of the Word*.

[97] See McCall, *Against God and Nature*, 207–18; and: "We are by nature 'children of wrath' (Eph 2:3) because the virus of sin has corrupted our inner being, but our lack of resistance to this virus is what renders us culpable before God. Our essential nature is good, for we are created in God's image; our existential nature is evil, for we have allowed the proclivity to sin to gain mastery over us. Guilt is not inherited, but the weakness that leads to sin is part of our human inheritance." Bloesch, *Jesus Christ*, 47.

When Can Sinners Repent and Believe?

The second question is addressed briefly: When can sinners repent of their sin and confess Jesus as Lord, to be saved? To answer that question, I will summarize and critique the doctrine of total depravity defined as total inability. If total depravity were defined only as humans are sinners in need of God's grace in Christ, then doctrinal differences would not emerge. However, total depravity is typically defined to include the views that all people are born spiritually dead and unable to repent of sin and call on the Lord unless they are first granted by God the gift of faith and the will to believe.[98]

Total Depravity as the Inability to Repent and Believe

The Canons of Dort is a document that resulted from the series of meetings held by the Dutch Reformed Church in the Netherlands in 1618–19 to address theological differences between the followers of Jacob Arminius and the followers of John Calvin. Three articles are quoted to support the definition above of total depravity.[99]

Article 3 stated, "Therefore, all people are conceived in sin and are born children of wrath, unfit for any saving good, inclined to evil, dead in their sins, and slaves to sin; without the grace of the regenerating Holy Spirit they are neither willing nor able to return to God, to reform their distorted nature, or even to dispose themselves to such reform."[100] The distinction in their view is that people do not become children of wrath due to their sinful acts, but they enter the world as children of wrath. Also, sinners are unable to return to God apart from the regenerating work of the Spirit. In other words, sinners must be saved to return to God.

Article 9 stated, "The fact that many who are called through the ministry of the gospel do not come and are not brought to conversion must not be blamed on the gospel, nor on Christ, who is offered through the gospel, nor on God, who

---

[98] Though it is possible to define total depravity without including total inability, the doctrine is not typically defined that way in the theological literature. Thus, the doctrine of depravity in this chapter includes inability.

[99] The articles are from the section titled, "The Third and Fourth Main Points of Doctrine: Human Corruption, Conversion to God, and the Way It Occurs." See the text in "The Canons of the Synod of Dort, 1618–19," in *Creeds and Confessions of Faith in the Christian Tradition*, ed. Jaroslav Pelikan and Valerie Hotchkiss, vol. 2, *Creeds and Confessions of the Reformation Era* (New Haven, CT: Yale University Press, 2003), 569–600.

[100] "Synod of Dort," 2:584.

calls them through the gospel and even bestows various gifts on them, but on the people themselves who are called."[101] Although the confession claimed sinners *cannot* return to God unless they are first regenerated, article 9 blames sinners when they are not converted.

Article 14 stated, "Faith is a gift of God, not in the sense that it is offered by God for man to choose, but that it is in actual fact bestowed on man, breathed and infused into him. Nor is it a gift in the sense that God bestows only the potential to believe, but then awaits assent—the act of believing—from man's choice; rather, it is a gift in the sense that he who works both willing and acting and, indeed, works all things in all people produces in man both the will to believe and the belief itself."[102] Other Christians view salvation as the gift of God and faith as the means for that salvation. The confession, however, views faith as the gift of God, which he gives to only some people. Thus, only those people who have been given a gift of faith will be saved.

The doctrine of total depravity is explained as total inability in the writings of some theologians. James Boice and Philip Ryken explained, "In this sad and pervasively sinful state we have no inclination to seek God, and therefore *cannot* seek him or even respond to the gospel when it is presented to us. In our unregenerate state, we do not have free will so far as 'believing on' or 'receiving' Jesus Christ as Savior is concerned."[103] They clarified that unbelievers "cannot" respond to the gospel by repenting and believing in Jesus when it is presented. Consistent with article 3 in the Canons of Dort, they taught that a person believes in Jesus *after* they are born again. Mark DeVine wrote, "Humanity's fall into sin results in a condition that must be described in terms of spiritual blindness and deadness and in which the will is enslaved, not free." DeVine continued, "We need to ask whether the Arminian insistence that the work of the Holy Spirit frees the will to either repent and believe or refuse to do so does not evidence a deeper misunderstanding of the nature of depravity itself."[104] John Piper wrote, "Faith is the evidence of new birth, not the cause of it."[105] "Regeneration precedes faith," R. C. Sproul explained. He added, "We do not

---

[101] "Synod of Dort," 2:585.

[102] "Synod of Dort," 2:587.

[103] James Montgomery Boice and Philip Graham Ryken, *The Doctrines of Grace: Rediscovering the Evangelical Gospel* (Wheaton, IL: Crossway, 2009), 30; italics in the original.

[104] Mark DeVine, "Total Depravity," in Barrett and Nettles, *Whomever He Wills*, 35 (see intro., n. 22).

[105] John Piper, *Desiring God: Meditations of a Christian Hedonist* (Sisters, OR: Multnomah, 1986), 50.

believe in order to be born again; we are born again in order to believe."[106] R. Albert Mohler Jr. also affirmed that regeneration precedes faith:

> In the mystery of the sovereign purposes of God and by his sheer grace and mercy alone, the Word was brought near to us. As a result, we were called, made alive, and regenerated. We then believed what we otherwise would never have been able to believe, and we grasped hold of it, knowing that it is the sole provision of our need. We came to know of our need and of God's response and provision for us in Christ, and then we came to know of our necessary response of faith, repentance, confession, and belief.[107]

According to these views of total depravity, spiritual blindness and deadness results in the enslavement of the human will so that people do not have the ability to repent and believe the message of the gospel unless they are first regenerated, or born again.

The Implications of Total Depravity as the Inability to Repent and Believe

If total depravity as the inability to repent and believe is true, then two implications follow. First, people are able to exercise faith in Christ only if and after God gives them the gift of faith through the grace of regeneration. Second, all commands and invitations in the Bible to repent and believe can be obeyed only by people to whom God first gives faith and who are first born again by the Holy Spirit. These implications are supported by those who affirm the doctrine. Loraine Boettner wrote, "The regeneration of the soul is something which is wrought in us, and not an act performed by us. It is an instantaneous change from spiritual death to spiritual life. It is not even a thing of which we are conscious at the moment it occurs, but rather something which lies lower than consciousness. At the moment of its occurrence the soul is as passive as was Lazarus when he was called back to life by Jesus."[108] Boettner described salvation as something that occurs to a spiritually dead person. He compared the passive nature of the salvation of a spiritually dead person as analogous to the physical resuscitation

---

[106] Robert C. Sproul, *Chosen by God* (Wheaton, IL: Tyndale, 1986), 72.

[107] R. Albert Mohler Jr., "The Power of the Articulated Gospel," in *The Underestimated Gospel*, ed. Jonathan Leeman (Nashville: B&H, 2014), 19.

[108] Loraine Boettner, *The Reformed Doctrine of Predestination* (1932; repr., Grand Rapids: Eerdmans, 1960), 165.

of a physically dead person. Thomas J. Nettles wrote, "Regeneration of sinners is like the birth of a baby, who is actually passive in the process and comes into life as a result of the work of outside forces. The child has nothing to do with being born. Being born again, according to Jesus, is like that."[109] Nettles compared being born again spiritually to being born physically; in both instances, he claimed, the person is passive in the process. Matthew Barrett clarified the reason why only some people are saved: "God promises that eternal life will be granted on the condition of faith. However, God never promises that He will bestow faith on everyone."[110] For Barrett, as well as others in this perspective, God saves only those people to whom he grants faith.

A Biblical Case for the Ability of Sinners to Repent and Believe for Salvation

A Biblical Theology of Repentance

In the Old Testament the primary word for repentance means "to turn back" (*šûb*).[111] Jeremiah used the term when he declared that Jerusalem "refused to repent" (Jer 5:3). God's people refused to turn away from their sinful actions and return to him. One resource described the Hebrew word this way: "The basic meaning of return or change in direction is used metaphorically to express repentance as a change in direction away from sinful actions toward obedience to God."[112] In the New Testament the key words are the noun "repentance" (*metanoia*) and the verb "to repent" (*metanoeō*). John the Baptist and Jesus began their public ministries by declaring that people should repent (Matt 3:2; 4:17). They used the imperative form of the word, which means they were issuing a command. Jesus denounced the cities that did not repent (Matt 11:20), which implies that they could repent but refused to do so. In his sermon at Pentecost, Peter identified Jesus as the crucified and risen Christ and commanded that people repent (Acts 2:38). In his sermon at Mars Hill, Paul declared that God

---

[109] Thomas J. Nettles, *By His Grace and For His Glory: A Historical, Theological, and Practical Study of the Doctrines of Grace in Baptist Life* (Lake Charles, LA: Cor Meum Tibi, 2002), 289.

[110] Matthew Barrett, "The Scriptural Affirmation of Monergism," in Barrett and Nettles, *Whomever He Wills*, "Monergism," 124 (see intro., n. 22).

[111] For a comprehensive biblical theology of repentance, see Mark J. Boda, *"Return to Me": A Biblical Theology of Repentance*, New Studies in Biblical Theology, ed. D. A. Carson (Downers Grove, IL: IVP Academic, 2015).

[112] Lesley DiFransico, "Repentance," in *Lexham Theological Wordbook*.

"commands all people everywhere to repent" (Acts 17:30b). Repentance has been defined as "the acknowledgement and condemnation of one's own sins, coupled with a turning to God."[113] Kenneth Keathley identified genuine repentance of the whole person—mind, body, and will—in the story of the prodigal son (Luke 15:11–24). The younger son evidenced a change in his thinking (v. 17), his emotions (v. 19), and his will (v. 18).[114] Godly sorrow leads to repentance, which results in salvation (2 Cor 7:10). In the Old and New Testaments, people who repent of their sin and turn to God receive healing, restoration, and salvation.

A Biblical Theology of Faith/Believing

The word *faith* rarely appears in the Old Testament as a noun.[115] The primary word used is a verb translated "to believe" (*'mn*). For example, Abram *believed* the Lord, and the Lord considered Abram's response as righteousness (Gen 15:6). Also, when Judah was threatened with invasion, King Jehoshaphat led his people to seek the Lord and his help. The prophet Jahaziel declared they would see the salvation of the Lord. Before the victory, the king told the people, "*Believe* in the LORD your God, and you will be established; *believe* in his prophets, and you will succeed" (2 Chron 20:20 CSB; emphasis added).[116] The people believed the Lord and the Lord delivered them. As a final example, upon hearing the prophet's warning that their great city would be overthrown in forty days, "the Ninevites *believed* God" (Jonah 3:5; emphasis added). Rather than referring to faith as a concept, Old Testament authors referred to people who believed, or trusted, God.

Believing in Jesus is a foundational concept in the New Testament. The concept of faith appears 243 times as a noun (*pistis*, "faith") and 241 times as a verb (*pistueō*, "to believe"). To have faith is to believe. In the New Testament, the Old Testament concept of believing God incorporates believing his Son. Jesus marveled

---

[113] Frank L. Cross and Elizabeth A. Livingstone, eds., *The Oxford Dictionary of the Christian Church*, 3rd ed. rev. (Oxford: Oxford University Press, 2005), 1393.

[114] Kenneth Keathley, "The Work of God in Salvation," in *A Theology for the Church*, rev. ed., ed. Daniel L. Akin (Nashville: B&H Academic, 2014), 575–76.

[115] The word *faith* appears only four times in the Old Testament in the NASB (Deut 32:51; Job 39:12; Ps 146:6; Hab 2:4).

[116] In a clever wordplay in the Hebrew, the verb forms *haaminu* ("trust") and *theamenu* ("you will be safe") come from the same root verb, *'mn* ("to believe"). *The NET Bible First Edition Notes* (n.p.: Biblical Studies, 2006), 2 Chron 20:20.

at the faith of the centurion (Matt 8:10), saw the faith of the paralytic's friends (Matt 9:2; Mark 2:5), and told the bleeding woman that her faith made her well (Matt 9:22; Mark 5:34). Paul described the message he preached to both Jews and Greeks, "They must turn to God in repentance and have faith in our Lord Jesus" (Acts 20:21). In John's Gospel, faith is never a noun (*pistis*, "faith") but always a verb (*pistueō*, "to believe"). The emphasis is striking because other biblical authors use both terms. John's exclusive use in his Gospel of the verb reveals a point that the author intended to make to his audience. John had no interest in mentioning faith or belief as a concept. However, John uses the verb "to believe" ninety-six times to emphasize the need for people to believe in Jesus.

The terms for belief can refer to knowledge or trust. Some people believe only in the sense that they know something to be true (knowledge). But mental assent *only* to theological truth will not save a person. Consider, as examples, that demons believe (*pisteuein*, "to believe") that there is one God (Jas 2:19), and demons addressed Jesus as Son of the Most High God (Mark 5:7). Those statements of theological truth were uttered by demons who were not and never will be saved. Salvation requires repenting of sin and believing Christ in the sense that one is personally entrusting themselves to Christ. Paul wrote that we are saved by grace through faith (Eph 2:8). Salvation is a gift of God that is received by faith or trusting in Christ. Keathley rightly stated, "Faith is the instrument by which we accept salvation."[117]

A Biblical Theology of Spiritual Death

Scripture reveals various metaphors for sinners who have not yet repented of their sin and trusted in Jesus for their salvation. They are referred to as sick (Matt 9:12), blind (Matt 15:14; 2 Cor 4:4), lovers of darkness (John 3:19), and dead (Luke 15:24; John 5:24; Eph 2:1). Some Christians misinterpret spiritual deadness to mean a person *cannot* repent of sin and believe in Jesus unless God first grants them faith. However, Scripture does not require that view.[118] Rather, such an interpretation says more than Scripture and is contrary to the plain meaning of several texts. Faith is

---

[117] Keathley, "God in Salvation," 577.
[118] See David L. Allen, "Does Regeneration Precede Faith?" *Journal for Baptist Theology & Ministry* 11, no. 2 (Fall 2014): 34–52.

the means of salvation.[119] To assert that God grants faith to only some people is to wrongly affirm that God desires only some people to believe in Jesus.[120]

Consider the metaphor of spiritual deadness. In the garden, Adam and Eve, who died spiritually when they ate the fruit, were able to hear from and respond to God (Gen 3:10–13). In the parable of the prodigal son, the spiritually dead person (the son) was able to return to his father (Luke 15:24). Like the two previous parables (vv. 7, 10), the son returning to the father depicts a sinner's repentance. The spiritually dead son was able to repent of his sin and return to his father. In John 5:24, a spiritually dead person is able to hear and believe in Jesus. In the story of the raising of Lazarus, Jesus raised his friend from *physical* death (John 11). As already noted, some Christians conflate the metaphor of being raised from *spiritual* death (Eph 2:1) with the story of Lazarus being raised from *literal* death. Ronnie W. Rogers noted, "I disaffirm that the technical meaning of being spiritually dead is adequately illustrated by using Lazarus or dead people in a cemetery, etc., in order to show that like them, the lost who are dead in sin cannot believe until they have been given life—regenerated. This picture is contrary to the panoply of Scripture. For example, Rom 10:9 says, 'If you confess . . . and believe in your heart' which no physically dead graveyard man can do, but a spiritually dead man, by the grace of God, can do."[121] Affirming that people are spiritually dead does not require a denial that sinners can repent and believe in Jesus.[122] In Scripture, spiritually dead people can and do respond to God.

Paul's remark in Acts 17:30 indicates who God commands to repent of sin. Paul declared, "In the past God overlooked such ignorance, but now he commands all people everywhere to repent." The preaching of the apostles included the call to repent of sin and believe in Jesus to be saved (see Acts 2:38; 3:19; 8:22; 20:21; 26:20). The command to repent implies that people are *able* to repent. It would be unjust for God to command a task then judge people who could not comply for failing to do that which he commanded.[123] God, who desires the salvation of every

---

[119] People are saved by grace *through* faith (Eph 2:8).

[120] For the case that God desires every person to be saved through faith in Jesus, see Allen, Hankins, and Harwood, *Anyone Can Be Saved.*

[121] Ronnie W. Rogers, *Reflections of a Disenchanted Calvinist: The Disquieting Realities of Calvinism* (Bloomington, IN: CrossBooks, 2012), 22.

[122] Rogers, 21; see also Rogers, *Does God Love All or Some? Comparing Biblical Extensivism and Calvinism's Exclusivism* (Eugene, OR: Wipf & Stock, 2019), 160–65.

[123] "If someone is going to be condemned because they personally failed to do something (in this case, to believe), then they must have been capable of doing it in the first place. Otherwise no guilt could attach to their action, and their condemnation would be unjust." John C. Lennox,

person and commands every person to repent and believe in Jesus, draws every person to himself (John 12:32).

Baptist confessions affirm both the sinfulness of humanity as well as the ability of sinners to repent and believe in Jesus. Article 6 of the New Hampshire Confession (1833), titled "Of the Freeness of Salvation," stated, "Nothing prevents the salvation of the greatest sinner on earth except his own voluntary refusal to submit to the Lord Jesus Christ, which refusal will subject him to an aggravated condemnation."[124] Rather than describing people as unable to respond to God, the confession claimed that "nothing prevents" a sinner's salvation except the sinner's "voluntary refusal." According to "The Faith of Free Will Baptists" (2013), "the call of the Gospel is coextensive with the atonement to all men, both by the word and strivings of the Spirit, so that salvation is rendered equally possible to all; and if any fail of eternal life, the fault is wholly his own."[125]

All Christians should affirm that sin separates them from the God whom Scripture declares to be "holy, holy, holy" (Rev 4:8). It was our sin combined with his love for us, the world, which resulted in God giving his Son to die on the cross so that whoever believes in him will be saved (John 3:16; Rom 5:8). All Christians must also affirm that people are saved by God's grace through faith, not by their works (Eph 2:8–9). The doctrine of total depravity, however, affirms much more than the sinfulness of humanity and the grace of God. The doctrine of total depravity, when defined as total inability, insists that people respond to God in repentance and faith only *after* they are born again. In other words, people repent and believe *because* they are born again. A better interpretation of the Bible, however, is that people are saved from sin and reconciled to God when and *because* they repent of their sin and believe in Jesus (see Mark 1:15; Acts 3:19; 20:21; 16:31).

Determined to Believe? The Sovereignty of God, Freedom, Faith, and Human Responsibility (Grand Rapids: Zondervan, 2018), 145.

[124] In 1853, J. Newton Brown added or changed the italicized portions: "Nothing prevents the salvation of the greatest sinner on earth *but* his own *inherent depravity and* voluntary *rejection of the gospel*, which *rejection involves him in* an aggravated condemnation." Though the 1853 edition mentions depravity, both editions indict the individual sinner for rejecting the gospel. See the New Hampshire Confession, art. 6, "Of the Freeness of Salvation," in Lumpkin, *Baptist Confessions of Faith*, 363.

[125] "The Gospel Call," chap. 8 in "The Faith of Free Will Baptists," pt. 2 in *A Treatise of the Faith and Practices of the National Association of Free Will Baptists, Inc.* (Antioch, TN: National Association of Free Will Baptists, 2013), 10.

Conclusion

In this chapter I presented two views of original sin and advocated for inherited corruption against inherited guilt. I also argued for total depravity as the inability to save oneself rather than the inability to repent and believe in Jesus. Though Christians differ on these details of original sin and total depravity, they are united on declaring that all people are sinners in need of God's grace that is available only through the death and resurrection of Jesus. As these doctrinal discussions continue, may we be faithful witnesses of the crucified, risen, and returning Son.

2

A Critique of Unconditional Election

—— Leighton Flowers ——

Election simply means a "choice." When we speak of "divine election," therefore, we are referring to the choice, or even choices, of God. Simple enough, right? Well, theologians have been known to overcomplicate relatively simple biblical concepts. My goal is to bring it back to the basics. All I ask of you is to be cognizant of your own theological presumptions and be willing to objectively set them aside to consider what may be a different perspective.

Systematic theology can be a wonderful tool to help navigate the many doctrines of the Bible by organizing them according to categories. A potential downside to the systematic approach, however, is overcomplication through the conflating of those categories and adding unbiblical philosophical baggage to the meaning of words, in an attempt to make one's own theological system fit within the whole of Scripture. I firmly believe this is what has happened with the *doctrine of divine election*, particularly influenced by Westernized individualism, and most clearly demonstrated by the theological system known as Calvinism.[1]

---

[1] "From Augustine of Hippo to the twentieth century, Western Christianity has tended to interpret the doctrine of election from the perspective of and with regard to individual human

The otherwise simple idea of God making choices has been systematized in such a way to align virtually all God's choices within one overarching soteriological category—thus limiting the biblical concept of *election* to the unilateral choice of God to save some people rather than others—regardless of the beliefs, choices, or behaviors of the individual, even from before the person was created.[2] According to this approach, the biblical doctrine of divine election has a hyperfocus on soteriology—the doctrine of salvation—and tends to make huge categorical errors when interpreting the Scriptures.[3] Therefore, my goal in this chapter is to uncover some of these perceived errors by going back to the basics of what the Scriptures teach regarding all that God has chosen to do in the redemption and reconciliation of fallen humanity.

More Than One Kind of Choice

The Bible talks about at least four different kinds of divine choices when it comes to the plan of redemption and the fulfillment of the gospel:

---

beings. During those same centuries the doctrine has been far less emphasized and seldom ever controversial in Eastern Orthodoxy. Is it possible that Augustine and later Calvin, with the help of many others, contributed to a hyper-individualization of this doctrine that was hardly warranted by Romans 9–11, Eph. 1, and I Peter 2? Is it not true that the major emphasis in both testaments falls upon an elect people—Israel (OT) and disciples or church (NT)?" James Leo Garrett Jr., *Systematic Theology: Biblical, Historical, and Evangelical,* 2 vols. (Grand Rapids: Eerdmans, 1995), 2:500.

[2] In John Calvin's words, "God foresaw no good in man, save that which he had already previously determined to bestow by means of his election." Calvin, *Institutes of the Christian Religion,* 2 vols., trans. Henry Beveridge (Grand Rapids: Eerdmans, 1975), 2:217 (3.22.5). Additionally, "We say, then, that Scripture clearly proves this much, that God by his eternal and immutable counsel determined once for all those whom it was his pleasure one day to admit to salvation, and those whom, on the other hand, it was his pleasure to doom to destruction. We maintain that this counsel, as regards the elect, is founded on his free mercy, without any respect to human worth, while those whom he dooms to destruction are excluded from access to life by a just and blameless, but at the same time incomprehensible judgment." Calvin, 2:210–11 (3.21.7).

[3] As Norman Geisler observed, "John Piper, widely held by extreme Calvinists to have the best treatment on Romans 9, makes this mistake. Piper claimed that 'the divine decision to "hate" Esau was made "before they were born or had done anything good *or evil*" (9:11).' But, as shown on the previous page, the reference here is not to something said in Genesis about the *individuals* Jacob and Esau *before they were born.* What Genesis 25 says is simply that the older would serve the younger. What is said in Malachi 1:2–3 about the nations of Jacob and Esau (Edom) is not only centuries after their progenitors had died, but it is also in regard to what the nation of Edom had done to the chosen *nation* of Israel." Geisler, *Chosen but Free: A Balanced View of Divine Election,* 2nd ed. (Minneapolis: Bethany House, 2001), 85; italics in the original.

1. the election of a nation,
2. the election of messengers from that nation,
3. the election of those who would hear their message, and
4. that which pertains to soteriology, the election to save those who believe that message.

All these choices of God can be said to be "unconditional" in that none of them are based upon the morality, strength, nationality, or other unique personal qualities of those being chosen (i.e., they are not chosen based upon the good or bad things they do in life). This is different, however, from an "arbitrary choice," which for the purpose of this chapter will be defined as:

> subject to individual will or judgment without restriction; contingent solely upon one's discretion; decided by a judge or arbiter rather than by a law or statute; having unlimited power; uncontrolled or unrestricted by law.[4]

A clear distinction must be drawn between the biblical choices of God, which are not conditioned upon the merits of those chosen, versus the Calvinist system, which logically entails the unbiblical principle that God secretly made *arbitrary* choices before the foundation of the world, unilaterally fixing the eternal destiny of every individual.[5] To this point, there is disagreement among Calvinists, as John Calvin[6]

---

[4] *Collins English Dictionary*, 2012 digital ed., s.v. "arbitrary," https://www.dictionary.com /browse/arbitrary.

[5] Some representative quotes from Calvin's *Institutes* (Beveridge trans.) suffice to illustrate this principle. Accordingly, "if we cannot assign any reason for his bestowing mercy on his people, but just that it so pleases him, neither can we have any reason for his reprobating others but his will" (2:224 [3.22.11]). "Many professing a desire to defend the Deity from an invidious charge admit the doctrine of election, but deny that any one is reprobated (Bernard, in *Die Ascensionis*, Serm. 2). This they do ignorantly and childishly since there could be no election without its opposite reprobation. . . . Those, therefore, whom God passes by he reprobates, and that for no other cause but because he is pleased to exclude them from the inheritance which he predestines to his children" (2:225–26 [3.23.1]). "Now, since the arrangement of all things is in the hand of God, since to him belongs the disposal of life and death, he arranges all things by his sovereign counsel, in such a way that individuals are born, who are doomed from the womb to certain death, and are to glorify him by their destruction" (2:231 [3.23.6]).

[6] As Calvin commented: "There are some, too, who allege that God is greatly dishonored if such *arbitrary power* is bestowed on Him. But does their distaste make them better theologians than Paul, who has laid it down as the rule of humility for the believers, that they should look up to the sovereignty of God and not evaluate it by their own judgment?" *The Epistles of Paul the Apostle to the Romans and Thessalonians*, in *Calvin's New Testament Commentaries*, 12 vols., trans.

and Jonathan Edwards[7] openly acknowledged the arbitrary nature of the Calvinist doctrine of unconditional election, while other Calvinists do not.[8] In fact, one notable Calvinist pastor, Sam Storms, candidly acknowledged the inherent nature of "partiality" or favoritism within Calvinism.[9]

Let us look at each of these four divine choices, one at a time, to avoid making this common error of conflating them with one another: the election of a nation, the election of messengers from that nation, the election of those to whom the message will be sent, and the election to grant entrance to all who believe the message.

1. The Election of a Nation

God chose the nation of Israel to be the people through whom all the families of the earth would be blessed (Deut 7:6–8; Acts 3:25). He did not choose Israel to the

---

R. MacKenzie, ed. David W. Torrance and Thomas F. Torrance (Grand Rapids: Eerdmans, 1995), 8:209–10; emphasis added.

[7] In his popular sermon, "Sinners in the Hands of an Angry God" (preached at Enfield, Connecticut, July 8, 1741), Jonathan Edwards referred to God's will in election as "arbitrary," as seen here: "The observation from the words that I would now insist upon is this.—'There is nothing that keeps wicked men at any one moment out of hell, but the mere pleasure of God.'— By the *mere* pleasure of God, I mean his *sovereign* pleasure, his *arbitrary will* [emphasis mine], restrained by no obligation, hindered by no manner of difficulty, any more than if nothing else but God's mere will had in the least degree, or in any respect whatsoever, any hand in the preservation of wicked men one moment." In *The Works of Jonathan Edwards*, 2 vols., rev. Edward Hickman (Edinburgh: Banner of Truth, 1992), 2:7; italics in the original.

[8] Robert A. Peterson and Michael D. Williams make this important distinction: "His gracious choosing ultimately transcends our reason, but it is *not arbitrary*." Peterson and Williams, *Why I Am Not an Arminian* (Downers Grove, IL: InterVarsity, 2004), 66; emphasis added. Calvinists who affirm that God's choice of persons in election is arbitrary mean that it is according to his good pleasure; those who deny God's choice is arbitrary mean that it is not arbitrary because it is not without reasons—God has his own reasons for his choices, i.e., his own good pleasure. So, the disagreement is largely peripheral. Both agree that election is simply out of God's good pleasure.

[9] Storms somewhat shockingly puts it: "So, does the Calvinistic doctrine of unconditional divine election and monergistic regeneration make God 'a respecter of persons, arbitrary, and morally ambiguous'? Or again, God is not impartial, say many Arminians, if he favors some with life but not all. He is guilty of showing partiality toward the elect. *Of course he is!* That is what unconditional election is all about. But we should refrain from saying that God is 'guilty' of being partial toward the elect because *this kind of partiality is a virtue, not a vice. It is a divine prerogative for which God should be praised, not vilified.*" Sam Storms, "Does Unconditional Election Make God 'A Respecter of Persons'?" (blog), Oklahoma City, OK, November 11, 2014, https://www.samstorms.org/enjoying-god-blog/post/does-unconditional-election-make -god-a-respecter-of-persons; italics in the original.

neglect of all the other nations in the world; on the contrary, he did so to bless (or bring the means of redemption) to them all (Gen 12:3). This text suggests that no aspect of divine election should ever be thought of as pitting those chosen against everyone else, as if God arbitrarily shows favoritism.[10]

Suppose a warden of a prison chose one undeserving prisoner to deliver gifts to all the other undeserving prisoners. Does the warden's choice reflect any unexplained bias or unilateral favoritism? No, of course not. His choice benefits all the prisoners and does not neglect any of them. So, too, God's choices concerning undeserving Israelites are for the benefit of all whom he has created, even though no one deserves the provision he graciously sends through Israel. As the psalmist wrote, "The LORD is gracious and compassionate, slow to anger and great in faithful love. The LORD is good to everyone; his compassion rests on all he has made" (Ps 145:8–9).

God's choice of the nation of Israel shows the corporate aspect of God's election, which involves his plan of redemption made available for all individuals. His election of this small nation is not based on their superior morality or innate worth as a people; the Jews were no more worthy of being selected than any other nation God could have chosen to fulfill his redemptive purposes (Deut 7:6–8). But a key fact must be noted here: God's choice of the nation did not ensure the salvation of any particular individual within that nation because the choice was not primarily a choice of *salvation* for any of the individuals. Instead, it was a choice of a people for a particular redemptive purpose to *serve* as his witness for the greater blessing of the world. So we must refrain from misapplying passages that speak of God's unconditional choice of Israel to be a blessing to the world (e.g., Gen 28:14) as some sort of proof text for the unbiblical concept that God arbitrarily chose to effectually save some individuals to the neglect of the rest of the world.[11]

---

[10] "Opening his mouth, Peter said: 'I most certainly understand now that God is not one to show partiality, but in every nation the man who fears Him and does what is right is welcome to Him'" (Acts 10:34–35 NASB1995).

[11] This error is committed by John MacArthur: "Deuteronomy 7:6 and 14:2 says, 'The Lord your God has chosen you to be a people for his own possession out of all the peoples that are on the face of the earth.' And God said it wasn't because you were better than any other people, it wasn't because you were more attractive than any other people. God said it is because I of my own free will predetermined to set my love upon you and for no other reason. Israel, mine elect. God calls them." John MacArthur, "The Doctrine of Election, Part 1," (sermon 90-273), Grace to You, September 19, 2004, https://www.gty.org/library/sermons-library/90-273/the -doctrine-of-election-part-1.

2. The Election of Messengers

God chose and appointed messengers (prophets in the Old Testament and apostles in the New Testament) to deliver his revealed truth to the entire world (John 15:16; Acts 10:41). These messengers, like the nation from which they came, were not chosen because they were more moral, significant, or impressive. In fact, they were often immoral, insignificant, and unimpressive (1 Cor 1:26). Once again, it should be noted that God's choice of Israelites to deliver a message of salvation was not equal to their being individually and arbitrarily chosen for effectual salvation before time began. And they certainly were not chosen to the neglect of all the rest of humanity. Quite the opposite is true; these messengers from Israel were chosen to bring the good news of God's love and provision for all people of the earth (Luke 2:10). So one should not pluck out proof texts relating to God's unconditional choice of messengers to support the unbiblical Calvinistic concept that God unilaterally chooses which individuals will or will not be effectually made to believe their message.

For example, does God's choice of the messenger Jonah, a servant chosen to carry invitations to Nineveh, equally represent his choice of any particular Ninevite who might respond willingly to this invitation? Does the fact that God used externally persuasive means, like a storm and a big fish, to convince Jonah to obey prove that God used internally irresistible means (like effectual grace) to cause preselected Ninevites to respond willingly to Jonah's invitation? If so, the text certainly never draws that conclusion and, therefore, neither should we. Likewise, some may be tempted to point to the calling of Paul on the road to Damascus as an example of God's *effectual calling* of some to salvation.[12] Others might be tempted to use passages such as John 15:16 ("You did not choose me, but I chose you") as proof texts for the Calvinistic belief of individual election to salvation, when clearly Jesus was speaking to his servants (Luke 6:13) who were being prepared to take the invitation to the rest of the world.[13]

---

[12] As is John MacArthur: "The conversion of the apostle Paul was abrupt, startling, shocking. The man was on his way to persecute Christians. He was supernaturally, divinely converted on the spot, transformed and called to be an apostle because God had chosen him to that before the world began." John MacArthur, "The Sovereignty of God in Salvation," (sermon 80-46T), Grace to You, June 22, 1980, https://www.gty.org/library/sermons-library/80-46/the-sovereignty-of-god-in-salvation.

[13] MacArthur succumbs to this temptation: "And in John 15:16, that wonderful statement of Jesus to the disciples in which He says: 'You did not choose Me, but I chose you and appointed you that you should go and bear fruit.' We didn't choose Him. He chose us. We didn't decide for Christ—in the truest sense—He decided for us." MacArthur, "Sovereignty of God."

3. The Election of Hearers

God chose to invite people of all tribes, nations, and tongues into a covenant with him through faith. This gospel invitation was first sent to the Jews and then to the Gentiles (Matt 22:9–10; Mark 16:15; Rom 1:16; 10:11–13). God sends his message of redemption to "both evil and good" people alike (Matt 22:10), as his mission is "to seek and to save the lost" (Luke 19:10). This truth demonstrates that "God doesn't show favoritism" (Acts 10:34), and his message is for all sinners who need a Savior (Rev 22:17).

Once again, this choice of God is not conditioned upon the morality, impressiveness, or significance of those being chosen. If anything, the condition for his choice is one's weakness and lack of qualification. As with the divine choices spoken of before, this is not about individuals being arbitrarily chosen before the foundation of the world to be effectually caused to believe unto salvation. This is about the redemptive choice of God to send his message of salvation to every man, woman, boy, and girl, regardless of their nationality, morality, or other seemingly worthy quality. Christians must be careful not to remove from their context passages that address God's desire to grant all sinners the means of reconciliation, to support the unbiblical Calvinistic idea that God unilaterally chooses to effectuate faith in some individuals while withholding that moral ability from all others.[14]

4. The Election of Believers

God chooses to grant entrance into his kingdom to whosoever comes clothed in the righteousness of his Son through faith (Matt 22:14; John 3:16). Those permitted to

---

Calvinists know that John 15:16 refers to an election to discipleship rather than salvation, especially since Judas was included, yet strangely insist that what applies to election to discipleship also applies to salvation. When Jesus emphasized that he is the caller, it was not to demean them but to emphasize his purposes for them, which Jesus had to do since their messianic expectations were not in line with what God had in store.

[14] Many Calvinists use passages that speak of God "granting" or "enabling" the lost to believe or repent to argue that God has given repentance or faith to some individuals but not others, yet these passages simply represent the King's sovereign choice to send his invitation first to the Jews (so they may believe and repent) and then to the Gentiles (so they too may believe and repent). Faith comes by hearing and thus "God has given (i.e., granted or enabled) repentance resulting in life even to the Gentiles" (Acts 11:18), by sending them the invitation to believe and repent. How can they believe in one they have not heard (Rom 10:14)? How can they come to the banquet without an invitation? By inviting all sinners, he is granting or enabling them the ability to come.

enter are not given this right because they are of noble birth or in any way more morally qualified than anyone else (1 Cor 1:26–30). If anything, their only "qualification"
is that they humbly confess their lack of qualification by putting their trust in the
qualification of another, namely, Christ Jesus. They are granted entrance based on his
goodness, not their own. This divine choice, just like the three before it, is not conditioned upon the morality of the individual being chosen, but that does not necessarily
mean it is an arbitrary choice without any condition, as the Calvinistic system asserts.
The biblical condition is faith in Christ—being clothed in his righteousness.[15]

As referenced above, these four choices are most clearly illustrated in Christ's
parable of the wedding banquet recorded in the Gospel of Matthew:

> "The kingdom of heaven is like a king who gave a wedding banquet for his son.
> He sent his servants to summon those invited to the banquet, but they didn't
> want to come. Again, he sent out other servants and said, 'Tell those who are
> invited: See, I've prepared my dinner; my oxen and fattened cattle have been
> slaughtered, and everything is ready. Come to the wedding banquet.'
>
> "But they paid no attention and went away, one to his own farm, another
> to his business, while the rest seized his servants, mistreated them, and killed
> them. The king was enraged, and he sent out his troops, killed those murder-
> ers, and burned down their city.
>
> "Then he told his servants, 'The banquet is ready, but those who were
> invited were not worthy. Go then to where the roads exit the city and invite
> everyone you find to the banquet.' So those servants went out on the roads
> and gathered everyone they found, both evil and good. The wedding banquet
> was filled with guests. When the king came in to see the guests, he saw a man

---

[15] Calvinists often argue that a libertarian free decision to repent in faith would somehow
earn or merit one's forgiveness and salvation, but this is simply an unfounded assertion. Did the
prodigal son earn, merit, or in any way deserve the reception of his father on the basis that he
humbly returned home, believing that his father would help him? Of course not. He deserved
to be punished, not rewarded. His father's acceptance was a choice of the father alone, and it
was all of grace. The father did not have to forgive, restore, and throw a party for his son on
the basis that he chose to come home. That was the father's choice alone. It must also be noted
that humiliation and brokenness is not considered "better" or "praiseworthy" and is certainly not
inherently valuable. In fact, one could argue that it was weak and pitiful of the son to return
home and beg his dad for a job instead of working his own way out of that pigsty. The only thing
that makes this quality "desirable" is that God has chosen to grace those who humble themselves, something he is in no way obligated to do (Isa 66:2). God gives grace to the humble, not
because a humble response deserves salvation, but because he is gracious.

there who was not dressed for a wedding. So he said to him, 'Friend, how did you get in here without wedding clothes?' The man was speechless.

"Then the king told the attendants, 'Tie him up hand and foot, and throw him into the outer darkness, where there will be weeping and gnashing of teeth.' For many are invited, but few are chosen." (Matt 22:1–14)

The main and concluding point of Christ's parable was "For many are invited, but few are chosen" (v. 14). How were they invited? It was by an unworthy nation of flawed messengers being sent to the good and bad throughout the entire world. Notice that not one of these divine choices is conditioned upon the superior worth or morality of those being chosen.

- The nation was not chosen based on its worth or morality.
- The servants from that nation were not chosen based on their worth or morality.
- The invitations were not sent to people based on their worth or morality.
- Those granted entrance to the banquet were not more worthy or moral.

All these choices are "unconditional" regarding the morality or worth of those chosen, but that in no way proves or even implies those granted entrance to the wedding banquet were chosen without regard to their faith in Christ (i.e., clothed in his garments). Being chosen without regard to one's own worth or morality is much different than being chosen without regard to one's trust in the worth and morality of another. Yet the Calvinist systematic approach mistakenly conflates the two as if they were one and the same.

God chose Israel to be the mouthpiece by which he would call the world to reconciliation. This is what Christ was referencing when he said, "many are called," but what did he mean by "few are chosen"? This is an unmistakable reference to those permitted entrance into the banquet, based not on their own merit, but solely on their being properly clothed in the right wedding garments through faith. Notice their entrance is not conditioned upon their own worth or morality, but on the worth and morality of the One who clothed them through faith.

The king elects to permit those appropriately clothed to come in, while the rest are cast out. Likewise, God will only permit those clothed in the righteousness of Christ through faith to enter heaven. The "few" who are "chosen" (or elect) were conditionally granted entrance based upon their garments, which represent not their own qualifications but the righteousness of Christ graciously imputed to them by faith. This is the foundational understanding of "corporate election to salvation." We are elect only insofar as we are connected with the Elect One, Christ (clothed in his righteousness or under his headship).

Unconditional Election

As already demonstrated, we can speak in biblical terms about an "unconditional election," given that the conditions of God's choices are not based on the morality or meritorious qualifications of those who are chosen. However, this is different than what our Calvinistic friends mean when they speak of "Unconditional Election" (the *U* in the Calvinistic acronym TULIP).

For the Calvinist, "unconditional election" means that God does not foresee any action or condition, *including faith*, that induces him to choose one individual over another. Rather, election rests on God's *arbitrary* decision to effectuate faith in whomever he is pleased to save. John Calvin expressed it in this way:

> By predestination we mean the eternal decree of God, by which he determined with himself whatever he wished to happen with regard to every man. All are not created on equal terms, but some are preordained to eternal life, others to eternal damnation; and, accordingly, as each has been created for one or other of these ends, we say that he has been predestinated to life or to death.[16]
>
> Some are predestined to salvation, others to damnation. . . . Regarding the lost: it was His good pleasure to doom to destruction. . . . Since the disposition of all things is in the hands of God and He can give life or death at His pleasure, He dispenses and ordains by His judgment that some, from their mother's womb, are destined irrevocably to eternal death in order to glorify His name in their perdition.[17]

Ironically, the Calvinist application of unconditional election reflects the erroneous perception of the unbelieving Jews in the first century, who supposed themselves to be born unconditionally elect, simply on account of being born as children of Abraham in the flesh. John the Baptist dealt with this issue as well:

---

[16] Calvin, *Institutes*, trans. Beveridge, 2:206 (3.21.5).

[17] These quotes include citations from both the Battles and Beveridge translations of *Institutes*. Calvin, *Institutes*, quoted in Gilbert VanOrder Jr., *Calvinism's Conflicts: An Examination of the Problems in Reformed Theology* (Morrisville, NC: Lulu, 2013), 99.

When he saw many of the Pharisees and Sadducees coming to his baptism, he said to them, "Brood of vipers! Who warned you to flee from the coming wrath? Therefore produce fruit consistent with repentance. And don't presume to say to yourselves, 'We have Abraham as our father.' For I tell you that God is able to raise up children for Abraham from these stones. The ax is already at the root of the trees. Therefore, every tree that doesn't produce good fruit will be cut down and thrown into the fire." (Matt 3:7–10)

Paul dealt with this same issue writing to the church at Rome when he stated that "not all who are descended from Israel are Israel. Neither is it the case that all of Abraham's children are his descendants. . . . That is, it is not the children by physical descent who are God's children, but the children of the promise are considered to be the offspring" (Rom 9:6–8). So, in the same way that John the Baptist and the apostles had to deal with the perceived unconditional election of all Jews in the flesh, modern-day Christian apologists must deal with the perceived unconditional election that Calvinists suppose upon themselves.

Conditional Salvation

Even our Calvinistic friends affirm that salvation itself is conditioned upon faith. They just believe that faith is a condition that is ultimately met by an effectual act of God upon those unilaterally chosen before the foundation of the world. So, while Calvinists agree that certain conditions must be met before one will enter heaven, they maintain God unilaterally decided before creation to cause certain individuals to meet those conditions, while leaving the rest innately incapable of meeting those same moral conditions, due to factors ultimately beyond their control.

This is an important distinction because some bring a critique against Calvinism by pointing to texts of Scripture that unequivocally demonstrate that humankind must meet certain conditions to be saved. For instance, when John wrote, "Everyone who believes in him will not perish" (John 3:16), or when the apostle Paul wrote that "Everyone who calls on the name of the Lord will be saved" (Rom 10:13), the Calvinist will gladly affirm these as biblical conditions for salvation, because for them it is election that is unconditional, not salvation itself.

Calvinists maintain that God, by means of an "irresistible grace,"[18] causally determines for elected individuals to meet those biblically stated conditions. In other

---

[18] Irresistible Grace is the "I" in the Calvinistic acronym TULIP; sometimes referred to as an "effectual calling" or the work of "regeneration."

words, God causes the elect ones to believe so they can be saved, thereby meeting the biblically stated condition for their salvation.[19] God not only sets the condition, but according to Calvinism, God also meets that condition by an effectual or irresistible work of grace granted only to those unilaterally chosen before creation.

The systematic approach of the Calvinist is not consistent with the biblical revelation. The Scriptures do not leave us wondering why God shows favor to some people and not others, as if it is a mystery hidden within his arbitrary will. Luke 1:50 tells us, "His mercy is from generation to generation / on those who fear him." Isaiah 66:2b says, "I will look favorably on this kind of person: one who is humble, submissive in spirit, and trembles at my word." It is not a secret or mystery to whom God reveals his truth, as the psalmist clearly stated: "He leads the humble in what is right and teaches them his way" (Ps 25:9). And God himself said, "'This is what the LORD God of Israel says: As for the words that you heard, because your heart was tender and you humbled yourself before the LORD when you heard what I spoke against this place and against its inhabitants, that they would become a desolation and a curse, and because you have torn your clothes and wept before me, I myself have heard'— this is the LORD's declaration" (2 Kgs 22:18b–19).

Again and again throughout the Scriptures, the Lord tells us what condition must be met to find favor in his eyes: "I tell you, this one [the humble tax collector] went down to his house justified rather than the other, because everyone who exalts himself will be humbled, but the one who humbles himself will be exalted" (Luke 18:14). And in Matt 23:12 we read Christ's words: "Whoever exalts himself will be humbled, and whoever humbles himself will be exalted."

Calvinists argue, "If a person becomes humble enough to submit to God it is because the Holy Spirit has given that person a new, humble nature."[20] Again, the TULIP model seems to confound an otherwise simple truth. *Humble yourself so as be saved* is taken to mean that God, by means of his Spirit, unilaterally causes some people to be humble enough for him to save. This exegesis removes any meaningful sense of human responsibility and makes these biblical passages virtually meaningless, given that no one has any real capacity to respond positively to its warnings and appeals.

---

[19] In R. C. Sproul's words, "Faith is a necessary condition for salvation, but not for election. The prescient view makes faith a condition of election; Reformed theology sees faith as the result of election." Sproul, *What Is Reformed Theology?* (Grand Rapids: Baker, 1997), 145.

[20] John Samson, "Is Faith the Gift of God? What Does Jesus Say?," *Reformation Theology* (blog), July 19, 2006, http://www.reformationtheology.com/2006/07/is_faith_the_gift_of_god _what.php.

Corporate Election in Christ

What is meant by *corporate election*? How does this tie in to the biblical concept of predestination? What has God predestined for the church; that is, the body of Christ and the bride of Christ? The foundation of corporate election in Christ is seen in Eph 1:3–4: "Blessed is the God and Father of our Lord Jesus Christ, who has blessed us with *every spiritual blessing in the heavens in Christ. For he chose us in him*, before the foundation of the world, to be holy and blameless in love before him" (emphasis added).

God has blessed "the faithful saints in Christ Jesus" (Eph 1:1), "us who believe" (v. 19), with every spiritual blessing in the heavenly places in Christ. What spiritual blessing exists apart from being in Christ? The answer is none. So, what exactly is a spiritual blessing in the heavenly places? In Eph 1:1–14, Paul listed several examples. They include the spiritual blessings of holiness, adoption, redemption, revelation, an inheritance, and the indwelling of the Holy Spirit. God predestined these spiritual blessings for the believer in Christ.

For the unbeliever, these things are all unavailable. That would mean that even if, hypothetically, there was such a thing as a Calvinistic form of unconditional election, or even an irresistible grace, then as spiritual blessings they could only be available for the believer in Christ. This is also why we can know that the spiritual blessing of regeneration is only for the believer. Calvinism needs regeneration as a mechanism for Calvinism's totally depraved, totally disabled elect-*unbelievers* to be effectually made to believe, but as we see from the principle of Eph 1:3, regeneration is unavailable to unbelievers. As a spiritual blessing, regeneration is only available to those who are corporately in Christ by faith. This is also why we find in Ephesians 1 that each of the spiritual blessings listed are carefully qualified as "in him" (v. 4), "in the Beloved One" (v. 6), "in him" (v. 7), "in Christ" (v. 9), "in Christ" (v. 10), and "in him" (v. 13).

Can a person be secretly in Christ without realizing it, only to discover it later upon becoming a Christian believer? This may be what John Calvin had in mind. Consider the following:

> Christ says that the elect always belonged to God. God therefore distinguishes them from the reprobate, not by faith, nor by any merit, but by pure grace; for while they are far away from him, he regards them in secret as his own.[21]

---

[21] John Calvin, *John*, The Crossway Classic Commentaries, ed. Alister McGrath and J. I. Packer (Wheaton, IL: Crossway, 1994), 393.

This way of speaking, however, may seem to be different from many passages of Scripture which attribute to Christ the first foundation of God's love for us and show that outside Christ we are detested by God. But we ought to remember, as I have already said, that the Heavenly Father's secret love which embraced us is the first love given to us.[22]

Such a proposition of a secret love would undoubtedly constitute a spiritual blessing, and since Eph 1:3 makes it clear that every spiritual blessing is in Christ, it makes one wonder whether John Calvin had in mind the notion that Calvinism's elect were "in Christ" from eternity past. This would seem to be contradicted by Paul's statement in Rom 16:7, "Andronicus and Junia . . . were also in Christ before me." How could that be, if Calvinism's elect reside in Christ perpetually from eternity past? These are quandaries the Bible does not address, and they seem quite forced, due to the obligations required by Calvinism's theological baggage.

The concept of an elect-unbeliever contradicts statements made in the Bible. For instance, Rom 8:1–2 tells us "there is now no condemnation for those who are in Christ Jesus, because the law of the Spirit of life in Christ Jesus has set you free from the law of sin and death." Those who are in Christ are free from condemnation. But notice that Jesus said "anyone who does not believe is already condemned, because he has not believed in the name of the one and only Son of God" (John 3:18). So, if a person is both an unbeliever and also secretly in Christ, then he is both "already condemned" and free from condemnation. Such a position is untenable.

The simple reality is there is a clear distinction between unbelievers, who remain condemned, and believers in Christ, who are corporately blessed with the spiritual blessing of being free from condemnation. It is a universal imperative for everyone to become "in Christ," which is the storehouse of all of God's predestined spiritual blessings. By the grace of God, he both desires this and has made a way for it to happen, by taking upon himself the sins of the world (John 1:29) so that anyone who believes in him will not perish but have eternal life (3:16).

Boasting

Our Calvinist friends are often greatly scandalized, and even righteously indignant, when we claim that we made a decision for Christ or accepted Christ apart from irresistible means. Calvinists insist that God must always make the decision—on our

---

[22] Calvin, 76.

behalf—to believe in him. However, when the apostle Paul raises the matter of boasting in Eph 2:8–9, it is made with respect to the works of the Law. This is because those who seek to establish their own righteousness through the works of the Law, or any other type of works, do not need God. They are already self-sufficient and good enough as they are without him, and their righteous life is the living proof of it—so they claim. Of course, when the books are opened on judgment day, a different verdict will be rendered. Conversely, the person who comes to God, hat in hand, asking for his forgiveness and mercy, obtains exactly what the person who was working for it was denied. This is because those who come to God with a request are admitting their own insufficiency and confessing that they are not good enough as they are. They are welcoming the help of someone else.

Boasting that God saved you is the kind of boasting that he actually encourages because it is boasting about what he has done for you—not what you have done for yourself. So, even if you claim to have believed in God by your own free will, apart from irresistible means, you are still bringing glory and honor to him because you are crediting him for saving you. Saying that you are trusting in someone else to save you does not speak of your own goodness, but instead speaks of the goodness of the One in whom you are placing your trust.

The Calvinistic argument that humbly accepting Christ's appeal to be reconciled might lead to boasting (if done freely, rather than by effectual means) has several fundamental flaws:

1. Is belief in Calvinistic soteriology also effectually brought about by God? If so, then why hasn't God effectually brought all believers to accept Calvinistic doctrine to prevent this inevitable boasting? If not, then why wouldn't the Calvinist boast in their free choice to accept Calvinism?

2. People who would have the audacity to boast in humbly believing in Christ did not really humbly believe in Christ. Their rotten fruit has revealed a fake root. True humility doesn't boast about itself. It boasts of the One in whom we place our trust (1 Cor 1:21). Jeremiah 9:24 explained this perfectly: "But the one who boasts should boast in this: that he understands and knows me—that I am the LORD, showing faithful love, justice, and righteousness on the earth, for I delight in these things." Humbly confessing your sin, humbly recognizing your inability to save yourself, and humbling yourself before the Savior who sacrificed himself for you on the cross is antithetical to that which would motivate

one to boast in anyone except the One who saves the humble. How can a view that is based on fulfilling a requirement of humility inevitably lead to boasting? Certainly, people are capable of all kinds of evils, including boasting in being humble, but such boasting violates the principle of humility upon which our view is built.

3. Every forthright Calvinist would admit they know at least one Calvinist who is proud and arrogant and one non-Calvinist who is humble and selfless. So why is one prideful and the other arrogant if the doctrine itself is not the ultimate cause of these characteristics? In Calvinism, all things are in accordance with God's sovereign decree, so those who act pridefully (regardless of their soteriological views) are ultimately doing so because that is how God decreed for them to behave. Why does the Calvinist lament God's decree? I believe pride "is not from the Father, but is from the world" (1 John 2:16).

God's Righteousness

Righteousness is thought to come from one of two sources. Some believe it can come from within, based on one's own merits, while others rightly understand that it can come only from God. Those who seek righteousness in themselves, either by works or bloodlines (such as through circumcision or being born elect as a child of Abraham) will not obtain righteousness, while those who seek righteousness from God (by placing their trust in him rather than themselves) will obtain the same righteousness that others are denied. The principle of trusting in God means that you are not trusting in yourself, thus acknowledging that your own works and bloodlines ultimately fall short, and that *you need God*.

A full vessel cannot be filled; thus, one must empty (humble) himself to be filled. In other words, when we come to God already full of our own righteousness, there is seemingly nothing left for God to add, but when we come to God empty, seeking mercy and forgiveness, then there is a vessel for God to fill with his own righteousness.

God's Sovereignty

Calvinists contend that if humankind could freely assent to God's mercy and forgiveness through his well-meant offer of the gospel, then salvation would no longer be at the sole discretion of the sovereignty of God. Instead, ratios of participation and "synergism" would necessarily follow, such as possibly 1 percent our contribution to "make a decision" for Christ and 99 percent God's contribution to bestow grace and mercy.[23] The reality, however, is that our choices are 100 percent our own choices, and God's choices are 100 percent his own choices.

It seems to me that in the well-meant effort of the Calvinists to ascribe all good things to God they have, maybe unintentionally, also ascribed all bad things to him. While Calvinists seem most concerned with making sure humankind takes no credit for their salvation, non-Calvinists seem more concerned with a recognizably good and holy God. I suspect both have a noble purpose in their pursuits, but as with most disputes the balance is somewhere in the middle. But this balance cannot be seen in vaguely divided percentages of what is to be ascribed to God and to humanity. Salvation is 100 percent from God. Merely affirming the responsibility of humankind to accept and/or reject God's appeals for reconciliation does not in any way affect that percentage. Only when a Calvinist conflates the human choice to humbly repent in faith with God's choice to save whoever does so are these types of dilemmas created. In other words, Calvinists have created a dilemma by conflating two choices as if they were one and calling them both "salvation."

Let us look at the parable of the prodigal son as an illustration. It was 100 percent the son's choice to ask to leave with his share of the inheritance, and it was 100 percent the father's choice to allow him to go and not hold him against his will. It was 100 percent the son's choice to squander his fortune and 100 percent the son's choice to return home in humiliation. Finally, it was 100 percent the father's choice to restore his place as a son.

Everyone is 100 percent responsible for their own choices. The father had no moral obligation to take his son back but did so out of the graciousness of his heart. He was pleased to find that his son had returned home, even after bearing the full financial cost and burden of his son's misadventure. In that day, the father had the right to have his son stoned to death or cast out into poverty for his misdeeds. Restoration was certainly not required and was not what the son expected. The son was merely hoping he could be added to the servant staff. The father's choice to be gracious and grant an unexpected, complete restoration was 100 percent the father's choice. He was not compelled to do so. He simply wanted to because he was gracious and merciful, and so is God, to all who similarly come to him seeking mercy and forgiveness.

---

[23] Sproul, *Chosen by God*, 115 (see chap. 1, n. 106).

Even if someone were to persuade you to make a decision for Christ, it is still your sole choice to make, just as it is God's sole, sovereign prerogative to set the terms for salvation. However, Calvinists object that if humankind have their own free choice, why does one sinner respond to the offer of grace positively and the other negatively?[24] In asking this, Calvinists beg the question by simply assuming a deterministic cause outside of the individual's own agency. How would God reasonably be able to ask humankind on judgment day why they did this or that, if the answer was ultimately rooted in something other than the individual's own agency? Both human responsibility and divine judgment require liberty of the creature's will.

John 10: The Sheep

Calvinists regularly point to John 10 and Christ's reference to his "sheep" to support the notion that God unilaterally chooses to effectuate faith in some individuals while passing by the rest, for reasons that Calvinists confess they do not know.[25]

> I am the good shepherd. I know my own, and my own know me, just as the Father knows me, and I know the Father. I lay down my life for the sheep. But I have other sheep that are not from this sheep pen; I must bring them also, and they will listen to my voice. Then there will be one flock, one shepherd. . . .
> But you don't believe because you are not of my sheep. (John 10:14–16, 26)

If one understands "my sheep" to be in reference to "those I have unconditionally elected for effectual salvation before the foundation of the world," then this passage certainly seems to support the Calvinistic doctrine. However, the passage simply does

---

[24] Sproul, *What is Reformed Theology?*, 187.

[25] Hence MacArthur remarks, "We are chosen unto salvation. We are chosen to belong to Him. When you look at your salvation, then thank God. Thank God! Because you are a Christian because He chose you. I don't understand the mystery of that. That's just what the word of God teaches. That is the most humbling doctrine in all of Scripture. I take no credit, not even credit for my faith. It all came from Him. He chose me. He selected people to be made holy in order to be with Him forever. Why he selected me, I will never know. I'm no better than anyone else. I'm worse than many. But He chose me. . . . To whom do you owe your salvation? You owe it to the God who chose you. You owe it to the God who predestined you. You owe it to the God who redeemed you, the God who forgave you, the God who wanted you to be His own because He wanted you to be His own. It doesn't give any other reason, even though we are so unworthy, so unworthy." MacArthur, "Sovereignty of God."

not support this reading. The audience were Israelites who had become calloused to the voice of God. Because they had grown calloused to the Father, they were now unable to hear the voice of his Son, who spoke the same truth. This is not because they were in a condition from birth where they could only hate and refuse God's appeals for reconciliation, as if God was withholding the sufficient grace they needed to believe. The Jews had *grown calloused* through persistent unbelief; otherwise, they might have seen, heard, understood, and turned (see John 12:39–41; Acts 28:23–28). Here is how Jesus described their condition in that context: "You pore over the Scriptures because you think you have eternal life in them, and yet they testify about me. But you are not willing to come to me so that you may have life" (John 5:39–40).

Notice the order: the Jews refused to come after hearing the Scriptures so they might have life. Jesus did not say, "I refused to give you life so that you'd certainly come to me." The Jews of Jesus's day (generally speaking) had grown hardened, or more resolved in their rebellion, which explains their inability to see, hear, and turn, even in response to their own Messiah. Those who had not grown hardened, but instead listened and learned from the Father and feared God (like Cornelius in Acts 10), would believe the Son and follow him, like a sheep who recognized the shepherd's voice (see also John 6:45).

If a person listened to the Father before the incarnation, then they would listen to his Son, because the Father and Son are one. If a person refused to listen to the Father before the incarnation, then they would likewise be calloused to all the Son's teachings. Followers of the Father (idiomatically called "sheep" in the first century) also followed the Son. Those who refused to follow the Father were not counted as his sheep, and that is why they refused to follow the Son. This explains why Jesus said to them, "You don't believe because you are not of my sheep" (John 10:26).

Jesus was essentially saying, "Because you refuse to follow the Father, you also refuse to follow me, his Son." "You are not of my sheep" means "you are not a follower of God, and you have not listened and learned from him (John 6:45), therefore you will not follow me, the Son, either. If you had been listening to the Father, then you would recognize my voice, because I'm the Shepherd he sent who speaks the exact same truth." This is reflected in the following statement by Jesus: "If God were your Father, you would love me, because I came from God and I am here. For I didn't come on my own, but he sent me" (John 8:42).

Jesus was not saying, "You refuse to believe because I and the Father rejected you before the foundation of the world and are withholding the grace you need to believe," which is the necessary implication of the Calvinistic doctrine. The Jews' unbelief was not because they were born in a condition that caused them to hate God beyond their control. That flies in the face of Luke 19:41–42, which speaks of Jesus weeping over Israel because the truth of his identity as their Messiah was now "hidden from [their] eyes."

If most Jews of Jesus's day were born helpless and hopeless to believe in Christ, then why the need for God to hide this truth by means of parables to keep them from believing in the Messiah?[26] Moreover, if they were born totally unable to believe the truth, why would Jesus encourage those who were not his sheep/followers to consider the implication of his miracles: "If I am not doing my Father's works, don't believe me. But if I am doing them and you don't believe me, *believe the works. This way you will know* and understand that the Father is in me and I in the Father" (John 10:37–38; emphasis added).

God was not withholding some special grace that was necessary for the Jews to believe. That gives them too much credit and makes them victims rather than morally accountable rebellious sinners, rejecting a loving God who declares, "All day long I have held out my hands" (Rom 10:21) and "wanted to gather your children together, as a hen gathers her chicks under her wings" (Matt 23:37).

Conclusion

The Calvinistic doctrine of unconditional election is the unilateral (or arbitrary) decision of God to destine some people to hell and others to heaven for factors completely beyond their control. This doctrine cannot escape falling under the same fatalistic logic of the overarching philosophical commitment to theistic determinism held to by most of its notable proponents. I believe this doctrine, when logically and consistently applied, can be dangerous for the believer and the overall mission of the church and thus must be firmly refuted and soundly rejected as unbiblical teaching.

One presupposition that is acceptable when attempting to discern the meaning of any passage of Scripture is that God's choices are always good and right. Therefore, any confusing systematic doctrine that leads many otherwise discerning

---

[26] Richard N. Soulen and R. Kendall Soulen state, "Messianic secret refers to a discernible phenomenon in the Gospels, most especially in the Gospel of Mark, in which Jesus explicitly conceals His Messianic character and power until the closing period of His ministry." *The Handbook of Biblical Criticism*, 4th ed. (Louisville: Westminster John Knox, 2011), 124. This purposeful hiding of divine revelation is also referred to as "judicial hardening" or "blinding" of already calloused and rebellious individuals.

Bible believers to fundamentally question the goodness of God's character and the righteousness of his choices should be highly suspect and thoroughly vetted, if not outright rejected, especially if that doctrine leads many well-intentioned believers to question the need and urgency for evangelism and mission efforts.

Years ago, when I was a five-point Calvinist, I was as active in sharing my faith with others as I am today. In my ministry, since leaving Calvinism behind, I have regularly strived to help my non-Calvinist friends understand that Calvinists are not typically anti-evangelistic and that every mainstream, modern-day Calvinist scholar or pastor I know of is very interested in spreading the gospel to all people. As logically inconsistent as that may appear to some, it is a verifiable fact.

This fact, however, does not negate the merit of some sound logical and biblical arguments raised against the Calvinistic belief system, nor does it negate the fact that throughout history there have been significant numbers of Calvinistic believers who exhibit anti-evangelistic and hyper tendencies.[27] There is a good reason that when believers are introduced to Calvinism their first objection is typically questioning the necessity of evangelism. This natural reaction to the teaching of Calvinism is evidenced by the volumes of work produced by Calvinistic scholars over the years to answer this objection: "If God has unchangeably determined who will and will not believe so as to be saved, then why evangelize the lost?"

Many Calvinists will answer this question by simply saying, "Because God told us to."[28] But should the law alone be the primary motivation for our evangelistic efforts, or should we be motivated by that which motivated Christ to die in the first place: *love*?

> But God proves his own love for us in that while we were still sinners, Christ died for us. (Rom 5:8)

> For God loved the world in this way: He gave his one and only Son, so that everyone who believes in him will not perish but have eternal life. (John 3:16)

In Rom 9:1–3 Paul expressed the self-sacrificial heart of Christ when he wished himself accursed for the sake of his fellow countrymen. Paul was clearly motivated by love, not merely some obligation of the law, in his desire to evangelize the lost. Paul

---

[27] For additional historical information, see Peter Toon, *The Emergence of Hyper-Calvinism in English Nonconformity* (London: The Olive Tree, 1967).

[28] Voddie Baucham, "Predestination and Election" (sermon), posted by Hannah Gremmels on February 4, 2015, YouTube video, 1:19:16, https://www.youtube.com/watch?v=DH31wuNoois.

was willing to give up his own salvation for these hardened Jews who were trying to kill him. Is Christ less self-sacrificially loving than the apostle he inspired to write these words? By no means!

Paul was expressing the very heart of God himself, whom he quoted in the very next chapter: "But to Israel he [God] says, 'All day long I have held out my hands to a disobedient and defiant people'" (Rom 10:21).

Paul expressed this same truth to Timothy in 1 Tim 2:3–6:

> This is good, and it pleases God our Savior, who wants everyone to be saved and to come to the knowledge of the truth.
>
> For there is one God and one mediator between God and mankind, the man Christ Jesus, who gave himself as a ransom for all, a testimony at the proper time.

Jesus himself explained it in Matt 23:37: "Jerusalem, Jerusalem, who kills the prophets and stones those who are sent to her. How often I wanted to gather your children together, as a hen gathers her chicks under her wings, but you were not willing!" This is an echo of what we read in Isa 30:15: "For the Lord GOD, the Holy One of Israel, has said: 'You will be delivered by returning and resting; your strength will lie in quiet confidence. But you are not willing.'" Ezekiel 18:31–32 expressly portrays God's heart toward Israel: "'Throw off all the transgressions you have committed, and get yourselves a new heart and a new spirit. Why should you die, house of Israel? For I take no pleasure in anyone's death.' This is the declaration of the Lord GOD. 'So repent and live!'"

Love, not law, is the motive of Christ, and it must be our motive as well if we, and future generations, have any hope of persisting in our efforts to win this lost world. The Calvinistic doctrine of unconditional election fundamentally undercuts the motive of God's universal divine love and provision for all people, thus potentially leading the church to lose the driving urgency, motivation, and focus on its mission to make the provision of salvation through faith in Christ known to all people everywhere.[29]

---

[29] I would like to express thanks to Richard Coords and Marlene Weeks for their assistance in the development of this manuscript.

A Critique of Limited Atonement

—— David L. Allen ——

L imited atonement is a doctrine in search of a text. No one can point to any text in Scripture that states clearly and unequivocally that Christ died for the sins of a limited number of people to the exclusion of others. Most Calvinists admit this. Alternatively, a dozen clear texts in the New Testament *explicitly affirm* Christ died for the sins of all people, and another half dozen plus that indirectly suggest it. We will consider these texts in part 3.

I have written on the question of the extent of the atonement over the past twelve years.[1] It is often the case that participants in this discussion utilize the same vocabulary but employ a different dictionary. Here are the theological definitions as I use them in this chapter:

---

[1] David L. Allen, "The Atonement: Limited or Universal?" in Allen and Lemke, eds., *Whosoever Will*, 61–107 (see intro., n. 20); Allen, *Extent of the Atonement* (see intro., n. 10)—this volume came to assume proportions of indecent corpulence, weighing in at 850 pages; and *The Atonement: A Biblical, Theological, and Historical Study of the Cross of Christ* (Nashville: B&H Academic, 2019).

- **atonement**—the propitiatory and expiatory act of Christ on the cross whereby sins were imputed to him and satisfaction for sin was accomplished.
- **extent of the atonement**—answers the question, For whose sins did Christ die? Or, for whose sins was Christ punished?
- **limited atonement**—Christ bore the punishment due for the sins of the elect *alone*. The imputation of sin to Christ, substitution for the sinner, and satisfaction for sin was limited to the elect alone. This term will be used most often to describe the position of those who affirm Christ died only for the sins of the elect.
- **unlimited atonement**—Christ bore the punishment due for the sins of *all* humanity, dead and living (not to be confused with universal salvation).
- **limitarian**—a Calvinist who affirms limited atonement.
- **moderate Calvinist**—a Calvinist who affirms unlimited atonement.
- **non-Calvinist**—anyone, with the exception of moderate Calvinists, who affirms unlimited atonement regardless of denomination.

Several important points are prerequisite to a careful assessment of the issue. First, when it comes to the question of the extent of the atonement, the essence of the debate has to do with Christ's death in relation to the sins of people. There are only two options: (1) Christ died for the sins of the elect *alone* (limited atonement); or (2) Christ died for the sins of *all* humanity (unlimited atonement).

Notice the important phrase "for the sins of." Most Calvinists who affirm limited atonement will say things like "Christ died for the world," or "Christ died for all people." However, they are not referring to a substitution for the *sins* of all people. What they mean by this is something along the following lines: (1) Christ died for the world to bring common grace to all people; (2) Christ died for the world where "world" is understood to be "the elect"; (3) Christ died for the world where "world" is understood as Jews and Gentiles collectively such that Christ only died for the sins of some Jews and some Gentiles; (4) Christ died for the world such that he died for the sins of "some of all kinds of people." None of these indicate anything more than, in some sense, it can be said Jesus died *for the world*, but *not in the sense that he died for the sins of every person in the world*. Many limitarians believe that Christ's death has "universal aspects" to it. But by such statements they *do not* mean Christ died *for the sins of* the world.

Second, many older and more recent treatments on the extent of the atonement exhibit confusion as to the actual state of the question. The question is often answered without properly defining the question or distinguishing between the *intent* of the atonement, the *extent* of the atonement, and the *application* of the atonement.[2]

Herman Bavinck asserted three things relative to the extent question: (1) everybody limits the atonement in one way or another; (2) the atonement is intrinsically sufficient for the sins of all only in terms of worth and value (its "substance"), not that it served as an actual sacrifice for the sins of all people (its "*form,* [Bavinck's emphasis] . . . considered not in isolation but with a view to the reprobates, can be called not only 'not efficacious' but also 'not sufficient'"); and (3) therefore, "the difference concerns *only* [my emphasis] the question whether it was God's will and *intent* [Bavinck's emphasis] that Christ made his sacrifice for the sins of all people without exception or only for the sins of those whom the Father had given him."[3] Bavinck concluded, "When it is framed in this manner, the question is hardly doubtful."[4]

But this is a misleading and erroneous way to frame the question. First, it is false to say everybody limits the atonement. All orthodox Christians limit the application of the atonement, not its extent.[5] Second, Bavinck is equivocating on the sense of intent, as his following statements and arguments illustrate. For many limitarians, the issue of the atonement's extent (in the sense of Christ's *intent in accomplishing redemption*) gets automatically conflated with Christ's *intent to apply redemption* (i.e., election) and not on direct statements in Scripture about the extent of Christ's satisfaction. Consequently, the sense of "intent" is defined by the limitarian in such a way that limited atonement is deductively determined to be the only alternative. Many recent treatments of the extent of the atonement by limitarians follow this path or one very similar.[6]

---

[2] See, for example, Adam Johnson, who edited and wrote the introduction and conclusion in *Five Views on the Extent of the Atonement* (Grand Rapids: Zondervan Academic, 2019). His ten-page introduction never gets around to defining the issue of the extent of the atonement. The title of the book itself is misleading—there are only two views on the *extent* of the atonement—a limited satisfaction for sins or an unlimited satisfaction for sins.

[3] Herman Bavinck, *Reformed Dogmatics,* 4 vols., ed. John Bolt, trans. John Vriend (Grand Rapids: Baker, 2006), 3:464.

[4] Bavinck's discussion evinces *no interaction* with Moderate Reformed scholarship on the question. Every argument Bavinck made for limited atonement had been answered by moderate Calvinists before him. Bavinck, 3:464.

[5] Universalists do not limit the atonement in extent or application. Universalism is not within the bounds of orthodox Christian doctrine, though the view seems to be growing in popularity, even among some evangelicals.

[6] David Gibson and Jonathan Gibson define limited atonement in a generic way that does not clearly articulate the heart of the concept as a limited substitution of Christ for the sins

A notable exception is Mark Snoeberger, editor of *Perspectives on the Extent of the Atonement: 3 Views*, who correctly understands the question of the extent of the atonement: "The primary question, thus, that this book addresses is not, For whose benefit did Christ die? But more specifically, For whom was Christ a substitute?"[7] The former question is the question of the *intent to apply* the atonement. The latter question is the question of the extent of the atonement.

When the question is properly asked as to the specific issue of the atonement's extent, there are only two possible answers: limited atonement or unlimited atonement.

Third, historically, it was the near-universal belief of the church until the late sixteenth century that the extent of the atonement was unlimited. With only rare exceptions before the Reformation, limited atonement was never espoused. It is not found in the Patristic era, even in Augustine.[8] Its only proponent in the medieval

---

of the elect only. Gibson and Gibson, eds., *From Heaven He Came and Sought Her: Definite Atonement in Historical, Biblical, Theological, and Pastoral Perspective* (Wheaton, IL: Crossway, 2013), 38–39. See Allen, *Extent of the Atonement*, 660–61. Notice their definition speaks to the "intent" and "application" of the atonement, but it does not specifically reference the "extent." This illustrates their confusion on the actual state of the question. Michael J. Lynch also noted the book's confusion about the proper state of the question, and said, "The most glaring deficiency of the book is its ambiguity over the definition of definite atonement. . . . [T]he book only obfuscates the real issue that advocates of definite atonement should be arguing, namely, that Christ made a satisfaction only for the sins of the elect. . . . Definite atonement should not be used as shorthand for *an intention to apply redemption* to the elect alone [i.e., an *intent to save*], but rather for *an intention to accomplish redemption* [i.e., the *extent* of the satisfaction] for the elect alone." Michael J. Lynch, review of *From Heaven He Came and Sought Her*, ed. D. Gibson and J. Gibson, *Calvin Theological Journal* 49, no. 1 (April 2014): 352–53; emphasis mine. Lynch's point equally applies to Vanhoozer's recent chapter on the atonement, where he confuses election (the intent to save only the elect) with atonement as an actual satisfaction for the sins of all people. Vanhoozer makes two other theological mistakes. He confuses Christ's work of atonement with Christ's work as High Priest in his intercession, and he confuses atonement with the application of the atonement. Atonement accomplished does not equal "salvation" apart from application. Kevin Vanhoozer, "Redemption Accomplished: Atonement," in *Oxford Handbook of Reformed Theology*, ed. Michael Allen and Scott R. Swain (Oxford: Oxford University Press, 2020), 490–92.

[7] Mark A. Snoeberger, introduction to *Perspectives on the Extent of the Atonement: 3 Views*, ed. Andrew David Naselli and Mark A. Snoeberger (Nashville: B&H Academic 2015), 6.

[8] See Allen, *Extent of the Atonement*, 16–22. Augustine asserted that Christ died for the sins of Judas, and in many places in his writings he asserted that Christ died for the sins of all humanity. Some have maintained that Prosper of Aquitaine, early in his career, taught "definite atonement," based on an early letter that he wrote to Augustine (e.g., Michael A. G. Haykin, "'We Trust in the Saving Blood': Definite Atonement in the Ancient Church," in Gibson and

period was the ninth-century Augustinian monk Gottschalk.[9] The first generation of Reformers, including Luther, Calvin, and Zwingli, all affirmed universal atonement.[10] It was not until Theodore Beza in the late sixteenth century that we find limited atonement being clearly articulated.[11]

Fourth, it has been the near-universal teaching of the church from the Patristic era to the present (excepting universalists, who believe all people will be ultimately saved) that the atonement is limited in its *application* only to those who believe, or after Augustine, limited only in its application to the elect (since Augustine was the first of the church fathers to advocate unconditional election).

This historical testimony is significant for several reasons. It illustrates the relative lateness of limited atonement in the theology of the church. Limited atonement arises historically more in tandem with the Reformed development and refinement of the doctrine of election in their late sixteenth- and early seventeenth-century debates with Lutherans and Arminians on the subject. This leads one to suspect that limited atonement is a doctrine that is system-driven rather than exegetically

---

Gibson, *From Heaven He Came*, 72–73). But they falsely assume that just because Prosper attributed to the Massilians (or the so-called Semi-Pelagians) the belief that "Our Lord Jesus Christ . . . has died for the whole of mankind [*pro uniuerso autem humano genere mortuum esse dominum nostrum Iesum Christum*]" (Prosper of Aquitaine, "Letter to Augustine," in *Defense of St. Augustine*, trans. P. De Letter [New York: Newman Press, 1963], 43; Letter 225.6), he therefore must have disagreed with it. This is clearly a false inference since he also attributed to them the belief that "every man has sinned in Adam, and no one is reborn and saved by his own works but by God's grace" (Prosper, *Defense of Augustine*, 36; Letter 225.3). Augustine and Prosper both believed that. John Davenant dealt with this erroneous inference long ago. See John Davenant, "A Dissertation on the Death of Christ," in *An Exposition of the Epistle of St. Paul to the Colossians*, 2 vols., trans. J. Allport (London: Hamilton, Adams, 1832), 2:328. See also Michael J. Lynch, *John Davenant's Hypothetical Universalism: A Defense of Catholic and Reformed Orthodoxy*, Oxford Studies in Historical Theology (New York: Oxford University Press, 2021), 38–40.

[9] Allen, *Extent of the Atonement*, 24–26.

[10] Allen, 36–40, 48–96.

[11] This is somewhat acknowledged even by many Calvinists who affirm limited atonement, at least in terms of it being explicitly debated. For example, Robert Letham stated, "However, the extent—or intent—of the atonement only became a major question at the Colloquy of Montbéliard in 1586, where Theodore Beza clashed with the Lutheran Jacob Andraeus. From then until the Synod of Dort (1618–1619), it was a live issue." Letham, *Systematic Theology* (Wheaton, IL: Crossway, 2019), 571. Letham, however, erroneously asserted that "Prosper of Aquitaine held to definite atonement," without any supporting evidence. Letham, 570.

discovered from the text of Scripture.[12] As we shall see, almost all the arguments in favor of limited atonement are logical and theological rather than biblical.

Fifth, among the Reformed since the late sixteenth century, limited atonement has always been a disputed doctrine and has been the single most disputed issue among Calvinists themselves to this day. It is frequently assumed that limited atonement has been the only orthodox position within Calvinism. Knowledgeable Calvinists recognize this is false.[13] I have covered this territory in detail in *The Extent of the Atonement: A Historical and Critical Review* (see note 1 above). Due to space limitations, I will not cover the historical ground in this chapter. Rather, my focus will be to address the biblical, theological, and logical issues related to the extent of the atonement.

Sixth, not all Calvinists who reject(ed) limited atonement are or have been lock-step in their explication of unlimited atonement. Some were English Hypothetical Universalists, some Amyraldian, some Baxterian, and some eclectic. They differed over decretal order and terminological issues, but they *all* affirmed universal atonement in the sense that Christ provided satisfaction for the sins of all people.

Seventh, among all Christians in the past and today, limited atonement has always been the minority view. It appears to be held by the majority of those who self-identify as Calvinists regardless of denomination, but is rejected by all moderate Calvinists regardless of denomination, Catholics, Eastern Orthodox, and all non-Calvinist Protestants including all Methodists, Lutherans, Church of Christ, Pentecostals, Assemblies of God, and the majority of Baptists.

Eighth, many Calvinists assert, as did Loraine Boettner, that "the nature of the atonement settles its extent."[14] The logic unfolds in this fashion: since Christ died as a substitute for sinners, and since this substitution is understood as some form of penal substitution, then the nature of the atonement is such that it redeems, ipso facto,

---

[12] In one of the latest multiauthored books on the extent of the atonement, Adam J. Johnson, ed., *Five Views on the Extent of the Atonement* (Grand Rapids: Zondervan, 2019), Michael Horton's response to Andrew Louth's chapter begins with the words "The Synod of Dort." Horton, "Response to Andrew Louth," in Johnson, ed., 50. Horton's own chapter in this volume is less a biblical argument for limited atonement and more an example of reliance on the Reformed "system" of theology to defend limited atonement.

[13] Richard Muller, G. Michael Thomas, and Jonathan Moore, among many other Reformed scholars, have provided irrefutable evidence concerning the historical diversity on the extent of the atonement within the Reformed camp. See Allen, *Extent of the Atonement*, xivn2.

[14] Loraine Boettner, *The Reformed Doctrine of Predestination* (Philadelphia: Presbyterian and Reformed, 1965), 152.

all those for whom it was made. Salvation is rendered certain by the nature of the atonement. Hence, logically, limited atonement must be true. If Christ died in a substitutionary fashion for the sins of all people, then universalism would supposedly result.[15] The problem here is these Calvinists have succumbed to a commercialist understanding of the atonement and its mechanism. I will point out the error of this logic below.

All non-Calvinists and many Calvinists assert the nature of the atonement does not entail limited extent. They believe that the exegetical data clearly affirm that Christ died for the sins of all people. Limited atonement is rendered false on the grounds of the exegetical data itself.

I shall proceed on four fronts. First, we must define and distinguish three crucial aspects of the atonement: its intent, extent, and application. Second, arguments for limited atonement will be listed and answered. Third, texts and arguments that assert unlimited atonement will be presented, along with arguments supporting their interpretation. Fourth, two key theological, logical, and practical topics related to the extent of the atonement will be surveyed, demonstrating the problems with limited atonement and further supporting unlimited atonement.

I. Intent, Extent, and Application of the Atonement

Some of the recent works on the extent of the atonement are surprisingly unhelpful and in fact confusing because they fail to carefully distinguish at the outset between the *intent* of the atonement, the *extent* of the atonement, and the *application* of the atonement. This distinction is vital to the issue and fundamental to an understanding of the proper state of the question.

The *intent* of the atonement asks the question What is God's (Christ's) saving *purpose* in providing atonement? This question is answered differently by Calvinists and non-Calvinists.

All Calvinists agree that the ultimate intent of the atonement is to save the elect. Some Calvinists, usually those who are limitarians, assert that this is the *only* purpose in the atonement. Others allow for multiple purposes or intentions with respect to the atonement. From the Calvinist perspective, the issue of God's intent in the atonement considers questions such as: Does Christ desire the salvation of all people? Does God have a "universal saving will" that extends to all people? Most Calvinists,

---

[15] J. I. Packer, "What Did the Cross Achieve? The Logic of Penal Substitution," *Tyndale Bulletin* 25 (1974): 3–45.

even those who affirm limited atonement, answer these questions with a yes.[16] They usually express the answer by invoking the notion of God's two wills (or rather two senses of his will, e.g., Deut 29:29): his revealed will and his secret or decretal will. God desires the salvation of all people in his revealed will, as stated in Scripture (Ezek 18:32; 33:11; 1 Tim 2:4–6), but in God's decretal will, he intends only to save the elect.

All mainstream Calvinists,[17] regardless of their views on the extent of the atonement, affirm that God has an unequal desire for the salvation of all people in the sense that he desires the salvation of all but decrees only the salvation of the elect. All moderate Calvinists affirm not only that God desires the salvation of all but also that God *intended* to provide an atonement for the sins of all people commensurate with his universal saving desire and his universal benevolence. Moderate Calvinists believe God's saving intent in the atonement was dualistic: (1) he sent Christ to open a way of salvation for all humanity so that his death paid the penalty for their sins, thus rendering all people savable (capable of being saved should they believe in Christ); and (2) Christ died with the special purpose of ultimately securing the salvation of the elect only. Limitarian Calvinists believe in a strictly limited saving intent, which they argue necessarily requires that Christ provided a satisfaction *only* for the elect, and thus he secures salvation only for the elect.

Non-Calvinists affirm that God *equally* desires the salvation of all people. They find the notion of God's "two wills" to be fraught with contradiction and do not see such a concept anywhere in Scripture. Like their limitarian and moderate Calvinist counterparts, they believe God's (Christ's) intent with respect to the atonement necessarily has a bearing upon the extent of his satisfaction for sins on the cross. Unlike their limitarian counterparts, all non-Calvinists and moderate Calvinists believe the intent of the atonement is that Christ died for all people equally with respect to the actual satisfaction for sins to make salvation possible for all. Unlike their moderate Calvinist counterparts, all non-Calvinists believe Christ equally desires all to be saved and intends to secure the salvation only of those who do freely believe.

---

[16] See, for example, John Piper, *Does God Desire All to Be Saved?* (Wheaton, IL: Crossway, 2013). The majority of Reformed theologians affirm God's universal saving desire, though some do not speak to the issue at all. Very few deny it.

[17] Calvinists usually consider those who reject God's universal saving will to be "hyper-Calvinists" and, on that point, outside the boundary of mainstream Calvinism.

The *extent* of the atonement answers the question, For whose sins did Christ die? or, For whose sins was Christ punished? Were the sins of all humanity imputed to Christ or only the sins of the elect? There are only two possible answers to the question of the extent of the atonement: (1) He died for the sins of all humanity, or (2) he died for the sins of the elect only.

All non-Calvinists and moderate Calvinists believe that Jesus died *equally* for the sins of all humanity, regardless of the latter's view of a special intent to save only the elect. All limitarian Calvinists assert Christ died *only* for the sins of the elect and that it was God's intent that Christ should so die *only* for their sins.

The *application* of the atonement answers the question, When is the atonement applied to the sinner? There are three possible answers to this question: (1) It is applied in the eternal decree of God. This is the view of many hyper-Calvinists. (2) It is applied at the cross to all the elect at the time of Jesus's death. This is called "justification at the cross" and is the position of some hyper-Calvinists and a few limitarians. (3) It is applied at the historical moment the sinner exercises faith in Christ. This is the biblical view and is held by most limitarians, all moderate Calvinists, and all non-Calvinists.[18]

In addition to these distinctions, it is vital to identify and distinguish between Christ's atonement as (1) an actual satisfaction for sins, and (2) the offer of salvation to humanity based on and grounded in the atonement.

The chart on the following page illustrates the distinction between the atonement's intent, extent, and application, as viewed by non-Calvinists, moderate Calvinists, and limitarians.

Here is the crucial point, one that seems to be missed in so many discussions of the extent of the atonement: *All non-Calvinists and moderate Calvinists believe the extent of the atonement is unlimited.* In their view, Christ became a substitute (some non-Calvinists would say, wrongly in my view, "representative" and not a "substitute")[19] for the sins of all people such that his atonement satisfied God's law and grounds God's justice (Rom 3:21–26) in saving sinners who repent and believe in Christ.

---

[18] The *ultimate cause* of the application is also in dispute, since Calvinists want to argue that the libertarian freewill view grounds the decisive cause of salvation in human will rather than in God's will, and non-Calvinists want to argue that the compatibilist view of freedom entails the loss of any genuine human freedom of the will and implicates God as the author of sin.

[19] Scripture affirms penal substitutionary atonement. For clear evidence of this biblically, theologically, and as historically advocated since the Patristic era, see Allen, *The Atonement* (see intro., n. 20).

TWO VIEWS ON THE INTENT, EXTENT, AND APPLICATION OF THE ATONEMENT

	NON-CALVINISTS	MODERATE CALVINISTS	LIMITARIAN CALVINISTS
Intent of the Atonement	*Equal intent* to save all people.	*Unequal intent:* universal desire to save all but special intent to save only the elect.*	Most limitarians teach a universal desire to save all with a special intent to save only the elect, while others (hyper-Calvinists) maintain an intent to save only the elect.
Extent of the Atonement	Christ died for the sins of all people.	Christ died for the sins of all people.	Christ died *only* for the sins of the elect.
Application of the Atonement	Application limited to only those who believe.	Application limited to the elect because of unconditional election.	Application limited to the elect because of unconditional election.

Shaded area in each row equals agreement.

II. Arguments for Limited Atonement

If we categorize all the evidence proffered by limitarians for limited atonement and against unlimited atonement, we find they constellate around seventeen key broad-based arguments. I will engage and respond to all seventeen below. All but one class of arguments in favor of limited atonement proceed on logical or theological grounds and not on exegetical grounds. Since theology is (or at least should be) predicated on exegesis of the biblical text, we begin with the biblical data itself.

   A. Some Calvinists appeal to a small number of verses alleged to directly support limited atonement:

   Matthew 1:21: Christ came to save his people.
   John 10:15: Christ lays his life down for his sheep.

Acts 20:28: Christ purchased the church with his own blood.

Ephesians 5:23: Christ gave himself for the church.

The argument proceeds as follows: these verses state Christ died *for* a specific group (his people, his sheep, the church). Therefore, the necessary implication is that he did *not* die for others not subsumed in these categories. This argument commits the negative inference fallacy which states that specificity in a statement does not entail exclusion of those not among the specified group. Bare positive statements that Christ died for his "sheep," "the church," or "his people" cannot be legitimately interpreted to mean he did not die for others not in these categories. For example, if I say, "I love my wife," that does not necessarily entail that I love *only* my wife and therefore do not love my son, daughter, or someone else. To assert such is to make a logical error. This is the mistake made by all who attempt to affirm limited atonement *from these texts.*

Calvinists take the phrase "his people" in Matt 1:21 and interpret it theologically to refer to those whom Christ has elected to salvation. According to limitarians, since Christ died only for those whom he has unconditionally elected to salvation, this verse is taken as confirmation of that view.

However, to interpret "his people" in Matt 1:21 as the elect is hermeneutically flawed and a gross anachronism. Nowhere in Scripture does the phrase "his people" refer to anyone or anything other than the nation of Israel. A simple concordance search of the phrase makes this evident. A survey of the major exegetical commentaries on Matthew reveals that no commentator interprets the phrase "his people" to refer to anyone other than the nation of Israel, including most Reformed commentaries on Matthew. I find it interesting that Reformed systematic theologians often use this text as evidence of limited atonement, but Reformed biblical exegetes seldom if ever do. They know better. "His people" may be theologically used to describe the elect in Reformed theology, but it is never so used in Scripture.[20] Again, the negative inference fallacy comes into play, since God saves more than Jewish people; he also saves Gentiles. No matter how one slices it, using Matt 1:21 to support limited atonement is problematic. The verse is a statement of purpose and does not speak to the extent of the atonement at all.

---

[20] Even if "his people" is used to refer to an elect group, it cannot refer to all of the elect, since people still in unbelief are never called "his people" in Scripture. Many Reformed theologians fail to distinguish carefully between all the elect as an abstract class and those elect who are alive but in a preconversion state of unbelief.

John 10:15 is a statement that occurs within a broader context of the eternal security of those who belong to Christ via salvation and the fact that Christ will never abandon them. John 10 is not an atonement context; much less does it address the issue of the extent of the atonement. The verse does not explicitly teach a limited atonement. That is a deduction not made based on the teaching of the text itself but on a logical fallacy—negative inference.

What cannot be demonstrated is where John 10:15 logically demands that Christ died only for the sheep. By what logic does one exclude Jesus's critics from the scope of his death by the revelation that they are not his sheep? There is nothing in Jesus's statement that limits the scope of his death. As long as the Pharisees and other unbelievers refused what Jesus was saying, they were incapable of receiving the saving benefits of his death. Even if Jesus's statement indicates that his critics are not now nor ever will be among his sheep, that does not affirm or entail limited atonement.

However, that is not the only error made by limitarians in their interpretation of John 10:15. To assert this verse teaches limited atonement is to take what applies to existing believers and extrapolate the predication to all the elect in the abstract—the unborn and currently unbelieving elect. What are the exegetical grounds for reading "sheep" in John's context as the abstract class of all the elect? There are none. Notice Jesus describes the "sheep" as those who hear his voice and follow him in obedience. That cannot be said for all the elect. Where is the term "elect" in the New Testament ever used for anyone other than believers? Nowhere.

Here is the logical argument limitarians desire to set out from John 10:15:

1. Christ died for his sheep (where "sheep" are understood as all the elect of all time).
2. Pharisees are not his sheep (since Jesus states this is the case).
3. Therefore, Christ did not die for them.

Most defenders of limited atonement attempt to employ this kind of logical argument without stating it explicitly. But the argument is invalid. The conclusion does not follow, and the syllogism is logically fallacious. Consider this parallel example from Donald A. Carson:

All orthodox Jews believe in Moses.
Smith is not an orthodox Jew.
Therefore, Smith does not believe in Moses.[21]

---

[21] Donald A. Carson, *Exegetical Fallacies*, 2nd ed. (Grand Rapids: Baker, 1996), 102.

No matter how you parse it, this is invalid logic, and no sound argument can be grounded in an invalid logical argument. It does not matter what interpretation of the sheep one takes in John 10; the argument is invalid. Limitarians wrongly conclude from John 10 that Christ died only for those given to him. Jesus's statements in John 10 in no way prove exclusivity. When we are told Jesus died for his "friends," does that prove he died only for them? Did he not die for his enemies as well? I would point out also that contextually, those who are given to Christ are in a believing state as the sense of "friends" connotes. The point here is that simple positive statements cannot logically be used to infer category negations. To attempt to sustain the case for limited atonement in this way is merely a circular argument.

The point of John 10 is not about the extent of Christ's death at all, but the faithfulness and loyalty of Christ to the sheep. The Pharisees are the hirelings who abandon the sheep. Jesus is saying to them something like this: "I am not like you, who run away, rather I will lay my life down for the sheep, defending them to the end." And by implication, we, the sheep, can truly know that Christ has effectually saved us. There is no limited atonement in John 10:15 or in John 10 at all.

Acts 20:28 speaks of the church of God, which Christ purchased with his own blood. Limitarians want to read this verse as asserting limited atonement. It does not, and for the same reason above—the negative inference fallacy.

Ephesians 5:23 occurs in the context of Paul's discussion of the marriage union and how it reflects the nature of the relationship between Christ and his church. Paul's purpose is not to address the issue of the extent of the atonement but rather to show how the sacrificial love of Christ for his church is the foundation for the love that a husband should have for his wife. Proponents of limited atonement are making an invalid logical deduction that this statement asserts Christ died *only* for the church. Paul makes no such assertion. The logical error here is again the negative inference fallacy.

Limitarians wrongly interpret each of these texts because they assume the verses address the extent of the atonement (a hermeneutical error), speak of the elect as an abstract class (a theological error), and unwittingly employ the negative inference fallacy (a logical error).

B. Some Calvinists interpret Isaiah 53:12; Matthew 28:28; Mark 10:45; 14:24; and Hebrews 9:28 as support for limited atonement. In these texts Christ is said to die for or ransom the "many." Since "many" is used and not "all," limitarians deduce limited atonement from these texts.

However, the above is a serious misreading of the text and fails to note that the English "many" is a translation of a common Hebraism that actually means "all." Martin Hengel correctly noted that Matt 28:28, Mark 10:45, and Mark 14:24 are "connected by the universal service 'for the many,' in the sense of 'for all.'"[22] Paul employs the word "many" to mean "all" in Rom 5:15 and 19. Notice also Paul's interpretive allusion to the Isaiah 53 passage in 1 Tim 2:6 where he refers to Christ's cross as a "ransom" for "all." Paul is simply interpreting the "many" in Isaiah 53 correctly to mean "all."[23] Limitarians want to argue that "all" in all atonement texts always means "many," but refuse to admit "many" in all atonement texts always means "all"!

C. Some Calvinists interpret John 17:9 deductively to support limited atonement. "I pray for them. I am not praying for the world but for those you have given me, because they are yours" (John 17:9).

The context is Christ's intercessory prayer for the apostles on the eve of his crucifixion. The limitarian argument is simple: The extent of the intercession delimits the extent of the atonement such that Jesus only died for those for whom he prays. Or, to put it another way, for all for whom Christ died, he effectually intercedes. Jesus intercedes only for the elect; therefore, he died only for the sins of the elect. Since Jesus did not intercede for the world, he did not die for the sins of the world. This argument has been rebutted by many, including Calvinists.[24]

---

[22] Martin Hengel, *The Atonement: The Origins of the Doctrine in the New Testament* (Philadelphia: Fortress, 1981), 73. See also pp. 50, 70.

[23] Joachim Jeremias pointed out, in the Hebrew text there is no difference between the "many" of Isa 52:14–15 and Isa 53:11–12. All Jews and Gentiles are included. "For many" is not exclusive ("many, but not all"), but inclusive ("the totality, consisting of many"). John 6:51 demonstrates this usage in that "for many" is paraphrased as "for the life of the world." Jeremias, *The Eucharistic Words of Jesus* (Philadelphia: Fortress, 1966), 228–29. This is how John Calvin understood the meaning of "many" as well, both in Isaiah 53 and Mark 10:45: "'Many' is used, not for a definite number, but for a large number, in that He sets Himself over against all others. And this is its meaning also in Rom. 5.15, where Paul is not talking of a part of mankind but of the whole human race." Calvin, "A Harmony of the Gospels Matthew, Mark, and Luke," in *Calvin's New Testament Commentaries*, 12 vols., ed. David W. Torrance and Thomas F. Torrance, trans. T. H. L. Parker (Grand Rapids: Eerdmans, 1995), 2:277.

[24] See Richard Baxter, *Catholick Theologie* (London: printed by Robert White, 1675), 2:68–69; Harold Dekker, "God's Love to Sinners: One or Two?," *Reformed Journal* 13 (1963): 14–15; Edward Polhill, "The Divine Will Considered in Its Eternal Decrees," in *The Works of Edward Polhill* (Morgan, PA: Soli Deo Gloria, 1988), 167–68, 170–71, 174; and William G. T. Shedd, *Dogmatic Theology*, 3 vols. (Nashville: Thomas Nelson, 1980), 3:420–21. All of these men are Calvinists.

First, the text does not assert limited atonement. Second, in the text Jesus is praying for his apostles specifically. Third, the context makes clear the purpose and content of his prayer: unity.

The limitarian argument is based in logic, not the actual context, and proceeds in a *modus tollens* fashion:[25]

1. If Christ died for a person, Christ will effectually pray for that person.
2. Christ does not pray for some people.
3. Therefore, Christ did not die for some people (those for whom he did not pray).

The problem is with the first (major) premise. A logically invalid inference is being drawn that cannot be sustained from Scripture. John 17:9 does not state or even imply that Christ only prays for some people, much less that these people for whom he prays are the "elect" according to Reformed theology. The text does not state that Jesus died only for the sins of those for whom he prays. Limitarians fall prey to two logical fallacies in their argument: (1) the negative inference fallacy, and (2) the generalizing fallacy (namely, election entails limited atonement). The mistake here is a collapsing of the intercession of Christ into his expiation for sins. This merely begs the question of the extent of the atonement.[26]

The ones who are "given" to Christ are the eleven apostles, according to the context. Moreover, Christ prays for future believers in v. 21 and finally for the "world" in v. 23. David Ponter pointed out how limitarians merely allege, assume, and assert without any evidence the following when it comes to John 17:

1. That this is a specific and effectual high priestly prayer on the part of Jesus.
2. That the "world" of v. 9 represents the world of the reprobate.
3. That those "given" in v. 9 represent the totality of the elect.
4. That the extent of the high priestly intercession delimits the scope of the satisfaction.

---

[25] *Modus tollens* is a form of logical argument stating: if a conditional statement is accepted (*if p then q*), and the consequent does not hold true (*not-q*), then the negation of the antecedent (*not-p*) can be inferred.

[26] See Allen, *The Atonement*, 171–75; Leon Morris, *The Gospel According to John*, NICNT (Grand Rapids: Eerdmans, 1971), 725; and Donald A. Carson, *The Gospel According to John*, PNTC (Grand Rapids: Eerdmans, 1991), 560–61.

5. That the two parallel clauses in vv. 21 and 23 are systemically overlooked or misread.[27]

In John 17 Jesus prayed for three groups: the disciples exclusively (v. 9); all future believers (v. 21); and finally, unbelievers—that is, the "world" in normal Johannine usage (v. 23). Jesus prayed for the world's salvation, as evidenced by the subjunctive mood in Greek: "that the world may believe" and "that the world may know." Jesus prayed for the unity of the apostles and all future believers (or for all disciples as such) for the stated purpose: that the world may believe and know that Jesus had been sent from the Father. Rather than supporting limited atonement, John 17 supports an unlimited atonement. Limited atonement is neither asserted nor can it be validly deduced from John 17:9.[28]

The same situation applies to Heb 7:25, another verse often used to assert limited atonement. Christ's intercession is for those who "come to" him. But the author of Hebrews does not say that all for whom Christ died he therefore intercedes for in prayer. The logical argument for limited atonement from these verses is flawed from the start.

D. Some Calvinists argue that the words "world" and "all" either do not mean or cannot mean "all who have lived, are alive now, or shall live in the future." Hence, texts that speak of Christ dying for the sins of the "world" or for "all" people do not teach unlimited atonement. From these texts, limited atonement is deduced.

The argument fails for several reasons. First, even if these texts are reinterpreted as limitarians wish to do, said texts cannot be logically interpreted to affirm limited atonement. Unless words like "only" or semantic equivalents are employed in atonement texts speaking of extent, to deduce limited atonement would be to invoke the negative inference fallacy once again.

Second, the issue is not whether these words can sometimes mean something less inclusive than every person currently living, or all people who have lived, live now, or will be alive in the future. That is not in dispute. The problem is, when "world" is used in contexts addressing the extent of the atonement, it is clear that "world" is all-inclusive, usually in the sense of *all unbelievers*, whether elect or not. Take, for

---

[27] David Ponter, "Revisiting John 17 and Jesus' Prayer for the World," *Calvin and Calvinism: An Elenchus for Classic-Moderate Calvinism* (blog), February 10, 2015, http://calvinandcalvinism .com/?p=15779.

[28] Allen, *The Atonement*, 171–75.

example, John 3:16. It is exegetically impossible to restrict the word "world" here to mean anything less than all humanity by application, or at least all *unbelieving* humanity in terms of meaning, since the disobedient "world," contextually, stands in need of salvation (v. 17). Francis Turretin spent four futile pages in a vain attempt to make "world" in John 3:16 refer only to the elect and finally acknowledged that his own interpretation differed from Calvin, who affirmed that "world" in this text means all humanity.[29] Calvin's treatment of John 3:16 should be read carefully. He made the salient point that because the atonement is unlimited in nature, those who reject Christ are "doubly culpable":

> Our Lord Jesus suffered for all and there is neither great nor small who is not inexcusable today, for we can obtain salvation in Him. Unbelievers who turn away from Him and who deprive themselves of Him by their malice are today *doubly culpable*. For how will they excuse their ingratitude in not receiving the blessing in which they could share by faith?[30]

Christ was offered as a sacrifice to all the world.[31] Calvin asserted that John 3:16 affirms Jesus "suffered for all." Furthermore, because salvation is obtainable for all on the grounds of an unlimited atonement, those who reject Christ are "inexcusable." Finally, these are "doubly culpable," because they "turn away" from Christ and have no excuse for "their ingratitude in not receiving the blessing in which they could share by faith."[32]

Third, limitarians attempt to get around the unlimited meaning of "all" and "world" by arguing that "all" means "some of all kinds of people" and "world" actually means "the world of the elect," or "all elect people without distinction," or "all kinds of elect people," or "elect Jews and Gentiles," or "all the elect within the nations."

---

[29] Francis Turretin, *Institutes of Elenctic Theology*, 3 vols., trans. George Musgrove Giger, ed. James T. Dennison Jr. (Phillipsburg, NJ: P&R, 1992), 1:405–8.

[30] John Calvin, *Sermons on Isaiah's Prophecy of the Death and Passion of Christ* (Geneva, 1559; repr., London: James Clark, 1956), 141; emphasis added.

[31] Contextually it is clear Calvin did not mean Christ is "offered" through the preaching of the gospel (though he certainly affirmed this), but rather referred to Christ's atonement. Moreover, in the context, Calvin seems to have unbelievers in mind in his conception of the "world."

[32] That Calvin held to unlimited atonement can no longer be doubted by any fair-minded inquirer. See Allen, *Extent of the Atonement*, 48–96, for a detailed discussion of Calvin's view of the extent of the atonement, including analysis of primary and secondary literature on the subject. See also Paul A. Hartog, *Calvin and the Death of Christ: A Word for the World* (Eugene, OR: Cascade Books, 2021).

Most modern limitarians have given up on interpreting "world" as the world of the
elect (an interpretation they inherited from John Owen), and seldom does one see
that argument today. They recognize that exegetically the word "world" is never
used for the "elect" in Scripture.[33] The standard approach is to go the "all without
distinction" route.

Fourth, we must watch the subtle but illegitimate hermeneutical shift limitarians
make at this point with "all" and "world" in atonement contexts. "All without distinction"
or "all kinds of people" is converted to mean "some of all kinds of people." "World" is
taken to mean "all people without distinction" or "all kinds of people," which is then
further interpreted to mean "some of all kinds of people." Thus, "all" becomes "some
of all sorts," an exegetically and hermeneutically unwarranted and illegitimate move.

With respect to the New Testament atonement texts that use universal
language, the bifurcation of "all without distinction" and "all without exception" is
ultimately a distinction without a difference. If I speak of all people without racial,
gender, or other distinctions, am I not speaking of all people without exception?
The distinction is artificial. Nothing in the lexicon of these words, or in the syntax
of the texts, or in the context supports such an interpretation. The interpretation
is solely driven by dogmatics—limited atonement is assumed to be theologically
correct, so the texts simply cannot be interpreted to mean what they appear to
mean on the surface.

Take 1 Tim 2:1–6 as an example. Limitarians essentially convert "all" in 1 Tim 2:6
to mean "some." In the Greek text, the word "all" (*pantōn*, 1 Tim 2:6) obviously refers
to people, and in conjunction with v. 5 (where Jesus is "the one mediator between
God and humanity," HCSB), the "all" of v. 6 clearly corresponds to "humanity" of v. 5.
The limitarian interpreter makes "all" refer to "all without distinction" (i.e., "all kinds
of people") and then makes this refer to "some of all kinds of people." But note that
with this maneuver, the modifier "all" no longer stands for "all people" but modifies
"kinds" of people.

Contextually, is Paul urging Christians to pray for all "kinds of people" or for
individual people in such a way that no concrete, particular person is to be excluded

[33] Commenting on John 3:16, Donald A. Carson notes how some take the "world" as the
elect. He rejects such a notion and says, "All the evidence of the usage of the word in John's
Gospel is against the suggestion." Carson, *The Difficult Doctrine of the Love of God* (Wheaton,
IL: Crossway, 2000), 17.

from prayer? The latter is obviously the case, and this is how Calvin (properly, I might add) interpreted the text.[34]

The phrase "all people" is unrestricted in v. 1 and is all-inclusive. Paul then asserted God's desire for "all" people to be saved. There is nothing restrictive in the word "all" here either. Finally, the ground for the possible salvation of "all" people is the atonement of Christ: "For there is . . . one mediator between God and humanity, the man Christ Jesus, who gave himself as a ransom for all" (vv. 5–6).[35]

With respect to 1 John 2:2, John Owen and all limitarians who follow his lead create a modus tollens argument for limited atonement based on how they read this verse:

1. If Christ has died for the sins of a given person, that person cannot fail to be saved.
2. Some people fail to be saved.
3. Therefore, Christ did not die for those who fail to be saved.

Thus, the atonement must be limited.

The problem is with the major premise. Nowhere in Scripture is this proposition ever stated, nor can it be obtained by valid inference from Scripture. This idea is a theological assumption injected into the text.

Nevertheless, limitarians attempt to find ways to limit the meaning of "the whole world" to something less than all unbelievers living on earth at the time of John's writing. Three different approaches are taken with respect to the meaning of "the whole world": (1) the elect, (2) the world of Gentiles and/or Jews and Gentiles, and (3) all kinds of people in the world—i.e., all people "without distinction" (race, ethnicity, gender, etc.), not all people "without exception." These interpretations overlap, and those who support limited atonement usually argue that for John (at least in 1 John 2:2) "world" means all the believing elect without distinction from among both Jews and Gentiles.

Contextually, none of the three suggested meanings for "the whole world" corresponds with what John says in the text. As to "world" signifying Gentiles, or

---

[34] Calvin, *Sermons on Timothy* (Edinburgh: Banner of Truth, 1983), 177. Here Calvin spoke of a group of people ("Turks") "which cast away the grace which was purchased for all the world."

[35] See the excellent treatment of this text in I. Howard Marshall, *A Critical and Exegetical Commentary on the Pastoral Epistles*, ICC (Edinburgh: T&T Clark, 1999), 425–33.

Jews and Gentiles—this meaning is, likewise, never found anywhere in the New Testament. But since the Jews divided all people into two groups, Jews and non-Jews (Gentiles), then even this distinction semantically is a reference to all unbelieving people without exception. Moreover, John cannot mean the "Gentiles" alone in 1 John 2:2 because in 1 John 5:19, both the unbelieving Gentile world and unbelieving Jews live under the power of Satan. As to "world" meaning "all kinds of people without distinction," the same holds true. This is a distinction without a difference.[36]

Finally, in the limitarian reading of 1 John 2:2, the argument converts the noun *hilasmos* into a past-tense verb. The claim is that if Christ has paid for the sins of an individual, that person cannot fail to be saved. However, in 1 John 2:2, *hilasmos* as a noun is timeless and references the provision of propitiation/expiation, which is not only available to the believer who has sinned, but also to every sinner in the "whole world."[37]

Passages like John 1:29, John 3:16, 1 Tim 2:4–6, and 1 John 2:2 simply cannot be shackled with the limiting lexical chains that restrict the meaning of "world" and "all" to something less than all unbelieving humanity. It is simply not exegetically possible to interpret "all" and "world" in the texts listed above, and several others, in a limited fashion.

The bottom line here is that "all people" becomes, for proponents of limited atonement, "some people of all kinds." *All* becomes *some*. In 1 Tim 2:4–6, Paul's intent is to say that Jesus is the Savior of all people without distinction, which simply also means all people without exception.

E. Some Calvinists interpret certain words or phrases in specific texts to imply limited atonement. The operative word here is *imply*. These texts do not assert limited atonement. No scriptural text does. For example, John 11:51–52 is compared with 1 John 5:2 and used to assert limited atonement. John 11:51–52 states that Caiaphas "prophesied that Jesus was going to die for the nation, and not for the nation only, but also to unite the scattered children of God." First John 5:2 states, "This is how we know that we love God's children: when we love God and obey his commands."

John speaks of Jesus as dying "for the nation," an obvious in-context reference to the nation of Israel. Furthermore, he also died with the purpose "to unite the

---

[36] Allen, *The Atonement*, 158–62.
[37] Allen, 160–61.

scattered children of God." Children of God is taken here by the limitarian to refer to all the elect among the nations of the world. Presumably, John's use of "for the nation" means something along the lines of "the elect within the nation of Israel," though the text does not state such. "God's children" in 1 John 5:2 refers again to the "elect," according to this reading. It is difficult to see how 1 John 5:2 can be used as any evidence for limited atonement, even when connected with John 11:51–52. In context, "the scattered children of God" is most likely a reference to the Gentiles who benefit from the death of Christ as well as the nation of Israel.[38] Since John spoke of the nation of Israel and not the elect among the nation of Israel, and since he spoke of the Gentiles and not the elect among the Gentiles, this text could be marshalled as indirect evidence supporting unlimited atonement.

F. Some Calvinists utilize John Owen's famous "trilemma" argument, which is based on his "double-payment" argument. Owen set up the following trilemma:

Christ died for either

1. all the sins of all people,
2. some of the sins of all people, or
3. all the sins of some people.[39]

Owen's assumption is this: if Jesus paid the penalty for the sins of a given person, then God cannot demand a second payment from that person. Owen wanted to prove the impossibility of the first major premise in his trilemma. To do so, he constructs a modus tollens argument:

1. If Christ died for the sins of someone, that person cannot fail to be finally saved.
2. Some people are not finally saved.
3. Therefore, Christ did not die for the sins of some people.

Thus, limited atonement must be true.

---

[38] Another possible interpretation is that the reference is to the Jews in the Diaspora. Andreas Köstenberger, *John*, BECNT (Grand Rapids: Baker, 2004), 353.

[39] John Owen, *The Death of Death in the Death of Christ*, in *The Works of John Owen*, 16 vols., ed. W. H. Goold (New York: Robert Carter and Brothers, 1852), 10:173.

Owen failed to acknowledge, or at least overlooked, the fact that the benefits of the atonement are only applied conditionally—one must believe in Christ to be saved. If this condition is not met, a person cannot be saved. Even on a Calvinist reading, Eph 2:1–3 makes this evident, as even the unbelieving elect are "children under wrath" before their salvation. The argument assumes the mechanism of the atonement operates like a commercial transaction where a debt is paid and thus discharged. We shall see more on this when we examine the double-payment argument below.

Owen's trilemma argument faces many of the same kinds of problems as the double-payment argument, two of which appear to be insurmountable. The first is the problem of the issue of original sin. Notice it is not original "sins" but original "sin." If Christ died for original sin, then he died for at least one of the sins of all people, including the non-elect. If this is the case, then the argument is defeated, as it would have to be admitted that Christ died for some of the sins (original sin) of all people.

The second problem concerns the issue of how imputation of sin works. Thinking of the imputation of sin to Christ as a transference of the guilt of specific transgressions is problematic in that it operates on a commercialistic mechanism. Limited atonement necessitates a quantifiable form of imputation of sin—and that is commercialism. Commercialism is not less than a conception of the death of Christ in literal debt categories with quantifiable suffering for so many sins. The atonement does not purchase things, such as commodities like faith, grace, and so forth, in any literal transactional sense. Redemption, in the sense of a ransom price, in Scripture should always be understood metaphorically. In Scripture, people are always the object of redemption, not commodities. No one is "paid" anything when it comes to the atonement and its application.[40]

The biblical approach to imputation is that Christ suffered sufficiently for all *categories* of human sin which, by definition, includes every human sin. The key is understanding imputation as transference in a metaphorical sense rather than a literal sense.

The triple choice argument undermines the true meaning of imputation and operates on the assumption of the transference of specific, quantifiable sins. This problem is explained in #7 below.

---

[40] For a more detailed discussion of commercialism and the atonement, see Allen, *The Atonement*, 227–33.

G. Some Calvinists utilize John Owen's double-payment argument. The argument proceeds as follows: If the ransom is paid, justice demands that those for whom it is paid must go free. It cannot be said to be paid for any who are not eventually freed. Or to put it another way, if God punished the sins of someone on the cross and then punished the sinner again in hell, this would be unjust on God's part. A related argument is called the "double-jeopardy" argument. In our system of law and justice, a person cannot be charged and punished twice for the same crime. Thus, limited atonement is deduced.

The assumption is that if Christ died for the sins of a given person, God cannot demand a second satisfaction from that person. The argument proceeds logically in a modus tollens fashion, attempting to prove the impossibility of the major premise:

1. If Christ died for a person, that person cannot fail to be finally saved.
2. Some people are not finally saved.
3. Therefore, Christ did not die for the sins of some people.

There are flaws in the double-payment argument. First, this argument is never made in Scripture. Second, the first premise is never asserted in Scripture. Third, the argument falsely assumes that the same person is being punished twice. There is no unilateral equivalence between Christ's punishment on the cross and the unbeliever's punishment in hell. It is never the case that the same person is charged and punished for the same crime, because in the one case it is the person of Christ who bore the punishment, and in the other case it is the person of the sinner who bears the punishment should he fail to believe.

Fourth, the argument is based on a commercial understanding of the atonement. It fails to understand that the language of debt and ransom is metaphorical and not literal. The argument assumes that if Christ died for someone, this is equivalent to saving that person. The mistake is viewing God as a creditor because sin is metaphorically described as a debt. Sin as debt is about obligation, not about the death of Christ being a payment to a creditor (God). Nowhere in Scripture is God ever viewed as the "creditor" who is paid a debt via the death of Christ.

The double-payment argument only works on the assumption that the death of Christ works transactionally and is commercial in nature such that it is comparable to a literal debt payment. The blood of Christ is metaphorically or analogically compared to commercial transactions in Scripture via the use of debt language, such as "ransom," "redemption," or "purchase." Such language is not meant to describe the actual mechanism of how atonement works. Christ's blood is not a literal commercial commodity. Sin is a debt, but it is more than a debt—it is a crime against God's law with moral implications. Criminal debt is not equivalent to commercial debt.

For example, suppose you and I are dining in a restaurant. When the bill arrives, I suddenly realize I have no money on me. In my embarrassing situation, you kindly agree to pay my bill. The restaurant owner does not care who pays the bill as long as the bill is paid. What I owed is settled because you paid my debt. This is an example of a commercial debt. But suppose, when the bill arrives and I lack the money to pay my debt, after you pay the bill for both of us, I get mad, lose my mind, rob the restaurant of $500 in cash, and abscond into the night. You, in your kindness, pay back the $500 I stole to the restaurant owner. Later, when I am apprehended, am I free to go because you paid my debt? No! Criminal debt is not equivalent to commercial debt.

Let us alter the scenario slightly. Suppose that after I steal the $500, you are suspected of the theft, charged, and serve six months jail time. Later, it is discovered that I committed the crime, and after being charged and found guilty, I am sent to jail to serve six months. I cannot say: "You can't send me to jail, the debt has been paid! Someone else has paid for my crime!" No, criminal "debt" obligations do not work that way. Just because the debt has been paid by one who did not commit the crime, it does not follow that I am liberated from my criminal obligation before the law. Sin is a violation of God's law, which renders the sinner criminally guilty before God.[41]

The argument does not, and in fact, cannot work on a penal model or on other noncommercial models. Scripture makes clear that God has annexed a condition that must be met before the atonement is applied: faith in Christ. Thus, the atonement is made for all people and its saving benefit is conditional, according to Scripture.

Fifth, the double-payment argument negates the principle of grace. Charles Hodge stated: "There is no grace in accepting a pecuniary satisfaction. It cannot be refused. It *ipso facto* liberates. The moment the debt is paid the debtor is free; and that without any condition. Nothing of this is true in the case of judicial satisfaction."[42] The double-payment argument undermines grace because salvation is then, by entailment, "owed" to the elect.[43]

---

[41] Allen, 163–66.

[42] Charles Hodge, *Systematic Theology*, 3 vols. (Grand Rapids: Eerdmans, 1993), 2:557.

[43] A point well made by Andrew Fuller: "But it [the view of Christ's death as a literal payment of a debt] would be equally inconsistent with the free *forgiveness* of sin, and with sinners being directed to apply for mercy as *supplicants*, rather than as *claimants*." "The Gospel Worthy of All Acceptation," in *The Complete Works of the Rev. Andrew Fuller*, ed. J. Belcher, 3 vols.

Sixth, the double-payment argument proves too much. The question must be asked, Why are the elect not justified at the cross? How can they be condemned (John 3:18)? Yet Eph 2:1–3 states that even the unbelieving elect remain under the wrath of God before their conversion. How can this be if the double-payment argument is valid?

Seventh, the argument undermines the role of faith by denying the need for any condition in salvation. Salvation was not purchased to be given to anyone absolutely, whether or not they believe, but only upon the exercise of faith. It is no injustice if salvation is not given to someone who fails to fulfill God's condition, even though a substitutionary satisfaction for their sins has been made. Instead of the "double payment" argument against unlimited atonement,[44] limitarians should ponder Calvin's "doubly culpable" argument for unlimited atonement.[45]

H. Some Calvinists attempt to deduce limited atonement by asking if the sin of unbelief is atoned for in the death of Christ. If Christ died for the sins of all, does that include the sin of unbelief? If so, universalism would result.

The above question is related to the previous question concerning double payment and John Owen's trilemma argument. Christ died for either (1) all the sins of all people, (2) some of the sins of all people, or (3) all of the sins of some people. Owen concluded that options 1 and 2 are problematic. If option 1 is true, Owen queried whether unbelief was a sin atoned for by Christ's death. If so, how can one suffer in hell for a sin already atoned for?

Owen's argument raises questions he did not answer. Is substitution conceived quantitatively in Scripture? It is not, but Owen conceived of it this way. If unbelief is atoned for, according to Owen's commercialistic method of arguing, why are the elect

---

(Harrisonburg, VA: Sprinkle, 1988), 2:373; italics in the original. See also Fuller, "The Gospel Its Own Witness," in *Complete Works*, 2:80–82.

[44] For a critique of the double-payment argument from a Calvinist, consult Oliver D. Crisp, *Deviant Calvinism: Broadening Reformed Theology* (Minneapolis: Fortress, 2014), 213–33. Crisp makes use of Robert Lewis Dabney's criticisms of the double-payment argument. See also Michael Lynch, "Quid Pro Quo Satisfaction? An Analysis and Response to Garry Williams on Penal Substitutionary Atonement and Definite Atonement," *Evangelical Quarterly* 89, no. 1 (2018): 51–70. Lynch correctly pointed out that the infallibility of the atonement's application to the elect is not found in the nature of the atonement itself because this would assume a commercialistic logic concerning the satisfaction for sins. Moreover, such an approach collapses the distinction between election and the atonement.

[45] Calvin, *Sermons on Isaiah's Prophecy*, 141.

not saved at the cross? What is the relationship of unbelief to the unforgivable sin? These are questions Owen never gets around to answering.

Owen's argument defeats itself by proving too much, as Neil Chambers argued.[46] If Christ died for all the sins of some people (the elect), then he must also have died for their unbelief. If this is the case, then why are the elect not saved at the cross? If Owen replies that it is because the benefits of Christ's death are not yet applied to them, then they remain in an unbelieving state and therefore cannot be spoken of as saved in any way. Paul confirms this in Eph 2:1–3 when he states that even the unbelieving elect remain under the wrath of God (or liable to damnation) in their unbelieving state. But, according to Owen, since their penalty has been paid, they cannot be punished for that unbelief, as he has already stated that God will not exact a second payment for the one offense (double-payment argument).

Owen has engaged in polemical reductionism in his consideration of "unbelief" because unbelief is not just an offense like any other; it is also a state, which must be dealt with not only by forgiveness but by regeneration. Chambers noted that Owen recognized this in relating the cross to the causal removal of unbelief as a state, but unbelief regarded as a sin and unbelief regarded as a state bear different relations to the cross. Sin bears a direct relation to the cross, which is the enduring of the penalty for sin; the change of state from unregenerate to regenerate (from being lost to being saved) bears an indirect relation to the cross and is dependent upon preaching and regeneration by the Spirit. Chambers then pointed out that for Owen to acknowledge that reality, he would have to say that Christ died for all the sin, including the unbelief, of those who believe and for none of the sins of those who don't believe. But for the polemical force of his argument, Owen ignored the distinction that would place too much weight on human response and expose his argument to criticism.

We turn now to consider several less-common arguments for limited atonement that are occasionally propounded.

I. Some Calvinists interpret Rom 5:8-10 and Rom 8:32 to imply limited atonement. The argument proceeds as follows: There is an intrinsic effectiveness

---

[46] See also Allen, *Extent of the Atonement*, 204–23, where I draw heavily on material from Calvinist Neil Chambers's dissertation, "A Critical Examination of John Owen's Argument for Limited Atonement in *The Death of Death in the Death of Christ*" (ThM thesis, Reformed Theological Seminary, 1998), 233–39. Chambers's critique of Owen's limitarian arguments is the most substantive of which I am aware.

within the atonement itself such that all for whom it is made receive the efficacious benefits of it, in other words, salvation.

The argument attempts to construct a logical link between atonement accomplished and atonement applied. The argument is derived via logical deduction:

1. The atonement is self-effectively applied to all for whom Christ was delivered up (to die).
2. The atonement is not applied to some people.
3. Therefore, Christ was not delivered up (to die) for some people.

Robert Some of Cambridge published a tract in 1596 listing arguments for limited atonement. One of his texts was Rom 8:33–34.[47]

Before we consider the syllogism above, note that both passages in Romans employ biconditionals: if A and B, then C. In other words, if Christ died for us, and if we have believed, then we shall be saved. This construction is biblical and valid logically. The error limitarians make is the false inference (logically) that if someone is not saved, then Christ did not make an atonement for their sins. The valid inference is that either Christ did not die for them or they have not believed. Since we have already eliminated the possibility that Christ did not die for them, it follows that the reason someone is not saved is because that person has not believed.

Whereas the biconditionals are overtly stated in Rom 5:8–10, the key to Rom 8:32 is wrapped up in the meaning of "us." Who are the "us"? Contextually from Paul's standpoint, clearly the "us" references "we who have believed" (Heb 4:3). Paul's argument in Rom 8:32 is enthymematic. An enthymeme is a particular means of expressing a syllogistic argument that has one proposition, usually a premise, left unstated. Most syllogistic arguments in ordinary oral or written language are enthymematic. Overt expression of each premise and conclusion would be rhetorically pedantic as one would be stating the obvious. In Rom 8:32, unlike Rom 5:8–10, Paul's premise of the intervening conditional of "faith" is left unstated. The "us" references those who have believed. To assert that the "us" can be interpreted to mean "all the elect of all time," including the unborn and unbelieving elect, has no exegetical grounds and is a purely theological move grounded in Reformed dogmatics, not careful exegesis of the text.[48]

---

[47] See Allen, 126.

[48] See my full treatment of Rom 8:32 here: David L. Allen, "Romans 8:31–34 Again . . . Responding to James White," https://drdavidlallen.com/romans-831-34-again-responding-to -james-white/. It is interesting to see how Calvin treated this text. He conflated John 3:16

J. Some Calvinists employ the purchase of faith argument for limited atonement. Faith is a condition of salvation, as Scripture clearly asserts. According to limitarians, this faith has been purchased for all those who have been predestined for salvation, and only for those so predestined. For their sins and theirs alone did Christ die. Philippians 1:29 is often used to support this claim.

The argument is syllogistic and unfolds in the following way:

1. Faith is purchased in the atonement and given to all for whom Christ died.
2. Faith is not purchased in the atonement and thus not given to some people.
3. Therefore, Christ did not die on behalf of some people.

The failure of the argument is in the first premise. All Phil 1:29 says is that those who believe have been granted some capacity to believe. There is no reference here to the extent of the atonement. The verse does not say that all for whom Christ died are granted faith, much less that all for whom Christ died have faith purchased on their behalf. Paul says nothing here about the so-called elect in an abstract class including all unborn and unbelieving elect.

Moreover, if this verse indicates a purchase of faith, then the verse ends up proving too much, as it would be necessary to assert that all suffering has also been purchased by the atonement since both infinitives in Greek, *pisteuein* (to believe) and *paschein* (to suffer), are equally governed by the same verb, *echaristhē* (given, granted).

Paul presents no mechanism or causal chain that the atonement purchases faith. This is an example of Reformed dogmatics being read into the text. One can see that in virtually all the exegetical commentaries, including those written by Calvinists, the purchase-of-faith argument is not mentioned in their discussions of Phil 1:29.

There is a sense in which faith is a gift from God. But faith is never said to be something "purchased" for the elect. The error is in thinking that faith as a gift is equivalent to faith as a purchase. In Owen's scheme, faith becomes something like a commodity instead of what it is: a relational response. "Gift" is the language of grace. "Purchase" is the language of rights. Owen even states that the elect are "owed" salvation.[49] This is contrary to Scripture and negates grace.

---

and Rom 8:32, thus demonstrating his adherence to unlimited atonement. Allen, *Extent of the Atonement*, 69–70.

[49] Allen, 213–14.

K. Some Calvinists appeal to Old Testament covenant typology in support of limited atonement. Limitation in the old covenant (benefits limited to the nation of Israel) entails a limitation in the new covenant (the elect).[50] The argument carries no weight and merely begs the question. This argument struggles to answer the rebuttal question of whether in the final analysis every Israelite received salvation. For the argument to hold, this would have to be asserted by the limitarian. But none assert this, as it is obvious that not every single person in Israel received ultimate salvation. Yet the old covenant sacrifice addressed the sins of the nation, as Isa 53:6 asserts, "We all went astray like sheep; we all have turned to our own way; and the LORD has punished him for the iniquity of us all."

Another problem for this line of argument is that many Gentiles were received into the people of God as proselytes. Did the old Mosaic covenant and sacrificial system not atone for their sins? The old Mosaic covenant and sacrificial system did indeed atone for their sins, in the sense that the actual atonement was grounded proleptically in the death of Christ on the cross, since Heb 10:1–4 makes clear it is impossible that the blood of bulls and goats should take away sin. Though the proselytes were not originally part of the old covenant, they became a part of that covenant, and their sins were atoned for.

The typology of the Old Testament indicates an unlimited atonement. First Corinthians 5:7 refers to the Old Testament Passover as a type of the death of Christ. According to Exodus 12, was the firstborn of the home protected from death merely because the lamb had been slain? No. God did not say, "When I see that the lamb has been slain, I will pass over you." Rather, He said, "When I see the blood [on the two doorposts and the lintel], I will pass over you" (Exod 12:7, 13). The lamb had to be slain to provide salvation for the firstborn, but the blood also had to be applied before the provision became effective on his behalf. Peter showed that being "sprinkled with the blood," in fulfillment of the type, speaks of the obedience of faith, the personal application, by faith, of Christ's death (1 Pet 1:2).[51]

L. Some Calvinists assert that the blood of Christ was "wasted" or "shed in vain" for those eternally lost as an argument for limited atonement. Some

---

[50] Hugh Martin developed this argument in detail. See Hugh Martin, *The Atonement: In Its Relations to the Covenant, the Priesthood, the Intercession of Our Lord* (1877; repr., Edinburgh: Banner of Truth, 2013).

[51] Allen, *The Atonement*, 156–57.

who argue for limited atonement assert that if some people for whom Christ died experience eternal punishment, then somehow the blood of Christ has been "wasted" or "shed in vain" for them. This was a common argument by John Owen.[52] The argument presupposes that if God wills that Christ die for the sins of all people, and all those for whom he died are not ultimately saved from their sins, then God is doing something in vain or is wasting his efforts to bring about an end that ultimately remains unfulfilled.

There are several problems with the "wasted blood" argument. First, one must distinguish between defect or failure in the atonement itself versus failure due to the fault of unbelievers to receive the benefit of the atonement because of lack of faith. The atonement itself is perfect and complete. It is sufficient to save anyone who meets God's condition of salvation: repentance of sin and faith in Christ.

Second, the argument fails to appreciate the benevolent nature of God as revealed in Scripture. He causes the rain to fall upon the just and the unjust (Matt 5:45). Third, who are we to tell God that Christ died in vain when God tells us that Christ died for all, even for those who ultimately reject him? As Richard Baxter said, we should "be afraid of blaspheming God" by suggesting that Christ died in vain.[53]

M. Some Calvinists assert that universal atonement leads to universalism (universalism argument). Does universal atonement entail universalism; that is, that all will therefore be eternally saved? The argument confuses the extent of the atonement with its application. The atonement, in and of itself, saves no one. Only when the atonement is applied does salvation occur.

Relatedly, the argument wrongly understands the nature of the atonement as a commercial transaction—if Christ died for someone's sins, then those sins are ipso facto forgiven. This is not how the atonement works. "Atoned for" does not equal "saved." The atonement does not secure its own application. God has annexed the condition of faith in Christ for the benefits of the atonement (salvation) to be applied. No one (of age) is saved apart from faith in Christ. Even the unbelieving elect (the

---

[52] See Owen, *The Death of Death*, 149, 238, 248, 413. Owen spoke of Christ's blood being spilled "in vain."

[53] Baxter, *Catholick Theologie*, 2:66–67. For more on this issue, see Allen, *The Atonement*, 223–25. It would be similarly absurd to argue that the tree of life in the garden was a waste (or put there in vain) because God, according to Reformed theology, did not ordain that Adam would eat from it. Surely it was an objective sign of the generosity and provision of God for Adam's eternal well-being, even though it was rejected.

elect in their unbelieving state) are still under the wrath of God, according to Eph 2:1–3, and should they die in that state would be eternally lost (as John Piper rightly acknowledged in his chapter in *From Heaven He Came and Sought Her*).[54]

N. Some Calvinists contend that unlimited atonement makes the atonement "potential" but not "actual" in that many for whom Jesus died never receive the benefits of the atonement (efficacy argument). At the heart of this argument is the belief in what is called the "efficacy of the atonement." Limitarians generally argue that somehow the atonement itself secures its own application for the elect. However, *the atonement in and of itself does not secure its own application.* Nowhere in Scripture is this taught. The *application* of the atonement *by the Holy Spirit* in regeneration serves as the efficacy for the atonement. The atonement is what legally grounds the salvation of any individual. The atonement itself does not make salvation "certain." God does that through the Holy Spirit at the point of regeneration when the benefits of the atonement (forgiveness of sins; salvation) are *applied* to the believer in Christ.

Limitarians attempt to impale their opponents on the horns of a dilemma: either the atonement is actual, or it is only potential. But such an argument engages in equivocation and a false dilemma. The equivocation is the substitution of "atonement" for actual "salvation" when the atonement is applied. Atonement accomplished must be distinguished from atonement applied, as Scripture does. The atonement is an actual, completed event. There is nothing "potential" about it. However, "salvation" in the sense of atonement applied is potential for all for whom atonement has been accomplished, *upon condition of faith.*

The limitarian errs by considering the atonement itself as a cause effected by God alone that brings about an effect (salvation for the elect) *without any intervening condition.* But this understanding of the atonement leaves out something important in the equation: the reality of intervening conditions (biconditionals). For example, take the statement "Jesus actually saves all who believe." This is how Scripture puts things. Never in Scripture are we told that the atonement itself saves anyone. Scripture knows of no salvation apart from belief.

Therefore, on the grounds of an accomplished atonement, Jesus is the potential Savior of all people. Salvation is not actualized until the mechanism of faith occurs.

---

[54] John Piper, "'My Glory I Will Not Give to Another!' Preaching the Fullness of Definite Atonement to the Glory of God," in Gibson and Gibson, *From Heaven He Came*, 633–67.

Before that point, salvation is, and in fact *has to be*, potential. According to Eph 2:3, even the unbelieving elect (thinking of election from a Calvinistic perspective) are under the wrath of God ("we were by nature children under wrath"). The atonement itself does not save anyone until faith is exercised.[55]

Limitarians collapse the potentiality into actuality—a major error. Their logic proceeds in this fashion:

1. Jesus can only be the potential Savior of the ones for whose sins he died.
2. Jesus did not die for the non-elect.
3. Therefore, there is no potential salvation for the non-elect.

Proposition 2 is the point of contention, and thus limitarians are merely begging the question. It is a false dilemma to assert that either Jesus is an actual Savior or he is only a potential Savior.

Jesus saves all who believe, based on an all-sufficient atonement accomplished for the sins of all people. This is the clear teaching of Scripture.

Non-Calvinists affirm that Christ died to make all people savable and with the special intention to save only those who believe (who are also the elect). It is false to say that non-Calvinists do not believe in effectual salvation. They just do not believe that God intends to save only the elect in the way the Calvinist defines election. Non-Calvinists believe that God purposes to effectually save all who believe in Christ. Limitarians mistakenly assume that when they prove the efficacy of the atonement, they disprove the universality of the atonement.

O. Some Calvinists argue that since the persons of the Trinity always work in harmony, unlimited atonement results in trinitarian disharmony. With respect to the notion of trinitarian disharmony, the argument of limitarians is that a separation of the atonement's extent from its especially intended application entails "a fatal disjunction" within the trinitarian work of salvation.[56] But where is this stated in Scripture? The argument seems to rest on assumptions and inferences rather than Scripture. It assumes the Reformed understanding of election. If God has designed the atonement to be unlimited, and at the same time has annexed a condition of faith in Christ for its benefits to be made available, then no trinitarian disunity ensues.

---

[55] Allen, *The Atonement*, 215–17.

[56] David Gibson and Jonathan Gibson, "Sacred Theology and the Reading of the Divine Word," in Gibson and Gibson, *From Heaven He Came*, 49.

Moreover, Scripture indicates the atonement is multi-intentional and is not limited only to the salvation of those who believe (or the elect in a Reformed framework). The atonement has implications for common grace for all humanity and cosmic dimensions whereby God effects eschatological reconciliation of all things by means of the cross (see Col 1:20). Limitarians overlook these aspects of the atonement when they argue unlimited atonement entails trinitarian disunity.

Though space prohibits a more in-depth discussion, limitarians should take a closer look at their concept of a covenant of redemption with the Father and Son entering into a pre-temporal pact where the Father is under obligation to grant salvation to the elect based on the Son's atonement. Talk about trinitarian disunity! No wonder Karl Barth critiqued the covenant of redemption, calling it "Christian mythology."[57]

P. Some Calvinists assert that the logical consistency of the TULIP acronym supports limited atonement. There are generally two variations: (1) All five elements of the TULIP stand or fall together; and (2) if you accept unconditional election, you must accept limited atonement.

One or more of the doctrines represented by the TULIP acronym may be biblically sound while others are not. Since the early seventeenth century, theologians have affirmed as many as all five points to as few as one or none of the five points. Moderate Calvinists reject limited atonement but still maintain the other four points are consistent within themselves. Either way, the consistency argument with respect to the TULIP acronym in no way is an argument for limited atonement.

Q. Some Calvinists assert that there is no verse in Scripture that when rightly interpreted affirms unlimited atonement.
Calvinists feel the weight of the universal texts and struggle to explain them. Their approach is to reinterpret words like "world" and "all" in these texts to mean something less than universal; or to argue that the texts don't speak of the extent of the atonement but rather the universal *offer* of the gospel to the world. This argument has been addressed above.

These seventeen arguments from limitarians constitute the arsenal against unlimited atonement. In summary, with only one exception, the arguments against unlimited atonement are developed either by implication or logical deduction.

---

[57] See my critique of the so-called covenant of redemption in Allen, *Extent of the Atonement*, 216–18.

Only a few texts are adduced to explicitly affirm limited atonement, and none of them, upon close examination, support the claim. Most of the hopelessly contrived arguments advanced for limited atonement illustrate the triumph of ingenuity over evidence. Once these seemingly Samson-like arguments are shorn of their faulty presuppositions, logical errors, and hermeneutical mistakes, the soft underbelly of limited atonement becomes vulnerable and cannot stand in the naked light of scriptural texts that affirm the unlimited extent of the atonement.[58]

III. New Testament Texts Affirming Unlimited Atonement

Here we segue into Part III, where we list and briefly discuss the key verses in the New Testament that affirm unlimited atonement.[59] Since limitarian arguments or exegesis of these texts are identified and answered in Part II above, I will not repeat them here. In Part III the focus is on positive exegesis and evidence supporting the view that these texts affirm unlimited atonement. Part III is divided into two sections: (1) texts that *assert* unlimited atonement, and (2) texts that *imply* unlimited atonement.

Fourteen Texts That Assert Unlimited Atonement

Matthew 20:28; Mark 10:45: These texts directly address the extent of the atonement. Christ gave himself as a ransom "for many." The word *many* in these two verses is the Greek word *pollon* and is a Hebraism from Isaiah 53 in the inclusive universal significance of the Greek word *polys*. The Hebrew term in Isaiah 53, *rabbim* ("the great," v. 12 KJV), is used in the sense of the Greek *pas*, meaning "all." As Martin Hengel noted, when Jesus spoke of his intent "to give his life as a ransom for many" he meant "all; everyone."[60] "The saying over the cup and the saying about ransom are connected by the universal service 'for the many,' in the sense of 'for all.'"[61] These texts overtly assert unlimited atonement.

---

[58] See Allen, 657–763, for a chapter-by-chapter evaluation and critique of all the arguments for limited atonement in *From Heaven He Came and Sought Her*.

[59] For space considerations, we will not deal with the key Old Testament text that affirms unlimited atonement, Isa 53:6, since I have discussed it elsewhere. See Allen, *The Atonement*, 40.

[60] Hengel, *The Atonement*, 50, 70. In Isaiah 53, as well as Matt 20:28 and Mark 10:45, Calvin understood the "many" to mean "all" people. See Calvin, "A Harmony of the Gospels," in *Calvin's New Testament Commentaries*, 2:277.

[61] Hengel, 73.

John 1:29: "The next day John saw Jesus coming toward him and said, 'Here is the Lamb of God, who takes away the sin of the world" (HCSB). This text speaks to the purpose of Jesus's coming into the world: to take away sin. It also addresses the extent of the atonement with the words "of the world." The Greek verb *airō*, "to take away," is associated with the Hebrew *kpr*, the common word in the Old Testament for the bearing of sin and the taking away of sin by means of sacrifice. The singular use of "sin" signifies the totality of the world's sin.[62] The word *world* here, by application, cannot be taken to mean anything less than the world of all humanity.[63] This is a generic statement of unlimited scope.

John 3:16: "For God loved the world in this way: He gave his one and only Son, so that everyone who believes in him will not perish but have eternal life." No text in the New Testament is any clearer regarding the extent of the atonement in connection with God's love for the world. Love is the motive for the giving of Jesus as an atonement for the sin of the world.

Scripture links the atonement with its primary motivating factor of God's love for lost humanity in texts such as Rom 5:8; 2 Cor 5:14–15; and 1 John 4:7–11. The question arises concerning limited atonement: If Christ died only for the sins of the elect, how can that be reconciled with texts that indicate the atonement was the result of God's love for all people and was in fact made for the sins of all people?

Calvinists differentiate between God's general non-salvific love for the non-elect and his "special" or "saving" love for the elect. This distinction is arbitrary. Calvinists simply state that God, for reasons known only to himself, has set his saving love on some people and not on others. Texts like John 3:16 would seem to indicate that no such distinction exists. Non-Calvinists believe that such a distinction impugns the character of God as revealed in Scripture.

It is true that God's love expressed as his method of relationship to and benefits toward all believers certainly differs from that of unbelievers. But it is a different matter to suggest, as all Calvinists do, that God places a saving love on some individuals and not on others. From a non-Calvinist perspective, Scripture does not make such a distinction *with respect to individual salvation*. This is not negated by the fact

---

[62] Rudolf Schnackenburg, *The Gospel According to St. John*, 3 vols., trans. C. Hastings et. al. (New York: Crossroad, 1990), 1:298; Köstenberger, *John*, 67.

[63] See Adolf Schlatter, *Der Evangelist Johannes*, 2nd ed. (Stuttgart: Calwer, 1948), 48–49.

that God places his special elective love on Israel in the Old Testament.[64] That is a national and corporate issue and should not be pressed by analogy into the New Testament as a paradigm for individual soteriology.

Second Peter 3:9 states that God does not desire any to perish but rather desires all to come to repentance. How could God be said to love, with a desire to save, in any meaningful sense of the term, those for whom he did not provide atonement for their sins? Since no one can possibly be saved apart from the atonement of Christ, it is simply contradictory to speak of God's universal love and his universal saving will on the limited atonement platform.[65]

John 3:16 speaks in universal terms: "world" and "whoever" (NKJV). The text affirms God's love for all people. His love is unrestrictive: the scope of his love is the entire world. John specifically says God gave Jesus to be an atonement for the sins of the world. "Just as God's love encompasses the entire world, so Jesus made atonement for the sins of the whole world (1 John 2:2)."[66] There is no limitation here.

There is, however, a condition for the benefits of Christ's atonement to be effective for any individual: "everyone who believes." God has annexed a condition on salvation: faith in Christ. The atonement is unlimited. The benefits of the atonement are limited to only those who believe. Note the use of "everyone who believes" in both vv. 15 and 16. In v. 15, the reference is to the lifting up of the serpent on the pole in the wilderness (Num 21:8–9). Köstenberger noted the phrase "everyone who believes" "strikes a markedly universal note."[67] It will not do to attempt to interpret the participle "everyone who believes" as somehow affirming limited atonement, especially with the universal language of "world." The participle semantically communicates the notion that all who meet the condition, belief in Christ, will have eternal life. The fact that the condition expressed by the participle is narrower than the provision of

---

[64] Israel was elected or chosen to bring salvation to the rest of the world (Gen 12:2–3; Exod 19:6), not to exclude the rest of the world from divine love or blessings.

[65] Allen, *The Atonement*, 188–92. Many in the history of the Reformed tradition have subordinated God's love to his sovereignty. In the section of the Westminster Confession of Faith that addresses the attributes of God—love is absent. See WCF, 2.1–2; as well as WLC, Q. 7; WSC, Q. 4. This is telling.

[66] Köstenberger, *John*, 129. The great Southern Baptist Greek scholar A. T. Robertson said that "world" in John 3:16 means "the whole cosmos of men, including the Gentiles, the whole human race." He adds that "this universal aspect of God's love appears also in II Cor. 5:19; Rom. 5:8." Robertson, *Word Pictures in the Greek New Testament*, vol. 4, *The Fourth Gospel and the Epistle to the Hebrews* (Nashville: Broadman, 1932), 50.

[67] Köstenberger, *John*, 128.

the atonement in no way intimates limited atonement. It merely indicates a limited application of a universal atonement. John 3:16 affirms unlimited atonement.

Romans 5:18–19: "So then, as through one trespass there is condemnation for everyone, so also through one righteous act there is justification leading to life for everyone. For just as through one man's disobedience the many were made sinners, so also through the one man's obedience the many will be made righteous" (vv. 18–19).

Romans 5:18–19 asserts four propositions:

1. Adam's sin brings condemnation for everyone.
2. Christ's atonement provides justification for all who believe.
3. Adam's sin made all people sinners.
4. Christ's obedience in his death provides righteousness for all who believe.

Paul's main point is there is a remedy for universal sin—a universal atonement. Everyone is affected by Adam's sin. Everyone is affected by Christ's atonement. In Rom 5:15, Paul asserts that Adam's sin led to spiritual death for "the many," where "many" here is the Hebrew idiom meaning "all," as we saw above. Adam's act that made all people sinners is counteracted by the atonement of Christ: "how much more have the grace of God and the gift which comes through the grace of the one man Jesus Christ overflowed to the many" (v. 15).

Romans 5:14–15, 18–19 assert unlimited atonement.

1 Corinthians 15:3–4: "For I passed on to you as most important what I also received: that Christ died for our sins according to the Scriptures, that he was buried, that he was raised on the third day according to the Scriptures." This text is the nearest thing to a definition of the gospel anywhere in the New Testament. Paul asserts he "received" this teaching, which highlights its traditional and hence authoritative nature. The text directly states, "Christ died for our sins." Paul is addressing the church at Corinth, but he is speaking about his consistent practice in preaching from the time of his first arrival at Corinth (Acts 18:1–18). He clearly affirms the content of the gospel he preached in Corinth included the fact that "Christ died for our sins." Notice carefully that Paul is saying this is what he preached pre-conversion, not post-conversion. Thus, the "our" in his statement cannot be taken to refer to all the elect or merely the believing elect, which is what limitarians are forced to argue. The entire pericope of 1 Cor 15:3–11 should be kept in mind. Notice how Paul comes back around to what he had said in verse 3 when he gets to verse 11: "Whether then it was I or they, so we preach and so you believed" (NASB). Paul's use of the customary present tense in Greek when he said "so we preach" (*kērussomen*) along with the aorist tense of "believed" (*episteusate*) makes it clear that he refers to a past point in time when they believed what it was his custom to preach. What did Paul preach to them in his evangelistic efforts to win all the unsaved to Christ? He preached the gospel, which included the proposition that "Christ died for our sins." First Corinthians 15:3–4 asserts the atonement is unlimited.

2 Corinthians 5:14-21: Several important aspects of the atonement are taught in this passage. First, Paul affirms the universal scope of the atonement: "one died for all" (v. 14). Second, Paul affirms that Christ's love is demonstrated in a universal atonement (vv. 14–15). Third, through the death of Christ, God reconciled the world to himself objectively (v. 19). What is this reconciliation? It is the providing of means whereby people can be reconciled via Christ's death. God is not in a state of full reconciliation (including subjective reconciliation) with all people. He is in a state of objective reconciliation with all people. Because of the atonement, there are no legal barriers on God's part hindering the salvation of any person. The death of Christ objectively reconciled the world to God in the sense that his justice is satisfied, and he stands ready to pardon. The subjective side of reconciliation does not occur until the atonement is applied when the individual repents and believes in Christ.[68] Scripture speaks of no full reconciliation between God and humanity except that which takes place at conversion. The passage, therefore, cannot refer to the full and completed reconciliation of the world to God. If so, there would be no need for Paul to exhort people to be reconciled to God, as he does in v. 20.

Fourth, in similar fashion to Rom 3:21–26, the result of this objective reconciliation for the unbelieving world is God's "not counting their trespasses

---

[68] Thomas Aquinas affirmed the "objective" aspect of reconciliation, as did Calvin, Luther, and other Reformers. Luther stated: "The Gospel is a proclamation of Christ, true God and man, who by His death and resurrection has atoned for the sins of all men and conquered death and the devil." *Selected Psalms III*, in *Luther's Works*, vol. 14 (St. Louis: Concordia, 1968), 88. See also the Lutheran theologians Franz Pieper, *Christian Dogmatics*, 4 vols. (St. Louis: Concordia, 1950), 2:347–51, and John T. Mueller, *Christian Dogmatics* (St. Louis: Concordia, 1955), 310–11. Methodist theologian Thomas Oden also asserted the necessity of viewing reconciliation as objective and subjective. Salvation does not occur until sinners "receive the reconciling event already accomplished and become reconciled to God." Oden, *Systematic Theology*, vol. 2, *The Word of Life* (San Francisco: HarperCollins, 1992), 2:356. See also Lewis Sperry Chafer, *Systematic Theology*, 4 vols. (Dallas: Dallas Seminary Press, 1971), 3:192.

against them" (v. 19) in the sense of his not condemning the world but rather seeking their salvation (John 3:17). This reference is to current unbelievers at the time of Paul's writing and expresses the state of affairs from the death of Christ on the cross to the present time for living unbelievers.

Fifth, though Christ died for all, only believers "in Christ" are subjectively reconciled with God and thus experience salvation (vv. 17–18). God has "reconciled us to himself" (v. 18). Sixth, the command to evangelize is grounded in a universal atonement (2 Cor 5:19b, 21). God has given to us the word of reconciliation (i.e., the mandate for evangelism). As ambassadors for Christ, we plead with people to be reconciled to God (v. 20).[69] Furthermore, Paul affirms that as ambassadors for Christ God appeals through us to all the unsaved. Seventh, God made Christ "to be sin for us" (v. 21). In his substitutionary atonement, Christ took our place and suffered the judgment of God for our sin.[70]

1 Timothy 2:1-6:

> First of all, then, I urge that petitions, prayers, intercessions, and thanks-givings be made for everyone, for kings and all those who are in authority, so that we may lead a tranquil and quiet life in all godliness and dignity. This is good, and it pleases God our Savior, who wants everyone to be saved and to come to the knowledge of the truth.
>
> For there is one God and one mediator between God and mankind, the man Christ Jesus, who gave himself as a ransom for all, a testimony at the proper time.

This passage explicitly teaches God's universal saving will and unlimited atonement. Paul links the death of Christ "for all" with God's stated desire for "everyone to be saved." The Greek sentence that is expressed in verses 5–6 is introduced by the subordinating conjunction "for" (*gar*), which semantically gives the grounds for the

---

[69] Some commentators understand 2 Cor 5:20–21 as Paul appealing to the Corinthian church to be reconciled to God. But this is contextually problematic. Paul includes himself with the church as appealing to those unbelievers outside the church to be reconciled to God, as rightly noted by Stanley E. Porter, "Peace, Reconciliation," in *Dictionary of Paul and His Letters*, IVP Bible Dictionary Series, ed. Gerald. F. Hawthorne, Ralph. P. Martin, and Daniel G. Reid (Downers Grove, IL: InterVarsity, 1993), 696.

[70] For a more detailed analysis of this text and its implications for unlimited atonement, see Allen, *The Atonement*, 96–101.

statement in verse 4. Jesus is said to be the "mediator" between God and humanity. Paul affirms Christ died "for all." First Timothy 2:6 is a rewording of the saying of Jesus in Mark 10:45, with "all" replacing "many" in that text. The "many" of Mark 10:45 has been re-expressed using more idiomatic Greek to clarify that the original saying, and Paul's intent, is to express unlimited atonement.[71]

1 Timothy 4:10: "For this reason we labor and strive, because we have put our hope in the living God, who is the Savior of all people, especially of those who believe." Here, Paul describes God as both "the Savior of all people" and "especially of those who believe." The implication is that the atonement accomplished by Christ on the cross was for all people, but its application is only to those who believe. Notice Paul says Christ is the Savior of two groups of people: "all" and "those who believe." He is not actually the Savior of all people in the sense that all people are actually saved (verbal idea). He *is* God's appointed Savior (his office) over all who may *potentially* be saved by virtue of his unlimited atonement. If the atonement is not unlimited, Jesus could not be the Savior of "all people."

Titus 2:11–14: "For the grace of God has appeared, bringing salvation for all people, instructing us to deny godlessness and worldly lusts and to live in a sensible, righteous, and godly way in the present age, while we wait for the blessed hope, the appearing of the glory of our great God and Savior, Jesus Christ. He gave himself for us to redeem us from all lawlessness and to cleanse for himself a people for his own possession, eager to do good works." Paul asserts the grace of God has appeared, which brings salvation for "all people," and that Christ "gave himself for us." If God's grace through the death of Christ brings salvation for all people, it stands to reason that Christ's death on the cross must be for all people. Otherwise, the intention expressed in v. 11 and the redemption that is accomplished do not match. This verse speaks to the purpose or intent of God in the atonement: to bring salvation for all people. The verse indicates that salvation is a possibility for all on the grounds of the atonement that has been accomplished for all.

Hebrews 2:9: "But we do see Jesus—made lower than the angels for a short time so that by God's grace he might taste death for everyone." In Heb 2:9, the author makes the connection between the necessity of the incarnation for the atonement.

---

[71] See Marshall, *Pastoral Epistles*, 425–33.

He explicitly states that Christ died "for everyone." The Greek word translated "for everyone" is *pantos*, meaning "all people" without restriction, and there is no reason why it should be limited to some people and not everyone.[72]

Hebrews 9:28: "So also Christ, having been offered once to bear the sins of many, will appear a second time, not to bear sin, but to bring salvation to those who are waiting for him." In Heb 9:28 the author asserts Jesus bore "the sins of many." We have already seen the Semitic idiomatic use of "many" to mean "all," and that is the case here.[73]

2 Peter 2:1: "There were indeed false prophets among the people, just as there will be false teachers among you. They will bring in destructive heresies, even denying the Master who bought them, and will bring swift destruction on themselves." The key phrase is "denying the Master who bought them." The word translated "bought" (Gk. *agorazō*, lexical form) connotes the purchase of a slave from the slave market to set him free. This redemption language is often used in the New Testament to speak of what Christ accomplished by his death on the cross. Such terminology would seem to indicate that Christ died for the sins of those false teachers. The "swift destruction" language indicates eternal punishment.[74]

Limitarians especially struggle with this text. Schreiner rejects the traditional interpretation that the word "bought" refers to Christ's death on the cross for the sins of false teachers. Schreiner opts for a "phenomenological" reading: "It appeared as if the Lord had purchased the false teachers with his blood (v. 1), though they actually did not truly belong to the Lord."[75] Schreiner feels the pinch of his own strained exegesis and asks, "Is this an artificial interpretation introduced to support a theological bias?"[76] It would seem such is the case.

1 John 2:1–2: "My little children, I am writing you these things so that you may not sin. But if anyone does sin, we have an advocate with the Father—Jesus Christ the

[72] See David L. Allen, *Hebrews*, NAC 35 (Nashville: B&H, 2010), 212.
[73] See Allen, 212, 488.
[74] Gene L. Green, *Jude and 2nd Peter*, BECNT (Grand Rapids: Baker, 2008), 241.
[75] Thomas R. Schreiner, "'Problematic Texts' for Definite Atonement in the Pastorals and General Epistles," in Gibson and Gibson, *From Heaven He Came*, 390. See also Schreiner, *1, 2 Peter, Jude*, NAC 37 (Nashville: B&H, 2003), 331.
[76] Schreiner, "Problematic Texts,'" 391.

righteous one. He himself is the atoning sacrifice for our sins, and not only for ours, but also for those of the whole world." First John 2:2 is one of the clearest verses in Scripture affirming a universal atonement. Whenever John uses the term "world" (Gk. *kosmos*) in any salvation passage dealing with God's intent of the atonement or the extent of the atonement, "world" means all people, by application; or to be more nuanced depending on the passage, "world" signifies either all people, inclusive of believers and unbelievers, or all unbelievers, exclusive of believers (as in 1 John 5:19).[77]

In only two places in John's letter does he employ the phrase in Greek *holos kosmos*, "whole world": 1 John 2:2 and 5:19. It could not be clearer in 5:19 that by "whole world," John means all living unbelievers at the time of his writing. He identifies two groups of people: living believers (5:19a) and all living unbelievers (5:19b). There is no reason to think that John's use of the phrase "whole world" in 1 John 2:2 means anything different or anything less than all living unbelievers at the time of his writing. Thus, 1 John 2:2 clearly teaches unlimited atonement.

1 John 4:14: "And we have seen and we testify that the Father has sent his Son as the world's Savior." As we have seen, John's use of "world" in his letter includes all humanity, or when contrasted with believers, all unbelieving humanity. Jesus is described as "the world's Savior," not in the sense that he actually saves all people (universalism), but he is the Savior of all people conditionally, such that if anyone believes, he or she shall be saved. The import here is similar to 1 John 2:2. This text supports unlimited atonement.

Texts That Imply Universal Atonement

Matthew 22:2–14; Luke 14:16–24: These texts record Jesus's parable of the wedding banquet. This parable has implications both for the extent of the atonement and the well-meant offer to all to respond to the gospel.

When the king's original invitees declined to come to the banquet, he informed his servants "the banquet is ready" (Matt 22:8) and sent them to invite "everyone you find to the banquet" (v. 9).

---

[77] For a detailed discussion, see also Allen, *The Atonement*, 158–63; Allen, *Extent of the Atonement*, 702–3. The most comprehensive online treatment of this text is David Ponter, "First John 2:2 and the Argument for Limited Atonement," *Calvin and Calvinism: An Elenchus for Classic-Moderate Calvinism* (blog), February 16, 2015, http://calvinandcalvinism.com/?p=15807. My discussion of this text in Allen, *The Atonement*, 158–63, is dependent on Ponter's treatment.

One implication from this parable is the gospel invitation from God extends to all people just as the king sent his servants to invite "everyone you find" to the banquet. Another implication is that the atonement (the provision for salvation for those who are invited) is complete, sufficient, and available for all who are invited and come to Christ by faith.

If limited atonement is true, there is no provision of salvation to those invited who are among the non-elect. This being the case, how can the invitation be considered genuine? On the unlimited atonement platform, there is no contradiction. There is a sufficient provision for all who are invited to salvation, whether or not they respond.

Luke 22:19-21: "And he took bread, gave thanks, broke it, gave it to them, and said, 'This is my body, which is given for you. Do this in remembrance of me.'

"In the same way he also took the cup after supper and said, 'This cup is the new covenant in my blood, which is poured out for you. But look, the hand of the one betraying me is at the table with me.'"

The significance of this text for the extent of the atonement is twofold: (1) The text indicates that Judas was at the table during this portion of the Lord's Supper, and (2) Jesus said the cup represents the new covenant in his blood, "which is poured out for you." Jesus included Judas in his plural use of "you." All are agreed that Judas died as a reprobate, yet Jesus said he shed his blood for the sins of Judas. This, by implication, confirms the atonement is unlimited.

Interestingly, both Augustine and Calvin interpreted the text in this fashion.

For Judas the traitor was punished, and Christ was crucified: but us He redeemed by His blood, and He punished him in the matter of his price. For he threw down the price of silver, for which by him the Lord had been sold; and he knew not the price wherewith he had himself by the Lord been redeemed. This thing was done in the case of Judas.[78]

Calvin in numerous places explicitly says Judas was at the table and that Christ died for his sins.[79]

---

[78] Augustine, "Exposition on the Book of Psalms," in NPNF[1], 8:309.
[79] See Calvin, *Tracts and Treatises*, 2:93, 234, 297, 370–71, 378; and his commentary on Matt 26:21 and John 6:56.

Acts 3:26: "God raised up his servant and sent him first to you to bless you by turning each of you from your evil ways." Calvinists often appeal to Paul's preaching in Acts to support the contention that the apostles never used such language as "Christ died for your sins." They conclude from this lacuna that Paul never employed such a phrase in evangelistic preaching or witnessing and this is evidence for limited atonement. But is such a conclusion valid?

First, this is an argument from silence. It does not conclusively prove Paul, Peter, or anyone else did not say it, nor is it a valid argument that they did not believe it. Second, all the sermons in Acts are condensations of the actual sermons given. Third, we have already seen how 1 Cor 15:3–4 indicate Paul's normal method of preaching when he first arrived at a city was to include in the gospel content the fact that "Christ died for our sins."

With respect to Peter's sermon in Acts 3, how else could he tell his hearers to "repent and be baptized . . . in the name of Jesus Christ for the forgiveness of your sins" (Acts 2:38) if he did not somehow connect the death of Christ on the cross as accomplishing the means for their forgiveness and salvation? Are we to think that Peter's hearers did not understand that what Peter was saying in essence was since Christ died for their sins, the door was opened for them to repent and believe? Furthermore, if Peter believed in limited atonement, how could he say, "God raised up his servant and sent him first to you to bless you by turning each of you from your evil ways" (Acts 3:26)? For any of the non-elect present in his audience, there was no atonement for them, so it would be impossible for them to be saved, even if they wanted to. It would also be disingenuous on Peter's part to give anyone such false hope.[80] Hence, we can deduce unlimited atonement from Acts 3:26 by implication.

Romans 14:15 and 1 Corinthians 8:11: "For if your brother or sister is hurt by what you eat, you are no longer walking according to love. Do not destroy, by what you eat, someone for whom Christ died" (Rom 14:15). "So the weak person, the brother or sister for whom Christ died, is ruined by your knowledge" (1 Cor 8:11).

Both these texts speak about someone for whom Christ died. Both texts deal with the subject of activity on the part of a Christian that is offensive in some way to someone with a weaker conscience. Paul exhorts believers to forgo any activity that is going to cause a weaker brother to stumble. Such restraint is an act of love for the weaker brother, who is someone for whom Christ died.

---

[80] Allen, *Extent of the Atonement*, 778.

At issue in these texts are two questions: (1) the identity of the "weak" brother or sister" (is he or she a believer or an unbeliever?), and (2) the meaning of "destroy." Many Calvinist interpreters identify the "brother or sister" as a fellow Christian, and then conclude that "destroy" means something less than eternal destruction. However, the Greek word translated "destroy" (*apollumi*) is found in both texts and is always used in the New Testament for eternal destruction, not merely to stumble or fall, as is often alleged.

If the Reformed doctrine of the perseverance of the saints is true (and I believe it is), then how can one who is truly a believer be eternally destroyed? On the other hand, if the "brother or sister" is not a believer, he remains "someone for whom Christ died." If this is the case, then unlimited atonement is the implication. If the "brother or sister" refers to a believer, then limited atonement is not established by virtue of the negative inference fallacy (one could not logically conclude Christ died only for the "brothers and sisters").

Calvin's comments on Rom 14:15 and 1 Cor 8:11 are of interest. He speaks of two groups of people: the brother or sister whom "God has adopted" and also those sinners in general who are "ignorant and weak." Calvin asserts both have been "redeemed by the blood of Christ."[81]

We have examined numerous New Testament texts explicitly or implicitly affirming universal atonement. Now we turn our attention to key theological issues that impinge on the extent question, serve to falsify limited atonement, and support unlimited atonement.

IV. Theological Issues that Impinge on the Extent of the Atonement

We shall consider two issues: (1) the sufficiency of the atonement; and (2) the "well-meant" or sincere offer of the gospel.

---

[81] John Calvin, "Romans and Thessalonians," in *Calvin's New Testament Commentaries*, 8:298; and "1 Corinthians," in *Calvin's New Testament Commentaries*, 9:179. Many of the Reformed in times past spoke of the atonement as "redeeming" all people in the sense of an objective atonement. If by a "most contemptible brother" (Calvin, "Romans and Thessalonians," 8:298) Calvin means someone who is an unbeliever, then obviously Calvin held to an unlimited atonement. For the argument that these texts can refer to unbelievers, see John Goodwin, *Redemption Redeemed: A Puritan Defense of Unlimited Atonement*, ed. John D. Wagner (Eugene, OR: Wipf & Stock, 2001), 83–94.

Sufficiency of the Atonement

Most limitarians maintain that Christ's atonement is sufficient for all people, even though it only satisfied for the sins of the elect. Others deny the atonement is sufficient for the sins of the non-elect. Much confusion exists on this topic. Let us begin with definitions:

> Sufficiency of the Atonement—whether the atonement is sufficient in and of itself to atone for the sins of all humanity. There are four aspects to consider on the question of sufficiency:
>
> 1. Infinite, Universal Sufficiency: (1) When used by limitarians, this terminology means, at least by entailment, that the death of Christ *could have been* sufficient or able to atone for all the sins of the world *if God had intended for it to do so*. However, since they think God did not intend for the death of Christ to satisfy for the sins of all but only for the sins of the elect, it is not *actually* sufficient or able to save any others. (2) When used by moderate Calvinists and non-Calvinists, the terminology means the death of Christ is of such a nature that it is actually able to save all people. It is, *in fact* (not hypothetically), a satisfaction for the sins of all humanity. Therefore, if anyone perishes, it is not for lack of atonement for his sins.[82]
> 2. Limited Sufficiency: the death of Christ only satisfied for the sins of the elect *alone*, thus it is *limited in its capacity to save* only those for whose sins Christ died.
> 3. Intrinsic Sufficiency: the atonement's *internal or infinite, abstract ability* to save all humanity (if God so intended), in such a way that it has no direct reference to the actual extent of the atonement.
> 4. Extrinsic Sufficiency: the atonement's actual infinite ability to save all and every individual, and this because God wills it to be so, such that Christ *in fact* made a satisfaction for the sins of all people. Extrinsic sufficiency enables the unlimited satisfaction to be truly adaptable to all people. Every living person is savable because there is blood sufficiently shed for him (Heb 9:22).

---

[82] The nineteenth-century Reformed systematic theologian Charles Hodge made this point in *Systematic Theology*, 2:556–57.

Discussions of the extent of the atonement inevitably lead to the famous "Lombardian formula," the statement made by the medieval theologian Peter Lombard. The formulaic section has been translated as follows: "He offered himself on the altar of the cross not to the devil, but to the triune God, and he did so for all with regard to the sufficiency of the price, but only for the elect with regard to its efficacy, because he brought about salvation only for the predestined."[83] This is popularly rephrased as: "Christ died sufficiently for all, but efficiently only for the elect."

Lombard's original intended meaning was to posit twin truths: the atonement is unlimited, but the application of the atonement is limited only to the elect. Before Theodore Beza and the late sixteenth century, the Lombardian formula was accepted by Calvin and all the Reformers. However, Beza's criticism of the Lombardian formula launched a movement to revise its meaning. Beza and others began to insert hypothetical language into the formula such that the meaning became "Christ's death *could have been* (instead of 'was') a ransom for the sins of all people." There are many examples of this revision in the writings of limitarians at the time.[84]

Lombard's formula is fraught with confusion today since it has been used by those on both sides of the post-Reformation extent debate to articulate and defend their position, often without the speaker specifying in what sense he is using the term. Whenever the formula is used, the question must always be asked: What is meant by the term "sufficient"? (hence the definitions and distinctions above). Is the term being used in a purely hypothetical way such that the sufficiency is *limited to intrinsic worth and value,* or is the term understood to refer to an *actual sufficiency* (universal and extrinsic), defined as Christ paying the price for the sins of all people?

---

[83] Peter Lombard, *The Sentences Book 3: On the Incarnation of the Word*, trans. Giulio Silano, Mediaeval Sources in Translation 45 (Toronto: Pontifical Institute of Medieval Studies, 2008), 86. See also Lombard's commentary on Heb 2:9 in *Patrologia Latina*, 222 vols., ed. J. P. Migne (Paris: Migne, 1855), 192:236 [Col. 0419B], wherein he said, "*Gustaret, dico, pro omnibus, scilicet pradestinatis qui per ejus mortem redempti sun et salvati. Vel pro omnibus, generaliter mortuus est, quia omnibus pretium suffecit,*" which, translated, says, "He might taste, I say, for all, that is, for the predestined who by his death are redeemed and saved. His taste of death was efficacious only for the elect who are actually saved by it. And/or he died generally for all men, because the price was sufficient for all." The *concept*, however, is *at least* as old as Ambrose (AD 338–97). "Although Christ suffered for all, yet He suffered for us particularly, because He suffered for the Church." Ambrose, *Exposition of the Holy Gospel according to Saint Luke*, trans. Theodosia Tomkinson (Etna, CA: Center for Traditionalist Orthodox Studies, 1998), 201–2.

[84] For the full discussion and evidence of the revision, see Allen, *Extent of the Atonement*, 27–31.

The sufficiency argument of limitarians proceeds in this fashion: the death of Christ is sufficient for all people *in the sense of its infinite worth and value*; however, it is not sufficient *as an actual atonement for all sins*. Therefore, we should preach the gospel to all people since it is sufficient and since we lack knowledge of who are the elect.

Here is the problem: How can Christ's substitutionary death be said to be sufficient for forgiveness of all the sins of the entire world when, according to limited atonement, no atonement for sins exists for the non-elect? What limitarians are actually saying is that the atonement *would* or *could be* sufficient for all *had God intended it to be sufficient* for them. But God did not intend the atonement to be a payment for sin on behalf of the non-elect; thus, there is no satisfaction made for their sins. The sufficiency can only be understood to be a statement about the atonement's *infinite intrinsic value*, such that it could hypothetically be satisfactory for all, but it is not "extrinsically" or "actually" sufficient for all.[85]

Limitarians cloud the issue of sufficiency when they tell us that Christ's death is sufficient in the sense that if anyone believes the gospel, he will find a sufficient atonement for his sins. Therefore, all people are savable, insofar that if anyone believes, he will be saved. That proposition is true as far as it goes because it only speaks to the causal relationship between faith and salvation: anyone who truly believes will certainly be saved. But limitarians exhibit their confusion on this issue when asked why this is so. Their response: because there is an atonement of *infinite value* able to be applied to the one who believes. But is "infinite value" capable of sustaining the claim of a sufficient atonement for all who believe? If we ask a clarifying question, it becomes clear that "infinite value" cannot be equated with "sufficiency" or render the atonement sufficient for the sins of all people. Here is the question: If one of the non-elect were to believe, could they be saved? The only consistent answer is no, from the perspective of limited atonement because, by definition, no satisfaction of sins exists for the non-elect.

The issue here is not the sufficiency of the atonement in terms of its worth or value—all agree the atonement is sufficient to atone for a thousand worlds in terms of its value—if God had so intended. The issue is the fact the atonement cannot be

---

[85] John Owen ("A Display of Arminianism," in *Works*, 10:89; *The Death of Death*, in *Works*, 10:295–97, 337) and Francis Turretin (*Elenctic Theology*, 2:458–59; 14.14.9) explicitly put it in hypothetical terms.

sufficient to save anyone for whom it does not exist—the non-elect. They cannot be saved, because there is no atonement for their sins—period.

If the sufficiency is only hypothetical, or if Christ only sustained a penal relationship with the sins of the elect, then there are no grounds for a sincere offer to the non-elect, as the non-elect are not savable in terms of the law. Therein lies the problem for all limitarians. For all who affirm limited atonement, by necessary entailment, the atonement can only be sufficient for those for whom it is efficient.[86]

On the grounds of Scripture, one should affirm universal sufficiency and conditional efficacy with respect to the atonement and its application. Aquinas noted: "Although Christ atoned sufficiently for the sins of mankind by his death . . . each one must seek the means of his own salvation [i.e., 'each one must seek to be regenerated by Christ']."[87]

Likewise, one should affirm that universal sufficiency is not negated by conditional acceptance of the gospel offer. Thomas Oden rightly noted: "As to sufficiency, the cross is for all, for the world. As to efficacy, the cross becomes effective for some, for the faithful. From this derives the distinction of universal sufficiency and conditional efficacy: as to sufficiency it is universal; as to efficacy it is limited to those who accept God's offer of salvation through Christ."[88] Oden appeals to Rom 3:25, "God presented him as the mercy seat by his blood, through faith." The atonement is for all people but must be appropriated by those who believe and thus are united to Christ.[89]

The "Well-Meant" or Sincere Offer of the Gospel

How does Scripture describe the offer of salvation to the unsaved by God and by human preachers? Scripture speaks of the gospel proclamation or presentation as a "call" to salvation. John in his Gospel employs various terms to express the notion of a call to respond to the gospel. One term John uses is "come," conveying the semantic concept of "invitation." "Jesus . . . cried out, 'If anyone is thirsty, let him come to me and drink. The one who believes in me, as the Scripture has said, will have streams of

---

[86] Allen, *The Atonement*, 177–81.

[87] Thomas Aquinas, "Summa Contra Gentiles: Books 3–4," in *The Works of Thomas Aquinas*, 60 vols., trans. Fr. L. Shapcote, ed. and rev., The Aquinas Institute (Green Bay, WI: Aquinas Institute, 2018), 12:479; *SCG*, IV.55.

[88] Thomas Oden, *Systematic Theology*, vol. 2, *The Word of Life* (Peabody, MA: Prince Press, 2001), 388.

[89] Oden, *Word of Life*, 390.

living water flow from deep within him'" (John 7:37–38). Notice here the invitation is to all people. The condition of salvation is stated to be faith in Christ.

Similar invitation terminology occurs in the book of Revelation: "Both the Spirit and the bride say, 'Come!' Let anyone who hears, say, 'Come!' Let the one who is thirsty come. Let the one who desires take the water of life freely" (22:17). The invitation expressed is connected to the call to come and it is given to all.

Other verses could be cited, all of which indicate that a person is *offered* or tendered something, and that person is *invited* to "come" or "receive" that which is offered, which will be *given* upon coming. Moreover, the offer of the gospel directs the offeree to place his or her faith directly in Christ himself and not just in a proposition about Christ. The offer is made to all who hear the gospel. The gospel content is outlined by Paul in 1 Cor 15:3–4 and includes "Christ died for our sins."

Scripture is clear: God offers salvation to all people on the grounds of an unlimited atonement and invites all people to respond to his offer: "One died for all. . . . That is, in Christ, God was reconciling the world to himself, not counting their trespasses against them, and he has committed the message of reconciliation to us. Therefore, we are ambassadors for Christ, since God is making his appeal through us. We plead on Christ's behalf, 'Be reconciled to God'" (2 Cor 5:14, 19–20).

If the atonement had been made for no one, there would in fact be no price paid for sin. If the atonement had been made for only some people, it was no price paid for those for whom it was not made. If Christ did not pay the price for the sins of all people, how can God's promises and proposals of salvation to all people who hear the call be true?

If some of those for whom there is no price paid should believe, could they be saved? The limitarian says yes, based on the intrinsic *value* of the death of Christ. But how can this be? They cannot be saved apart from a price paid for them, and for them no atonement has been made. Only unlimited atonement grounds and guarantees the truth of the promises made by God in the gospel call to all people. Otherwise, the promises are rendered untrue.[90]

---

[90] See, for example, John Piper's attempt to justify the well-meant offer on the limited atonement platform without ever even mentioning the connection of the well-meant offer with the extent of the atonement. John Piper, *Does God Desire All to be Saved?* (Wheaton, IL: Crossway, 2013). Michael Horton sidesteps the extent question early on and appeals to the well-meant offer, claiming its validity without ever addressing its connection with the actual extent of the atonement and the logical problems that are endemic to his system. Horton,

If there is no atonement for some people, then those people are not savable. If no atonement exists for some, how is it possible that the gospel can be *offered* to those people for whom no atonement exists? *If anyone is not savable, he is not offerable.* One cannot offer salvation in any consistent way to someone for whom no atonement exists. Limitarians are caught in a logical dilemma from which they cannot escape. They cannot have it both ways—either Christ has substituted for the sins of all people, or he has not. Universal atonement alone grounds the sufficiency of the atonement and the free offer of the gospel to all people.[91]

If limited atonement is true, and limitarians want to argue that all people are savable, then they are left with only two possibilities: (1) either those for whom Christ did not die may be saved without an atonement for their sins, or (2) they cannot be saved at all. Both options are contrary to Scripture.

Limitarians might respond by arguing that no one of the non-elect will be saved anyway. This argument presumes the Reformed doctrine of unconditional election is biblical, which all non-Calvinists would dispute. But that is a secondary issue and does not absolve limitarians of criticism. Whether anyone does believe, or whether they can believe, is beside the point. The promise of the gospel must be true (because it is the promise of God), and it must be *antecedently* true to the faith or unbelief of any person (because otherwise it could not be the genuine or real object of faith). For a promise to be true, there are necessary preconditions grounding the reality of the promise so that its fulfillment is possible and guaranteed should the conditions be met. These preconditions must exist in the real world and not in some other possible world, and they must exist antecedently to whether someone for whom Christ did not die believes or does not believe.[92]

When God offers salvation to one of the non-elect by saying to him, "If you believe, you will be saved," then on the limited atonement scheme, this offer *cannot* be genuine, and is, in fact, false. One would have to deny limited atonement in order

---

"Traditional Reformed View," in *Five Views on the Extent of the Atonement*, ed. Adam J. Johnson and Stanley L. Gundry (Grand Rapids: Zondervan Academic, 2019), 112–33.

[91] Allen, *The Atonement*, 177–81. Classic hyper-Calvinists, such as Gospel Standard Baptists (see art. 29 in their *Articles of Faith and Rules* [Harpenden, UK: Gospel Standard Trust, 2008], 35), saw this logic as well, and therefore consistently rejected Gospel "offers," though they, like most hyper-Calvinists, affirmed the need to preach to all.

[92] So argued by Calvinist Edward Polhill, "The Divine Will Considered in its Eternal Decrees," in *The Works of Edward Polhill* (Morgan, PA: Soli Deo Gloria, 1998), 164–65.

to affirm the conditional statement "if you believe, you will be saved." On the limited atonement platform, to affirm both the condition and the promise is an unavoidable contradiction. God cannot genuinely offer to anyone something he does not have available to give. Limited atonement undermines and falsifies the well-meant and sincere offer of the gospel.

This dilemma has never been answered coherently by limitarians.

We can summarize the logical dilemma limitarians create for themselves in the following twelve-point reasoning chain. I suspect all limitarians would agree with these first four statements:

1. For one to be saved (i.e., have his or her sins forgiven), one would have to be "forgivable"; that is, able to be forgiven in the sense of capable of having forgiveness conferred upon him or her by God.
2. No sin can be forgiven apart from the atonement of Christ, which functions as a legal basis for forgiveness.
3. Forgiveness of sins is an act of God grounded in the atonement of Christ.
4. Only sins actually imputed to Christ on the cross are forgivable.

By definition and necessity, all limitarians also agree with this statement:

5. Only the sins of the elect are imputed to Christ.

Necessarily, all limitarians must also agree with this statement:

6. Therefore, only the sins of the elect are forgivable.

This statement is necessarily true because there is no atonement for the sins of the non-elect, according to the limitarian. To deny this statement, the limitarian would have to deny substitutionary atonement and claim that God can and would forgive the sins of people for whom Jesus did not die (i.e., for whom there is no atonement). No limitarian would deny substitutionary atonement.

All limitarians (with the exception of hyper-Calvinists) would agree with the following statement:

7. God offers forgiveness of sins to all humanity in the preaching of the gospel.

Based on point 7, the implication or presupposition is twofold:

8. God must be able to confer what he offers.
9. The sins of those being offered forgiveness are indeed forgivable.

Therefore, it follows that

10. All offers of forgiveness of sins necessarily entail those sins are forgivable.
11. God offers forgiveness of sins to all people provisionally (i.e., if they believe).

Therefore,

12. The sins of all people must be forgivable.

Here is the problem for all limitarians: point 6 directly contradicts point 12.[93]

Scripture teaches that God does indeed offer salvation to all people. The following passages demonstrate this: Isa 1:18; Isaiah 55; Luke 24:47; Acts 2:38–39; 13:38.

As I have argued elsewhere, several consequences flow from the question of the sufficiency of the atonement, its extent, and the well-meant gospel offer:

1. If limited atonement is correct, Jesus did not substitute himself on the cross for the sins of the non-elect.
2. Therefore, it is impossible that the non-elect could ever be saved since there is no atonement made for their sins. They are in the same unsavable state they would be if Jesus had never come at all. Or, as others have argued, they are no more savable than fallen angels.[94]
3. It is impossible that the atonement can ever be described as sufficiently able to save the non-elect in any way other than hypothetically: something can't be sufficient for anyone for whom it is nonexistent. To suggest otherwise is simply to engage in semantic word games, obfuscation, or equivocation.
4. Further complications emerge concerning the preaching of the gospel. How can preachers universally and indiscriminately offer the gospel in good faith to all people, which clearly includes many who are non-elect, when there is no gospel to offer them; that is, when there is no satisfaction for all their sins? The usual response from limitarians is that we don't know who the elect are,

---

[93] This twelve-point logical analysis is an abbreviated and modified presentation originally presented by David Ponter, "Limited Atonement and the Falsification of the Sincere Offer of the Gospel," *Calvin and Calvinism* (blog), March 27, 2012, http://calvinandcalvinism.com/?p=11670.

[94] If there is not a universal sufficiency in the atonement, then those for whose sins Jesus did not die are being invited to what is naturally impossible for them. However, if there is universal sufficiency in the atonement (unlimited atonement), there is no impossibility of anyone believing the gospel except his own unbelieving heart.

so we offer the gospel to all. But this misses the point and the problem. The issue is not that we don't know who the elect are. That is a given. The issue is we are offering something to all people, including those who turn out to be non-elect, that indeed does not exist for all to whom the offer is made. An offer made to all sinners entails contradiction as the preacher knows that the satisfaction for sins by Christ on the cross was not made for all to whom the gospel comes, but pretends and speaks as if there is a legitimate offer to all to whom the gospel is preached.

5. The problem is even more acute with respect to the gospel offer when it is understood that it is God himself making the offer through us. Second Corinthians 5:18–20 makes it clear that it is God offering salvation to all people through the church *on the grounds of the atonement of Christ*. If he himself has limited that substitution to only the elect, how can he make such an offer genuinely to all people?

6. If Christ did not die for the sins of all people, what exactly is it unbelievers are guilty of rejecting? There is no atonement for their sins for them to reject. Unbelief of the gospel, by its very definition, involves rejection of God's provision of grace through Christ's death.

7. Scripture makes use of universal exhortations to believe the gospel. Limited atonement deprives these commands of their significance.[95]

For God's offer of salvation to be genuine, limited atonement cannot be true.

Unlimited atonement guarantees the genuineness of the offer of salvation made to all people through the preaching of the gospel. Without belief in the universal saving will of God, a universal extent in Christ's sin-bearing (thus a universal sufficiency of the atonement), there can be no well-meant offer of salvation from God to the non-elect who hear the gospel call.[96]

Conclusion

Looking at all the evidence in Scripture, and attempting to construct a theology of the intent, extent, and application of the atonement, what does unlimited atonement

---

[95] Allen, *Extent of the Atonement*, 773–75.

[96] Allen, *The Atonement*, 182.

mean specifically, and what does it entail? Let me answer the question by means of a series of denials and affirmations.

First, the denials. This chapter denies that

1. Christ died for the sins of any one group or section of humanity (the elect) to the exclusion of all other members of humanity.
2. Christ died *sufficiently* for all humanity such that only the *value or merit* of the atonement is or *could have been* sufficient for the sins of all humanity.
3. God's (Christ) intended both *antecedently and consequently* the salvation of all humanity through the atonement.
4. Christ died on such terms that all humanity in the end will be eternally saved (universalism).
5. God's (Christ's) intent in the atonement is dualistic such that he desires the salvation of all humanity in his revealed will but intends only to save the elect in his decretal will.
6. Christ purchased by the atonement the gift of faith for all humanity, or for any group of humanity, or for any individual person.
7. Christ purchased by the atonement *unconditional forgiveness* of sins for all humanity, for any group of humanity, or for any individual person.
8. Christ's atonement is only *hypothetically* able to save all sinners since it is only a satisfaction for the sins of some sinners.
9. The atonement *in and of itself* somehow contains its own efficacy such that it must be applied to those for whom it is made, whether viewed as all humanity or the elect.
10. The atonement's extent is determined by the doctrine of election, regardless of how election is defined.

This chapter affirms that

1. Christ died as a *sacrifice* and *substitute* for the sins of all humanity, past, present, and future such that the atonement is unlimited in extent.
2. God (Christ) *intended* to die for the sins of all humanity such that the atonement was an actual sacrifice, propitiation, and expiation of the sins of all humanity, whether or not any individual believes.
3. God (Christ) *antecedently* desired and intended the salvation of all people by the atonement, but *consequently* only intended the salvation of those who believe in Christ.

4. Christ died for the sins of all humanity with the intention of providing an *objective reconciliation* of the entire world of humanity such that the law of God is fully satisfied.

5. The atonement is *extrinsically sufficient* for all people and for all the sins of humanity because it is an actual atonement for all people and for all the sins of humanity.

6. Christ's death on the cross atoned for the sins of all humanity *and* provides other universal benefits to all humanity such as general or common grace.

7. Christ's death atoned for original sin such that the condemnation brought on by Adam's sin to all humanity has been taken away; thus, if any individual is eternally lost, it is due to his own sin.

8. The atonement is efficacious for all who believe in Christ the moment the Holy Spirit applies the benefits of the atonement (regeneration, justification, and so forth) to the believer.

9. All to whom the benefits of the atonement are efficaciously applied by God, and each individual to whom the benefits of the atonement are applied, receive(s) eternal salvation *by grace through faith in Christ* such that their salvation is *grounded* in the atonement itself.

10. The final salvation (glorification) in heaven of all who believe is *guaranteed* by the Holy Spirit's regeneration, justification, sanctification, and ultimate glorification, which are all grounded in the atonement.

I take it the reader will agree, whatever side he is on concerning the extent of the atonement, that the issue is not much ado about nothing, nor are chapters like this just so much brabbling. On the contrary, the topic is a titan issue in theology. Here we are on holy ground at the foot of the cross.

The burden of proof is on the advocates of limited atonement to demonstrate from Scripture that Christ died *only* for the sins of the elect and not merely that he intends to only save the elect. Simple positive statements in Scripture such as "Christ died for the church," or Paul's statement in Gal 2:20 that Christ "gave himself for me" cannot logically entail a universal negation: "Christ did not die for other people's sins," or "Christ did not die for all people's sins." It simply cannot be demonstrated exegetically from Scripture that Christ died *only for some people's sins* (a limited imputation of sin), in light of passages that employ terms like "world" and "all" in the various extent passages.[97]

---

[97] Allen, *Extent of the Atonement*, 790.

Advocates of limited atonement misread Scripture. Limited atonement is a doctrine that is hermeneutically flawed, theologically unsound, and logically defective. Ultimately, it is a concept that is system-driven. The systematic grid for many limitarians has so hardened in concrete that there is no possibility of considering any alternative. It is difficult to understand why some Calvinists cling so tightly to limited atonement when faced with the exegetical data coupled with the testimony of the church until the late sixteenth century. I am reminded of Irving Kristol's statement: "When we lack the will to see things as they really are, there is nothing so mystifying as the obvious."[98]

> Christ died for the sins of all, because of His and the Father's love for all, to provide a genuine offer of salvation to all, and His death not only makes salvation possible for all, but actually grounds the salvation of all who believe through the regenerating work of the Holy Spirit. There is a provision of forgiveness for all to whom the gospel comes. There is a provision of forgiveness for all who come to Christ through the gospel.[99]

J. I. Packer once wrote that belief in limited atonement was "necessary to the recovery of the gospel."[100] The irony is that limited atonement denies and distorts a crucial aspect of the gospel: that Christ died for the sins of all humanity, providing an unlimited atonement as evidence of his unlimited love and grace to a lost and dying world.

---

[98] Irving Kristol, "'When Virtue Loses All Her Loveliness'—Some Reflections on Capitalism and 'The Free Society' (1970)," in *Classics of American Political and Constitutional Thought: Reconstruction to the Present*, ed. Scott J. Hammond, Kevin R. Hardwich, and Howard L. Lubert, vol. 2 (Indianapolis: Hackett, 2007), 758.

[99] Allen, *Extent of the Atonement*, 791.

[100] J. I. Packer, "Introductory Essay," in Owen, *Death of Death*.

Is God's Grace Irresistible?
A Critique of Irresistible Grace

—— Steve Lemke ——

The Background of the Issue

Irresistible grace is so crucial to Calvinism that B. B. Warfield described the "I" of the TULIP as the very "hinge of the Calvinistic soteriology" and monergism (the belief that there is no human element in salvation) the "hall-mark" of Calvinism.[1] What is the background of this doctrine of irresistible grace?

The doctrine of irresistible grace was addressed most famously at the Dutch Reformed Synod of Dort, which offered a response to the concerns voiced by the Remonstrants. The Remonstrants perceived themselves to be Reformed followers of Calvin in that they were members of the Dutch Reformed Church, and they affirmed two well-known Calvinist doctrinal statements—the Belgic Confession and the Heidelberg Catechism. This difference of opinion was echoed in Baptist

---

[1] Benjamin B. Warfield, "Calvin and Calvinism," in *The Works of Benjamin B. Warfield*, 10 vols. (Grand Rapids: Baker, 2003), 5:359.

history in the distinction between General Baptists (who generally agreed with the Remonstrants on these points) and Particular Baptists (who generally agreed with the Synod of Dort on these points). While both the Remonstrants and the Dortians agreed that humans are all depraved and totally helpless to save themselves apart from God's grace, they mainly argued whether God's grace is resistible. In articles 3 and 4 of their "remonstrances" (or statement of concerns), the Remonstrants expressed their conviction that some of their fellow Reformed brethren had become so extreme in their beliefs they had departed from scriptural teachings. In particular, while affirming that salvation comes only by God's grace, the Remonstrants were concerned about the teaching that God forces his grace on sinners irresistibly. The Remonstrants affirmed

> that this grace of God is the beginning, continuance, and accomplishment of all good, even to this extent, that the regenerate man himself, without prevenient or assisting, awakening, following and cooperative grace, can neither think, will, nor do good, nor withstand any temptations to evil; so that all good deeds or movements, that can be conceived, must be ascribed to the grace of God in Christ. But as respects the mode of the operation of this grace, it is not irresistible; inasmuch as it is written concerning many, that they have resisted the Holy Ghost. Acts 7, and elsewhere in many places.[2]

In other words, the Remonstrants taught that the only way for anyone to be saved is for God's grace to come before, during, and after justification because even the best-intentioned human being can "neither think, will, nor do good" apart from God's grace.[3] They said that all good "that can be conceived, must be ascribed to the grace of God in Christ."[4] But the questions are, Why is this saving grace of God not appropriated or experienced by everyone? Has God failed in some way? Does God not truly love all persons? Does God not desire the salvation of all persons? The Remonstrants refused to blame this failure on God but rightfully assigned it to the rebellion and resistance of fallen human beings. God created human beings with the freedom either to cooperate with God and receive his grace or to reject finally God's gracious gift. Again, human beings would have no salvation at all apart from the grace of God; but

---

[2] Schaff, "Five Arminian Articles," 3:547 (see intro., n. 3).
[3] Schaff, 547.
[4] Schaff, 547.

God refuses to actualize that salvation in the life of anyone who continually resists his grace, refuses to humbly receive it, and finally rejects it.

The Synod of Dort, however, strenuously objected to the Remonstrants' denial of irresistible grace:

> VII. Who teach that the grace by which we are converted to God is nothing but a gentle persuasion, or (as others explain it) that the way of God's acting in man's conversion that is most noble and suited to human nature is that which happens by persuasion, and that nothing prevents this grace of moral suasion even by itself from making natural men spiritual; indeed, that God does not produce the assent of the will except in this manner of moral suasion, and that the effectiveness of God's work by which it surpasses the work of Satan consists in the fact that God promises eternal benefits while Satan promises temporal ones. . . .

> VIII. Who teach that God in regenerating man does not bring to bear that power of his omnipotence whereby he may powerfully and unfailingly bend man's will to faith and conversion, but that even when God has accomplished all the works of grace which he uses for man's conversion, man nevertheless can, and in actual fact often does, so resist God and the Spirit in their intent and will to regenerate him, that man completely thwarts his own rebirth; and, indeed, that it remains in his own power whether or not to be reborn.[5]

The Problem of Defining Irresistible Grace

The term "irresistible grace," then, came initially as a view denied by the Remonstrants and defended by the Dortian Calvinists. The Synod of Dort rejected the notion that God's grace was limited to exerting strong moral persuasion on sinners by the Holy Spirit to lead them to salvation. The Calvinists also rejected the notion that a person can "resist God and the Holy Spirit, when God intends man's regeneration and wills

---

[5] "The Synod of Dort (1618–1619)," Heads III and IV, Rejection of Errors, Articles VII and VIII, available online at https://www.apuritansmind.com/creeds-and-confessions/the -synod-of-dordt-1618-1619-a-d/. For a different translation, see James T. Dennison Jr., ed., "The Canons of Dort (1618–1619)," in *Reformed Confessions of the 16th and 17th Centuries in English Translation*, 4 vols. (Grand Rapids: Reformation Heritage Books, 2008–14), 4:142–43 (III–IV, Rejection of Errors, pars. 7–8).

to regenerate him."[6] Instead, the Dort statement asserted that God brings to bear the "powers of His omnipotence as potently and infallibly [to] bend man's will to faith and conversion."[7]

To understand how Calvinists say God effects irresistible grace, one must understand the important distinction they draw between what is variously known as the "general" or "outward" call from the "special," "inward," "effectual," or "serious" call. Steele, Thomas, and Quinn equate the "efficacious call" with irresistible grace, based on this distinction between these proposed two different callings from God:

> The *gospel invitation extends a call* to salvation to everyone who hears its message. . . . But this outward general call, extended to the elect and the non-elect alike, will not bring sinners to Christ. . . . Therefore, the *Holy Spirit*, in order to bring God's elect to salvation, extends to them a *special inward call* in addition to the outward call contained in the gospel message. Through this special call the Holy Spirit performs a work of grace within the sinner which inevitably brings him to faith in Christ [italics in the original]. . . .
>
> Although the general outward call of the gospel can be, and often is, rejected, the special inward call of the Spirit never fails to result in the conversion of those to whom it is made. This special call is not made to all sinners but is issued to the elect only! The Spirit is in no way dependent upon their help or cooperation for success in His work of bringing them to Christ. It is for this reason that Calvinists speak of the Spirit's call and of God's grace in saving sinners as being "efficacious," "invincible," or "irresistible." For the grace which the Holy Spirit extends to the elect cannot be thwarted or refused, it never fails to bring them to true faith in Christ![8]

As this statement indicates, some contemporary Calvinists seem to be a little embarrassed by the term "irresistible grace" and have sought to soften it or replace it with a term like "effectual calling." They also object when others criticize that

---

[6] Dennison, *Reformed Confessions*, 4:143 (III–IV, Rejection of Errors, par. 8), accessed December 3, 2021, https://www.apuritansmind.com/creeds-and-confessions/the-synod-of-dordt-1618-1619-a-d/.

[7] Dennison, 4:143.

[8] David N. Steele, Curtis C. Thomas, and S. Lance Quinn, *The Five Points of Calvinism: Defined, Defended, Documented*, 2nd ed. (Philadelphia: P&R, 2004), 52–54. See also Barrett, "The Scriptural Affirmation of Monergism," in Barrett and Nettles, *Whomever He Wills*, 127–46 (see intro., n. 22); and Piper, *Does God Desire* (see chap. 3, n. 16).

"irresistible grace" suggests that God forces persons to do things against their wills. Instead, they insist, God merely woos and persuades. Ironically, this is precisely what the Synod of Dort denied to the Remonstrants (see earlier quotation from the Synod).

Calvinists thus sometimes sound disingenuous in affirming a strong view of irresistible grace while simultaneously softening the language about it to make it more palatable. For example, John Piper and the Bethlehem Baptist Church staff affirm that irresistible grace "means the Holy Spirit can overcome all resistance and make his influence irresistible. . . . The doctrine of irresistible grace means that God is sovereign and can overcome all resistance when he wills."[9] Yet, just a few paragraphs later, they affirm that "irresistible grace never implies that God forces us to believe against our will. . . . On the contrary, irresistible grace is compatible with preaching and witnessing that tries to persuade people to do what is reasonable and what will accord with their own best interests."[10] Note the striking contradiction—God will "overcome all resistance and make his influence irresistible," and yet "irresistible grace never implies that God forces us to believe against our will." No attempt is made in the article to reconcile these apparently contradictory assertions.

Likewise, R. C. Sproul argued at great length that John 6:44 ("No one can come to Me unless the Father who sent Me draws him" [HCSB]) does *not* refer merely to the necessity that God "woo or entice men to Christ," such that humans can "resist this wooing" and "refuse the enticement."[11] In philosophical language, Sproul said, this wooing is a necessary but not sufficient condition for salvation "because the wooing does not, in fact, guarantee that we will come to Christ."[12] Sproul stated that such an interpretation is "incorrect" and "does violence to the text of Scripture."[13]

Instead, Sproul insists, the term "draw" is "a much more forceful concept than to woo" and means "to compel by irresistible superiority."[14] However, in discussing irresistible grace, Sproul tells of a student who, hearing a lecture on predestination by John Gerstner, rejected it. When Gerstner asked the student how he defined

---

[9] John Piper and the Bethlehem Baptist Church staff, "What We Believe about the Five Points of Calvinism: Position Paper of the Pastoral Staff of Bethlehem Baptist Church (TULIP)" (Minneapolis: Bethlehem Baptist Church, 1997), March 1, 1985, http://www.desiringgod.org /ResourceLibrary/Articles/ByDate/1985/1487_What_We_Believe_About_the_Five_Points _of_Calvinism/#Grace, 10.

[10] Piper and staff, 12.

[11] Sproul, *Chosen by God*, 69–70 (see chap. 1, n. 106).

[12] Sproul, 69.

[13] Sproul, 69.

[14] Sproul, 69.

Calvinism, the student described it as the perspective that "God forces some people to choose Christ and prevents other people from choosing Christ." Gerstner then said, "If that is what a Calvinist is, then you can be sure that I am not a Calvinist either."[15] What is the difference between compelling "by irresistible superiority" and "forcing" people to do something? Sproul likewise chastised a Presbyterian seminary president for rejecting the Calvinist doctrine that "God brings some people, kicking and screaming against their wills, into the kingdom." Sproul described this Presbyterian theologian's view as "a gross misconception of his own church's theology," as a "caricature," and "as far away from Calvinism as one could possibly get."[16] So which way is it? If God compels people with "irresistible superiority," in what way is it inaccurate to say that God forces people to choose Christ? The Synod of Dort insisted that such attempts at moral persuasion of unsaved persons was wasted time. The irresistibility of God's grace (and not merely the use of strong moral persuasion) was *precisely* what the Synod of Dort rejected and the Remonstrants affirmed. While the Remonstrants affirmed that the compelling grace of God persuades the lost to receive Christ as Lord and Savior, the Synod of Dort insisted that this was not going far enough. Note their explicit denial that a person can "resist" God. The language used in the Synod of Dort describes God's omnipotence as being such that God can "potently and infallibly bend man's will to faith and conversion."[17]

Bending the will of a fallible being by an omnipotent Being powerfully and unfailingly is not merely sweet persuasion. It is forcing one to change one's mind against one's will. Calvinists often describe their position as *monergism* as opposed to *synergism*. In monergism, God works entirely alone, apart from any human role.[18] In synergism, on the other hand, humans cooperate with God in some way in their own regeneration and conversion, usually simply putting their trust in Christ in response

---

[15] Sproul, 122.

[16] Sproul, 122.

[17] Dennison, *Reformed Confessions*, 4:143 (III–IV, Rejection of Errors, par. 8).

[18] R. C. Sproul expressed this monergistic view of salvation in this unambiguous way: "What predestination means, in its most elementary form, is that our final destination, heaven or hell, is decided by God not only before we get there, but before we are even born. It teaches that our ultimate destiny is in the hands of God. Another way of saying it is this: From all eternity, before we even existed, God decided to save some members of the human race and to let the rest of the human race perish. God made a choice—He chose some individuals to be saved into everlasting blessedness in heaven and others He chose to pass over, to allow them to follow the consequences of their sins into eternal torment in hell." Sproul, *Chosen by God*, 22. See also Barrett, "Monergism," 120–87.

to the work of the Holy Spirit in their lives. None of us non-Pelagians would affirm for a minute that we can achieve salvation apart from God. The question is whether humans have any role at all in regeneration and accepting or receiving their own salvation. The Calvinists say, "No! Your salvation is monergistic, provided only by the grace of God."[19] When a critic says this response means that God imposes irresistible grace against a person's will or that humans do not have a choice in the matter, the Calvinists protest that they are being misunderstood and caricatured. When challenged that irresistible grace goes against someone's will, most Calvinists reply that it is not against a person's will at all. God changes their will through regeneration invincibly, such that the person is irresistibly drawn to Christ. Calvinists call this human willing, which is externally driven, *compatibilist volition*, as opposed to the more common view, *libertarian freedom*. In libertarian freedom a person does not have absolute freedom (a frequent Calvinist stereotype), but a person chooses between at least two alternatives. In every case a person could have, at least hypothetically, chosen something else. But in compatibilism, people always choose their greatest desire. They have no alternative but to will to do what they want to do. So when God changes their will through irresistible grace or enabling grace, they really have no choice. They will what God has programmed them to will. Irresistible grace affirms that it is *logically impossible* for the elect to resist God's saving grace, just as impossible as two plus two equaling five.

A Calvinist system that advocates both monergism (God is the only actor) and compatibilism (persons do what God wants them to do after he changes their will through preconversion regeneration) leaves little room for human volition in response to God's grace. Calvinists cannot insist that an omnipotent God overwhelms and bends human will powerfully and unfailingly, and then transform this doctrine into something other than it is. Sometimes Calvinists attempt to soften the hardness of irresistible grace with more palatable language such as "effectual calling." The effectual calling means precisely the same thing as irresistible grace; effectual calling just sounds nicer. At the end of the day, in Calvinism, people have no choice but to do what God has programmed them to do. Nonetheless, Calvinists often attempt to sidestep criticism by asserting that the doctrine has been misunderstood, even when

---

[19] Ironically, Sproul acknowledged that after God gives the monergistic "operative grace of regeneration . . . the rest of the process is synergistic," including belief in God, responding to God, and living the Christian life. *Willing to Believe: The Controversy over Free Will* (Grand Rapids: Baker, 1997), 73. Logically, Sproul's teaching would seem to affirm that one could lose salvation after regeneration.

non-Calvinists have quoted or paraphrased what Calvinists themselves have said in describing their own doctrine.[20] No matter how modern-day Calvinists may attempt to gloss over the hardness of irresistible grace with word games or equivocations to project it in a softer, gentler light, the doctrine remains what it is. This study will examine irresistible grace as it is described and defined in standard Calvinist doctrinal teachings.

The Bible and Irresistible Grace

What does the Bible say about irresistible grace? The easy answer is the Bible does not specifically address it. The phrase "irresistible grace" does not appear anywhere in Scripture. Neither can one find such important Calvinist words as "monergism," "compatibilism," or *ordo salutis*. This absence alone does not mean irresistible grace might not be a reality. Other doctrines such as the Trinity are described in Scripture but not with the theological name that we now give them. So let us examine Old Testament texts, New Testament texts, and the ministry and teachings of Jesus to see if they support irresistible grace. We will also see how the repeated all-inclusive invitations to salvation throughout Scripture and the descriptions of how to be saved argue against irresistible grace.

Key Texts Affirming Resistible Grace

Old Testament Texts—Some Scripture texts appear to deny irresistible grace and to affirm resistible grace explicitly. For example, in Proverbs 1, the wisdom of God personified speaks to those whom "I called" (Prov 1:24 NASB), to whom "I will pour out my spirit on you" (v. 23b), and to whom wisdom has made "my words known to you" (v. 23c). Nevertheless, no one regarded God's truth, for the hearers refused God's message and disdained wisdom's counsel (vv. 22–26). Some might claim this message merely exemplifies the resistible outward call. The problem becomes complicated because these are God's elect people, the Jews, with whom God had entered into covenant: "I called and you refused" (v. 24a). God makes them the offer: "I will pour out my spirit on you" (v. 23b), but they would not

---

[20] For an example of Calvinists not accepting the implications of their own definition of irresistible grace when a non-Calvinist quotes it back to them, see Steve Lemke, "A Biblical and Theological Critique of Irresistible Grace," in *Whosoever Will*, 115–17 (see intro., n. 20).

turn and instead refused to accept the message (v. 24). The grace that was so graciously offered was ungraciously refused. The proffered grace was conditional on their response. Acceptance of God's Word would have brought blessing, but their rejection of it brought calamity upon themselves.

In the Prophets and the Psalms, God responds to the Israelites' refusal to repent and their rejection of his Word:

> "When Israel was a child, I loved him, and out of Egypt I called My son. As they called them, so they went from them; they sacrificed to the Baals, and burned incense to carved images. I taught Ephraim to walk, taking them by their arms; but they did not know that I healed them. I drew them with gentle cords, with bands of love, and I was to them as those who take the yoke from their neck. I stooped and fed them. He shall not return to the land of Egypt; but the Assyrian shall be his king, because they refused to repent. And the sword shall slash in his cities, devour his districts, and consume them, because of their own counsels. My people are bent on backsliding from Me. Though they call to the Most High, none at all exalt Him. How can I give you up, Ephraim? How can I hand you over, Israel? How can I make you like Admah? How can I set you like Zeboiim? My heart churns within Me; My sympathy is stirred. I will not execute the fierceness of My anger; I will not again destroy Ephraim. For I am God, and not man, the Holy One in your midst; and I will not come with terror." (Hos 11:1–9 NKJV)

> They did not keep the covenant of God; they refused to walk in His law. (Ps 78:10 NKJV)

> "But My people would not heed My voice, and Israel would have none of Me. So I gave them over to their own stubborn heart, to walk in their own counsels. Oh, that My people would listen to Me, that Israel would walk in My ways!" (Ps 81:11–13 NKJV)

> They have turned their backs to Me and not their faces. Though I taught them time and time again, they do not listen and receive discipline. (Jer 32:33 HCSB)

New Testament Texts—One of the most direct references to the resistibility of grace in the New Testament is in Stephen's sermon in Acts 7:2–53, just before his martyrdom in vv. 54–60. In confronting the Jews who had rejected Jesus as Messiah,

Stephen said, "You men who are stiff-necked and uncircumcised in heart and ears are always resisting the Holy Spirit; you are doing just as your fathers did" (v. 51 NASB). The Remonstrants referenced this specific Scripture, as do most scholars who reject the notion of irresistible grace. Stephen is not speaking to believers but to Jews who have rejected Christ. He not only accuses them of "resisting the Holy Spirit" but observes that many of their Jewish ancestors resisted God as well. The word translated as "resist" (*antipiptō*) means not "to fall down and worship," but to "oppose," "strive against," or "resist."[21] Clearly this Scripture teaches that the influence of the Holy Spirit is resistible. A similar account in Luke describes the Pharisees' response to the preaching of John the Baptist: "But the Pharisees and lawyers rejected the counsel of God against themselves, being not baptized of him" (Luke 7:30 KJV).

Another example of resistance occurs in Paul's salvation experience in Acts 26. As Saul was on the road to Damascus to persecute Christians, a blinding light hit him, and a voice out of heaven said, "Saul, Saul, why are you persecuting Me? It is hard for you to kick against the goads" (Acts 26:14 HCSB). Saul had resisted the conviction of the Holy Spirit in events such as the stoning of Stephen, but after his dramatic experience with the risen Christ, Saul did believe. Even so, some time lapsed before Ananias arrived and Paul received the Holy Spirit (Acts 9:17). However, in both the Old and New Testaments, other people saw miracles yet continued to resist God's grace.[22]

What do Calvinists say about these texts? First, Calvinists do not deny that people can resist the Holy Spirit in some situations. Unbelievers can resist the "outward call" of the gospel, but the elect cannot resist the "effectual call." John Piper has said, "What is irresistible is when the Spirit is issuing the effectual call."[23] However, Calvinistic explanations do not appear to help in this instance. The Jews, after all, were God's chosen people, and the entirety of the Jewish people were covered under

---

[21] William E. Vine, *An Expository Dictionary of New Testament Words* (Old Tappan, NJ: Revell, 1966), 286; Joseph H. Thayer, *A Greek-English Lexicon of the New Testament* (Nashville: Broadman, 1977), 51; *BDAG*, 90.

[22] John Chrysostom said in a sermon on 1 Cor 1:4–5, "But some man will say, 'He ought to bring men in, even against their will.' Away with this. He doth not use violence, nor compel; for who that bids to honours, and crowns, and banquets, and festivals, drags people unwilling and bound? No one. For this is the part of one inflicting an insult. Unto hell He sends men against their will, but unto the kingdom He calls willing minds." John Chrysostom, *The Homilies of St. John Chrysostom on the First Epistle of St. Paul the Apostle to the Corinthians*, homily 2, point 9 (Oxford: John Henry Parker, 1854), 17.

[23] Piper and staff, "Five Points of Calvinism."

the covenant, not just individual Jews. Calvinist covenantal theology sees the entire nation of Israel as being God's chosen people. The elect, after all, are supposed to receive the effectual call. Calvinists often quote, "Jacob I have loved, but Esau I have hated" (Rom 9:13 NKJV) as strong evidence for election.[24] But these divinely elected people have not only rejected Jesus as Messiah but resisted the Holy Spirit through many generations in history. Therefore, it would seem God's grace is resistible, even among the elect who are eligible to receive the effectual call.

Resistible Grace in the Ministry and Teachings of Jesus

Throughout his teaching ministry, Jesus taught and ministered in ways that seem to be inconsistent with the notion of irresistible grace. In each of these occasions, he appears to advocate the idea that God's grace is resistible. For example, hear again Jesus's lament over Jerusalem: "Jerusalem, Jerusalem! [The city] who kills the prophets and stones those who are sent to her. How often I wanted to gather your children together, as a hen gathers her chicks under her wings, *yet you were not willing!*" (Matt 23:37 HCSB, emphasis added; cf. Luke 13:34). What was Jesus lamenting? He was lamenting that despite God's gracious love for "Jerusalem" (by metonymy including *all* Jews, not merely the leaders) and his desire to gather them to eternal security under his protection, and the many prophets and messengers he sent them with his message, they rejected the message that was sent them and "were not willing" to respond to God. In fact, the Greek sets the contrast off even more sharply than the English does because forms of the same Greek verb *thelō* (to will) are used twice in this verse: "I willed . . . but you were not willing."[25] Gottlob Schrenk described this statement as expressing "the frustration of His gracious purpose to save by the refusal of men."[26] Note also that his lament concerned the entire city of Jerusalem, not just a small number of the elect within Jerusalem. Indeed, Jesus's "how often" signified even his preincarnate salvific concern about not only the persons living in Jerusalem at that time but for many previous generations of Jerusalemites.

Again, one might suggest that the prophets were merely the vehicles for proclaiming the general call, and thus these Jerusalemites never received the efficacious

---

[24] Israel's election to service as a chosen people and individual election to salvation for Christians are interwoven in Romans 9–11. Calvinists often do not give adequate attention to the former. See the article by William Klein in this volume.

[25] Gottlob Schrenk, s.v. "*theō, theleōma, theleōsis*," in *TDNT*, 3:48–49.

[26] *TDNT*, 3:48–49.

call. However, this argument will not do. First, the Jerusalemites were God's chosen people. As the elect, they should have received the efficacious call, but in fact, they were still unwilling to respond. Some Calvinists might make this argument: the election of Israel included individuals within Israel, not all of Israel as a people. Only a remnant of physical Israel, not all of it, will be saved. But the proposal that God sent the efficacious call to just a portion of Israel nevertheless does not match up well with this text or numerous other texts.

Even so, the greater issue is that if Jesus believed in irresistible grace, with both the outward and inward calls, his apparent lament over Jerusalem would have been just a disingenuous act, a cynical show because he knew that God had not and would not give these lost persons the necessary conditions for their salvation. His lament would have been over God's hardness of heart, but that is not what the Scripture says. Scripture attributes the people's not coming to God to their own unwillingness, that is, the hardness of their own hearts.

What is generalized in Jesus's lament over Jerusalem is personalized in the incident with the rich young ruler (Luke 18:18–23). The ruler asked, "What must I do to inherit eternal life?" (v. 18 HCSB). If Jesus were a Calvinist, one might have expected him to answer, "Nothing!" and admonish the young ruler for the impertinence of his question, particularly the idea that he could do anything to inherit eternal life, as if to steal glory from God's monergistic salvation. Instead, Jesus told him what he *could do*: he could go and sell all his possessions and give them to the poor. This instruction was not just about the young ruler's money; it was about his heart. He loved his money and the privileges it gave him, and he just could not live without it. In other words, Jesus would not grant him eternal life unless he was willing to make a total commitment of his life to God, but the young ruler was unwilling to do so. Jesus let him walk away and face the solemn consequences of his decision.

Noting the rich young ruler's unwillingness, Jesus then commented about how hard it is for a rich person to enter heaven—indeed, as hard as a camel going through the eye of a needle (Luke 13:24–28). Of course, if Jesus were a Calvinist, he never would have suggested that it was harder for rich people to be saved by God's irresistible grace than for poor people. Their wills would be changed immediately and invincibly upon hearing God's effectual call. It would be no harder for a rich person to be saved by God's monergistic and irresistible calling than it would be for any other sinner. But the *real* Jesus was suggesting that their salvation was tied in some measure to their *response and commitment* to his calling.

The same idea of resistible grace arises frequently in the parables of Jesus's teaching ministry. In the parable of the two sons (Matt 21:28–32), Jesus described their differing responses. One son initially refused to do the work he was told to do, saying "I don't want to!" but later "changed his mind" and did it (v. 29 HCSB). Meanwhile, the other son said he would do the work, but later he did not do the work. What was the main point of this parable? The point was that tax collectors and prostitutes were going to enter the kingdom of heaven before the chief priests and elders who resisted Jesus's teaching (vv. 31–32). The distinction between the two was *not* that one was a son and one was not, for they both were sons from whom the father desired obedience. The distinction between them is the *response* of each son—resistance from one, repentance and obedience from the other. Evidently Jesus thought that a personal response to the Father's will is important!

A similar teaching follows in the parable of the vineyard (Matt 21:33–44). Using the familiar Old Testament symbol of a vineyard to represent Israel, Jesus told of the owner of the vineyard going away and leaving it in the hands of the tenants. He sent back a series of messengers and finally sent his own son to instruct the tenants about running the vineyard, but they rejected each messenger and killed his son in the hope of seizing the vineyard for themselves. The owner then returned and exacted a solemn punishment on the rebellious tenants. Jesus then spoke of the cornerstone, the rock that was rejected by the builders but became the chief cornerstone, obviously speaking of himself (vv. 42–44). Jesus then told the Pharisees that the kingdom of God would be taken from them and "given to a nation producing its fruit" (v. 43 HCSB). Again, the key differential was whether persons were willing to be *responsive* to the Word of God.

The parable of the sower (or of the soils) in Matt 13:1–23; Mark 4:1–20; and Luke 8:1–15 highlights the issue of personal responsiveness to the Word of God. The *invariable element* is the seed, which represents the Word. The *variable factor* is the receptiveness of the soil on which the sower sowed the seed. The seed on the path, on the rocky ground, and among the thorns never became rooted enough in the soil to flourish. The seed on the path was snatched away by the evil one. The rocky ground represents the person who "hears the word" and "receives it with joy" (Matt 13:20 HCSB) but does not flourish because "he has no root in himself" (v. 21). The seed that fell among thorns represents the person who also hears the Word of God, but the message becomes garbled by worldly interests. Only the seed that fell on good, receptive ground flourished. Again, the variable is not the proclamation of the Word but the *response* of the individual.

Resistible Grace in the All-Inclusive Invitations in Scripture

One of the most off-repeated themes throughout many genres of Scripture is the broad invitation of God to "all" people. This invitation parallels in many ways David L. Allen's discussion on the issue of a limited atonement in this volume and in other works.[27] However, the question relating to irresistible grace is why, when receiving irresistible grace is the only way persons can be saved, would God choose only a small number of people to be saved? In essence, Calvinists blame God for those who do not come. These lost souls cannot come because God did not give them irresistible grace, the only way they can be saved. Roger Olson compared the roles of Satan and God in Calvinism: "Satan wants all people damned to hell and God wants only a certain number damned to hell."[28] While Calvinists would insist that the sinners who reject the message of salvation merely receive their just deserts, there is really more to it than that. Calvinists affirm that God elected some for his own reasons from before the world began, and he gave them irresistible grace through his Spirit so they inevitably would be saved. Obviously, those whom he did not choose to give the irresistible effectual call but merely the resistible outer ineffectual call can never be saved. These are no more or less sinners than others, but God for no obvious reason does not love this group (Calvinists call this "preterition," or intentionally overlooking some persons), while he loves the other group through election. God chose not to give them the means of salvation, and thus they have zero chance of being saved. The alternative perspective that I affirm is that God does extend the general call to all persons and unleashes the Holy Spirit to persuade and convict them of their need for repentance and faith. The Holy Spirit, however, does not impose his will irresistibly. At the end of the day, *response* to the grace of God determines whether the call is effectual.

The key issue, then, is whether salvation is genuinely open to all people or just to a few who receive irresistible grace. What does the Scripture say concerning this issue? First, Scripture clearly teaches that God desires the salvation of all people. The Bible teaches that:

> He Himself is the propitiation for our sins, and not only for ours, but also for those of the whole world. (1 John 2:2 HCSB)

---

[27] Allen, *The Atonement* (see intro., n. 20); Allen, *Extent of the Atonement* (see intro., n. 10); David L. Allen, "Commentary on Article 3: The Atonement of Christ," in Allen, Hankins, and Harwood, *Anyone Can Be Saved*, 55–64 (see intro., n. 20).

[28] Roger Olson, *Against Calvinism* (Grand Rapids: Zondervan, 2011), 159.

"It is not the will of your Father who is in heaven for one of these little ones to perish." (Matt 18:14 NASB)

"The Lord is . . . not willing that any should perish, but that all should come to repentance." (2 Pet 3:9 KJV)

"[God] wants everyone to be saved and to come to the knowledge of the truth." (1 Tim 2:4 HCSB)

The Greek word *pas* (πᾶς) and its similar cognate synonym words (*pantes, panta*, and *hos an*), meaning "all" or "everyone," such as in 1 Tim 2:4 and 2 Pet 3:9, in all the standard Greek dictionaries means "all" without exception![29]

Those who would like to translate the word *pas* as something other than a synonym for "all" should ponder the theological cost of such a move merely because it disagrees with their theological system. For example, Paul used the same term in 2 Tim 3:16, when he declared that *"all* Scripture is given by inspiration of God" (2 Tim 3:16 KJV, emphasis added). He did not mean that God inspires merely some selected portions of Scripture but that God inspires *all* Scripture. Likewise, the Greek word *pas* ("all"), used in the prologue to John, makes the enormous claim about creation that *"all* things were made by him; and without him was not any thing made that was made" (John 1:3 KJV, emphasis added). Jesus was not involved in merely creating a few trees and hills here and there, but *all* things were created by him. We see the word again in Ephesians when Paul looked toward the eschaton and claimed that in the fullness of time will be gathered *"all* things in Christ, both which are in heaven, and which are on earth" (Eph 1:10 KJV, emphasis added). Thus, an accurate doctrine of the creation of the world, the inspiration of Scripture, and the consummation of the world hinges on an accurate rendering of the Greek word *pas* as "all." So does the doctrine of salvation—that God desires the salvation of all people and has made an atonement through Christ that is sufficient for *all* people.

This same all-inclusive Greek word *pas* (translated as "everyone," "all," or "whosoever") is used repeatedly in the New Testament to offer an invitation to all people who will respond to God's gracious initiative with faith and obedience (italics in the following Scripture passages are mine):

---

[29] Bo Reicke, s.v. *"pas," TDNT*, 5:886–96; Thayer, *"pas," Greek-English Lexicon*, 491–93; *BDAG*, 782–84. Danker noted that *pas* pertains "to totality" with a "focus on its individual components." *BDAG*, 782. Johannes P. Louw and Eugene A. Nida similarly observe that *pas* denotes "the totality of any object, mass, collective, or extension" (L&N 1:597).

"Therefore *whoever* [*pas hostis*] hears these sayings of Mine, and does them, I will liken him to a wise man who built his house on the rock." (Matt 7:24 NKJV; see Luke 6:47–48)

"*Whosoever* [*pas hostis*] therefore shall confess me before men, him will I confess also before my Father which is in heaven. But *whosoever* [*hostis an*] shall deny me before men, him will I also deny before my Father which is in heaven." (Matt 10:32–33 KJV; see Luke 12:8)

"Come to Me, *all* [*pantes*] who are weary and heavy-laden, and I will give you rest." (Matt 11:28 NASB1995)

John the Baptist "came as a witness, / to testify about the light, / so that *all* [*pantes*] might believe through him." (John 1:7 HCSB)

Jesus is "the true light, who gives light to *everyone*" [*panta*]. (John 1:9 HCSB)

Whoever [*pas*] believes in Him should not perish but have eternal life. For God so loved the world that He gave His only begotten Son, that *whoever* [*pas*] believes in Him should not perish but have everlasting life. (John 3:15–16 NKJV)

"*Everyone* [*pas*] who drinks of this water will thirst again; but whoever [*hos an*] drinks of the water that I will give him shall never thirst; but the water that I will give him will become in him a well of water springing up to eternal life." (John 4:13–14 NASB1995)

"For this is the will of My Father, that *everyone* [*pas*] who beholds the Son and believes in Him will have eternal life, and I Myself will raise him up on the last day." (John 6:40 NASB1995)

"*Everyone* [*pas*] who lives and believes in Me will never die. Do you believe this?" (John 11:26 NASB)

"I have come as Light into the world, so that *everyone* [*pas*] who believes in Me will not remain in darkness." (John 12:46 NASB1995)

And it shall be that *everyone* [*pas, hos an*] who calls on the name of the Lord will be saved. (Acts 2:21 NASB)[30]

---

[30] Note the commentary on Acts 2:21 by John Calvin himself: "He [God] says, all things are in turmoil and possessed by the fear of death, *only call upon Me and you shall be saved.* So

"Of Him [Jesus] all [*pantes*] the prophets bear witness that through His name *everyone* [*panta*] who believes in Him receives forgiveness of sins." (Acts 10:43 NASB1995)

As it is written: "Behold, I lay in Zion a stumbling stone and rock of offense, and *whoever* [*pas*] believes on Him will not be put to shame." (Rom 9:33 NKJV)

For the Scripture says, "*Whoever* [*pas*] believes in Him will not be disappointed." (Rom 10:11 NASB1995)

Whoever [*pas*] denies the Son does not have the Father; the one who confesses the Son has the Father also. (1 John 2:23 NASB)

Whoever [*pas*] believes that Jesus is the Christ is born of God, and whoever loves the Father loves the child born of Him. (1 John 5:1 NASB1995)

Many more of these broad invitations are found throughout Scripture than space permits to list here. In addition, the New Testament often uses a form of *hostis*, which when combined with *an* or *ean* is an indefinite relative pronoun best translated as "anyone," "whosoever," or "everyone" and refers to the group as a whole, with a focus on each individual member of the group.[31]

An All-Inclusive Invitation in the Prophets

In the famous prophecy of Joel, the prophet commented on whom God delivers:

And it shall come to pass, that *whosoever* shall call on the name of the LORD shall be delivered: for in mount Zion and in Jerusalem shall be deliverance,

---

however much a man may be overwhelmed in the gulf of misery there is yet set before him a way of escape. We must also observe the universal word, 'whosoever'. For God himself admits all men to Himself without exception and by this means invites them to salvation, even as Paul deduces in Rom. 10, and as the prophet had earlier recorded. 'Thou Lord who hearest prayer, unto Thee shall all flesh come' (Ps. 65.2). Therefore since no man is excluded from calling upon God the gate of salvation is set open to all. *There is nothing else to hinder us from entering, but our own unbelief*." Calvin, "The Acts of the Apostles 1–13," in *Calvin's New Testament Commentaries*, 12 vols., trans. J. W. Fraser and W. J. G. McDonald, ed. David W. Torrance and Thomas F. Torrance (Grand Rapids: Eerdmans, 1995), 6:61–62, emphasis added. Evidently Calvin does not always agree with Calvinists.

[31] Thayer, "*hostis*," *Greek-English Lexicon*, 33–34, 454–57; BDAG, "*hostis*," 56–57, 725–27, 729–30. Danker noted that *hostis* means "whoever, everyone, who, in a generalizing sense," and when combined with *an* "the indefiniteness of the expression is heightened." *BDAG*, 729.

as the LORD hath said, and in the remnant whom the LORD shall call. (Joel 2:32 KJV)

Note that the "whosoever" (translated "everyone" in NASB and HCSB) refers to "the remnant whom the Lord shall call." These are not two distinct groups but are one and the same.

All-Inclusive Invitations Offered by Jesus

Jesus offered an all-inclusive invitation in the Sermon on the Mount and throughout his teaching ministry. Note that Jesus did not say "whoso-*elect*" in these invitations; the invitation is always addressed to "whoso*ever*."[32]

"And blessed is he, *whosoever* [*hos ean*] shall not be offended in me." (Matt 11:6 KJV; see Luke 7:23)

"For *whosoever* [*hostis an*] shall do the will of my Father which is in heaven, the same is my brother, and sister, and mother." (Matt 12:50 KJV; cf. Mark 3:35)

"If *any* man [*tis*] will come after me, let him deny himself, and take up his cross, and follow me. For *whosoever* [*hos an*] will save his life shall lose it: and *whosoever* will lose his life for my sake shall find it." (Matt 16:24–25 KJV; cf. Mark 8:34–35; Luke 9:23–24)

"I am the living bread that came down out of heaven; if *anyone* [*ean tis*] eats of this bread, he will live forever; and the bread also which I will give for the life of the world is My flesh." (John 6:51 NASB1995)

"If *anyone* [*ean tis*] is willing to do His will, he will know of the teaching, whether it is of God or whether I speak from Myself." (John 7:17 NASB1995)

Now on the last day, the great day of the feast, Jesus stood and cried out, saying, "If *anyone* [*ean tis*] is thirsty, let him come to Me and drink." (John 7:37 NASB)

"Truly, truly, I say to you, if *anyone* [*ean tis*] keeps My word he will never see death." (John 8:51 NASB1995)

---

[32] See also Mark 8:38/Luke 9:26; Mark 9:37/Luke 9:48; Mark 10:15; and Luke 14:27.

All-Inclusive Invitations in the Proclamation and Epistles of the Early Church

"And it shall be that *everyone* [*pas, hos an*] who calls on the name of the Lord will be saved." (Acts 2:21 NASB)

"Of Him [Jesus] all [*pantes*] the prophets bear witness that through His name *everyone* [*panta*] who believes in Him receives forgiveness of sins." (Acts 10:43 NASB1995)

For *everyone* [*pas, hos an*] who calls on the name of the Lord will be saved. (Rom 10:13 HCSB)

Whoever [*hos an*] confesses that Jesus is the Son of God, God abides in him, and he in God. (1 John 4:15 NASB1995)

All-Inclusive Invitations in John's Revelation

"Behold, I stand at the door and knock; if *anyone* [*ean tis*] hears My voice and opens the door, I will come in to him and will dine with him, and he with Me." (Rev 3:20 NASB)

And the Spirit and the bride say, Come. And let him that heareth say, Come. And let him that is athirst come. And *whosoever will*, let him take the water of life freely. (Rev 22:17 KJV)

To be sure, Calvinists attribute all these verses to the "general call" or "universal call" that God gives to all people although he has no intention of actually saving many of them. But in so doing they impose their own theological beliefs on the text. These verses mention no difference between a "general call" and "specific call," or between "common grace" and "enabling irresistible grace." Therefore, when we see the same all-inclusive invitation over and over again in the various genres of Scripture, the question must be asked if the Calvinist theological system is doing justice to the biblical text. Calvinists should take seriously Paul's admonition in Rom 9:20 (NIV): "But who are you, a human being, to talk back to God?" In Romans 9 Paul was addressing believers from a Jewish background who believed they were among the elect people, the "frozen chosen." But much to their surprise, God in his sovereignty extended salvation to others—the Gentiles whom they hated. If God has chosen to save those who come to him by faith in Christ, as Romans 9–11 repeatedly assert, who are we to disagree with his sovereign choice? Just so, if God says he desires the salvation of all people, I believe he means it, not just in his revealed (for Calvinists, evidently deceptive) will, but also in his secret (real) will. The call is indeed universal or general for everyone to be saved. But the elect are not limited to a select group that God has chosen because he especially and savingly loves them and rejects by preterition all others, but are coterminous with those who have trusted Christ as Savior and Lord.

Resistible Grace in Descriptions of How to Be Saved

Another line of evidence in Scripture that supports the idea that grace is resistible is in biblical descriptions of how to be saved. Whenever anyone in the New Testament asks a direct question about how to be saved, the answer never refers to election. The answer always calls for an action on the part of the person to receive the salvation that God has provided and offers to each person. In Scripture, eternal life is proffered to all those who hear the gospel, not just to a few select persons who receive effectual grace irresistibly. What do the New Testament salvific formulas say is required to be saved?

The Teachings of Jesus

Jesus directly tied salvation to faith in him realized through human response to the proclamation of the gospel:

> "And as Moses lifted up the serpent in the wilderness, even so must the Son of Man be lifted up, that whoever believes in Him should not perish but have eternal life. For God so loved the world that He gave His only begotten Son, that whoever believes in Him should not perish but have everlasting life. For God did not send His Son into the world to condemn the world, but that the world through Him might be saved.
>
> "He who believes in Him is not condemned; but he who does not believe is condemned already, because he has not believed in the name of the only begotten Son of God." (John 3:14–18 NKJV).

The Need for Persuasion

At the end of the sermon at Pentecost, some of the hearers "were pierced to the heart and said to Peter and the rest of the apostles, 'Brethren, what shall we do?'" (Acts 2:37

NASB1995). Peter's answer was not, "Are you elect or not?" His answer was, "Repent, and each of you be baptized in the name of Jesus Christ for the forgiveness of your sins; and you will receive the gift of the Holy Spirit" (v. 38). Even after this, "with many other words he [Peter] solemnly testified and kept on *exhorting* them, saying, 'Be saved from this perverse generation!'" (v. 40, emphasis added). The word translated "exhorting" in the NASB1995 is variously translated in other Bible versions as "strongly urged" (HCSB), "entreated" (Weymouth), "pleaded" (NIV), or "begged" (NCV). The word that is translated "exhort" is *parekalei*, meaning to invite or summon someone to a decision, to beseech or implore someone, or to plead with or call someone to a decision.[33] The same meaning applies to all six other usages of *parekalei* in the New Testament. Of course, had Peter known that grace was irresistible, he wouldn't have wasted his time with such a solemn exhortation, knowing that God had already regenerated them by irresistible grace. What persuasion is necessary for one who is already convinced?

Likewise, Paul wrote that his preaching was an effort intended to "persuade" people (2 Cor 5:11 NIV). The word Paul used here is *peithō*, meaning to persuade or convince someone, to try to win someone over to your point of view.[34] Why would there be a need to persuade someone who had already been regenerated by irresistible enabling grace?

The Appeal to the Philippian Jailer. When the Philippian jailer saw the miraculous intervention of God in releasing Paul and Silas from his jail, he fell at their feet and asked the salvation question in the most direct way possible: "Sirs, what must I do to be saved?" (Acts 16:30 NASB). Peter did not respond by talking about election. Instead, he answered, "*Believe* in the Lord Jesus, and you will be saved, you and your household" (v. 31; emphasis added). Being saved was conditional on his belief.

The Appeal to the Ethiopian Eunuch. After Philip had witnessed to the Ethiopian eunuch from the Old Testament prophecies, the eunuch exclaimed, "'Look! Water! What prevents me from being baptized?' And Philip said, 'If you believe with all your heart, you may.' And he answered and said, 'I believe that Jesus Christ is the Son of God'" (Acts 8:36–37 NASB1995). And so he was baptized. Note that his being baptized was conditional upon his trust in Christ.

---

[33] Otto Schmitz, s.v. "*parakaleō*," *TDNT*, 5:773–79, 793–94.

[34] Rudolf Bultmann, s.v. "*peithō*," *TDNT*, 6:8–9.

The Teaching of Paul. "If you confess with your mouth, 'Jesus is Lord,' and believe in your heart that God raised Him from the dead, you will be saved. One believes with the heart, resulting in righteousness, and one confesses with the mouth, resulting in salvation" (Rom 10:9–10 HCSB). Again, salvation is conditional on trusting in Christ.

To summarize, the Scriptures contain significant evidence against irresistible grace. The Bible specifically teaches that the Holy Spirit can be resisted. It repeatedly calls upon all people to respond to God's gracious invitation. The descriptions of how to be saved focus on the requirement for a positive human response to God's initiative. The texts do not seem to support irresistible grace, but they call upon persons to respond to the grace of God in specific ways. The plain reading of these texts tends to support the belief that God's grace, by his own intent and design, is *resistible*, and choosing Christ is *voluntary* (guided by the conviction and convincing of the Holy Spirit).

Assessing Calvinist Arguments and Proof Texts for Irresistible Grace

In the previous version of this article in *Whosoever Will*, I explored seven theological concerns about irresistible grace.[35] While I still affirm those concerns, in this article I have chosen to address some arguments and proof texts proffered by Calvinists to defend the notion of irresistible grace. Specifically, we will examine Calvinist proof texts in John 6 and 12; Rom 8:29–30; and Eph 2:1 in the light of the best hermeneutics.[36] Then we will examine two theological arguments made by Calvinists—that irresistible grace is required for God to be sovereign, and it is necessary for God to receive glory.

Calvinist Argument #1: John 6:37–44, 65 and 12:32

Probably the Scripture most frequently cited by Calvinists regarding irresistible grace is John 6:44, along with related verses in John 6 and 12:

---

[35] Lemke, "Critique of Irresistible Grace," in *Whosoever Will*, 109–62.

[36] For more on sound hermeneutics, see Steve Lemke, Grant Lovejoy, and Bruce Corley, eds., *Biblical Hermeneutics: A Comprehensive Introduction to Interpreting Scripture*, 2nd ed. (Nashville: B&H Academic, 2002).

"All that the Father gives Me will come to Me, and the one who comes to Me I will certainly not cast out. For I have come down from heaven, not to do My own will, but the will of Him who sent Me. This is the will of Him who sent Me, that of all that He has given Me I lose nothing, but raise it up on the last day. For this is the will of My Father, that everyone who beholds the Son and believes in Him will have eternal life, and I Myself will raise him up on the last day. . . . No one can come to Me unless the Father who sent Me draws him; and I will raise him up on the last day." . . . And He was saying, "For this reason I have said to you, that no one can come to Me unless it has been granted him from the Father." (John 6:37–40, 44, 65 NASB1995)

"And I, if I am lifted up from the earth, will draw all men to Myself" (John 12:32 NASB1995).

John Frame,[37] R. C. Sproul,[38] Matthew Barrett,[39] Loraine Boettner,[40] William Hendrikson and Simon J. Kistemaker,[41] and Robert Yarbrough[42] (among others) list these verses as among the primary proof texts for irresistible grace. To make their case, several of them referred specifically to a citation in Kittel's ten-volume *Theological Dictionary of the New Testament.*[43] As Sproul noted, one translation for the word "draws" (*helkuō*) is "to compel by irresistible superiority."[44] Barrett waxed eloquent to infer from that one definition that John 6:44 teaches God's drawing is "indefectible, invincible, unconquerable, indomitable, insuperable, and unassailable summons,"[45] words which appear neither in this text or any other biblical text regarding God's grace, but appear only when Calvinistic presuppositions color the reading of Scripture. Calvinists like to appeal to other New Testament references in which

[37] John Frame, *Salvation Belongs to the Lord* (Phillipsburg, PA: P&R, 2006), 184.
[38] Sproul, *Chosen by God*, 69; *Grace Unknown: The Heart of Reformed Theology* (Grand Rapids: Baker, 1997), 153–54.
[39] Barrett, "Monergism," 141.
[40] Loraine Boettner, *The Reformed Faith* (Philadelphia: P&R, 1984), 11.
[41] William Hendriksen and Simon J. Kistemaker, *Exposition of the Gospel according to John*, 2 vols., New Testament Commentary (Grand Rapids: Baker, 2002), 1:238.
[42] Robert Yarbrough, "Divine Election in the Gospel of John," in *Still Sovereign: Perspectives on Election, Foreknowledge, and Grace*, ed. Thomas R. Schreiner and Bruce A. Ware (Grand Rapids: Baker, 2000), 50n10.
[43] Albrecht Oepke, s.v. "*Elkō*," *TDNT*, 2:503.
[44] Sproul, *Chosen by God*, 69; *Grace Unknown*, 153.
[45] Barrett, "Monergism," 141.

the word "draw" is used literally, such as Acts 16:19 and Jas 2:6, in which prisoners are being physically dragged against their wills by authorities.

The Calvinist use of *helkuō* in Jas 2:6, Acts 16:19, and other places as justification for understanding *helkuō* in John 6:44 as meaning "to compel by irresistible superiority," or a "forceful [irresistible] attraction," commits a word-study fallacy known as "word loading" or "illegitimate totality transfer."[46] Word loading occurs when an interpreter takes a meaning of a word in one context (physical) and then seeks to apply that same meaning into a different context (spiritual). A simple example of this fallacy is to overlook the fact that the same word "spirit" (*pneuma*) that refers to the human spirit can also refer to the divine Holy Spirit. It is the same Greek word with two very different meanings, depending on the context. "The *immediate context* always determines the meaning for any word—no matter how many times a word carries such a meaning in another context."[47]

Perhaps more embarrassingly for the Calvinists' exegesis of John 6:44, the article on *elkō* in the abridged one-volume *TDNT*, which focuses more on biblical interpretation than general usage, was authored by the same Albrecht Oepke who authored the article in the ten-volume edition. Oepke noted that *helkein* in the Old Testament "denotes a powerful impulse . . . [that] expresses the force of love." Oepke's specific interpretation of John 6:44 deals a stunning blow to the Calvinist interpretation of that would-be proof text:

> This is the point in the two important passages in Jn. 6:44; 12:32. There is no thought here of force or magic. The term figuratively expresses the supernatural power of the love of God or Christ which goes out to all (12:32) but without which no one can come (6:44). The apparent contradiction shows that both the election and the universality of grace must be taken seriously; *the compulsion is not automatic.*[48]

By no means is the abridged version of Kittel the only lexigraphical reference favoring a non-Calvinist reading of John 6:44. Note how the following well-respected lexicons address "draw" in John 6:44 to be interpreted metaphorically or figuratively rather than literally:

---

[46] See Carson, *Exegetical Fallacies*, 53 (see chap. 3, n. 21); and Moisés Silva, *Biblical Words and Their Meaning* (Grand Rapids: Zondervan, 1995), 25–27.

[47] Steve Witzki, "Free Grace or Forced Grace?" *The Arminian* 19, no.1 (Spring 2001): 2.

[48] Albrecht Oepke, s.v. "*elkō*," *TDNTa*, 227; emphasis added.

A Greek-English Lexicon of the New Testament and Other Early Christian Literature, 3rd ed., by Bauer and Danker: "to draw a pers. in the direction of values for inner life, *draw, attract*, an extended fg. [figurative] mng. [meaning] . . . J[ohn] 6:44 . . . J[ohn] 12:32."[49]

The Analytical Lexicon to the Greek New Testament by Mounce: "met. [metaphorically] *to draw* mentally and morally, John 6:44; 12:32."[50]

Greek-English Lexicon to the New Testament by Hickie: "met., *to draw*, i.e. *to attract*, Joh. 12:32. Cf. Joh. 6:44."[51]

Analytical Lexicon of the Greek New Testament by Friberg, Friberg, and Miller: "figuratively, of a strong pull in the mental or moral life *draw, attract* (JN 6.44)."[52]

Greek and English Lexicon to the New Testament by Robinson: "*to draw*, by a moral influence, John 6:44. 12:32."[53]

The New Analytical Greek Lexicon by Perschbacher: "met. *to draw* mentally and morally, John 6:44; 12:32."[54]

Note that these respected lexicons all take "draw" in John 6:44 to be a figurative or metaphorical usage when applied to spiritual issues within persons. In short, these standard lexicons provide no support for the Calvinist reading of John 6:44.[55]

Other exegetical points can be raised to show the error of the Calvinist interpretation of John 6:44,[56] but one more must be mentioned here. Who is it that the

---

[49] *BDAG*, 251.

[50] William Mounce, *The Analytical Lexicon to the Greek New Testament*, Zondervan Greek Reference Series (Grand Rapids: Zondervan Academic, 1993), 180.

[51] William J. Hickie, *Greek-English Lexicon to the New Testament* (New York: Cosimo, 2007), 13.

[52] Timothy Friberg, Barbara Friberg, and Neva Miller, *Analytical Lexicon of the Greek New Testament* (Bloomington, IN: Trafford, 2006), 144.

[53] Edward Robinson, *A Greek and English Lexicon to the New Testament* (Charleston, SC: Bibliolife, 2009), 240.

[54] Wesley J. Perchbacher, ed., *The New Analytical Greek Lexicon* (Peabody, MA: Hendrickson, 2009), 135.

[55] Furthermore, if "draws" meant irresistible drawing, John 12:32 would affirm universal salvation.

[56] For this detailed analysis, see Steve Witzki, "Calvinism and John 6: An Exegetical Response, Part One," *The Arminian* 23, no. 1 (Spring, 2005): 4–7; Steve Witzki, "Calvinism

Father draws? Is it some arbitrary choice he makes in his "secret will"? Schreiner and Ware asserted that the "drawing" in John 6:44 is only for the elect:

> Is [this an] unlimited or common grace, given to all? Or is it a particular grace, an efficacious grace given only to some? The second half of verse 44 answers our question, for there we find that . . . the one who is given grace (who is drawn by the Father) is actually saved (raised up). The drawing of the Father, then, is not general, but particular, for it accomplishes the final salvation of those who are drawn. God's grace, without which no one can be saved, is therefore an efficacious [irresistible] grace, resulting in the sure salvation of those to whom it is given.[57]

Who are "all that" the Father will draw (John 6:37 NASB1995)? Woven throughout John 6 (and prior chapters) are repeated references to the necessity of *believing* in Jesus as Savior and Lord to receive eternal life (John 3:16, 18, 36; 6:27–29, 40, 54). Schreiner and Ware also acknowledged that those who are "coming" to Christ (John 6:35, 37, 44, 45) are essentially synonymous with those "believing" in Christ. John 6:39–40 are verses woven together with the preposition "for," and these verses mirror the structure of each other in an ABCCBA pattern ("A" being the repeated phrase "raise them up," for example).[58] What this makes clear is that the identity of those whom the Father gives to Jesus are precisely identical with *those who believe*. Calvinist F. F. Bruce supported this reading of John 6:37–40: "In the first part of verse 37 the pronoun 'all' is neuter singular (Gk. *pan*), denoting the sum-total of believers. In the second part ('the one who comes') each individual of the sum-total is in view. This

---

and John 6: An Exegetical Response, Part Two," *The Arminian* 23, no. 2 (Fall 2005): 4–7; and Witzki, "Free Grace or Forced Grace?" *Arminian* 19, no. 1 (Spring 2001): 1–5.

[57] Thomas Schreiner and Bruce Ware, introduction to *Still Sovereign*, 15. Schreiner and Ware thus interpret John 6:44 to mean, "No one can come to me unless the Father who sent me draws him, and I will raise the one whom the Father draws up on the last day." However, John 6:44 must be read in light of a preceding verse with a parallel construction, John 6:40: "For this is the will of My Father, that everyone who sees the Son and believes in Him will have eternal life, and I Myself will raise him up on the last day" (NASB). Therefore, the proper interpretation of John 6:44 should be, "No one can come to me unless the Father who sent me draws him, and I will raise up on the last day the one who comes to me (through faith)." As noted above, the lexical definition of "draw" does not mean the irresistible drawing that Calvinists try to make it mean to suit their theology. This promise of the resurrection is given to believers who respond to the gracious invitation of God.

[58] Witzki, "Calvinism and John 6, Part One," 4–5.

oscillation between the [believing] community and its individual members reappears in verses 39 and 40."[59]

Likewise, Lenski noted that those who are given by the Father to the Son sum up "the whole mass of believers of all ages and speaks of them as a unit."[60] Vincent described it as "all believers regarded as one complete whole."[61] Jesus stated God's will clearly and unequivocally: "For this is the will of My Father, that *everyone who sees the Son and believes in Him* will have eternal life, and I Myself will raise him up on the last day" (John 6:40 NASB). To be sure, because of human depravity, it is essential that the Father must draw humans unto himself through the convicting and convincing of the Holy Spirit. God's grace is a necessary condition of our salvation, but God's saving grace does not become operational in our own lives until we place our faith in Jesus Christ.

Ben Witherington pointed out the necessity of both God's grace and human response by faith in addressing this passage:

> Both God's sovereign grace and human response play a role in human salvation, but even one's human response is enabled by God's grace. God's role in the relationship is incomparably greater than the human one, but the fact remains that God does not and will not save a person without the *positive human response, called faith*, to the divine leading and drawing.[62]

Richard Lenski affirmed that both God's grace and human response are voiced in John 6:37 and 6:44:

> But in these expressions, "all that the Father gives," and, "all that he has given," Jesus speaks of all *believers* of all ages as already being present to the eyes of God, he also thus is giving them to Jesus. . . . God's grace is universal. He would give all men to Jesus. The only reason he does not do so is because so many men obdurately refuse to be part of that gift. . . . "Him that comes to me" makes the matter individual, personal, and *a voluntary act*. The Father's

---

[59] F. F. Bruce, *The Gospel of John* (Grand Rapids: Eerdmans, 1983), 154.

[60] Richard C. H. Lenski, *The Interpretation of St. John's Gospel* (Minneapolis: Augsburg, 1961), 463.

[61] Marvin Vincent, *Vincent's Word Studies in the New Testament*, 4 vols. (Peabody, MA: Hendrickson, 1886), 2:150.

[62] Ben Witherington III, *John's Wisdom: A Commentary on the Fourth Gospel* (Louisville: Westminster John Knox, 1995), 158, emphasis added.

drawing (v. 44) is one of grace alone, thus it is efficacious, wholly sufficient, able to change the unwilling into the willing, but *not by coercion, not irresistibly. Man can obdurately refuse to come. . . .*[63]

Here [in John 6:44] Jesus explains the Father's "giving" mentioned in v. 37 and 39: he gives men to Jesus by drawing them to him. This drawing [*helkuō*] is accomplished by a specific power, one especially designed for the purpose, one that takes hold of the sinner's soul and moves it away from darkness, sin, and death, to Jesus, light, and life. No man can possibly thus draw himself to Jesus. The Father, God himself, must come with his divine power and must do this drawing; else it will never be effected. . . . The drawing is here predicated of the Father; in 12:32 it is predicated of Jesus, "And I will draw all men unto myself." . . . The power by which these Jews are at this very moment being drawn is the power of divine grace, operative in and through the Word these Jews now hear from the lips of Jesus. While it is power (Rom. 1:16), efficacious to save, *it is never irresistible* (Matt. 23:37, "and ye would not"). Nor is this power extended only to a select few, for in 12:32 Jesus says, "I will draw all men." The power of the gospel is for the world, and no sinner has fallen so low but what this power is able to reach him effectually.[64]

Therefore, we need not speculate about what God's "secret will" *might be*, because Jesus clearly revealed what his will *actually is*: "For this is the will of My Father, that *everyone who sees the Son and believes in Him will have eternal life, and I Myself will raise him up on the last day.*" (John 6:40 NASB; emphasis added). The Father draws those whom he has foreseen will believe in his Son as Savior and Lord! God's grace is necessary for salvation, but God's grace does not become operational in our own lives until we respond by placing our faith in Jesus Christ.

Calvinist Argument #2: Romans 8:29–30

Another proof text cited by many Calvinists is Rom 8:29–30, sometimes called the "Golden Chain of Redemption":

For those He foreknew He also predestined to be conformed to the image of His Son, so that He would be the firstborn among many brothers. And those

---

[63] Lenski, *Interpretation of St. John's Gospel*, 464–65; emphasis added.
[64] Lenski, 475–76; emphasis added.

He predestined, He also called; and those He called, He also justified; and those He justified, He also glorified. (Rom 8:29–30 HCSB)

For example, Matthew Barrett argued that Rom 8:29–30 is an ideal example of the "effectual calling."[65] He cited Doug Moo in arguing that the links in the chain are all connected by the demonstrative pronoun "these" (*toutous*): "This leaves little room for the suggestion that the links in this chain are not firmly attached to one another, as if some who were 'foreknown' and 'predestined' would not be 'called,' 'justified,' and 'glorified.'"[66]

The Priority of Divine Foreknowledge

I absolutely agree with Moo's assertion. But it is ironic to me that Calvinists consider Rom 8:29–30 to favor their position. I cite it as a text favoring a non-Calvinist interpretation, so it obviously depends on the proper interpretation of the text. Note that the first link in that chain of redemption is not predestination, but *foreknowledge*. God does not first predestine the elect and then foreknow them. Rather, God's foreknowledge of human responses comes first, with God's election, calling, and justification flowing from his foreknowledge. The entire discussion of election in Romans 9–11 is framed by references to foreknowledge, both as a prologue to the discussion in Rom 8:29–30 and near its conclusion in Rom 11:1–2: "I say then, God has not rejected His people, has He? May it never be! For I too am an Israelite, a descendant of Abraham, of the tribe of Benjamin. God has not rejected His people whom He *foreknew*" (Rom 11:1–2 NASB1995; emphasis added).

Who are these people whom God foreknew? The apostle Paul made it very clear in Romans 9–11 that God will save whosoever will come to Him *by faith*:

What shall we say then? That Gentiles, who did not pursue righteousness, attained righteousness, even the righteousness which is *by faith*; but Israel, pursuing a law of righteousness, did not arrive at that law. Why? Because they did not pursue it *by faith*, but as though it were by works. They stumbled over the stumbling stone, just as it is written, "Behold, I lay in Zion a stone

---

[65] Barrett, "Monergism," 128–30.
[66] Douglas J. Moo, *The Epistle to the Romans*, NICNT (Grand Rapids: Eerdmans, 1996), 535; cited in Barrett, "Monergism," 129.

of stumbling and a rock of offense, and he who *believes* in Him will not be disappointed." (Rom 9:30–33 NASB1995; emphasis added)

But what does it say? "The word is near you, in your mouth and in your heart"—that is, the word of *faith* which we are preaching, that if you confess with your mouth Jesus as Lord, and *believe in your heart* that God raised Him from the dead, you will be saved; for with the heart a person *believes*, resulting in righteousness, and with the mouth he confesses, resulting in salvation. For the Scripture says, "*Whoever believes* in Him will not be disappointed." For there is no distinction between Jew and Greek; for the same Lord is Lord of all, abounding in riches for *all who call on Him*; for "*Whoever will call on the name of the Lord* will be saved." (Rom 10:8–13 NASB1995; emphasis added)

Exegetical Evidence

God's foreknowledge is consistently affirmed in the Bible (Ps 139:1–10; Acts 2:23; Rom 8:29; 11:2; 16:27; 1 Pet 1:2). The Greek word translated "foreknew" is the verb *proginoskō*. In any standard lexicon, the root Greek word for "foreknew" (*proginoskō*) simply means knowing something before it happens.[67] In his classic commentary on the letter to the Romans, Frederic Godet noted that "knowledge" is the "first and fundamental meaning" of *prognosis*.[68] In his commentary on Romans, R. C. H. Lenski likewise affirmed that "both linguistically and doctrinally *the knowing* cannot be eliminated and an act of *willing*, a decree, be substituted. . . . 'Foreknew' ever remains eternal advance knowledge, a divine knowledge that includes all that God's grace would succeed in working in us."[69] Ben Witherington also distinguished God's foreknowledge from predestination:

---

[67] Rudolf Bultmann, s.v. "*proginoskō, prognosis*," *TDNT*, 1:715–16.

[68] Frederic L. Godet, *Commentary on Romans* (Grand Rapids: Kregel, 1977), 325. Godet notes that "the act of *knowing*, exactly like that of seeing, supposes an object perceived by the person who knows or sees. It is not the act of seeing or knowing which produces this object; it is the object, on the contrary, which determines this act of knowing or seeing. And the same is the case with divine provision of foreknowledge; for in the case of God who lives above time, foreseeing is seeing; knowing what shall be is knowing what to Him already is. And therefore it is the *believer's faith* which, as a future fact, but in His sight already existing, *which determines His foreknowledge*" (emphasis added).

[69] Richard C. H. Lenski, *The Interpretation of St. Paul's Epistle to the Romans* (Columbus, OH: Lutheran Book Concern, 1936), 558–59.

Paul distinguishes between what God knows and what God wills or destines in advance. Knowing and willing are not one and the same. The proof of this is of course that God knows very well about human sin but does not will it or destine it to happen.[70]

The belief that divine election is based upon his foreknowledge of a believer's faith is not a new idea. This understanding of Scripture goes back to the earliest days of Christianity. Lenski noted of the earlier church fathers, "The older dogmaticians interpreted: *quos credituros praevidit*, 'whom he foresaw as believers.'"[71] Gerald Bray and Ben Witherington also have documented that the belief in divine foreknowledge is seen in both Judaism and in the early church fathers, including Diodore of Tarsus, Theodoret of Cyrrhus, Ambrosiaster, Cyril of Alexandria, and John Chrysostom.[72] Election based on divine foreknowledge is also affirmed by Molinism, in which God's foreknowledge is described as "middle knowledge."

The Requirements for Salvation

What requirements has God sovereignly established for salvation? The Bible makes it abundantly clear that God requires *repentance and faith* for salvation. As noted earlier, every formulaic statement of what is required for salvation makes the necessity of repentance and faith crystal clear (Matt 10:32–33; Mark 16:15–16; John 3:14–17; 6:40; 11:26; 12:46; Acts 2:21, 27–30; 10:43; 16:30–31; Rom 9:33; 10:9–11; 1 John 5:1). The question is not what God *could* or *might* have done, but what he *has* done. God does foreknow, elect, and predestine a particular type of person from before the foundation of the world—and that is *believers*! Based on his foreknowledge of those who will (under the conviction of the Holy Spirit) repent of their sins and trust Christ as their personal Lord and Savior, God elects, predestines, justifies, and glorifies (Rom 8:29–30).

Since the traditional interpretation of Rom 8:29–30 as God electing based on his foreknowledge of the future faith of believers does not square with Calvinist

---

[70] Ben Witherington III, with Darlene Hyatt, *Paul's Letter to the Romans: A Socio-Rhetorical Commentary* (Grand Rapids: Eerdmans, 2004), 230.

[71] Lenski, *Romans*, 559.

[72] Gerald Bray and Thomas Bray, eds., *New Testament VI: Romans (Revised)*, Ancient Christian Commentary on Scripture (Downers Grove, IL: InterVarsity, 1998), 233–44; Witherington, *Romans*, 227–28. Additional early church fathers who endorsed this perspective on human freedom and foreknowledge include Origen, Irenaeus, Tertullian, and Jerome.

theology, they reinterpret Rom 8:29–30 in various ways. Calvinist scholars have raised at least three challenges to the traditional interpretation of Rom 8:29–30: that "foreknew" really means "foreloved," that God's foreknowledge is not chronologically and logically before God's predestination, and that genuine human freedom would violate God's foreknowledge and sovereignty. What is wrong with each of these alternative explanations?

Does foreknew mean foreloved? No. As noted earlier, standard lexicons make it clear that the primary meaning of "foreknew" is "fore*knew*," not "foreloved." Witherington pointed out that the next reference to foreknowledge in Romans, Rom 11:2, makes this distinction between God foreknowing believers and election even clearer:

> Love for God can be commanded, but it cannot be coerced, compelled, or engineered in advance, or else it loses its character as love. The proof that this line of thinking, and not that of Augustine, Luther, or Calvin, is on the right track is seen clearly in 11:2, where Paul says plainly that God foreknew his Jewish people, and yet not all of them responded positively to his call. Indeed, only a minority have as he writes this letter. God's foreknowledge, and even God's plan of destiny for Israel, did not in the end predetermine which particular individual Israelite would respond positively to the gospel call and which would not. In 10:8–15 Paul will make clear that the basis of that response is faith and confession.[73]

Does God's predestination precede his foreknowledge? Some Calvinists suggest that foreknowledge is an overarching summary, so that the first link in the "Golden Chain of Redemption" is really predestination. However, although this view squares with Calvinist theology, it does not square with Rom 8:29–30. As noted earlier, the "Golden Chain of Redemption" is intended as a series of events, one following after the other, linked in each case by the Greek word *hous*, translated, "whom." God foreknowing believers is clearly the first link in that chain.[74] Witherington commented, "*Hous*, 'whom,' at the beginning of v. 29 must refer back to 'those who love

---

[73] Witherington, *Romans*, 229–30.

[74] F. F. Bruce noted that these phrases are also connected in what is called a *sorites* construction, in which the predicate of one clause becomes the subject of the next clause. Bruce, *The Epistle of Paul to the Romans*, Tyndale New Testament Commentary (Grand Rapids: Tyndale, 1963), 176.

God,' that is, Christians, in v. 28. The discussion that follows is about the future of believers."[75] Witherington lamented that what some commentators "seem to have clearly missed is that we continue to have reference to the same *hous*: once in v. 29, and three times in v. 30. . . ." One implication of this series of connected statements is that

> since vv. 29–30 must be linked to v. 28, the "those who" in question are those about whom Paul has already said that they "love God"—i.e., Paul makes perfectly clear that he is talking about Christians here. The statement about them loving God *precedes* and determines how we should read both *hous* in these verses and the chain of verbs. God knew something in advance about these persons, namely that they would respond to the call of God in love. For such people, God goes all out to make sure that in the end they are fully conformed to the image of Christ.[76]

Does human freedom obviate God's sovereignty? Calvinists question how God could foreknow all things before the foundation of the world and yet allow us genuine libertarian free will. If he knows for sure what we are going to choose to do before we do it, do we really have a choice? How could God foreknow that we are going to change our minds? Once God knows what we are going to do, does it not become fixed and determined so that we have no real free choice—we can choose nothing else?

The fundamental problem with these objections is that they put nonlogical limitations on God's omniscience and foreknowledge. Human choices reflect our God-given creaturely freedom, and God foreknows the future free choices of individuals. As an omniscient being, God timelessly knows all future human choices (not only the actual choices, but also the possible choices in any conceivable circumstance). To deny the complete foreknowledge of God is to deny the omniscience of God.

Second, from a logical perspective, the claim that God's foreknowledge takes away any real human choices *fundamentally confuses the difference between knowledge and causation*. Two plus two is not four because I know it; it is true because it is true in reality. In fact, two plus two equals four whether or not I believe it. *Knowing* something does not *cause* it to happen, even for God. Knowledge, no matter who holds

---

[75] Witherington, *Romans*, 227.
[76] Witherington, 229, n. 28.

it, is causally indeterminative. Therefore, it is a misconception to think that God's foreknowledge of future human choices *causes* a person's acceptance or rejection of faith in Christ.

Third, the claim that God's foreknowledge takes away any real human choices *fundamentally confuses the important distinction between necessity* (what *must* happen) and *certainty* (what *will* happen). Since God's omniscient knowledge does not *cause* future events, his (fore)knowledge does not make these events *necessary*. God knows future events with certainty, but that does not mean that those events had to happen by logical necessity. Future events are contingent on the future decisions of his free creatures.[77] As explained earlier, God simply knows before we make those choices what our choices are going to be.

Ponder this analogy, although human analogies about God are inherently limited because he is not bound to our limitations of time and imperfect knowledge. Jim and Rusty were fans of a basketball team playing a game that would determine the league championship, but their schedules did not permit them to watch the game. So they taped it to watch later. Jim got out of the meeting early and witnessed the team making a remarkable comeback to win in the last seconds of the game. When Rusty came in, he did *not* know the outcome of the game (or that Jim had seen it). As their team trailed the opponent for most of the game, Rusty kept lamenting that their team was going to lose, but Jim told Rusty that he is confident that they could come back and win. Jim encouraged Rusty to have faith in their team. Sure enough, as Jim foreknew, the team came back in the last seconds of the game and won a dramatic victory. Rusty was amazed that Jim seemed so sure that their team would rally and win the game. In truth, of course, Jim did not really have "faith"—he had knowledge of what would actually happen that was inaccessible to Rusty.

The point is this: Jim's certain knowledge of what would happen at the end of the game had exactly *nothing* to do with his team winning the game. His knowledge did not predetermine the fouls, the plays, or the last-second shot that won the game. Jim knew the result with *certainty*, but not of *logical necessity*. He simply knew ahead of time what would actually happen without causing what happened. Likewise, God knows our future choices with certainty without making them logically necessary. So

---

[77] For more on the confusion of contingency and necessity, see Kenneth D. Keathley, *Salvation and Sovereignty: A Molinist Approach* (Nashville: B&H Academic, 2010), 8–9, 31–38; and Robert E. Picirilli, *Grace, Faith, Free Will—Contrasting Views of Salvation: Calvinism and Arminianism* (Nashville: Randall House, 2002), 36–63.

the compatibility of divine foreknowledge and human freedom is coherent, and more importantly, it aligns with the description of God's foreknowledge of human choices in the pages of Scripture.

Calvinist Argument #3: Ephesians 2:1

Calvinists see the need for irresistible grace arising from their interpretation of Eph 2:1 that those who are lost are "dead in trespasses and sins": "And you were dead in your offenses and sins, in which you previously walked according to the course of this world, according to the prince of the power of the air, of the spirit that is now working in the sons of disobedience" (Eph 2:1–2 NASB).

Reformed thinkers typically use the analogy of Jesus raising Lazarus from the grave, overlooking the fact that Lazarus's resuscitation regarded physical death, while death in Eph 2:1 refers to spiritual death. But Calvinists take spiritual deadness not as a metaphor but literally, and build the rest of their theological superstructure on it. For example, in a sermon on Ephesians 2, John MacArthur said that "spiritual death is an inability to respond to stimulus." A sinner "has no capacity to respond to God. . . . Spiritually dead people are like zombies—they don't know they're dead and they're still going through the motions of living."[78] Since unsaved people are like a "corpse" that cannot respond to God, irresistible grace is necessary. Calvinists reason people must be regenerated through irresistible grace before they can become alive enough spiritually to respond to God. For example, Barrett expressed this view: "Man is dead, lifeless, rotting away. . . . He is like Lazarus, dead in the tomb. He stinketh. What Lazarus needed was the resurrection."[79]

Exegetical Evidence

However, there are good exegetical reasons to believe that "dead" in Eph 2:1 should not be taken with such wooden literalism but in fact is a much richer concept. First, the Calvinist interpretation of Eph 2:1 is another example of the exegetical fallacy of word loading;[80] that is, applying a word as it is used in one setting (physical) to a different setting (spiritual). In such cases, the word addressing the spiritual setting

---

[78] John F. MacArthur, "Coming Alive in Christ," February 26, 1978, a sermon available online at https://www.gty.org/library/sermons-library/1908/coming-alive-in-christ.

[79] Barrett, "Monergism," 121.

[80] Steve Witzki, "Free Grace or Forced Grace?," 2.

is normally understood metaphorically or symbolically. Physical death is the body's separation from the soul; spiritual death is the soul's separation from God. Neither of these deaths imply a loss of human freedom.

Second, within a few verses in Ephesians 2, Paul also spoke of the lost as "foreigners" and "strangers" (Eph 2:12, 19). Foreigners do not enjoy citizenship and are far from God, but foreigners are still *alive*. Ephesians 2:1 is further qualified by 1 Cor 1:18 ("the word of the cross is foolishness to *those who are perishing*"; NASB1995, emphasis added); 2 Cor 2:15 ("For to God we are the fragrance of Christ among those who are being saved and among *those who are perishing*"; HCSB, emphasis added); and 2 Cor 4:3 ("And even if our gospel is veiled, it is veiled to *those who are perishing*"; NASB, emphasis added). The metaphorical concept of spiritual deadness is present in all three passages, but the *deadness is not yet complete*. The lost are perishing but not yet dead.

Opportunity remains for a response that can result in a different destiny. The prodigal son is described as having been "dead" (separated) from his father, but after he repented he was "alive" (Luke 15:24, 32). The boy was not physically dead; he was metaphorically and relationally dead. The New Testament also applies the word "dead" to the church. The church in Sardis is warned that they are "on the point of death" (Rev 3:2 NRSV). Is this church of elect members spiritually dead? Of course not. Romans 6:2, 11 and 1 Pet 2:24 proclaim that believers are "dead" to sins. Does that mean they have total inability to sin? The New Testament affirms that Christians continue to sin (Rom 7:21–25; 1 John 1:8), so these Scriptures cited earlier cannot mean we are unable to sin. James 2:17 affirms that faith without works is "dead." Does that mean that good works are required for salvation? No. We are saved by faith, not good works, although a believer's faith should produce good works (Eph 2:8–10). Through these many Scriptures we see that the concept of spiritual deadness in the New Testament at times is obviously used metaphorically.

A third hermeneutical red flag that "dead" should not be taken literally is raised by Jesus, who said of unbelievers, "Unless you repent, you will *all likewise perish*" (Luke 13:3, 5 NASB; emphasis added). What possible threat would there be to a corpse that it would be dead in the future? Jesus spoke of perishing as a future event, not a past event. Again, this is an obvious clue that something real but metaphorical is at work here.

A fourth hermeneutical clue is that what Paul meant by "spiritual death" would seem to parallel how the Bible describes being spiritually alive. Jesus taught in John

6:54 (just ten verses after John 6:44, the alleged Calvinist proof text for irresistible grace) that believers *already have* eternal life as a present possession. Theologians often describe John 6:54 as elucidating "realized eschatology" or as a "proleptic" of a future full realization of eternal life. Obviously, we do not now have eternal life completely—we have a foretaste of the more complete eternal life fulfilled by glorification in heaven. Ephesians 1:13–14 speaks of the Holy Spirit as the down payment of our salvation "until the redemption of the purchased possession" (NKJV) when we receive our full heavenly inheritance. So we have eternal life, and yet we don't—at least, not yet fully.

Might this give us an insight into what Paul was saying about spiritual death? Unbelievers are dying in their trespasses and sins, on an inevitable track for the second death apart from claiming Christ as their Savior. Even if the language might suggest a completed status, we use past tense language at times to refer to a present reality. Teenagers jokingly say to someone who has teased them, "You're dead!" Although by tense it literally means the person is already dead, what is really being said is that the person is *just as well as* dead. "Death row" at Angola Prison, the maximum-security prison in Louisiana that houses the men under a death sentence, is highlighted in the movie *Dead Man Walking*, which addresses capital punishment. These prisoners are called "dead men" because they were under a sentence of death unless a reprieve was given. Indeed, Thayer's lexicon described "death" in Eph 2:1 and other places in the New Testament as being a metaphor for being "destitute of a life that recognizes and is devoted to God, because it has been given up to trespasses and sins," or "inactive as respects doing right."[81] So "lost" persons are *headed* for death unless they repent of their sins and turn to Jesus, but the final sentence has not yet been executed.

Therefore, we have good hermeneutical reasons to believe that caution should be utilized in interpreting Eph 2:1 in an overly literal way. Yes, all people are sinful. Yes, we cannot be saved without the assisting grace of the Holy Spirit. Yes, life without God is walking death, perishing spiritually. But we retain enough of the image of God that we can respond to the work of the Holy Spirit. We do not have total inability; we have limited ability through God's prevenient grace to respond as God requires of us in all the formulas defining salvation. We cannot save ourselves; salvation is completely of God. But God has required that only believers should receive salvation (John 6:40).

---

[81] Thayer, *Greek-English Lexicon*, s.v. "*Nekros*," 423–24.

Irresistible Grace "Makes" God Sovereign

Clearly, Reformed theology is associated with a high view of the sovereignty of God. This reputation is well deserved. Calvinists were among those who pointed out the errors of the low-sovereignty approach of the Openness of God theology. We join Calvinists such as Bruce Ware in opposing the diminished-sovereignty view of Open Theism, especially because of its denial of exhaustive divine foreknowledge.[82] Several excellent books affirming a high view of divine sovereignty have been published recently by Calvinist scholars.[83] These beliefs are hardly doctrines that are unique to Calvinism. Acknowledging the sovereignty of God is a simple, basic Christian belief—no controversy there. Calvinists are not the only Christians who believe in the sovereignty of God, although at times they suggest that they are. Non-Calvinists acknowledge God's sovereignty just as much as Calvinists do.

Problems with Divine Determinism. Since we all agree that God is sovereign, the question arises, *How* does God express his sovereignty? The contention here is, contrary to Calvinists, irresistible grace does not accord God maximal sovereignty, while resistible grace does. For example, John Feinberg defends the deterministic dictum that "God ordains *all things*."[84] John Calvin taught that "*not one drop of rain falls without God's sure command*."[85] As noted earlier, he asserted that God "at his own good pleasure arranged" the fall of Adam and his posterity,[86] and that "it was his [God's] pleasure to doom to destruction" all to whom he did not choose to give irresistible grace.[87] Wayne Grudem claimed that God "exercises an extensive, ongoing, sovereign

---

[82] Ware's devastating critique is in *God's Lesser Glory: The Diminished God of Open Theism* (Wheaton, IL: Crossway, 2000).

[83] See Bruce Ware, *God's Greater Glory: The Exalted God of Scripture and the Christian Faith* (Wheaton, IL: Crossway, 2004); and Schreiner and Ware, *Still Sovereign.* The title of the latter book seems a bit misleading in that it suggests multiple perspectives, but in fact the book is written entirely from a Calvinistic perspective.

[84] John Feinberg, "God Ordains All Things," in *Predestination and Free Will: Four Views on Divine Sovereignty and Human Freedom*, ed. David Basinger and Randall Basinger (Downers Grove, IL: InterVarsity, 1986), 17–60; emphasis added.

[85] John Calvin, *Institutes of the Christian Religion*, 2 vols., ed. John T. McNeill, trans. Ford Lewis Battles, LCC 20 (Philadelphia: Westminster Press, 1960), 1:204 (1.16.5); emphasis added.

[86] Calvin, *Institutes*, 2:232; emphasis mine. For translation by Battles, see Calvin, *Institutes*, trans. Battles, 2:955 (3.23.7).

[87] Calvin, *Institutes*, 2:931, trans. Beveridge.

control over all aspects of His creation."[88] John Frame defined God's "decretive will" as his "highly mysterious" purpose that "*governs whatever comes to pass.*"[89] John Piper asserted that even catastrophic airplane crashes killing many people are caused directly by God.[90]

If God is in total control of everything that happens, then he is responsible for all the evil and suffering in the world as well as those who face reprobation for all eternity. This divine determinism within Calvinism led Roger Olson to address this issue in a chapter titled "Yes to God's Sovereignty; No to Divine Determinism."[91] Scripture denies that God is the author of evil: "Let no one say when he is tempted, 'I am being tempted by God'; for God cannot be tempted by evil, and He Himself does not tempt anyone. . . . Do not be deceived, my beloved brethren. Every good thing given and every perfect gift is from above, coming down from the Father of lights, with whom there is no variation or shifting shadow" (Jas 1:13, 16–17 NASB1995).

It is one thing to say that God reigns over the universe, that nothing is impossible for him, that he can do and has the right to do anything he chooses to do (although we know that he will not act against his nature), and that nothing in the universe is outside his control.[92] We affirm all these things. But we do not affirm that God exercises his control over the universe such that he causes everything that happens. He *allows* many

---

[88] Wayne Grudem, *Systematic Theology: An Introduction to Biblical Doctrine* (Grand Rapids: Zondervan, 1994), 355; emphasis added.

[89] John Frame, *Apologetics to the Glory of God: An Introduction* (Phillipsburg: P&R, 1994), 175; emphasis added.

[90] Piper has unambiguously attributed causal origin of disasters such as aircraft crashes to God alone. For example, regarding a well-publicized airline crash, Piper states that "the crash of flight 1549 was designed by God." According to Piper, God precisely guided the geese into both engines of the plane, but also assisted the captain's hands in the amazing landing of the flight in the Hudson River. Piper opines that the reason God did this was to provide a parable for the impending inauguration of President Obama. See John Piper, "The President, the Passengers, and the Patience of God," Desiring God, January 21, 2009, http://www.desiringgod.org/ResourceLibrary /TasteAndSee/ByDate/2009/3520_The_President_the_Passengers_and_the_Patience_of_God. Piper apparently did not provide an explanation of God's purpose (nor does any sensible explanation come to mind) for crashing a Continental Airlines flight into a house in Clarence Center (near Buffalo), New York, the next month (Feb. 13, 2009), killing all 49 persons on board and one in the house that was hit. For details, see http://www.cnn.com/2009/US/02/13/plane.crash.new.york/.

[91] Olson, *Against Calvinism*, 70–101.

[92] We know from Scripture that God *will not* do some things because they are counter to his nature. However, I believe so strongly in the freedom and sovereignty of God that I hesitate to say he *cannot* do anything.

evil things to happen, but he does not *cause* them. He *allows* people to accept or reject Christ, but he does not *cause* them to be the elect or reprobates (apart from affirming their own acceptance or rejection of Christ, his requirement for salvation). God is sovereign. He can intervene anywhere to do whatever he wills. But he allows natural processes and human choices, all of which he perfectly foreknows, to be included as a part of his overall plan. This is a higher view of sovereignty than that proposed by Reformed theology. In Calvinism, God micromanages a universe of puppets; in what we understand to be the biblical perspective, God is so great that he can be in control of the universe even with human choices and natural cause and effect. Apart from its impersonal implications, one might liken God to a giant computer that can anticipate every move that an opponent might make in the game of chess and what the best counterpoint to that action is—except that God also foreknows all the moves before anyone makes them! God can intervene whenever he sees fit. The universe is never out of his control.

In the final analysis two possible answers explain why there is so much evil in the world and why so many people do not become Christians and will receive eternal torment in hell. The Calvinist answer is that God willed it to be that way. Since God ordains and causes all things, he is responsible for all the suffering and pain in our world. Since God is the only one who can save, and because he is all-loving, all-powerful, and all-knowing, he could save everybody. But he does not even save the majority of people. Most people go to hell for all eternity. Why? Some deep, mysterious, secret will in the character of God is the reason given. That approach, I believe, is neither the most honoring approach to God nor the truest to Scripture. But what if we take human responsibility more seriously? Then most of the suffering in the world is our own doing. Those who reject Christ are only getting the just desserts of their own choices. God's honor is vindicated. He is holy, loving, and righteous. He does love all people and desires the salvation of all people. He does save all those who come to faith through grace unto salvation. This approach gives God the greatest glory and honor—the approach that the Bible teaches.

God's Sovereignty and Human Choices. Since Calvinists believe that God causes all things, it also entails that God decides everything that a person does. Calvin affirmed that "God by His secret bridle so holds and governs (persons) that they cannot move even one of their fingers without accomplishing the work of God much more than their own."[93] Feinberg followed Richard Taylor's definition of determinism

---

[93] John Calvin, *A Defence of the Secret Providence of God, by Which He Executes His Eternal Decrees*, trans. H. Cole (London: Sovereign Grace Union, 1927), 238; emphasis added.

"that for everything that happens there are conditions such that, given them, *nothing else could happen*," and thus "for every decision a person makes, there are causal conditions playing upon his or her will so as to decline it decisively or sufficiently in one direction or the other. Consequently, the *agent could not have done otherwise*, given the prevailing causal influences."[94] Likewise, Paul Helm affirmed that "God controls all persons and events equally" because "God could hardly exercise care over them without having control over it."[95] However, although persons do not have the ability to choose from among various alternatives, we are willing to do what is done: "He [God] exercises his control, as far as men and women are concerned, not apart from what they want to do, or (generally speaking) by compelling them to do what they do not want to do, but through their wills."[96]

This Calvinist account of divine determinism of human actions is labeled as *compatibilism*. Developed largely by Jonathan Edwards,[97] compatibilism claims that we always act according to our greatest *desire*. When God changes our wills and desires through irresistible grace, the Holy Spirit regenerates our spiritual life, making us genuinely desire to trust Christ. But we did not have the ability to choose or do anything else. Compatibilism, in any standard definition, affirms the compatibility of *human freedom and determinism*.[98] The discussion about compatibilism has been muddled by some theologians who define compatibilism as something that it is *not*—that is, the compatibility of human freedom with divine sovereignty or God's will.[99] Compatibilism is *not* the compatibility of human freedom with the sovereignty of God or God's will. The compatibility of God's sovereignty and/or God's

---

[94] Feinberg, "God Ordains All Things," 21, citing the definition in Richard Taylor, "Determinism," in *The Encyclopedia of Philosophy*, 8 vols., ed. Paul Edwards (New York: Macmillan, 1967), 2:359; emphasis added.

[95] Paul Helm, *The Providence of God*, Contours of Christian Theology, ed. Gerald Bray (Downers Grove, IL: InterVarsity, 1994), 20–21.

[96] Helm, 22.

[97] Jonathan Edwards, *Freedom of the Will* (New York: Cosimo, 2007). For contemporary advocates of compatibilism, see Helm, *Providence of God*; Helm, "Classical Calvinist Doctrine of God," in *Perspectives on the Doctrine of God: 4 Views*, ed. Bruce Ware (Nashville: B&H, 2008), 5–75; John Feinberg, "A Case for a Compatibilist Specific Sovereignty Model," chap. 14 in *No One Like Him: The Doctrine of God*, Foundations of Evangelical Theology (Wheaton, IL: Crossway, 2001); Feinburg, "God Ordains All Things," 17–60.

[98] Galen Strawson, s.v. "Free Will," in *Routledge Encyclopedia of Philosophy*, 10 vols., ed. Edward Craig (New York: Routledge, 1998), 3:743–53.

[99] For examples of this confusion, see Donald A. Carson, *How Long, O Lord? Reflections on Suffering and Evil* (Grand Rapids: Baker, 1990), 200–204; Ware, *God's Greater Glory*, 73–85;

will with human freedom is noncontroversial for believers, though we might struggle to explain it. The issue in compatibilism is whether human choices are compatible with divine determinism.

Strictly speaking, compatibilist "freedom" is really not freedom at all; it is *voluntary* but not *free*—that is, just being willing to do something does not mean that a person is free. One must have a choice to have freedom. Acts under compulsion are not really free. God changing our will invincibly in irresistible grace brings to mind phenomena such as hypnotism or brainwashing. Obviously, this sort of mind control is not appropriate when applied to God. If someone is pointing a gun at you, you might be willing to hand over your wallet to him, but that does not mean that you do so freely. You give him the wallet because you are under compulsion. To truly be free, there must be a choice between at least two alternatives (even if the only alternatives are yes or no).

The popular alternative to the compatibilist willing account is *soft libertarian freedom*.[100] In soft libertarianism, limited choices are available in almost every aspect of life. Absolute freedom, of course, is just a myth. Time does not permit a more thorough discussion of this issue, but soft libertarian freedom has at least the following advantages over compatibilist willing:[101]

(a) Soft libertarianism squares with our experience of decision making in real life. Almost universally, we think that when we make decisions, we are genuinely deciding something between real alternatives, not just doing what we most desire.

Ware, "A Modified Calvinist Doctrine of God" in *Perspectives on the Doctrine of God*, 98–99. Helm pointed out Ware's inconsistent use of these terms in *Perspectives*, 44.

[100] I say "soft libertarian freedom" to distinguish it from stronger views of freedom, which do not adequately account for our human limitations or how powerful forces can be brought to bear on our decisions. For more details, see Steve Lemke, "Agent Causation, or How to Be a Soft Libertarian," (paper, Southwest Regional meeting of the Evangelical Philosophical Society, n.d.), https://www.nobts.edu/about/institutional-effectiveness1/LemkeSW-files/libertarian%20 agent%20causation.pdf; and "Agent Causation and Moral Accountability: A Proposal of the Criteria for Moral Responsibility," (paper, 2009 annual meeting of the Evangelical Philosophical Society, New Orleans, November 19–21, 2009), https://www.nobts.edu/_resources/pdf/Faculty /lemkesw/ETS%20Agent%20Causation%20and%20Moral%20Accountability.pdf; cf. Alfred R. Mele, "Soft Libertarianism and the Flickers of Freedom," in *Moral Responsibility and Alternative Possibilities: Essays on the Importance of Alternative Possibilities*, ed. David Widerker and Michael McKenna (Burlington: Ashgate, 2003), 251–64.

[101] For more on this concern, see Lemke, "Soft Libertarian"; Lemke, "Moral Accountability"; and chapter 12 in this book by John Laing.

(b) We do not always do what we desire the most, as compatibilism claims. We often do what we do *not* desire to do, as Paul expressed in Rom 7:15–16.

(c) In libertarian freedom, we are morally accountable for our choices. In compatibilism, it is difficult to hold us morally accountable because we really had no choice.

(d) Only libertarian freedom offers the real choice required to accept, receive, or respond actively to the gracious offer of God through the Holy Spirit.[102]

Allow me to add one important caveat. The affirmation of soft libertarian freedom is *not* motivated by any effort to detract from God's power or glory, or to anthropocentrically elevate human effort as autonomous or as a competitor for God. Rather, it is a corollary of a proper doctrine of God which, in line with Scripture, affirms the character of God as righteous, holy, and loving. Because humans do have a measure of creaturely freedom, the evils that we see in our world can be rightfully attributed to human sinfulness rather than to God. But if God controls *all things*, it logically entails that God *causes* evil (an entailment not necessary if humans have real freedom). However, again, asserting human freedom is not to elevate humans, but to lift up the righteous and loving character of God.

Let me be clear. We do not deny a high view of divine sovereignty. God is God and he can do anything he wants. Nothing can limit God. His kingdom is going to come, and his will is going to be done, whether anybody on earth likes it or not. So it makes sense from our vantage point that God has the *right* and the *ability* to reign in this way. Likewise, we tend to equate sovereignty with power and control. If, for example, you were a tyrannical despot in a late-medieval European city, you might well think that being sovereign means to have total control, to banish, exile, torture, and kill those who disagree with you. But is this the way of Christ? Does this notion of sovereignty as total control bring glory to God? No. Nothing could possibly force God to do that. He obviously could force irresistible grace on us, but he does not. That is not the way an all-loving Being works. He could have written all of Scripture with his own fingers (anthropomorphically speaking), as he did with the

---

[102] A version of libertarian freedom was held by virtually all the early church fathers. For example, see Joseph P. Farrell, *Free Choice in St. Maximus the Confessor* (South Canaan, PA: St. Tikhon Seminary Press, 1989); Origen, *De Principiis*, bk. 3, chap. 1 in *The Ante-Nicene Church Fathers*, ed. A. Roberts, J. Donaldson, and A. C. Coxe; trans. Frederick Crombie (Buffalo, NY: The Christian Literature Company, 1885).

Ten Commandments, but he did not. He worked through human authors to write down his inerrant Word. He could have sent angels as his messengers so that the message was accurate. But he chose to work through the "foolishness of preaching" (1 Cor 1:21 KJV) of earthen vessels such as prophets and preachers to communicate God's infinitely valuable message. He could have saved us by irresistible grace, but I do not believe that he does. He requires us to respond.

Exegetical Evidence. The three parables in Luke 15 are instructive about human response. The lost sheep and the lost coin must be sought out and rescued by the owner. But in the parable of the prodigal son, the one parable dealing with a human being who is lost, the account differs. The prodigal son wandered into the far country out of his own lust and arrogance. Not until he had "wasted his substance with riotous living" and was "in want" did he come "to himself" (Luke 15:13–14, 17 KJV). The waiting father eagerly hoped for the son's return but did not go and find him and compel him to come home.

In Mark 10:15 (see Luke 9:48; 18:17), Jesus described receiving the grace of God as being such that unless you receive the kingdom of God like a little child, you will never enter it. The Greek word is *dechomai*, which means "to receive," "to take up," "to take by the hand."[103] Likewise, in John 1:12, "As many as *received* him, to them gave he power to become the sons of God, even to them that believe on his name" (KJV; emphasis added). Here, the Greek word for "received" is *paralambanō*, meaning "to take to oneself," "to join an associate to oneself," "to accept or acknowledge one to be such as he professes to be," "not to reject," or "to receive something transmitted."[104] In John 3:11 we see the negative, "You do not accept Our testimony" (HCSB), again using *lambanō*, "to receive."[105] Throughout Scripture we have one imperative command after another—hundreds of imperatives. Each of these imperatives calls on us to respond. Why do you think God put so many imperatives in his Word if he did not require a response from us?

Choose you this day whom ye will serve. (Josh 24:15 KJV)

Seek the Lord and His strength; seek His face continually. (1 Chr 16:11 NASB)

---

[103] Thayer, *Greek-English Lexicon*, 130, ref. 1209.
[104] Thayer, 484, ref. 3880.
[105] Thayer, 870–971, ref. 2983.

Seek the Lord. (Zeph 2:3 HCSB)

"Come to Me, all who are weary and heavy-laden, and I will give you rest." (Matt 11:28 NASB1995)

"Repent, and each of you be baptized in the name of Jesus Christ for the forgiveness of your sins; and you will receive the gift of the Holy Spirit." (Acts 2:38 NASB)

"Believe in the Lord Jesus, and you will be saved, you and your household." (Acts 16:31 NASB)

Why does God offer so many conditional promises if he does not intend to keep his word?

"If my people, who are called by my name, will humble themselves and pray and seek my face and turn from their wicked ways, then will I hear from heaven, and I will forgive their sin and will heal their land." (2 Chr 7:14 NIV)

"If you seek Him, He will be found by you." (2 Chr 15:2 HCSB)

If any man will come after me, let him deny himself, and take up his cross, and follow me. For whosoever will save his life shall lose it: and whosoever will lose his life for my sake shall find it. (Matt 16:24–25 KJV; cf. Mark 8:34–35; Luke 9:23–24)

If you confess with your mouth, "Jesus is Lord," and believe in your heart that God raised Him from the dead, you will be saved. One believes with the heart, resulting in righteousness, and one confesses with the mouth, resulting in salvation. (Rom 10:9–10 HCSB)

"Behold, I stand at the door and knock; if anyone hears My voice and opens the door, I will come in to him and will dine with him, and he with Me." (Rev 3:20 NASB)

And the Spirit and the bride say, Come. And let him that heareth say, Come. And let him that is athirst come. And whosoever will, let him take the water of life freely." (Rev 22:17 KJV)

Why does God give promises to those who seek him if he does not intend to honor them?

You, LORD, have not forsaken those who seek You. (Ps 9:10 NKJV)

They who seek the LORD shall not be in want of any good thing. (Ps 34:10 NASB1995)

Men and brethren, children of the stock of Abraham, and whosoever among you feareth God, to you is the word of this salvation sent (Acts 13:26 KJV).

Granted, in and of themselves, people's choices accomplish nothing. Perhaps the best model is the account about Naaman in 2 Kings 5. Naaman, the commander of the Aramean army, had leprosy. He asked for help. The prophet Elisha told him to go wash in the Jordan River seven times. Naaman initially rejected that notion, complaining about having to bathe in the dirty Jordan River. Finally, after his servants prevailed upon him, he did it, and his leprosy was cleansed. What was it that cleansed Naaman's leprosy? Was it his dunking himself in the Jordan River seven times? Of course not! Without God, he could have dunked himself in the river a thousand times and nothing would have happened. On the other hand, what happened when he did not go bathe? Nothing! God allowed him to suffer the results of his own rebellion. But when Naaman responded obediently to God's direction through the prophet, Naaman was healed. So it is with our salvation. Humans do not do anything to earn or deserve salvation, and are too sinful in nature to seek God independently or take the initiative in their own salvation. Humans come to salvation only as they are urged by the conviction of the Holy Spirit, and they are drawn to Christ as he is lifted up in proclamation. Cooperation contributes absolutely nothing to human salvation. God's grace provides the necessary condition for salvation. However, God in his freedom has sovereignly decided that he will only give the gift of salvation to those who believe, who trust Jesus Christ as Savior and Lord.

The Necessity of Responding to God. If God truly is sovereign, does he not have the right to determine the criterion for salvation? Absolutely! I have one son. I cannot imagine me sacrificing him, even to save someone else's life (particularly people who are my enemies). But God sent his only begotten Son so that *those who believe* may be saved (John 3:16). Is God asking too much to require a faith response as a condition for the salvation provided in Christ to apply in their lives? Absolutely not! If that is the criterion that God has chosen for salvation, and Scripture repeatedly says it is (see previous sections), our sovereign God has every right to require our response to the sacrifice of his Son! Making salvation dependent on a personal response does nothing to take away from the sovereignty of God; *it results from the sovereign decree of God!*

In my youth, the necessity of responding to God's gracious initiative was communicated to me by Dr. Gray Allison, a lifelong evangelist who was a member of my home church. He was then a faculty member of New Orleans Baptist Theological Seminary, and later was founder and president of Mid-America Baptist Theological Seminary. In illustrating with this group of young people how to be saved, he showed us some money and asked for a volunteer to help him illustrate salvation. He told the young volunteer that he (Dr. Allison) wanted to give him this money, but continued holding it in his hand. He asked whose money it was. Everyone said it was Dr. Allison's money. He held it out, and the young man grasped the money in his hand. Then Dr. Allison asked again whose money it was. Everyone said it was now the volunteer's money. Like most illustrations, this one can be misunderstood. But the point Dr. Allison was making was that for one to appropriate salvation into their own lives, the person must accept it, receive it, and take hold of it. Had the young man not taken hold of it, it never would have been his. Yet the money was a completely free gift provided entirely by Dr. Allison. Salvation is a free gift of righteousness (John 5:15–17), a gift received only by those who believe.[106]

The Alternative of Prevenient or Assisting Grace. What alternative is there to affirming irresistible grace? The most common alternative to irresistible grace is usually called *prevenient* or *assisting* grace.[107] In *assisting* or *enabling grace*, God through the Holy Spirit convicts, convinces, and impels the unsaved toward repentance and faith. God can exert powerful influences through the Holy Spirit to incline unbelievers toward faith and obedience without literally forcing them to do so or changing their wills (John 15:26–27; 16:7–15; 1 Thess 1:5).

Humans cannot save themselves. This situation was depicted powerfully in an 1850 painting by Ivan Aivazovsky, "The Ninth Wave," which hangs in the Russian

---

[106] Some Calvinists might allege that believing is thus a "work" that takes away God being responsible alone for our salvation. This does not follow logically, as Richard Cross makes clear: "Person *x* freely promises to do action *a* if person *y* acts in way *w*. We would not, I think, say that *y* causes *a* in the case that *y* acts in way *w*. We would say that *x* causes *a*. So, as a case of such a promise or covenant, if God freely promises to justify me in the case that I satisfy certain moral requirements, justification is caused not by me but by God." Cross, "Anti-Pelagianism and the Resistibility of Grace," *Faith and Philosophy* 22, no. 2 (April 2005): 201.

[107] Although "prevenient grace" is the term most often used in the non-Calvinist tradition, I prefer to use the term "assisting grace," "enabling grace," or to simply use the biblical language as in John 16:7–15. For further exploration of the concept of prevenient grace see W. Brian Shelton, *Prevenient Grace: God's Provision for Humanity* (Wilmore, KY: Francis Asbury Press, 2014).

Museum in St. Petersburg. The painting on an enormous canvas depicts the aftermath of a sunken sailing ship. Only the mast of the ship remains afloat. The survivors of the sunken ship cling to the mast of the ship, buffeted by high waves. Like much of earlier Russian art, the painting communicates a powerful spiritual message. Like most sailing ship masts, this mast is in the shape of a cross. Only those who cling to the cross will be saved. No one can save themselves. It is only by the grace of God that the mast can save them, though they must take hold of it.

While driving home from preaching one Sunday night years ago, I experienced a terrible wreck. The car rolled off the road out of my control, making me feel as if I was being tossed round and round like clothes in a dryer. The airbag crushed my glasses, so I could not find the brake as the vehicle rolled. Since I knew I had been going at interstate highway speed and never touched the brake, I simply waited for the last crash that I thought would end my life. However, when the vehicle stopped rolling, I was alive but in pain. I crawled out of the car into the ditch. I was hurting and alone on this cold night in a remote area. But drivers who saw the wreck called 911, and an ambulance came to get me. I couldn't even get up myself because of the pain. They put me on a stretcher and took me to the hospital. There the doctors ministered to me, diagnosed the problem, and put me on a path toward healing. But before the medical staff helped me, they first asked me to sign a *consent* form. I had to consent before I could receive care. I was delighted to receive from them what I could not do for myself![108]

Eternal salvation has some similarities to my physical rescue. We cannot save ourselves. We can do no good "works" to rescue ourselves (Eph 2:8–9). The only thing humans can do is assent to be rescued, or at least not resist being rescued. Giving one's assent to be saved is not a "good work." Unfortunately, in the world of salvation, all too many refuse to *accept* Jesus's gracious offer of salvation. Most do not even recognize they are drowning and reject all efforts to warn them. Some foolishly think they can save themselves, but they cannot. In the end, because of their rejection of the persistent witness of the Holy Spirit and the salvation proffered through Christ, God reluctantly allows them to drown eternally in their own sins (Matt 12:32; Mark 3:29; Luke 12:10; Rom 1:21–32; 5:6–21).

---

[108] For another version of this "ambulatory" model, see Cross, "Resistibility of Grace," 199–210; and Keathley, *Salvation and Sovereignty*, 103–5. Cross and Keathley use this example to argue that one can affirm both that salvation is monergistically brought about by God and that God's grace is resistible. My position adds to their view that a *positive response* is necessary, which, regarding salvation, requires responding in faith to Jesus Christ.

Billy Graham put it so well:

There is also volitional resolution. The will is necessarily involved in conversion. People can pass through mental conflicts and emotional crises without being converted. Not until they exercise the prerogative of a free moral agent and will to be converted are they actually converted. This act of will is an act of acceptance and commitment. They willingly accept God's mercy and receive God's Son and then commit themselves to do God's will. In every true conversion the will of man comes into line with the will of God. Almost the last word of the Bible is this invitation: "And whosoever will, let him take of the water of life freely" (Rev 22:17). It is up to you. You must will to be saved. It is God's will, but it must become your will, too.[109]

We have it from God's own Word—God *chooses* how he wants to exercise his sovereignty. We should understand sovereignty from God's perspective, not from a sinful human perspective. *If we truly believe in the sovereignty of God*, we must be obedient to the criteria he has laid down. We should let God be God and rule the world and bring about salvation as *he* has sovereignly established in his Word.

Irresistible Grace Gives God More Glory

Non-Calvinists are happy to affirm the strong emphasis that glorifying God should be our primary vocation, as John Piper has articulated so well.[110] However, while agreeing that God's people should give him the praise he rightfully deserves, we should be mindful that (a) God does not need our praise, and (b) our praise does not make God more glorious. God *is* glorious! His *shekinah* glory radiates from him every moment of eternity. There is nothing you or I could do to make him more glorious. We can and should simply join in the heavenly chorus giving him the praise and glory he rightfully deserves. Praising God is one of our responsibilities and privileges as believers, but he is already perfectly glorious. The key question is, *what* gives God maximal glory?

Moral Problems with Monergism. Many Calvinists believe that only monergistic salvation gives God the maximal glory. According to Matthew Barrett, "Monergism preserves God's glory":[111]

---

[109] Billy Graham, *The World Aflame* (Minneapolis: Billy Graham Evangelistic Association, 1967), 134.

[110] John Piper, *God's Passion for His Glory: Living the Vision of Jonathan Edwards* (Wheaton, IL: Crossway, 1998).

[111] Barrett, "Monergism," 186.

If God's work in calling and regenerating the sinner is conditioned upon man's will, then God cannot receive all the glory in salvation. But if God works alone, effectually to call and regenerate dead sinners, then He does receive *all* of the glory in our salvation. . . . [O]nly monergism can do justice to the glory of God in salvation.[112]

Let there be no doubt what monergism entails. It entails God's culpability for reprobation because he predestines a few to heaven and most to hell. Hear the words of John Calvin himself:

God not only foresaw the fall of the first man, and in him the ruin of his posterity, but *also at His own pleasure arranged it.*[113]

We say, then, that Scripture clearly proves this much, that God by his eternal and immutable counsel determined once for all those whom it was his pleasure one day to admit to salvation, and those whom, on the other hand, *it was his pleasure to doom to destruction.*[114]

First, how do Calvin's words align with God's Word? Calvin's words stand in sharp contrast to the words of God recorded in Ezek 33:11: "Tell them, 'As I live— this is the declaration of the Lord God—I take no pleasure in the death of the wicked, but rather that the wicked person should turn from his way and live. Repent, repent of your evil ways! Why will you die, house of Israel?'" as well as the repeated assertions in the New Testament that God desires that all persons be saved (Matt 18:14; 1 Tim 2:4; 2 Pet 3:9; 1 John 2:2).

Second, is God's refusal to save the majority of persons praiseworthy for God? I think not! Imagine a fireman who goes into a burning orphanage to save some young children because they are unable to escape by themselves and can be saved only if he rescues them. Only the fireman can save them because he has an asbestos suit. He comes back in a few minutes, bringing out three of the thirty children; but rather than going back in to save more children, the fireman goes over to the news media and brags about how praiseworthy he is for saving the three children. He believes he should be glorified for saving a few. Indeed, saving the three children was a good, heroic deed. But the pressing question on everyone's mind is, What about the other

---

[112] Barrett, 120–21.

[113] Calvin, *Institutes*, trans. H. Beveridge, 232 (3.23.7); emphasis added.

[114] Calvin, 210 (3.21.7); emphasis added.

twenty-seven children? Since he has the means to rescue the children and, indeed, is the only one who can save the children since they cannot save themselves, do we view the fireman as morally praiseworthy? We would not. In fact, probably he would be charged with depraved indifference homicide. He had the means to help them, but he would not. If we do not find that praiseworthy in a human, why would we find it praiseworthy in God? If God deliberately decided *not* to save (i.e., give irresistible grace to) anyone in your family (your parents, siblings, spouse, or children), indeed, if he took a pernicious pleasure in dooming them to destruction, would that make him more glorious for you? For most of us, it would make him *less* glorious.

As I write these words, we are in the grip of a pandemic that has surpassed 4.6 million deaths worldwide. Vaccines that promise to prevent the disease are now available. Suppose the drug companies decided they would only produce vaccines for 10 percent of the world's population and allow the local government leaders to determine who was among the elect to get the lifesaving vaccine. What would be the result of such decisions? There would be rioting and destruction! To have a life-giving means and refuse to provide it for more than a few people is impossible to defend. If people *chose* not to take the vaccine, that would be a different matter. But if the means to saving lives is reserved for a chosen few when many more lives could easily be saved, it is immoral. But Calvinists say that irresistible grace, which only God provides, is the only way people can receive eternal life. How can one defend God giving the lifesaving means to just a few? Monergism and irresistible grace do more to besmirch God's glory than praise him.

Questions about Conflict within God's Will. Second, the notion of irresistible grace also creates questions about the character of God that present him as less glorious. The two callings (the outward and inward, effectual and ineffectual, serious and not serious callings) correspond to two apparently contradictory wills within God (the revealed and secret wills of God). The revealed will of God issues the Great Commission that the gospel should be preached to all nations, but the secret will is that only a small group of elect will be saved through irresistible grace. The revealed will commands the general, outward call to be proclaimed, but the secret will knows that only a few will receive the effectual, serious calling from the Holy Spirit. The God of hard Calvinism is either disingenuous, cynically making a pseudo-offer of salvation to persons whom he has not given the means to accept, or there is a deep inner conflict within the will of God. If he has extended a general call to all persons to be saved, but has given the effectual call irresistibly to just a few, the general call seems rather misleading. This conflict between the wills of God portrays him as having a divided mind.

In response to this challenge, Calvinists appeal to mystery. Is that a successful move? No, because God's revealed will is not a mystery; it is revealed in his Word.

The Remonstrants, against whom the Synod of Dort was directed, raised the concern that the hard Calvinist perspective advocated by the Synod of Dort portrayed God as riddled by inner conflict. The Remonstrants later affirmed in a response written after the Synod of Dort:

> 8. All those whom God calls to salvation, those he calls seriously, that is, with an upright and altogether unfeigned purpose and will to save. And we do not agree with those who hold that God externally calls some whom He does not will to call internally, that is, does not will that they be actually converted, even before they have rejected the grace of the calling.

> 9. There is not in God such a hidden will which stands over against His will which is revealed in the Word, that He according to that will (that is, the hidden will) does not will the conversion and the salvation of the greater part of those whom He through the Word of the gospel, and according to the revealed will, is seriously calling and inviting unto faith and salvation; neither do we here acknowledge, as some speak, a holy dissimulation, or a double person in God.[115]

Some Calvinists attempt to downplay this criticism by advocating the "well-meant offer" or "free offer" of the gospel to the lost. As the Synod of Dort affirmed in Doctrine 2, article 5:

> Moreover, the promise of the gospel is, that whosoever believes in Christ crucified shall not perish, but have everlasting life. This promise, together with the command to repent and believe, ought to be declared and published to all nations, and to all persons promiscuously and without distinction, to whom God out of His good pleasure sends the gospel.[116]

---

[115] "The Opinions of the Remonstrants," Responses to article 3 of the Synod of Dort, comments 8–9, in Vance, *The Other Side of Calvinism*, rev. ed. (Pensacola, FL: Vance Publications, 1999), appendix 3, 604; also available online at "C. The Opinion of the Remonstrants regarding the third and fourth articles, concerning the grace of God and the conversion of man," The Arminian Opinions (Heretical), A Puritans Mind, https://www.apuritansmind.com/creeds-and-confessions/the-remonstrants-arminian-documents/the-arminian-opinions/.

[116] "The Canons of the Synod of Dort," in Schaff, *Creeds of Christendom*, 3:586 (II, art. 5); available online at https://ccel.org/ccel/schaff/creeds3/creeds3.iv.xvi.html.

However, such a claim appears to be not only logically contradictory but also mean-spirited to proclaim a false offer of salvation to persons who have no possible chance to receive it because they were not one of the lucky ones to get irresistible grace. Obviously, portraying God as having a divided mind and will is not the way we want to go. It seems disingenuous for God to offer a definitive, serious calling to some but not at all offer a serious calling to others. This does *not* make God appear more glorious!

Irresistible Grace Is Impersonal. The biblical image of God is based on God as love (1 John 4:7–8) and God as holy (1 Pet 1:16). A God who says he loves all people and desires to save all people but intentionally saves just a few is not the God of the New Testament. The God of the Bible deals with persons as persons, as F. Leroy Forlines articulated; for us to be in a relationship with God, we must be dealt with as persons rather than as machines:

> In the relationship of the physical to the physical, or the relationship of the parts of a machine to one another, we are dealing with *cause* and *effect* relationships. . . . When a hammer hits a nail, the hammer is active and the nail is passive. The hammer *causes* the nail to be driven into the wood. The nail had no choice. A force outside the nail caused the nail to be driven into the wood.
>
> Interpersonal relationships do not submit to such a simple analysis. *Influence* and *response* provide more appropriate terms. . . . [T]he inability of one person to *cause* another person to do something grows out of the nature of what it means to be a *person*. . . . There is no such thing as a person doing or not doing something *without having made a decision*. . . . [I]t has been a mistake over the centuries to focus the conflict between Calvinists and Arminians on whether fallen or redeemed man has a *free will.* The real question is: Is fallen man a personal being, or is he sub-personal? . . . . Human beings are personal beings, by God's *design*, and were made for a *personal relationship* with a personal God. God will not violate His own plan.[117]

The same concern pertains to the distinction that Calvinists make between the "universal" (ineffective) call and the "particular" (effective) call. Suppose we had a "will changer" machine or pill that turned its victim into a mindless robot who always did what he or she was instructed. The 1975 cult movie *The Stepford Wives* told this story, often repeated with variations in various science fiction story lines. The Stepford,

---

[117] F. Leroy Forlines, *The Quest for Truth: Answering Life's Inescapable Questions* (Nashville: Randall House, 2001), 313; italics in the original.

Connecticut Men's Association had the technology to turn their wives into subservient, robotic women who existed only to please their husbands. If taken to court, the Men's Association members would definitely not be held up for praise. They would be accused and tried for crimes such as kidnapping, enslavement, and brainwashing. We would not consider the men to be glorious. We would consider them to be depraved. Is this not how Calvinists are portraying God? He is changing people's will so they will glorify him? Why would the omnipotent Lord of the universe even care about that? To even suggest such a thing is to view the Bible from a radically anthropocentric point of view in which God desperately needs people to give their approval to him, even if he has to force them to do so. Love is only meaningful when it is chosen. Therefore, if we are concerned about God's greater glory, it would be in a world of free persons, not persons whose will was mechanically overridden.

What understanding of sovereignty gives God greater glory? Does this notion of sovereignty as total control bring the greatest glory to God? No. Suppose a couple desires to have a baby. They have at least two options. Option one is that they can go down to Walmart and purchase a doll. That plastic doll, for every time they pull its string, will say, "Daddy, I love you!" Now that is total control. They can have that doll say, "I love you" anytime they want. They just pull its string; the doll has no decision but to react the way it has been programmed to react. Option two, however, is to have a real baby. Now, they know from the beginning that the baby is going to be more trouble. Babies do not come home from the hospital housebroken. They cry all night. They break their toes, and they break your hearts. But when that child of his or her own volition says, "Daddy, I love you," it really means something. The parents are more glorified with a real child than with a doll that could not have praised them had they not pulled its string. So, then, which gives God the greater glory—a view that the only persons who can praise God are those whose wills he changes without their permission, or the view that persons respond to the gracious invitation of God and the conviction of the Holy Spirit to praise God truly of their own volition?

God's Concept of Glory. Not surprisingly, God does not think about things the way we do. He says in his Word, "For as the heavens are higher than the earth, so are my ways higher than your ways, and my thoughts than your thoughts" (Isa 55:9 KJV). Hear again God's statement in Hosea 11:

> "How can I give you up, Ephraim? How can I hand you over, Israel? How can
> I make you like Admah? How can I set you like Zeboiim? My heart churns
> within Me; My sympathy is stirred. I will not execute the fierceness of My

anger; I will not again destroy Ephraim. For I am God, and not man, the Holy One in your midst; and I will not come with terror." (vv. 8–9 NKJV)

If you or I had omnipotent power and were faced with a stubborn and rebellious people, perhaps we would just torch them in our anger. We might feel not only that we were exercising greater sovereignty and authority, but in so doing we might deem ourselves more glorious. But God said, "I am God, and not man, the Holy One in your midst" (Hos 11:9 NKJV). Evidently, God's ways are truly not like our ways. Jesus taught us that God sees greatness in a different light—doing things God's way involves not total control or the arbitrary use of power, but a servant spirit:

> But Jesus called them to Himself and said, "You know that the rulers of the Gentiles lord it over them, and those who are great exercise authority over them. Yet it shall not be so among you; but whoever desires to become great among you, let him be your servant. And whoever desires to be first among you, let him be your slave—just as the Son of Man did not come to be served, but to serve, and to give His life a ransom for many." (Matt 20:25–28 NKJV; cf. Mark 10:42–45; Luke 22:25–28)

In Luke's account, Jesus mentions that these Gentile authorities were called "benefactors" (Luke 22:25), persons who dispensed gracious acts on which subjects they chose. But Jesus said it should not be so for God's people, and he grounded that on nothing other than himself—"just as the Son of Man did not come to be served, but to serve, and to give His life a ransom for many" (Matt 20:28 NKJV).

Although God truly has the right and ability to do whatever he wants whenever he wants, he does not normally choose to express his sovereignty in that way or act against his loving nature. God evidently sees servanthood and allowing the free choices of his creatures as more glorious than the arbitrary exertion of power and authority. The plan that some of Jesus's disciples had to glorify Christ was for him to overthrow the Romans, seize the throne of Israel, and exercise control as king; but God had a better plan. He sent Jesus to the shameful cross. It is hard for humans to understand sovereignty and glory in this way, but we are truly to have the mind of Christ Jesus,

> who, being in the form of God, did not consider it robbery to be equal with God, but made Himself of no reputation, taking the form of a bondservant, and coming in the likeness of men. And being found in appearance as a man,

He humbled Himself and became obedient to the point of death, even the death of the cross. Therefore God also has highly *exalted* Him and given Him the name which is above every name, that at the name of Jesus every knee should bow, of those in heaven, and of those on earth, and of those under the earth, and that every tongue should confess that Jesus Christ is Lord, to the *glory* of God the Father. (Phil 2:6–11 NKJV; emphasis added)

We have it from God's own Word—that is the way he wants to exercise sovereignty, and that is what he finds to be glorious. We should understand sovereignty and glory from God's perspective, not from a human perspective. We believe God deserves more than the lesser glory and sovereignty of open theism and even more than the greater glory and sovereignty offered by Calvinism. Let us give God the maximal glory that he deserves!

Conclusion

This essay has raised significant biblical and theological issues that challenge the viability of the doctrine of irresistible grace. I believe the cumulative case that has been raised against irresistible grace is compelling. Certainly, high Calvinists have their own explanations for some of these concerns. I encourage each believer, like the Bereans encountered by Paul (Acts 17:10–11), to search what the Scriptures say concerning these issues, under the guidance of the Holy Spirit who leads us into all truth (John 16:7–15).

A Critique of Perseverance of the Saints

—— **Ken Keathley** ——

Blessed assurance, Jesus is mine!
Oh, what a foretaste of glory divine!

Fanny Crosby

At a symposium honoring Dale Moody,[1] I. Howard Marshall recited the old saw that Arminians know they are saved but are afraid they cannot keep it, while Calvinists know they cannot lose their salvation but are afraid they do not have it.[2]

---

[1] This chapter was previously published as the article "Does Anyone Really Know If They Are Saved? A Survey of the Current Views on Assurance with a Modest Proposal," *Journal of the Grace Evangelical Society* 15, no. 1 (Spring 2002): 37. Used with permission.

[2] See I. Howard Marshall, "The Problem of Apostasy in New Testament Theology," in *Kept by the Power of God: A Study of Perseverance and Falling Away*, 3rd ed. (London: Paternoster, 1995), 267.

Aside from being witty, this highlights the two components of the question about assurance. First, is it possible to know absolutely or even confidently that one is saved; and second, is it possible for those who currently believe they are saved to have assurance that they will remain in a state of grace until the day of redemption? It is more than just a little ironic that though they travel different routes, many Arminians and Calvinists arrive basically at the same answer—assurance is based on evidence of sanctification.[3] Michael Eaton pointed to the nineteenth-century preacher Asahel Nettleton as a good example of this odd state of affairs when he quoted Nettleton who stated, "The most that I have ventured to say respecting myself is, that I think it possible I may get to heaven."[4] Words perhaps expected from an Arminian, but Nettleton was a Calvinist.

The Biblical Tension

Scripture presents us with a seeming tension. On the one hand, a plethora of texts assure that believers are secure and that they will be preserved. On the other hand, a significant number of other passages warn against falling away and stress the necessity of persevering. Disagreement about the best way to approach reconciling and integrating these two disparate sets of texts has produced much division among evangelicals.

Passages That Promise Security and/or Give Assurance

Scripture texts offering security or assurance can be grouped under four categories. First, certain verses promise believers that everlasting life is a present reality (e.g., John 3:16, 18, 36; 5:24; 11:25–26). Jesus declared, "Most assuredly, I say to you, he who hears My word and believes in Him who sent Me has everlasting life, and shall not come into judgment, but has passed from death into life" (John 5:24 NKJV).[5] Eternal life is not merely something that waits for believers after physical death. For the Christian, eternal life is not only a future hope; it is enjoyed now.

---

[3] Both Marshall and D. A. Carson made this observation. See D. A. Carson, "Reflections on Christian Assurance," *Westminster Theological Journal* 54, no. 1 (1992): 21. Carson stated, "Thus at their worst, the two approaches meet in strange and sad ways."

[4] Cited by Michael Eaton, *No Condemnation: A New Theology of Assurance* (Downers Grove, IL: InterVarsity, 1995), 3.

[5] Unless otherwise noted, all Scripture references in this chapter are from the New King James Version.

Second, numerous texts promise believers that they are secure; that is, that they will continue to be saved (e.g., John 10:27–29; Rom 8:31–39; Eph 4:30; Heb 13:5; 1 Pet 1:5; Jude 24). Many consider John 10:27–29 to be the locus classicus concerning the surety of a believer's final salvation. Jesus promised, "My sheep hear My voice, and I know them, and they follow Me. And I give them eternal life, and they shall never perish; neither shall anyone snatch them out of My hand. My Father, who has given them to Me, is greater than all; and no one is able to snatch them out of My Father's hand." Our Savior made this pledge without qualification. Christians are secure in the hands of the triune God. We cannot lose our salvation because it is not ours to lose. We are "kept by the power of God" (1 Pet 1:5) and "sealed for the day of redemption" (Eph 4:30).

A third set of texts teaches that believers can have confident knowledge, that is, full assurance that they are saved (e.g., 1 John 2:3; 3:19–21; 4:13–16; 5:13, 18–20). The apostle John declared, "These things I have written to you who believe in the name of the Son of God, that you may know that you have eternal life, and that you may continue to believe in the name of the Son of God" (1 John 5:13). Christians are not just saved; they can be certain they are saved. The Bible promises believers the existential experience of certainty. This conviction can be rightly described as a form of knowledge. A person trusting Christ for salvation can know he or she is saved. This life of confident trust can serve as a powerful witness to non-Christians.

But what about Christians who serve the Lord poorly or fail spectacularly? A fourth set of texts teaches that less-than-perfect believers are still saved (e.g., 1 Cor 3:15; 5:5; 2 Pet 2:7–9). For example, the Bible does not present Lot (Abraham's nephew) as an exemplar of sainthood. If anything, Genesis presents him as a cautionary tale. Yet he was rescued from Sodom by angels who told him they could not bring judgment on the wicked cities as long as he was there (Gen 19:21–22). Similarly, when the apostle Peter used Lot as an example, he made the point to repeatedly describe him as a "righteous man" (2 Pet 2:7–9). This is not the characterization we might expect of one whose life seemed to oscillate between spiritual compromise and moral failure. Lot appears to be the type of believer who will experience great loss at the day of judgment and still be saved, "yet so as through fire" (1 Cor 3:15).

Passages That Warn and/or Require Perseverance

If the Bible gave only promises and assurances about salvation, there would be no tension to resolve. But some of the most disturbing verses in Scripture are those that demand continued obedience from believers and give serious warnings to those who do not endure. Like the assurance texts, these warning passages can be grouped under four headings.

First, Scripture warns that some who think they are saved actually are not (e.g., Matt 7:21–23; 13:24–30; 25:11–12). Jesus cautioned that many on judgment day will tragically discover they are not ready: "Not everyone who says to Me, 'Lord, Lord,' shall enter the kingdom of heaven." Rather he or she must be a person who "does the will of My Father." The protests of the unprepared are disturbing in that their self-description seems quite commendable. They prophesied, engaged in spiritual warfare and served—all in the name of Christ. Jesus said that he will reject them, declaring that he never knew them and that their deeds were evil (Matt 7:21–23). In addition, Jesus taught cautionary lessons such as the parable of the ten virgins. One disturbing aspect of this parable is the similarity of the characters, not their differences. They were not five virgins and five harlots; all ten were virgins.

Second, the Bible warns that some who profess faith will not persevere (e.g., Matt 13:20–22; Acts 8:22–23; 2 Pet 2:1, 20–22; 1 John 2:19). The phenomenon of apostasy is a challenge to every soteriological system. What exactly is happening in and to a person who, by outward appearances, gave a sincere profession of faith yet later abandons Christ? Regardless of how challenging the occurrences of falling away may be, Scripture itself warns that recantations are going to happen. In the parable of the sower, some seed fell on shallow ground, sprang up, and then quickly withered away (Matt 13:5–6). Our Lord explained that the shallow ground signified the type of person who professes faith, even "with joy," only to later quit when difficulties come (vv. 20–22). Even during Jesus's ministry "many of his disciples went back and walked with Him no more" (John 6:66). Today, as we see several famous "de-conversions," Christ's question to the disciples seems very relevant: "Do you also want to go away?" To which we can only give Simon Peter's poignant reply, "Lord, to whom shall we go? You have the words of eternal life" (vv. 67–68).

A third set of texts seems to teach that ultimate salvation depends on perseverance (e.g., Matt 10:22; 24:13; 1 Cor 9:27; Phil 2:12; Col 1:21–23; Rev 3:5). Paul seems to offer a qualified promise to the Christians in Colossae that was contingent on their persistence. They could count on all the benefits of the gospel "if indeed you continue in the faith, grounded and steadfast, and are not moved away from the hope of the gospel which you heard" (Col 1:23). Elsewhere the apostle expressed the personal concern that after he had preached to others "I myself [might be] disqualified" (1 Cor 9:27). On more than one occasion Jesus flatly declared, "He who endures to the end shall be saved" (Matt 10:22; 24:13). He warned that we should "take heed" to ourselves lest we are distracted with "carousing, drunkenness, and cares of this life, and that Day come on [us] unexpectedly." We are to "watch . . . and pray always" so that we "may be counted worthy" when we stand before him (Luke 21:34–36).

Last, a fourth set of passages warns that judgment awaits those who apostatize (Heb 2:3; 3:7–4:13; 6:4–8; 10:26–31; 12:25–29; 2 Pet 2:1–3). The author of Hebrews made this point no fewer than five times. Those who neglect their great salvation shall not escape (Heb 2:3), but a certain and fearful judgment awaits them (10:26–27). Apostasy appears to be unforgivable. The author explained that

> it is impossible for those who were once enlightened, and have tasted the heavenly gift, and have become partakers of the Holy Spirit, and have tasted the good word of God and the powers of the age to come, if they fall away, to renew them again to repentance, since they crucify again for themselves the Son of God, and put Him to an open shame. (Heb 6:4–6)

Clearly there is an abundance of biblical passages that both offer assurance and require perseverance. In this chapter I endeavor to show how to understand both sets of text as a unified whole. I will argue that a believer's assurance is found in Christ alone and that the warning passages serve as tests of genuineness.

In 2001 Thomas Schreiner and Ardel Caneday presented an updated version of the provocative position set forth earlier by Louis Berkhof and G. C. Berkouwer. They attempt to reconcile the biblical passages that promise unconditional assurance with passages that warn of divine judgment (particularly the five warning passages in the book of Hebrews) by positing "that adhering to the warnings is the means by which salvation is obtained on the final day."[6] The believer's salvation is not merely manifested by perseverance, but rather, eschatologically speaking, a believer is saved through perseverance. However, Schreiner and Caneday deny that the elect will apostatize, claiming the warning passages are the means by which God has chosen to preserve the elect. The "means-of-salvation" position, seems to be, as a practical

---

[6] Thomas Schreiner, "Perseverance and Assurance: A Survey and a Proposal," *Southern Baptist Journal of Theology* 2, no. 1 (Spring 1998): 53. See Thomas Schreiner and Ardel Caneday, *The Race Set before Us: A Biblical Theology of Perseverance and Assurance* (Downers Grove, IL: InterVarsity, 2001); G. C. Berkouwer, *Faith and Perseverance* (Grand Rapids: Eerdmans, 1958), 88–124; Louis Berkhof, *Systematic Theology*, rev. ed. (Grand Rapids: Eerdmans, 1996), 548. John Piper takes a similar position in *Future Grace* (Sisters, OR: Multnomah, 1995), 231–59.

matter, a melding of Arminian and Calvinist soteriology.[7] Critics respond that if they are correct, then perhaps we should be honest enough to admit to our Catholic counterparts that the Council of Trent was right after all.

This chapter will first address the two main questions about assurance with a brief survey of the proposed answers. Second, additional attention will be given to the means-of-salvation position of Schreiner and Caneday, which has been the topic of much discussion in evangelical circles. Third, it will be contended that, though Schreiner and Caneday have made a positive contribution to the discussion about assurance, a variation of the test-of-genuineness position best explains the tension between the biblical texts that assure and those that admonish.

How Does One Know He Is Genuinely Saved?

Three schools of thought have provided three different answers to the question of how an individual believer knows if he or she is genuinely saved. The first view, held by the Roman Catholic Church, regards the claim of assurance of salvation to be a demonstration of spiritual arrogance. Roman Catholic soteriology does not separate sanctification from justification and therefore does not present assurance as something currently available. The second view is that of the Reformers. Flying the banner of *sola fide*, they trumpeted a certainty to salvation that made saving faith and assurance virtual synonyms. The post-Reformation Calvinists and Puritans held to a third view that saw assurance as a grace given after conversion and discerned by careful self-examination. The second and third answers still predominate evangelicalism today.

The Roman Catholic View: Assurance Is Not Possible

If salvation is a lifetime process that may or may not be successfully completed, then assurance of salvation is not possible. Following Augustine, official Catholic doctrine views justification as a process that occurs within the individual Christian over the course of his lifetime and perhaps even continues after death. No one can know for

---

[7] Hicks used this point to argue that the respective positions of the Arminian and the Calvinist on the economy of redemption are essentially the same and that a truce, or at least the calling of a draw, between the two sides is in order. See John Mark Hicks, "Election and Security: An Impossible Impasse?" (paper presented at the annual meeting of the Evangelical Theological Society, Colorado Springs, CO, Nov. 14–16, 2001), 12–17.

sure how far along he is on the journey of faith or if he will continue the difficult task of walking in the Way. Seen from this light, the Reformed doctrine of justification by faith alone seems to present a truncated soteriology. The Council of Trent condemned all who claim to have assurance of salvation, declaring, "If any one saith, that a man, who is born again and justified, is bound of faith to believe that he is assuredly in the number of the predestinate; let him be anathema."[8] The Tridentine Council reasoned that since only the elect will persevere, and since only God knows who is and who is not elect, then special revelation would be required for someone to have assurance of salvation.[9] Calvin responded by declaring that for the elect to have assurance, the Word of God was all the special revelation needed.[10]

The Reformers: Assurance Is the Essence of Faith

So how does one know if she is saved? The answer of the Reformation was that this knowledge is a part of salvation itself. Calvin defined faith as "a firm and certain knowledge of God's benevolence toward us, founded upon the truth of the freely given promise in Christ, both revealed to our minds and sealed upon our hearts through the Holy Spirit."[11] The very nature of conversion and regeneration ensures that the believer will know when she has believed. Anyone can know whether she has believed in Jesus Christ, and all who believe in him are saved. Therefore, assurance is the essence of saving faith.[12]

Having certain knowledge at the time of conversion does not exclude the possibility that a believer may have doubts after her salvation, nor does it mean that only those with absolute certainty are saved. Luther stated:

---

[8] "Canons Concerning Justification," in *The Teaching of the Catholic Church*, ed. Karl Rahner (Cork: Mercer, 1966), 400 (canon 15; DS 1565).

[9] "Canons Concerning Justification," 400 (canon 16; DS 1566). For a Catholic perspective on the Council's view on assurance, see Avery Dulles, *The Assurance of Things Hoped For* (New York: Oxford University Press, 1994), 48–50.

[10] Calvin asked, "What else, good Sirs, is a certain knowledge of our predestination than that testimony of adoption which Scripture makes common to all the godly?" John Calvin, "Acts of the Council of Trent with the Antidote," in *Selected Works of John Calvin*, 7 vols. (Grand Rapids: Baker, 1983), 3:155.

[11] Calvin, *Institutes*, trans. Battles, 1:551 (3.2.7) (see chap. 4, n. 85).

[12] Hebrews 11:1 states, "Now faith is being sure of what we hope for, being convinced of what we do not see" (NET). Both Zane Hodges and Thomas Schreiner hold that assurance is the essence of saving faith. At least on this point they are agreed.

Even if my faith is feeble, I still have the selfsame treasure and the selfsame Christ that others have. There is no difference. Faith in Him makes us all perfect, but works do not. We might compare this to two persons who possess a hundred guldens [gold or silver coins]. The one may carry them in a paper sack, the other may keep them in an iron chest. But for all that, both possess the entire treasure. Thus the Christ whom you and I own is one and the same, regardless of the strength or the weakness of your faith or of mine.[13]

Both Luther and Calvin realized that many genuine believers have subsequent doubts. Nevertheless, this view does contend that when a person is saved, she knows it, and this core conviction, though buffeted, will never die.

However, certain doctrines advocated by the Reformers for the purpose of establishing assurance often produced the opposite effect. The doctrines of the absolute decree of election and reprobation made within the hidden will of God, limited atonement, and temporary faith created a tension in later Calvinist theology and made assurance of salvation very difficult to obtain. This difficulty manifests itself particularly in the theology and practice of the Puritans.

The Puritans: Assurance Is Logically Deduced

Theologians debate intensely about whether the struggles later Calvinists and Puritans had over assurance of salvation were the result of their departure from the teachings of Calvin or if they simply took Calvin's theology to its logical conclusion. R. T. Kendall and Charles Bell argued that Calvin held to a doctrine of unlimited atonement and to a Christocentric doctrine of assurance. Their "Calvin vs. the Calvinists thesis" is that later Calvinism, beginning with Beza, departed from Calvin by adhering to a doctrine of limited atonement and to a doctrine of assurance that begins with the absolute decree of the hidden God as its starting point.[14] Others have responded that the confusion begins with Calvin himself and that his followers'

---

[13] Martin Luther, "Sermons on the Gospel of St. John: Chapters 6–8," in *Luther's Works*, 55 vols., ed. Jaroslav Pelikan, Hilton C. Oswald, and Helmut T. Lehmann (St. Louis: Concordia, 1999), 23:28.

[14] R. T. Kendall, *Calvin and English Calvinism to 1649* (New York: Oxford University Press, 1979); and M. Charles Bell, *Calvin and Scottish Theology: The Doctrine of Assurance* (Edinburgh: Handsel, 1985).

works simply highlighted his confusion.[15] Either way, it is a historical fact that much of the Puritan's life was defined by his search for assurance. This concern about assurance would mystify the average evangelical of today.

Post-Reformation Calvinists stressed the doctrines of double predestination and limited atonement to emphasize that the believer's salvation is completely by grace and is as secure as the nature and character of God himself. But the doctrine of limited atonement implies that the anxious inquirer cannot presume that Christ died for him; Christ died for an individual if and only if that person is one of the elect. How does one know if he is elected? The electing decree is part of the hidden will of God, so the only way a person knows that he is elect is if he truly believes in Jesus Christ for salvation. But how does one know if his faith is genuine or if he is deceived? A genuine faith manifests itself by persevering in doing good works. In the final analysis, the basis of assurance in Post-Reformation Puritan Reformed theology was sanctification, not justification.

The doctrine of temporary faith, a notion first formulated by Calvin but later developed by Beza and Perkins, further intensified the problem of assurance in Calvinist and Puritan theology. According to them, God gives to the reprobate, whom he never intended to save in the first place, a "taste" of his grace. Based on passages such as Matt 7:21–23, Heb 6:4–6, and the parable of the sower, Beza and Perkins attributed this false, temporary faith to an ineffectual work of the Holy Spirit. Perkins propounded a system in which the reprobate might experience five degrees of ineffectual calling that to him is indistinguishable from a genuine conversion experience. Those who profess to be believers are encouraged to examine

---

[15] Zachman and Thomas argued that the trouble began with the inconsistencies of Calvin's formulation of the doctrine of assurance and that the later Calvinists are closer to Calvin than Kendall or Bell wanted to admit. Thorson concluded that "Calvin is not just complex, but inconsistent." See Randall Zachman, *The Assurance of Faith: Conscience in the Theology of Martin Luther and John Calvin* (Minneapolis: Fortress, 1993); G. Michael Thomas, *The Extent of the Atonement: A Dilemma for Reformed Theology from Calvin to the Consensus (1536–1675)* (Carlisle: Paternoster, 1997); and Stephen Thorson, "Tensions in Calvin's View of Faith: Unexamined Assumptions in R. T. Kendall's *Calvin and English Calvinism to 1649,*" *JETS* 37, no. 3 (September 1994): 423. Beeke and Hawkes defend the Puritan's approach to assurance, calling it a thoroughly trinitarian model and "especially elegant." See Joel Beeke, *The Quest for Full Assurance: The Legacy of Calvin and His Successors* (Edinburgh: Banner of Truth, 1999); and R. M. Hawkes, "The Logic of Assurance in English Puritan Theology," *Westminster Theological Journal* 52, no. 2 (Fall 1990): 247–61.

themselves, lest they are found to possess only this temporary faith.[16] Beza declared that the reason God gives temporary faith to the reprobate is so that "their fall might be more grievous."[17] In Olmsted's opinion, Beza's teaching "comes perilously close to ascribing the matter to divine sadism."[18]

History shows that these doctrines produced a crippling anxiety in the later Calvinists and Puritans that drove them to an introspection that an objective observer might describe as pathological. John Bunyan's *Pilgrim's Progress* has blessed multitudes of Christians, but his spiritual autobiography, *Grace Abounding to the Chief of Sinners,* is disturbing. He recounts how, in his seemingly endless search for assurance of salvation, he was haunted by the question, "How can I tell if I am elected?"[19]

Kendall and Bell document the pastorally damaging results of the Puritan approach to assurance. Even those who disagree with Kendall's thesis concede that his "devastating critique" of the miserable travails produced by Puritan theology and practice is more or less "on the mark."[20] Kendall recounted the life and work of William Perkins (1558–1602), who is often called the father of Puritanism. Perkins wrote extensively and almost exclusively on the subject of assurance, devoting 2,500 pages to the topic. Unfortunately, the preaching and teaching of Perkins on assurance often had the opposite effect, creating more doubts than were resolved. Ironically, Perkins, like so many other Puritans of his day, died without a clear assurance of his own salvation.

In a similar fashion, Bell chronicled the struggle for assurance among the Scottish Calvinists. He said:

---

[16] See Richard Muller, "Perkin's *A Golden Chaine:* Predestinarian System or Schematized *Ordo Salutis?*" *Sixteenth Century Journal* 60, no. 1 (1978): 75. Perkins devised an elaborate chart that expounded a supralapsarian view of salvation. Under the heading of "A Calling Not Effectual," Perkins listed five evidences of the ineffectual work of the Holy Spirit: (1) an enlightening of the mind; (2) a penitence accompanied by a desire to be saved; (3) a temporary faith; (4) a taste of justification and sanctification that is accompanied by the heartfelt sweetness of God's mercy; and (5) a zeal for the things of religion. See also Kendall, *Calvin and Calvinism,* 67–76. Kendall quoted Perkins as saying that the quest for assurance ultimately requires a "descending into our own hearts" (Kendall, *Calvin and Calvinism,* 75), which is a type of introspection that Calvin warned against.

[17] Cited in Kendall, *Calvin and Calvinism,* 36.

[18] Richard H. Olmsted, "Staking All on Faith's Object: The Art of Christian Assurance According to Martin Luther and Karl Barth," *Pro Ecclesia* 10, no. 2 (May 1, 2001): 140–41.

[19] John Bunyan, *Grace Abounding to the Chief of Sinners* (Chicago: Moody, 1959), 26.

[20] George Harper, "Calvin and English Calvinism to 1649: A Review Article," *Calvin Theological Journal* 20.2 (November 1985): 257.

It is well known, for example, that for generations many in the Scottish Highlands have refused to receive the communion elements because of the want of personal assurance of their salvation. Although believing that Jesus Christ is the Savior and the Son of God, self-examination fails to yield sufficient evidence of their election to salvation. Fearing that apart from such assurance they may eat and drink in an unworthy manner, and thereby incur the judgment of God, they abstain from receiving the Lord's Supper.[21]

The later Calvinists and Puritans employed two syllogisms, the practical syllogism and the mystical syllogism, in their attempt to ascertain assurance by way of logical deduction. They used the practical syllogism (*syllogismus practicus*) to determine whether they had believed and the mystical syllogism (*syllogismus mysticus*) to search for evidence of true faith.[22] The practical syllogism is as follows:

Major premise: If effectual grace is manifested in me by good works, then I am elect.
Minor premise (practical): I manifest good works.
Conclusion: Therefore, I am one of the elect.

But how does one know the minor premise of the practical syllogism is true for him? The Puritans attempted to answer this question by an introspective self-examination using the mystical syllogism. The mystical syllogism is as follows:

Major premise: If I experience the inward confirmation of the Spirit, then I am elect.
Minor premise (mystical): I experience the confirmation of the Spirit.
Conclusion: Therefore, I am one of the elect.

Beza concluded, "Therefore, that I am elect, is first perceived from sanctification begun in me, that is, by my hating of sin and my loving of righteousness."[23] The post-Reformation Calvinists and the Puritans believed that the basis of assurance is sanctification.

Of the three answers given to the question, "How does one know that he is genuinely saved?" only the second option, "Assurance is the essence of saving faith,"

---

[21] Bell, *Calvin and Scottish Theology*, 7.
[22] Beeke, *Quest for Full Assurance*, 132–39.
[23] Theodore Beza, *A Little Book of Christian Questions and Responses*, Q.209 (Allison Park, PA: Pickwick, 1986), 96–97.

provides certainty of salvation. Assurance of salvation must be based on Jesus Christ and his work for us—nothing more and nothing less.

How Secure Is One's Salvation?

Even if a believer knows he is saved, the question of perseverance is still unanswered. This brings us to the second aspect of assurance—how secure is one's salvation? Arminians have traditionally answered that apostasy is possible for the believer, while Calvinists have affirmed the perseverance of the saints. Some scholars have offered mediating positions that argue while the Scriptures warn against the danger of apostasy, the possibility of apostasy does not exist. Thomas Schreiner and Ardel Caneday's means-of-salvation position is one such midway proposal, and this chapter will give additional attention to it.

Apostasy Is Possible	Apostasy Is Not Possible	Apostasy Is Threatened, but Not Possible
Non-elect believers fall—Luther *Non-persevering believers fall*—Moody	*Implicit Universalism*—Barth *Once Saved, Always Saved*—Grace Evangelical Society *Test of Genuineness*—Demarest	*Irreconcilable Tension*—Carson *Means of Salvation*—Schreiner and Caneday *Middle Knowledge*—Craig

Lutheran and Arminian Views: Apostasy Is Possible

Two positions accept the possibility that a believer may lose his salvation. Many Lutherans argue that non-elect believers may fall from grace, while traditional Arminians argue that all believers are at risk of apostasy.

Non-Elect Believers Fall

According to many Lutherans, only elect believers persevere and only God knows which believers are the elect.[24] God has not elected every believer whom he regenerates. A believer can lose his salvation and be placed back under the wrath of God by

---

[24] Bruce Demarest, *The Cross and Salvation* (Wheaton, IL: Crossway, 1997), 437–38. This paragraph depends on Demarest.

committing mortal sins. As examples, Luther made a contrast of David and Peter from Saul and Judas. He held up the first pair as examples of saints who lost their salvation but regained it by their repentance, but he viewed the second pair as formerly regenerate saints who experienced eventual damnation.[25] God grants repentance and perseverance to his elect. Since election is part of the hidden will of God, all believers must strive to endure until the end. On a practical level, the Lutheran perspective operates much like the Arminian one.

Non-Persevering Believers Fall

Arminians interpret the assurance passages in the light of the warning passages and understand salvation to be a present condition that a believer enjoys but could lose. Two recent proponents of this position, Dale Moody and I. Howard Marshall, argued that the Scriptures are filled with explicit warnings to believers that they must persevere if they are to be saved.[26] Moody claimed that because of preconceived theological positions, the full impact of these verses has been muted. He lamented, "Yet cheap preaching and compromise with sin have made such texts forbidden for serious study."[27] He argued, "Eternal life is the life of those who continue to follow Jesus. No one can retain eternal life who turns away from Jesus."[28]

Schreiner pointed out that Moody solved the tension between the assurance passages and the warning passages by denying there is a tension.[29] Moody asserted that Calvinists have put so much emphasis on the assurance passages that they have bleached out the full force of the warning passages' meaning. However, Moody appears to have committed the same error in reverse when he ignored the unconditional nature of the promises of preservation and made them subordinate to the warning passages.

Calvinist and Dispensational Views: Apostasy Is Not Possible

Three positions argue apostasy is not possible and the believer's eventual salvation is guaranteed. The first position is the implicit universalism of Karl Barth based on his

---

[25] Luther, "Lectures on Galatians, 1535, Chapters 1–4," in *Works*, 26:94.

[26] Marshall, *Kept by the Power of God*; and Dale Moody, *The Word of Truth: A Summary of Christian Doctrine Based on Biblical Revelation* (Grand Rapids: Eerdmans, 1981).

[27] Moody, 350.

[28] Moody, 356. Moody defended his position by claiming that it was also the position of A. T. Robertson, the famed New Testament scholar at Southern Seminary.

[29] Schreiner, "Perseverance and Assurance," 33.

view of election. The Grace Evangelical Society advocates the second view—the once saved, always saved position—as a major plank of their doctrinal platform. Wayne Grudem argued for a third view, the test-of-genuineness position, which argues that saving faith manifests itself by perseverance.

Implicit Universalism

In a famous discussion in his *Church Dogmatics*, Karl Barth demonstrated that the Reformers' formulation for assurance stands on an unstable platform. Beginning the search for certainty with the electing decree that is hidden in the secret will of God dooms the enterprise from the start. He argued that the Reformers erred when they attempted to develop a doctrine of assurance with a Christological beginning and an anthropological ending.[30]

Barth resolved the question of assurance by utilizing his idiosyncratic view of election. According to Barth, Jesus Christ is both the electing God and the elected Man. God relates to the elect only through Christ, but Christ is also the rejected Man of the reprobate. Therefore, God relates to all, both elect and rejected, through Christ, with the result that God rejects the rejectedness of the reprobate. Barth solved concerns about assurance by placing all humankind in Christ.[31]

Barth never conceded that his position implied universalism. J. I. Packer observed that this was "a conclusion that Barth himself seems to have avoided only by will power."[32] However, his approach seems to conclude that a reprobate is someone who is elect but does not yet know it.

Once Saved, Always Saved

The once-saved-always-saved position rejects the traditional Reformed doctrine of the perseverance of the saints in favor of the doctrine of eternal security. Proponents of the view include Zane Hodges, Charles Stanley, and Charles Ryrie.[33] Advocates of

---

[30] Karl Barth, *Church Dogmatics*, 13 vols., ed. G. W. Bromiley and T. F. Torrance, trans. G. W. Bromiley et al. (Edinburgh: T&T Clark, 1956–75), vol. II/2: *The Doctrine of God, Part 2*, 333–40.

[31] Barth, II/2, 344–54. Randall Zachman and G. Michael Thomas currently advocate Barth's position. See Zachman, *Assurance of Faith*, viii, 244–48; and Thomas, *Extent of the Atonement*, 252–53.

[32] J. I. Packer, "Good Pagans and God's Kingdom," *Christianity Today* 30.1 (January 17, 1986): 22–25.

[33] See Zane Hodges, *Absolutely Free!* (Grand Rapids: Zondervan, 1989); Charles Ryrie, *So Great Salvation: What It Means to Believe in Jesus Christ* (Wheaton, IL: Victor,

the once-saved-always-saved position, while not accepting Barth's view on election, agree with him that any attempt to arrive at assurance of salvation that involves looking at the believer's life for evidence or support will not succeed.

Assurance of salvation comes only by trusting the promises of the Word of God. The believer should manifest the fruits of salvation, but there is no guarantee that he will. At best, works provide a secondary, confirmatory function.[34]

Critics argue that this position has three weaknesses. First, it either ignores or explains away the real meaning of the warning passages directed to the saints. Second, it encourages laxity in Christian commitment. Third, it gives false comfort to those who walk in disobedience to the commands of Scripture and who in fact really may not be saved.[35]

The advocates of the once-saved-always-saved position argue that the Bible provides plenty of motivation for Christian service without threatening the believer with eternal damnation.[36] First, the believer is moved to service by a sense of gratitude for his salvation. Second, the believer who fails to follow the Lord faithfully experiences the chastening hand of God, even to the point of death, if necessary. Third, in addition to divine chastening in this life, the disobedient believer experiences the loss of rewards at the judgment seat of Christ. The carnal believer enjoys the preservation of God even if he does not persevere in the faith.[37]

Test of Genuineness

The test-of-genuineness position, traditionally understood as the doctrine of the perseverance of the saints, agrees with the once-saved-always-saved view that the believer's salvation is eternally secure. They also agree that good works are not necessary to procure salvation. However, unlike those who advocate the doctrine of eternal security, the advocates of the test-of-genuineness position contend that the fruits of salvation will always and eventually manifest themselves in the life of a believer.[38]

1989); and Charles Stanley, *Eternal Security: Can You Be Sure?* (Nashville: Thomas Nelson, 1990).

[34] See "Assurance," What We Believe, Grace Evangelical Society, accessed December 8, 2021, http://www.faithalone.org/beliefs/.

[35] Moody, *Word of Truth*, 361–65.

[36] See "Motivation," What We Believe, Grace Evangelical Society, accessed December 8, 2021, http://www.faithalone.org/beliefs/.

[37] Stanley, *Eternal Security*, 92–100.

[38] Demarest, *Cross and Salvation*, 439–44.

The test-of-genuineness proponents base their doctrine of perseverance on God's promises in Scripture that he will complete his work of salvation in the individual believer.[39] Even though a believer may fail miserably and sin terribly, he cannot remain in that condition. A Christian may fall totally, but his fall will not be final. The true believer will persevere.

The warning passages serve as litmus tests, according to the test-of-genuineness position.[40] Those who are not genuinely converted will eventually show their true colors. Therefore, the judgments threatened in those passages are not directed toward believers but are intended for false disciples, who for one reason or another are deliberately masquerading as real Christians.

Schreiner and Caneday agree with the advocates of the test-of-genuineness position that true believers will persevere, but they believe that the test-of-genuineness advocates have misinterpreted the warning passages in the New Testament. Schreiner and Caneday argued the warning passages are oriented toward the future, while the test-of-genuineness position turns the warnings into tests of past behavior.[41]

Mediating View: Apostasy Is Threatened, but Is Not Possible

Some scholars understand the warning passages to be admonishing believers about the danger of eternal judgment, while at the same time they hold the Scriptures teach that a believer cannot apostatize. Three positions attempt to reconcile these two seemingly contrary concepts. The first view, the irreconcilable tension position, argues that the two types of passages are irresolvable and that a compatibilist approach must be taken. Second, the means-of-salvation position argues that the warnings are how the believer is preserved. Third, William Lane Craig argued the means-of-salvation view is a middle-knowledge approach.

Irreconcilable Tension

Certain scholars have given up any attempt to reconcile the assurance passages with the warning passages and have ascribed the whole matter to mystery. In his book

---

[39] "Being confident of this very thing, that He who has begun a good work in you will complete it until the day of Jesus Christ" (Phil 1:6).

[40] See Wayne Grudem, "Perseverance of the Saints: A Case Study from the Warning Passages in Hebrews," in Schreiner and Ware, *Still Sovereign*, 133–82 (see chap. 4, n. 42).

[41] Schreiner and Caneday, *Race Set before Us*, 29–35.

Assurance and Warning, Gerald Borchert concluded the two types of passages are in irreconcilable tension and must be held in a "delicate balance."[42]

D. A. Carson took a similar tack when he argued for taking a compatibilist approach to the issue at hand. He defined compatibilism as

> the view that the following two statements are, despite superficial evidence to the contrary, mutually compatible: (1) God is absolutely sovereign, but his sovereignty does not in any way mitigate human responsibility; (2) human beings are responsible creatures (i.e., they choose, decide, obey, disobey, believe, rebel, and so forth), but their responsibility never serves to make God absolutely contingent.[43]

Since we do not know how God operates in time, how God operates through secondary agents, or how God is both sovereign and personal at the same time, then we are not going to know how the two types of passages interface. In the end, we are left with a theological antinomy. Carson concluded, "So we will, I think, always have some mystery."[44]

Neither Schreiner nor Hodges is impressed with Carson's appeal to compatibilistic mystery. Schreiner cautioned against appealing to mystery too quickly; otherwise, he contends we may be simply avoiding the hard labor and hard choices of doing theological work. He suspected that Borchert and Carson are using "tension" and "mystery" as code words for "contradiction."[45] Likewise, Hodges argued that an assurance based on a mystery is not much of an assurance at all. He said, "If 'assurance' were indeed a mystery, then it would be a deeply disquieting mystery to those who need assurance the most. Does Dr. Carson know beyond question that he himself is regenerate? If so, let him tell us *how* he knows. The compatibilist cannot have a mystery and a confident answer too!"[46]

Means of Salvation

In their book *The Race Set before Us,* Thomas Schreiner and Ardel Caneday presented a provocative position they label the means-of-salvation view. They agree with

---

[42] Gerald Borchert, *Assurance and Warning* (Nashville: Broadman, 1987), 194.

[43] Carson, "Reflections on Christian Assurance," 22.

[44] Carson, 26.

[45] Schreiner, "Perseverance and Assurance," 52.

[46] Zane Hodges, "The New Puritanism Part 1: Carson on Christian Assurance," March 1, 1993, http://www.faithalone.org/journal/1993i/Hodges.htm.

the advocates of the test-of-genuineness position that a believer cannot apostatize. However, they argued that the warning passages, such as those found in Hebrews, threaten believers with eternal damnation in hell if they fail to persevere. They rejected the way proponents of the once-saved-always-saved position interpret 1 Cor 9:27 to mean that Paul was concerned about losing his fitness for the ministry when he spoke of keeping his body in subjection so that he would not be cast away. Rather, they agreed with Dale Moody that Paul, despite all his service to Christ, was genuinely concerned he still might not go to heaven.[47]

They argued that obtaining eternal life requires great effort. Only by diligent perseverance can the believer obtain eventual justification on the final day. They stated:

> We have insisted throughout this book that the New Testament directs its admonitions and warnings to believers. We have also argued that these warnings do not merely threaten believers with losing rewards but that eternal life itself is at stake. Biblical writers frequently warn believers that if they turn away from Jesus Christ they will experience eternal judgment. If believers apostatize their destiny is the lake of fire, the second death, hell. These warnings cannot be waved aside and relegated to those who are not genuine Christians. They are directed to believers and must be heeded for us to be saved on the last day. We will win the prize of eternal life only if we run the race to the end. If we quit during the middle of the race, we will not receive eternal life.[48]

Curiously, Schreiner and Caneday argued that though the threats of damnation to the saints are real, the possibility of apostasy is not. This is because God uses the warnings as the means to cause the believer to endure. They explained, "[C]onditional warnings in themselves do not function to indicate anything about possible failure or fulfillment. Instead, the conditional warnings appeal to our minds to conceive or imagine the invariable consequences that come to all who pursue a course of apostasy from Christ."[49] In assessing the warnings, they make a distinction between that which is conceivable and that which is possible. They likened the warnings to road signs and concluded, "Road signs caution against conceivable consequences, not probable consequences."[50]

---

[47] Schreiner and Caneday, *The Race Set before Us,* 178–83.
[48] Schreiner and Caneday, 267.
[49] Schreiner and Caneday, 199.
[50] Schreiner and Caneday, 208.

The way Schreiner and Caneday saw it, rather than causing consternation in the elect, the threats of damnation produce encouragement and confidence: "The admonitions and warnings of the Scriptures threaten believers with eternal judgment for apostasy, but these warnings do not violate assurance and confidence regarding final salvation. . . . The warnings do not rob us of assurance. They are signposts along the marathon runner's pathway that help us maintain our confidence."[51]

Schreiner and Caneday argued that the advocates of the other positions have overlooked a primary interpretative principle to the New Testament, which is the "now—not yet" tension of an inaugurated eschatology.[52] With the resurrection of Christ, the end of the age has begun, so all the blessings of the kingdom of God and its salvation are an accomplished fact. However, our Lord has not returned, so the full enjoyment of our salvation is not yet accomplished. This sets up a tension in the world, the church, and in the hearts of individual believers that is expressed in the biblical record. Schreiner and Caneday argued that the once-saved-always-saved position is particularly guilty of an overrealized eschatology. They contended that those like Hodges and Stanley have emphasized the conversion event to the point of making salvation a past event. The means-of-salvation view teaches that saving faith is not a one-time event but rather a lifetime journey. All the components and aspects of salvation have a "now—not yet" orientation—even justification. They agreed that justification is primarily forensic, but they also argue that final justification is obtained by perseverance.[53]

The means-of-salvation position contends that the New Testament is always referring to the gift of salvation when it speaks of the believer's reward.[54] Passages that exhort the elect to pursue crowns of life, glory, and righteousness are making reference to salvation itself, not to any subsequent reward that the believer may earn in addition to salvation.

As an aid to understanding the basis of assurance, Schreiner and Caneday presented a three-legged stool.[55] They argued the first leg is the promises of God, the second leg is the evidence of a changed life, and the third leg is the inward witness of the Holy Spirit. They admitted the analogy is an imperfect one, since the promises

---

[51] Schreiner and Caneday, 269.
[52] Schreiner and Caneday, 46–86.
[53] Schreiner and Caneday, 77–79.
[54] Schreiner and Caneday, 89–95.
[55] Schreiner and Caneday, 276–305.

of God are primary for assurance, but they deny that there can be a discontinuity between the first leg and the other two.

Schreiner and Caneday presented a most intriguing proposal in the means-of-salvation view. They made a compelling argument that the New Testament utilizes the "now—not yet" motif in its discussion of soteriology. It seems the biblical witness, in fact, often does use the terminology of reward to describe the gift of eternal life.

However, serious questions remain. First, when they stated that the warnings are means by which the elect are enabled to persevere, just what did they mean? How real is the possibility of apostasy for the believer? In 1 Cor 9:27, when Paul spoke of his fear of being cast away, was he genuinely expressing concerns and doubts about his eternal destiny? If so, what kind of confidence is that? Their position seems to be unclear at this point.[56] Dale Moody scoffed at the means-of-salvation view as Arminianism that has lost its nerve. In his opinion it ultimately "reduces the warnings to bluffing."[57]

Second, Schreiner and Caneday nuanced the point that the warning passages caution against conceivable or imaginable consequences rather than possible or probable consequences. But are the consequences even conceivable? They affirmed that the believer experiences forensic justification, full adoption, and divine regeneration as present realities. How, then, is it conceivable that a believer so positioned in Christ is in any danger of damnation?[58] This objection does not arise merely from an over-

---

[56] Over the years Schreiner has changed his position concerning the purely forensic nature of justification. In his *Romans* commentary (Grand Rapids: Baker, 1998), Schreiner argued that justification was not only forensic, but also transformative. However, a few years later, in his *Paul, Apostle of God's Glory in Christ* (Grand Rapids: InterVarsity, 2001), he repudiated that position (192). He explained: "I have had a Romans-7-type experience with the theme of righteousness in Paul's theology. I argued in my law book that the term was forensic, then in my Romans commentary I changed my mind and maintained that it was both forensic and transformative. Now in my Pauline theology I have shifted back to the forensic view. Here is a good example of my fallibility as an interpreter! I cannot be right in all three books!" ("A New Pauline Theology," *Academic Alert* 10, no. 3 (Autumn, 2001): 2. *The Race Set before Us* was published between those two books and seems to have been written during Schreiner's transformative phase. Schreiner is to be commended for his willingness to publicly acknowledge this shift.

[57] Moody, *Word of Truth*, 361.

[58] In a response to an earlier edition of this chapter, Schreiner wrote, "Keathley also misunderstands what Caneday and I mean by 'conceivable.' It doesn't mean that we think damnation is possible for believers. It means that believers think about what would happen if they were to apostatize, and reflecting on the danger always keeps believers from apostasy. I would suggest that Keathley doesn't understand our position because he can't imagine threats being genuine without apostasy being truly possible." Schreiner, "Promises of Preservation and Exhortations

realized eschatology, as they contend. There is a "now" component to the "now—not yet" tension.

Third, what happens to those who do not persevere? Many who at one time professed faith in Christ later renounced their faith (the list includes everyone from Julian the Apostate to gospel recording artist Derek Webb, who now describes himself as a Reformed atheist). If their failure to persevere indicates an absence of salvation, then the warnings were not given to the elect after all, and the means-of-salvation position collapses into the standard test-of-genuineness view held by most Calvinist evangelicals.[59] If the failure to persevere results in a loss of salvation for the non-elect, then the means-of-salvation hypothesis really is Arminian after all, whether they admit it or not.

Fourth, as the first section of this chapter demonstrated, the Puritans employed an approach very similar to the means-of-salvation position and found it to be pastorally disastrous. Schreiner and Caneday acknowledged the experience of the Puritans but give little reason to believe the same problems would not reoccur if the means-of-salvation view were to become widespread again.[60] The subtitle to their book is *A Biblical Theology of Perseverance and Assurance*, but the work seems to be long on perseverance and short on assurance.

Fifth, at times it appears the means-of-salvation proposal comes dangerously close to a works-salvation position. Graciously enabled works are still works. Most evangelicals agree that true saving faith works, but it is still faith that is the means of salvation. But this is not Schreiner and Caneday's position. They stated, "Perseverance is a necessary means that God has appointed for attaining final salvation."[61] However, Calvin addressed this approach in his response to the Council of Trent. He stated:

---

to Perseverance," in *Whomever* He *Wills*, 196–97 (see intro., n. 22). Actually, I think I understand what they mean by "conceivable." The question is whether the New Testament authors understood themselves to be warning about consequences that were merely conceivable, but not possible. I believe their argument is incoherent. I would argue that the warning passages alert us to repercussions that are very possible. Making the cautionary passages only about apostasy (something we both agree is not possible) bleaches out the force of the warnings.

[59] This is, in fact, the position that Schreiner and Caneday take about those who lapse. See Schreiner and Caneday, *The Race Set before Us*, 243.

[60] Schreiner and Caneday, 277–78.

[61] Schreiner and Caneday, 152. In his response to an earlier edition of this chapter, Schreiner expressed agreement with my concern that perseverance defined in terms of good works and great effort dismantles the Reformation. He stated, "Now I know what he is worried about, and I share the same concern. . . . We must beware of overreading the necessity of works, as Keathley

Here there is no dispute between us as to the necessity of exhorting believers
to good works, and even stimulating them by holding forth a reward. What
then? First, I differ from them in this, that they make eternal life the reward;
for if God rewards works with eternal life, they will immediately make out
that faith itself is a reward which is paid, whereas Scripture uniformly proclaims that it is the inheritance which falls to us by no other right than that
of free adoption.[62]

Even though they are careful to insist that the works done by the believer are actually accomplished by the grace of God, their position is difficult to reconcile with the
Reformation principle of *sola fide*.

Middle Knowledge

Does the means-of-salvation view inadvertently abandon the traditional Reformed
understanding of divine sovereignty? William Lane Craig believes that it does. He
argued that the means-of-salvation position implicitly employs middle knowledge.[63]
Craig asked why, if the believer's will is so overwhelmed by God's grace, does God
give the warnings at all? And, if the warnings themselves bring about perseverance,
does this mean the believer is capable of apostasy, even if he does not apostatize?
Hypothetically, at least, the elect can fall away, but God, using middle knowledge,
has chosen to actualize a world in which scriptural warnings will operate as means
to keep his children from apostasy. This is a novel understanding of perseverance,

---

rightly cautions. Certainly works are not the basis of eternal life, but they are the necessary fruit
of faith." Schreiner, "Promises of Preservation," 197. Schreiner here helpfully described works as
"the necessary fruit of faith." If he would consistently express the nature of necessity in this way,
then we would have very little disagreement. However, he also said, "Many texts can be adduced
in the NT which teach that works are necessary for eternal life. Keathley worries that I may
teach salvation by works. . . . Further, Caneday and I make clear that works are not the *basis* of
salvation. . . . Caneday and I make it clear that works are not the *ground* of righteousness, but
we show in text after text that works are *necessary* for final salvation." Schreiner, 197. Actually,
Caneday and Schreiner have not made themselves very clear at all. They are using the word
"necessary" in an idiosyncratic way. In addition, when Schreiner said that works are necessary
for "final salvation," he slipped in a concept that he left undefined.

[62] John Calvin, "Antidote," 144–45.

[63] The middle knowledge position attempts to affirm a high view of divine sovereignty
while at the same time holding to a libertarian view of human free will. By way of middle
knowledge, i.e., knowledge of what free creatures would do in a certain situation, God ordains
scenarios that eventuate in free persons doing his will.

but it appears to be the view argued by those who hold to the means-of-salvation.[64] Craig stated:

> The classical defender of perseverance must, it seems, if he is to distinguish his view from Molinism, hold to the intrinsic efficacy of God's grace and, hence, the causal impossibility of the believer's apostasy. But in that case, the warnings of Scripture against the danger of apostasy seem to become otiose and unreal.[65]

Craig concluded that the means-of-salvation view is, in fact, a Molinist perspective and represents an abandonment of the classic Reformed doctrine of perseverance.

Schreiner and Caneday's response to Craig's article seems to indicate they miss the point to his argument. In an appendix to their book *The Race Set before Us*, they contended that Craig misunderstood the difference between his view of how God's grace works in the human will and the view of Reformed theology.[66] Since Craig assumed a "false disjunction" between God's grace that overwhelms the believer's will and the warnings themselves, he thought the efficacy of the warnings resides merely in themselves. Schreiner and Caneday claim Craig wrongly attributes his own view to the proponents of the means-of-salvation position, and "thus his whole argument against the Reformed view takes a trajectory that will miss its mark."[67]

However, Craig does fully realize the difference between the Reformed view and the Molinist view of God's use of means. That is exactly his point, which seems to be lost on Schreiner and Caneday. If God is using the warnings as the means to ensure perseverance, then either the saints would fall without the warnings (which is contrary to how Reformed theology understands God's grace working in the believer) or the saints would persevere even without the warnings (which would make the warnings superfluous). Either way, the means-of-salvation position is a departure from Reformed soteriology.

---

[64] William Lane Craig, "'Lest Anyone Should Fall': A Middle Knowledge Perspective on Perseverance and Apostolic Warnings," *International Journal for Philosophy of Religion* 29, no. 2 (1991): 65–74, https://www.jstor.org/stable/40036651.

[65] Craig, 72.

[66] Schreiner and Caneday, *The Race Set before Us*, 332–37.

[67] Schreiner and Caneday, 337.

A Modest Proposal: A Variation of the Test-of-Genuineness Position

The position offered over the next few pages is very close to the once-saved-always-saved view. However, it differs in that it simultaneously affirms both God's preservation of the redeemed and their persistent, persevering faith, so it is more accurately described as a variant of the test-of-genuineness view. This position has four points. First, the only basis for assurance is the objective work of Christ. Second, assurance is the essence of saving faith. Saving faith perseveres is the third point, and the fourth point is that there are rewards offered by God to the believer subsequent to salvation.

First, the only basis for assurance is the objective work of Christ. Any doctrine of assurance that includes introspection as a component will produce anxiety in the hearts of the very people it is intended to encourage. Barth was right when he pointed out that no system that has a Christological beginning and an anthropological ending can provide genuine and sustained assurance.

This is why Schreiner and Caneday's analogy of a three-legged stool for assurance fails. They admit the analogy is imperfect, because they view the leg of God's promises as preeminent over the other legs of sanctification and the inward testimony of the Spirit. Nevertheless, a stool with one leg that is longer, stronger, and sturdier than the others is an inherently unstable platform. To change metaphors, when it comes to providing assurance, the provision of Christ is the soloist and evidences are just members of the backup choir.

A close corollary to the premise that Christ is the only basis for assurance is the necessity to reaffirm the doctrine of *sola fide*. Perseverance cannot be understood in terms of good works and great effort without having the result of dismantling the Reformation. The doctrine of perseverance must be formulated so that it does not create the impression that the Scriptures contradict themselves about grace and works.[68]

Second, assurance is the essence of saving faith. The very nature of conversion and regeneration guarantees that certain knowledge of salvation is simultaneous with being saved. Subsequent doubts and fears may come, but a core conviction about one's relationship with God will remain.

Good works and the evidences of God's grace do not provide assurance. They provide warrant to assurance, but not assurance itself. Perhaps a good analogy is how a Christian knows the love of God. He experiences the love of God every day

---

[68] Romans 11:6 states, "And if by grace, then it is no longer of works; otherwise grace is no longer grace. But if it is of works, it is no longer grace; otherwise work is no longer work."

in a myriad of ways. However, all those countless blessings merely affirm what the Christian already knows—God loves him in Christ, according to the objective testimony of Scripture. Even during those times when the good favor of God seems to be circumstantially absent and that Christian's confidence is tested, he still knows that God loves him the same way he has always known this—by the promises of God. So it is with the assurance of salvation. Good works play the mere supporting role of confirmation.

Third, saving faith perseveres or remains until the day when it gives way to sight. Perseverance should be understood as a faith that cannot be annihilated and therefore persists. This persistent faith inevitably and eventually exhibits itself in the believer's life in a way that brings glory to God. The point of Hebrews 11 is that saving faith manifests itself by the journey of discipleship. One may stumble and falter but never leave the trail. Perseverance should be viewed more as a promise than a requirement.

I cannot agree with Schreiner and Caneday when they contend that the test-of-genuineness position makes the mistake of turning the forward-looking warning passages into retrospective tests. Rather, the warning passages that look forward (such as those found in the letter to the Hebrews) are pointing out the obvious: genuine belief will not turn back. Warnings about future behavior can be tests of genuineness without being retrospective.

Some passages teach that past behavior can be an indicator of genuineness. The genuinely saved person hungers and thirsts for righteousness, even when he is struggling with temptation or even if he stumbles into sin. In fact, I am not overly concerned with the destiny of those who struggle nearly as much as I am about those who do not care enough to struggle. Indifference is more of a red flag than weakness.

The absence of a desire for the things of God clearly indicates a serious spiritual problem, and a continued indifference can possibly mean that the person professing faith has never been genuinely converted. God is infinitely more dedicated to our salvation than we are, and he will not fail to finish that which he has begun. If a believer engages in willful disobedience or deliberate indifference, our heavenly Father promises him decisive and appropriate action. The indwelling of the Holy Spirit ensures that no peaceful backslider exists.

Fourth, there are rewards that are subsequent to salvation for the believer to win or lose. One of the great weaknesses of the Schreiner and Caneday proposal is the necessity to deny that there are any subsequent rewards available for the believer and that all promises of reward must be references to salvation itself. Their position is difficult to reconcile with many biblical passages. For example, 1 Cor 3:12–15 speaks of one Christian's work remaining while another Christian's work burns. The believer whose work remains receives a reward while the other believer suffers loss. Schreiner and Caneday admitted the passage teaches "some will be saved that have done shoddy work."[69] This admission undermines the major plank of their position—that persevering in good works is the necessary means by which our salvation is completed. A better understanding of the role of works in believers' lives is to hold that we will be judged and rewarded according to our service.

In the end, assurance comes from depending on Christ alone. I agree with Calvin's retort to the Catholic controversialist Albert Pighius, "If Pighius asks how I know I am elect, I answer that Christ is more than a thousand testimonies to me."[70]

---

[69] Schreiner and Caneday, *Race Set before Us*, 51.

[70] John Calvin, *Concerning the Eternal Predestination of God* (Louisville: Westminster John Knox, 1997), 130.

SECTION TWO

Historical Issues with Calvinism

Calvinism Is Augustinianism

—— Kenneth Wilson ——

Calvinism can boast of its extremely logical systematic theology, along with an impressive pedigree of adherents over the centuries who argue for its biblical foundation. However, does it have a firm foundation historically? Some Calvinists claim to have found Calvinistic theology in the early church fathers.[1] But for the last four centuries, scholarly Calvinists have freely admitted that Augustine was the first Christian to lay the foundations for a theology of divine determinism and its corresponding anthropology. Alister McGrath explained, "The pre-Augustinian

---

[1] See John Gill, *The Cause of God and Truth, in Four Parts* (1735–1738; London: Collinridge, 1855), 220–315; C. Matthew McMahon, *Augustine's Calvinism: The Doctrines of Grace in Augustine's Writings* (Coconut Creek, FL: Puritan Publications, 2012); James White, "Dividing Line" podcast, April 13, 2020 at https://www.aomin.org/aoblog/general-apologetics /story-time-with-uncle-jimmy/ (stamp 1.14.58–1.20.49) then rebutted by Kenneth Wilson on Leighton Flowers, "Soteriology 101" podcast, April 25, 2020 at https://youtu.be/LatpdNAnH4g (stamp 1:49.02–1:59.0).

theological tradition is practically of one voice in asserting the freedom of the human will."[2] In AD 412, Augustine disrupted that unified voice by denying free will. John Calvin was Augustine's ardent disciple.

John Calvin admitted his dependence on Augustine's novel theology. This fact heightens the gravity of performing this historical research, seeking to understand why Calvinists think as they do. When he read Scripture, Calvin's own interpretations followed Augustine's interpretations: "Augustine is so wholly within me, that if I wished to write a confession of my faith, I could do so with all fullness and satisfaction to myself out of his writings."[3] In his *Institutes of the Christian Religion*, Calvin quoted Augustine many more times than any other author, at least 373 times (by my count). These facts have compelled the Calvinist Matthew McMahon (whose ThD dissertation was *Augustine's Calvinism*) to write:

> The filtered systemization of the five points of Calvinism which have been brought to the modern churches as the doctrines of grace were originally systematized and widely written on, not by Calvin, but by Augustine. This is why one finds that every four pages written in the *Institutes of the Christian Religion* John Calvin quoted Augustine. Calvin, for this reason, would deem himself not a Calvinist, but an Augustinian. . . . [I]nstead of calling one who believes the doctrines of grace a Christian Calvinist, should they be more likely deemed an Augustinian-Calvinist?[4]

Likewise, Loraine Boettner admitted, "The Reformation was essentially a revival of Augustinianism."[5] Therefore, these Calvinist authors appropriately used terms like "Augustinian-Calvinism" and "Augustinianism" to designate modern Calvinism.[6]

---

[2] Alister McGrath, *Iustitia Dei: A History of the Christian Doctrine of Justification*, 3rd ed. (1998; repr., Cambridge: Cambridge University Press, 2005), 34. See also Loraine Boettner, *The Reformed Doctrine of Predestination* (Phillipsburg, NJ: P&R, 1932), chap. 28.1, 365; and Benjamin Warfield, *Studies in Tertullian and Augustine* (Oxford: OUP, 1930; repr., Westport, CT: Greenwood, 1970), 129.

[3] John Calvin, "A Treatise on the Eternal Predestination of God," in *Calvin's Calvinism*, trans. H. Cole (Grandville, MI: Reformed Free Publishing, 1987), 38.

[4] McMahon, *Augustine's Calvinism*, 7–9.

[5] Boettner, *Predestination*, chap. 28.2, 365.

[6] See also Paul Helm, "The Augustinian-Calvinist View," in *Divine Foreknowledge: Four Views*, ed. James K. Bielby and Paul R. Eddy (Downers Grove, IL: InterVarsity, 2001), 161–89; see Phillip Cary, *Inner Grace: Augustine in the Traditions of Plato and Paul* (Oxford: Oxford University Press, 2008), 122–24 for "Augustinianism."

Calvinism is Augustinianism. For this reason, we must understand how Augustine developed and in critical ways departed from traditional Christian doctrine, especially in his writings on divine determinism, human depravity, and the loss of free will.

Augustine of Hippo was brilliant in his writings on the Trinity and other doctrines. But he was also the only major figure in Christian history who could boast of being discipled within all three of the ancient world's most severely deterministic pagan systems—Stoicism, Neoplatonism, and Gnostic-Manichaeism. All prior Christian bishops and authors had rejected this pagan determinism:

> Throughout the early centuries of the church, theology was marked by an emphasis upon the compatibility of divine foreknowledge and human freedom largely to combat Stoic determinism and astrological fatalism. . . . God's control over the future is determined by a foreknowledge of human choices. Divine election is in part a function of this foreknowledge. The manner in which God will determine and govern a human life is fixed by an awareness of the ways in which freedom will be exercised.[7]

Although rejecting divine determinism in his early writings, Augustine, in his later years, reverted to his prior pagan ideas and thereby contradicted all previous Christian authors, himself included. Therefore, we must examine the historical foundation of Calvinism laid by Augustine of Hippo in AD 412.[8] After spending decades being trained in pagan philosophies and religions, Augustine became a Christian: he championed human free will against Manichaean determinism. Nevertheless, in the final eighteen years of his life, Augustine's Stoic view of micromanaging sovereignty caused him to revert to teaching the pagan determinism of his early training. The story of his conversion then reversion is fascinating. Moreover, it is critical for us to understand the profound impact his reversion to his early pagan concepts would have on later Christian thought.

Augustine Was Trained in Pagan Providence

Augustine of Hippo (AD 354–430) is the most famous theologian in Western Christianity. Before his Christian baptism in AD 386 at the age of about thirty-two

---

[7] David Fergusson, s.v. "Predestination," in *The Oxford Companion to Christian Thought*, ed. Adrian Hastings, Alistair Mason, and Hugh S. Pyper (Oxford: Oxford University Press, 2000).

[8] The traditional date in scholarly works has been AD 396 when writing *Ad Simplicianum*, but that has been disproven, as will be subsequently explained.

years, Augustine studied philosophy and taught rhetoric. He was trained in Stoicism's meticulous providence and also spent ten years as a Gnostic-Manichaean, believing in a micromanaging and specific providence. *On Providence* was his first published book (AD 386). His God controlled every minuscule event in the universe, including the precise muscle movements in rooster's necks as they fight and the falling of a leaf from a tree to its exact resting place on the ground (*Ord.*1.12–25). Augustine was also heavily influenced by the rigid determinism of Plotinus and Porphyry (Neoplatonism), as well as by Cicero.[9]

He retained this pagan view of meticulous providence even after becoming a Christian, confessing that he never doubted this micromanaging view (*Conf.* 6.5, 7; cf. *Ord.*2.12). Augustine taught it is impossible for a person to be killed unjustly, even if "wrongly" sentenced by an unjust judge. Why? Because he must have deserved to die since micromanaging providence and God's justice are perfect—things could not be better than they are (*Quant.*73).[10] His God experiences absolutely nothing against his desires, and they are absolute: all God's desires will be fulfilled (*Gen. Man.*2.29).[11] Augustine taught, "Whatever occurs by chance occurs accidentally; whatever occurs accidentally does not occur by providence. If, then, some things occur by chance in the world, the universe is not governed by providence" (*Div. quaest.*24). "There is nothing in the universe that is disordered and nothing that is unjust" (*Div. quaest.*27).

This particular view of Stoic providence continues after AD 411. "Let us therefore have no hesitation in believing that what seems to be messy and disordered in human affairs is governed, not by no plan at all, but by an altogether loftier one, and by a more all-embracing divine order" (*Serm.*D29.7, AD 412). "So nothing happens unless the Almighty wills it, either by allowing it to happen or by doing it himself" (*Enchir.*24, 95; AD 422). This sentence suggests Augustine may have intuitively realized that

---

[9] Gerard O'Daly, *Platonism Pagan and Christian: Studies in Plotinus and Augustine*, Variorum Collected Studies Series 719 (Farnham, UK: Ashgate, 2001); and Augustine Curley, "Cicero, Marcus Tullius," in *Augustine Through the Ages: An Encyclopedia*, ed. Allan D. Fitzgerald (Grand Rapids: Eerdmans, 1999), 190–93. Neoplatonism's determinism is nuanced since fatalism (astrological fatalism) is denied.

[10] English translations are from *The Works of Saint Augustine: A Translation for the 21st Century*, ed. and trans. Edmund Hill (Hyde Park, NY: New City Press, 1992–2009). A complete list of Augustine's works comparing English and Latin titles may be found in the New City Press Catalog 2021, 16–19, https://www.newcitypress.com/media/downloads/The_Works_of_Saint_Augustine_Catalog.pdf.

[11] Robert O'Connell, "The *De Genesi contra Manichaeos* and the Origin of the Soul," *Revue des Études Augustiniennes* 39, no. 1 (1993): 129–41.

his Stoic providence and Christian views were not compatible. He required at least some provision for God's "allowing it to happen" (permissive will). The fact that all prior Christians taught God's general sovereignty while rejecting Stoic, Gnostic, and Manichaean meticulous providence did not dissuade him.[12] Augustine never refuted the rigid pagan determinism of his Stoic and Neoplatonic philosophies. Assimilating Neoplatonism's tactic, Augustine restricted "fatalism" to mean a meticulous control by the stars (astrology). This way, God can foreordain and micromanage the universe without the accusation of fatalism.[13]

Augustine Also Taught Christian Free Will (AD 396–411)

For twenty-five years Augustine embraced the nearly unanimous consensus, Christian view that all humans retained freedom of choice to accept or reject God's offer of salvation (free choice/free will). For fifteen years as Bishop of Hippo, he wrote and preached against the pagan views of *Divine Unilateral Predetermination of Eternal Destinies* (DUPED, unconditional election). The Manichaeans taught unconditional election. God unilaterally chose and infused grace and faith into the elect (the "pneumatics" or spiritual ones), while the damned (the "hylics" or earthy ones) had total inability to respond to God's offer of salvation.[14] In contrast, Augustine's Christian God did not decide who would go to heaven or hell based upon his own desire or will (monergism). The Christian God was relational.

The Christian relational God interacted with humans, with God deciding eternal destinies through foreknowledge of every person's own choice (conditional election). Augustine had been indoctrinated for ten years as a hearer within the monergistic Manichaean sect, but after leaving the sect he championed the traditional Christian view of a relational God and human free choice against this Manichaean fatalism.

---

[12] Kenneth Wilson, *Augustine's Conversion from Traditional Free Choice to "Non-Free Free Will": A Comprehensive Methodology* (Tübingen: Mohr Siebeck, 2018), 41–94.

[13] Eugene TeSelle, *Augustine the Theologian* (New York: Herder and Herder, 1970; repr., Eugene, OR: Wipf and Stock, 2002), 313.

[14] Gedaliahu Stroumsa, "Titus of Bostra and Alexander of Lycopolis: A Christian and a Platonic Refutation of Manichaean Dualism," in *Neoplatonism and Gnosticism*, ed. Richard T. Wallis (New York: SUNY Press, 1992), 337–49; Geo Widengren, *Der Manichäismus* (Darmstadt: Wissenschaftliche Buchgesellschaft, 1977), 63–65. See *Cologne Mani-Codex*, M.7.82–118, Mir. M. III, p. 27.

So Augustine held in tension his contradictory concepts of pagan providence and Christian free will.

Augustine's Traditional Early Theology (AD 396–411)

Calvinists are not anxious to explore or admit to Augustine's early theology of twenty-five years when he taught this traditional free choice defense (based upon God's foreknowledge of human choices and actions). Augustine rejected Manichaean total inability. Adam's sin passed to his progeny physical death, moral weakness, and a sinful propensity. There was no sign of Manichaean inherited guilt that damns persons to hell from total inability (*Ver. rel.*25, 29, 68; *Gen. Man.*2.19, 21). When writing his commentary on Romans, Augustine did not consider Rom 5:12 worthy of mention. Instead, he wrote, "For by his free will man has a means to believe in the Liberator and to receive grace"; and, "Through foreknowledge God chooses believers and damns unbelievers" (*Exp. prop. Rm.*44.3, 62.15). "For this reason both punishment and reward would be *unjust*, if man *did not* have free will" (*Lib. arb.*2.3; emphasis added). Augustine the Christian sidelined his prior Neoplatonic and Manichaean view of total inability and absence of free will.

Even as descendants of Adam who inherit his sinful nature, humans could still respond to God's invitation that called everyone equally to salvation. Why? Because all persons remain capable of a positive response to God's grace for salvation (*Gen. Man.*1.17; *Util. cred.*79; *Ver. rel.*65). All persons also retain the ability to change their own "wills," which Augustine proved by citing Matt 12:33 (*Adim.*26.1). The "evil will" is not a hindrance to receiving God's truth. It is merely a pollution that can be removed (*S. Dom. m.*2.69). Augustine taught unconditional election: God in his universal love has given every human freedom of will with the capacity to respond to him and the right to become God's child (*Vera relig.* 27, 65).[15]

Augustine rebutted the Manichaean interpretations of Eph 2:3 and 2:8–10. The Manichaean interpretation was a divine, deterministic, unilateral bestowal of grace to a spiritually dead human (incapable of a positive response). He argued the Ephesians 2 verses "clearly reveal free choice" (*Fort.*16–17). Rejecting the Manichaean doctrine of alienation from God by natural birth, Augustine viewed this "nature of wrath" (Eph 2:3–4) as what we form within ourselves by our walk/actions. Our behavior, not our birth, creates our corrupted natures (*Fort.*21). This freedom to form our choices

---

[15] This is incorrectly cited as *Util. cred.* 27 in my Oxford thesis and *Augustine's Conversion*.

and behaviors applies to every human currently, not merely Adam (*Fort.*22; cf. *Fid.*10; *Immort. an.*17). So, all individuals determine their own fates by their own behaviors (*Ver. rel.*10, 31).

Augustine accused Felix and Manichaeism of abusing the phrase "free will" by rendering it meaningless since those who are *not willing were incapable* of willing good. Augustine accused Manichaeans of cleverly disguising this lack of free will. The Manichaeans denied that their fatalistic teaching amounted to overt "compulsion" by their shockingly cruel God (*Fel.*2.5; *Faust.*22.22).

Augustine was adhering to the unanimous traditional doctrine of Christian free will by refuting pagan unilateral determinism in salvation. But his Christian view of free will indirectly contradicted his own Stoic meticulous providence. His meticulous providence defined omnipotence as God ordaining and receiving everything he desires. Augustine proclaimed, "He does whatever He wills: that itself is omnipotence" [by definition] (*Symb.cat.*2). Yet Augustine preached that the answer to Gnostic/Manichaean unilateral assignment to heaven or hell was the Christian God's relational foreknowledge of human freewill choices, following the lead of all prior early Christian authors.[16]

For example, Irenaeus (ca. AD 180) had argued that the Manichaean god was puny because he could only achieve his goals by micromanaging all events and persons. In contrast, the Christian God allowed humanity freedom, yet was so powerful he could still accomplish his plans. It requires a more omnipotent and sovereign God to allow human freedom. "The essential principle in the concept of freedom appears first in Christ's status as the sovereign Lord, because for Irenaeus man's freedom is, strangely enough, a direct expression of God's omnipotence, so direct in fact, that a diminution of man's freedom automatically involves a corresponding diminution of God's omnipotence."[17] Christians wholeheartedly and consistently opposed pagan divine sovereignty that eliminated human free choice for salvation. For decades, Augustine taught this traditional Christian free will that refuted Manichaean monergistic determinism in salvation.

---

[16] See Augustine's *S. Dom. m.*1.72 and *Adim.*17; and earlier authors' writings such as *1 Apol.*43–44 and 61.9–10, *Dial.*103, 140.4, 141.2; *Adv. haer.*1.1.14, 1.18, 2.29.1, 3.12.2–11, 4.4.3, 4.29.2, 4.37.2–5, 5.28.1; *Strom.*1.1, 4.24, 5.14, 6.7.4, 6.16, 7.7 and *Quis dives Salvetur* 21.1–2.

[17] Gustaf Wingren, *Människan och Inkarnationem enligt Irenaeus* (Lund: C.W.K. Gleerup, 1947); *Man and the Incarnation: A Study in the Biblical Theology of Irenaeus*, trans. R. Mackenzie (London: Oliver and Boyd, 1959), 36–37.

Augustine held in tenuous tension his two contradictory views—his pagan view of a meticulous Stoic providence and his Christian view of free will (within God's general sovereignty).[18] The universal Christian response to pagan meticulous and heretical monergistic sovereignty was summarized by the famous early church scholar, Henry Chadwick: "For in rejecting the Gnostic way the Christians thereby rejected as inauthentic adulteration and corruption any theology of pure revelation teaching salvation by an arbitrary predestination of the elect and the total depravity of the lost, and possessing no criteria of rational judgment."[19] This was Chadwick's point: Gnostic and Manichaean unilateral determinism was heresy. But they were using Christian Scriptures to prove their theology.

Gnostics and Manichaeans Abused Christian Scriptures to Prove Determinism

Gnostics and Manichaeans usurped Christian Scriptures to argue for their deterministic theologies. They were able to interpret certain passages through their own deterministic lenses and discover their own doctrines (eisegesis). Irenaeus (ca. AD 180) warned Christians about these heretical misuses of Scripture by Gnostics in his major book *Against All Heresies*.

Gnostics/Manichaeans had cited Rom 9:18–31 to prove DUPED with humans having no choice (Augustine, *Gen. litt.*11.10–12 and Origen, *P. Arch.*3.1.21). Gnostics taught that divine foreknowledge proved pagan absolute determinism (Origen, *Cels.*2.20; *Philoc.*23.7). They used Phil 2:13 to teach God gifted the "good will" only to the unilaterally chosen elect, resulting in salvation (*P. Arch.*3.1.20). The Valentinian Gnostics taught divine determinism without human free choice by using Romans 11 in a Stoic interpretation of sovereignty (Clement, *Exc. Theod.*56.3–27).[20]

The Manichaeans appealed to John 6:44–45 and 14:6. "No one can come to me unless the Father who sent me draws him" (6:44) proved DUPED devoid of human

---

[18] Kenneth Wilson, "Early Christians Unanimously Opposed Augustine of Hippo's Divine Providence," Oxford 18th International Conference on Patristic Studies, 2019; *Studia Patristica* (Leuven: Peeters, 2021), forthcoming.

[19] Henry Chadwick, *Early Christian Thought and the Classical Tradition* (Oxford: Clarendon, 1966), 9.

[20] Jeffrey Bingham, "Irenaeus Reads Romans 8: Resurrection and Renovation," in *Early Patristic Readings of Romans*, Romans Through History and Culture Series, ed. Kathy L. Gaca and L. L. Welborn (London: T&T Clark, 2005), 114–32.

choice/will (*C. litt. Petil.*2.185–186; *Fort.*3; *Fort.*16–22). Manichaeans used Psalm 51:5 to prove all humans were damned at birth due to Adam's sin (that Augustine refuted in *C. litt. Petil.*2.232). The 1 John 2:2 text had been used to argue Christ died only for the elect (Origen, *Comm. Ev. Jo.*6.59; *Comm. Rom.*3.8.13). Fortunatus the Manichaean cited Eph 2:3, 8–10 to support meticulous providence. Since spiritually dead persons cannot respond positively, God must unilaterally choose only the elect in rigid determinism by infusing faith (*Fort.*14–21). Augustine, however, following the lead of all prior Christian authors, refuted the fatalistic determinism of Fortunatus and these Manichaean abuses of Scripture for twenty-five years. But, as we will now discover, he later reverted to his prior Manichaean deterministic interpretations.

Augustine's Transition Did Not Occur in AD 396 from Reading Scripture

Scholars have long claimed Augustine's move toward his later determinism and "non-free free will" theology began with his letter to Bishop Simplicianus of Milan about AD 396. Allegedly, after reading Galatians, Romans, and Corinthians, Augustine used these Scriptures to modify traditional Christian doctrine.[21] The problem with this simplistic theory is that it claims Augustine introduced a dozen novel doctrines in the course of writing one short letter; then, he developed total amnesia on his new doctrines for the next fifteen years.[22] In fact, for another fifteen years after writing this letter he continued to defend election based upon God's foreknowledge and the traditional view of original sin as physical death, moral weakness, and a propensity to sin (without guilt). After 1,600 years, no cogent explanations have been forthcoming to explain this disturbing contradiction.

---

[21] James Wetzel, "Simplicianum, Ad," in *Augustine through the Ages*, 798–99; Peter Brown, *Augustine of Hippo: A Biography* (London: Faber and Faber, 1967; rev. Berkeley, CA: University of California Press, 2000), 147–48; Ernest Evans, *Tertullian's Homily on Baptism* (London: SPCK, 1964), 101; Paul Rigby, "Original Sin," in *Augustine through the Ages*, 607–14; Carol Harrison, *Rethinking Augustine's Early Theology: An Argument for Continuity* (Oxford: Oxford University Press, 2006).

[22] Patout Burns, "From Persuasion to Predestination: Augustine on Freedom in Rational Creatures," in *In Dominico Eloquio—In Lordly Eloquence: Essays on Patristic Exegesis in Honour of Robert Louis Wilken*, ed. Paul M. Blowers, Angela R. Christman, David G. Hunter, and Robin D. Young (Grand Rapids: Eerdmans, 2002), 294–316; Kenneth Wilson, *The Foundation of Augustinian-Calvinism* (Montgomery, TX: Regula Fidei Press, 2019), 33–49.

Compelling evidence now demonstrates that in AD 412, Augustine revised his second part of *Ad Simplicianum* (2.5–22), as well as *Lib. arb.*3.47–54, bringing his earlier letter and work in line with his later theology.[23] The gradual development of his later theology can be definitively traced when his entire massive corpus is read chronologically without presuppositions.[24] Augustine's novel theology (novel for Christianity) began appearing simultaneously in his works, sermons, and letters in AD 412.[25] Augustine's conversion from his traditional Christian "free choice" (conditional election) to his Stoic "non-free free will" determinism (unconditional election) did not occur as previously accepted in AD 396. It occurred in AD 412 during his polemic against the Pelagians.

Why Did Augustine Revert to Pagan Salvific Determinism in AD 412?

The major influence on Augustine's AD 412 reversion to his prior deterministic Manichaean interpretations of Scripture was the arrival of Pelagius and Caelestius near his North African home in late AD 411. Augustine previously admitted (AD 405) he did not know why infant baptism was practiced (*Quant.*80). But the conflict with Caelestius and Pelagius forced him to rethink the church's infant baptismal tradition and precipitated his reversion to his pagan DUPED.[26] Caelestius had argued that infants did not receive baptism for salvation from sin but only for inheritance of the kingdom. Augustine's polemical response to Caelestius in AD 412 was logical: (1) Infants are baptized by church tradition; (2) water baptism is for forgiveness of sin and reception of the Holy Spirit; (3) some dying infants are rushed by their Christian parents to the bishop for baptism but die before baptism occurs, while other infants born of prostitutes are found abandoned on the streets by a church virgin who rushes them to the baptismal font where the bishop baptizes them; (4) these infants have no "will" and no control over whether or not they are baptized to receive the Holy Spirit to become Christians. Therefore, God must unilaterally and unconditionally predetermine which infants are saved by baptism and which are

[23] Wilson, *Augustine's Conversion*, 134–64. Augustine revised many works, including *Mus.*6, *Doctr. chr.*3.36–4.46, *Pecc. merit.*3, *Gen. litt.*1.3b–12.37, and *Trin.*13–15.

[24] This methodology was used for my Oxford doctoral thesis, *Augustine's Conversion*.

[25] Wilson, *Augustine's Conversion*, 215–40.

[26] Wilson, 285. See also Chadwick, *Early Christian Thought*, 110–11.

eternally damned without baptism (unconditional election).[27] God's election must be unconditional since infants have no personal sin, no merit, no good works, no functioning free will (incognizant due to the inability to understand at their age), and therefore, no choice.

In his next work that same year, Augustine concluded if this is true for infants, then unbaptized adults also have no choice or free will (*Sp. et litt.*54–56). The Holy Spirit was received in water baptism, transforming the person into a Christian with a free will. Since humans have no free will before baptism, God must unilaterally choose who will be saved and infuse faith into those persons. Augustine taught even when "ministers prepared for giving baptism to the infants, it still is not given, because God does not choose [those infants for salvation]" (*persev.*31). Infant baptism became the impetus for Augustine's novel theology when he reinterpreted that church tradition and reached a logical conclusion. By doing this he abandoned over three hundred years of church teaching on free will. According to the famous scholar Jaroslav Pelikan, Augustine departed from traditional Christian theology by incorporating his prior pagan teachings and thereby developed inconsistencies in his new anthropology and theology of grace, especially his "idiosyncratic theory of predestination."[28]

Augustine Reverted to His Prior Pagan Philosophies in AD 412

The controversy over infant baptismal regeneration propelled Augustine to revert to his pagan training. Augustine's reading of the Neoplatonism of Plotinus (*Enneads*) and Porphyry provided vital concepts he would incorporate from philosophy into his new theology.[29] Evil produced an incapacitating fall with a total loss of the image of God in humans (*Enn.*1.1.12; 1.8.5; 4.3.12). In Neoplatonism, all humans were created as pure spirits (no physical body). Their voluntary choice to become physical resulted in the loss of free will.

By this choice humanity lost the "good will" and became inextricably chained in universal wickedness from an "evil will" (*Enn.*3.2.10; cf. Stoicism). This required

---

[27] Augustine, *Pecc.mer.*1.29–30. In contrast, ca. AD 200, Tertullian had rejected infant baptism, stating one should wait until personal faith was possible (*De bapt.*18).

[28] Jaroslav Pelikan, *The Christian Tradition: A History of the Development of Doctrine*, vol. 1, *The Emergence of the Catholic Tradition* (100–600) (Chicago: University of Chicago Press, 1975), 278–327, quotation at 325.

[29] O'Daly, *Platonism Pagan and Christian*, 719.

the Spirit to implant the desired love and restore the "good will" by divine infusion (*Enn.*3.5.4; 1.7.9; 3.2.9.1; 2.3.1.1; 3.3.19–21; 4.8.5.1–4). Although human souls do not possess genuine free will, (somehow) neither do they act by compulsion (*Enn.*4.3.13).[30] The Neoplatonic "Reason-Principle" (god) purposefully created only a few individuals to whom he would gift a "good will" but created many more evil individuals who would remain devoid of personal choice. These evil persons were created as predestined to damnation. Nevertheless, those created for damnation remain inexcusably culpable and guilty, because the universe is just and good when each person accepts his or her god-imposed role, including those eternally tortured screaming in pain (*Enn.*3.2.17). Because "The One" (god) can only do good, he is exonerated by doctrinal definition from committing any injustice. These pagan philosophical teachings were the warp and woof of Augustine's earlier studies, and these buttressed his theological answers to the Pelagian challenge.

Augustine utilized all these Neoplatonic doctrines after AD 411: (1) humanity's fall resulted in total inability to respond with loss of free will (leaving only an evil will); (2) individuals were created for the purpose of damnation unto God's glory; (3) individuals were culpable despite the lack of any choice to do good or respond positively; and (4) God was just, despite deliberately creating persons for eternal torture. After AD 412 Augustine regurgitated these pagan doctrines. "This absolutely obvious truth by which we see that so many are not saved because God does not will this, though human beings do" (*Ep.*217.19). God purposefully created persons to damn them eternally (*Nupt. et conc.*2.31–32). We possess no writings from any prior Christian author who held such pagan views.

Similarly, in AD 412, Manichaean Divine Unilateral Predetermination of Eternal Destinies (DUPED) invaded Christianity through Augustine. Foreknowledge now resulted from God unilaterally predetermining the elect (in other words, divine foreordination preceded divine foreknowledge). This was a Gnostic requirement. "Present a command to us to see Thee, so that we may be saved. Knowledge of Thee, it is the salvation of us all! Present a command! When Thou dost command, we have been saved" (*The Three Steles of Seth*, 125). Augustine wrote a similar line: "Give what you command, and command what you will" (*Conf.*10.40).

---

[30] This equivocation was also practiced by the ardently deterministic Stoics, since a total absence of free will was untenable to many among the ancient populace.

Thus, Augustine abandoned the unanimous consensus of the earlier Christian view and reverted to his Gnostic-Manichaean deterministic interpretations of Christian Scripture in AD 412. This can be best visualized by examining the following chart that compares the different interpretations of key Scripture passages by early Christians, Gnostic-Manichaeans, and Augustinian-Calvinists.

Scripture	Early Christian	Gnostic-Manichaean	Augustinian-Calvinist
Rom 5:12	physical death	spiritual death	spiritual death
Rom 9–11	temporal benefits	election to salvation	election to salvation
Eph 2:3	self-formed nature	created nature by birth	fallen nature from Adam
Eph 2:8–9	salvation is the gift	faith is the gift	faith is part of the gift
John 6:44	God's Word draws all persons equally	only the elect are drawn	only the elect are drawn effectually
John 6:65	granted to all who believe	DUPED	DUPED
John 14:6	Christ is an open door for all persons	closed door DUPED	closed door DUPED
Phil 2:13	favor/good pleasure*	God gives the "good willer"	God gives the "good willer"
Ps 51:5	hyperbole for sinner	physical birth damns	Adam's guilt damns at physical birth

*Greek *eudokias*; the five other texts (Ps 5:13, 68:14, 144:16; Sir 15:15; Luke 2:14) containing *eudokia* refer to favor, acceptance, or good pleasure; "good willer" is my pejorative term for the pagan concept of a formal faculty that can "will good" (Stoic/Neoplatonic/Manichaean). It must be gifted by god/the One to overcome the "evil will" in spiritually dead persons incapable of a positive response to god/the One's offer of salvation. The same passages the Gnostics and Manichaeans had interpreted as deterministic are now used by modern Calvinists to prove total depravity and unconditional election (the essential elements of Divine Unilateral Predetermination of Eternal Destinies, DUPED).

Gnostics and Manichaeans had used these same Christian Scriptures (listed above) for centuries to promote their unilateral determinism. Before Augustine, orthodox Christians had refuted heretical Gnostic and Manichaean DUPED and "interpreted *proorizō* [election] as depending upon *proginoskō* (foreknow)—those whom God foreknew would believe he decided upon beforehand to save. Their chief concern was to combat the concept of fatalism and affirm that humans are free to do what is righteous."[31]

Augustine's move toward DUPED was recognized by his peers, so he was accused of reverting to his prior Manichaean theology.[32] But as a splendid rhetorician, Augustine defended himself brilliantly by creating a subtle distinction. He modified Gnostic/Manichaean "*created* human corrupt nature" (producing damnation) into a Christianized "*fallen* human corrupt nature" in Adam with inherited guilt (producing damnation; *Nupt. et conc.*2.16). Augustine's novel nuanced "fallen" nature borrowed a key Gnostic/Manichaean and Neoplatonic doctrine: humans have total inability to respond to God until divinely awakened from spiritual death.

Furthermore, to avoid violating centuries of unanimous Christian teaching, Augustine had to redefine the Christian meaning of free will. He concluded God must micromanage and manipulate the circumstances that guarantee a person would "freely" respond to the invitation of God's calling to eternal life.[33] This should be compared to placing a mouse in a maze, then opening and closing doors so the mouse could "freely" reach the cheese. (In Christian theology that emphasized free will, all doors remained open for the maze traveler to choose his or her own path.) Augustine's redefined free will was Stoic "non-free free will." A millennium later, Calvinists would label this divine manipulation of the human free will by the term *irresistible grace* (God forcing a person to "love" him).

---

[31] Carl Thomas McIntire, "Free Will and Predestination: Christian Concepts," in *The Encyclopedia of Religion*, 15 vols., ed. Lindsay Jones, 2nd ed. (Farmington Hills, MI: Macmillan Reference USA, 2005), 5:3206–9.

[32] *C. Jul. imp.*1.52. His ordination as a bishop was blocked and almost prevented due to his prior Manichaeism. See Jason D. BeDuhn, "Augustine Accused: Megalius, Manichaeism, and the Inception of the *Confessions*," *Journal of Early Christian Studies* 17, no. 1 (2009): 85–124; and Henry Chadwick, "Self-Justification in Augustine's Confessions," *English Historical Review* 178 (2003): 1168. As in the chart above, see Augustine's Manichaean interpretations of Romans 9–11 (*Pecc. merit.*29–31, *Spir. et litt.*50, 60, 66; *Nupt.*2.31–32, *C. du ep. Pelag.*2.15, *Enchir.*98, *C. Jul.* 3.37,4.15, *Corrept.* 28); Eph 2:8–10 (*Spir. et litt.*56, *C. du ep. Pelag.*, *Enchir.*31, *Praed.*12); John 14:6 and 6:44, 65 (*C. du ep. Pelag.*1.7, *Grat.*3–4,10); and Phil 2:13 (*Spir. et litt.*42, *Grat. Chr.*1.6, *C. Jul.*3.37, 4.15, *Grat.*32, 38).

[33] Burns, "From Persuasion to Predestination," 307.

Augustine's Three Stages of Grace

Three stages comprised Augustine's understanding of God's grace. In stage one (AD 386–395), he espoused that humans could merit salvation by their choices and actions as they improved themselves.[34] In stage two (starting AD 395–96), Augustine learned about grace from Jerome and Victorinus with their understandings of Eph 2:8–10 and from the writings of Tichonius on human free will. This resulted in Augustine's new emphasis on God providing power and assistance because good works cannot earn justification (*Exp. quaest. Rom.*20).[35] He now taught that God gives grace to persons without merit who humble themselves and request it (*ex. Gal.*15, 24, 54). Augustine quotes 1 Tim 2:4, affirming God "desires all men to be saved" (NASB1995), where "all men" means every individual since all are capable of becoming God's children (*ex. Gal.*26.4, 30.3). However, people can resist God's grace (*ex. Gal.*63). Guilt must be personal with no hereditary guilt from Adam (*Exp. quaest. Rom.*45–46, 49; *Exp. Rom. inch.*8, 10). God's foreknowledge is not causal as a result of foreordination but is relational by incorporating human free choices into his plan (*Lib. arb.*3.6–8). In stage three (AD 412–430), Augustine reverted to his pre-Christian Manichaean view of radical grace. Grace is divinely forced upon persons, thereby determining human wills and eternal destinies. He reverted to his Manichaean view of universal spiritual death due to physical birth "in Adam," nuanced as inherited guilt. Philip Lee concluded Augustine's new Christianized view of original sin mimicked the Gnostic [and Manichaean] view of inherited eternal damnation from Adam at physical birth.[36] As in Gnostic-Manichaeism, God now had to infuse grace and faith into the dead sinner for that person to believe.

Near the end of his life, Augustine ridiculed his fellow monks at Marseilles for not understanding that God-given perfect faith will persevere (*Ep.*225). This resulted from Augustine's deterministic eisegesis of Phil 1:6. He altered the "good work" into perseverance unto salvation (not in the context) instead of the Philippians' financial

---

[34] Wilson, *Augustine's Conversion*, 96–101.

[35] Jerome, *Comm. Eph.*1.2.8–9; Victorinus, *Ep. P. Eph.*1–2.9; Henry Chadwick, "Tyconius and Augustine," in *A Conflict of Christian Hermeneutics in Roman Africa: Tyconius and Augustine*, ed. Charles Kannengiesser and Pamela Bright (Berkeley: Center for Hermeneutical Studies, 1989), 49–55.

[36] Philip J. Lee, *Against the Protestant Gnostics* (Oxford: Oxford University Press, 1987), 50–52.

gift to Paul (cf. Phil 1:6–7 with 4:10–19).[37] He argued his case for his deterministic theology by using the exact same scriptural interpretations he had learned as a Manichaean (*Grat.*10, 17, 32–33, 44–45; *Nupt. et conc.*2.31–32; *Serm.*26, 30.10, 131.1, 3, 6; *Ep.*225) and that he had refuted as heresy after becoming a Christian bishop.[38]

Augustine's Final Theology (AD 412–430)

Augustine's final theology closely resembled a modern Calvinist's acronym of TULIP—representing Total inability, Unconditional election, Limited atonement, Irresistible grace, and Perseverance of the saints.

Total Depravity (Inability)

Newborn humans have no ability to understand intellectually, so they cannot choose God or choose salvation through water baptism. No human will or response is possible or required in babies, so none is required in adults.

Unconditional Election

God unilaterally determined which babies would reach the baptismal font to receive salvation versus which dying babies would be divinely blocked from baptismal salvation, and, therefore, sent to hell.

Unconditional election and total depravity (inability) both resulted from Augustine's logic invented in his novel theology of infant baptism. His move has defamed biblical predestination. Biblical predestination has been incorrectly viewed as being the same concept as pagan unilateral determinism, continuing even into our modern era. "Moderns believe predestination is but another word for strict determinism."[39]

---

[37] David Black, *Linguistics for Students of New Testament Greek* (1988; repr., Grand Rapids: Baker, 1995), 170–96. Perseverance must be assumed (out of context).

[38] Kenneth Wilson, "Reading James 2:18–20 with Anti-Donatist Eyes: Untangling Augustine's Exegetical Legacy," *Journal of Biblical Literature* 139, no. 2 (2020): 389–410.

[39] Kyle Pasewark, "Predestination as a Condition for Freedom," in *Human and Divine Agency: Anglican, Catholic, and Lutheran Perspectives*, ed. F. M. McLain and W. M. Richardson (Lanham, MD: University Press of America, 1999), 50. His remark is accurate but not in the way he meant it. Its Calvinistic abuse is the reason moderns believe it is the same concept.

Limited Atonement

Limited atonement was a logical deduction from Augustine's Stoic view of providence. God predetermines to bring about every event in the universe and only those events he desires. Augustine's Neoplatonic God would not have wasted Christ's precious blood on those whom he created only for damnation. Heracleon the Gnostic had apparently limited Christ's propitiation for the whole world (1 John 2:2) to only the elect Church (*Com.Ev.Joan* 6.59; 6.38 in English). Origen refuted this heresy (*Com.Rom.*3.8.13; 4.11.1–2). Augustine never overtly stated this doctrine but implied it. After his reversion to his prior pagan doctrines in AD 412, Augustine implicitly abandoned the traditional Christian doctrine that Christ died for all humans. With five different explanations over many years, he kept trying to explain how God desires all persons to be saved (1 Tim 2:4), yet all persons are not saved. This could not logically fit his Stoic and Neoplatonic view of sovereignty. According to Henry Chadwick, Augustine's alteration forced God's sovereignty to trump (trample) God's justice.[40]

Irresistible Grace

This doctrine is implied but not stated in those terms. Augustine concluded God must micromanage and manipulate the circumstances that would guarantee a person would "freely" respond to the invitation of God's calling to eternal life.[41] The mouse in the maze example "freely" choosing as maze doors are closed and opened should be remembered here. But only in AD 421 (*c.Jul.*4.8.42) did Augustine alter the text to mean "all who are saved," meaning those who are saved are only saved by God's will (cf. *Ench.*97, 103). People fail to be saved, "not because they do not will it, but because God does not" (*Ep.*217.19). God makes other Christians desire and pray earnestly for the salvation of their family and friends who are nevertheless hopelessly damned (*Corrept.*15, 47). John Rist rightly identified this as "the most pathetic passage."[42]

---

[40] For God's sovereignty trumping God's justice, see Henry Chadwick, "Freedom and Necessity in Early Christian Thought about God," in *Cosmology and Theology*, ed. David Tracy and Nicholas Lash (Edinburgh: T&T Clark, 1983), 8–13; Donato Ogliari, *Gratia et Certamen: The Relationship between Grace and Free Will in the Discussion of Augustine with the So-Called Semipelagians* (Leuven: Leuven University Press, 2003).

[41] Burns, "From Persuasion to Predestination," 307.

[42] John M. Rist, "Augustine on Free Will and Predestination," in *Augustine: A Collection of Critical Essays*, ed. R. A. Markus (New York: Doubleday, 1972), 239.

By AD 429, Augustine quoted 1 Cor 1:18, adding "such" to 1 Tim 2:4, redefining *all* to mean as "all those elected," and thus forced it to imply an irresistible calling. Alexander Hwang noted, "Then the radical shift occurred, brought about by the open and heated conflict with the Pelagians. 'Desires' took on absolute and efficacious qualities, and the meaning of 'all' was reduced to the predestined. 1 Timothy 2:4 should be understood, then, as meaning that God saves only the predestined. All others, apparently, do not even have a prayer."[43]

Perseverance of the Saints

Augustine did not invent this doctrine until three or four years before his death. He had to explain why many infants who had been regenerated through water baptism and who possessed the Holy Spirit did not persevere in faith and good works as adults. He invented the extra gift of perseverance, using this logic: (1) some baptized infants would mature into responsible Christians while other baptized babies would fall away from the faith and perhaps live immoral lives; (2) both possessed the Holy Spirit; (3) therefore, God must give a second gift of grace called "perseverance" only to some *specially elected Christians*. By removing Phil 1:6 from its context, Augustine incorrectly concluded, "By this gift they cannot fail to persevere" (*Corrept.*34, AD 426–27). Without this second gift of grace called perseverance, a baptized Christian—who possesses the Holy Spirit—will not persevere and ultimately will not be saved (*Corrept.*18). Modern Calvinists must modify the obvious deficiency in this Augustinian doctrine by denying that the person was ever a Christian.

A Critique of Augustine's Reversion to Pagan Concepts

When he redefined Christian terms and concepts, Augustine misrepresented earlier Christian authors. Lewis Ayres politely noted, "Augustine was an attentive reader of his forebears, but one whose interpretations of them were frequently very much his own."[44] As a result, Luther and Calvin mistakenly believed that Augustine was merely teaching what all of the earlier church fathers had taught.[45] But in fact,

---

[43] Alexander Hwang, "Augustine's Various Interpretations of 1 Tim. 2:4," *Studia Patristica* 43 (2006): 137–42.

[44] Lewis Ayres, *Augustine and the Trinity* (Cambridge: Cambridge University Press, 2010), 86.

[45] See Martin Luther, "To George Spalatin—Wittenberg, October 19, 1516," in *Luther's Works*, 48:23 (see chap. 5, n. 13); Luther, "Lectures on Romans: Glosses and Scholia," in *Luther's*

Augustine himself admitted that he had tried but failed to continue in the Christian doctrine of free will of the first four centuries. He consistently utilized the same Christian terms but inserted new meanings into those terms.[46] Roger Haight wrote, "Grace for Augustine was delight in the good, a new form of liberty that required an internal modification of the human will. No one [Christian] prior to Augustine had really asserted anything like this need for an inner working of God within human freedom."[47] Augustine redefined free will, utilizing Stoic concepts, deformed original sin with Manichaean dualism, and mutilated faith into a divine gift to match Gnostic and Manichaean unilateral election.[48] Augustinian scholar Eugene TeSelle noted:

> Augustine always reacted vigorously to the suggestion that he taught what amounted to a doctrine of *fate*. Now it is undeniable that he did hold to something like what is usually meant by fate. . . . To him fate meant something precise: the doctrine that external occurrences, bodily actions, even thoughts and decisions are determined by the position of the heavenly bodies [*C. dua*

Works, vol. 25; Calvin, *Institutes*, trans. Battles, 1:158–59 (I.xiii.29) (see chap. 4, n. 85); Harry Wolfson, *Religious Philosophy: A Group of Essays* (Cambridge, MA: Belknap Press of Harvard University Press, 1961), 158–76, in which he explained the centuries-old traditional Judeo-Christian understanding of free will (despite the sinful inclination) that persisted until the "later Augustine" introduced Stoic ideas into Judeo-Christian theology, and especially Augustine's misunderstanding of *concupiscentia* in his Latin translation of *Wisdom of Solomon* 8:21.

[46] This included the terms original sin, grace, predestination, free will, and so forth. "For example, in the early patristic writers we find references to the *origin of sin*, to a *fall*, and to the *inheritance of sin*, but what is meant is often different from the meaning given to those terms in the later classical tradition influenced by Augustine." Tatha Wiley, *Original Sin: Origins, Developments, Contemporary Meanings* (New York: Paulist Press, 2002), 53; italics in the original; Ralph Mathiesen, "For Specialists Only: The Reception of Augustine and His Teachings in the Fifth Century Gaul" in *Collectanea Augustina: Presbyter Factus Sum*, ed. Joseph Lienhard, Earl Muller, and Roland Teske (New York: Peter Lang, 1993), 30–31; Rebecca Weaver, s.v. "Predestination," in *Encyclopedia of Early Christianity*, 2nd ed., ed. Everett Ferguson (New York: Garland, 1998): "The now centuries-old characterization of the human being as capable of free choice and thus accountable at the last judgment had been retained, but the meaning of its elements had been considerably altered"; Peter J. Leithart, "Review of *Adam, Eve, and the Serpent*" by Elaine Pagels, *Westminster Theological Seminary Journal* 51, no. 1 (Spring 1989): 186. "Augustine's concept of free will certainly differs from that of earlier theologians."

[47] Roger Haight, *The Experience of Language of Grace* (New York: Paulist, 1979), 36.

[48] In Stoicism, fate controls every minute occurrence in the universe (Cicero, *Div.*1, 125–26), and although a person has no possibility of actuating an opportunity, "free will" remains solely by definition (Cicero, *Fat.*12–15). See Margaret Reesor, "Fate and Possibility in Early Stoic Philosophy," *Phoenix* 19, no. 4 (1965): 285–97, esp. 201; Stoics, "took elaborate precautions to protect their system from rigid determinism." Neoplatonists did the same.

ep Pel., II,6,12] or more broadly, universal material determinism [*C. dua ep Pel.* II, 6,12; *De Civ. Dei.* IV.33, V.1,8].[49]

Augustine said if anyone "calls the will of God or the power of God itself by the name of fate, let him keep his opinion but correct his language" (*C. dua ep. Pel.*1.2.4). Over a thousand years later, Augustine's novel and syncretistic reinterpretations of Christian Scripture (TULIP) would be faithfully replicated by Calvin and his followers.

Similarly, modern Calvinists (such as the contributing authors of *Whomever* He *Wills*) vehemently defend their theology using Scripture. But they refuse to admit their own interpretations are based on the pagan philosophies and Manichaean religion deeply imbedded into their current syncretistic scriptural interpretations by Augustine.[50] God as micromanager of the universe (Stoic sovereignty) stands foremost and paramount: total depravity (Manichaean) follows logically from it (using the same pagan arguments).[51] For Calvinists like Andrew Davis, "Romans 9:11–13 is the mortal wound for conditional election."[52] This replicates the "biblical" arguments by Gnostics and Manichaeans for unconditional election (determinism); but all pre-Augustinian Christian writings opposed this pagan doctrine. Thomas Schreiner claimed all Christians will inevitably persevere. This assumes the perfect divine gift of faith unilaterally infused by (the Gnostic/Manichaean) God cannot fail, because ultimate salvation requires perseverance—faith plus works (i.e., not our own but fruit God produces, per Augustine). This includes Schreiner's appeal to Phil 1:6, repeating Augustine's tortured interpretation.[53] Bruce Ware's chapter on the compatibility of determinism and freedom could have been argued by a Stoic or Manichaean who was familiar with Scripture. His argument for compatibility was unnecessary in

---

[49] TeSelle, *Augustine the Theologian*, 313; emphasis in the original.

[50] Barrett and Nettles, *Whomever* He *Wills* (see intro., n. 22).

[51] Steven Lawson, "Our Sovereign Savior," 3–15; and Mark DeVine, "Total Depravity," 16–36, in *Whomever* He *Wills*.

[52] Andrew Davis, "Unconditional Election: A Biblical and God-Glorifying Doctrine," in *Whomever* He *Wills*, 51.

[53] Thomas Schreiner, "Promises of Preservation and Exhortations to Persevere," in *Whomever* He *Wills*, 188–211, esp. 192. His "biblical" arguments all rest on those pagan assumptions inherited from Augustine. Distinguishing works as necessary fruit for final salvation but not the basis of it mimics Roman Catholicism's theology. Calvinists merely replace (Faith + Works ➡ Salvation) with (Faith ➡ Works ➡ Salvation). Neither Roman Catholics nor Calvinists believe in faith alone for salvation—both require good works.

pre-Augustinian Christian theology.[54] Likewise, Stephen Wellum repeated Augustine's appeal to "mystery" that was not required until his Stoic god unilaterally desired, predetermined, and ordained all things, including monstrous evils (such as genocide, rape, torture, and child sacrifice).[55] Matthew Barrett's "The Scriptural Affirmation of Monergism" would have shocked all pre-Augustinian Christians, while making the ancient monergistic Manichaeans proud.[56]

For Calvinists, the only reasonable theological choice must be Calvinism, since in Arminianism, "God is robbed of his glory at the expense of demanding libertarian freedom."[57] This false disjunction (limited to two poor choices of Calvinism and Arminianism) ignores the centuries of unanimous pre-Augustinian Christian theology on human free will and God's general sovereignty. Calvinism's God is puny. Calvinism limits God's sovereignty.

Calvinists must either ignore these facts or attempt to marginalize them. The vast majority of Christianity—Catholics, Orthodox, Protestants, and other Christian groups—have been unsuccessful in using these facts to convince Calvinists of their errors. We cannot seem to break through the resilient barrier of indoctrinated self-deception to reach adherents of modern Calvinism. In Calvinism, tradition has triumphed over truth.

Conclusion

Augustine of Hippo subverted Christian theology in AD 412 by incorporating his prior Stoic view of meticulous providence and his prior Manichaean doctrine of Divine Unilateral Predetermination of Eternal Destinies (DUPED). All prior Christians had fought against Stoic meticulous providence and Gnostic/Manichaean DUPED. They taught the Christian God is relational and exercises *general* (not specific) sovereignty for the purpose of allowing human freedom. The Christian God chooses persons for salvation based upon his foreknowledge of *their* free choices. Augustine reverted to his Manichaean deterministic interpretations of Scripture

---

[54] Bruce Ware, "The Compatibility of Determinism and Human Freedom," in *Whomever He Wills*, 212–30. There was no Christian tension between general sovereignty and free will for centuries before Augustine; Fergusson, s.v. "Predestination," *Oxford Companion*.

[55] Stephen Wellum, "God's Sovereignty over Evil," in Barrett and Nettles, *Whomever He Wills*, 256.

[56] Barrett, "Monergism," 120–87 (see intro., n. 22).

[57] Barrett and Nettles, introduction to *Whomever He Wills*, xxvi.

when attempting to explain infant baptism against the Pelagians. For twenty-five years he had refuted those interpretations as heresy.

After AD 411, Augustine's final eighteen years of theology was DUPED as the Manicheans had claimed—monergistic, to the glory of Augustine's new inscrutable sovereign God who creates then damns innocent babies to hell.[58] He confessed, "I cannot find a satisfactory and worthy explanation—because I can't find one, not because there isn't one" (*Serm*.294.7). After 1,600 years, no philosopher or theologian has found a "satisfactory and worthy explanation" to salvage Augustine's syncretism of pagan ideas into Christianity that damns innocent babies to hell. It will forever remain a "mystery."

Cicero (ca. 50 BC), one of Augustine's favorite authors, had argued for the incompatibility between divine omniscience and human free will. Augustine's final answer was to claim that divine foreknowledge of the future occurs only through God's unilateral predetermination and ordaining of every event, both good and evil (*Civ*.5). By this move he departed from all prior Christian teaching and syncretized a concept common in Stoicism: "God foreordains human wills."[59] The Stoic scholar John Rist concluded that Augustine's novel Christian determinism produced "a theology which fails to do justice to his own theory of God's love."[60] In contrast, Jerome succeeded in refuting the Pelagians without adopting the extremes of Augustinianism (*Against the Pelagians* 3) and retained the traditional Christian beliefs in God's general sovereignty, grace, and free will.[61]

Harry Wolfson, historian and philosopher at Harvard University's Judaic Studies Center, concluded, "Augustine's doctrine of grace is only a Christianization of the Stoic doctrine of fate."[62] Because of Augustine's AD 412 reversion to pagan ideas, the

---

[58] See Augustine, *Serm*.294.7: "Here too I like to exclaim with Paul, *Oh the depths of the riches!* (Rom 11:33). Unbaptized infants go to damnation; they are like the apostles' words, after all: *From one to condemnation* (Rom 5:16). I cannot find a satisfactory and worthy explanation . . . [he cited all of Rom 11:33–36]." See *The Works of Saint Augustine*, III/8, 196n8, with Hill's comments: "Babies who die unbaptized therefore go to hell. . . . It is precisely this assumption that renders his whole argument weak, and his conclusion highly questionable."

[59] Christopher Kirwan, *Augustine*, The Arguments of the Philosophers (New York: Routledge, 1989), 98–103.

[60] John Rist, *Augustine: Ancient Thought Baptized* (Cambridge: Cambridge University Press, 1994), 307.

[61] See Vít Hušek, "Human Freedom According to the Earliest Latin Commentaries on Paul's Letters," *Studia Patristica* 44 (2010): 385–90.

[62] Harry Wolfson, *Religious Philosophy: A Group of Essays* (Cambridge, MA: Belknap Press of Harvard University Press, 1961), 176. See also Michael Frede and Halszka Osmolska, *A Free*

exalted justice of the relational Christian God (used to combat pagan philosophies and heresies) was instantly transformed into inscrutable theology—deformed theology. Augustine overtly wrote of God's predestination of the ones he purposefully created for damnation in eternal torment ("double predestination"; *Nat. orig.*1.14, *Civ.*14.26, 15.1; *Serm.*229S, *Serm.*260D.1; *An.et or.*4.16).[63] Augustine borrowed his prior Neoplatonic inscrutable mystery as his defense for this horrendous divine injustice (*Serm.*D.29.10 and *Serm.*294.7). Neoplatonism (ca. AD 250) had invented this crucial theodicy by appealing to the inscrutable secret counsels of God, who is fair by definition, regardless of whatever apparent evils he desires and ordains. Prior Christians had never required this implausible and disingenuous attempt at a defense for their God.

Modern Calvinists teach Augustine's theology. Calvinists appeal to the same deterministic interpretations of the same Scripture passages taught by Manichaeans. Calvinism's historical foundation is dangerously unstable. Its foundation relies on the Manichaean interpretations of Scripture by a single man in the ancient church who rejected three hundred years of unanimous church teaching of free will, a teaching that had refuted Stoic and Gnostic/Manichaean determinism. This man was indoctrinated for decades in extremely deterministic pagan philosophies and heretical Manichaeism. Augustine admitted he changed his theology regarding free will: he abandoned the Christian rule of faith regarding free choice. "In the solution of this question I struggled in behalf of free choice of the will, but the grace of God won out" (*Retr.*2.1).

But the grace that "won out" was not Christian grace: it was Manichaean grace. According to Augustine (*Conf.*7.5), he only escaped the philosophical prison of Manichaean DUPED by accepting Christian free choice. This freed him from viewing God as punishing unjustly. But ironically, after finally escaping, Augustine's later "inscrutable justice" of Christianized pagan DUPED reimprisoned both himself and his followers.

In contrast, the prior nearly unanimous Christian teaching (that God offers his grace to every human equally) persisted throughout the Patristic period into the eighth century with John of Damascus (d. ca. AD 760): "We ought to understand that while

---

Will: Origins of the Notion in Ancient Thought (Berkley, CA: University of California Press, 2011), especially 153–174, "Chapter Nine—Augustine: A Radically New Notion of a Free Will?"

[63] Gerard O'Daly, "Predestination and Freedom in Augustine's Ethics," in *The Philosophy in Christianity*, ed. Godfrey Vesey (Cambridge: Cambridge University Press, 1989), 90.

God knows all things beforehand, yet He does not predetermine all things. . . . So that predetermination is the work of the divine command based on foreknowledge" (*Exp. fid.*44). Eleonore Stump astutely concluded, "Unless Augustine is willing to accept that God's giving of grace is responsive to something in human beings, even if that something is not good or worthy of merit, I don't see how he can be saved from the imputation of theological determinism with all its infelicitous consequences."[64]

A willingness to return to the universal Christian theology that God gives grace as a response to human choice would never come for Augustine. The famous rhetorician never looked back in his resolve to win his debate against the Pelagians at all costs. William Frend explained, "Augustine could not concede a single point to his adversaries and this was his undoing."[65] Augustine died eighteen years after reverting to his pagan monergistic determinism, still trusting in his self-crafted syncretistic theology.

As we observed in the introduction, Calvinists address the blatant absence of their theology in the pre-Augustinian centuries in one of two possible ways. The less scholarly Calvinists invent proto-Calvinists among early Christian authors. Scholarly Calvinists claim Augustine was the first theologian since the apostle Paul to interpret Scripture correctly. Benjamin Warfield opined Augustine's "doctrine was not new" but was lost for four centuries between the time the apostle Paul wrote it and Augustine "recovered" it for the church (the Calvinist Gap Theory).[66] These scholars appear oblivious to the enormous chasm separating Paul from Augustine. This formidable chasm is Augustine's Stoicism, Neoplatonism, and Manichaeism. It separates Paul from Augustine by hundreds of years and thousands of miles. Calvinists attempt to bridge this insurmountable gap by using the "hermeneutical" lens of Augustine's Manichaeism to reinterpret Pauline (and other) Scriptures within their own paradigm.

Calvinism's alleged "biblical foundation" rests on Augustine's deterministic interpretations of Scripture from his decade of Gnostic/Manichaean training (John 6:44–66; 14:6; Rom 9–11; Eph 2:1–3, 8–9; Phil 2:13; etc.). Such a dangerous foundation requires a precarious "faith" in Augustine's "Sovereign God," caricatured through syncretism with Stoic and Neoplatonic philosophy and the heretical

---

[64] Eleonore Stump, "Augustine on Free Will," in *The Cambridge Companion to Augustine*, ed. Eleonore Stump and Norman Kretzmann (Cambridge: Cambridge University Press, 2001), 124–147 at 142.

[65] William H. C. Frend, "Doctrine of Man in the Early Church: An Historical Approach," *Modern Churchman* 45, no. 3 (1955): 227.

[66] Warfield, *Tertullian and Augustine*, 129.

Manichaean religion.[67] He baptized his prior pagan philosophies and religion into Christianity, resulting in an unrecognizable doctrinal conglomeration. Calvinism is Augustinianism. Augustinianism is Christian theology scrambled with Gnostic/Manichaean theology and Stoic/Neoplatonic philosophy. As John Rist concluded, Augustinianism is *"Ancient* [pagan] *Thought Baptized."*[68]

Nevertheless, these serious syncretistic errors did not make Augustine a heretic or a non-Christian. Augustine still embraced the essential doctrines of the Christian faith. Modern Calvinists also embrace the major tenets of Christianity regarding Jesus Christ as God in the flesh and Savior from sin. Despite their divergent views (sovereignty, total depravity/inability, and DUPED determinism) imported from Augustine's paganism, Calvinists remain Christian brothers and sisters worthy of respect, love, and fellowship—contrary to the opinion of one extreme evangelical sect.[69] In this anti-Christian period of history, Christians of all persuasions must be unified, despite our internal disagreements.

---

[67] Wilson, *Foundation of Augustinian-Calvinism*, 97–103. Translated into Spanish—*Fundación del Calvinismo Agustiniano*; into German—*War Augustin der erste Calvinist?*; and into Portuguese—*Fundamento do Calvinismo-Agostiniano.*

[68] See note 60. Rist's focus was pagan Stoicism.

[69] Some Christian groups can press anti-Calvinism too far, so much that they themselves violate the limits of historical orthodoxy. See, e.g., Kenneth Wilson, *Heresy of the Grace Evangelical Society: Become a Christian without Faith in Jesus as God and Savior* (Montgomery, TX: Regula Fidei Press, 2020). Bob Wilkin and his Grace Evangelical Society teach "assurance is of the essence of saving faith." Calvinists *cannot* have assurance of their own eternal security because Calvinists teach perseverance in faith and works until physical death is required for final salvation. Therefore, Calvinists are not Christians. This GES heresy requires absolute assurance in Jesus's promise of personal eternal security to become a Christian, yet does not require faith in Jesus as God and Savior.

7

Dissent from Calvinism in the Baptist Tradition

—— J. Matthew Pinson ——

For the first three centuries of the Baptist tradition, most Baptists were Calvinists. However, for most of that period, various movements of dissent arose, and in the second half of the nineteenth century and throughout the twentieth century, traditional forms of Calvinism receded. Dissent from Calvinism in the first three centuries of the Baptist experience took place on two fronts: (1) confessionally Arminian movements among Baptists who descended from, or identified with, the English General Baptists and (2) dissent from, and the decline of, Calvinism among Baptists who descended from the English Particular Baptists.

A knowledge of the origins of the Baptist movement helps one understand this dynamic. The English Baptists of the seventeenth century coalesced into two groups: General Baptists and Particular Baptists. The first Baptists, under the leadership of Thomas Helwys, were General Baptists. They were thus named because they subscribed to the Arminian doctrine known as general redemption, which holds that God desires everyone's salvation, sent Christ to die for everyone's sins, and sent the

Holy Spirit to call everyone to himself. The reason people are not converted is their resistance to this *gratia universalis*, this "general" redemptive calling, not that they have been left outside the scope of divine grace.

The Particular Baptists, who arose a generation after Helwys, were thoroughgoing Calvinists. Most of them taught not the *gratia universalis et resistibilis* (universal and resistible grace) of the general redemption teaching but rather the *gratia particularis et irresistibilis* (particular and irresistible grace) of Calvinism: God wants certain individuals to be elect and certain individuals to be non-elect. These non-elect individuals remain outside the scope of Christ's atoning death and the Spirit's internal gracious calling to salvation (though many Particular Baptists believed that an external call goes out to everyone).[1]

Modern Baptist bodies descend from, or have identified with, one of these two groups. The confessionally Arminian groups either descended directly from the English General Baptists or arose spontaneously and identified themselves with that tradition. The Free Will Baptists of the American South, for example, consisted of English General Baptists who sailed across the Atlantic in the seventeenth century and whose descendants decades later were dubbed "Free-Willers" by their detractors. The Freewill Baptists of the North, a group associated with Benjamin Randall that was separate from the Southern Free Will Baptists, merged with the Northern Baptists in 1911.[2] They did not descend organically from the English General Baptists but identified with that movement in the nineteenth century. The same can be said about the General Association of General Baptists, an Arminian Baptist denomination that originated in the early nineteenth century with congregations largely in the American Midwest.

All other Baptists have, for all intents and purposes, descended from the English Particular Baptists. This includes Baptists in English-speaking countries—or congregations and associations established around the world as a result of Baptist mission work—who are not General Baptists. In the United States, for example, it includes

---

[1] Recent scholarship has demonstrated that not all Particular Baptists held to limited atonement. A minority affirmed unlimited atonement, though they maintained all other elements of Calvinistic soteriology. See Allen, *Extent of the Atonement* (see intro., n. 10), 463–506; and David Wenkel, "The Doctrine of the Extent of the Atonement among the Early English Particular Baptists," *Harvard Theological Review* 112, no. 3 (2019): 358–75.

[2] A minority of this group consisted of fundamentalists in the Midwest and Southwest who remained aloof from the 1911 merger but later united with Free Will Baptists in the South to form the National Association of Free Will Baptists in 1935.

the old Northern Baptist (now American Baptist) and Southern Baptist Conventions and their descendants and African American or fundamentalist denominations or fellowships of independent churches that broke with these bodies. It also includes Regular and Separate Baptists who remained aloof from those conventions, particularly in Appalachia, as well as Primitive and other Particular Baptist groups that maintained their autonomy after the Anti-Mission Controversy.[3]

This brings up the issue of what to call Baptists whose roots are in the Particular Baptist heritage yet who have moderated or modified their Calvinism to the point where it is only a "two-point Calvinism" (total depravity and perseverance of the saints).[4] Some have recently wished to be referred to as Arminian; the Society of Evangelical Arminians, for example, has members who fit this description. Most wish to be referred to as simply traditional Baptists, saying they are neither Arminian nor Calvinist but Baptist.[5] Some of their confessionally Arminian friends have referred to them as "pseudo-Calvinists" or "sub-Calvinists."[6] Some simply call themselves "non-Calvinists." I have sometimes referred to them as "post-Calvinists." Nomenclature notwithstanding, most of these individuals believe that it is inappropriate for them simply to take on the moniker "Arminian." The reason for this reluctance is not hard to understand. The moniker carries four centuries of confessional baggage that is not easily discarded, including the universal tendency for confessional Arminian bodies to affirm the possibility of apostasy.

A related difficulty is the way Baptist authors have historically used the word *Calvinism*. Often, until very recently, there has been a tendency to include under the rubric of "mild Calvinism" an approach that would agree with Calvinists that humanity is totally depraved and believers cannot commit apostasy. This chapter, in considering Baptist dissent from Calvinism, will first discuss Baptists in confessionally

---

[3] Some fellowships of European Baptist immigrants sprang up spontaneously but have tended to identify with this tradition.

[4] As will be discussed below regarding H. C. Thiessen, E. Y. Mullins, and Herschel Hobbs, "once-saved, always-saved" Baptists traditionally affirmed a strong doctrine of total depravity and natural inability apart from divine prevenient grace.

[5] David L. Allen et al., "Neither Calvinists nor Arminians, but Baptists," *Journal for Baptist Theology and Ministry* 7, no. 1 (Spring 2010): 57–63, https://www.nobts.edu/baptist-center -theology/journals/journals/JBTM_7-1_Spring_2010.pdf.

[6] Leroy Forlines, following J. Oliver Buswell, uses "pseudo-Calvinists," while Robert Picirilli uses "sub-Calvinists." F. Leroy Forlines, *Classical Arminianism: A Theology of Salvation* (Nashville: Randall House, 2011), 280; Robert E. Picirilli, *Grace, Faith, Free Will: Contrasting Views of Salvation—Calvinism and Arminianism* (Nashville: Randall House, 2002), 194–95.

Arminian Baptist denominations. It will then consider those who have emerged from the non-General Baptist stream of the Baptist tradition yet have softened their Calvinism considerably, often beyond recognition.

Confessionally Arminian Baptist Bodies

The Early English General Baptists

The first Baptists were Arminian. They originated under the leadership of Thomas Helwys, who had broken with his compatriot John Smyth, with whom he had been exiled in Holland, to come back to England to establish the first Baptist church on English soil.[7] In reality, Helwys, not Smyth, was the first Baptist, since he left Smyth because the latter had become a Mennonite before the Baptist movement ever got off the ground. Some of this involved matters of orthodoxy, ecclesiology, and culture: Helwys demurred from Smyth's embrace of the Hoffmanite Christology of the Waterlander Mennonites. He also disagreed with the Mennonite view that Christians could not be magistrates or fight in just wars and that there had to be a sort of "baptismal succession" to have a true church.

Much of Helwys's rationale for his split from Smyth, however, was soteriological in nature. He criticized Smyth's recent denial of original sin, total depravity, and the imputation of the righteousness of Christ in justification. In short, Helwys affirmed an Arminianism much like that of the Dutch Reformed scholar Jacobus Arminius, thus diverging from the overt semi-Pelagianism and moralism of Smyth and the Waterlanders. Some modern scholars have referred to Helwys as a Reformed Arminian. Helwys agreed with Smyth and the Mennonites on *how one comes to be* in a state of grace (e.g., conditional election, resistible grace before and after conversion). Yet he differed with them on *what it means to be* in a state of grace (e.g., the nature of atonement, justification, sanctification).[8]

---

[7] For more information on these two figures, see Joe Early Jr., *The Life and Writings of Thomas Helwys* (Macon, GA: Mercer University Press, 2009); Marvin Jones, *The Beginning of Baptist Ecclesiology: The Foundational Contributions of Thomas Helwys* (Eugene, OR: Pickwick, 2017); and Jason K. Lee, *The Theology of John Smyth: Puritan, Separatist, Baptist, Mennonite* (Macon, GA: Mercer University Press, 2003).

[8] For a full argument for this, see J. Matthew Pinson, "Sin and Redemption in the Theology of John Smyth and Thomas Helwys," in *Arminian and Baptist: Explorations in a Theological Tradition* (Nashville: Randall House, 2015).

The mainstream of seventeenth-century General Baptist soteriology provided an alternative to predestinarian Calvinism and its denial of libertarian freedom. Helwys reasoned that if God desires everyone's salvation, provides atonement for everyone through Christ, and calls everyone to himself through the Spirit, then he would never withhold his grace from the reprobate. Yet, he said:

> This is the whole substance of what they [Calvinists] say. That God hath decreed to forsake and leave those that he hath appointed to condemnation, to themselves, and withholdeth his grace from them, leaving them to sin, and so to perish for their sin. We will not put them to prove this because we know they cannot, but we will show, by the mercy of God, that it is an old, conceived imagination and hath no ground of truth."[9]

For Helwys, the reason people are reprobated is their resistance to the *gratia universalis*, not a divine secret will that only a few be given salvific grace. In short, Helwys, like Arminius, believed in conditional, individual election and conditional, individual reprobation. God elects for eternal salvation those whom he knows from eternity in Christ through faith. He reprobates those whom he knows from eternity resist Christ in unbelief.[10] Helwys argued:

> This lamentable opinion of particular *redemption* and *reprobation* saith they [the reprobate] can have no part nor portion in Christ. So is their judgment enlarged for not receiving Christ, with whom they have nothing to do. And thus do they make Christ to offer himself to them that he would not have receive him, and which he hath decreed shall not receive him, nor believe him, and make the words of the Lord feigned words, and words of dissimulation.[11]

While General Baptist theology agreed with other non-Calvinists on the doctrines of universal, resistible grace and conditional election, it diverged in many

---

[9] Thomas Helwys, *A Short and Plaine Proofe by the Word and Workes of God that Gods decree is not the cause of anye Mans sinne or Condemnation. And That all Men are redeamed by Christ. As also, That no Infants are Condemned* (Amsterdam: 1611), sig. A7v–r. These quotations are from the original. For a modern critical edition of Helwys's works, see Early, *Thomas Helwys*. The spelling, punctuation, etc., of early modern English works quoted in this chapter have been modernized.

[10] Thomas Helwys, "A Declaration of Faith of the English People Remaining at Amsterdam," reprinted in J. Matthew Pinson, *A Free Will Baptist Handbook: Heritage, Beliefs, and Ministries* (Nashville: Randall House, 1998), 125.

[11] Helwys, *Short and Plaine Proofe*, sig. B2v.

ways from typical Arminianism. Many non-Calvinists of Helwys's day tended, like Smyth, to downplay original sin and the total depravity of humanity. Most Arminians demurred from penal substitutionary atonement and justification by the imputation of Christ's righteousness alone. They advocated moralistic or perfectionist views, as well as understandings of perseverance that have to do with maintaining salvation through penitence rather than being justified by union with Christ through faith.

Rather, similarly to Arminius, Helwys affirmed Reformed concepts of original sin and depravity as well as justification by the imputation of Christ's righteousness through faith alone. Smyth had averred that justification "consists partly of the imputation of the righteousness of Christ apprehended by faith, and partly of inherent righteousness, in the holy themselves."[12] Helwys responded that "man is justified only by the righteousness of Christ, apprehended by faith."[13]

Later General Baptists such as Thomas Grantham picked up these themes. Grantham affirmed Reformed conceptions of original sin, human depravity, and total inability. He also advanced Reformed doctrines of penal substitutionary atonement and justification by the imputation of the active and passive obedience of Christ. Yet he remained Arminian in his understanding of how one comes to be in a state of grace, affirming the necessary, divine drawing grace of the Holy Spirit that is nonetheless resistible as well as election conditioned on divine knowledge of one's persistent union with Christ through faith.[14]

Grantham's Reformed categories of justification and union with Christ came together with his Arminian view of falling away in a manner that was distinct from many other Arminians of his day. Because divine grace is resistible, he taught, it must continue to be so after conversion. Yet because believers, in union with Christ through faith, are justified only by the imputed righteousness of Christ, continued faith alone is what guarantees their perseverance. One falls from grace only when one "destroys a state of faith," the state Grantham believed was described in Heb 6:4–6. Such apostasy is "irrecoverable." Those who have apostatized "cannot, (as Chrysostom notes

---

[12] "Short Confession of Faith in 20 Articles by John Smyth," in Lumpkin, *Baptist Confessions of Faith*, 101 (see chap. 1, n. 76).

[13] Helwys, "Declaration of Faith," 125.

[14] Thomas Grantham, *A Dialogue between the Baptist and the Presbyterian* (London: 1691), 19–20. See Pinson, *Arminian and Baptist*, chap. 5, for details on Grantham's soteriology.

upon the place) be twice made Christians; and there being but one sacrifice for sin, there remains no more for such."[15]

Helwys's and Grantham's Reformed Arminian soteriology was reflected in confessional documents such as the Standard Confession of 1660, the confessional document of the General Assembly of General Baptists, as well as confessions such as the Orthodox Creed. These confessions take the *gratia universalis et resistibilis* as their starting point for understanding the divine salvific plan. Election is conditional; those who resist divine prevenient grace are condemned, but those whom God knows in Christ, through their belief, are chosen for eternal salvation:

> That God hath even before the foundation of the world chosen (or elected) to eternal life, such as believe, and so are in Christ, John 3. 16. Ephes. 1. 4, 2 Thess. 2. 13. Yet confident we are, that the purpose of God according to election was not in the least arising from foreseen faith in, or works of righteousness done by the creature, but only from the mercy, goodness, and compassion dwelling in God, and so it is of him that calleth, Rom. 9. ii."[16]

Divine salvific grace continues to be resistible after conversion:

> Such who are true believers, even branches in Christ the Vine, (and that in his account, whom he exhorts to abide in him, John 15. 1, 2, 3, 4, 5.) or such who have charity out of a pure heart, and of a good conscience, and of faith unfeigned, 1 Tim. 1. 5. may nevertheless for want of watchfulness, swerve and turn aside from the same, vv. 6, 7. and become as withered branches, cast into the fire and burned, John. 15. 6. But such who add unto their faith virtue, and unto virtue knowledge, and unto knowledge temperance, &c. 2 Pet. 1 5, 6, 7. such shall never fall, vv. 8, 9, 10. 'Tis impossible for all the false Christs, and false prophets, that are, and are to come, to deceive such, for they are kept by the power of God, through faith unto salvation, 1 Pet. 1. 5.[17]

The Orthodox Creed articulated these same doctrines: universal, resistible grace before and after conversion, and thus the conditional election of individuals. (The

---

[15] Thomas Grantham, *Christianismus Primitivus: Or, the Ancient Christian Religion* [. . .] (London: Printed for Francis Smith [. . .], 1678), 2:2.155 (b. 2.2, c. 11, §5). See also Helwys, "Declaration of Faith," 125–26.

[16] Standard Confession, 1660, art. 8, repr. in Pinson, *Free Will Baptist Handbook*, 134.

[17] Standard Confession, 1660, art. 18, repr. in Pinson, 137.

General Baptists never say anything about election being corporate. They mention only conditional election, which is of necessity of individuals, since Christ's *corpus*, the church, against which the gates of hell cannot prevail, is unconditionally, not conditionally, elect.) The Orthodox Creed, a lengthier confession of faith, fleshes out the Reformed doctrines of total depravity and the utter graciousness of God in salvation, ruling out the allegation of semi-Pelagianism.

The following quotation encapsulates the Reformed Arminian thrust of the creed, which emphasizes *sola fide* and *sola gratia* while maintaining basic Arminianism: "We are chosen in Christ before the foundation of the world. Now faith is necessary as the way of our salvation, as an Instrumental Cause: but the Active and Passive Obedience of Christ, is necessary as a Meriting Cause of our Salvation; therefore God's Eternal Decree doth not oppose his revealed Will in the gospel, it being but one, not two diverse or contrary Wills."[18] Christ's work is the meritorious cause of election, not our faith. Yet our faith is what apprehends the merit of Christ, which God considered in his foreknowledge. This is in line with the Lutheran scholastic maxim, with which Arminius concurred, *intuitu Christi meriti fide apprehendi*: Divine election is "in consideration of the merit of Christ apprehended by faith." This, the creed insists, is the only way to conceive of election that does not posit two contradictory wills in God—a revealed will that everyone be saved and a secret will that only the elect be saved.

Some have thought article 36 of the Orthodox Creed teaches certain perseverance, but this fails to recognize the subtleties of seventeenth-century Arminian and Lutheran thought. The creed affirmed that the elect will persevere, which Arminius and most Arminians and Lutherans of the time taught. However, God elects for eternal salvation only those believers who persevere in Christ to the end of life. So, while all the elect will persevere, not all true believers will. Rather, the creed says in its article on reprobation that God "hath decreed to punish all those wicked, or ungodly, disobedient, and unbelieving or impenitent sinners, that have, or shall despise his grace, love, and wooings, or strivings of the Holy Ghost, or long-suffering, whether by a total and continued rejection of grace, or by a universal and final apostasy."[19] It cites verses such as Heb 10:26–30 and Jude 4, which are always associated with the Arminian doctrine of apostasy.

---

[18] *An Orthodox Creed: Or, A Protestant Confession of Faith* [. . .] (London: 1679), 11–12 (art. 9). An online version transcribed by Madison Grace can be found at http://baptiststudiesonline.com /wp-content/uploads/2007/02/orthodox-creed.pdf (Center for Theological Research, 2006).

[19] *An Orthodox Creed*, 13 (art. 10).

Like the Anglicans and Presbyterians, the General Baptists in England struggled with heresy and decline in the eighteenth century until Dan Taylor reorganized the General Baptists in England in the late eighteenth century in the form of the New Connexion of General Baptists. Taylor's efforts resulted in a reaffirmation of the basic Arminian distinctives of the denomination.[20]

The General (Free Will) Baptists in the American Colonies

In the American colonies, the General Baptists thrived in the early eighteenth century. While eschewing the more extreme revivalism in the Great Awakening, they grew through evangelism and church planting, spreading the news of the "Six Principles of the Christian Religion" from Heb 6:1–2. This is why people often referred to them as "General Six-Principle Baptists."

Paul Palmer, whose father-in-law Benjamin Laker, a friend of Thomas Grantham, had signed the 1663 edition of the General Baptist Standard Confession, exemplified this evangelistic and church planting thrust. A convert from Quakerism, Palmer became convinced of General Baptist doctrine, especially of Arminianism, as indicated by the fact that he wrote a book about it, which is no longer extant, entitled *Christ the Predestinated and Elected*.[21] Palmer, considered by both the Southern Free Will Baptists and the Baptists of North Carolina as their founder, preached the Six Principles of the Christian Religion and Arminianism and planted many churches according to that pattern.[22]

Yet this movement clashed with the strongly Calvinistic Philadelphia Association in the mid-eighteenth century and was nearly snuffed out of existence by that body. During most of the colonial period, the General Baptists were growing rapidly. In the first half of the eighteenth century, they were planting churches and having such evangelistic success that Southern Baptist historian William Whitsitt later said they

---

[20] See Richard T. Pollard, *Dan Taylor (1738–1816), Baptist Leader and Pioneering Evangelical* (Eugene, OR: Pickwick, 2018).

[21] C. Edwin Barrows, ed., *The Diary of John Comer* (Providence: Rhode Island Historical Society, 1893), 102.

[22] For more information on this early period, see Pinson, *Free Will Baptist Handbook*, 6–11; and E. Darrell Holley, "Without a Monument: The Life of Elder Paul Palmer," accessed December 6, 2021, https://fwbhistory.com/?p=603.

"dominated in America" from 1639 to 1740 and that Palmer's movement was "the most prosperous body of Baptist people at that time in the world."[23]

Thomas Kidd, who lauds the Philadelphia Association and its proselytization of the General Baptists of North Carolina, was partly right when he said the General Baptists in the 1750s "mostly opposed the new revivalism."[24] Many Calvinist Baptist historians have repeated the mistaken views of John Gano and the Philadelphia Association Calvinists of the 1750s, painting the General Baptists as cold, rationalistic, and not interested in spiritual fervor. This caricature, however, is belied by their evangelistic zeal and church planting success in difficult fields dominated by established churches.[25]

Some General Baptist pastors in Carolina in the 1750s had surreptitiously accepted Calvinism and were slowly and secretly leading their congregations down that path, while maintaining the appearance of being General Baptists. These pastors called on the Philadelphia Association for its help. So that association sent "missionaries" down to help these ministers proselytize and assume control of as many of the General Baptist churches as possible. (Thus, in the opening line of Kidd's article—"Calvinists once dominated Baptist life in America"—the word "dominated" is aptly chosen.)

These agents of the Philadelphia Association claimed that the General Baptist churches were filled with false converts, because those congregations did not require their members to go through a long, drawn-out litany of their conversion experience. Instead, the General Baptists simply ensured that their new members had been converted, and admitted to church membership, according to the Six Principles of the Christian Religion. The Six Principles were deeply imbedded in General Baptist piety and constituted the General Baptists' own scripturally rooted "order of

---

[23] Quoted in George Washington Paschal, *History of North Carolina Baptists*, 2 vols. (Raleigh: The General Board, North Carolina Baptist State Convention, 1930), 1:528.

[24] Thomas S. Kidd, "Calvinism Is Not New to Baptists: Grace Unleashed in the American Colonies," Desiring God, June 13, 2015, https://www.desiringgod.org/articles/calvinism-is -not-new-to-baptists.

[25] The definitive account of this sad tale is Jesse Owens's essay "When General Baptists Became Particular Baptists," written for a doctoral seminar on American Religious History at Southern Baptist Theological Seminary, posted August 3, 2015, http://www.helwyssociety forum.com/when-general-baptists-became-particular-baptists/. Other recent tellings of the story appear in William F. Davidson, *The Free Will Baptists in History* (Nashville: Randall House, 2002); Michael R. Pelt, *A History of the Original Free Will Baptists* (Mount Olive, NC: University of Mount Olive Press, 1996).

conversion." New believers must have—to use the language of the Geneva and King James Bibles—repented from dead works, placed their faith in Christ, been baptized, had the elder(s)'s hands laid on them symbolizing the reception of the Holy Spirit (which, incidentally, the Philadelphia Association also required as a Christian ordinance), and acknowledged that as believers they would one day be resurrected with Christ and stand at the judgment.

The Calvinist Baptists required an often lengthy and highly emotional rendition of how believers came to be converted and see themselves as elect. This also happened in non-Baptist circles, where "New Light" Congregationalist and "New Side" Presbyterian churches began to require these experiential exercises for admission to church membership—with the "Old Lights" objecting that this was adding things to the ordinary means of grace and to the sufficiency of Scripture.[26] This is similar to what the General/Free Will Baptists said, as exemplified by nineteenth-century Free Will Baptist Rufus K. Hearn, who stated in his *Origin of the Free Will Baptist Church of North Carolina*:

> These early churches took the Bible for their guide, they practiced its sacred teachings, and as the Apostles never required [the recounting of an "experience of grace"], and as it was nowhere authorized in Holy Writ, they practiced what they found the gospel required, that is, faith in the Lord Jesus Christ, repentance towards God, and baptism by immersion; and baptized their members on a profession of their faith in the Lord Jesus Christ. . . . Every Free Will Baptist will see that this is his doctrine, and the true doctrine of the New Testament, and it is our practice to the present day to baptize members on their profession of faith in the Lord Jesus Christ. They may call it lax in discipline, if they choose; we cannot, for we find no warrant in the New Testament for an experience of grace, as they term it.[27]

One of the most famous episodes in the annals of Free Will Baptist history was when John Gano, the most well-known of the proselytizers from the Philadelphia Association, intruded uninvited into a meeting of General Baptist ministers gathered

---

[26] Sherman B. Cranfield, "Reunion of the Synods of New York and Philadelphia, (Second Article)" *Presbyterian Quarterly Review* 7, no. 28 (January 1859): 543. See J. Matthew Pinson, *Free Will Baptists and the Sufficiency of Scripture* (Antioch, TN: Historical Commission, National Association of Free Will Baptists, 2014).

[27] Rufus K. Hearn, "Origin of the Free Will Baptist Church of North Carolina" in *General Baptist History*, ed. D. B. Montgomery (Evansville, IN: Courier, 1882), 169–70.

in a meeting house, about two years after the Philadelphia Association began working surreptitiously to take over these congregations. Gano forced his way into the
pulpit and said, "Jesus I know, and Paul I know, but who are ye?"

As Hearn said, "Most ministers, on being regarded as intruders, would probably have ceased from further effort at proselyting, and departed from the place, but
Mr. Gano took a different course. He went to a meeting of those who, as he well
knew, had met for consultation, and did not desire his presence. Not content with
this, he obtrusively entered the pulpit."[28] After Gano returned from his tour, the
Philadelphia Association sent more ministers down to continue the work of proselytization. This episode nearly killed what is now known as the Free Will Baptist
movement. However, the churches that survived would later blossom into the Free
Will Baptist movement of the South.

As the renowned Southern Baptist historian William Whitsitt said, "I am a
Particular Baptist throughout, but I have sometimes been moved to tears by the sad
fate of Paul Palmer, when his flourishing field—the most prosperous body of Baptist
people at that time in the world—was overrun and trampled down by his enemies.
Paul Palmer excites my imagination and evokes my sympathy. He was a great and
worthy man, and ought to have a monument somewhere."[29]

The remnant that survived the Philadelphia Association incursion went on to
foster a strong movement of churches in North and South Carolina that migrated
south and west into the frontier. By 1812, when they condensed the 1660 General
Baptist Standard Confession into the 1812 Abstract, they were becoming known as
"Free Will Baptists," having been dubbed "Free Willers" by their detractors.

The 1812 Abstract communicated the same general-redemption Arminianism
that had been taught by their forebears: Because of "the great love wherewith he
loved the world," God sent his Son, who "freely gave himself a ransom for all, tast-
ing death for every man" (art. 2).[30] Original sin brings on humanity the fall and
misery (art. 4). Yet God wants everyone to be saved through the knowledge of the
truth, which means the gospel should be preached to everyone (art. 5). The theme of
the *gratia universalis et resistibilis*, the "doctrine of General Provision made of God

---

[28] Hearn, 153.

[29] Quoted in Paschal, *History of North Carolina Baptists*, 1:528.

[30] These articles from the 1812 Abstract are found in Pinson, *Free Will Baptist Handbook*,
144–45.

in Christ, for the benefit of all mankind" (art. 8), is encapsulated in article 6 of the Abstract, which repeats the Standard Confession of 1660 almost verbatim:

> We believe that no man shall suffer in hell for want of a Christ that died for him, but as the scripture has said for denying the Lord that bought them; because they believe not in the name of the only begotten Son of God. Unbelief therefore being the cause why the just and righteous God of Heaven, will condemn the children of men, it follows against all contradiction, that all men at one time or another are found in such a capacity as that through the grace of God, they may be eternally saved.

Article 9 also bears witness to this universal prevenient grace in an original article written in 1812:

> We believe that sinners are drawn to God the Father, by the Holy Ghost, through Christ His Son, and that the Holy Ghost offers His divine aid to all the human family, so as they might all be happy, would they give place to His divine teaching; whereas such who do not receive the Divine impressions of the Holy Spirit, shall at a future day, own their condemnation just, and charge themselves with their own damnation, for willfully rejecting the offers of sovereign grace.

The article on election quoted verbatim from the above-mentioned article from the Standard Confession, but the article on justification was newly written: "We believe that no man has any warrant in the holy scriptures for justification before God through his own works, power, or ability which he has in and of himself, only as he by Grace is made able to come to God, through Jesus Christ; believing the righteousness of Jesus Christ to be imputed to all believers for their eternal acceptance with God."[31]

Thomas Kidd's story of the meteoric rise of the Calvinistic Baptists in American religious life is met with the reality of their rapid decline.[32] He asked, "How did Calvinism lose its dominant position among Baptists?" His answer is that the

---

[31] Curiously, the 1812 Abstract appears to teach certain perseverance. This occurrence of this article, which disappeared from later editions of the confession, does not receive comment in the sparse extant literature of the day and remains a mystery.

[32] See also Thomas S. Kidd and Barry Hankins, *Baptists in America: A History* (New York: Oxford University Press, 2015), 88.

"American Revolution, with its focus on liberty, gave new life to 'free will' theology in traditionally Calvinist denominations."[33] There is likely some truth to that. However, what H. Leon McBeth once said about the Free Will Baptists is also true: They exerted an influence on larger Baptist life that caused Baptists to moderate their strict Calvinism in favor of a milder form of Calvinism which many people have termed three-point Arminianism or Arminianism with unconditional perseverance.[34]

Benjamin Randall and the Northern Freewill Baptists

One of these movements was the Freewill Baptists in the North. This movement, though similar in name to the southern movement, was never in organic union with the Free Will Baptists of the South who descended from the English General Baptists. Historians often refer to the northern Freewill Baptists as the Randall movement because they originated with the ministry of Benjamin Randall. Randall was a product of the Great Awakening. Converted as a result of the ministry of George Whitefield, Randall forged a New Light version of Arminianism that was somewhat less Reformed than that of his southern counterparts on the doctrines of atonement, justification, and sanctification.

Scott Bryant convincingly argued that Randall did not go through a Calvinist phase, as historians (including myself) have concluded. Bryant quoted Randall as saying, "As the doctrine of Calvin had not been in dispute among us, I had not considered whether I believed it or not." When asked on one occasion early in his ministry why he did not preach Calvinist doctrine, Randall responded plainly, "Because I do not believe it." Randall and his colleagues gave birth to a growing Arminian denomination centered in New England, which upset the equilibrium of New England Calvinism. On the one hand, New England Baptists who were inclined toward Calvinism became more rigorous in their Calvinism in reaction to the Freewill Baptists. On the other hand, many New England Baptists felt the need to soften their Calvinism.[35]

The Freewill Baptist Treatise, to which all Freewill Baptist ministers subscribed, is a mixture of Reformed elements with quasi-Wesleyan doctrine. It said that "Christ

---

[33] Kidd, "Not New to Baptists."

[34] H. Leon McBeth, *The Baptist Heritage: Four Centuries of Baptist Witness* (Nashville: Broadman, 1987), 210–11, 714.

[35] Scott Bryant, *The Awakening of the Freewill Baptists: Benjamin Randall and the Founding of an American Religious Tradition* (Macon, GA: Mercer University Press, 2011), 83.

gave his life a sacrifice for the sins of the world and thus made salvation possible for all men." The confession also affirmed penal substitutionary atonement: "He died for us, suffering the penalty of the law in our stead to make known the righteousness of God." The atonement provided "satisfaction for the violation of [God's] law"; and "the power to believe is the gift of God." Yet the confession's doctrine of sanctification was more like Wesleyanism's and differed strongly from that of the southern Free Will Baptists: "The attainment of entire sanctification in this life is both the privilege and duty of every Christian."[36] By the 1860s, the General Conference had revised the treatise to exclude the doctrine of entire sanctification.

The *gratia universalis et resistibilis* is the theme of the confession's Arminian doctrine: "The grace of God, the influences of the Holy Spirit, and the invitations of the gospel are given to all men, and by these they receive power to repent and obey all the requirements of the gospel. Hence it appears a perfect inconsistency to suppose that God would provide salvation for a less number than he really loved." God loves everyone, Christ died for everyone, the Holy Spirit "reproves" everyone, the gospel "invites" everyone, and "by virtue of these all men have the ability to repent and believe." Therefore, the treatise asks, "What other conclusion can be drawn than that the salvation of all is possible?" The confession stressed that everyone's salvation is merely possible, "for though in its provision it is free and absolute, yet in its application it is expressly conditional. Salvation then being freely provided and man being capable through grace of obtaining it if he perish, whom can he blame but himself? The charge must fall upon him with aggravated weight: '*Thou hast destroyed thyself.*'"[37]

The confession affirmed that divine salvific grace continues to be resistible even after conversion. Thus perseverance is not "certain." Though believers are "kept by the power of God through faith unto salvation," this power is "only used to keep the saints *through their faith*," but Scripture teaches that "some have put away faith and a good conscience and concerning faith made shipwreck."[38] The movement's primary systematic theologian John J. Butler explained these doctrines systematically in his

---

[36] "A Treatise on the Faith of the Freewill Baptists (1834)," reprinted in William J. McGlothlin, ed., *Baptist Confessions of Faith* (Philadelphia: American Baptist Publication Society, 1911), 317, 319, 321.

[37] *A Treatise on the Faith of the Free-will Baptists* (Dover, NH: Free-will Baptist Printing Establishment, 1848), 55–58.

[38] *Treatise* (1848), 75–76.

book *Natural and Revealed Theology*.[39] That book was revised later in the century by Ransom Dunn.[40]

The General Association of General Baptists

The General Association of General Baptists arose spontaneously in the nineteenth-century American Midwest.[41] A minister named Benoni Stinson embraced Arminian tenets, which led to his and his wife's break with New Hope Baptist Church and the Calvinistic Wabash District Association of Baptists in Indiana in 1823.[42]

Stinson strongly taught an anti-Pelagian doctrine of original sin, depravity, and the need for a radical intervention of divine grace. Yet he affirmed that God made provision for this grace to reach everyone, and if people are not saved, the fault is their own; it is not because God is withholding his grace. The only remedy to this fallen condition is the necessity of atonement as penal satisfaction. When Adam sinned, Stinson argued, "all the posterity of man was involved in this transgression." They were all "subject to the condemnation, by virtue of their relation to the parental head." Man, therefore, lost the "moral image of God," thus becoming "corrupt, fallen, depraved and ruined," and thus "under condemnation and without help" and "unable to extricate himself from his fallen state by any ability he possessed in his ruined condition."[43]

Stinson described the salvific remedy: "When he was lost and condemned, help could only be communicated in a way consistent with the honor of that law and dignity of God's character." God by grace, "unsolicited," sends Christ to make "that necessary atonement to the law and satisfaction to justice." Thus, believers can be "released from the guilt of original sin" and saved "through the merits of Jesus Christ, which make it possible for everyone "to be delivered from personal or actual transgression." Stinson averred, "We look upon [Christ] to be of that spotless holiness that would be calculated not only to satisfy justice, but atone to the law, and to magnify it and make it honorable."[44]

---

[39] John J. Butler, *Natural and Revealed Theology: A System of Lectures* (Dover, NH: Freewill Baptist Printing Establishment, 1861).

[40] John J. Butler and Ransom Dunn, *Lectures on Systematic Theology* (Boston: Morning Star, 1892).

[41] David B. Montgomery, *General Baptist History* (Evansville, IN: Courier, 1882), 138, 182.

[42] Montgomery, 180–81.

[43] Benoni Stinson and Joel Hume, *A Debate on the Doctrine of the Atonement* (Cincinnati: E. Morgan, 1863), 5, 41.

[44] Stinson and Hume, 5–6.

The possibility to partake in the merits of Christ is not limited to the elect but is offered to all; otherwise, they would "make Christ their own, contrary to their will and choice." God and his decrees are not responsible for one's damnation. Rather, "the damnation of the sinner is upon his own head. . . . Man, by failing to do what he might have done (repent and believe), subjects himself to just condemnation." God gives everyone "sufficient ability to obey the commandment" to repent and believe.[45]

When several regional General Baptist associations gathered in 1870 in Gallatin County, Illinois, to form the General Association of General Baptists, they agreed on some brief "Articles of Faith." These articulated a general atonement, that everyone had to repent and believe to be saved, with the exception of "infants and idiots," who were included in the covenant of grace. They eschewed semi-Pelagianism and affirmed the possibility of apostasy in the statements that "we are fallen and depraved creatures, and cannot extricate ourselves from our fallen situation by any ability we possess by nature." Instead, the whole of grace and salvation is rooted in Christ's "life, death, resurrection, ascension, and intercession." The possibility of apostasy from salvation is taught in the simple Scripture quotation from Mark 13:13, "He that shall endure unto the end, the same shall be saved."[46]

The Decline of Calvinism among Baptists of Particular Baptist Origins

The late eighteenth and nineteenth centuries marked a period of the decline of Calvinism among Baptists who originated with the English Particular Baptists. One sees this among the Baptists of Great Britain as well as those of North America.

British Baptists

The softening of strict Calvinism among British Baptists in the late eighteenth century began with the move away from the high Calvinism of leaders such as John Gill and John Brine and the move toward new leaders such as Andrew Fuller, John Collett Ryland, John Ryland Jr., and Robert Hall of Arnesby.[47] In contrast to

---

[45] Stinson and Hume, 130, 163–66.

[46] "General Association Articles of Faith (1870)," https://www.nobts.edu/baptist-center
-theology/confessions/General_Association_Articles_of_Faith_1870.pdf.

[47] William H. Brackney, *Historical Dictionary of the Baptists* (Lanham, MD: Scarecrow, 2009), 572.

the strict Particular Baptists, these young leaders, spurred on by the revival fervor of the day, emphasized the free offer of the gospel and the death of Christ for all people, yet they were still Calvinist in their espousal of unconditional election and irresistible grace. Andrew Fuller even forged a friendship and made common cause with Dan Taylor, the principal leader of the New Connexion of General Baptists. While the two friends debated controverted points of doctrine, the cordial spirit between them differed from the more hostile tension between Fuller and the hyper-Calvinists and Antinomians.[48]

This softening gave way to full-blown dissent from orthodox Calvinism among the British Baptists as the nineteenth century progressed, to the point where W. T. Whitley could say in 1928, "The great mass of Baptists no longer attend to the question at all. . . . For the majority the truth or falsity of Calvinism is a vanished condition."[49] As Gerald Parsons said of English Nonconformity in general, "The decline of the old high Calvinism" exemplified "the impact of the evangelical revival upon the Old Dissent. . . . Old theological distinctions between Arminians and Calvinists, or between varieties of Calvinism, became less central and less decisive in shaping the pattern of nineteenth-century Nonconformity." This was seen in the revised constitution of the loosely united Baptist Union in Great Britain in 1832.[50]

The erosion of Calvinism among British Baptists is evidenced by the formation of new Particular Baptist associations that separated from the mainstream Baptist movement in Great Britain. In the 1840s, for example, groups of strict Particular Baptists organized new associations such as the New London Strict Association (1845) and the New Suffolk and Norfolk Association of Strict Baptists (1848). They formed these new associations to separate from Baptists who were de-emphasizing Calvinism in their alliances with General Baptists. These associations even tried to establish a national strict Particular Baptist body but failed. Robert Torbet explained that in the 1840s London was the center of this controversy between stricter and milder Calvinists, but it moved north in the 1850s. Some congregations, for example,

[48] Chris Chun, *The Legacy of Jonathan Edwards in the Theology of Andrew Fuller* (Leiden: Brill, 2012), 33–34. See also John H. Y. Briggs, "Evangelical Ecumenism: The Amalgamation of General and Particular Baptists in 1891," *Baptist Quarterly* 34, no. 3 (1991): 101.

[49] William Thomas Whitley, *The Baptists of London, 1612–1928* (London: Kingsgate, 1928), 27.

[50] Gerald Parsons, *Religion in Victorian Britain*, vol. 1, *Traditions* (Manchester, UK: Manchester University Press, 1988), 72.

separated from the Lancashire and Cheshire associations, stating that the associations were "on the 'down-grade' from strict Calvinism and close communion."[51]

One sees the same trend among Scottish Baptists from the 1840s through the 1860s. Calvinism began declining among Scottish Baptists just as it was declining in the Reformed churches generally.[52] This deterioration began to occur in the 1840s through the influence of Baptist Union of Scotland leaders such as Francis Johnston, William Landels, and Thomas Milner, who were influenced by the theology and practices of Charles Finney. The Baptist Union ceased to exist in 1853, but by the time it was relaunched in 1869, Talbot explained, Calvinism's ascendancy "was now over. An era in which evangelical Arminianism predominated was now about to take place."[53]

The decline of Calvinism in Great Britain continued into the late nineteenth century as Baptists moved toward a more formal union of their Calvinist and Arminian branches in 1891. The desuetude of Calvinist orthodoxy among English Baptists is illustrated no more vividly than in an 1868 article in the *General Baptist Magazine*, which celebrated the fact that the Particular Baptists had "become wiser" in shedding their strong Calvinism:

> There is no need now that we should be distinct from the other section of the Baptist body. The extravagant Calvinism of years gone by in Particular Baptist churches has been discarded or moderated and rendered agreeable. Our existence has been necessary as a protest. Our existence now is necessary as a friend and an ally. Our views of the atonement are held in so-called Particular Baptist churches, and a moderate Calvinism exists even among our own. Now we are really one with the other body. General and Particular are words which might be disused. Our greater brother has become wiser; we need not now protest but may walk and prosper with him.[54]

British Baptists were taking part in a broader deterioration of Calvinism in other denominations. In 1876, for example, the *General Baptist Magazine* noted the same slippage among the Independents (Congregationalists), citing R. W. Dale to the

---

[51] Robert G. Torbet, *A History of the Baptists* (Philadelphia: Judson, 1950), 110.

[52] Brian Talbot, *The Search for a Common Identity: The Origins of the Baptist Union of Scotland, 1800–1870* (Milton Keyes, UK: Paternoster, 2003), 15.

[53] Talbot, 16. See also Torbet, *History of the Baptists*, 87.

[54] Charles Clarke, "The Present State of the General Baptist Denomination," *General Baptist Magazine* (London: E. Marlborough & Co., 1868), 101.

effect that "Calvinism is almost an obsolete theory amongst Independents," and that "the doctrine of 'general redemption' . . . is generally accepted and preached amongst them."[55] By 1891 the Particular and General Baptists came together in formal union, and, as Robert Torbet said, "only a few Baptist churches in the northern counties still remained outside the fellowship; they were either Scotch or Strict Particular Baptists."[56]

Baptists in the American North and Canada

Baptists in the Northern States

Bryan Bademan correctly argued, "One of the central narrative strands in the traditional historiography of American religion is the nineteenth-century Americanization and decline of Calvinism."[57] By 1891, Baptist historian Henry Clay Vedder, of New York and Pennsylvania, could say that "modifications in Baptist faith and practice during the last two centuries" included "a less rigidly Calvinistic theology." He averred, "That both Calvinism and Arminianism have been so modified as to bear little relation to the systems once passing under these names is so well understood, and so little likely to be questioned, that it is not worth while to waste space in more than a statement of the fact." Anyone who compares published sermons a century earlier to the ones in the 1880s and 1890s, Vedder said, "must be struck by this fact. . . . Whether these changes have been for the better or for the worse, they are undeniable and they are permanent."[58]

This state of things, however, was by no means new in 1891. In 1860 the eminent New England Calvinist Baptist minister and premier Baptist historian of his day, David Benedict, lamented the decline of Calvinism over the course of his ministry in his book *Fifty Years among the Baptists*. He explained that the New England Baptists in the late eighteenth and early nineteenth century, while Calvinistic in their

---

[55] John Clifford, "Scraps from the Editor's Waste Basket," in *General Baptist Magazine* 78:66, quoted in Briggs, "Evangelical Ecumenism," 111–12.

[56] Torbet, *History of the Baptists*, 138.

[57] See Bademan's list of authors who support this thesis. Bademan rightly went on to argue that Calvin had a strong influence on American thought in many significant ways. R. Bryan Bademan, "The Republican Reformer: John Calvin and the American Calvinists," in *Sober, Strict, and Scriptural: Collective Memories of John Calvin, 1800–2000*, ed. Johan de Niet, Herman Paul, and Bart Wallet (Leiden: Brill, 2009), 267.

[58] Henry C. Vedder, *A Short History of the Baptists* (Philadelphia: American Baptist Publication Society, 1891), 221–23.

doctrines of predestination and irresistible grace, "were not in the habit of enforcing them so strongly as were those in New York, Philadelphia, and further South." The Baptists who identified with the "New Light" movement that emerged from the Great Awakening were even milder in their Calvinism than before, Benedict said. "Indeed, their orthodoxy was often called in question by the old school party. . . . These zealous reformers, in their public performances, dwelt mostly on the subjects of Christian experience and practical religion, while the strait Calvinists labored much to explain and defend the strong points of their system."[59]

Benedict explained that in his youth the Baptists were largely Calvinistic, but the Freewill Baptist movement associated with Benjamin Randall, and to a lesser extent the Seventh Day Baptists, were "then coming into notice." These Arminian preachers, along with the Methodist circuit riders "who often came in contact with the Baptists" and seemed as if they "considered themselves predestined to preach against Predestination," influenced the larger Baptist movement.[60] Soon, hostility between Freewill Baptists and other Baptists was "mollified, so that the differing men can meet together without taunting each other with their offensive creeds," and this movement toward conciliation aided in the weakening of Calvinism among New England Baptists: "On this subject I lately remarked to a Freewill Baptist minister, 'Your side has been coming up, and ours has been going down, till the chasm between the two parties is by no means so great as formerly.'"[61]

Benedict explained that by the late eighteenth and early nineteenth centuries, a more moderate Calvinism, which he called "the Fuller system," had already softened the older Calvinism, teaching that Christ died for all and all are called to salvation. Since then, Benedict lamented, "so greatly has the standard of orthodoxy been lowered, even among those who are reputed orthodox, from former times, and so little attention do most of our church members of the present day pay to the doctrines which are advanced by their ministers," that most present-day Baptists, except the older ones, would not realize that Calvinism used to be ascendant among the Baptists. Writing in the late 1850s, Benedict lamented that now, "nothing that will sound harsh or unpleasant to very sensitive ears [will] come from the preachers; the old-fashioned doctrines of Predestination, Total Depravity, Divine Sovereignty, etc., if referred to at all, must be by way of circumlocution and implication." He quoted

---

[59] David Benedict, *Fifty Years among the Baptists* (New York: Sheldon, 1860), 137–38.
[60] Benedict, *Fifty Years*, 139.
[61] Benedict, 140.

one layman as saying that "our minister . . . never mentions [election] openly." Most Baptists "would sit very uneasy under discourses in which the primordial principles of the orthodox Baptist faith should be presented in the style of our sound old preachers of bygone years."[62]

Even in areas where the confession of faith remained Calvinistic, "this moderating still goes on, in theological training, in ministerial functions, and in public sentiment, and to what point of moderation we shall in time descend, it is difficult to foretell." Benedict feared more Baptists were becoming like John Leland, who, although a Calvinist, "was not one of the straitest class. Two grains of Arminianism, with three of Calvinism, he thought would make a tolerably good compound." Benedict quoted an English statesman who once said of his own church, "'We have a Calvinistic creed, a Roman ritual, and an Arminian clergy.' This in time may apply to us, minus the ritual, in some cases."[63]

Benedict's prediction was more accurate than he may have realized. By 1890, New York pastor Edward Hiscox could say, in his widely read Baptist church manual, that Baptists were broadly Calvinistic, but most only "moderately so, being midway between the extremes of Arminianism and Antinomianism. . . . The freedom of the human will is declared, while the sovereignty of divine grace, and the absolute necessity of the Spirit's work in faith and salvation are maintained."[64]

The deterioration of Baptist Calvinism throughout the North and Canada is evinced by the cooling of hostilities between Freewill Baptists and their wider Baptist counterparts, which concluded in a full, formal merger between them, both in Canada and the United States, in the early twentieth century. In 1908 Northern Baptist C. H. Spalding highlighted the crucial role of the New Hampshire Confession of Faith in this development:

> During this century and a quarter the Baptists have been greatly modified. The yielding of the rigid Calvinistic feeling recorded itself in New England when in 1832 the New Hampshire confession was adopted by the New Hampshire

---

[62] Benedict, 141–43. Steve Lemke quoted the New England Baptist Francis Wayland, president of Brown University, as saying in 1857 that strict Calvinism had been considerably softened over the previous fifty years. Steve W. Lemke, "History or Revisionist History? How Calvinistic Were the Overwhelming Majority of Baptists and Their Confessions in the South until the Twentieth Century?" *Southwestern Journal of Theology* 57, no. 2 (2015): 235–36.

[63] Benedict, *Fifty Years*, 144.

[64] Edward T. Hiscox, *The Standard Manual for Baptist Churches* (Philadelphia: American Baptist Publication Society, 1890), 57–58; See also Lemke, "History or Revisionist History?," 236–37.

state convention. In the middle states where the old Philadelphia confession is nominally held it has either been expurgated of its strong expressions, or allowed to fall into "innocuous desuetude." The Baptists today have little, if any, more sense of restriction in their Calvinism than Benjamin Randall had in 1780.[65]

As Peter Thuesen argued, by 1833, after the Philadelphia Confession had held sway for nearly a century, "weariness among some Baptists with the Arminian-Calvinist struggle" led to the publication of the New Hampshire Confession of Faith (NHC), which "avoided the most contentious predestinarian issues."[66] The "effect" of the NHC, according to Mark Noll, was to "soften . . . the Calvinistic doctrines of unconditional election and limited atonement."[67] Thus James Leo Garrett said of the NHC, "Although called 'moderately Calvinistic,' it could as well be denominated 'moderately Arminian.'"[68]

Benedict, a strong Calvinist himself, criticized this shift away from what he called the "high authority" of the Philadelphia Confession. The meat of Calvinism was being lost to the "mere water and milk" of Arminianism. Thus, as Douglas Weaver has emphasized, the NHC's soteriological shift demonstrated "the growing influence of Arminianism in Baptist life."[69] J. Newton Brown first published the 1833 NHC in his widely publicized *Encyclopedia of Religious Knowledge* in 1835.[70] Numerous Baptist bodies throughout the United States began to use this version of the confession, leading it to become "the most influential Baptist confession in America."[71] The confession's popularity received large boosts when Brown, by that time editorial secretary of the American Baptist Publication Society, revised and republished it in

---

[65] Charles Hubbard Spalding, "Baptists and Free Baptists: Proposed Union of the Two Denominations in Missionary Service," *The Standard* 55, no. 35 (May 2, 1908): 12.

[66] Peter J. Thuesen, *Predestination: The American Career of a Contentious Doctrine* (New York: Oxford University Press, 2009), 193.

[67] Mark A. Noll, *A History of Christianity in the United States and Canada* (Grand Rapids: Eerdmans, 1992), 178–79.

[68] James Leo Garrett, *Baptist Theology: A Four-Century Study* (2009; repr., Macon, GA: Mercer University Press, 2019), 151.

[69] C. Douglas Weaver, *In Search of the New Testament Church: The Baptist Story* (Macon, GA: Mercer University Press, 2008), 97–98.

[70] "Baptists," in J. Newton Brown, ed., *Encyclopedia of Religious Knowledge, or, Dictionary of the Bible, Theology, Religious Biography, All Religions, Ecclesiastical History, and Missions* (Brattleboro, VT: Fessenden, 1835), 191–92.

[71] Weaver, *New Testament Church*, 97–98.

The Baptist Church Manual. Its impact took another leap forward when the influential Landmark leader J. M. Pendleton included it in his *Church Manual Designed for the Use of Baptist Churches* in 1867.[72]

Minor wording differences distinguish the 1835 and 1853 editions of the NHC, but both versions diverge significantly from the Calvinism of the Philadelphia Confession. According to these editions of the NHC, because of the fall "all mankind are now sinners . . . by nature utterly void of that holiness required by the law of God." Salvation is "wholly of grace, through the mediatorial offices of the Son of God." Christ "honored the law by his personal obedience, and made atonement for our sins by his death." Justification is "bestowed not in consideration of any works of righteousness which we have done, but solely through his own redemption and righteousness." In the 1853 edition Brown added, "His perfect righteousness is freely imputed to us of God."[73]

The "blessings of salvation" are "made free to all by the gospel," and it is the "immediate duty of all to accept them by a cordial and obedient faith; . . . nothing prevents the salvation of the greatest sinner on earth, except his own voluntary refusal to submit to the Lord Jesus Christ." The 1853 version added "inherent depravity" and "voluntary rejection of the gospel" to the words "voluntary refusal." Neither edition specified whether regeneration occurs before or after faith. Election, "the gracious purpose of God, according to which he regenerates, sanctifies, and saves sinners," is "perfectly consistent with the free agency of man" and "comprehends all the means in connection with the end." While it "utterly excludes boasting," it "encourages the use of means in the highest degree." "Such only are real believers as endure unto the end."[74]

Why did this decline in Calvinism, not just among Baptists, but in other denominations, occur? Scholars mostly conjecture that it coincided with the New Light revivalism of the Great Awakening, exemplified by the Separate Baptist movement, as well as what Nathan O. Hatch termed the "democratization of American Christianity."[75] As James Tull noted, a "striking effect" of the influences of the New Light revivalism of the Great Awakening was "an erosion of the old Calvinist consensus which

---

[72] See J. Newton Brown, *Baptist Church Manual* (Philadelphia: American Baptist Publication Society, 1853); James Madison Pendleton, *Church Manual Designed for the Use of Baptist Churches* (Philadelphia: American Baptist Publication Society, 1867).

[73] Brown, *Encyclopedia of Religious Knowledge*, 191; Brown, *Baptist Church Manual*, 7–13.

[74] Brown, *Baptist Church Manual*, 7–13.

[75] Nathan O. Hatch, *The Democratization of American Christianity* (New Haven, CT: Yale University Press, 1991); see particularly the section of the book entitled, "The Crusade against Calvinist Orthodoxy and Control," 170–79.

had obtained since the Puritan era." Despite the efforts of Isaac Backus to combine Calvinism and revivalist-pietism, the Separate Baptists "lost a considerable number of adherents to the Freewill Baptist movement," which "eventually swept away many Separate Baptists on the northern frontier."[76] Many Separate Baptists became full Arminians, uniting with the Freewill Baptists. Some Separate Baptists, Tull said, "became more Arminian than the Arminians."[77]

Douglas Weaver agreed that over the first half of the nineteenth century, even in places where Calvinism remained Baptists' "formal theology," the spread of "revivalism and democratic idealism, which expressed considerable confidence in the abilities of a free common people, softened or 'Arminianized' the practice of Calvinism. . . . Some Baptists tied to the lower end of the social scale found no warmth in predestination."[78] This process was helped along by the northern Freewill Baptists, who helped erode Calvinism among northern Baptists, particularly in New England, prompting the publication of the NHC.[79]

Canadian Baptists

One sees this same dynamic of the softening and decline of Calvinism at work among Canadian Baptists. Daniel Goodwin's study of the process that led to the union of the Arminian and (formerly) Calvinist Baptists of the Maritime Provinces exemplified the softening of Calvinism among Canadian Baptists. He argued that these Baptists came to experience "a heightened sense of free moral agency that was spread by the emergence of market capitalism and responsible government. This in turn led to the modification and decline of Calvinism among the Regular Baptists."[80] One Baptist author wrote in the *Religious Intelligencer* in 1884: "Today it is a well-known fact of experience that the very high views as to limited atonement and election have undergone considerable change. It can safely be said that more liberal views prevail approaching to beliefs of Free Baptists [the term Freewill Baptists began to use of

---

[76] James E. Tull, *Shapers of Baptist Thought* (Valley Forge, PA: Judson, 1972), 73.

[77] Tull, 76.

[78] Weaver, *New Testament Church*, 97.

[79] Weaver, 97–98. Regarding the influence of the Freewill Baptists in this process of decline, see also McBeth, *Baptist Heritage*, 210–11; Lumpkin, *Baptist Confessions of Faith*, 360; Gilbert R. Englerth, "American Baptists and Their Confessions of Faith" (PhD diss., Temple University, 1969), 282.

[80] Daniel Goodwin, "The Meaning of 'Baptist Union' in Maritime Canada, 1846–1906," in *Baptist Identities: International Studies from the Seventeenth to the Twentieth Century*, ed. Ian M. Randall, Toivo Pilli, and Anthony R. Cross (Milton Keyes, UK: Paternoster, 2006), 153–54.

themselves in the latter nineteenth century].” This narrative of Calvinism's modification and decline in the Baptist experience, which mirrors "the general decline of
Calvinism among Anglo-American Protestants in the nineteenth century," provided
the main thrust of Goodwin's story.[81]

The same thing that occurred in England and Scotland occurred in the Maritime
provinces. An ultra-Calvinist group split from the other Regular Baptist churches to
form the Particular Dependent Close-Communion Baptists. Goodwin said this group
"siphoned off some of the more traditionally Reformed churches and leaders among
the Regular Baptists in New Brunswick and facilitated the decline of Calvinism among
the mainstream Regular Baptists in the region." This group's formation showed that
"some of the more extreme forms of Calvinism" were moving toward the periphery
of Baptist life in the Maritimes in the mid- to late-nineteenth century. This "pav[ed]
the way for a broadly-defined Maritime Baptist culture that left little room for dogmatically held theological extremes. It was this middle ground that came to dominate
Regular and Free Baptist life and facilitated union in 1905 and 1906."[82]

An 1899 editorial in the *Messenger and Visitor* testified to this middle ground,
arguing that the distinction between Calvinism and Arminianism "no longer has the
significance for church relationship [between the Baptist and Free Baptist churches]
that it once had. The acceptance of Calvinistic doctrine is not now, if it ever was,
a condition of admission into a [Regular] Baptist church, and we suppose that no
Christian would be in any danger of exclusion from Free Baptist communion because
of being a Calvinist."[83]

Baptists in the American South

The process of the softening of Calvinism took the same course in the South as it
did in the North, if a little later. Over the course of the nineteenth century, southern Baptists gradually moderated and modified the Calvinism of their Particular
Baptist heritage. This moderated Calvinism was well-entrenched in the grass roots of
Southern Baptist churches by the 1880s. This is illustrated in a quotation in John A.
Broadus's 1893 biography of James Petigru Boyce, the staunchly Calvinistic president
of Southern Baptist Theological Seminary who died in 1888. Broadus quoted Edgar

---

[81] Goodwin, "'Baptist Union' in Maritime," 161–62.
[82] Goodwin, 163.
[83] Goodwin, 163.

E. Folk of Tennessee, editor of the widely read *Baptist and Reflector*, as reminiscing, "You had to know your Systematic Theology, or you could not recite it to Dr. Boyce. And though the young men were generally rank Arminians when they came to the Seminary, few went through this course under him without being converted to his strong Calvinistic views."[84]

Far from embracing a less-Reformed understanding of depravity and redemption, like many of the Anti-Calvinists associated with the Methodists and Disciples of Christ and Churches of Christ around them, "post-Calvinistic" Baptists in the South would not part with the classic Reformed doctrines of *sola gratia* (original sin and total depravity) and *sola fide* (the imputation of the righteousness of Christ alone in justification). Furthermore, they held strenuously to the Calvinist doctrine of the certain perseverance of the saints. Because of this *via media* between Calvinism and Arminianism, some referred to their views as mild Calvinism, while others termed it mild Arminianism.[85]

The perspective of this essay will differ on this point from distinguished scholars such as Tom Nettles, whose work I have long appreciated. Until I undertook the study of this subject, I simply assumed—because I knew that Southern Baptists arose from the Particular Baptist rather than General Baptist stream of the Baptist family—scholars such as Tom Nettles were right when they said things like: "Only slight, isolated, and idiosyncratic declines from Calvinism entered Southern Baptist theology prior to the 20th century. No one of trend-setting influence seriously challenged the Calvinistic hegemony before the arrival of E. Y. Mullins as president of The Southern Baptist Theological Seminary in 1899." As a Free Will Baptist who remains outside the loop of the Southern Baptist Convention (SBC), I did not see myself as having a "dog in this hunt" and basically agreed with Nettles, Tom Ascol, and others who have advanced this view. As the reader will note, my study of the subject has caused me to change my mind on this.[86]

---

[84] John A. Broadus, *Memoir of James Petrigru Boyce, D.D., LL.D.* (New York: A. C. Armstrong and Son, 1893), 265; Lemke, "History or Revisionist History?," 237.

[85] Hosea Holcombe, *A History of the Rise and Progress of the Baptists in Alabama* (Philadelphia: King and Baird, 1840), 50.

[86] Tom Nettles, "The Rise and Demise of Calvinism among Southern Baptists," *Founders Journal* 19/20 (1995), 28–29. See also Tom Ascol, "Southern Baptists at the Crossroads: Returning to the Old Paths," in the same journal issue, as well as "Faith of our Founders: An Interview with Tom Ascol," July 1, 2012, http://www.ligonier.org/learn/articles/faith-of-our-founders-an-interview-with-tom-ascol/.

Peter Thuesen summarized the tug-of-war between Calvinism and Arminianism in nineteenth-century Southern Baptist life—a tension more and more Southern Baptists became comfortable maintaining as the century progressed:

> Most Southern Baptists had been influenced enough by the Calvinism of the convention's founders that they rejected the Arminian notion that a genuinely converted person could later backslide and lose his salvation. Baptists called this "eternal security" rather than perseverance, and they used it as an apologetic weapon against Methodists and Pentecostals. Nevertheless, the non-Calvinist faction shared Arminians' profound unease with the Calvinist doctrines of unconditional election, limited atonement, and irresistible grace. The non-Calvinists were in many respects the heirs of a revivalistic tradition in the South, which was first institutionalized during the Great Awakening by the Sandy Creek Baptist Association in North Carolina and was anti-creedal and voluntaristic in outlook. This quasi-Arminian faction was also highly biblicistic, often railing against the tyranny of "man-made" dogmas.[87]

Writing as early as 1813, Calvinist David Benedict chronicled, and lamented, the softening of Calvinist soteriology among Baptists in the South as they migrated out from Virginia. These Baptists were divided into Regular and Separate Baptists, with the Separate Baptists being "much more numerous." The Regular Baptists were "very highly Calvinistick," and while a majority of the Separate Baptists started out as moderate Calvinists, they were "far from being unanimous in their doctrinal sentiments." Thus, many of them were "much inclined to the Arminian side of the controversy; and some of the most distinguished among them, in opposing the high strains of Calvinism, which were incessantly and in many instances dogmatically sounded by their orthodox brethren, had gone nearly the full length of Arminius." When the Separate Baptists migrated into Kentucky, the Calvinistic-leaning ones united with the Regular Baptists in the Elkhorn Association, while those "inclined to the Arminian system, as well as those who adopted some of the Calvinistick creed in a qualified sense," united with the South Kentucky Association.[88]

The prevailing Separate Baptist view is summed up in the words of John Leland, who in 1791 quipped:

---

[87] Thuesen, *Predestination*, 201.

[88] David Benedict, *A General History of the Baptist Denomination in America* (1813; repr., Morrisville, NC: Lulu, 2005), 237.

I conclude that the *eternal purposes* of God, and the *freedom of the human will*, are both truths; and it is a matter of fact, that the preaching that has been most blessed of God, and most profitable to men, is *the doctrine of sovereign grace in the salvation of souls, mixed with a little of what is called Arminianism.* These two propositions can be tolerably well reconciled together; but the modern misfortune is, that men often spend too much time in explaining away one or the other.[89]

Sydney Ahlstrom averred that while Arminian and strongly Calvinist parties persisted in the Baptist churches, most Baptists blended "revivalistic and 'orthodox' tendencies along the lines suggested by John Leland's compromise." Ahlstrom remarked that this "majority view" of American Baptists in the nineteenth century found expression in the NHC.[90]

Robert Baylor Semple, in his history of Virginia Baptists, concurred that "the Regulars complained that the Separates . . . kept within their communion many who were professed Arminians." To this, the Separates replied that "if there were some among them who leaned too much towards the Arminian system, they were generally men of exemplary piety and great usefulness in the Redeemer's kingdom, and they conceived it better to bear with some diversity of opinion in doctrines than to break with men whose Christian deportment rendered them amiable in the estimation of all true lovers of genuine godliness. . . . To exclude such as these from their communion would be like tearing the limbs from the body."[91] Thus R. B. C. Howell, writing in 1857, referred to the Sandy Creek Association, in a context as early as the 1760s, as a "Separate, or Arminian, association."[92]

An example of the incessant Arminian-leaning minority report among southern Baptists from a Particular Baptist heritage is the incident of Separate Baptist leader Jeremiah Walker in the 1790s. Walker, a well-known Baptist minister with ties to North Carolina, Georgia, and Virginia Baptists, became an Arminian, writing a

---

[89] John Leland, "A Letter of Valediction on Leaving Virginia, 1791," in *The Writings of the Late Elder John Leland*, ed. L. F. Green (New York: G. W. Wood, 1845), 172. Italics in the original.

[90] Sydney Ahlstrom, *A Religious History of the American People*, 2nd ed. (New Haven, CT: Yale University Press, 2004), 322. See also Lemke, "History or Revisionist History?," 233.

[91] Robert Baylor Semple, *A History of the Rise and Progress of the Baptists in Virginia* (Richmond: Pitt & Dickinson, 1894), 100.

[92] Robert Boyle C. Howell, *The Early Baptists of Virginia* (Philadelphia: Bible and Publication Society, 1857), 45–46, quoted in Lemke, "History or Revisionist History?," 246.

highly publicized pamphlet entitled *The Fourfold Foundation of Calvinism Examined and Shaken*. In 1791 a debate took place in the form of two sermons preached from the Calvinist and Arminian perspectives, hosted by the General Committee of the Baptists of Virginia, between Walker and Jesse Mercer's father, Silas Mercer. Mercer had brought charges against Walker in the Georgia Baptist Association, which had excluded Walker and some of his followers in 1790.[93] This large meeting of Virginia Baptists was hosting a discussion on Calvinism and Arminianism between two Baptists all the way from Georgia, one of whom had been excommunicated at the behest of the other.[94]

Semple said, "Mr. Mercer was a decided Calvinist, and Mr. Walker as decided an Arminian; though it must be confessed that neither of them carried their system to such extremes as they have been carried by many. Mr. Mercer denied the doctrine of eternal reprobation, and Mr. Walker acknowledged that of imputed righteousness." What he said next, however, is what is most revealing about the mixture of opinions in this large gathering of Baptist ministers in the early 1790s: "In the General Committee each had a respectable party, though the Calvinist side was much the largest. It is hard to say which of the two had the advantage in point of talents. . . . As it respected address, either in or out of the pulpit, Walker had greatly the superiority."[95]

After the General Committee meeting, Walker and Mercer "both traveled and preached extensively throughout the State, creating wherever they went much conversation and agitation of mind among the people." Semple said that Walker's pamphlet "was thought to have made temporary impressions upon many strong Calvinists. . . . The ultimate consequence of this investigation of principles was a decrease of Arminianism among the Baptists of Virginia, and a much greater uniformity in the doctrines of grace. Some were thought also, after these events, to have pushed the Calvinistic scheme to an Antinomian extreme."[96]

Efforts in the late eighteenth century toward the union of Regular and Separate Baptists met with conflict, because the Separate Baptists were averse to confessions of faith and "the Regulars were unwilling to unite with them, without something of the kind." Finally, in 1801, with the Awakening's "softening influence on the minds of the saints," these different soteriological expressions were "intermixed" among the

---

[93] Anthony L. Chute, *A Piety above the Common Standard: Jesse Mercer and Evangelistic Calvinism* (Macon, GA: Mercer University Press, 2004), 20–24.

[94] Semple, *Baptists in Virginia*, 107–8.

[95] Semple, 108.

[96] Semple, 110.

Baptists, who were more willing to unite. Thus, for example, the terms of union between the Elkhorn and South Kentucky Associations held that "the preaching *Christ tasted death for every man*, shall be no bar to communion."[97]

The terms of union also "did not list grace's irresistibility or predestination," explains Richard Traylor.[98] Benedict bemoaned that "it soon appeared that in the southern department of the Old Separate community, there were a number who had gone far into doctrinal errors. Some were decided Arminians."[99] This episode led Thomas Kidd and Barry Hankins to conclude that with the "phenomenal growth among frontier Baptists, distinctively Calvinist theology began to wane."[100]

The Separate Baptists were the main conduit of non-Calvinist theology into the Baptist experience in the South. Using Walter Shurden's labels of the "Charleston" (Regular) and "Sandy Creek" (Separate) traditions, Wayne Flynt stated, "If Charleston, South Carolina, provides the clearest ancestry for Calvinism, Sandy Creek, North Carolina, lays firmest claim to the revival tradition. Ardent, charismatic, emotional, independent, biblicist, the Sandy Creek tradition merged elements of both Calvinism and Arminianism."[101] Steve Lemke pointed out that most of the growing Baptist movement on the frontier in the nineteenth century identified with the Sandy Creek tradition, most of which was "neither fully Calvinist nor Arminian, but somewhere between those polar positions."[102]

As Albert Henry Newman argued, Methodism influenced the Separate Baptists in the Carolinas in the 1770s. In the South Carolina General Association of Separate Baptists, Newman said, a "small majority decided in favor of the Calvinistic position, although the Arminian side had the abler supporters." The two groups united, but the Arminians wished to retain "liberty" regarding the "construction" or wording of the doctrine of election. This Arminianizing tendency waned. While some ministers "continued to lean toward Arminianism" at this early period, "the denomination as a

---

[97] Semple, 239–40.

[98] Richard C. Traylor, *Born of Water and Spirit: The Baptist Impulse in Kentucky 1776–1860*, America's Baptists (Knoxville: University of Tennessee Press, 2015), 116.

[99] Benedict, *General History*, 239–41. Similarly, in 1894, Albert Henry Newman remarked that some of the "Separates had . . . a leaning toward Arminianism." Albert Henry Newman, *A History of the Baptist Churches in the United States* (New York: Christian Literature, 1894), 334–35.

[100] Kidd and B. Hankins, *Baptists in America*, 88.

[101] Wayne Flynt, *Alabama Baptists: Southern Baptists in the Heart of Dixie* (Tuscaloosa: University of Alabama Press, 1988), 27.

[102] Lemke, "History or Revisionist History?," 233.

whole was so decidedly Calvinistic that they felt it necessary in the interest of peace to keep their Arminian views somewhat in the background."[103]

However, the fact that Arminianizing arose this early in the South and continued to crop up illustrates the decline of Calvinism among Baptists in the South. In the Carolinas, the Baptists who adopted the Philadelphia Confession also approved a statement that said, "To prevent its usurping a tyrannical power over the consciences of any: We do not mean that every person is bound to the strict observance of everything therein contained." The greatest impediment to union from the Regular Baptists' perspective, Newman argued, was "the guarded way in which the Confession of Faith had been adopted by the Separates and their toleration of Arminianism."[104]

This Arminianizing trend among Baptists in the South continued into the early nineteenth century, though Calvinism was still by far in the ascendancy. Gregory Wills noted the complaints by this time that, owing to the unpopularity of Calvinism outside the church, "Baptists nowadays are afraid to preach the doctrines of Grace," with congregants murmuring about "the doctrine of eternal and particular election." One Calvinist minister worried that "some of the Pedobaptists are saying that Baptists are becoming ashamed of Predestination and Election, and that they will soon quit preaching it."[105]

Wayne Flynt's research on Alabama Baptists in the nineteenth century illustrated the ubiquity of this current of dissent from Calvinism as early as the 1830s that grew into a full-blown moderation of it later in the century. Elder Daniel Bestor exemplified this. He started out as a strict Calvinist, but he moved to Alabama from Connecticut and as he ministered on the Alabama frontier his theology gradually shifted. One of Bestor's Calvinist colleagues said he "verged on Arminianism." Another pastor, Sion Blythe, was criticized by one Calvinist as having "little analytical ability" and being "better at winning sinners to faith in Christ than in training them in doctrine, and was 'somewhat of an Arminian.'"[106]

As early as the 1830s, well-known Calvinists such as Hosea Holcombe, while critical of the Arminianizing tendencies among Alabama Baptists, were "tolerant and

---

[103] Newman, *History of the Baptist*, 299–301. Incidentally, unions of the Regular and Separate Baptists usually resulted in the gradual laying aside of ordinances the latter had previously practiced, such as love feasts, anointing of the sick, feet washing, etc. (Newman, 302).

[104] Newman, 302.

[105] Gregory A. Wills, *Democratic Religion: Freedom, Authority, and Discipline in the Baptist South, 1785–1900* (New York: Oxford University Press, 1997), 107.

[106] Flynt, *Alabama Baptists*, 27.

broad-minded toward deviation from what [they] considered orthodoxy."[107] Holcombe thought the first generation of Alabama Baptist ministers held a "middle ground" in the Calvinist-Arminian debate, while their views were "considerably diverse," including everything from Old School Calvinism to some who "leaned to Arminianism." He lamented that "a considerable number of ministers" had "departed from the old Baptist foundation. . . . The doctrine of election and predestination is dreaded by many young preachers. They cannot reconcile those sublime points of doctrine with their views; and with the use of the means—the agency, and the accountability of man." Still, Holcombe maintained that "in the main," he believed these Arminian-leaning ministers "advance good doctrine." Telling a story from John Wesley's ministry, the Calvinist Holcombe encouraged Baptists across the soteriological spectrum to "cordially unite in the things wherein we agree." Even at this early period, he said, it was hard to know what to call Baptists who expressed these different soteriological opinions: "What is called Calvinism with some, is denominated Arminianism with others."[108]

The tendency toward Arminianism among Alabama Baptists caused many Calvinists to make compromises for the sake of harmony among the brethren. The Tuscaloosa Association was in turmoil for many years over this issue. In 1849 the distinguished Calvinist minister Basil Manly Sr. "was asked to prepare a sermon on the subject of sovereign grace and free will." He preached what Flynt called a "masterful compromise," which eventually allowed both sides to coexist and affected other Alabama associations as well.[109]

The strong Calvinist Jesse Mercer of Georgia noted that "low Calvinism" and even "Arminianism" were in evidence among the early Baptists of Georgia: "It seems to be taken for granted that all those venerable fathers, who founded the Baptist denomination in this state, were . . . stern calvinistic preachers. . . . But this is altogether a mistake." He then described some ministers whom he called "low Calvinists" and others whom he said "were thought rather Arminian; some quite so. . . . And here it may not be amiss to add, that the Baptists in the upper parts of South Carolina, in those days, comprehended mostly, it is believed, in the Bethel Association, were general provisionists."[110]

---

[107] Flynt, 27.

[108] Holcombe, *Baptists in Alabama*, 50–52.

[109] Flynt, *Alabama Baptists*, 29. Flynt gave several other examples of the Arminianizing trend among Alabama Baptists in the early-to-mid-nineteenth century.

[110] Charles Dutton Mallary, *Memoirs of Elder Jesse Mercer* (New York: John Gray, 1844), 201–2.

As Peter Lumpkins has chronicled, this gradual move away from Calvinism began quite early. The establishment of the Broad River Association in North Carolina in 1800, for example, marked a clear shift away from strict Calvinism. Broad River diverged from the neighboring Yadkin Association, whose articles of faith affirmed "the doctrine of eternal, particular election." Instead, Broad River drafted new articles of faith that did not affirm unconditional election and irresistible grace, let alone limited atonement. Instead, they alluded to 2 Thess 2:13, saying, "We believe in the doctrine of *Election* through sanctification of the Spirit and belief of the truth." Many associations added to this statement another biblical phrase popular among Arminians: "election . . . according to the foreknowledge of God."[111]

One surmises that their mere quoting of Scripture in the article on the election was a move designed to accommodate individuals who had rejected the doctrine of unconditional election, but since it was Scripture, a Calvinist could also affirm it. This shift in the Broad River Association in 1800 is a major part of the story of the waning of Calvinism among the Baptists of the South whose heritage was Particular Baptist. At least seventy-two Baptist associations across the South in the nineteenth century would adopt some variation of the Broad River Association articles of faith. Those articles were in use in associations in every southern state except one.[112]

The articles of faith based on the Broad River Association illustrated the Southern Baptist *via media* between Calvinism and Arminianism. While eschewing unconditional election, they affirmed the "doctrine of original sin" and total depravity: "man's impotency to recover himself from the fallen state he is in by nature, by his own free will and holiness." They also noted that justification is "only by the merits of Jesus Christ" and that "the saints shall persevere in grace, and not finally fall away." The articles of faith of the French Broad Association, another early North Carolina association in the Broad River tradition, left out election altogether, but affirmed original sin, total depravity and inability, justification by the imputation of Christ's righteousness, and certain perseverance, using the same language as Broad River on original sin and depravity but substituting the words "imputed righteousness" for "merits." The language of imputed righteousness was

---

[111] E. Peter Frank Lumpkins, "The Decline of Confessional Calvinism among Baptist Associations in the Southern States during the Nineteenth Century" (PhD diss., University of Pretoria, 2018), 67, 166, 174, 175, https://repository.up.ac.za/bitstream/handle/2263/67778/Lumpkins_Decline_2018.pdf?sequence=1&isAllowed=y.

[112] Lumpkins, 344–45, 386.

common in Southern Baptist confessional documents regardless of whether or not they were Calvinist.[113]

The NHC was even more influential among Baptists in the South than the Broad River articles of faith. Especially popular among Landmark Baptists, the confession's influence on Southern Baptists in every southern state in the latter half of the nineteenth century is undisputed. This influence resulted in the heavy dependence of the 1925 Baptist Faith and Message on the NHC. Some scholars, however, have assumed that the confession did not begin to influence Southern Baptists until its 1853 publication in J. Newton Brown's widely read *Baptist Church Manual*. However, Lumpkins established that at least forty Baptist associations in the South used the first edition of the confession, published in Brown's *Encyclopedia of Religious Knowledge* in 1835.[114]

Another seventy-five Baptist associations in the South in the nineteenth century either wrote their own confessions of faith that were not Calvinistic on the doctrines of unconditional election, limited atonement, and irresistible grace (while still retaining total depravity and certain perseverance) or just did not refer to or define election at all.[115]

The delegates to the original session of the SBC in Augusta, Georgia in 1845 reflected this diversity. Many of the primary leaders of the convention were strict Calvinists who affirmed the Philadelphia Confession. Yet this original session, having been convened so quickly, was not geographically representative, and many of the poorer farmer-preachers could not afford to attend. Only around 13 percent of Southern Baptist associations were represented. Even Virginia, the most highly represented state, had only around 18 percent of its associations represented, and around 71 percent of its delegates were from a single association. Still, many associations were represented at the original session of the convention that embraced a milder "two-point" moderation of Calvinism.[116]

---

[113] Lumpkins, 408–9.

[114] Lumpkins, 118. For more on the influence of the NHC among Southern Baptists, see Lemke, "History or Revisionist History?," 251–54.

[115] Lumpkins, 149–77. Lumpkins argued that these associational confessions did not affirm total depravity, but I believe that at least some of the associations did clearly affirm total depravity and inability without the intervention of special prevenient grace. One must be careful to read neither contemporary debates nor strict Calvinist interpretations of total depravity into these statements.

[116] Lumpkins, 178–282.

In all, out of 424 associations surveyed, only 96 had full-fledged Calvinist confessions of faith articulating the doctrine of unconditional election, limited atonement, or irresistible grace.[117] Even if Calvinism was formally in the ascendancy in 1845 at the founding session of the SBC, which is debatable, in the second half of the nineteenth century, it was modified and moderated to the point that it had lost most of its influence over Southern Baptists. This would lay the groundwork for what I call a "post-Calvinist" mainstream in Southern Baptist theology that would accompany the explosive growth of the denomination from the late nineteenth century forward.

Non-Calvinism among Baptists in the Twentieth Century

Despite the debate among Southern Baptist scholars about how much Calvinism was in the ascendency in the nineteenth century, there is no debate that the milder soteriology that held to total depravity and certain perseverance but rejected unconditional election, limited atonement, and irresistible grace constituted the overwhelming mainstream in Baptist theology from the early twentieth century forward.

Meanwhile, the Randall movement of Free Baptists in the North merged with the Northern Baptist Convention in 1911 and abandoned their insistence on the possibility of apostasy. Yet the National Association of Free Will Baptists—founded in 1935 when some midwestern Free Baptists who stayed out of the 1911 merger united with the much larger contingent of Free Will Baptists in the South—continued their confessional adherence to a full-blown Arminian theology, including the possibility of apostasy. The same can be said of the American General Baptists in the Midwest.

Five theologians exemplified the Baptist dissent against strong Calvinism in the twentieth century. Leroy Forlines and Robert Picirilli consolidated the General–Free Will Baptist tradition in a Reformed Arminian movement that matured from the mid-twentieth through the early twenty-first century. Henry C. Thiessen was representative of the *via media* between Calvinism and Arminianism in Northern Baptist circles. E. Y. Mullins and Herschel Hobbs typified this approach among Southern Baptists.

---

[117] Lumpkins, 440–45.

Free Will Baptists: Leroy Forlines and Robert Picirilli

During their student days at Welch College in the late 1940s and early 1950s, Leroy Forlines and Robert Picirilli began to develop a system that would later be termed Reformed Arminianism. Their interest was sparked particularly by a course entitled "Arminian Theology" taught by the college's founding president, Linton C. Johnson.[118] Forlines's thought in this area would develop more in the direction of systematic theology, whereas Picirilli's would develop more toward exegetical theology, though each had his own unique mixture of the two disciplines.

Forlines's thought in these early years was shaped by his reading of the *Works of Jacobus Arminius* against the backdrop of the American scholastic Calvinism of authors such as William G. T. Shedd and Charles Hodge, in which he steeped himself. His reading of Arminius's "Oration on the Priestly Office of Christ" made a profound impact on his thinking. This led him to emphasize the way the "penal satisfaction" Christ made in his atonement, and the resultant "active and passive obedience of Christ" imputed to believers in justification, were necessary to deal with the total depravity of the human mind and heart, which could be counteracted only by "enabling grace," the "necessity of the enlightening and drawing power of the Holy Spirit."[119]

Through his teaching and his books such as *Systematics*, his commentary on Romans, and his larger systematic *The Quest for Truth*, Forlines trained two generations in a Reformed Arminianism that uniquely reflected the Arminianism of English General Baptists such as Thomas Helwys and Thomas Grantham in the seventeenth century.[120] Robert Picirilli provided undergirding for this perspective in his numerous New Testament commentaries and mediated the school of thought to a larger evangelical readership in books such as *Grace, Faith, Free Will* and *Free Will Revisited*.[121] What

---

[118] F. Leroy Forlines, *Classical Arminianism*, 246.

[119] Forlines, *Classical Arminianism*, 24. "Enabling grace" is from Robert E. Picirilli, *Grace, Faith, Free Will*, 155–57. Forlines stated that his reading of Lorraine Boettner's *Studies in Theology*, in connection with Arminius while taking the aforementioned course, impressed on him the importance of the imputation of the active and passive obedience of Christ (*Classical Arminianism*, 246n6).

[120] F. Leroy Forlines, *Systematics* (Nashville: Randall House, 1975); F. Leroy Forlines, ed., *Romans*, The Randall House Bible Commentary (Nashville: Randall House, 1987); *The Quest for Truth: Theology for Postmodern Times* (Nashville: Randall House, 2001).

[121] Robert E. Picirilli, *Free Will Revisited: A Respectful Response to Luther, Calvin, and Edwards* (Eugene, OR: Wipf and Stock, 2016).

struck readers about their type of Arminianism was how it was Reformed on what it means to be in a state of grace (Reformed views on penal substitutionary atonement, imputation, sanctification, and the Christian life), and on the radical depravity from which grace rescues sinners. Thus, it diverged from much Arminianism. Yet it was fully Arminian on how one comes to be in a state of grace (universal grace that is resistible before and after conversion as well as conditional election).

Evangelical Baptists in the North: Henry Clarence Thiessen

Henry Clarence Thiessen was likely the most influential Baptist systematic theologian in the northern evangelical movement in the early-to-mid-twentieth century.[122] A professor at Wheaton College and later president of Los Angeles Baptist Theological Seminary, Thiessen came to exemplify the middle course between Calvinism and Arminianism most Baptists espoused in the twentieth century. Heavily influenced by the Northern Baptist theologian Augustus H. Strong, Thiessen retained Strong's conservative four-point Calvinist instincts while jettisoning the latter's doctrines of unconditional election and effectual calling. "By election," Thiessen said, "we mean that sovereign act of God in grace, whereby from all eternity He chose in Christ Jesus for Himself and for salvation, all those whom He foreknew would respond positively to prevenient grace."[123]

Thiessen, however, retained the classic Calvinist understanding of the certain perseverance of the saints, saying that "all who are by faith united to Christ, who have been justified by God's grace and regenerated by His Spirit, will never totally nor finally fall away from the state of grace, but certainly persevere therein to the end."[124] Yet he articulated that doctrine and the doctrine of sanctification in a more classically Calvinist fashion: the true believer will persevere in holiness, and individuals for whom a pattern of sin is the norm indicate thereby that they were never truly regenerate.[125] Furthermore, Thiessen emphasized the total depravity of sinners and a classic Augustinian doctrine of original sin. Because "the sin of Adam and Eve

---

[122] Carl F. H. Henry surpassed Thiessen in influence after the 1950s, but throughout his career Henry remained aloof from soteriological concerns, though he seems to have held moderate views. See Carl F. H. Henry, *God, Revelation and Authority*, 6 vols. (Waco, TX: Word Books, 1976–83), 6:106.

[123] Henry Clarence Thiessen, *Introductory Lectures in Systematic Theology* (Grand Rapids: Eerdmans, 1949), 156.

[124] Thiessen, 385.

[125] Thiessen, 388–89.

constituted all their posterity sinners," being "imputed, reckoned, or charged to every member of the race," all humanity is totally depraved, which produces "a total spiritual inability in the sinner in the sense that he cannot by his own volition change his character and life so as to make them conformable to the law of God."[126]

Thiessen also eschewed governmental and other theories of atonement that most Arminians of his day articulated, embracing instead the Reformed view of theologians such as Strong, as well as the imputation of the active and passive obedience of Christ as the sole ground of the individual's justification. God "cannot free the sinner until the demands of justice are satisfied." Because "Christ's death fully satisfied these demands," God "restores us to favor by imputing to us Christ's righteousness."[127] Curiously, this mediating system that was so evident in his 1949 book *Introductory Lectures in Systematic Theology*, which was published in nineteen editions in three languages and used as a systematics text in hundreds of seminaries, colleges, and Bible institutes across the world, was revised after his death to teach four-point Calvinism.[128]

Southern Baptists: E. Y. Mullins and Herschel Hobbs

E. Y. Mullins, the president of Southern Baptist Theological Seminary from 1899 until his death in 1928, looms large in the story of the move from strict Calvinism to the Southern Baptist soteriological *via media*. Mullins's footprint in Southern Baptist theology is also seen in his being the major figure behind the 1925 Baptist Faith and Message, the confession of faith of the SBC. Calvinist Baptist historian Tom Nettles, who asserted a "Calvinist hegemony" among Southern Baptists in the nineteenth century, said that Mullins's arrival as president of Southern Seminary in 1899 helped break that hegemony. Mullins, according to Nettles, was a linchpin in the formal theological breakdown of Calvinism in the SBC.[129]

Mullins's soteriology is sometimes difficult to discern for the reader steeped in traditional theological systems. He presents a *via media* between traditional Calvinism and traditional Arminianism, and, unlike both systems, his explanation posits mystery and holds the poles of election and universal grace in tension. Perhaps the reason

---

[126] Thiessen, 260, 268.

[127] Thiessen, 324, 364.

[128] Henry Clarence Thiessen, *Lectures in Systematic Theology*, rev. ed., ed. Vernon D. Doerksen (Grand Rapids: Eerdmans, 1979), 107–8.

[129] Nettles, "Calvinism among Southern Baptists," 28–29.

for this is so, as R. Albert Mohler Jr. averred, "he could transcend the Calvinism/Arminianism controversy."[130] Thus Mullins said that "Arminianism overlooked certain essential truths about God in its strong championship of human freedom. As against it, Calvinism ran to extremes in some of its conclusions in its very earnest desire to safeguard the truth of God's sovereignty. We are learning to discard both names and to adhere more closely than either system to the Scriptures, while retaining the truth in both systems."[131]

Nettles said Mullins "rejected the view of God's sovereignty that defined election in terms of his mere will or good pleasure. He concluded that predestination conforms to the character of God as righteous love." Although Mullins still agreed that individuals owe their salvation solely to the divine initiative, Nettles explained, "he denied that God's eternal purpose is to save only his elect individuals. Rather, God desires the salvation of all men."[132]

---

[130] R. Albert Mohler Jr., "E. Y. Mullins: The Axioms of Religion," Albert Mohler website, July 16, 2009, https://albertmohler.com/2009/07/16/e-y-mullins-the-axioms-of-religion.

[131] Mullins, *Doctrinal Expression*, vii (see chap. 1, n. 78).

[132] Thomas J. Nettles, *By His Grace and for His Glory: A Historical, Theological, and Practical Study of the Doctrines of Grace in Baptist Life* (Grand Rapids: Baker, 1986), 246. While the subject below is beyond the scope of this essay, Calvinists such as Nettles identify a decline of Calvinism and a rise in ultra-revivalism with decline in orthodoxy, identifying Mullins in this narrative as setting the stage for more liberal trends. Yet there are too many counterarguments to this for it to be valid. In some cases, there is some truth to this narrative. However, many non-Calvinist Baptists share J. Gresham Machen's concerns about Mullins's experientialism (see Sean Michael Lucas, "Christianity at the Crossroads: E. Y. Mullins, J. Gresham Machen, and the Challenge of Modernism," *Southern Baptist Journal of Theology* 3, no. 4 [Winter 1999]: 58–78). However, the situation is much more complicated than the simple narrative one often hears about revivalistic Arminianism being simply a precursor to liberalism. For one thing, the early General Baptists were not revivalistic *enough* for the New Light Calvinist Baptists. The General Baptists were standing against what they saw as excesses in Great Awakening revivalism. Yet even in Baptist groups with Particular Baptist origins, some of the most orthodox, fundamentalist groups in the Northern and Southern Baptist orbits were non-Calvinist revivalists. These included small fundamentalist denominations as well as Independent Baptists. Indeed, it is easy to argue that the resurgence of Calvinism in the SBC is not a cause but rather a result of the resurgence of conservatism, which was brought about primarily by individuals from the more non-Calvinist wing of that denomination. Furthermore, in other non-Calvinist movements outside the Baptist tradition, whether Anabaptist or Wesleyan or Stone-Campbell/Restorationist, there are more liberal wings but also staunchly conservative, even fundamentalist, groups. However, the same can be said of historically Calvinist bodies in the Presbyterian and Reformed communities.

Mullins argued that the universal conviction of the Spirit and call of the gospel constitute a sincere calling, both externally in preaching and internally to all humanity: "Nothing can be clearer from the teaching of Scripture than the fact that the call and invitation are universal and that there is a free offer of salvation to all who hear and repent and believe." Yet he taught that election is based on divine foreknowledge and that the "responsibility for rejection is upon those who reject the gospel offer . . . [not] upon God himself." The Spirit's conviction "is a conviction of hope for all who yield to it and turn from their sins."[133]

Mullins militated against the traditional Calvinist conception of irresistible grace. "God cannot take the soul by sheer omnipotence" because he has imposed on himself certain limitations. He is "limited by human freedom. He made us free. He will not coerce man in his choices. If he did so he would destroy our freedom."[134] Mullins averred, "He [man] would not have made the choice if left to himself without the aid of God's grace. But when he chooses, it is his own free act. God's grace is not 'irresistible' as a physical force is irresistible. Grace does not act as a physical force. It is a moral and spiritual and personal power."[135]

Any mystery or ambiguity in E. Y. Mullins was absent by the time of Herschel Hobbs, the quintessential representative of mid-to-late-twentieth century Southern Baptist theology. Herschel Hobbs spent most of his career as pastor of First Baptist Church of Oklahoma City. From that post he wrote numerous works of New Testament exegesis (his PhD from Southern Baptist Theological Seminary was in New Testament) and Baptist doctrine. His most enduring legacy was that of chairman of the committee that drafted the Baptist Faith and Message (1963).

Hobbs self-consciously rooted himself in the thought of E. Y. Mullins, even publishing an edited version of Mullins's *Axioms of Religion* that commingled his and Mullins's ideas. Hobbs's soteriology, however, cleared up any ambiguities in Mullins's *via media*, presenting a perspicuous middle ground between Calvinism and Arminianism. On the Calvinist side, Hobbs affirmed original sin, total depravity, penal substitutionary atonement, the imputation of the righteousness of Christ in justification, a Reformed view of sanctification and assurance, and the traditional Calvinist understanding of certain perseverance of genuine believers. Thus, he

---

[133] Mullins, *Doctrinal Expression*, 365–67.
[134] Mullins, 348.
[135] Mullins, 344.

affirmed two of the traditional five points of Calvinism, demurring to unconditional election, limited atonement, and irresistible grace.

Some have thought that because Hobbs used the language of "inclined" to sin in the 1963 Baptist Faith and Message rather than "in bondage to sin" (BFM 1925), he did not affirm total depravity or that sinners were in bondage to sin.[136] However, Hobbs's view of sinful humanity as being in bondage to sin is evident throughout his writings. One sees his embrace of the classic Augustinian doctrines of original sin and total depravity in his book *Fundamentals of Our Faith*, in which he wrote, "Adam was the head of the race, and through him sin and death were bequeathed to all men," resulting in a "sentence of spiritual separation from God."[137]

Hobbs wrote that in Romans 1–3, "this truth of total depravity is clearly set forth." Our "sinful nature makes [it] impossible" to "live up to" the knowledge of God that Romans 1 discusses. Unregenerate humanity "substitutes idols for God," and because of a "rebellious mind," always makes "the wrong decision as to what is right." "Conscience is not sufficient" because, though the human "heart hungers for God," a "warped moral judgment leads men to worship and serve 'the creature more [rather] than the Creator.'" Everyone is "equally guilty before God" having "reprobate minds" as well as "perverted moral judgment," which "leads them astray."[138]

Furthermore, far from embracing the view that humanity possesses an innate natural ability to believe the gospel, Hobbs affirmed the necessity of what has traditionally been known as prevenient grace, though he used the language of the Holy Spirit's universal "conviction" and "God's overtures of grace," both of which can be freely resisted by the sinner. Yet there is no hint in Hobbs's writings of natural ability to seek after God, which he said total depravity makes impossible. Human beings in their depraved state can seek only after idols and can never respond positively to the true God.[139]

One way Hobbs strikes out in a new direction in terms of historic Baptist understandings of election is in a fledgling account of election as the corporate choice of the body of Christ, to which he referred in several places throughout his career. Historically, Baptists, whether Calvinist or Arminian or somewhere between, had always affirmed individual election. Those tending toward Arminianism had affirmed *conditional*

---

[136] Baptist Cameos: "Herschel Hobbs," The Reformed Reader, accessed November 6, 2020, http://www.reformedreader.org/hobbs.htm.

[137] Herschel H. Hobbs, *Fundamentals of our Faith* (Nashville: Broadman, 1960), 70–71.

[138] Hobbs, 71–73; brackets original.

[139] Herschel H. Hobbs, *What Baptists Believe* (Nashville: Broadman, 1964), 51, 68; *Fundamentals of Our Faith*, 59, 71.

election, which necessitated individual election. (The corporate election of the body of Christ—the church—is, after all, unconditional by definition. One can speak of conditional election only with respect to individuals. All Christians—Calvinists and Arminians alike—believe the church is unconditionally, corporately elect.)

The broad outlines of Hobbs's theology of election tend toward what is now known as *corporate election*. "The doctrine of election is two-fold: God has chosen a plan of salvation and has elected a people to propagate that plan."[140] Thus, he argued, the Greek word *proorizo*, for "predestined," means "to set a boundary beforehand," and election consists of God setting a boundary around his corporate body, his people. That is how Hobbs defined the "elect in Christ" of Ephesians 1, which speaks of "God's election of a people to propagate His plan," which "refers to the church."[141]

Epilogue

Much has changed and much has stayed the same in Baptist soteriology over the past half century. Most Baptists all over the world hold to the *via media* between Calvinism and Arminianism that increasingly became the dominant Baptist soteriological posture over the course of the nineteenth century. Calvinism, however, has experienced a resurgence. At the end of the twentieth century, the Founders movement began to foster an interest in Calvinism in the SBC. With the repristination of Southern Baptist thought following the renewal of conservative theology in that movement, there has been an attempt to return to the sources of Baptist historical identity. Many in this movement have recovered the strong Calvinism of the Charleston tradition that dominated the formal, written theology of the early SBC. This has resulted in vibrant resurgence of strict Calvinism in the SBC that has spilt over into other Baptist groups, including the Independent Baptists, the vast majority of whom have affirmed a soteriology similar to Thiessen's described above.[142] It has commonalities with movements in northern Baptist denominations associated with Baptists such as Minnesota pastor John Piper. Calvinism has also become ascendant among the faculties, staffs, and members of many SBC ministries and educational institutions.

---

[140] Herschel H. Hobbs and E. Y. Mullins, *The Axioms of Religion*, rev. ed. (Nashville: Broadman, 1978), 71; see also Hobbs, *Fundamentals of Our Faith*, 95–97.

[141] From a 1995 article in *The Alabama Baptist* reprinted at Peter Lumpkins, "Calvinism: Hershel Hobbs & Timothy George" (blog), December 4, 2006, https://peterlumpkins.type pad.com/peter_lumpkins/2006/12/calvinism_hersc.html.

[142] See, e.g., John R. Rice, *Predestined for Hell? No!* (Murfreesboro, TN: Sword of the Lord, 1958); Laurence M. Vance, *The Other Side of Calvinism* (Pensacola, FL: Vance Publications, 1999).

This development has produced strong response in various Baptist communions. In the SBC, the primary response has come from the "traditional Baptist" quarter. Like Calvinism, "traditional Baptist" soteriology has exceeded the borders of the SBC and affected Baptists in other communions. Some in this movement have emphasized the human ability to respond to the gospel without prevenient grace, and others have found refuge in some form of Molinism. The majority of this movement, however, seem to have held, like Mullins and Hobbs, to the traditional Baptist *via media* described in this chapter, which holds to a doctrine of total depravity and prevenient grace similar to that of traditional Arminians and Lutherans who espouse universal, resistible grace and thus conditional election. They have also agreed with Reformed Arminians on the Reformed doctrines of penal substitutionary atonement, and its implications in the imputation of Christ's righteousness in justification, as well as a broadly Reformed understanding of sanctification and spirituality. In contradistinction to Reformed Arminians, however, they have continued a tenacious affirmation of the Calvinist doctrine of the certain perseverance of regenerate believers.

Thus, many in the "traditional Baptist" group have made common cause with Reformed Arminians among the Free Will Baptists, American General Baptists, and those interspersed throughout other denominational communions, with the exception of the basic difference on whether a true believer can apostatize. This is perhaps the primary reason most in this movement have eschewed the Arminian label, claiming to be "neither Calvinists nor Arminians but Baptists,"[143] though some have called themselves Arminians, even joining the Society of Evangelical Arminians.

Reformed Arminianism continues to be the dominant soteriological expression of confessional Arminian Baptist groups such as Free Will Baptists and American General Baptists. Scholars such as Leroy Forlines, Robert Picirilli, Stephen Ashby, and I, in agreement with many of the more Reformed emphases of non-Baptist Arminians such as Thomas Oden and I. Howard Marshall, have mounted a vigorous defense of Arminianism. This approach has gained steady traction as Arminians and post-Calvinists alike have sought resources for the theological understanding and undergirding of the classic teaching of the *gratia universalis et resistibilis* that has characterized the mainstream of Christian thought for twenty centuries.

---

[143] See "Neither Calvinists nor Arminians but Baptists" (white paper 36, Center for Theological Research, 2010), http://www.baptisttheology.org/baptisttheology/assets/File/NeitherCalvinistsNorArminiansButBaptists.pdf.

8

A Wesleyan Critique of Calvinism

—— Ben Witherington III ——

While sometimes one still hears the caricature of John Wesley as being a "folk theologian," because he is chiefly known today through his *Standard Sermons* and voluminous *Journal* and not through his theological treatises such as *Predestination Calmly Considered* (a rebuttal to Augustus Toplady of "Rock of Ages" fame, among others), such a caricature cannot be made of Richard Watson. No one who has carefully read the 1,200 pages of Watson's *Theological Institutes* could fail to see that he was an extraordinary systematic theologian, and much of his efforts in those *Institutes* was directed apologetically to critiquing Calvin's similar volumes in various ways, as we shall see.

At the outset it should be made clear that Wesleyan Arminianism, while akin to the work of Jacob Arminius in some ways,[1] is by no means a rerun of Arminius's

---

[1] Regarding Arminius's work, see the helpful studies by Keith D. Stanglin and Thomas H. McCall, *Jacob Arminius: Theologian of Grace* (New York: Oxford University Press, 2012); and Roger E. Olson, *Arminian Theology: Myths and Realities* (Downers Grove, IL: InterVarsity, 2006).

work. Arminius, it is fair to say, was basically revising the Reformed theology of Calvin, Beza, and the later Dutch Calvinists. This is not in fact what Wesley and his successors were doing. Wesley and Watson believed there were some fundamental flaws in Calvin's theology, which could not be remedied by tweaking certain points along the way.

A second preliminary point that needs to be stressed is that Wesley's theology, including its further exposition by Watson, is neither Pelagian nor semi-Pelagian when it comes to the issue of original sin. Both agreed that fallen human beings were *non posse non peccare* (not able not to sin) apart from the grace of God. This distinguished their work from later Methodists or Methodist-influenced theologians in the nineteenth century such as Daniel Whedon, John Miley, and Charles Finney, who had drunk too deeply from the American well of voluntarism, even to the point of arguing that fallen human beings still had some form of "free will." Wesley and Watson strongly disagreed with this. Their optimism lay in the grace of God and its genuine ability to transform fallen human nature, not in some concept of native free will. What Wesley found especially odd about Luther and some Calvinists was, for all their talk about the sovereignty of God and his almightiness, they did not really believe that God's grace was powerful enough to "entirely sanctify even in an instant" or radically change human beings' bent natures.[2]

The fact that few Calvinists even to this day know *anything* about Richard Watson's *Institutes,* having never read them, is partly the fault of various Methodist theologians who in the twentieth century allowed the work to go out of print, and instead became enamored with German theology, which led in turn to "Boston personalism" and other modern theologies being taught in Methodist seminaries and graduate schools.

Personally, I was shocked, when I taught Wesley's *Standard Sermons* at Duke Divinity for two summers in the early 1980s, that most of the theologians there appeared to have at best a nodding acquaintance with Watson's work and had never really studied his *Institutes* in depth, so far as I could tell. All this is by way of saying that it is largely Methodism's own fault that it allowed Watson's work to disappear

---

[2] On this point see my introductory essay in the recently republished edition of Watson's *Theological Institutes,* 2 vols. (Bellingham, WA: Lexham, 2018). This republication is of the original 1831 work, and not of the later nineteenth-century edition done in 1850, which includes a helpful 90-page precis of the whole work by John McClintock that extended the life of Watson's *Institutes* throughout the rest of the nineteenth century.

into obscurity in the twentieth century, thereby losing the classic orthodox Wesleyan critique of Calvinism. But it was not so in the nineteenth century. Watson's *Institutes* was the *required* textbook for all Methodist ministers, including circuit riders, along with Wesley's *Standard Sermons*. Furthermore, they also had as a resource Watson's very useful *A Biblical and Theological Dictionary*, published in 1833, only two years after his *Institutes*.

In that dictionary is a very concise but detailed critique of Calvin's theology of predestination, and perhaps it will be wise to start there, before moving on to some of the arguments in the *Institutes*.[3] One final preliminary comment: this essay will deal at some length with Watson's representation of Wesleyan Arminian theology; and to this I will add some of my own exegesis of the relevant texts, based on the study of New Testament scholars over the last half century. Drawing on Watson's logical and theological reasoning, and on recent exegesis of the critical texts, a very compelling case can be made in favor of the Wesleyan Arminian reading of Scripture and against the way Calvinism has tended to read it.

Do You Know Your Predestination?

Focusing on chapters 21 and 22 of book 3 of Calvin's *Institutes*, Watson stressed Calvin's flat denial that God's election of some to everlasting life and reprobation of others to damnation is based on God's foreknowledge of how they would respond to the gospel if given the opportunity. No, it is based solely in the "secret counsel" of God and in God's will. Basically, God knows with certainty how people will respond to the gospel because he had already willed the outcome, and who are we to question God's will or secret reasons?

Watson found this whole line of argument unbiblical in light of what Romans 8–11 *actually* says, that those who love God are destined in advance to be conformed to Christ's image and the vessels of wrath have fit themselves for destruction. They were not made that way by God's predetermination.[4] And Watson would have nothing to do with the illogic of single predestination of the saved. Single predestination

---

[3] This article can now be conveniently found at http://evangelicalarminians.org/richard
-watson-calvinism-defined/ in a February 19, 2008 reprint of the original article. It in turn was taken from the online version of Watson's work at http://www.imarc.cc/apolg/history7.html

[4] Here a careful attention to the Greek is in order—the vessels of mercy have been prepared (by God) in advance for glory, which is much the same as what is said in Rom 8:28, whereas the vessels of wrath have prepared themselves (a middle-passive form of the verb) for destruction.

of the saved implies double predestination necessarily, as Calvin said. Calvin himself put it this way:

> Indeed many, as if they wished to avert a reproach from God, accept election in such terms as to deny that anyone is condemned. But they do this very ignorantly and childishly, since election itself could not stand except as set over against reprobation. God is said to set apart those whom he adopts into salvation; it will be highly absurd to say that others acquire by chance or obtain by their own effort what election alone confers on a few. Therefore, those whom God passes over, he condemns; and this he does for no other reason than that he wills to exclude them from the inheritance which he predestines for his own children.[5]

In his rebuttal of this whole approach, Watson did not spare the rhetoric. Here I quote him in full:

> Thus he [Calvin] assumes the very thing in dispute, that God has willed the destruction of any part of the human race, "for no other cause than because he *wills it*;" of which assumption there is not only not a word of proof in Scripture; but, on the contrary, it ascribes the death of him that dieth to his own will, and not to the will of God. 2. He pretends that to assign any *cause* to the divine will is to suppose something antecedent to, something above God, and therefore "impious;" as if we might not suppose something IN God to be the rule of his will, not only without any impiety, but with truth and piety; as, for instance, his perfect wisdom, holiness, justice, and goodness; or, in other words, to believe the exercise of his will to flow from the perfection of his whole nature; a much more honorable and Scriptural view of the will of God than that which subjects it to no rule, even though it should arise from the nature of God himself. 3. When he calls the will of God, "the highest rule of justice," beyond which we cannot push our inquiries, he confounds the will of God, as a rule of justice *to us*, and as a rule to himself. This will is our rule; yet even then, because we know that it is the will of a perfect being: but when Calvin represents *mere will* as constituting God's own rule of justice, he shuts out knowledge, discrimination of the nature of things, and holiness; which is saying something very different from that great truth, that God cannot will

---

[5] Calvin, *Institutes*, trans. Battles, 2:947 (3.23.1) (see chap. 4, n. 85).

anything but what is perfectly just. It is to say that blind will, will which has no respect to anything but itself, is God's highest rule of justice; a position which, if presented abstractedly, many Calvinists themselves would spurn. 4. He determines the question by the authority of his own metaphysics, and totally forgets that one *dictum* of inspiration overturns his whole theory,— God "*willeth* all men to be saved;" a declaration, which in no part of the sacred volume is opposed or limited by any contrary declaration.[6]

Watson could have also pointed out that the sequence of statements in Rom 8:28–30 in fact does not support Calvin's interpretation of those verses. Consider the following: (1) Paul seldom talks about our love for God, rather focusing again and again on God's love for humanity especially as expressed in Christ and through his death on the cross for sinners, indeed even for God's enemies. But here in Romans 8 he does indeed explain that God works all things together for those who love him, which provides a preview of v. 29 where he explains that this includes our sanctification, conformity to Christ's image, and our glorification. (2) The phrase "those whom he foreknew" has as its *only* antecedent "those who love God." This necessarily means that there is a clear connection between what God knows about persons and his consequent predestination. It is those who love God whom God destines in advance to be conformed to Christ's image. In short, this text is *not about God predestining some from a mass of unredeemed humanity to be Christians, but rather about God destining those who love him to a glorious future.* (3) Nothing in this text suggests that God knows something because he first wills it. To the contrary, Paul distinguished God's foreknowing and his predestining by saying "those whom he foreknows he *also* predestines." Foreknowledge clearly does not mean or necessarily imply predestining, because God foreknows human sin, evil, and a myriad of things that God does not will at all.[7] God is light, and in him is no darkness at all. It is simply not true that God knows all things because he has antecedently willed them, any more than it is true that whatever God wills is necessarily good or just *simply because God wills it.*

---

[6] Richard Watson, *A Biblical and Theological Dictionary* (New York: Published by B. Waugh and T. Mason [. . .], 1833), s.v. "Calvinism," 196; emphasis original.

[7] Sometimes one will also hear that foreknowing means foreloving unto salvation, but this hardly works because elsewhere in the New Testament God's foreknowledge includes the behavior of lawless human beings who are not being converted but rather are the executioners of Jesus in Acts 2:23. Notice as well in that verse the very clear distinction between God's predetermined plan and God's foreknowledge.

No—what makes it good or just is that it comports with God's nature, which is good and just, but also compassionate and merciful.

Herein is uncovered what is perhaps one of the most important objections of Wesleyan Arminian theology to Calvin; namely, Calvinism besmirches the very character of God who is not merely just but also loving; not merely righteous but also compassionate; not merely fair but also merciful; and, most important, who does indeed desire the salvation of all fallen human beings.

I have expounded at some length the statement "God is love" (1 John 4:8, 16) in my most recent small theological book *Who God Is*,[8] and one of the things that comes to light in that discussion is the close connection between love and freedom. Love, the *agape* love there referenced, is inherently self-sacrificial and self-giving like Christ on the cross. It must be freely given and freely received and responded to. If it is indeed true that God freely loves the world, and that he wants humanity to respond to him by loving him with their whole being and by loving their neighbor as themselves, this in turn requires that somehow the human responders must be free to do so. Wesley and Watson would say this freedom comes from God's universal prevenient grace that enables such a response. Love cannot be predetermined, manipulated, or coerced. It has to be freely given and freely responded to, or it ceases to actually be love. And Wesley and Watson agreed with Augustine when he prayed, "Give what Thou commandest, and command what Thou wilt" (*Da quod jubes, et jube quod vis*).[9] It is God's enabling grace that allows the response of love and loving obedience to God's commandments.

What Watson found especially besmirching of God's character is that ultimately Calvin's view makes God the author of sin and evil, since everything is predetermined by God's secret counsel or hidden will (which in turn leads to a further contradiction that God's revealed will, desiring none should perish, is at odds with God's secret or hidden will). Here is how Watson dealt with Calvin's attempt to have it both ways, at once exonerating God from being the author of sin and evil, and at the same time affirming absolute and double predestination. He began with a further quote from Calvin and then rebutted it as follows:

---

[8] Ben Witherington, *Who God Is: Meditations on the Character of Our God* (Bellingham, WA: Lexham Press, 2020); see esp. chap. 1.

[9] Augustine, "Confessions," in NPNF[1], 1:153 (10.29.40), 155 (10.31.45), 159 (10.37.60); "On the Gift of Perseverance," in NPNF[1], 5:547 (*De Dono Perseverantiæ*, chap. 53).

"Their perdition depends on the divine predestination in such a manner, that the *cause* and *matter* of it are found *in themselves*. For the first man fell because the Lord had determined it should so happen. The reason of this determination is unknown to us.—Man, therefore, falls according to the *appointment* of divine providence; but he falls by *his own fault*. The Lord had a little before pronounced everything that he had made to be 'very good.' Whence, then, comes the depravity of man to revolt from his God? Lest it should be thought to come from creation, God approved and commended what had proceeded from himself. By his own wickedness, therefore, man corrupted the nature he had received pure from the Lord, and by his fall he drew all his posterity with him to destruction" [Calvin, *Institutes*, 3.23.8]. It is in this way that Calvin attempts to avoid the charge of making God the author of sin. But how God should not merely *permit* the defection of the first man, but *appoint* it, and *will* it, and that his will should be the "necessity of things," (all which he had before asserted,) and yet that Deity should not be the author of that which he *appointed, willed,* and *imposed a necessity upon,* would be rather a delicate inquiry. It is enough that Calvin rejects the impious doctrine; and even though his principles directly lead to it, since he has put in his disclaimer, he is entitled to be exempted from the charge;—but the logical conclusion is inevitable.[10]

The logical conclusion is that Calvin is forced to affirm an inherent contradiction to his own logic, and the result is a further besmirching of God's character as both just and loving.

Watson brought home the point more forcefully in what follows:

These propositions manifestly fight with each other; for if the reason of reprobation be laid in man's corruption, it cannot be laid in the mere will and sovereign determination of God, unless we suppose him to be the author of sin. It is this offensive doctrine only, which can reconcile them. For if God so wills, and appoints, and necessitates the depravity of man, as to be the author of it, then there is no inconsistency in saying that the ruin of the reprobate is both from the mere will of God, and from the corruption of their nature, which is but the result of that will. . . . But if it be denied that God is, in any

---

[10] Watson, "Calvinism," 197; emphasis original.

sense, the author of evil, and if sin is from man alone, then is the "corruption of nature" the effect of an independent will; and if this corruption be the "real source," as he says, of men's condemnation, then the decree of reprobation rests not upon the sovereign will of God, as its sole cause, which he affirms; but upon a cause dependent on the will of the first man: but as this is denied, then the other must follow.[11]

Watson is also not persuaded by the argument that the church fathers before Augustine were all Augustinians and thence Calvinists before their day. No, says Watson, this is not a fair reading of either the Bible or subsequent church history leading up to Augustine. Indeed, it is not even a fair reading of Calvin himself! He put it this way:

> On one topic, however, Calvin and the older divines of that school were very explicit. They tell us plainly, that they found all the Christian fathers, both of the Greek and the Latin church down to the age of St. Augustine, quite unmanageable for their purpose; and therefore occasionally bestow upon them and their productions epithets not the most courteous. Yet some modern writers, not possessing half the splendid qualifications of those veterans in learning, make a gorgeous display of the little that they know concerning antiquity; and wish to lead their readers to suppose, that the whole stream of early Christianity has flowed down only in their channel. Everyone must have remarked how much like Calvin all those fathers speak whose words are quoted by Toplady in his "Historic Defence." Nor can the two Milners [Joseph and Isaac], in their "History of the Church," entirely escape censure on this account, though both were excellent men, and better scholars than Toplady. But from the manner in which they "show up" only those ancient Christian authors, some of whose sentiments *seem* to be nearly in unison with their own, they induce the unlearned or half informed to draw the erroneous conclusion, that the peculiarities of Calvinism are not the inventions of a comparatively recent era, and that they have always formed a prominent part of the profession of faith of every Christian community since the days of the Apostles.[12]

[11] Watson, 197–98.
[12] Watson, 204; emphasis original.

What of Election, Salvation, and Imputed Righteousness?

Richard Watson was quite explicit about the notion of imputed righteousness, that it was unbiblical and based on a misreading of Romans 3–5. This reading goes all the way back to a faulty Latin translation of these chapters that Augustine relied on, not knowing even as much Greek as my first-year graduate students who are taking Greek.[13] Watson's fundamental objections to imputed righteousness, other than the observation that it is not in Romans, are: (1) it involves a legal fiction; and (2) it obviates the need to obey God's command to be holy as he is holy.[14]

Watson pointed out at length from Romans 4 that it does not say Christ's righteousness was credited to Abraham as his own righteousness, but rather that Abraham's faith was credited as Abraham's righteousness, and Christ is not mentioned in that context. Then, Paul held up Abraham as the example of what is the case with Christian believers as well—their faith is reckoned for righteousness. But there is an issue with how to interpret the meaning of the word *dikaiosunē*. In the first place, the language of Paul here is not legal language; it is the language of business, of credits and debits. This language Paul knew well as a maker of tents. So Paul was not talking about some legal status, or some legal fiction here, he was talking about one real thing being credited as another, like when a check is credited the same as cash. The second issue is that the story of Abraham in Genesis 12–15 has to do with the establishment of a relationship between the living God and Abraham, who, by the way, was a pagan before that relationship was established, whose family worshipped pagan gods. Probably what Paul was talking about here was Abraham being put into right relationship with God, through his trusting of God.

Watson further stressed that if Christ is viewed as having completely fulfilled the law of God, then "this doctrine of the imputation of Christ's obedience makes his sufferings superfluous. For if he has done all that the law required of us, and if

---

[13] On all this, see my discussion in Witherington and Hyatt, *Romans*, 121–23, 146–48 (see chap. 4, n. 70).

[14] There are of course other major objections to the notion of imputed righteousness; Paul himself said that believers become the righteousness of God, not merely are counted as righteous or have the benefits of imputed righteousness (see 2 Cor 5:21). And then, too, a correct reading of the Greek of 1 Cor 1:30 does not support the interpretation that Christ is our righteousness—it reads literally "but from Him **you are** in Christ Jesus (who was made our wisdom from God) righteousness, and holiness, and freedom/redemption." The subject of those traits at the end of the sentence is not Christ, but rather "you are."

this is legally accounted our doing, then we are under no penalty of suffering, and his suffering in our stead was more than the case required."[15] What Watson wanted to avoid is the notion that Christians are not required to obey God's law. In short, he was concerned about various forms of antinomianism in Protestantism, which he traced back to some of the things Luther said about the law. Watson followed Wesley quite strictly at this point and quoted him to good effect:

> "The judgment of the all-wise God is always according to truth; neither can it ever consist with his unerring wisdom to think that I am innocent, to judge that I am righteous or holy because another is so. He can no more confound me with Christ than with David or Abraham" [Wesley].[16] But a contradiction is involved in another view. If what our Lord was and did is to be accounted to us in the sense just given, then we must be accounted never to have sinned, because Christ never sinned, and yet we must ask for pardon, though we are accounted from birth to death to have fulfilled God's law in Christ.[17]

Admittedly, not all Wesleyans understood this as clearly as John Wesley and Richard Watson. For example, in Charles Wesley's classic hymn, "And Can It Be," we find these lines in verse 5: "No condemnation now I dread; / Jesus and all in Him is mine! / Alive in Him, my living Head, / and clothed in righteousness divine. / Bold I approach the eternal throne / and claim the crown, through Christ my own." Perhaps Charles had been listening too much to the sermons of that Calvinistic Methodist, George Whitefield, when he wrote these lines.

Watson was also clear that there is a difference between election and salvation. Election in the Bible is by and large corporate—it is in Israel in the Old Testament, and in Christ and his body the church in the New Testament. Indeed, I would go further and say, if one reads Ephesians carefully it becomes clear that Christ is depicted as the Elect One chosen and destined before the foundation of the universe to be our Savior (not least because he existed back then, and no human beings did), and as the Elect One of God, Jesus himself *never needed to be saved!* Election therefore must have to do with God's historical purposes for Israel, and then for the

---

[15] Watson, *Institutes*, 2:182.

[16] John Wesley, "Sermon V.—Justification by Faith," in *The Works of the Reverend John Wesley, A. M.*, 7 vols. (New York: J. Emory and R. Waugh [. . .], 1831), 1:47.

[17] Watson, *Institutes*, 2:272.

Messiah of Israel and his people, the church, *not* with the individual salvation of particular persons.

Ephesians is perfectly clear that salvation is by grace and through faith, and the latter has to be exercised by the receiver of the gift of salvation. Watson had much to say about corporate election, and he believed that since some genuine believers commit apostasy and fall away, we have clear enough proof that initial salvation or justification does not guarantee final salvation or eternal security. Indeed, the Wesleyan perspective understands Hebrews 6 to warn believers that they are not eternally secure until they are securely in eternity. Salvation has three tenses—I have been saved, I am being saved (sanctification), and I shall be saved.[18]

Furthermore, it is now clear from the majority of evidence in early Jewish literature that the concept of election was corporate and had to do with the historical purposes God had for his people to be a light to the nations about the one true living God. It did not guarantee anyone's personal everlasting salvation.[19] Part of the problem since the Reformation has been the overreading of the Old Testament and Gospel references to "salvation," which seldom refer to what Paul meant by the term.

Normally, "salvation" in the Old Testament, including in Psalms, has to do with rescue from danger or enemies, or healing from some disease; in other words, it does not have a purely spiritual meaning, nor does it refer to "conversion." This is often what the term *saved* means in Gospel passages as well. When Jesus said to the woman healed of her continuous blood flow, "Your faith has saved you," what is meant is, "Your faith has healed you" (Mark 5:21–34).[20] And this reveals another underlying problem with Protestant approaches to these issues—anachronism, the failure to read these texts in light of their immediate historical contexts, and instead reading these texts in light of later Protestant theology, particularly Lutheran and post-Lutheran readings of Paul. It is fair to say that the Wesleyan tradition, along with other forms of Protestantism, has sometimes been guilty of this mistake. However, it was less prone to read the New Testament in light of Augustine, Luther, and Calvin than the Lutheran and Reformed traditions.

---

[18] See Watson, *Institutes*, 2:366–67, 384–85.

[19] See the lengthy discussion I had with Chad Thornhill on this matter in Ben Witherington, *Biblical Theology: The Convergence of the Canon* (New York: Cambridge University Press, 2019), 349–85.

[20] For a detailed examination of the salvation language, specifically in antiquity in general and in Luke-Acts in particular, see Ben Witherington, *The Acts of the Apostles: A Socio-Rhetorical Commentary* (Grand Rapids: Eerdmans, 1998), 821–43.

Covenantal Thinking and Covenant Love?

Since the Reformation and eighteenth-century English Revival movements, including Methodism, we know a great deal more about the nature and scope of ancient covenants than the Reformers did. For instance, we know that ancient Near Eastern covenants or treaties are similar to what we find in the Old Testament, particularly if we are talking about the Mosaic covenant. The kind of covenants we find in the Bible are like ancient lord-vassal treaties where all the terms are dictated by the lord, and the vassal simply has to accept them. They are not parity agreements or deals struck between equals. Furthermore, such covenants had provisions for what happened if the vassal failed to keep the covenant. In these covenants, there are both blessings offered and curse-sanctions if the agreement is kept or alternately broken. Such covenants are *not* unconditional. If the covenant is broken, the lord can simply invoke the penalties or curse-sanctions and the covenant relationship is over. Or the lord can begin a new covenant with his vassals, if he so chooses. The only covenant in the Bible that is "everlasting" is the new covenant, which is not merely a renewal or continuation of the Mosaic or Abrahamic covenants.

Paul told us clearly in Galatians 4 that the new covenant is the fulfillment of the Abrahamic covenant, and it is the *sequel* to the Mosaic covenant.[21] Christ came to redeem those under the Mosaic law; "out from under the Mosaic Law" is how Paul put it (Gal 4:5, author's translation).[22] While the Wesleyan tradition rightly understood that there were commandments and law in the new covenant, commandments that had to be obeyed, by and large they took the position that Puritans and others took: that while the Old Testament ceremonial law had been fulfilled by Christ, the moral law was carried over into the new covenant. This is why, for instance, in City Road Chapel in London, Wesley posted the Ten Commandments on one side, and some of the Sermon on the Mount on the other side, of the pulpit.

---

[21] Clearly enough, Jer 31:31–33, where we find the only full reference to a new covenant in the Old Testament, made a distinction between the old covenant and a new covenant written on the human heart. Note the statement that the new covenant will *not* be like the old one! Paul, in the chronologically earliest place in the New Testament where we hear about the Mosaic covenant being called the old covenant (2 Corinthians 3, written in the AD mid-50s), drew on Jeremiah 31 to make clear the difference between the Mosaic ministry, with a law written on tablets of stone, and his own for the sake of the gospel and the new covenant involving the Spirit inscribing it on human hearts.

[22] The relevant passages in Galatians are Gal 3:15–4:4 and 4:21–31, which make clear Paul's covenantal theology.

The problem with this approach is the failure to recognize that the new covenant is not a continuation of the Mosaic one, even though there is some overlap in commandments in those two covenants. The new covenant involves what Paul called the law of Christ. This includes some portions of the previous Mosaic law that Christ reaffirmed, plus some new teaching of Jesus himself (see the Sermon on the Mount), which goes beyond and indeed annuls some of the previous laws (for instance, food laws), as well as some of the apostolic teaching based on these two sources (see, e.g., Galatians 6 and Romans 12–14). Wesley and Watson were not wrong that there is law in the new covenant and that God expects obedience, nor were they wrong that obedience or disobedience affects one's relationship with God. In the latter case it grieves the Holy Spirit in the believer.

Another Calvinistic notion that Wesleyan Arminians reject is the idea that the Hebrew term *hesed* refers purely to God's covenant love, a special love that God has for the elect and only owes and directs towards them, a love not for everyone. Let us consider first the fact that throughout the Greek translation of the Old Testament, when the word *hesed* shows up in a text, it is translated as "mercy," not covenant love. This should have prevented us from thinking it has something to do with an exclusive covenant love only promised and directed towards God's people. No, God has mercy on whomever, as Paul was later to emphasize in Romans 9–11. In some Old Testament texts, such as Psalms 42–43, it seems clearly to mean simply compassion. The term is used of persons other than God. For example, Jacob asked Joseph to deal with him with compassion (*hesed*), not according to some sort of owed covenant love (Gen 47:29). Even more telling is Rahab's pleading with the Hebrew spies to have *hesed* on her in Josh 2:12–14; she was no member of the covenant community at all. Or consider Ruth 1:8, where Naomi commended Ruth for dealing with her with *hesed* even after her sons had died and Ruth had no covenant or contract with Naomi even indirectly. In texts like Num 14:18 it is used to stress God's constant compassion and mercy, or his loving-kindness in spite of his people's sin. The point is to reveal something about God's ongoing character, especially expressed toward those who love him and keep his commandments, but not exclusively so.

The term *hesed* does not *mean* "covenant love," not least because it is sometimes used of relationships that do not involve God's covenant with his people. Rather, it is a relational term referring to God's unchanging character to have mercy, compassion, and loving-kindness, both toward those with whom he has a covenant relationship and those he does not. It comes as no surprise when we later hear a text like John 3:16

that tells us that God loves *the world*—not merely the elect with whom he has a covenant relationship.[23]

Ḥesed is not a term defining God's distinctive love for his covenant people. It is a term describing his character to be merciful and compassionate and slow to anger, even toward those with whom he does not have a covenant relationship. Calvinism's penchant for limiting the scope of God's love, even in various cases to the point of limiting by divine design the scope of Christ's atoning death, does not comport with what the Bible says about God's loving-kindness or with what the New Testament teaches about the scope of Christ's death on the cross. As Wesley and Watson both stressed, Christ's death was sufficient to atone for the sins of the world, but only effective for those who accept Christ's benefits by grace through faith in Christ.

The phrase "the righteousness of God" does not mean the covenant faithfulness of God. Sometimes the phrase is used in a context where God already has a relationship with a covenant people, but John Barclay was right to emphasize that the phrase itself does not *mean* "God's covenant faithfulness."[24] The context determines how the phrase is used. Most often it is a comment on God's character, his own righteousness. Thus, in Romans 1, after offering his thesis statement about God's righteousness, Paul proceeded in Rom 1:18–32 to lay out what could be called the "wrath" side of that righteousness, God's judgment on human idolatry and immorality. The attempt to redefine key terms such as *ḥesed* or "righteousness" in terms of a certain kind of Reformed covenantal theology does not do justice to the actual meaning of the terms in their original biblical contexts. And the same can be said about the Reformed reconfiguration of the meaning of the word *charis* or "grace," particularly in Paul. We need to talk about the atonement and God's grace next.

Atonement and Grace

Both Calvinists and classic Wesleyan Arminians agreed that the atonement provided by Christ's death on the cross was limited, in the sense that not everyone got the benefits of Christ's death. Neither group were universalists, or those who believe in the end everyone will be saved. The question that kept being raised, however, was who or what limited the benefits of the atonement? The Calvinist answer, going

---

[23] On *ḥesed*, see Witherington, *Biblical Theology*, 27–29, 290–91.
[24] See John M. G. Barclay, *Paul and the Gift* (Grand Rapids: Eerdmans, 2015), 562–74.

back to Calvin himself, was that God limited the benefits of the atonement by divine design, because he only elected some to be saved.

Interestingly, on some aspects of atonement theology there was clear agreement between the two groups. For example, Watson stressed that the death of Christ indeed involved both propitiation and expiation, because God's demands for accountability for sin, justice, and righteousness had to be met.[25] In short, penal substitutionary atonement is what the New Testament teaches. This view was based on 1 John 1; 2 Cor 5:21; and Romans 3–5, among other texts. God could not pass over sin forever if he were to be reconciled to human beings. Where the two views diverge is regarding why that atonement had limited saving efficacy.

Wesleyans like Watson pointed to texts such as 1 Tim 2:4–5, which says explicitly that God wants all human beings to be saved, and that Christ's death provided a ransom for all, "revealing God's purpose at his appointed time" (NET). For Watson, it could hardly be clearer that God did not limit the saving benefits of Christ's atoning death. To the contrary, it was human beings rejecting those benefits that provided the limitation. If a Calvinist pointed to Mark 10:45 ("[I] did not come to be served but to serve, and to give [my] life as a ransom for many"; NET) as evidence that Christ intended the atonement to benefit only some, this view was quickly countered by pointing out that Jesus was contrasting the one person who provides the ransom, with the "many," which includes everyone else. He was not contrasting "many" with "all" in this saying. Further, it was pointed out that 1 Tim 2:4–5 seems clearly enough to be a Pauline further explanation of what Mark 10:45 meant.

Clearly, both classic Calvinism and classic Wesleyan Arminianism were agreed that the death of Jesus was absolutely necessary for the salvation of anyone at all, and ultimately the necessity lay in the fact that God's moral character was immutable, unchangeable. He could not take a pass forever on his holiness, righteousness, or justice. What he could do is provide a sacrifice that lovingly provided a substitute for God's judging human wickedness so that forgiveness could be provided. Both sides of the argument agreed that forgiveness does not involve ignoring righteousness or overruling justice. Rather, it involves providing in love a means by which sins could be dealt with, forgiveness could be offered, and God remains the same just and merciful, righteous and compassionate, holy and loving God that he had always been.

For the Wesleyan Arminian, it was always seen as something of a mystery why evangelism's message of Christ crucified and of repentance and forgiveness was so

---

[25] Watson, *Institutes*, 2:148–52.

essential to human salvation, *if in fact* before the foundation of the universe some had already been destined to be saved and some to be lost. Couldn't God have just made a declaration of who was saved and who was lost and not require the Great Commission? Why would Paul tell us in Romans 10 that preaching, hearing, and responding to the gospel was absolutely necessary if some were to be saved, if in fact God could have done it otherwise?

It was not enough for Watson and others to hear that God graciously chose preaching as the means by which he worked out his already predetermined plan. To the contrary, the New Testament itself suggested over and over again that God had enlisted human beings to be an essential part of saving the world, such that missionaries and evangelists became coworkers with God, as Paul called himself. Behind all this was a belief that while God was certainly sovereign and almighty, he had chosen to empower angels and human beings with a modicum of ability to make their own choices in life, even to choose sin, which was against God's will. Wesleyans emphasized this was not some native ability called "free will" but rather human or angelic will enabled by God's universal prevenient grace. The issue was not whether God was sovereign but how he had chosen to exercise his sovereignty, and whether he had enabled viable secondary causes and choices by humans and angels, which could either freely be in accord with God's will or even go against it. In other words, God is not the only actor in the universe who causes things to happen. And behind all this was a belief that God loves human beings and treats them as persons, not as things or robots. Human beings are not chess pieces being moved around God's chess board by him toward a predetermined end. Professor Dennis Kinlaw used to say that God was a loving Father before he was sovereign. What he meant by that was that before the creation of anything God was love and in a loving relationship with his Son. So, love is an essential attribute of God. However, sovereignty is a relational and secondary attribute that refers to how God relates to his creation and his creatures. Were sovereignty the key to understanding God at all, it would be hard to explain why he never needed to exercise it from all eternity before he created the universe and its inhabitants.[26]

But what about God's grace? Was it irresistible or not? Was God like the Godfather making humans an offer they could not refuse, or was he more like a lover who woos those he seeks to win? For Arminians, saying God is love meant he

---

[26] Thanks to my colleague Ken Collins for pointing this out and reminding me of what Professor Kinlaw used to say.

treated persons personally, and he wanted them to freely respond to the gospel, freely respond to the commandment to love God with all one's heart.

Watson himself took issue with the great American Reformed theologian Jonathan Edwards in his treatise "Freedom of the Will." Edwards argued that what freedom meant when applied to fallen human beings in bondage to sin is that they merely did not feel compelled to respond to or reject the gospel, and yet the outcome of their fate could not be otherwise. As Watson put it, the upshot of Edwards's approach is that "man can neither will nor act otherwise than they do . . . being inevitably disabled by an act of God [or] bound by a chain of events established by an almighty power."[27] In either case, there is no power of contrary choice by human beings. But if that is the case, then at a minimum God has destined some to be sinners, and it is hard to escape the conclusion that this makes God the ultimate author of evil as well as good. Again, for the Wesleyan Arminians this ends up maligning the good moral character of God and denying such Scriptures as "God is light and in Him is no darkness at all" (1 John 1:5 NKJV). What then of God's grace—is it resistible or irresistible? How does God's grace work?

In perhaps the most important book written by a New Testament scholar in this century, John Barclay explained in his *Paul and the Gift* that what has happened in the Protestant discussion of God's grace since the Reformation is that different groups have prioritized or emphasized some possible reading of the language of God's grace in the Bible, at the expense of other readings.[28] Barclay made clear that certain modern notions of grace are not in fact biblical. One example is the notion that God's grace is "given with no thought of return." To the contrary, God's grace is given to begin a relationship with persons in which God desires and expects to be loved and served in return. Another example is the notion that the most meritorious form of giving or grace is anonymous giving that requires no response or acknowledgement of the giver. As Barclay pointed out, the whole point of God's gracious approach to human beings is so that we might know and love God.

Barclay went on to stress that "the word *charis* itself does not have the specific sense of an undeserved or incongruous gift. It takes on that nuance in Paul but only because it there refers to God's gift given in the Christ event."[29] As Barclay pointed out, frequently the term is used when someone gives a gift to a worthy recipient. In

---

[27] Watson, *Institutes*, 2:536.
[28] Barclay, *Paul and the Gift*.
[29] Barclay, 562–74.

itself the word does not imply the gift is undeserved or the recipient unworthy. It is only when the term is used in the context of discussing God's gift of salvation to sinners that it takes on the notion of a gift given to those who have not earned, merited, or deserved it. The term itself can be used variously. Indeed, it was most frequently used of human beings gifting other human beings and thereby setting up a relationship that involved an ongoing reciprocity cycle.

Further, Barclay pointed out that as for the efficacy of God's grace the following can be said: "There is a tendency in a line of interpretation from Augustine through Calvin to Jonathan Edwards to 'perfect' (radicalize or absolutize) the efficacy of grace, to the point where it causes, constrains or compels our own wills. This is to turn God's agency/will and our agency/will into a zero-sum game: the more of one, the less of the other. But God's will is not on the same level as ours, working in the same causal nexus." He then added: "It would be problematic for Paul as for us, if our response to grace could not be considered in any sense voluntary (i.e., truly willed) . . . Now voluntary in Paul's eyes does not mean 'free from any external influence' . . . he does not labor under our illusion that we can and should act as completely autonomous individuals. But he does expect that God's work in us generates our own willing (Phil 2:12–13), as *freed* agents who could do otherwise (it is possible in Paul's eyes, to fall out of grace)."[30] This is exactly right. God's grace is powerful but not irresistible, and in the Wesleyan tradition apostasy is possible even for the most devout Christian. What then about the beautiful ending to Romans 8, where we are told that nothing can separate us from the love of God? It actually says that no outside force or power or person (human or angelic) or set of circumstances can separate us from God's love.[31]

Both Watson and Wesley believed that no good work could be done without the aid of God's grace. However, the moral seriousness of the exhortations to persevere in the faith, behave in holy ways, and work out one's salvation would be pointless if in fact the believer had been predestined to do such things *and could not do otherwise*. All the warnings in the New Testament about apostasy, about quenching or grieving the Spirit, and about behaving in such an immoral way as to prevent one from entering the eschatological kingdom of God (see Gal 5:19–20) are not just directed towards the

---

[30] John Barclay, email exchange with the author, September 2015.

[31] The one thing not included in that list is the believer himself. From the Wesleyan perspective, apostasy is a deliberate, willful rejection of the work of God in the life of a believer by that believer. Since apostasy is deliberate and intentional, it is never a matter of "losing one's salvation." It is a matter of throwing salvation away.

non-elect; indeed, they are directed time and again to the whole audience, including all the devout believers. From a Wesleyan Arminian point of view there would be no point in warning an audience against such behaviors if it was impossible for them to do otherwise. The moral seriousness of the ethics of the New Testament is undercut by either the notion that the elect *cannot* finally act in such ways, or by the notion that the non-elect are the only ones being warned but they cannot help but be that way.

But what about this whole concept called "prevenient" grace? It is true the phrase itself is not found in the Bible, but what of the idea? W. B. Shelton, in a detailed full-length study, has provided the necessary evidence that the idea behind the phrase is certainly found in Scripture.[32] John Wesley regularly pointed to John 1:9, which though likely a reference to Christ himself coming into the world, nonetheless says that all persons have been illuminated by that coming. Shelton quoted Wesley himself, who put it this way: "There is a measure of free-will supernaturally restored to every man, together with that supernatural light which 'enlightens every man.'"[33] One could have gotten there as well from a careful reading of what is said about the role of the Holy Spirit in relationship to the world in John 14–17: the Spirit convicts sinners of sin, convinces them of righteousness, and converts them to Christ. Now, clearly, some of this involves the work of the Spirit before they have responded positively to Christ. While the term *grace* does not show up in those chapters, the gracious work of God does, and it must be remembered that this is the Gospel that tells us in various ways that God loves the world (*kosmos*), a term that means the world of fallen humanity, and he desires that none of them should perish but rather have everlasting life. Further, Christ was not sent into the world to condemn human beings or to tell them that many of them were doomed not only from before their birth but from before the foundation of the universe! It should be clear when one reads Watson and Wesley that they are not talking about the modern secular notion of free will. They are talking about the human will renovated by God's prevenient grace and enabled to respond to the gospel. This is hardly Pelagianism in any form.

In my book *The Problem with Evangelical Theology*,[34] I pointed out how all the Protestant theologies, whether Reformed, Arminian, Pentecostal, or Dispensational,

---

[32] Shelton, *Prevenient Grace* (see chap. 4, n. 107).

[33] John Wesley, *Predestination Calmly Considered*, 3rd ed. (London: Printed by Henry Cock [. . .], 1755), 33–34.

[34] Ben Witherington, *The Problem with Evangelical Theology: Testing the Exegetical Foundations of Calvinism, Dispensationalism, Wesleyanism, and Pentecostalism*, 2nd ed. (Waco, TX: Baylor University Press, 2015).

have their strengths and weaknesses, and I freely admitted that Wesleyan Arminian theology has some exegetical weaknesses. The notion of instantaneous entire sanctification, especially if one wants to call it Christian perfection, is one of those weaknesses. As I noted in that book, it is not an accident that it is precisely the distinctive features of each of these theologies that are exegetically the weakest. Put another way, it is precisely in the places where they vary from the shared orthodoxy of the whole Christian tradition that they find the least scriptural support.

If one reads Wesley's *A Plain Account of Christian Perfection*, it quickly becomes obvious he is talking about the ability to avoid conscious active sin on the one hand, and about having an experience of the perfect love of God that casts out all fear (and sin?) from the human heart on the other hand. In other words, a particular narrow definition of sin is required to allow for Christian perfection here and now, but this ignores sins of omission, accidental sins, and so forth. One can have a genuine experience of the perfect love of God and not be "made perfect in love" thereby. And merely avoiding deliberate, willful sin is not all that the New Testament means by "sin." Nevertheless, the worse that can be said about Christian perfection is that Wesley's optimism about what God's grace can accomplish even in this life is the basis of this thinking, not some optimism about human nature inherently, or left to itself. As so often, the attempt to find adequate theological language to describe a genuine Christian experience or biblical reality leads to hyperbole or inadequate terminology. Wesley realized this and especially in later years talked about "entire sanctification" rather than Christian perfection, as he realized the latter term could confuse those not in the know.

And So?

John Wesley never claimed that Wesleyan theology was a perfect reading of Scripture, but he was utterly convinced that it was the reading that does best justice to the complexities of both the nature of a gracious God and the doctrine of salvation. I agree with him about that. It is interesting that Wesley was well familiar with earlier exegetes like Origen and Chrysostom, as was Watson, and they knew that such early church fathers were not Calvinists before their time. Wesley believed he was returning to pure scriptural Christianity, or as he preferred to call it, plain scriptural views of primitive Christianity shorn of later anachronisms. That in any case should be the goal. Wesley called himself a *homo unius libri*, a man of one book, even though he had studied thousands of books and had written hundreds of books or treatises or journal entries or letters. The litmus test for the Christian must be the Scriptures themselves, not later theologies, however helpful or useful.

In this essay I have attempted to give a glimpse, both ancient and modern in character, to how a Wesleyan Arminian critique of Calvinism looks. This is of course not the only way the matter could be approached, but I do think it deals with the major fault lines that divide Arminians and Calvinists. While, as Wesley once said, his views were only a hair's breadth from Calvinism on things like original sin or that salvation was of grace from start to finish and at no point a human self-help program, at the end of the day his view of God's character, God's sovereignty, the scope of the atonement, the way God's grace works, the nature of election, and various other topics varied considerably from Reformed theology. Perhaps someday we will find out who was more nearly right; but for now we must remember that we know in part, and we see in part, which should lead not to hubris but to humility in discussing the verities of our faith.

SECTION
THREE

Crucial Theological, Biblical, and Ecclesiological Issues with Calvinism

9

Romans 9 and Calvinism

—— Brian J. Abasciano ——

Romans 9 is often touted as validating Calvinism, specifically its view of un-conditional individual election.[1] Well-known Calvinist pastor and scholar John Piper once wrote in reference to his previous belief in free will, "Romans 9 is like a tiger going about devouring free-willers like me." And in regard to the doctrines of unconditional election and irresistible grace, he testified that "Romans 9 was the watershed text and the one that changed my life forever." Piper found that his non-Calvinist worldview could not stand against Romans 9.[2] Non-Calvinist evangelicals have heard similar testimonies over and over from numerous Calvinists who claim that they were practically forced by Romans 9 to become Calvinists.

---

[1] Thomas R. Schreiner, "Does Romans 9 Teach Individual Election unto Salvation? Some Exegetical and Theological Reflections," *JETS* 36 (1993): 25–40 (25), noted this phenomenon.

[2] John Piper, "The Absolute Sovereignty of God: What Is Romans Nine About?" Desiring God, November 3, 2002, https://www.desiringgod.org/messages/the-absolute -sovereignty-of-god.

What are we to make of this? Must we all become Calvinists if we are going to be honest and faithful to Scripture? Does Romans 9 demand Calvinism? Does it really teach unconditional individual election unto salvation? In this essay, I will argue that Romans 9 neither demands Calvinism nor teaches unconditional election but that it contains a corporate and conditional view of election unto salvation. First, I will discuss the nature of election in Romans 9. Second, I will situate Romans 9 in the context of the letter. Third, I will present a brief exegesis of Romans 9 with an eye on the doctrine of election and Calvinist interpretation of the passage.[3]

Election in Romans 9

While Calvinists typically think Romans 9 teaches unconditional individual election, many scholars now think Paul rather had corporate election in mind.[4] Corporate election was the view of the Old Testament and Second Temple Judaism; Paul and the rest of the New Testament only used corporate language when speaking explicitly of election unto salvation; and the sociohistorical context of Paul and the early Church was collectivist.[5] Speaking of Rom 9:10–13 and corporate election, distinguished Calvinist scholar Douglas Moo conceded that corporate election is what one would expect Paul to have in mind, "an expectation," he pointed out, "that seems to be confirmed by the OT texts that Paul quotes."[6] But it is important to specify the

---

[3] Romans 9 is a notoriously difficult passage with an immense amount of secondary literature. Space does not allow for a detailed treatment here. For further detail and substantiation of the exegesis presented in this essay, see my series of books on the passage: Abasciano, *Paul's Use of the Old Testament in Romans 9:1–9: An Intertextual and Theological Exegesis*, JSNTSup/ LNTS 301, ed. Mark Goodacre (London: T&T Clark, 2005); Abasciano, *Paul's Use of the Old Testament in Romans 9:10–18: An Intertextual and Theological Exegesis*, JSNTSup/LNTS 317, ed. Mark Goodacre (London: T&T Clark, 2011); and Abasciano, *Paul's Use of the Old Testament in Romans 9:19–33: An Intertextual and Theological Exegesis*, JSNTSup/LNTS (London: T&T Clark, 2015).

[4] A phenomenon observed by Schreiner, "Election," 25, 34; Douglas Moo, *The Epistle to the Romans*, 2nd ed., NICNT (Grand Rapids: Eerdmans, 2018), 591.

[5] For explanation of these points, see Brian J. Abasciano, "Corporate Election in Romans 9: A Reply to Thomas Schreiner," *JETS* 49, no. 2 (June 2006): 351–71 (esp. 353–58), and the literature cited there.

[6] Moo, *Romans*, 605. Moo went on to argue that Paul (unexpectedly) spoke of individual election, but his arguments do not stand against the type of view of corporate election discussed in this chapter.

nature of the corporate election in view, because various conceptions of it have been posited by scholars as Paul's view in Romans 9.[7]

The best view of corporate election recognizes that the election of God's people in the Old Testament was a consequence of the choice of an individual who represented the group, the corporate head and representative. In other words, the group was elected in the corporate head, as a consequence of its association with this corporate representative (Gen 15:18; 17:7–10, 19; 21:12; 24:7; 25:23; 26:3–5; 28:13–15; Deut 4:37; 7:6–8; 10:15; Mal 1:2–3). Moreover, individuals (such as Rahab and Ruth) who were not naturally related to the corporate head could join the chosen people and thereby share in the covenant head's and elect people's identity, history, election, and covenant blessings.

There was a series of covenant heads in the Old Testament—Abraham, Isaac, and Jacob—and the choice of each new covenant head brought a new definition of God's people based on the identity of the covenant head (in addition to the references in the previous paragraph, see Rom 9:6–13). Finally, Jesus Christ came as the head of the new covenant (Romans 3–4; 8; Gal 3–4; cf. Heb 9:15; 12:24)—he is the Chosen One (Mark 1:11; 9:7; 12:6; Luke 9:35; 20:13; 23:35; Eph 1:6; Col 1:13; and numerous references to Jesus as the Christ/Messiah, which essentially means the anointed/chosen one)—and anyone united to him comes to share in his identity, history, election, and covenant blessings (we become coheirs with Christ: Rom 8:16–17; cf. Gal 3:24–29). Thus, election is "in Christ" (Eph 1:4 NET), a consequence of union with him by faith. Just as God's people in the old covenant were chosen in Jacob/Israel, so God's people in the new covenant are chosen in Christ.

Since those in Christ share in his identity, history, and covenant blessing, generally what is true of Christ the covenant head is true of those who are in him. Christ is the Son of God (Rom 1:3–4), holy (Acts 13:35), the Holy One (Mark 1:24; Luke 4:34; John 6:69; Acts 2:27; 13:35; 1 John 2:20), beloved (Eph 1:6), righteous (Acts 22:14; 1 John 2:1), the heir to all God's promises (Rom 8:17; Heb 1:2), and the possessor and dispenser of the Holy Spirit (Acts 2:33), who is the bestower and marker of election

---

[7] Cf. Brian J. Abasciano, "Clearing Up Misconceptions about Corporate Election," *Ashland Theological Journal* 41 (2009): 59–90 (81n3). The published version of this article has some misprinting and uses endnotes. A more accurate version using footnotes may be found at http://evangelicalarminians.org/brian-abasciano-clearing-up-misconceptions-about-corporate -election/. In the notes to this chapter, I will include references to the single-spaced footnotes version in brackets after references to the published version; that reference for the above citation is p. 2, n. 3.

(Acts 2:33; Rom 8:1, 9–11, 14–17; Gal 3:2–5; Eph 1:13–14). So, those who are in Christ—who therefore share in his history, identity, and blessings—are sons of God (Gal 3:26), holy (1 Cor 3:17; Eph 2:19–22; Col 3:12), holy ones (Eph 1:1), beloved (Eph 5:1), righteous (Rom 3:22; 2 Cor 5:21), heir to God's promises with and because of Christ (Rom 4:13–17; 8:16–17; Gal 3:29), and indwelt by the Holy Spirit (Acts 2:33, 38–39; 11:15–17; Rom 8:9–11, 14–17; Gal 3:2–5; Eph 1:13–14). As those in Christ, they even share in his death, resurrection, and heavenly rule (Rom 6:1–11; Eph 2:4–7; Col 2:11–13). Every spiritual blessing is bestowed in Christ (Eph 1:3), which is a way of saying that every spiritual blessing is given to those in Christ *because* they are in Christ—that is, every spiritual blessing is given as a consequence of union with Christ. Thus, election is "in Christ" (Eph 1:4), a consequence of union with him, which makes election conditional on union with Christ. That also makes election conditional on faith in Christ since union with Christ is by faith, in Paul's theology.[8] Election is conditional on union with Christ, and union with Christ is conditional on faith. Therefore, election is conditional on faith in Christ.

Paul's olive tree metaphor later in his argument (Rom 11:17–24; n.b. Romans 9–11 is a united section) exemplified corporate election perfectly. The olive tree represents the elect people of God.[9] But individuals get grafted into the chosen people and share in election and its blessings by faith in Christ or get cut off from God's elect people and their blessings because of unbelief. The root of the olive tree (God's people) is the covenant heads/patriarchs.[10] And the elect status of the chosen people is rooted in the election of the covenant heads; they share in the covenant heads' election. Christ is the head of the new covenant, the final definer of God's people, *the* seed of Abraham to whom the covenant promises were made (Gal 3:16) and in whom believers also become the seed of Abraham and heirs to the covenant promises (Romans 4; Galatians 3–4). That is, in him they become the elect people of God, which is also to say, by faith in him they become elect. Membership in the chosen people (i.e., election) is by faith in Christ, and exclusion from the chosen people is due to unbelief.

---

[8] For faith as uniting us with Christ, see John 14:23; Romans 6; 1 Cor 1:30; 2 Cor 5:21; Gal 3:26–28; Eph 1:13–14; 2; 3:17 and the literature cited in Abasciano, "Misconceptions," 82n13 [8n12].

[9] Thomas R. Schreiner, *Romans*, 2nd ed., BECNT 6 (Grand Rapids: Baker, 2018), 451–52, 469, 565–66; Moo, *Romans*, 715, 724n747.

[10] Cf. Schreiner, *Romans*, 562, 567; Moo, *Romans*, 717–18, 722.

The focus of election in the olive tree metaphor is clearly the corporate people of God, which spans salvation history. The olive tree itself is a corporate figure for the people of God. Nevertheless, individuals are part of the picture. They are elect secondarily as members of the elect people. They share in the elect status of the people, and most fundamentally, of the covenant heads. As Paul metaphorically puts it, they "share in the nourishing root of the olive tree" (Rom 11:17 ESV).[11]

Both corporate and individual election perspectives afford a place to a corporate and an individual dimension to election. They differ on which dimension is primary and so leads to the other, whether union with Christ and consequent sharing in the election of Christ and his people leads to the individual's election, or whether the discrete election of multiple individuals leads to there being an elect group.[12] This invalidates perhaps the most frequent and fundamental objection to corporate election, that it excludes individuals. It does not exclude individuals but recognizes that the election of individuals is rooted in union with Christ and thus derives from his election; the individual is elect as a part of the elect people. New Testament texts portraying individuals as elect or as entering or exiting from the people of God do not imply individualistic election but fit perfectly well with the corporate election model, which always included individuals with a primary focus on the group.

Calvinist scholars Thomas Schreiner and Douglas Moo both surprisingly agreed that those who are grafted into the olive tree basically share in the election of the patriarchs (Rom 11:17).[13] It is not surprising that they interpret the imagery this way—it is clearly the right interpretation. But it is surprising that they do not seem to realize the strong, inescapable implication that this demands corporate, conditional election. The concept of election of the people as a sharing in the election of the corporate head is the definition of corporate election. Moreover, the text explicitly indicates that membership in the people and sharing in the election of the covenant heads and chosen people is conditional on faith.

---

[11] All Scripture quotations in this chapter are from the ESV unless otherwise noted. I have chosen the ESV because it currently seems to be the translation of choice among Calvinists.

[12] Some might reason that individuals must first be chosen and gathered for a chosen group to exist, but this is an individualistic way of looking at it that misses the corporate perspective of the biblical text and the scriptural fact that Christ is a corporate figure as well as an individual figure. As a corporate figure, Christ sums up and embodies his people in himself. See further note 17 below, and much more extensively, Abasciano, "Misconceptions," 64–72 [12–30].

[13] See note 12 above and note additionally that Schreiner identified the fatness/richness (*piotētos*) of the root as "the electing grace of God" (Schreiner, *Romans*, 588).

The corporate approach to election is confirmed by another passage in Romans 11, starting with v. 7. In 11:7, those whom Paul called "the rest" (*hoi loipoi*) are manifestly not elect. Now according to Calvinism, God elected certain individuals from eternity for salvation, making a static group that can never change; no one can be added to it or taken away from it. However, Paul believed that individuals from "the rest" could yet believe, and he hoped to bring as many of them to Christ as he could (vv. 11–24).

But this is incompatible with a Calvinistic view of election and in line with corporate election. Rather than the elect referring to those who were chosen to believe and be saved in eternity past, and therefore including all unbelievers who will eventually believe, Paul's viewpoint here evinced a dynamic view of the elect in the new covenant as referring only to those who are actually in Christ by faith and allows for departure from and entry into the elect as portrayed in the olive tree metaphor.[14] Individuals are not elect until they believe and come to share in the election of Christ the covenant head, and they remain elect only as long as they believe, that is, only as long as they remain united to Christ by faith.[15] The number of the elect changes

---

[14] Non-Calvinists who deny that true believers can forsake saving faith might balk at the notion of the possibility of departing from the elect people. Though I would argue that Rom 11:17–24 demands the possibility, it is not an essential point regarding Romans 11's definition of the elect. For even if one holds that God will not allow genuine believers to forsake their faith and therefore be cut off from the elect people, there can be no question that the text portrays those who come to faith as being grafted into the chosen people.

[15] Non-Calvinists who deny that true believers can forsake saving faith can still affirm this definition of the elect because it would remain true that individual believers remain elect only as long as they continue to believe; it is just that they think all genuine believers will continue to believe. One might question this corporate definition of the elect because Eph 1:4 says that believers were chosen in Christ before the foundation of the world. But the phenomenon of union with Christ (indicated by the phrase "in Christ") bringing the church to share in Christ's identity, history, and election best explains Eph 1:4's reference to the prehistoric election of the church. Because the church is identified with Christ (it is his body after all) and shares in his history and election, his election is their election. His being chosen before the foundation of the world was their being chosen before the foundation of the world. We can see this sort of dynamic at work in various biblical texts, such as Gen 25:23 indicating that the nation of Israel was in the womb of Rebekah because Jacob was; Mal 1:2–3 saying that God loved/chose Israel by loving/choosing Jacob; Heb 7:9–10 stating that Levi paid tithes to Melchizedek in Abraham; various OT passages telling contemporary Israel that God chose them in the past in reference to his choice of the patriarchs and/or his choice of Israel as his covenant people at Sinai (e.g., Deut 4:37; 7:6–7; 10:15; 14:2; Isa 41:8–9; 44:1–2; Amos 3:2); Romans 6 indicating that we died with Christ; and Eph 2:4–6 stating that in Christ we were made alive with him, raised with Christ, and seated in the heavenlies with him. Individuals come to share in this

depending on who is united to Christ by faith because the election of God's people is derivative of Christ's election, a result of union with Christ by faith, and thus a sharing in his election. Even though the elect in Rom 11:7 had obtained right standing with God, Paul sought to reach the non-elect to bring them to faith in Christ and to become part of the elect. All of this coheres with the fact that the terminology of the elect always referred in the New Testament to believers and not lost sinners who will eventually believe.[16] Nor does the Old Testament provide any sort of precedent for the elect referring to people in the world who are not part of the people of God but will eventually be among them.[17]

The corporate focus of the biblical concept of election unto salvation is at odds with the Calvinist view of election as God choosing this or that individual to believe and thus to be saved. Biblical election unto salvation in the New Testament is covenantal election. It is God's choice of the church as his covenant people (something we will see in Rom 9:6–9), the continuation and fulfillment of his choice of Israel as his covenant people as seen in Rom 11:17–24 discussed above (see also Eph 2:11–22).[18] To use another covenantal relationship as an illustration, it is not like a man choosing a woman as the one he intends to marry (illustrative of the Calvinist view), but it is like a man choosing a woman as his wife in the very act of marrying her (illustrative of the corporate view). His saying, "I do," enacting the covenant of marriage, is his choice of her as his covenant partner. It is in this sense that God chose Israel at Sinai, in his making a covenant with them.

Some have mistakenly taken Paul's appeal in Romans 9 to the discretionary election of the former covenant heads to be an indication that the election of God's people for salvation is individual and unconditional. But the election of the covenant head is unique, entailing the election of all who are identified with him. Each

---

corporate election when they believe in Christ and are therefore united to him. This is akin to how, upon becoming an American citizen but not before, a naturalized American citizen can say that we (America) won the Revolutionary War when that victory took place before he or any American alive today was ever born.

[16] The main possible exception is 2 Tim 2:10, but see Marshall against this being an exception. I. Howard Marshall, "Universal Grace and Atonement in the Pastoral Epistles," in Clark H. Pinnock, ed., *The Grace of God and the Will of Man* (Minneapolis: Bethany House, 1989), 51–69 (65–66).

[17] Marshall, 66.

[18] Hence, most precisely, election is not so much directly to salvation, but to covenant partnership/relationship. However, salvation is a blessing of the new covenant, and so it may be said that election is unto salvation.

individual member of the elect is not chosen as an individual to become part of the elect people in the same manner as the corporate head was chosen to be the corporate head. Rather, individual members of the covenant people share in the election of the covenant head. In harmony with his great stress in Romans on salvation/justification being by faith in Christ, Paul appealed to God's discretionary election of Isaac and Jacob to defend God's right to make election to be by faith in Christ rather than works or ancestry, as his conclusion to the section bears out, referring to the elect state of righteousness: "What shall we say, then? That Gentiles who did not pursue righteousness have attained it, that is, a righteousness that is by faith; but that Israel who pursued a law that would lead to righteousness did not succeed in reaching that law. Why? Because they did not pursue it by faith, but as if it were based on works" (Rom 9:30–32b).

The Context of Romans 9

To exegete Romans 9 properly, we must take account of its context, both the context of the letter as a whole and the context of the section of the epistle in which it is found, chapters 9–11.[19] Regarding the letter as a whole, we begin with the observation that Paul wrote to a mixed church of a minority of Jews and a majority of Gentiles that was marked by some tension and conflict between the two groups. Paul intended to take the gospel to Spain and desired the support of the Roman church. Thus, his main purpose in writing the letter was to unite the church in Rome behind his gospel in order that they might together support his future mission to Spain, which would aim to convert both Jews and Gentiles but would prioritize Jews first before turning to Gentiles.

With this purpose in mind, Paul, in Romans 1–11, explained and defended his gospel of justification by faith, which grants covenant membership with all its blessings (including salvation) to all who believe, whether Jew or Gentile, but excludes unbelieving Jews (see esp. Romans 3–4). As N. T. Wright pointed out, by the end of Romans 8 Paul had "systematically transferred the privileges and attributes of 'Israel' to the Messiah and his people."[20] And as Brendan Byrne noted, Paul had described

---

[19] For an assessment of the letter and chaps. 9–11 as the context of Romans 9, see Abasciano, *Romans 9:1–9*, 27–44.

[20] Nicholas T. Wright, *The Climax of the Covenant: Christ and the Law in Pauline Theology* (Edinburgh: T&T Clark, 1992), 250; cf. 237.

"the extension of Israel's privileges to Gentile believers and the inclusion of those Gentiles within the eschatological people of God."[21] Paul ended Romans 8 with an exalted, glorious celebration of the blessing and security of this new covenant people of God made up of Jews and mostly Gentiles.

But ironically, the celebratory climax of Romans 1–8 naturally leads to consideration of the most compelling objection to Paul's gospel—that it would make God unfaithful to his covenant promises to Israel, since most Jews had not received the fulfillment of those promises while the church of Jews and Gentiles had. It was such a critical objection that Paul had already discussed it briefly in Rom 3:1–8, but now comes back to it for an extended treatment in chapters 9–11,[22] which is a lengthy, unified section of the letter defending the faithfulness of God to his promises to Israel in light of Paul's gospel.

Romans 9:1–5

Paul's rejoicing over the church's possession of all the blessings of God for his chosen people (Romans 8) led him to face the grievous state of the vast majority of his kinsmen, the Jewish people, who were excluded from the fulfillment in the new covenant of the Old Testament promises made to Israel. In Rom 9:1–3 Paul expressed severe grief over their cursed state, that they are cut off from Christ, excluded from the elect covenant people, and slated for the eschatological wrath of God.[23] Verses 4–5 ground Paul's grief by observing that the Jewish people are the very people to whom the promises most fittingly belong as the historic chosen people. The terrible truth entailed by Paul's gospel that unbelieving ethnic Israel has not received the fulfillment of God's covenant promises to Israel but believing Gentiles have received them calls God's faithfulness into question, and therefore, Paul's gospel too for being a message that allegedly demands the conclusion that God is unfaithful. Paul offered his defense of God's faithfulness in his gospel in the rest of Romans 9–11.

---

[21] Brendan S. J. Byrne, *Romans*, Sacra Pagina 6 (Collegeville, MN: Liturgical Press, 1996), 282.

[22] Most scholars view Rom 3:1–8 as a brief discussion that is resumed at length in Romans 9–11. An extensive list of scholars supporting the view may be found in Brian J. Abasciano, "Paul's Use of the Old Testament in Romans 9:1–9: An Intertextual and Theological Exegesis" (PhD diss., University of Aberdeen, 2004), 84n125.

[23] In 9:3, Paul implied that unbelieving ethnic Israel was "*anathema* from Christ," a phrase that most scholars take as indicating eternal condemnation, as noted by Jack Cottrell, *Romans*, 2 vols., College Press NIV Commentary (Joplin, MO: College Press, 1998), 2:47.

Before looking at the first leg of Paul's defense (vv. 6–33), we should note that an appeal to vv. 1–5 serves as a key element of Piper's case for individualistic election and against corporate election in Romans 9. He argued that the text shows Paul's focus was on individuals, as he was concerned that many individual Israelites were not saved but damned.[24] However, as we have seen, attention to individuals does not demand nor even hint at individualistic election. Corporate election always included individuals as elect by sharing in the election of the corporate head and his people (see the section on election earlier in this chapter). It always allowed for attention to individuals, mention of the elect state of individuals, and the addition of individuals to, or the cutting off individuals from, the elect people without shifting election to a choice about whether or not the individual would join the elect people.[25]

Romans 9:6–13

Paul responded in Rom 9:6a to the challenge to God's faithfulness presented by unbelieving ethnic Israel's exclusion from the new covenant and its blessings (vv. 1–5) with his main thesis for all of Romans 9–11: the word of God has not failed. The rest of Romans 9–11 supports that contention. "The word of God" especially includes the promises of God to Israel spoken in the Scriptures and reflected in the privileges of Israel listed in 9:4–5 as well as the theme of promise found in vv. 8–9 (that includes "the promise" mentioned in v. 9; cf. also "the sayings of God" in 3:2, my translation). Verse 6b then encapsulates Paul's primary point in support of his declaration of God's faithfulness: "For not all who are descended from Israel belong to Israel." That is, not all ethnic Israelites/Jews are part of true Israel/the true covenant people of God, the Israel to whom God made his covenant promises. As Paul made clear in Romans 4 (see esp., vv. 13, 16, and 18), the covenant promise was made to Abraham *and his seed*. Paul now clarified 9:6b in the first part of the next verse (v. 7a): "nor [is it] that all [who are his] children are the seed of Abraham,"[26] confirming that belonging

---

[24] John Piper, *The Justification of God: An Exegetical and Theological Study of Romans 9:1–23*, 2nd ed. (Grand Rapids: Baker, 1993), 64–65.

[25] For further response to Piper on this point, see Abasciano, "Misconceptions," 64 (11–12), and Abasciano, *Romans 9:1–9*, 183–89.

[26] My translation; cf. similarly, NET; Moo, *Romans*, 590, 595–96n133; James D. G. Dunn, *Romans*, 2 vols., Word Biblical Commentary 38 (Dallas: Word, 1988), 2:538, 540, though most side with the ESV, which has "children" as referring to Abraham's covenantal descendants (see Schreiner, *Romans*, 469–70, for the case for the majority translation; my translation avoids his

to the Israel to which God made covenant promises has to do with being the seed of Abraham, an identity that Romans 4 has already established as conditional on faith in Christ.

The second half of v. 7 quoted Gen 21:12 as positively summing up the negatively stated point of 9:6b–7a: "but 'Through Isaac shall your offspring be named.'" This Old Testament quotation indicates that inclusion in the covenant would not be based on physical descent from Abraham but on association with Isaac; otherwise, Isaac's brother Ishmael would have been included in the covenant. While this might seem still to involve physical descent as determining covenant membership, it shows God's authority to define the covenant people based on the condition he lays down, and Paul found a deeper principle at work in God's choice of who his people are, which he will reveal in v. 8. But before looking at that, we should note two points that are relevant to the focus of our concern in this chapter.

First, we see here the phenomenon of corporate election mentioned in our earlier discussion of election. The covenant people of God were defined by association with the covenant head, Abraham. But with God's choice of a new covenant head, Isaac, the covenant people of God (i.e., the seed of Abraham) were redefined based on association with Isaac. The significance of the language of being named (or chosen or some other verb) "in *x*" (i.e., "in" some person, be it Isaac or Christ or whomever) can be seen here: it refers to being named (or whatever the action is) because of connection to the person in whom the action is said to take place, in this case, Isaac. But we know from what Paul said previously in Romans (and later for that matter; remember the olive tree of Romans 11) that the seed of Abraham, who are heirs to the covenant promises, are those who are in Christ by faith, whether Jew or Gentile. The covenant people of God are those who believe in Christ, and covenant membership is granted by faith. In other words, election is by faith; it is conditional on faith in Christ. This is in essence what Paul is defending in Romans 9–11 as compatible with God's faithfulness.

Second, Paul's quotation of Gen 21:12 spoke of God naming certain people Abraham's seed in the sense of identifying them as Abraham's seed or descendants, God's covenant people, who are heir to the covenant promises. The word for naming here (*kaleō*) is the same word often translated "to call," as it is translated in the rest of

---

grammatical criticism of the alternative view). The primary basis for my translation is that it sticks with Paul's use of the word *sperma* ("seed") earlier in the letter as a label for Abraham's covenantal descendants and especially this usage clearly seen in the next verse (Rom 9:8).

Romans 9 by most translations (see vv. 12, 24–26). This is Paul's concept of calling in this chapter, God's naming those who believe as his own covenant people, which in fact makes them his own people and the recipients of his covenant promises.

Calvinists tend to deny the naming sense here in favor of their doctrine of effectual calling, God's effective summons to faith that irresistibly brings about saving faith in the one who receives the summons. But calling in Romans 9 refers to naming. Even Schreiner admitted that naming is the meaning in the original context of Paul's quotation (Gen 21:12).[27] Moreover, the naming sense is certain in 9:25–26 because those verses use a construction called a double accusative that demands the naming sense with the term "to call."[28] The naming sense is obvious from a simple look at the verses whether or not one knows about double accusatives. It is also certain in v. 24, since its reference to calling is supported and explained by vv. 25–26 with their clear use of the naming sense. This is all part of a calling/naming theme in the chapter, introduced in v. 7. Moo even saw calling as the topic of vv. 6–29, highlighted at the beginning and ending of the passage.[29] That is largely correct, but the topic serves the larger theme of God's faithfulness (v. 6a); Paul is defending God's calling of his new covenant people as consistent with his Old Testament promises to Israel. Calvinist insistence on calling in Romans 9 as an effective summons that irresistibly causes faith seems very much like reading Calvinist theology into the text to conform the text to Calvinist theology rather than letting the text define our theology.

The naming sense of calling in Romans 9 undermines the Calvinist interpretation of the passage because it means the effective call of God that Paul is defending in the chapter is either roughly equivalent to election (the corporate view) or directly reflective of it (the Calvinist view) and is conditional on faith. God names those who believe as his children. That is what has called God's faithfulness to his promises to Israel into question, for he does not name unbelieving Jews as his children and his heirs to his covenant promises.

---

[27] Schreiner, *Romans*, 470.

[28] See, e.g., Charles E. B. Cranfield, *A Critical and Exegetical Commentary on the Epistle to the Romans*, 2 vols., ICC (Edinburgh: T & T Clark, 1975–79), 2:500. A double accusative is not necessary for the naming sense, but when present, it requires the naming sense. On the phenomenon of double accusatives in the Greek of the NT, see Daniel B. Wallace, *Greek Grammar beyond the Basics: An Exegetical Syntax of the New Testament* (Grand Rapids: Zondervan, 1996), 181–89.

[29] Moo, *Romans*, 589.

The phenomenon of calling as naming in Romans 9 undermines not only Calvinist interpretation of Romans 9, but also a key tenet of Calvinism known as "effectual calling," which conveys the famous irresistible grace Calvinism teaches.[30] Scholars typically regard the language of the calling of Christians to be technical language that bears the same meaning everywhere it occurs. If it means naming in Romans 9, then it likely means naming everywhere else in the New Testament. And indeed, a naming sense works just as well, and often better, than a summoning sense of the language elsewhere in the New Testament. For example, when Paul introduced himself to the Roman church as "a called apostle"[31] in Rom 1:1, the idea of naming/designation/appointment fits the context even better than does summoning since Paul is indicating that God has in fact made him an apostle by appointing him, not by merely summoning him to be one.

The strongest and most common evidence Calvinists typically give in favor of their doctrine of effectual calling is that the theological language of calling almost always refers to those who have responded positively to the gospel summons (i.e., Christians) and seems to refer to an effectual act. Romans 8:30 is most frequently cited as an example because it is alleged that it indicates that all who are called are justified,[32] which would mean that everyone who is called in the way envisioned in the verse believes, since justification is by faith. But this line of argument fails to support calling as effectual summoning over effectual naming because the point is totally consistent with both; both perspectives hold to calling as effectual. Showing that calling is effectual does not address the question of whether it refers to summoning or naming. This eliminates the strongest argument for the Calvinist conception of effectual calling if it is considered against the notion of effectual naming.

Romans 9:8 interprets the quotation of Gen 21:12 and sums up the significance of all the statements of 9:6b–7: "This means that it is not the children of the flesh who are the children of God, but the children of the promise are counted as offspring [lit. seed]." This verse is critical to understanding Romans 9. It gives the governing principle that refutes the charge that God is unfaithful for (allegedly) breaking his

---

[30] On effectual calling as an essential element of Calvinism and inextricably intertwined with irresistible grace, see Bruce A. Ware, "Effectual Calling and Grace," in Schreiner and Ware, *Still Sovereign*, 203–27 (see chap. 4, n. 42), who argued in favor of the doctrine.

[31] This is a more literal translation of the Greek, as noted by footnotes in the NASB and NET versions. Paul used the adjectival form of the terminology *klētos* rather than the verb.

[32] But for a contrary view, see F. Leroy Forlines, *Romans*, Randall House Bible Commentary (Nashville: Randall House, 1987), 239–40.

promises to Israel as his covenant people due to rejecting unbelieving ethnic Israel from enjoying the fulfillment of those promises. That principle is that the covenant people who are heirs to the promises (the children of God) are not defined by ancestry (the children of the flesh) but by promise (the children of the promise). This is a way of saying that God considers those who believe to be his covenant people; election is based on faith. From the beginning, God's promises were not for ethnic Israel based on its character as *ethnic* Israel but for true, spiritual Israel, those who would believe.

That Paul spoke about God calling/choosing believers as his covenant people is suggested by the context of the letter as we have been explicating it to this point. It is also indicated most immediately by the identification of the seed of Abraham (= the covenant people = the heirs of the promises) as "the children of the promise." The phrase is rich in meaning, including designating its referents as the seed/offspring God promised to Abraham and especially as believers in Christ and God's promise (Christ and the promise are two sides of the same coin), and consequently, as heirs to the promise through faith.[33] Romans 4 has already made clear that those who believe in Christ become the promised seed of Abraham by faith, who receive the promise by faith.

In Rom 9:9, Paul supported his interpretation of Gen 21:12 (articulated in Rom 9:8) with a quotation of the promise given to Abraham (Gen 18:10, 14), showing that the covenant people would come about through promise. This leaves 9:8 as Paul's main point so far in supporting his declaration of God's faithfulness in v. 6a. To the allegation that God is unfaithful for not giving the fulfillment of his covenant promises to unbelieving ethnic Israel, Paul replied that God never gave the promises to Israel as defined by physical ancestry but to Israel as defined by God's promise and God's call (naming), which, in the context of Romans, referred to those who believe in Christ. That is who is named by God as the seed of Abraham, the new covenant people, and the heirs to the covenant promises.

Romans 9:10–13 adds to v. 9's support of the principle enunciated in v. 8 (God has not chosen his children by ancestry, but by faith). It provides an even stronger example of the principle by using two brothers (twins) with the same mother and father (Isaac and Ishmael had different mothers). Moreover, it expands the principle by highlighting Jacob's election as the covenant head to have been before birth and so not constrained by Jacob's or Esau's actions. Furthermore, Esau had the natural right

---

[33] For a full accounting of the phrase, see Abasciano, *Romans 9:1–9*, 196–98.

as the firstborn to inherit the covenant and its promises. But God overrode that, sovereignly choosing Jacob rather than Esau as the covenant head in whom the covenant people would be identified.

Calvinist interpreters typically take the election of Jacob before he was born to be evidence of Paul teaching unconditional individual election unto salvation in this passage. But this is out of step with the nature of the election in the Old Testament text Paul quoted. As we observed in the last paragraph of the section on election earlier in this chapter, the election of the covenant head is unique, entailing the election of all who are identified with him, while the election of individual members of the covenant people comes to them through sharing in the election of the covenant head rather than being chosen directly to become part of the elect people. Jacob's election to covenant headship does not provide the pattern for the election of individual covenant members. It shows God's sovereignty over who the covenant people are by his election of the covenant head (and by implication, over any conditions he has set for union with the covenant head) since their membership in the chosen people is conditional on connection to the covenant head. God's choice of Jacob as the covenant head was not constrained by Jacob's ancestry or works.

This reading is corroborated by Paul's assertion that God announced his choice of Jacob before Jacob and Esau had done anything good or bad "in order that the purpose of God in election would continue not by works, but by the one who calls" (9:11b–c).[34] The purpose of God to which Paul referred is best construed as God's purpose to save the world in harmony with Paul's concern in Romans to argue for the inclusion of Gentiles in the covenant people (see esp. chaps. 2–4, 9–11, 15); the Old Testament background of Rom 9:7–9, in which we see that the purpose of Abraham's election was to bless the world in him (e.g., Gen 18:18–19 located in the broader context of Paul's quotation of Gen 18:10, 14); and 9:10–13's role as support for v. 8 and its principle that the chosen people are not identified by physical ancestry but by promise/faith. The call of God referred to in v. 11 used the same word for naming as in v. 7 and surely carries the same import—God's naming of his chosen people based on faith. C. K. Barrett commented insightfully: "Works and calling are coordinated here, just as, earlier in the epistle, works and faith are coordinate. Evidently calling and faith correspond . . . Not works but faith leads to justification;

---

[34] My translation; cf. similarly, the NIV and NET. See Abasciano, *Romans 9:10–18*, 46–49, for a detailed discussion of the grammatical issues relevant to the main question of translation in Rom 9:11, the key phrase *hē kat'eklogēn prothesis* ("the purpose of God in election").

not works but God's call admits to the promise. These are different ways of expressing the same truth."[35]

But how does God's purpose to save the world, his choice of Jacob as the covenant head based on his own unconstrained sovereign will, and his sovereign decision to base covenant membership on faith rather than works or ancestry relate? God's unconstrained choice of Jacob shows his right to choose who his people are according to his own good pleasure through his election of the covenant head, which allowed for him to choose Jesus Christ as the head of the new covenant and faith as the condition for union with him. Faith is the condition of union with Christ and membership in the covenant people. Basing the fulfillment of God's purpose to bless the world on his sovereign call rather than on works or ancestry facilitates that fulfillment, for it enables God to call his people based on faith rather than works or ancestry and thereby include Gentiles in addition to Jews in the blessings of Abraham. However, this also entails the heartbreaking rejection of unbelieving ethnic Israel from the covenant.

Paul closed this section with a citation of Mal 1:2–3 ("Jacob I loved, but Esau I hated"), which gives further substantiation of God's election of Jacob over Esau and consequently, of God's election of Israel and rejection of Edom based on his sovereign will (the language of love and hate here refers to covenantal election and rejection). We have another instance here of corporate election. In the context of Malachi 1, God's election of Jacob entails the election of Israel. In the new covenant, the election of Christ entails the election of those who believe in him. With the condition for membership in the new covenant being faith in Christ, Paul's argument based on these Old Testament texts places unbelieving ethnic Israel in the present in the place of those who are physically descended from the former covenant head but rejected from the covenant (Ishmael and Esau), while the church is in the place of covenant partnership.

Romans 9:14–18

Romans 9:14–18 now supports vv. 10–13 (which join vv. 7–9 in supporting 6b) by addressing an objection to Paul's demonstration of sovereign divine election in the form of God choosing his people by faith without regard to works or ancestry. The objection is that this would make him unrighteous through violation of his covenant

---

[35] Charles K. Barrett, *A Commentary on the Epistle to the Romans*, 2nd ed., Black's New Testament Commentary (London: A & C Black, 1991), 171.

promises to Israel.[36] How could God not have regard for works and ancestry in light of the Old Testament? Paul has already answered the objection to a substantial extent through his argumentation in vv. 6–13, but he now expands and strengthens his answer.

Paul vehemently denied the charge of unrighteousness (v. 14) and supported his position further with two quotations of Scripture. First, in Rom 9:15 he quotes Exod 33:19b, "I will have mercy on whom I have mercy, and I will have compassion on whom I have compassion." In its original context, the quotation reveals the nature of God in relation to sinful humanity and refers most specifically to the divine mercy of the corporate covenantal election of the people of God. In the Exodus context, this is part of God's reply to Moses's request for God to reinstate Israel's election after it had been forfeited due to their forsaking of the Lord in their idolatrous sin with the golden calf.[37] It means that God has mercy on (i.e., chooses as his covenant people) whomever he chooses based upon whatever conditions he establishes. The statement emphasizes God's merciful character and his sovereign freedom in bestowing his mercy of covenant election as he pleases.

Calvinists tend to see this as a clear statement of unconditional election.[38] But the wording itself does not demand that in the least. In itself, the wording is consistent with either conditional or unconditional election, though the construction appears always to be used of conditional action when signaling freedom of action.[39] Regarding God's declaration—"I will have mercy on whom I have mercy"—as applied to the time of the new covenant, the question is, on whom does God choose to have mercy? The answer provided by the letter to the Romans is, those who believe. In

---

[36] Having (mistakenly) found unconditional election in 9:6–13, Calvinist interpreters tend to take the objection to be that unconditional individual election to salvation would make God unrighteous in the sense of being unfair. But our exegesis has not found unconditional election of individuals to salvation in vv. 6–13, but corporate election to salvation on the condition of faith. Moreover, Paul has been defending God's faithfulness to his promises to Israel, and this specific objection arises from God's choice of one people over another apart from works or ancestry; Paul has specified these two concerns. Furthermore, even if Jacob's election was unconditional, which is debatable, we have already noted that the election of the covenant head is unique and that the election of the covenant people is inherently conditional on union with the covenant head.

[37] That is the import of Moses's request to which Exod 33:19 responded; see Abasciano, *Romans 9:1–10*, 63–65.

[38] See, e.g., Piper, *Justification*, 82–83.

[39] See Abasciano, *Romans 9:10–18*, 177.

accordance with our tracing of Paul's argument to this point, the quotation is used here to support God's right to name his covenant people by faith rather than works or ancestry. It does so by revealing that God's nature in relation to sinful humanity is to be merciful and to bestow mercy according to his own good and sovereign pleasure. It is God's prerogative if he wants to disregard works and ancestry as a basis of covenant membership and to have faith as the condition for it.

The situation is much the same with 9:16: "So therefore, [it is] not of the one who wills nor of the one who runs, but of the mercy-bestowing God."[40] This is Paul's interpretation of his quotation of Exod 33:19b in Rom 9:15. God's bestowal of mercy, specifically in this instance, his election of his covenant people, is at his discretion as the one who bestows that mercy. He can have mercy on whom he chooses. He can disregard works and ancestry and choose those who believe in Christ as his covenant people. This obvious truth, inferred from Exod 33:19b, upholds Paul's denial of unrighteousness in God for naming his new covenant people by faith rather than works or ancestry in Rom 9:14.

In 9:17 Paul gave a second Old Testament quotation to support v. 14's claim of God's righteousness in his sovereign election: "For this very purpose I have raised you up, that I might show my power in you, and that my name might be proclaimed in all the earth" (quoting Exod 9:16). In Rom 9:18 he then sums up the thrust of his argument based on Exod 33:19b and Exod 9:16, with the first half of Rom 9:18 summing up the former—"So then he has mercy on whomever he wills"—and the second half of v. 18 summing up the latter and giving Paul's interpretation of Exod 9:16: "and he hardens whomever he wills."

In accordance with the unconditional election they believe Paul to have taught in the previous verses, Calvinists tend to take the allusion to the hardening of Pharaoh's heart to teach unconditional hardening as well, backed up by the claim that God unconditionally hardened Pharaoh. But we have not found Paul to be teaching unconditional election in the previous verses. Moreover, attention to the Old Testament background reveals that God's hardening of Pharaoh was not unconditional but a judgment against him for his wicked treatment of Israel and his

---

[40] My translation, which is more literal than the popular level translations; cf. similarly, Moo's (*Romans*, 613) translation, which is still less literal than the one I provide here. Most translations use the word "depend," which is not necessarily wrong or a critical difference, but it could mistakenly be taken to indicate that human actions have nothing to do with God's decision to show mercy, and it might obscure the most likely sense of the language here, which is to speak of the origin of God's mercy.

rebellion against the Lord and in answer to Israel's prayers (see, e.g., Exod 2:23–25; 3:7–10; 5:1–23).[41] Furthermore, a close reading of Exodus reveals that the divine hardening of Pharaoh's heart was not typically a direct, supernatural work in his heart, but rather indirect and natural, often in the form of strategic actions God took (such as withdrawing a plague) that inspired boldness in Pharaoh to do what he already freely wanted to do.

This accords with the vocabulary of hardening used in Exodus, which most fundamentally refers to the strengthening of a person's already freely formed will.[42] In the context of Exodus, hardening is connected to the signs (mostly plagues) performed by Moses that would normally overwhelm Pharaoh and force him to yield to God's demand. In this context, the language of hardening/strengthening Pharaoh's heart takes on the nuance of emboldening Pharaoh to do what he already really wanted to do but would not otherwise do because of the pressure of God's mighty power in the plagues. Hence, the hardening of Pharaoh's heart was not irresistible. It did, however, ironically make Pharaoh's own sinful free will its own punishment in God's execution of poetic justice upon him as his emboldened will repeatedly chose actions that brought additional judgment down on him and his people.

With Rom 9:17 and 18b, Paul is addressing the negative side of God's sovereignty in election—covenantal rejection—and the uncomfortable truth that God's sovereign decision to choose his people by faith apart from works or ancestry hardened ethnic Israel to the gospel. The very means by which God fulfilled his promises to Israel (especially the promise to Abraham to bless the world in him) also hardened ethnic Israel to faith in Christ. As Paul says later in the chapter, (ethnic) Israel did not

---

[41] This undercuts typical Calvinist appeals to God's prediction that he would harden Pharaoh's heart before Moses approached Pharaoh, for this precedes the earliest prediction of hardening (4:21). Such appeals falter on other grounds as well, but there is no need to address them further because this point keeps them from even getting out of the gate. The best Calvinistic response to this point is to appeal to Ps 105:25; see esp. G.K. Beale, "An Exegetical and Theological Consideration of the Hardening of Pharaoh's Heart in Exodus 4–14 and Romans 9," *Trinity Journal* 5 NS (1984): 129–54 (136). For a rebuttal of Beale, see Abasciano, *Romans 9:10–18*, 112–14.

[42] The most fundamental and prevalent word for hardening in the Exodus hardening passages is the Hebrew verb *ḥzq*, which most basically means "to be strong, strengthen." It can also mean "to have courage." The Greek word for harden that Paul uses in Rom 9:18 is the same word the LXX normally uses to translate *ḥzq* in the hardening passages of Exodus, *sklērunō*, which most basically means "to harden," but can mean "to strengthen," as it should be taken in the LXX of Exodus and in Romans 9 in light of the Exodus context. For an extensive treatment of the vocabulary of hardening in Exodus, see Abasciano, *Romans 9:10–18*, 92–108.

attain righteousness, "Because they did not pursue it by faith, but as if it were based on works. They have stumbled over the stumbling stone, as it is written, 'Behold, I am laying in Zion a stone of stumbling, and a rock of offense; and whoever believes in him will not be put to shame'" (vv. 32–33). And as he says of ethnic Israel a little further on, "For I bear them witness that they have a zeal for God, but not according to knowledge. For, being ignorant of the righteousness of God, and seeking to establish their own, they did not submit to God's righteousness. For Christ is the end of the law for righteousness to everyone who believes" (10:2–4). The great offense of election apart from works or ancestry to Jews in Paul's time can be seen in Acts 22, where we read that a group of Jews tried to kill Paul because they perceived him to be teaching against the law and to be defiling the temple by bringing a Gentile into it. After calming down, they were willing to listen to Paul, tolerating testimony to the resurrection of Christ, but flew into a murderous rage at the mere mention of mission to the Gentiles.

In 9:17 Paul quotes an Old Testament text that bears witness in its original context to the Lord hardening rebellious Pharaoh as the means for bringing judgment on him for his sin and as part of the process of fulfilling his covenant promises, bringing about the renewed election of God's people, and blessing the world with the knowledge of God by the proclamation of his name. God's sovereign decision to name his people based on faith rather than works or ancestry facilitates all of this in the new covenant with ethnic Israel in the place of Pharaoh. Through election by faith, God brought a general, corporate judgment on ethnic Israel for the ethnocentrism, pride, and self-reliance that would lead them to seek to establish their own righteousness (10:3), take offense at Christ (9:32–33), and stubbornly resist the gospel of salvation by faith. Yet this did not ensure that any particular Jews rejected the gospel. God would prefer that Jews believe in Christ, and Paul revealed later in his argument (chaps. 10–11) that God is pursuing their faith and consequent salvation. Any of them could accept the gospel by God's grace, and some did (like Paul!). But they must come on God's terms and in submission to his chosen means of salvation. Just as with Pharaoh, God made ethnic Israel's own freely formed will serve as its own punishment in ironic, poetic justice.

At the same time, election by faith in Christ apart from works or ancestry fulfills God's covenant promises to Abraham and his seed (i.e., the true Israel, the children of the promise), for (1) it grants fulfillment of the promises to anyone who believes, whether Jew or Gentile (remember the climactic promise to Abraham that all nations would be blessed in him), and (2) it is inherently connected to that which actually brings about the fulfillment of the promises, the death and resurrection of Christ. It also brings about the renewed election of God's people as the condition for membership in the new covenant and sharing in its election. Finally, it is essential to the new covenant proclamation of God's name, which, given the Old Testament background (esp. Rom 9:15/Exod 33:19), is multifaceted but entails God's judgment and especially his mercy. These are both proclaimed in the gospel of justification by faith. Indeed, election/sonship/justification by faith are the mercy proclaimed by the new covenant that manifests God's glorious name/character.

Romans 9:19–29

Paul has shown from Scripture that God has every right to have mercy on whomever he wills and to harden whomever he wills, specifically in context, to name those who believe in Christ apart from works or ancestry as his covenant people and to reject unbelieving Jews (those with works and Jewish ancestry but without faith in Christ), and even to establish a condition for covenant membership that was so offensive to Jewish sensibilities that it was bound to harden many of them to Christ and the gospel. Now in 9:19–29 Paul addresses an objection to what he has argued in vv. 14–18, especially aimed at the side of hardening and judgment entailed in God's sovereign decision to choose his people by faith rather than works or ancestry. The objection is articulated in v. 19: "You will say to me then, 'Why does he still find fault? For who has resisted his purpose?'"[43]

Calvinists tend to point eagerly at v. 19 and the verses that follow as strong evidence that Paul taught unconditional election and hardening in Romans 9. But they assume that the hardening Paul spoke of in vv. 17–18 is unconditional as well as deterministic/irresistible. Based on that assumption, the objection of v. 19 seems aimed straight at the notion of an unconditional, irresistible hardening combined with judgment for sin caused by the hardening. Paul's reply then seems to affirm unconditional election and especially unconditional hardening by sharply rebuking the objection ("But who are you, O man, to answer back to God?"; v. 20a) and appealing to God as Creator while leaving out any mention of his actions being conditional

---

[43] My translation. The ESV strays from a more literal rendering by speaking of ability ("who can resist") while most other translations follow the Greek more closely by speaking of what has happened ("who has resisted" or the like). Most translations use the term "will" in this verse where I have used "purpose," but the latter is the more specific nuance of the Greek word used here (*boulēma*); see, e.g., Dunn, *Romans*, 556; Gottlob Schrenk, "βούλημα," *TDNT*, 1:636–37.

on human actions (vv. 20b–21). Calvinists commonly argue that Paul would have surely appealed to the conditionality of God's actions on human decisions if hardening was conditional, because that would refute the objection. Indeed, they insist that the question of v. 19 would not arise if hardening was conditional.

At first blush this is a powerful argument and probably the strongest argument for a Calvinistic reading of Romans 9. However, it is based on false assumptions. Our exegesis has concluded that the hardening in vv. 17–18 is neither unconditional nor irresistible.[44] Rather, the objection in v. 19 is best understood in view of Rom 3:5, 7.

In Romans 9 Paul resumed the relatively brief discussion of Rom 3:1–8 for fuller discussion that extends through chap. 11.[45] In fact, in 9:1–13 Paul reached back to the passage immediately preceding Romans 3, picking up 2:17–29's theme of God's approval apart from works or ancestry. In 9:3–5 he picked up 3:1–2's theme of Jewish privilege despite God's judgment on unbelieving ethnic Israel, and in 9:6 he picked up 3:3's question of whether Jewish unfaithfulness nullifies the faithfulness of God. Paul's answer to that question in 3:4 is no; and as Moo put it, "God's faithfulness, or 'righteousness,' is manifested even through the sin of his people"[46] by God's judgment. Paul basically repeated that answer again in a different form in 9:17–18. Romans 3:5 considers an objection to that principle, and 3:7 repeats the objection by using a specific example. In its essence, the objection is that it would be unrighteous of God to condemn Jews, whose sin manifests his righteousness. In 9:19, Paul picked up the objection articulated in these earlier verses.[47] Displaying them together will help show the parallel:

> 3:5: "But if our unrighteousness serves to show the righteousness of God, what shall we say? That God is unrighteous to inflict wrath on us?"

---

[44] Even if one is inclined to regard hardening as irresistible in Exodus and Romans 9, the objection of Rom 9:19 still makes sense with conditional election, especially considering the OT background to vv. 20–21, which we will discuss. It makes good sense that even if election is conditional, there might be objection to irresistible hardening and consequent judgment even if it is temporary and reversible.

[45] So, e.g., Schreiner, *Romans*, 448; Moo, *Romans*, 189–90, 570; see further note 25 above.

[46] Moo, 189.

[47] See Peter Stuhlmacher, *Paul's Letter to the Romans: A Commentary*, trans. S. J. Hafemann (Louisville: Westminster John Knox, 1994), 150; Joseph A. Fitzmyer, *Romans: A New Translation with Introduction and Commentary*, Anchor Bible 33 (New York: Doubleday, 1993), 568; Craig S. Keener, *Romans: A New Covenant Commentary* (Eugene, OR: Cascade, 2009), 120.

3:7: "But if through my lie God's truth abounds to his glory, why am I still being condemned as a sinner?"

9:19: "You will say to me then, 'Why does he still find fault? For who has resisted his purpose?'" (author's translation)

After implying that God hardened ethnic Israel to accomplish his purpose of showing his power (in judgment and salvation) and proclaiming his name in all the earth (making his mercy and salvation available to all), the objection now arises, why does God still find fault (with Jews for their sin when he uses it to accomplish his purpose, especially when he has provoked them to hardheartedness with an offensive means of salvation)?[48] The clear implication is that God should not find fault in such circumstances with Jews who reject Christ.

The second question in 9:19, "For who has resisted his purpose?" (author's translation), grounds or supports the charge and implies that no one has prevented God's purpose of showing his power and proclaiming his name, but that it has been accomplished. The argument is that God should not judge Jews for their sin (rejecting Christ) because God accomplished his purpose through their sin. He has gotten what he wanted and benefited from Jewish sin. So what does he have to complain about or to blame them for? Paul answered this basic objection in 3:6 by pointing out that it undermines God's role as Judge of the world, and indeed, the very notion of divine judgment. Now, in 9:20–21, Paul will complement that answer by pointing to God's role as Creator.

Paul replied with a sharp rebuke to the objection that God should not judge Jewish sin because he accomplishes his purpose by it: "But who are you, O man, to answer back to God?" (Rom 9:20a). In other words, who do you think you are! Paul then used a classic biblical metaphor to address the objection, that of God as the

---

[48] One might wonder how God uses Jewish sin to show his power and proclaim his name. First, just as in Rom 3:4–7, it is through God's judgment on it, showing his power in judgment and the justice of his character/name. Second, hardening and election by faith apart from works or ancestry are so intertwined in this context that to speak of one of them is to speak of the other, since election by faith is what hardens (keep in mind that such hardening is resistible). Speaking of them is also to speak of Israel's sin, for hardening from the human side is stubborn rebellion against the Lord and his gospel and is itself sin. Thus, hardening from the divine side in the form of the proclamation of election by faith apart from works or ancestry, which brings along with it hardening from the human side in the form of resistance to the gospel on the part of many Jews, brings about the display of God's power in judgment on the hardened and in salvation for those who believe. Similarly, it also brings about the declaration of God's name/ character in the judgment and mercy of the gospel.

potter and his people as the clay: "Will the thing molded really say to the molder, 'Why did you make me like this?' Or does the potter not have right over the clay to make from the same lump one a vessel unto honor and another unto dishonor?" (vv. 20b–21).[49] As applied to the objection in the context of Romans 9 as we have detailed it in this chapter, the significance of the metaphor is obvious on its face.

As the Creator, does God not have the right to exclude from his people Jews who refuse to submit to his requirements for new covenant membership and to bring judgment on them for their rebellion against him (even if he glorifies himself through their rebellion and provoked their rebellion by choosing a means of salvation they would find exceedingly offensive)? And as the Creator, does God not have the right to name whom he desires as his people and to give them his blessings? Of course he does. To say otherwise is to arrogantly, and even blasphemously, put oneself in the place of the Creator God and to put the Creator God in the place of the creature. It is a denial of God's right as God and as Creator. It is as foolish as the notion of a pot complaining about how the potter made it.

The Old Testament background to Paul's potter/clay metaphor is illuminating, though we only have space to skim some key elements of its deep waters. Paul quoted from Isa 29:16 as well as alluded to Isa 45:9 and Jer 18:6.[50] All these passages are corporate in their focus. They all have to do with God's dealings with Israel as a nation,[51] supporting the corporate focus we have observed in Romans 9.

---

[49] My translation, which I have used here because the ESV and most other major contemporary translations speak of being made for honorable versus dishonorable use, whereas the Greek is more literally "unto honor" versus "unto dishonor." Translating with the language of usage might comport well with the metaphor, but it obscures a point that most Calvinists rightly hold: that Paul is most likely thinking of eschatological glory/blessing versus eschatological dishonor/condemnation.

[50] There is debate over what passages Paul had in mind and whether any shaped his thought in 9:20–21. Suffice it to say here that most scholars do think that Paul alluded to these texts and that they shaped his thought in this passage. See Shiu-Lun Shum, *Paul's Use of Isaiah in Romans: A Comparative Study of Paul's Letter to the Romans and the Sybilline and Qumran Sectarian Texts*, Wissenschaftliche Untersuchen zum Neuen Testament, 2.156 (Tübingen: Mohr Siebeck, 2002), 204–5. My book on 9:19–33 argues in detail for this majority position.

[51] Piper, *Justification*, 194–95, admitted that Isa 45:9 and Jer 18:1–6 have to do with Israel as a nation, but he tried to argue that Isa 29:16 is not about Israel as a corporate whole but about some men in Israel acting perversely. However, Piper missed the point that the rebellion of these men to God's treatment of them was rooted in God's treatment of Israel as a whole and a rebellion against God's plan for Israel. Thus, Leon Morris, *The Epistle to the Romans* (Grand Rapids: Eerdmans, 1988), 365, simply characterized the passage as having to do with Israel as a nation.

The Isaiah passages both have to do with objection to God's chosen means of salvation for his people, which we have already seen that Romans 9 is addressing up to this point. Isaiah 29:16 employs the potter/clay metaphor after the previous verse warns those who object to God's chosen means of salvation and try to avoid his judgment. What was the chosen means of salvation to which they objected? Faith, reliance upon the Lord, which prohibited reliance on other nations for well-being, such as Egypt.

In the context of Isa 45:9, God's chosen means of salvation to which Israel objected was the deliverer he chose for them. What was the problem with God's choice of a deliverer? He was a Gentile king (Cyrus). It was his Gentile ethnicity and all that went with it that hardened Israel to God's plan of salvation and provoked Israel's rejection of it.[52] Part of God's purpose in choosing Cyrus was to bring the world to know he is the only true God (Isa 45:6). Israel's resistance to God's choice of a savior for them was, in effect, resistance to God's plan of salvation for the Gentiles. The objection Paul is dealing with in Romans 9 is similar to God's chosen means of salvation (faith in Christ) and his chosen Savior (Christ), which opens up covenant membership and its salvation to the Gentiles.

Jeremiah 18:6 and its context is even more striking in its relevance. It uses the potter/clay imagery to argue for God's right to judge Israel, and Paul alluded to it in response to an objection that is most directly against God's right to judge Israel. Moreover, it depicts God as desiring Israel to repent; the potter/clay metaphor is used to call Israel to repentance (indeed, it is used similarly in the Isaiah passages as well). Furthermore, it depicts God's treatment of Israel as strongly conditional. It is almost as if the passage was meant to counter a Calvinistic reading of Romans 9.

In Jeremiah 18, God argues that he has the right to treat Israel as he sees fit, which means that he has the right to change his intention toward them from blessing to judgment if they walk in rebellion or from judgment to blessing if they repent. This supports a conditional election interpretation of Romans 9. Indeed, it suggests that the hardening in Romans 9 is reversible, that hardened Jews can become unhardened and believe in Christ. But that contradicts Calvinistic election[53] as well as the Calvinistic conception of hardening in Romans 9 advanced by some leading Calvinist

---

[52] For explanation, see J. Alec Motyer, *The Prophecy of Isaiah: An Introduction and Commentary* (Downers Grove, IL: InterVarsity, 1993), 361; cf. John N. Oswalt, *The Book of Isaiah: Chapters 40–66*, New International Commentary on the Old Testament (Grand Rapids: Eerdmans, 1998), 208.

[53] See the discussion of Romans 11 in the section on election earlier in this chapter.

commentators, who hold that the hardening of Romans 9 is normally irreversible and unto damnation.[54] Our reading coheres with Romans 11's portrayal of the hardening of Israel, where Paul explained that he tried to win hardened Jews for Christ.

The figure of God as a potter creating pots out of clay might give the impression that Rom 9:20–21 is talking about God creating individuals in the sense of bringing them into existence as human beings for the purpose of glory or dishonor. But that is not how the figure is used in the Old Testament background. In all three Old Testament background texts, the language of molding and making primarily refers to God's shaping the situation of Israel, whether in the form of being subject to the conditions of his plan of salvation (the Isaiah texts) or consignment to judgment versus blessing (Jeremiah 18). Both forms of molding/making are probably in view here in Romans 9: the condition for salvation in the new covenant that hardened ethnic Israel, and to which they objected (the objection Paul is responding to in Romans 9), and especially God's judgment upon unbelieving Jews in rejecting them from the new covenant and consigning them to eternal condemnation (a provisional consignment that becomes final if unbelief persists to the end) versus his saving mercy on believing Gentiles.

Romans 9:22–24 interprets and applies vv. 20–21: "What if God, desiring to show his wrath and to make known his power, has endured with much patience vessels of wrath prepared for destruction, in order to make known the riches of his glory for vessels of mercy, which he has prepared beforehand for glory—even us whom he has called, not from the Jews only but also from the Gentiles?" These verses are riddled with important questions of interpretation that we do not have space to explore here, and I can only give a bare sketch of my views. The vessels of wrath are those who reject Christ, whether Jew or Gentile (though the argument has a special focus on unbelieving Jews), and who are therefore under God's wrath.

Paul indicated that God wants to pour out his wrath and make his power known in judgment and salvation, and because of this desire he bears patiently with those who are "prepared for destruction," that is, as in Jeremiah, consigned to God's wrath. How does withholding their ultimate destruction accomplish God's wrath/judgment and salvation? As with Pharaoh, forestalling final judgment results in the

---

[54] Piper, *Justification*, 178n31; Schreiner, *Romans*, 485. Moo took this position in the first edition of his commentary (Douglas Moo, *The Epistle to the Romans*, NICNT [Grand Rapids: Eerdmans, 1996], 599, but has backed off from it in the second edition [cf. Moo, *Romans*, 618–19]).

multiplication of God's wrath as sinners store up wrath against themselves for the final judgment (Rom 2:5). But forestalling final judgment also gives sinners a chance to repent and go from being vessels of wrath to vessels of mercy, for "God's kindness is meant to lead [them] to repentance" (2:4). This latter purpose comes out as God's more primary purpose in 9:23.[55]

God's purpose for patiently enduring the vessels of wrath is now more clearly and directly asserted in v. 23 as being "to make known the riches of his glory for vessels of mercy, which he has prepared beforehand for glory." This refers to the bestowing of eschatological glory/ultimate blessing on those under God's mercy in the new covenant. God prepared them for glory in that, like in Jeremiah, he slated them for blessing (in this case, eschatological glory/blessing) in response to their faith and undertook the work of sanctification in their lives that goes along with that consignment to blessing. The ultimacy of this purpose among the purposes in 9:22–23 is also reminiscent of Jeremiah 18 (cf. Ezek 18:23, 32). While God desires to punish the wicked for their sin, and even to bring their punishment to full expression, he would rather they repent and become vessels of mercy instead. But if they will not repent, then he desires to pour out his wrath upon them, as is his right.

Thus, Paul has interpreted and applied the potter/clay metaphor in relation to the objection to God's naming of believers as his people, and especially, the objection to his judgment against unbelieving Jews based on his purpose being fulfilled through their sin and his hardening of their hearts through his offensive means of salvation. These two streams of God's sovereign plan are two sides of the same coin. And, of course, God the Creator, Namer, Judge, and Elector has the right to choose who his people are based on any conditions he chooses and to judge those who rebel against him. Surely he has the right to display his judgment and his mercy. Unquestionably he has the right to name his people by faith in Christ apart from work or ancestry and to reject even Jews who refuse to submit to God's righteousness (cf. 10:4). Objecting to this is like a clay pot objecting to the potter's molding of it. It is absurd.

Verse 24 brings the interpretation and application of vv. 20–21 and its potter/clay metaphor to a climax by explicitly stating the most offensive part of the gospel Paul has been defending: that God has called/named Gentiles as well as Jews who believe in Jesus as his own people, vessels of mercy (recall our earlier discussion of calling/naming in discussion of 9:7). The point is again that God has the right to do this

---

[55] Piper, *Justification*, 188–89, 213–14; Moo, *Romans*, 627; and Schreiner, *Romans*, 493, all agreed that the purpose articulated in 9:23 is the more primary of the purposes in vv. 22–23.

and that he is perfectly righteous in doing so. Verses 25–29 support this controversial claim with Old Testament texts.

Romans 9:30-33

The final verses of Romans 9 confirm the conditional election reading we have offered, with faith as the condition of covenant membership/election. Paul inferred from the preceding verses a prominent feature of his argument: "What shall we say, then? That Gentiles who did not pursue righteousness have attained it, that is, a righteousness that is by faith but that Israel who pursued a law that would lead to righteousness did not succeed in reaching that law" (vv. 30–31). The general sense of Paul's question is, what should be said now based on what he has been saying in Romans 9? What can be concluded from what Paul wrote in Rom 9:6b–29, especially vv. 24–29, including that Gentiles have attained righteousness *by faith*, while unbelieving Jews have not attained the law and its righteousness? Critically, Paul indicated that Gentiles attaining the elect status of righteousness by faith and unbelieving Jews not attaining that elect status summarized a primary feature of his argument in the preceding verses; it is in fact God's right to grant election based on faith apart from works or ancestry and to reject law-observant Jews without faith in Christ that Paul defended in Romans 9.

Paul asked why unbelieving Jews have failed to attain righteousness. Now, if Paul had been teaching Calvinism and its unconditional election in Romans 9, we would expect him to answer something like, because God did not (unconditionally) choose Israel but unconditionally hardened them. But if Paul has been teaching election conditional on faith, then we would expect him to answer something like, because they did not believe. And if we have been right to suggest that what hardened Israel to the gospel was its principle of election by faith *in Christ* apart from works or ancestry, then we might expect him to add, in connection with faith, something like, because they were offended at Christ. And lo and behold, this is exactly how Paul answered: "Why? Because they did not pursue it by faith, but as if it were based on works. They have stumbled over the stumbling stone, as it is written, 'Behold, I am laying in Zion a stone of stumbling, and a rock of offense; and whoever believes in him will not be put to shame'" (vv. 32–33). We have come to another passage that practically sounds as if it were meant to affirm conditional election and deny unconditional election in Romans 9.

Conclusion

While Calvinists tend to tout Romans 9 as proving unconditional election and demanding Calvinism, we have weighed those claims and found them wanting. Calvinistic interpretation of Romans 9 is too divorced from the chapter in the context of the letter and often seems to assume unconditional meaning for ambiguous language. Indeed, Calvinist interpreters often seem to try and squeeze unconditional meaning out of language that is just as much if not more consistent with a conditional meaning. At times, Calvinist interpreters even seem to require the text to address issues they bring to the text, which are foreign to it. That happens in part because they do not correctly grasp the Old Testament and Jewish background to Paul's thought in Romans 9, including the nature of corporate election and its relationship to individuals.

On the other hand, our exegesis of Romans 9 has found it to reflect a corporate and conditional election based on faith. At issue in the chapter is the most pressing objection to Paul's gospel of justification by faith, that it would make God unfaithful to his promises to Israel due to its exclusion of unbelieving Jews from the covenant people. Paul argued that according to his gospel God is faithful to his promises to Israel (v. 6a) because the promises were made to the seed of Abraham/the children of the promise, whom God names/identifies by faith, rather than to physical Israel or based on works or ancestry (vv. 6b–13, esp. v. 8), with scriptural support provided throughout. Election by faith apart from works or ancestry is ironically the way God fulfills his covenant promise—the promise to bless the world through Abraham—because it enables both Jews and Gentiles to be part of the new covenant and share in its promises/blessings (vv. 11–12), though it excludes Jews who refuse to believe. Verses 14–18 support vv. 9–13 with scriptural argumentation, and verses 19–24 support verses 14–18 with scriptural argumentation. Verses 25–29 support v. 24 with scriptural argumentation, and vv. 30–33 provide a conclusion to the chapter while introducing chap. 10, the next major section of the argument. All that follows 9:8 ultimately supports the verse, which is an explanatory restatement of 9:6b. Finally, 9:8 fundamentally supports 9:6a, the faithfulness of God to his promises to Israel.

Corporate and Personal Election

—— William W. Klein ——

"Context! Context! Context!" In so many realms of life, context is everything. In real estate, context is location. The same is true for understanding the meaning of words. What does the word *leaf* mean? Without more context you cannot give me an answer because "leaf" may refer to part of a plant, a thin foil (gold leaf), or a removable part of a table, among other meanings. "Leaf," like so many words, covers a range of meaning, or what we know as a *semantic field*. In biblical and theological studies, the words *elect* and *election* are controversial, even for those who believe they are referring to the same action: God's election of people. The word *predestination* suffers from the same confusion.

In the Bible, the concept of election occurs in various contexts and, like "leaf," to understand how the biblical writers understood the concept, we need to investigate those various contexts. When we look at the contexts in which election terminology occurs, we find that the writers present us with a range of meanings. To answer the question, What does election mean? requires a careful analysis of the various contexts in which the word occurs. As we will see, biblical writers use election with several meanings, and I will argue that part of the misunderstanding that Calvinists suffer from is a failure to understand the range of meanings.

Engaging in proper word studies also requires that we do not impose the meaning of a word from one context onto a use of that word in another context.[1] Simply because the dome of the capitol building in Denver is overlaid with gold leaf does not mean that every "leaf" is gold in color or results from hammering out a metal into a thin skin. A maple leaf is green and grows on a tree. Gold leaf is a very specific meaning of leaf that cannot be transferred to other contexts. For this reason, we need to carefully study the contexts in which "election" occurs and determine the meaning employed in each context. This is crucial: we must avoid assuming that what election means in one context can be transferred to a use in another and different context.[2]

Our task is more complicated when we realize that several words convey the concept of election. Using English translations, terms such as "choose," "appoint," "select," "name," or "be pleased to," among others, also convey the idea of election.[3] We need to study the semantic field, that is, the concept or meaning itself, which can be conveyed by a variety of terms.[4] Also, we will see that the task of understanding election involves challenging improper uses or misunderstandings of terms. One is especially pernicious. In many popular uses, "predestination" means "God has predestined who will be saved," so that "predestination" is equivalent to "election." Often this is coupled with a misunderstanding of God's sovereignty—God is in control of everything, including determining who will be saved. We will see that Paul's use of "predestination" has a decidedly different meaning and ought not be co-opted into the debate about how to understand election.

Before we engage in the analysis of the key New Testament (NT) texts, we must make some basic distinctions clear. Here, I am anticipating what our exegeses will uncover. Identifying these distinctions will help us understand the contexts in

---

[1] On various word study fallacies that interpreters may fall into, see Carson, *Exegetical Fallacies*, 27–64 (see chap. 3, n. 21). See also Silva, *Biblical Words*, 35–52 (see chap. 4, n.46).

[2] This fallacy is cumbersomely called "illegitimate totality transfer." See Carson, *Exegetical Fallacies*, especially word study fallacies #9 and #13, on pages 31 and 36. Also see Silva, *Biblical Words*, 25–27.

[3] We need to investigate the occurrences of the original language terms, not their English translations.

[4] For example, *sofa*, *settee*, *divan*, and *couch* all convey a similar meaning to many English speakers. One standard tool that aids in this task for the NT is Eugene Nida and Johannes P. Louw, *Greek-English Lexicon of the New Testament Based on Semantic Domains* (New York: United Bible Societies, 1988). For the domain "To Choose, to Select, to Prefer" they list well over a dozen different Greek terms (see 1:360–62).

which election terminology occurs and clarify how the biblical writers answer our central question: *How* and *to what* has God chosen people? Simply stated, we must distinguish between *corporate election* and *individual election* (answering *how?*). And we must distinguish between *election to salvation* and *election to a task* (answering *to what?*). Now we proceed to assess the biblical data.

Election in the Old Testament

In both the Old Testament (OT) and NT, the writers speak of election in both corporate and in individual terms.

Individual and Corporate

God's choice of individuals is the less common way the OT authors speak of election. God elected key figures in the history of Israel: Abraham (Neh 9:7), Jacob (Ps 135:4; Mal 1:2), Moses (Num 16:5, 7; Ps 106:23), David (1 Sam 13:13–14; 2 Sam 6:21; Ps 78:70), and Zerubbabel (Hag 2:23). God chose some individual prophets to serve; for example, Jeremiah (Jer 12:4–8) and Amos (Amos 7:14–15). Samuel referred to Saul as "the one the LORD has chosen" (1 Sam 10:24). Likewise, David himself insisted that God chose him to be king (2 Sam 6:21; cf. 1 Sam 16:8–10; 1 Kgs 8:16; 11:34; 1 Chr 28:4; 2 Chr 6:6) and that Solomon was God's choice to succeed him (1 Chr 28:5; 29:1). God even chose pagan kings such as Cyrus (Isa 45:1, 13) and Nebuchadnezzar (Jer 25:9; 27:6; 43:10; Ezek 29:19–20) to perform special tasks. The apostle Paul asserts that God chose (literally, "raised up") Pharaoh to serve him (Rom 9:17).

Far more commonly the OT writers employ election corporately.[5] For example, God chose Eli's family to serve as priests (1 Sam 2:27–28). The Levites as a group are objects of God's elective choice (1 Chr 15:2; 2 Chr 29:11; Deut 18:5; 21:5). God chose to use the monarchy to lead the nation. The dominant corporate use, however, is God's choice of the nation Israel. Numerous texts affirm that "the LORD your God has chosen you to be his own possession out of all the peoples on the face of the earth" (Deut 7:6; cf. 10:15; 14:2; Isa 41:8–9; Ps 132:13–14, among many other texts).

Now note the needed distinction between election to a task versus to salvation. Even following this brief survey, we can see that neither God's choice of individuals to serve him, nor God's choice of the nation Israel to be his treasured possession,

---

[5] For a more comprehensive survey of the dominant corporate use of election in the OT, see William W. Klein, *The New Chosen People: A Corporate View of Election*, rev. ed. (Eugene, OR: Wipf & Stock, 2015), 5–18.

guaranteed eternal salvation for these chosen ones. Their eternal salvation was not at issue here; God chose individuals and corporate entities for service.

Election to a Task versus Election to Salvation

Considering the previous section, the OT writers understood election primarily as a *task* or *function* that God has placed upon individuals, special groups, and the nation Israel. Whether the priesthood, monarchy, or the guild of the prophets, as corporate entities they were chosen to perform a task among the people. Likewise, individual priests, kings, or prophets were elected for a task, not for their eternal salvation. As such, these individuals could forfeit their election due to their failure to perform their tasks faithfully. For example, God chose Saul as king (1 Sam 10:24), but because of Saul's sins, God rejected his kingship (1 Sam 13:13–14; 15:10–11, 23, 26–29). Ordinary Jews were in the same situation. If they followed God's will and the terms of God's covenant with Israel—that is, faithfully discharged their duties—they enjoyed God's favor and blessing. However, the question of whether individual Jews were "saved" depends on their faithfulness to God's covenant and will, not to their election as members of the nation Israel, or even their election to specific tasks or functions within that people.

God chose the nation Israel to be a light to the nations. The prophet proclaimed, "Pay attention to me, my people, and listen to me, my nation; for instruction will come from me, and my justice for a light to the nations" (Isa 51:4); and "Nations will come to your light, and kings to your shining brightness" (60:3). The election of Israel was a call to serve God in the world. God's choice of Israel was election to a task, or election for service—the mission of God in the world. However, in contrast to the election of individuals who could forfeit their election, God's choice of his people Israel was an abiding election (1 Sam 12:22; Jer 31:27–28; Ezek 16:59–60).

Conclusions

Space precludes a survey here of Jewish views of election outside of the OT.[6] A survey of the OT leads to the following conclusions: (1) Israel as a nation was God's chosen

---

[6] For further discussion of the other Jewish literature that is antecedent to the NT—namely, the Apocrypha, Pseudepigrapha, Qumran, and the rabbis—see Klein, *New Chosen People*, 19–40. Essentially, these writers confirm what we discover in the OT, though events after the writing

people. (2) God's choice of Israel was God's sovereign choice, motivated solely by his love, not as a reward.[7] (3) God's choice of Israel constituted no blanket approval of the nation, nor did it guarantee blessing. Obedience was key to God's ongoing favor; disobedience, especially idolatry, resulted in judgment. (4) Corporate election of Israel did not assure the eternal salvation of individual Jews. Only the righteous remnant would be saved, and faith in Yahweh enabled the inclusion of Gentiles into the people of God.[8] (5) God chose subsets—corporate groups—to serve in various capacities: the monarchy, priesthood, and prophets. (6) God chose individuals to perform specific tasks or functions—some individuals within the groups of kings, priests, prophets—as well as the patriarchs (e.g., Abraham, Isaac, and Jacob), and even pagan rulers such as Pharaoh, Cyrus, and Nebuchadnezzar. (7) No texts assert that God chose individuals for eternal salvation.

Corporate election is the dominant usage in the OT. God chose his people Israel as his special possession primarily for service: that they would serve as his ambassadors in the world to bring to the nations the light of his salvation. God also chose individuals to serve him, performing various functions or tasks. Individual election is restricted to this use—election for service. Individuals are not chosen to be saved.

Election in the New Testament

Jesus and the writers of the NT emerged into a Jewish world dominated by this OT understanding of election. The NT authors were Jewish (Luke excepted) and OT-influenced Christians who believed they had inherited God's promises to Israel. The early Christians' mining of the OT to understand Jesus and what God was now doing in the world demonstrates how much they valued their inclusion into the people of God. Jesus himself explained how the OT Scriptures pointed to him as Messiah (Luke 24:27; cf. Acts 1:3). The church was the "Israel of God" (Gal 6:16); all who believed in Jesus were "Jew[s]" (Rom 2:28–29). Even Gentiles, formerly not members of the people of God, had now joined the people of God through faith in Christ (Rom 9:24–26).

---

of the OT led some writers to make some departures from the OT. These need not concern us here.

[7] Deuteronomy 10:15 emphasizes God's love as the basis for his choice. Some later Jewish literature suggests that Israel's foreseen obedience was a basis for God's choice while concurring that Israel was not worthy of God's loving choice.

[8] We may include here such figures as Rahab and Ruth.

In what follows I will take primarily a canonical approach, moving through the NT documents systematically by authors while keeping together the Synoptic Gospels and the Johannine literature for obvious reasons. The semantic field that concerns us is "election" or God's choosing.[9] We seek to understand how the writers present the ways in which God elects, selects, chooses, determines, appoints, or effects his salvific purposes for people.

Election in the Synoptic Gospels

Our survey will proceed topically or better, following a biblical theology of election—which is our ultimate objective in this essay.

God's Election of His People

Jesus refers to God's people as his "chosen ones" (Gk. *eklektoi*) in his parable of the unjust judge and widow (Luke 18:7 NIV). In his Olivet Discourse Jesus referred to believers experiencing tribulation as his "elect" (Gk. *eklektous*; Matt 24:22, 24, 31; pars.), whom he will rescue at the Parousia. Though God invites or calls many to enjoy his banquet, only those who respond to his invitation have the title "chosen" ones (Gk. *eklektoi*; Matt 22:14). Many Jews were called, but their failure to heed the call to believe in Jesus (see Matt 21:45–46; 22:15, 23) prevented them from entering the company of the "chosen."[10] None of these texts specify God as taking the initiative in choosing certain ones. In fact, in the text from the wedding banquet, we see that people acquire their chosenness by exercising faith in Jesus, heeding God's invitation to join his banquet. Similarly, when the King separates the sheep from the goats (Matt 25:31–46), he consigns them to their fates based on whether or not they exhibited active social concern "for one of the least of these brothers and sisters of mine" (Matt 25:40, 45). The criterion of what they had done (or failed to do) determines their fate; the outcomes were not predetermined.[11]

---

[9] Recall footnote 4 above. Many Greek terms occur within this semantic field.

[10] Edmund F. Sutcliffe concluded, "The parable makes it plain that if the others were not among the chosen, it was solely because they themselves refused the call. It was in their power to be among the chosen but they preferred to remain aloof." Edmund F. Sutcliffe, "Many Are Called but Few Are Chosen," *Irish Theological Quarterly* 28, no. 2 (April 1961): 130.

[11] This criterion is also present in Rom 2:6–10; Jas 2:14–17; and Rev 20:12–13. A genuine faith will demonstrate its existence and reality in the performance of "good works."

God's Will for People's Salvation

Some argue that God's will determines who is saved, such that he wills to save some but not others. Let us have a look. Initially we note that God's will is not always done. Jesus urged his disciples to pray that God's will (*thelēma*) might be done (Matt 6:10). God desires or wills (*thelō*) mercy, not sacrifice, but people do not always demonstrate mercy (Matt 9:13; 12:7; cf. Hos 6:6). God wills (*eudokia*; pleasurable will) to reveal things (knowledge of God's saving purposes) to those who humbly seek him as children (Matt 11:25–27 and parallels), though not all seek him. Jesus invited *all* to come to him for rest (Matt 11:28), but not all do. In his parable of the lost sheep Jesus explained the reason behind his invitation to all to enjoy his rest: "Your Father in heaven is not willing (*thelēma*) that any of these little ones should perish" (Matt 18:14 NIV). God wills the salvation of all his little ones, but God's will is not always accomplished.

Jesus desired for his fellow Jews to find salvation through belief in him. In Matt 23:37 he stated, "Jerusalem, Jerusalem, who kills the prophets and stones those who are sent to her. How often I wanted [*thelō*] to gather your children together, as a hen gathers her chicks under her wings, but you were not willing!" The Jews' wills clashed with Jesus's; they rejected him and suffered the consequences of their unbelief (Matt 23:38–39). On the other hand, to those who believe in Jesus rather than seek earthly possessions or treasure, God is pleased (*eudokeō*; God's pleasurable, willful resolve) to give the kingdom (Luke 12:32). We learn here that God wills that all be saved, not some selective group of his choosing.

Jesus Chooses

Several texts describe Jesus's selection of the twelve apostles. For example, we see "summoning"/"summoned" (*proskaleō*; Matt 10:1; Mark 3:13–14; *prosphōneō*; Luke 6:13); "summoned" (*prosphōneō*; Luke 6:13); "appointed" (*poieō*, "to make"; Mark 3:14); and "chose" (*eklegomai*; Luke 6:13). Jesus selected these individuals for a task—to serve him as apostles. Jesus also "appointed" (*anadeiknymi*)[12] seventy-two evangelists. These examples of election parallel the election of special individuals we noted in the OT. Here, this is election for service or to a task, not election to salvation.[13]

---

[12] *BDAG*, 62: "to assign to a task or position, appoint, commission."

[13] Election language regularly designates Christ as God's Elect One, particularly in the baptismal and transfiguration narratives. God appointed Jesus for his role as Messiah—this is

Conclusion

To summarize, first, the writers apply the label "elect ones" or "chosen ones" to those who belong to God as his people. This is the corporate group of Jesus's own followers, the ones who believe in him. They have responded to God's invitation on God's terms (Matt 22:14). No evidence suggests that God has predetermined these individuals to be among this elect body. People make their own choices to believe in Jesus or reject him. Jesus calls sinners to repent (Luke 5:32). God excludes from the kingdom those who deny Jesus—and they bear the blame for their exclusion (Matt 13:22; Mark 4:18–19; Luke 8:12–14).

Nor do the writers use the concept of God's "will" as the basis for anyone's membership in his saved body. We find no indication that God wills only some, or some select group, to be saved. In fact, God wills to save all (Matt 18:14; cf. 11:28–30); Jesus reveals the Father to all who approach him as children (Matt 11:25–27).

As to the election of individuals, the evidence is sparse but also clear-cut. God chose Jesus for his role as the Messiah; he is the Elect One, chosen for service—to undertake God's mission in the world. As part of his mission, Jesus chose or appointed the twelve apostles (Mark 3:13–14) and then seventy-two to serve in preaching and exorcising demons. No texts assert that God or Jesus selected specific individuals for salvation.

Election in Acts

Understandably, the occurrences in Acts overlap Luke's usage in his Gospel. Acts adds an interesting dimension to what we noted earlier, God's determination of certain events, though these are not prominent nor especially pertinent to our discussion of God's election of people.[14]

Corporate Election Uses

Acts records God's elective role with various corporate groups. In Acts 13:48 the author spoke of those who were appointed[15] (*tassō*) to eternal life. In this con-

---

election to a task or for service. See Matt 3:17; 12:18; 17:5; 26:24; Mark 1:11; 9:7; Luke 2:34; 3:22; 9:35; 23:35.

[14] For example, the Father has *set* certain periods of time (Acts 1:7); God *determined* times and locations of nations (17:26); and God *chose* a certain course of action (15:7).

[15] The NRSV and NJB translate the verb as "destined." Yet L&N allow for a sense of the verb *tassō* as "to do something with devotion" (1:662). That would suggest the sense: "All who were devoted [or disposed] to eternal life believed."

text, some Jewish leaders were threatened by the gospel message, but the listening Gentiles grasped its significance and embraced it with joy and praise to the Lord. These "appointed" ones believed. The form of the Greek verb could be middle or passive voice. Some argue that it is passive and that God is the agent of the appointment: God appointed some to be saved, and they subsequently believed.[16] Others argue that it is middle. In that case the sense would be, "As many as arranged eternal life *for themselves*, believed," or "As many as set *themselves* to eternal life believed."[17]

Though interpreters array themselves on both sides, it is very doubtful that Luke intended to point to God's pretemporal choice of some Gentiles for salvation here. In the context, the Jews fail to obtain eternal life because they reject the word of God, not because God did not elect them for salvation. That point is clear: Paul and Barnabas say, "It was necessary that the word of God be spoken to you first. Since you reject it and *judge yourselves* unworthy of eternal life, we are turning to the Gentiles" (Acts 13:46; emphasis added). It is God's plan to bring the message of salvation to the ends of the earth (v. 47), which Paul and Barnabas are in the process of doing. People must call upon the name of the Lord to be saved, as Peter asserted earlier (2:21). That is precisely what the Gentiles do when they hear Paul's message of good news: they believe. Believers are "the elect," or put another way, "the appointed ones," a title that has obvious parallels to "the chosen ones" (cf. Mark 13:20, 22, 27; parallels) and "the called."

Does God enable only some to embrace the message of salvation, as some Calvinists allege? When Luke says that God had "opened (*anoigō*) the door of faith to the Gentiles" (Acts 14:27), he meant that God created the opportunity for mission work and the potential for believing.[18] Paul worked to open the eyes of the Gentiles

---

[16] David G. Peterson, *The Acts of the Apostles*, PNTC (Grand Rapids: Eerdmans, 2009), 399, termed this "as unqualified a statement of absolute predestination—'the eternal purpose of God' (Calvin)—as is found anywhere in the NT." On the other hand, I. Howard Marshall said, "It could also refer to those who had already put their trust in God in accordance with the Old Testament revelation of his grace and were enrolled in his people, or perhaps it means that the Gentiles believed in virtue of the fact that God's plan of redemption included them." Marshall, *The Acts of the Apostles*, Tyndale New Testament Commentaries (Grand Rapids: Eerdmans, 1980), 231.

[17] In my translations, the words in italics show the special nuance of the middle voice. In other words, "and they believed, all who set eternal life for themselves."

[18] Joachim Jeremias, "θύρα," *TDNT* 3:174, said, "In relation to God the expression finds a place in missionary usage in the two-fold sense that God opens a door for the missionary . . . through which he can enter, by giving him a field in which to work . . . and also that he opens a door of faith to those who come to believe . . . by giving them the possibility of believing."

(26:18), but not all Gentiles responded. When Luke says, "he [God] . . . opened the door of faith," he does not deny the need for human response (13:39). The good news now goes out to all, even Gentiles, because God himself has *opened* the way. No evidence is here that God grants faith only to some.

Individual Election Uses

The author of Acts gives space to God's choice of individuals—some of which overlap his use in the Third Gospel, and some that pertain to the emerging Christian church. First, Jesus chose twelve apostles (Acts 1:2) and then the replacement for Judas (v. 24). God chose the apostles to be witnesses to Jesus's resurrection (10:41). These examples of election to a task parallel the author's references to God's choice of the patriarchs of Israel (13:17; cf. Neh 9:7; Ps 106:23). God "called" Barnabas and Saul for mission (Acts 13:2); namely a task, a point that Paul makes in Acts 16:10 in evangelizing Macedonia.

In Acts 16:14 we learn that God opened Lydia's heart for salvation.[19] As in the prior use discussed above (14:27), it is doubtful Luke intended here that God specifically elected Lydia so she was able to believe.[20] Luke used the language of mission—God "opens" doors for people to respond to the gospel. God opened a door for Lydia through Paul's preaching; Lydia made the decision to walk through by her faith. Subsequently, in Philippi, Paul gave his jailor this same open door (16:31).[21] The one who hears the message that God has opened to them must repent and believe.

Acts records God's choice of Paul as an apostle. Paul is a "chosen instrument" (9:15; 22:14; 26:16); this is election to a task or function. God made Paul a light for the Gentiles (13:47), one appointed for his task as an apostle (22:10). Extending Jesus's choice of his apostles, and the election of Paul, the Holy Spirit appointed elders for the churches the apostles planted (20:28). God also elected ("appointed,"

---

[19] Luke also used this verb *dianoigō* at Acts 17:3, where the CSB (and most versions) translated it as "explaining." Paul engaged in "explaining" so the Jews would grasp the truth. See also Luke 24:32 for Christ's *explaining* the Scriptures to the disciples. Then in v. 45 Luke reports that "[Jesus] opened their minds" so they could understand the significance of the OT messianic prophecies.

[20] This appears to be the conclusion of Peterson, *Acts of the Apostles*, 461, when he referred to "God's sovereignty in the process of conversion." See also Darrell L. Bock, *Acts*, BECNT (Grand Rapids: Baker, 2007), 534: "God creates the initiative to faith from within."

[21] Marshall, *Acts of the Apostles*, 267, said, "Luke underlines that conversion is due to the action of God who opens the hearts, *i.e.* the minds, of men and women to receive his Word."

"chose") Christ for his mission of redemption (3:20). He is God's chosen agent—providing another example of election to a task or role.

Conclusion

The author of Acts centered his discussion of election primarily in a theology of mission. For the mission of redemption, God elected an individual—his Son, Jesus—his chosen Messiah. To propagate the good news of the salvation that Christ secured, Jesus chose his apostles—including a replacement for the traitor Judas. Most significantly in Acts, God appointed Paul, a chosen instrument, to proclaim the message of salvation to the Gentiles to whom God had now opened the door of salvation. Those who respond to the invitation to believe are the "called" ones—they bear the name and identity of the God to whom they belong. Individual election is task oriented; people are divinely chosen to serve God in specific tasks or roles. I never stated that God has chosen certain ones to enable them to believe.

Election in the Johannine Writings

The Fourth Gospel dominates our survey here, though we note several points in the Johannine Epistles and Revelation. The first datum to consider is God's "love" (*agapaō*) for the entire world. That love motivated the provision of eternal life to all who would believe in Jesus (John 3:16). Moreover, God loves Jesus's disciples, the Christian community (17:23). God's love for his own and for the world finds parallels in the Johannine Epistles (1 John 4:9–11, 16, 19). Jesus *knows* his sheep and they know him (John 10:14, 27), a knowledge that parallels the reciprocal knowing between Jesus and the Father (v. 15). For neither verb, *love* or *know*, do we find evidence of election—that God chose to love or to know only some individuals.

John used the verb "choose." John the Baptist was chosen for a specific task, to pave the way for Jesus (John 3:27). Jesus reacted to Peter's confession that Jesus is "the Holy One of God" (6:69) by affirming that he had chosen the twelve apostles to serve him (v. 70). Again, this is election to a task, not salvation, for even Judas (a devil, *diabolos*) was among the chosen ones. Later, in the upper room, Jesus said, "I know those I have chosen" (13:18). Though Judas had every opportunity that the other disciples had to trust in Jesus, he decided not to. Jesus chose him, as the others, to serve him. Judas squandered his opportunity.

After Judas departed the scene, Jesus again affirmed his choice and appointment of the disciples to serve him (15:16, 19). The purpose for the disciples' election was ministry and mission, as is clear from the reference to "fruit" that should remain. This is not election to salvation.

John also stresses God's election of Jesus to be Savior of the world—election to a task or function. John presents Jesus as the *unique*, one and only Son (John 1:14, 18; 3:16, 18; 1 John 4:9), using the term *monogenēs*. Three of John's uses of God's "will" also highlight Jesus's appointment by the Father (John 4:34; 5:30; 6:38).

In addition to its use for determining Christ's role as Savior, we also find God's or Jesus's "will" used in connection with the salvation of people. John records Jesus as saying that "the Son also gives life to whom he wants" (*thelō*; John 5:21). The "life" of which he speaks is eternal life—a regular use of *zoē* in the Fourth Gospel (e.g., 3:15–16, 36; 4:14, 36; 5:24, 29, 39–40; 6:40, 54, 68; 10:28; 11:25), though here John uses a compound verb, "to give life" (*zōopoieō*). While some assume that Jesus's will to give life implies that he selects only some for this gift, the context argues against such an individual election. We learn that Jesus wills to give life to those who receive it on his terms; that is, those who "honor the Son" (5:23), which the Jews in this encounter were not doing (vv. 16–18). One must believe Jesus (v. 38) and come to him for life (v. 40; cf. v. 24). Faith in Jesus (v. 46) is the prerequisite for salvation. To these ones God "wills" to give life. No evidence is here that Jesus exercised some determinative (perhaps hidden) will and gives life only to some select group whom he has previously chosen. In addition, in John 6:38–40 we learn that God wills (*thelēma*) to incorporate all who believe in Jesus into the body of those he raises to eternal life on judgment day. Those who fail to believe have only themselves to blame (v. 36).

What role does God have in applying salvation to people? God "gives" (*didōmi*) salvation to people who believe (John 6:37–40). While Calvinists see here God's election of only some individuals, the context argues that the group to whom God gives salvation comprises those who exercise faith in Jesus. God provides salvation, which he freely gives to all those with faith (cf. 7:37–38). Indeed, "everyone who sees the Son and believes in him shall have eternal life" (6:40). Later in the Gospel, Jesus prayed for his disciples, those whom the Father had *given* to him (17:2, 6, 9, 24). Barnabas Lindars said, "Those whom you have given to me" equals "those who have been receptive, as explained in the prologue (John 1:12)."[22]

We draw a similar conclusion to Jesus's use of the verb "give" found earlier: "No one can come to me unless it is granted (*didōmi*) to him by the Father" (John 6:65). To argue that God *gives* this ability to only some misconstrues the context of Jesus's

---

[22] Barnabas Lindars, *The Gospel of John*, New Century Bible (London: Oliphants, 1972), 521.

words. These words do not explain why specific people come to Jesus, but rather why anyone at all is able to come. God alone provides salvation, and one must come on his terms—through faith in Jesus. Jesus has spoken "Spirit" words to his audience; he has given them revelation, the truth (v. 63). "But there are some among you who don't believe" (v. 64). This is John's consistent conclusion. Some reject the truth about Jesus, and their unwillingness to believe explains why many desert him. The Father has *given* Jesus to them to believe, but they refused to accept the demands and implications of following Jesus, so they "turned back and no longer accompanied him" (v. 66).

Speaking of God's salvific activity, Jesus affirmed that without the Father's "drawing," none can come to him (John 6:44). The obvious question follows: Does God draw only some, and not others? The word "draw" (*helkō*) occurs eight times in the NT with the sense of drag, draw, or attract.[23] Some things, like a net or person, can be *dragged* literally. Or metaphorically, a person may be *drawn* to a viewpoint or position by arguments or reasons that are persuasive, or even *attracted* to another person by features one finds in her or him. Calvinists typically argue that God draws some people to faith in Christ, and not others.

But any idea of divine selective and effectual drawing is alien to this context. John described various people who encounter Jesus. On one hand, some Jews persist in unbelief and disqualify themselves from eternal life. Nowhere does the text say that God has not drawn (i.e., chosen) them. Others are attracted to the message of Jesus and decide to believe in him. Individuals must decide whether to heed the *drawing* and learn from God (John 6:45). Certainly no one can come to Jesus apart from God's "pull"; what this text does *not* say is that God pulls only some.

At this point we must observe what Jesus said about *drawing* in John 12:32. Jesus declared, "And I, when I am lifted up from the earth, will draw [*helkō*] all people to myself" (NIV). God's drawing is not selective; in fact, it is universal. God demonstrated his love for humanity by sending Christ. The paramount demonstration of that love was Jesus's crucifixion—an event that Jesus said would be a *draw* to all. Attempts to limit "all people" to all the elect, or some elect Gentiles as well as some elect Jews, or all who believe, fall flat and border on special pleading to evade the clear sense here. Beasley-Murray says it well, "The term πάντας, 'all men,' expresses the universal scope of the eschatological event disclosed in ὑψωθῶ ('if I be lifted up');

---

[23] *BDAG*, 318. It occurs thirty-four times in the LXX.

the saving sovereignty is for *all* humankind."[24] God's "drawing" does not obviate the need for the required response. The cross draws all, but not all find salvation. Sadly, "even though he had performed so many signs in their presence, they did not believe in him" (John 12:37).

There are two instances of "calling" language in the Johannine corpus. The believers are "called children of God" (1 John 3:1). This is their name or identity, a usage we noted earlier, and one we will discover in Paul. Jesus's followers are "called," "chosen," and "faithful" (Rev 17:14). Certainly, these are labels or ways of describing the corporate people of God. We cannot read into these uses any sense of particular election.

In Revelation, John referred to the book of life in which the names of the saints are inscribed (3:5; 13:8; 17:8; 20:12, 15; 21:27; cf. Phil 4:3). Negatively, the names of the unsaved are not in this book. Jesus urges the church to remain faithful to him lest their names be removed from the book (1 John 3:5; cf. Exod 32:32–33). Fidelity to Jesus, rather than any sense of pretemporal election, explains the use of this book of life metaphor. But what about the phrase "from the creation of the world" (Rev 17:8 NIV)? Keeping to a metaphorical understanding, this likely alludes to God's omniscience. God knows who belong to him, and they can be confident in him. Yet, Jesus issued a warning to persevere, for God will not turn a blind eye to unfaithfulness (see Rev 2:5, 16, 23; as well as 3:5). Any "erasure" (again, a metaphor) from the company of the people of God owes to their unfaithfulness, not God's failure to elect them.

In the Second Epistle of John, the elder wrote to an "elect lady" (v. 1) and brought greetings from her "elect sister," adjectives that describe local church congregations (v. 13). Here is a corporate use, one that merely describes the status of these local churches: they are chosen. This parallels the description of Israel as an elect people that we saw in our study of the OT uses.

Conclusion

John highlighted God's love for people that motivated him to send his beloved and unique Son to give his life to redeem sinners. This love is personal and relational, not elective (as if he chooses to love some savingly and not others). God "knows" his people, and they know him, but with no determinative sense—in other words, Jesus's knowledge does not determine a response in them. Jesus chose the disciples,

---

[24] George R. Beasley-Murray, *John*, Word Biblical Commentary (Nashville: Nelson, 1999), 214. For a more complete defense see Klein, *New Chosen People*, 116–18.

an election to service. Even Jesus's choice of Judas played a role in fulfilling Scripture (John 13:18). God also appointed Jesus, the Beloved Son, to fulfill his messianic role. God wills to save sinners, and that salvific desire extends to all. God will save all who come to him through faith in his Son, Jesus. Christ was lifted up on the cross, the means of attracting people to his salvation. Yet this attracting or drawing is neither selective (he draws only some) nor irresistible (many do reject Jesus). Those who believe are the called, the chosen, the faithful, the ones whose names are inscribed in the book of life. However, those who reject Jesus may find their hearts hardened because of their unbelief. They will not find their names in the book.

Election in Paul's Writings

People often gravitate to Paul's writings when pondering the intricacies of election issues because of the detailed attention he pays to these issues.

God Foreknows

Paul stated that God "foreknows" or has "foreknowledge" of his people, both the nation Israel (Rom 11:2) and believers in Christ (8:29). In the first instance (11:2), Paul affirmed that God did not reject the historical people Israel when the body of Christians came into existence. While some commentators confidently assert that "to foreknow" means "to elect," the first meaning in the lexicons points to the verb and noun as prescience, knowing something beforehand.[25] That makes perfect sense in Rom 11:2. Israel is the object of God's prior knowledge. In fact, he has always known corporate Israel; God has had prior knowledge of a people, the nation Israel. Of course, God also elected the nation Israel!

But when we come to Romans 8, the plot thickens. Here, "those who love God" (v. 28) are now said to be "foreknown," as well as possessing four other attributes (vv. 29–30). It is important to state right at the outset: those foreknown comprise a corporate entity—the body of believers. While virtually all translations render the verb *proginosko* as foreknow,[26] many interpreters insist that this means "elect," even though Paul knew words for "elect" and used one a few verses later (v. 33). Calvinist

---

[25] See *BDAG*, 866; L&N, 1:334 (28.6); 1:362 (30.100); LSJ, 1473; Franco Montanari, Madeleine Goh, and Chad Schroeder, eds., "προγιγνώσκω," *The Brill Dictionary of Ancient Greek* (Leiden: Brill, 2015), 1752.

[26] The NLT and CEB render it, "God knew . . . in advance."

interpreters typically assert that "foreknow" equals "elect" based on an alleged *elective* sense of the Hebrew verb "know" (*yāda*),[27] which they then transfer to the Greek verb "know" (*ginoskō*).[28] After that questionable step, they transfer all that election baggage onto *proginoskō* and confidently assert that God has chosen specific *individuals* to be saved![29]

But as I noted, Paul spoke here of the corporate people of God, the church—not of individual believers. And while the notion of the church as the elect people of God is well-represented on the pages of Scripture, that is not Paul's point here. More likely, we should retain the face-value meaning of prior knowledge. The people of God are *foreknown*, and they will enjoy all the advantages God will implement for them, as the succeeding terms in Rom 8:29–30 affirm. God's intimate and eternal knowledge and high regard for his people leads to his loving and gracious outcomes for them—which he predestines.[30]

God Predestines

Much confusion surrounds this next term, *predestination*, for many deem it a synonym for election. Paul employs the verb "predestine" (*proorizō*) in five of its six occurrences in the NT.[31] In addition, one instance of the verb "prepare ahead of time" (*proetoimazō*) seems synonymous to *proorizō*. Paul's uses confirm the essential sense of this concept: to mark out or determine something beforehand. Paul identified several "somethings." In Rom 8:29–30, God predestines that his people become conformed to the image of his Son—God's *goal* for the foreknown ones, not God's *choice* of them. God also predestined ultimate glory for his people (1 Cor 2:7). Predestination concerns not whom God chooses, but what God has predetermined for his people.

That theme is continued in Ephesians. Those whom God *chose* he *predestined* (they are distinct actions) to be adopted as his children (Eph 1:5). This predestination results in the praise of God's glory (vv. 11–12). God determined beforehand that the church

---

[27] For the range of meanings of *yāḏa'*, see Willy Schottroff, "עדי *yd'* *to perceive, know*," *TLOT*, 1:508–21; Rudolf Bultmann, "γινώσκω," etc., *TDNT*, 1:689–716; and Moisés Silva, "γινώσκω," etc., *NIDNTTE*, 1:575–89. While "know" in the OT can point to intimate knowledge, it does not by itself and without further contextual support mean "elect." For a defense of this point, see Klein, *New Chosen People*, 7–8.

[28] Recall the fallacy "illegitimate totality transfer" mentioned in n. 2.

[29] Space prevents me from unpacking all the word study fallacies committed along the way here. See again Carson, *Exegetical Fallacies*.

[30] Marshall, *Kept by the Power of God*, 102 (see chap. 5, n. 2).

[31] Rom 8:29–30; 1 Cor 2:7; Eph 1:5, 11.

that becomes his inheritance sing the praises of his glory. In Eph 2:10, Paul used the verb "prepare ahead of time" (*proetoimazō*) with similar overtones. God has determined beforehand that the people whom he saves will perform good works. In summary, predestination describes, not *how* people become part of God's people, but *what* God has foreordained on their behalf because of his transforming work in their lives.

God Elects

While Paul covers a range of God's elective activity, we focus on several key words that Paul employed: the verb *eklegomai* (to choose, select) in four of its twenty-two occurrences in the NT; *eklektos* (chosen), six of its twenty-two uses; and *eklogē* (choice), five of its seven uses, in addition to relevant uses of words like *kleroō* (appoint) and *haireomai* (choose). First, Paul affirmed, in keeping with the OT record, that God chose Israel, the corporate people of God. Israel's lineage as a people comes through Jacob, not Esau (Rom 9:11). Using a Semitic contrast, Paul added that God loved Jacob and hated Esau, again, a reference to their descendants as people, not Jacob or Esau's personal salvation (v. 13). Throughout Romans 9–11, the fate of national Israel (not anyone's personal salvation) dominated Paul's thinking (see Rom 11:28).

Paul also affirmed that God elects Christians. The corporate sense dominates. Paul spoke of Jewish believers as a "remnant chosen by grace" (Rom 11:5, 7), clearly a subset of the entire nation, Israel. These are the saved ones out of the larger nation that pursued righteousness incorrectly, as if by works (9:30–33). Paul labeled believers as God's elect (*eklektos*; "those whom God has chosen"; 8:33 NIV). This adjective is a descriptive label, here and in the other places he uses it (Rom 16:13; Col 3:12; 1 Tim 5:21; 2 Tim 2:10; Titus 1:1). Paul's use underscores their "chosenness." Like Israel, now the church is God's corporate elect body. Paul told his Thessalonian readers that he knew "your election," that is, that God has chosen them (1 Thess 1:4 HCSB). In fact, God chose them as "firstfruits" of those to be saved, a salvation obtained via two means or instruments: the sanctifying work of the Spirit and their belief in the truth (2 Thess 2:13 NIV).[32] Their belief is set in contrast to those who believed a lie and remain unbelievers (vv. 10–12). While election is corporate here, Paul makes clear that individuals enter that body via both the Spirit's work and their faith.

---

[32] As Gene L. Green put it, "Although the divine decision and activity in bringing about salvation are the primary focus, the apostle does not lose sight of human responsibility in this process, which is indicated by the word *belief*." Green, *The Letters to the Thessalonians*, PNTC (Grand Rapids: Eerdmans, 2002), 327; italics in original.

Paul repeated the corporate label "the elect" or "chosen ones" in other places, for example, "God's chosen people, holy and dearly loved" (Col 3:12 NIV; cf. Titus 1:1). Paul labored as an apostle so that God's "elect" might obtain salvation (2 Tim 2:10). While some aver these elect ones were individually (and pre-temporally) chosen by God,[33] more likely Paul spoke of their "final salvation." Persevering in the true faith better captures the emphasis of the following verses (vv. 11–13). Paul suffered so that those who have believed (the elect) will arrive at the final eschatological destination: salvation.[34] We find no hint in these texts that God chose specific individuals to populate that body.

God has chosen "foolish things," a cryptic reference to the Christians at Corinth (1 Cor 1:27–28 NIV). God's wisdom differs from human wisdom, and he chooses as he wills, not according to human expectations. God saves those who believe (v. 21); as such they are in Christ Jesus (v. 30).

God's election of the church occurred before the creation of the world (Eph 1:4). Paul, as well as all believers, constitute God's chosen people—corporate election.[35] Many Calvinists, while agreeing that the reference here is corporate, insist that individual election is implied in what Paul said here. The argument runs as follows: if the entire body is chosen, then the individuals within it must be chosen.[36] But there exists no warrant for this, especially within a letter that focuses on the corporate church. Here Paul said that God chose "us"—that is, the church—"*in* Christ," not that God chose individuals *to be in* Christ. Snodgrass said it well: "Individuals are not elected and then put in Christ. They are in Christ and therefore elect."[37] Christ is the Elect One (recall the Synoptics); the church is elect by virtue of its incorporation in him. Before the foundation of the world God determined that those in Christ would be his people. Furthermore, the church obtains its inheritance, all God's blessings; or, as

---

[33] As say, e.g., George W. Knight III, *The Pastoral Epistles*, NIGTC (Grand Rapids: Eerdmans, 1992), 399; and John N. D. Kelly, *A Commentary on the Pastoral Epistles*, Black's New Testament Commentary (London: A. & C. Black, 1963), 178.

[34] Philip H. Towner, *The Letters to Timothy and Titus*, NICNT (Grand Rapids: Eerdmans, 2006), 504, agrees.

[35] William W. Klein, "Ephesians," in *The Expositor's Bible Commentary: Ephesians–Philemon*, rev. ed., 13 vols., ed. Tremper Longman III and David E. Garland (Grand Rapids: Zondervan, 2006), 12:48–49.

[36] Peter T. O'Brien, *The Letter to the Ephesians*, PNTC (Grand Rapids: Eerdmans, 1999), 99.

[37] Klyne Snodgrass, *Ephesians*, NIV Application Commentary (Grand Rapids: Zondervan, 1996), 49.

some prefer, the church becomes God's inheritance (v. 11).[38] In either case, the election here is corporate: God's people in Christ.

God Appoints

Several of Paul's examples of divine appointment shed light on our subject. God *appointed* (*horizō*) Jesus "the Son of God in power by his resurrection from the dead: Jesus Christ our Lord" (Rom 1:4 NIV). This is election to an exalted function or role (cf. Phil 2:9). God *set forth* Jesus as a sacrifice of atonement (Rom 3:25). God *was pleased* that all his fullness dwelled in Christ (Col 1:19), where the verb *eudokeō* possesses an elective sense.[39]

God also appointed Paul as his apostle—individual election to a task or function. God *set* Paul *apart* (*aphorizō*) to be a preacher of the gospel (Rom 1:1), indeed, set him apart for this role from his mother's womb (Gal 1:15). God chose (*eudokeō*) to reveal himself to Paul so that he might serve as an apostle to the Gentiles (cf. Acts 22:10, 14; 26:16–18). F. F. Bruce said, "Before ever he was born, Paul means, God had his eye on him and set him apart for his apostolic ministry."[40] Paul also designated himself as one *called* or named as an apostle (Rom 1:1; 1 Cor 1:1; Gal 1:15). Paul noted that God's grace was given to him, speaking of his apostolic office (Rom 12:3; 15:15–16; 1 Cor 15:10; Eph 3:7–8). He envisioned that office as a duty or stewardship (*oikonomia*) entrusted to him (1 Cor 9:16–17; cf. Eph 3:2; Col 1:25). He owed his apostleship to God's will (1 Cor 1:1; 2 Cor 1:1; Eph 1:1; Col 1:1; 2 Tim 1:1). In fulfilling that commission Paul asserted that God assigned (*merizō*) the arenas in which he ministers (2 Cor 10:13). While others preach with differing motives, Paul was set (*keimai*) or appointed for the defense of the gospel (Phil 1:16). He goes so far as to say his apostleship owes itself to the command (*epitagē*) of God (1 Tim 1:1; Tit 1:3). Using still another verb, God considered him faithful by appointing (*tithēmi*) him for ministry (1 Tim 1:12; 2:7; 2 Tim 1:11).

In addition to Paul, God also appoints others to various *roles* or *tasks* in his service. God also appoints ("gives"; *edōken*) other apostles to serve in various capacities (1 Cor 3:5). God places (*tithēmi*) other gifted people in various ministries in the church, endowed with the requisite gifts for service (1 Cor 12:28; cf. Eph 4:7—grace

---

[38] The NIV uses "chosen" to translate *kleroō*, rendered in many other versions as "obtained an inheritance" or "received an inheritance" (CSB).

[39] Paul used the verb with an elective sense also at 1 Cor 1:21 and Gal 1:15–16.

[40] F. F. Bruce, *The Epistle of Paul to the Galatians*, NIGTC (Grand Rapids: Eerdmans, 1982), 92.

is given). God made (*tithēmi*) Abraham a father of many nations (cf. Gen 17:5 LXX). God chose (*eklogē*) Jacob over Esau to continue the line of promise—election for service irrespective of either one's personal salvation. God chose Pharaoh to perform redemptive purposes in the history of his people Israel (Rom 9:17, 21). God gives spiritual gifts—a kind of appointment—so people can function in specific ministries (12:6). God appoints (*tassō*) governing authorities and calls believers to submit to their oversight (13:1).

God Calls

Paul used the words for "call" [verb *kalein* (to call), the noun *klēsis* (calling), and the adjective *klētos* (called)] numerous times, but we focus our attention on his uses pointing to the call to become a Christian.[41] The idea of "calling" can have two senses in the NT: to name or give a title to (as in "We called our daughter Alison") or to summon or invite (as in "We called her, but she did not come").[42]

Paul termed the Christians in Rome as "called" of Jesus Christ and "called" saints (Rom 1:6–7). The called ones are the saved, the members of the people of God (2 Thess 2:14). It is a call to eternal life (1 Tim 6:12). In other words, believers find their identity as God's called ones, which Paul further clarified as "called . . . holy" (as also in 1 Cor 1:2 NIV). God is the one who calls believers (Gal 5:8; 1 Thess 2:12; 5:24).

God has *named* Christians as his own (they belong to him), and he has *invited* them to live holy lives. Probably the first naming dominates Paul's calling language, but holiness is a common goal of God's call on his people's lives. Paul called Christians the "called" in Rom 8:28—a calling to fulfill God's salvific purposes. He then speci-fied that God *called* the ones he foreknew and predestined (v. 30). In this sequence, "called" points to their conversion—when God *named* them as his own.[43] When God "calls," Gentiles become "my people" (9:25–27); that is, he names or designates them as his own, the children of the living God. Paul asserted that God "called" believers

---

[41] In passing we note that Paul speaks of God's "call" of Israel that cannot be revoked (Rom 11:29). He called the nation as his own, beloved people (v. 28).

[42] On the various words for calling see Silva, "χαλέω," etc., *NIDNTTE*, 2:601–6; *BDAG*, 502–4, 549; Karl L. Schmidt, "χαλέω," etc., *TDNT*, 3:487–501. These two basic senses can also be detected in secular Greek literature, the LXX, and early Christian writings. For a defense that the naming sense dominates Paul's uses, see William W. Klein, "Paul's Use of *kalein*: A Proposal," *JETS* 27, no.1 (March 1984): 53–64.

[43] Dunn, *Romans*, 1:485, agreed this points to their conversion. See also Douglas J. Moo, *The Letter to the Romans*, NICNT, 2nd ed. (Grand Rapids: Eerdmans, 2018), 557, who under-stood "calling" as an effectual summons.

into fellowship with Jesus (1 Cor 1:9). Paul can simply refer to believers as the "called" with no further modifiers (v. 24); they possess a calling simply by virtue of their identity in Christ (1 Cor 1:26; 7:18, 21–22, 24).[44]

For Paul, to be "called" implies that believers have an obligation to live in ways that reflect their identity in Christ. Paul addresses the Corinthian Christians as "called as saints" (1 Cor 1:2; NIV: "called to be his holy people"). Again, God calls his people to live in holiness (1 Thess 4:7), to a holy calling (2 Tim 1:9). God calls them to peace (1 Cor 7:15; Col 3:15); to freedom (Gal 5:13); to live in and with hope (Eph 1:18); to a walk (lifestyle) worthy of their calling (their status as belonging to God; Eph 4:1, 4; 2 Thess 1:11). God's call comes graciously (Gal 1:6).

In all this language of calling, we find it is primarily descriptive, not prescriptive. That is, God *calls* believers, they possess the name or status of *called ones*, and their *calling* implies a way of life that reflects both that status and the One who called them. God's call names people as members of his holy family and describes their status: called ones. Paul's words ring out: "As it also says in Hosea, 'I will call Not My People, My People, and she who is Unloved, Beloved. And it will be in the place where they were told, you are not my people, there they will be called sons of the living God'" (Rom 9:25–26).

God's call does not enable or empower specific ones to join his body. Calling language in Paul gives us no warrant for saying that God calls specific individuals to salvation and grants them the ability to believe.

God's Will and Salvation

While Paul discussed many aspects of God's will in his letters, we isolate only a few that directly contribute to our discussion of election, whether individual election to a task or election to salvation. As to the first, God presented (*protithēmi*) Christ as an atoning sacrifice (Rom 3:25), which indicates election to a task. Christ's death for human sin was due to God's will (*thelēma*; Gal 1:4).

As to their salvation, corporately, believers are called—named as his own—based on God's purpose (*prothesis*; Rom 8:28). God wills (*thelō*) to show mercy to some and harden others, a will (*boulēma*) that cannot be resisted (9:15, 18–19). God displays his wrath based on what he wills (v. 22, *thelō*). Who are these objects of

---

[44] Paul's use of "calling" in 1 Cor 7:20 is an outlier, referring to the vocation or situation in life people were in when the salvific call came to them. Paul's point, however, is not that God calls people to specific vocations or jobs.

God's mercy and wrath? Paul did not say that God has chosen specific individuals to whom he will show mercy or harden and demonstrate wrath. In the context of Romans 9, Paul's concern is the elect people of God, a corporate entity. Entrance into that body is through faith in Christ (vv. 30–33; 10:9–13; contrast unbelieving Israel—9:31–32; 10:1–4, 21)

When it comes to determining who God saves, Paul says that God "was pleased" (*eudokēsen*) to save those who believe through the foolishness of preaching (1 Cor 1:21). This is his sovereign and pleasurable desire. Paul did not say that God saves those whom he has chosen to believe, but rather that God has chosen to save those who believe. For this reason, God willed (*thelō*) to reveal the riches of his glorious mystery among the Gentiles—so they might believe (Col 1:27). The provision of salvation is an act of God's will (*thelēma*). What was formerly a mystery, now God "purpose[s]" (*protithēmi*) to reveal through his pleasurable will (*eudokia*) in Christ (Eph 1:9).[45] God's will or purpose (*prosthesis*) determined what he predestined for his people (v. 11). Salvation is available to people only because of God's own purpose (*prothesis*) and grace (2 Tim 1:9).

Paul explained why God provided salvation: God wills (*thelō*) that all find salvation (1 Tim 2:4). However, given the evidence in the NT, it is clear that God's will is not fulfilled—many fail to obtain salvation. As Paul said everywhere, people must trust in Christ to be saved. Nowhere does Paul intimate that God wills to save only certain people, much less that such a will might be irresistible or determinative of their personal faith. God wills the salvation of all, but he saves only those who embrace Christ as Savior (1 Tim 4:10).

Conclusions

Paul's data provide the fullest picture of election to salvation. God *foreknows* his people. In the case of foreknown Israel, that knowledge is not salvific, for not all members of Israel are saved (Rom 9:6). However, since Christ, all Christian believers constitute the saved people of God whom he foreknows. To foreknow is to have prescience, to know beforehand; it does not mean to choose or elect. God established a destiny for his people in full (and prior) knowledge of who they are and would become because of his saving grace. That destiny has been *predestined*, along with blessed benefits: present and future conformity to the image of Christ, glory, adoption into God's family, the ability to praise God's glory, and the capacity to perform

---

[45] Klein, "Ephesians," 51.

good works. Paul never used the concept of predestination to infer that God selects some for salvation. Predestination concerns what God has predetermined for those who belong to him.

God has chosen or elected his people. Jacob and his descendants—the nation Israel—are elect. This is corporate election, but it does not mean that all individual Israelites are saved; only the remnant who believe find salvation. Two points stand out: election is corporate (Israel) and election is for service. This corporate election of Israel parallels the election of the church, but unlike corporate Israel, in the church election and salvation coincide. Before the world's foundation God chose the church "in Christ"; as his elect body, the church finds its identity in he who is the Chosen One. No one individual is elected by God to be saved, much less irresistibly. Rather, when individuals choose to place their faith in Christ through the sanctifying enablement of the Holy Spirit,[46] they enter the company of the elect. Election leads to mission, for the church as well as its individual members. The elect ones obtain eschatological salvation as they persevere through life's trials.

God *appoints* people to serve him in various roles, what we have termed election to tasks or functions. Paul noted that God chose Abraham, Jacob, and Pharaoh—for various tasks or functions. Jesus was God's Elect One—chosen to secure redemption. Paul viewed his apostleship as the result of God's appointment; he was a "marked man." God also appoints others whom he gifts for service. God even appoints governmental authorities who rule nations. Paul never used the idea of appointment to convey that God designates who will be saved.

God *calls* when he gives his people the name or status of the people of God, and to them he issues a *calling* to serve him and to reflect who they are and whose they are. The *called ones* are the saved people of God. When people call upon the name of the Lord (trust in Christ), God responds by enrolling them in the company of the saved and called.

The provision of salvation rests solely in the gracious and purposeful *will* of God. He *purposed* to send Christ to accomplish redemption. He *desires* that all come to salvation, and he made provision in Christ to effect that salvation. But he also wills to save only those who place their faith in Christ. Those who reject his offer of salvation will not be saved, but they have only their own unbelief to blame for their plight.

---

[46] Recall John 12:32—Jesus's drawing—and Acts 14:27—God's opening the door of faith—for corroboration of God's preparatory work so people have the opportunity to believe. Wesleyans often call this prevenient grace.

Election in the Remaining Letters

Hebrews

Using the verb "to call" (*kalein*), the anonymous author of this homily affirms that only God can appoint one to the office of high priest (Heb 5:4). Appointment to a task figures significantly in the author's portrayal of Christ's election. God "appointed" (*tithēmi*) Jesus heir of all things. God appointed Jesus as Messiah and High Priest (1:5; 5:5). In that vein, God "designated" (*prosagoreuō*) Christ to be a Melchizedekian high priest (5:10). God's oath "appoints" (*kathistēmi*) the Son (7:28; 8:3). All these uses reflect the idea of election to a task or role.

The author also employs calling language in the Pauline sense of the calling to be a Christian, a "heavenly calling" (3:1). While the description "heavenly" may point to their vocation—to live by heaven's values—it might also point out the originator of the call on their lives, God. Those who are called will receive an eternal inheritance (9:15). Previously the author affirmed that the readers are heirs of God's salvation (6:17) and also used "call" in the naming sense, as the following translation reflects: "Through Isaac shall your offspring be named" (11:18 ESV).

The dominant idea is Jesus's status as God's Chosen One, one under divine appointment as the only Son and as High Priest securing the salvation of his people. This underscores our previous findings of individual election to a task or function.

James

James affirmed that God "wills" (*boulomai* [47]) to give birth to Christians (Jas 1:18). This "will" expresses what God determined to accomplish—to bring forth a regenerated and redeemed people. James affirmed God's choice or purpose in providing salvation—in birthing the people of God—not the choice of specific individuals to be saved. The tenor of this is corporate.

Speaking of the rich, James asked, "Are they not the ones who blaspheme the honorable name by which you were called?" (2:7 ESV). Using the naming sense of "call" (*epikaleō*),[48] James reminded believers that they bear a special name, probably the name of Christ. They bear his name and so must act as Christ does and not show partiality.

---

[47] English versions translate *boulomai* here in various ways: "will" (NASB; KJV); "chose" (NIV; CEB; NLT); "choice" (CSB; NJB); "sovereign plan" (NET); and "purpose" (NRSV).

[48] To call upon or give a surname (*BDAG*, 373).

James asserted that God has chosen (*eklegomai*) the poor to be rich in faith and to inherit the kingdom (2:5). This is election to salvation; this is the choice of a corporate group: the poor, not specific individuals. James can hardly mean that all the poor of this world will inherit eternal salvation, for certainly many of them reject the gospel. And surely some rich will be saved. Because of their disadvantageous circumstances in life, the poor more readily see their need and turn to the gospel of Christ. James does not say that God has selected individual poor people to save.

1 Peter

Peter's uses match what we have previously uncovered. God's people have experienced God's call (1 Pet 1:15). God called them (2:9; 5:10), a reference to their conversion, when God named them as his own. As such, they possess a "calling" to endure suffering even when it results from doing good (2:21). In fact, "you were called for this, so that you may inherit a blessing" (3:9).

Peter also spoke of Christ's appointment as Savior. Christ was "foreknown" (*proginoskō*) by God before the world's creation, but now has been revealed in these last times (1:20).[49] God had prior knowledge of Christ's career; beyond that, God determined the salvific events in Jesus's life (cf. Acts 2:23; 4:28; 13:29). In using "foreknow" Peter drew attention to God's prior knowledge of the Messiah's coming—which the prophets saw only sketchily—but which in these last times God then made known and effected. Taken together, this is election to a task or function. Peter described Jesus as the living Stone, "chosen" (*eklektos*; 1 Pet 2:4, 6; cf. Isa 28:16; 42:1) by God.

Peter began his letter (1:1–2) by affirming that his readers are "chosen" (*eklektos*) according to "foreknowledge" (*prognōsis*). How does foreknowledge relate to their election?[50] Those interpreters who take "know" (*yāḏaʿ*) in the OT to have elective meaning (and who transfer that elective sense to the Greek words for knowledge and

---

[49] *BDAG*, 866, cite two senses for the verb: to have foreknowledge of, and to choose beforehand. They prefer the second meaning for the use at 1 Pet 1:20. Silva, "προγινώσκω," *NIDNTTE*, 4:139, and Alexander Sand, "προγινώσκω," *EDNT*, 3:153–54, concur. Most commentators prefer "foreordain" rather than "choose." However, the face-value sense of foreknowledge makes good sense here. Since God foreknew his plan, it was foreordained, so both senses coalesce here. Peter points to Jesus's task or role as redeemer.

[50] Virtually all English versions translate *prognōsis* here as foreknowledge, not predestination or election (see, e.g., CSB, NIV, NET, NASB, ESV, CEB, NAB, and Phillips). An outlier is the NRSV, which has "destined."

foreknowledge) typically posit that Peter's use of "foreknowledge" also has elective significance. But that results in a strange redundancy here: Are the readers elect ones according to election? It makes more sense grammatically to see that the readers are "elect" on the basis of God's "prior knowledge" (the face value sense of *prognōsis* found in Acts 26:5 and 2 Pet 3:17). Peter affirmed that the readers are elect either because God foresaw their eventual faith in Jesus (though this is not evident in Peter's words) or, more likely, in full knowledge of his plans for them (cf. our discussion about Rom 8:29 and 11:2). Peter's readers' status as elect refugees depends on God's active and concerned knowledge of them, a knowledge he has always had and which will work out for their well-being.

Peter described the chosen people of God with a variety of terms that emphasize his understanding of the corporate nature of the elect body (1 Pet 2:9): elect "race, people" (*genos*), a royal "priesthood" (*hierateuma*), a holy "nation" (*ethnos*), and God's own "people" (*laos*). All in all, Peter has repurposed these descriptors of the OT people of God and applied them to the Christian body of believers. At the end of his letter, Peter also described the church from which he wrote (likely in Rome) as "chosen together with you" (5:13), confirming the corporate usage.

Christ is God's elect Son (2:4, 6), foreknown before creation (1:20) but revealed now for his redemptive mission. So is the church God's called and elect people. While their calling may entail suffering as Christ's did (2:21; 3:9), they have the confidence of belonging to God as his special people—ones also chosen and foreknown (1:1–2; 2:9).

2 Peter

Peter affirmed Jesus's appointment to his task (2 Pet 1:17), paralleling the synoptic accounts of Jesus's transfiguration (Matt 17:5; Mark 9:7; Luke 9:35). As seen previously, the verb "to be well pleased" (*eudokein*) adds an elective component to the citation.

Peter affirmed that God does not will (*boulomai*) that any perish (2 Pet 3:9). Rather, God wills that "all" or "everyone" comes to repentance. In this section (2:3–9), Peter affirmed that God patiently stays the day of judgment so that more people can escape God's "destruction of the ungodly" (3:7).[51] While there are many thorny issues surrounding this contested text, it seems apparent that some perish because of their own resistance to God's call to repent, *not* because God prevents them or failed to

---

[51] Gene L. Green, *Jude and 2 Peter*, BECNT (Grand Rapids: Baker, 2008), 328, said, "He [God] does not wish that anyone 'perish' eternally."

choose them. Rather, they thwart God's will for their salvation. This is what the false teachers are guilty of; they scoff and reject God's offer of salvation.

Believers are those who are "called" (1:3), a common designation of their status. Yet the readers must "make every effort to confirm your calling and election, because if you do these things you will never stumble" (v. 10). Peter sounded a note of urgency like James's "faith without works is dead" (Jas 2:26). Words such as *calling* and *election* can be mere labels if they reflect an empty profession that bears no fruit, the kinds he outlines in 2 Pet 1:5–7. The readers must give tangible evidence in their lives, "for in this way, entry into the eternal kingdom of our Lord and Savior Jesus Christ will be richly provided for you" (v. 11).[52]

Jude

Jude wrote, "To those who are the called, loved by God the Father and kept for Jesus Christ" (Jude 1). As previously seen, the called are those whom God has *named* his own people. Gene Green put Jude's use in line with the other uses of this descriptor: "God's call . . . is corporate and constitutes them together as the people of God."[53] Jude affirmed they are loved and kept, the status of all God's called ones.

Conclusions

We have surveyed the data systematically and canonically. What remains is to summarize how the Bible, especially the NT, presents the nature of God's election.

The Corporate Nature of Election to Salvation

God chooses or elects both corporate groups and individuals. That said, the NT presents *election to salvation* in only corporate terms. Simply put, God has chosen the church in Christ as the ones he will save. The OT sets the precedent: God chose Israel

---

[52] Daryl J. Charles, "2 Peter," *The Expositor's Bible Commentary: Hebrews–Revelation*, rev. ed., ed. Tremper Longman III and David E. Garland (Grand Rapids: Zondervan, 2006), 13:391, stated it clearly: "The burden clearly rests on the shoulders of the readers to hold up their end of the covenantal agreement. If they are *willing*, they will never stumble. The guarantee is not that they will not sin, only that they will not *fall*."

[53] Green, *Jude and 2 Peter*, 47. As a reminder of what we saw at the outset, Richard Bauckham, *Jude, 2 Peter*, Word Biblical Commentary (Waco, TX: Word, 1983), 26–27, argued that the title *klētoi* (called) was transferred to Christians from OT Israel through such texts as Isa 41:9; 42:6; 48:12, 15; 49:1; 54:6; and Hos 11:1.

as his people—a corporate choice—though in the case of OT Israel not every individual within the nation will be saved, but only those who place their trust in Yahweh. In the apostle Paul's verbiage, "Not all who are descended from Israel are Israel" (Rom 9:6). God chose the nation or physical Israel, but he also chose the subset of spiritual Israel—the saved. Faith or trust is the key for entrance into the "people of God."

Election language in the NT parallels the OT pattern of a chosen people, but unlike the physical nation Israel, in the NT the elect people are all saved. They constitute the church, that body of people who place their trust in Jesus, the Messiah—both Jews and Gentiles. The church is spiritual Israel. This fulfills Jesus's mission to seek and save the lost (Luke 19:10). It climaxes the grand narrative of redemption.

All sectors of the New Testament affirm that salvific election is corporate. God chose the church as a body before the world's foundation (Eph 1:4). The New Testament writers never present election as God's choice of specific individuals (and not others) to populate that body. Christ is God's Elect One; all who enter into Christ (the church is the body of Christ) participate in his election. Christians benefit from what Christ accomplished because they are "in Christ," an especially pervasive formulation in Paul's writings. Individuals can rightfully be labeled as "elect" only because they are members of Christ's elect body, the church.

Individual Election to a Task

The Bible explains that God chooses people to perform tasks or serve in various roles. When the New Testament writers present the election of individuals, they see it as election to a task, not election to salvation. First, God chose Jesus; Jesus is God's Chosen or Appointed One. The Heavenly Voice says, "This is my Son, the Chosen One; listen to him!" (Luke 9:35). God chose Jesus for his messianic mission to secure salvation for all who trust in him. In the Gospels we find that Jesus chose his twelve apostles (Matt 10:1–5; Mark 3:13–19; Luke 6:12–16), and he also appointed seventy-two (Luke 10:1) to engage in ministry in his name. To repeat: these are examples of election to a task or function (apostleship or mission), not salvation, for Judas was among those elected (Luke 6:13–16; John 6:70). Paul was also a chosen apostle, a point he repeated in most of his letters. God appointed him to serve in the role or function as a steward of the glorious gospel message, especially to the Gentiles. This is individual election to a task, not his personal salvation.

The NT writers also speak of God's appointment of others to serve God in various capacities or to perform various functions or tasks. Paul named Pharaoh as God's chosen instrument; God appointed Roman government officials (Rom 9:17, 21; 13:1). Judas also played a role in the redemptive scheme (Acts 1:16). God appoints elders to serve in the churches (Acts 20:28) and calls missionaries to spread the gospel (Acts 13:2; 16:10). God gifts persons with spiritual capacities so they can function in various ministry positions (Rom 12:6; 1 Cor 12:28; Eph 4:7). The NT writers affirm that God (or Jesus) chooses individuals, but this is always election to service, never individual election to salvation.

God's Calling to Salvation

When speaking of salvation, the NT writers, particularly Paul, use "calling" language primarily in a naming sense. Believers in Christ are "the called" (e.g., Rom 1:6; 8:28; 1 Cor 1:24). This is equivalent to saying they are the saved ones, the people of God, or the elect of God. As Brian Abasciano put it, "For Paul, calling and election are closely related. Calling is the application and appellation of election, the act of designating a group as God's elect people."[54] These called or elect ones then have a "calling" that grows out of their identity in Christ and that they need to embrace (1 Cor 1:26; Eph 4:1, 4; Phil 3:14; 2 Thess 1:11; 2 Tim 1:9).

God's Foreknowledge

Foreknowledge and to foreknow (noun and verb) refer to God's prescience or prior knowledge, not to God's prior election of some to be saved. The sense of prior knowledge is clear in these words used outside the NT,[55] and it is the best gloss of the few uncontroversial instances in the NT (Acts 26:5; 2 Pet 3:17). Employing this face-value sense, we can say that God foreknew the course of Christ's redemptive career (Acts 2:23; 1 Pet 1:20), as he did his people Israel (Rom 11:2). Likewise, God foreknew Christians as a corporate body (Rom 8:29; 1 Pet 1:2). Foreknowledge does not mean election.

God's Predestination

The sovereign God has the capacity to determine events or states of affairs ahead of their occurrence and can assure they come about. While predestination may account

---

[54] Abasciano, *Romans 9.1–9*, 201 (see chap. 9, n. 5).

[55] See "προγιγνώσκω," *Brill Dictionary of Ancient Greek*, 1752; and "προγιγνώσκω," LSJ, 1473.

for a variety of different actions (e.g., Acts 1:7; 14:27; 15:7; 17:26; Heb 4:7), in the realm of salvation God predestines future outcomes or benefits for his saved ones. These include conformity to the image of his Son (Rom 8:29–30), their future glory (Rom 9:23; 1 Cor 2:7; Eph 1:11–12), and their adoption into his family (Eph 1:5). Contrary to much popular use, the NT writers never employ "predestination" to denote God's choice of who would become his people.

God's Will and People's Salvation

God may "will" outcomes in a determinative or definitive way: they occur without fail. Within that broad category, God may even will (allow) that his people suffer (1 Pet 3:17; 4:19). Regarding God's provision of salvation, God willed in this determinative sense a plan that would enable disobedient humans to find forgiveness and enter into his redeemed people—a plan that included appointing Jesus to secure salvation.

In other uses, what God wills may *not* occur. The term God's "will" may denote what God desires, wishes, or prefers, but which he does not determine. People may thwart his will, because in his sovereign design, he determined to allow that option (as in Adam and Eve's disobedience in the garden). Jesus encouraged his disciples to pray that God's *will* be done on earth, though it does not always happen. God *wills* that Christians be sexually pure (1 Thess 4:3) and do what is good (1 Pet 2:15), though God's people violate his desire for them. God also "wills" that all people be saved. The Bible is amply clear that not all people find salvation despite what God desires for them. We found no evidence to support a view that God wills only particular ones to be saved and gives only to them the capacity to believe. In a nutshell, God's universal, salvific will (the first sense) determined to provide salvation for all (John 3:16).[56] But God saves only those who embrace Christ by faith and who by so doing fulfill God's will (the second sense) that all be saved.

Because God wills that all be saved (1 Tim 2:4) and that none perish (2 Pet 3:9), Jesus was lifted up on the cross to draw all people to God (John 12:32). As a result, "*everyone* who calls on the name of the Lord will be saved" (Acts 2:21; emphasis added; cf. Rom 10:13; Joel 2:28–32). No view positing that God chose only some individuals for salvation is compatible with these clear statements as well as the overwhelming use of election to salvation as a corporate reality.

---

[56] See Vernon C. Grounds, "God's Universal, Salvific Grace," in *Grace Unlimited*, ed. Clark Pinnock (Minneapolis: Bethany Fellowship, 1975), 21–30, on God's desire for all to be saved.

11

The Character of God in Calvinism

—— Roger E. Olson ——

Calvinism is impossible. According to Charles Hodge, one of the greatest and most influential Calvinist theologians of modern times, some things are simply impossible.[1] In his influential three-volume *Systematic Theology*, the Princeton Seminary theologian wrote that some principles of thought are necessary. One is that "the impossible cannot be true."[2] Hodge fleshed out this principle with four specific subprinciples about what is impossible:

(1.) That is impossible which involves a contradiction; as, that a thing is and is not; that right is wrong, and wrong right. (2.) It is impossible that God should do, approve, or command what is morally wrong. (3.) It is impossible

---

[1] See David Wells, "The Stout and Persistent 'Theology' of Charles Hodge," *Christianity Today* 18.23 (August 30, 1974): 10–15. Wells taught theology at Gordon-Conwell Theological Seminary for many years and, like many other American evangelical Calvinists, considered Hodge one of the greatest of all evangelical theologians.

[2] Charles Hodge, *Systematic Theology*, 3 vols. (Grand Rapids: Eerdmans, 1973), 1:51. Hodge's three-volume *Systematic Theology* was first published in 1873–74.

that He should require us to believe what contradicts any of the laws of belief which He has impressed upon our nature. (4.) It is impossible that one truth should contradict another.[3]

In other words, I conclude—contrary to what Hodge concluded, that Calvinism—in its classical and most consistent form, is impossible. However, I will lay that here as my thesis and reach it as a conclusion after elucidation and argumentation.

Fleshing out my thesis a bit more fully, I believe that classical and consistent Calvinism, insofar as Calvinism can be self-consistent, is impossible because it includes beliefs, affirmations of fact, that violate Hodge's second principle (above) and necessarily make God a moral monster. It also includes beliefs, affirmations of fact, that violate Hodge's fourth principle (above) because it includes beliefs, affirmations of fact, that contradict one another. I assume that all classical, consistent Calvinists agree with the first principle—that God cannot do what is wrong. Unfortunately, some Calvinists do *not* agree with the second principle—that it is impossible that one truth should contradict another.[4] It is impossible to debate with such a person because logic does not matter to him or her. Fortunately, most scholarly Calvinists affirm Hodge's fourth principle while admitting that theology always includes mystery but not sheer logical contradiction.

Here I will argue that—contrary to classical, consistent Calvinists—Calvinism *does* make God the author of sin and evil, and that violates Hodge's second principle stated above—one with which the vast majority of Calvinists agree. *Classical, consistent Calvinism does affirm, implicitly, anyway, that God does what is morally wrong*. It makes God a moral monster unworthy of worship. It also empties the meaning of "God is good" in one of two ways. Either "good" becomes so ambiguous when applied to God that "God is good" is not informative, or "God is good" becomes a mere tautology because whatever God does is good just because God does it.

Now, obviously, no classical, consistent Calvinist scholar or theologian, *believes* these things about his or her Calvinist beliefs and affirmations. That is irrelevant here, because what I am looking at, attempting to point out, is the *good and necessary consequences* of what classical, consistent Calvinism affirms. Even if no Calvinist ever

---

[3] Hodge, *Systematic Theology*, 1:51.

[4] One example is Edwin H. Palmer, author of *The Five Points of Calvinism*, enlarged edition (Grand Rapids: Baker, 1972) who wrote of "the Calvinist" that "he realizes that what he advocates is ridiculous. . . . The Calvinist freely admits that his position is illogical, ridiculous, nonsensical, and foolish" (85).

believed or affirmed that God is the author of sin and evil and a moral monster, those conclusions are the good and necessary consequences of what they believe insofar as they are classical, consistent Calvinists.

Before continuing it is important to stop and explain what I mean by "classical, consistent Calvinism/Calvinists." After this brief explanation I will mostly drop "classical" and "consistent" and refer simply to "Calvinism" and "Calvinists," meaning not every "flavor" of Calvinism and not every individual Calvinist but that system of theology generally known as Calvinism and those believers who adhere to it.

One approach to defining a category such as "Calvinism" and "Calvinists" is to look at *prototypes*. In this case they include John Calvin, Jonathan Edwards, Charles Hodge, and John Piper. These theologians and others like them *define* what "Calvinism" means in its classical and most consistent form. That is not to say they all agree with each other about everything; it is only to say that theologians who study Calvinism generally agree that they stand out as normative examples of it.

Another, compatible approach to defining a category such as "Calvinism" and "Calvinists" is to look at *durable, coherent systems with "staying power."* This approach is not very different from the prototypes approach but differs in its focus on *systems* over *people*. The great, classical Calvinist *systems of thought* that strive for coherence include Calvin's *Institutes of the Christian Religion*, Edwards's *Freedom of the Will*, Hodge's *Systematic Theology*, and Piper's *The Pleasures of God*. A careful reader of these classic expositions of Calvinist theology will find impressive consistency between them. A *system of thought* runs through them, and it is generally recognized as classical, consistent Calvinism.

Here I will leave aside theologians and writings that are considered idiosyncratic or revisionist by the majority of Calvinist scholars. I address and criticize *only* those great theologians and writings that are generally and widely considered by all theologians to be examples of classical, consistent (or would-be consistent) Calvinist thought—especially about *God's sovereignty in providence and predestination*.

Because Calvinism is a system of thought and not just random, unrelated ideas, its two distinctive doctrines must be consistent with each other. These two are *providence* and *election*. (The word *predestination* is sometimes used for both and sometimes used solely for the latter.) Providence is, in Christian theology, any account of God's *governance* of created reality. Election, sometimes called "predestination," is, in Christian theology, any account of God's *choice* of whom to save. Calvinism presents one clear and distinct idea of providence and one clear and distinct idea of election, and the two *must* be consistent with each other. That sometimes they are not counts against Calvinism.

All Calvinist theologians, informed pastors, and laypersons believe (1) that God is absolutely, unconditionally sovereign over all things and people, foreordaining the course of nature and history exhaustively and comprehensively, and (2) that God unconditionally selects certain people to be saved and leaves others to eternal punishment. I will demonstrate this account of Calvinist theology with clear examples.

One problem immediately presents itself and it is that these two beliefs fall into contradiction with each other insofar as Calvinists believe that for some reason God *cannot* save all people. For Calvinists, God's sovereignty includes his omnipotence; God's power is unlimited (except by logic). If God is absolutely almighty over all creation and meticulously sovereign, there cannot be any reason why he *could* not save everyone. As we will see, however, Calvinists believe that God *does* not save everyone because that would undermine God's purpose in creation and salvation—the manifestation of his glory. This response I will explain more fully later.

First, then, an account of the prototypical Calvinist doctrine of providence, and then, second, an account of the prototypical Calvinist doctrine of *election/ predestination*.

Calvinism's doctrine of divine providence is sometimes called "meticulous providence" to distinguish it from general providence. According to Calvinism, all that happens, without exception, is willed by God. Lying in the background of Calvinism is fifth-century North African church father Augustine (AD 354–430). In 420 he wrote a handbook of Christian doctrine variously known as the *Enchiridion* or *Faith, Hope, and Charity*. There he declared that "Nothing . . . happens unless the Omnipotent wills it to happen."[5] Augustine wrote of evil as *permitted* by God, as opposed to bringing it about himself, but the context makes clear that even what God permits is part of God's plan. Augustine wrote here that "man's will" cannot prevent God from carrying out his own will. The gist is that although God does not actually *do* evil, evil is part of God's willing plan and permission for a good purpose.

My reason for mentioning Augustine is to show that the prototypical Calvinist account of God's providence did not begin with Calvin, although Calvin surely added a certain dimension to it. Before Calvin, Swiss reformer Ulrich Zwingli (1484–1531) wrote a treatise entitled *On Providence* in which he expressed the strongest possible notion of divine government and control over all events in creation. Some call this

[5] Augustine, *Faith, Hope, and Charity*, trans. L. A. Arand (Westminster, MD: Newman Press, 1953), 89.

idea "divine determinism." Most modern Christians trace it back to Calvin, but it predates him.

So, what of Calvin's account of God's providence? The following sentence expresses it in a nutshell: "Men can accomplish nothing except by God's secret command . . . they cannot by deliberating accomplish anything except what he [God] has already decreed with himself and determines by his secret direction."[6] Also, "God by the bridle of his providence turns every event whatever way he wills."[7] To make his position as clear as possible, Calvin offered an illustration about a merchant who is killed by robbers, thieves, while riding through a forest. "His death was not only foreseen by God's eye, but also determined by his decree."[8] Also, "God so attends to the regulation of individual events, and they all so proceed from his set plan, that nothing takes place by chance."[9] What about evil? Calvin did not hesitate to attribute even evil to God's plan and decree, even though he denied that any guilt thereby accrued to God because God's *intention* in foreordaining evil is good. "Since God's will is said to be the cause of all things, I have made his providence the determinative principle for all human plans and works, not only in order to display its force in the elect . . . but also to compel the reprobate to obedience."[10] In other words, even wicked people destined for hell because of their wickedness and lack of repentance do what God compels them to do.

These statements express the classical, consistent belief of true Calvinism, even if some later Calvinists are embarrassed by them and choose to soften them. There can be no question that, for Calvin, as for Augustine before him, God is the all-determining reality who plans, decrees, and renders certain everything that happens in creation without exception.

Here, to save space, I will add only a few confirming statements about God's providence from later Calvinist theologians.

The great Puritan preacher, scholar, and theologian Jonathan Edwards (1703–1758) affirmed meticulous providence in his treatise *Freedom of the Will*. According to him, there is "an infallible previous fixedness of the futurity of [every] event" following from God's "universal, determining providence" which implies "some kind

---

[6] Calvin, *Institutes*, trans. Battles, 1:229 (1.18.1) (see chap. 4, n. 85).

[7] Calvin, 1:209 (1.16.9).

[8] Calvin, 1:209 (1.16.9).

[9] Calvin, 1:203 (1.16.4).

[10] Calvin, 1:232 (1.18.2).

of necessity of all events."[11] Does this "universal, determining providence" and its consequent "necessity" include sin and evil? Edwards's clearest response lies also in *Freedom of the Will*:

> If by "the author of sin," is meant the permitter or not hinderer of sin; and at the same time, a disposer of the state of events, in such a manner, for wise, holy and most excellent ends and purposes, that sin, if it be permitted or not hindered, will most certainly and infallibly follow: I say, if this be all that is meant, by being the author of sin, I don't deny that God is the author of sin.[12]

Of course, Edwards qualified this admission by arguing that God never actually *causes* sin or evil but renders them certain by "withholding his action and energy" that the sinner needs not to sin or do evil.[13] And he asserted that by willing evil God does not do evil because God's *intention* in willing evil and rendering it certain is good.[14]

Charles Hodge (1797–1878) was almost certainly the most influential American conservative theologian of the nineteenth century. In his *Systematic Theology*, still in print more than a century after it was first published, the Princeton professor averred that "God foreordains whatsoever comes to pass. . . . The doctrine of the Bible is, that all events, whether necessary or contingent, good or sinful, are included in the purpose of God, and that their futurition or actual occurrence is rendered absolutely certain."[15] The context makes crystal clear that, for Hodge, it is God who renders them "absolutely certain." This is another expression of meticulous providence.

What, then, of sin and evil? Hodge clearly included them in his account of God's providence, but very cautiously—one might even say slyly—he denied that God is either their "author" or "approver."[16] And yet, he insisted that God *decreed* and *rendered certain* both sin and evil.[17] Something is amiss, logically, in Hodge's assertions about God's all-determining providence and denials that God "authors" or "approves" sin and evil.

Although many modern Calvinists have not heard of him, theologian Loraine Boettner (1901–1990) was one of the most influential Calvinists of modern times.

---

[11] Jonathan Edwards, *The Works of Jonathan Edwards*, vol. 1, *Freedom of the Will*, ed. Paul Ramsey (New Haven, CT: Yale University Press, 1957), 431 ("The Conclusion").

[12] Edwards, 1:399 (Part IV, §9.2).

[13] Edwards, 1:404 (Part IV, §9.3).

[14] Edwards, 1:411–12 (Part IV, §9.4).

[15] Hodge, *Systematic Theology*, 1:542.

[16] Hodge, 1:547.

[17] Hodge, 1:547.

He lived between Hodge and our next Calvinist example, R. C. Sproul. Boettner wrote his classic *The Reformed Doctrine of Predestination* in 1948; and, by all accounts among people who study modern Calvinism, he and that book stand out as especially clear examples of the Calvinist teaching about divine providence.

According to Boettner, "The world as a whole and in all its parts and movements and changes was brought into a unity by the governing, all-pervading, all-harmonizing activity of the divine will, and its purpose was to manifest the divine glory."[18] Also, according to him, God "very obviously predetermined every event which would happen" in creation.[19] "Even the sinful acts of men are included in this plan."[20] Boettner wrestled with the problems raised by this belief in meticulous providence. He argued that sin and evil arise from the human person's own nature but that "God so presents the outside inducements that man acts in accordance with his own nature, yet does just exactly what God plans for him to do."[21] How this solves anything with regard to God's goodness remains problematic, to say the least. What are "outside inducements" if not temptations? How does God, then, remain good? Because the ultimate good is God's glory and everything that happens—including sin, evil, and innocent suffering—happens because God decrees it for his glory.[22]

One of the most influential Calvinists of the twentieth century was the evangelical theologian and apologist R. C. Sproul Sr. (1939–2017). He authored numerous books and lectured to numerous audiences—strongly defending classical Calvinism and attacking alternative views of God's providence and election. Here is his most famous expression of God's providence: "If there is one single molecule in this universe running around loose, totally free of God's sovereignty, then we have no guarantee that a single promise of God will ever be fulfilled. . . . Maybe that one molecule will be the thing that prevents Christ from returning."[23] Also, Sproul added, "The movement of every molecule, the actions of every plant, the falling of every star, the choices of every volitional creature, all these are subject to his [God's] sovereign will."[24] For him, everything that happens is the will of God, even if not in the same

---

[18] Loraine Boettner, *The Reformed Doctrine of Predestination* (Grand Rapids: Eerdmans, 1948), 14.

[19] Boettner, 24.

[20] Boettner, 24.

[21] Boettner, 38.

[22] Boettner, 14.

[23] Sproul, *Chosen by God*, 26–27 (see chap. 1, n. 106).

[24] Sproul, *What Is Reformed Theology?*, 172 (see chap. 2, n. 19).

way.[25] That is, God actively decrees some things and decrees to permit other things.[26] Yet, even the things he decrees to permit, such as sin and evil, are part of God's sovereign plan and will; he foreordained them,[27] and he renders them certain. On the other hand, Sproul insisted, "One thing is absolutely unthinkable, that God could be the author or doer of sin."[28]

Again, as with Hodge, Edwards, and Calvin, something is logically amiss in Sproul's account of God's providence in relation to sin and evil. It is universally true in human experience that if a person plans, designs, foreordains, and renders certain some evil action, even if that action is carried out by another, he or she is responsible for and guilty of it.

Paul Helm (b. 1940) was not mentioned here earlier, but he is one of the most influential, intellectual Calvinist theologians. His name is not "household," but through his many writings and lectures, and through his teaching at evangelical educational institutions, he has influenced many Christians to adopt Calvinism. His book *Providence* (1994) is one of the clearest expressions and defenses of Calvinism published in recent decades. What is his view of God's providence?

According to Helm, "not only is every atom and molecule, every thought and desire, kept in being by God, but every twist and turn of each of these is under the direct control of God."[29] The clear implication is that sin and evil are directly controlled by God. Helm made clear that this does not mean merely that God keeps them under control; it means that God wills them: "To put it paradoxically, the breaking of his will became part of the fulfilling of his will."[30] "We know from Scripture that God's providence extends to evil human acts"[31] because "the providence of God is fine-grained; it extends to the occurrence of individual actions and to each aspect of each action."[32] Just in case anyone does not understand, Helm nailed it down: "God controls all events and yet issues moral commands which are disobeyed in some of the very events which he controls. For example, he commands men and women to love their neighbours while at the same time ordaining actions which are malicious

---

[25] Sproul, 172.
[26] Sproul, 172.
[27] Sproul, *Chosen by God*, 31.
[28] Sproul, 31.
[29] Helm, *The Providence of God*, 22 (see chap. 4, n. 95).
[30] Helm, 48.
[31] Helm, 100.
[32] Helm, 104.

or hateful."[33] And yet, Helm averred, God never actually *causes* sin or evil. How, then, does God control them? First, according to him, God *allows* evil and does not *do* evil.[34] Second, God determines sin and evil actions by "divine withholding." "God withholds his goodness or grace, and forthwith the agent forms a morally deficient motive or reason and acts accordingly."[35]

Who can be blamed for thinking his or her head is spinning at such mental gymnastics? This is why I said at the beginning that *Calvinism is impossible.* These subtle distinctions are devoid of real differences. If Calvin, Edwards, Hodge, and Helm are right, then God is the *ultimate cause* of sin and evil, including innocent suffering, the sufferings of children, even if only by planning, designing, foreordaining, and rendering them certain! Helm spoke for them all when he stated unequivocally that God's manifestation of his own glory in creation and redemption justifies his control over sin and evil.[36] This, he said, is "God's one end"[37] or purpose in everything, with the strong implication being that sin and evil are necessary to the accomplishment of that end. Many critics (I include myself) believe this makes God the ultimate malicious narcissist, which is impossible. Even Helm said that God's goodness "must bear some positive relation to the sorts of human actions we regard as good. Otherwise, why ascribe *goodness* to God?"[38] The problem, however, is that *none of these Calvinists' accounts of God's relation to sin and evil, or innocent suffering, bear any positive relation to human actions we regard as good.*

The last Calvinist theologian I will quote and examine is John Piper (b. 1946), retired pastor, author, and speaker. For any who may not be familiar with him, he was and remains one of the most influential Christian theologians (he has a doctoral degree in New Testament from the University of Münich) in the world. His books have sold by the hundreds of thousands, many in translations in countries such as Brazil and South Korea. He is a convinced Calvinist who "pulls no punches" when it comes to proclaiming and defending God's absolute, meticulous sovereignty.

Piper was the main speaker at the annual Passion Conferences, where as many as sixty-five thousand Christian young people gathered in the first two decades of the twenty-first century. At that conference in January 2005, in Nashville, Tennessee,

---

[33] Helm, 133.
[34] Helm, 171.
[35] Helm, 171.
[36] Helm, 23.
[37] Helm, 23.
[38] Helm, 167.

he spoke about "God's God-Centeredness" and claimed that the recent tsunami in Southeast Asia was from God in the sense that God designed it, even as he designs all things. Then he said that even if a "dirty bomb" leveled downtown Minneapolis (where his church was located), it would be from God.

These oral statements are entirely consistent with what Piper wrote about God's sovereignty and providence in *The Pleasures of God*. There he taught that God is in some sense the cause of all suffering.[39] He offered an example of what he believes about God's sovereignty in meticulous providence; it is about his own mother's death in an accident. According to him, she was riding in a car, in the passenger seat, when a wood four-by-four escaped the back of a truck and rammed through the window, killing her. Piper attributed this to God and explained that "I take no comfort from the prospect that God cannot control the flight of a four-by-four. For me there is no consolation in haphazardness. Nor in giving Satan the upper hand."[40]

What shall we conclude from these teachings of classical, prototypical, consistent Calvinists?[41] Calvinism includes the strongest doctrine of divine providence conceivable. God is the all-determining reality who designs, ordains, and renders certain everything that happens. Nothing—including sin, evil, and innocent suffering—escapes his control. It is all foreordained and rendered certain, even if indirectly through secondary causes. When it comes to sin and evil especially, God renders it certain, as part of his plan, by withholding the goodness and grace, the agent, whether Satan or Adam or anyone, would need not to sin. The question this view raises is troubling, to say the least.[42] I believe this view of providence cannot avoid making God the author of sin and evil as well as all innocent suffering, even the kidnapping, rape, and murder of a child, even the Holocaust. This makes the statement "God is good" meaningless. Either "good" means something entirely different than in any other context or it only means that whatever God does is good just because God does it. In either case, "God is good" is not informative.

What about Calvinism's doctrine of election? This doctrine is popularly called "predestination," but that can also refer to meticulous providence—that everything is predestined. So here I will use the term *election* for this Calvinist doctrine of salvation.

---

[39] John Piper, *The Pleasures of God* (Portland, OR: Multnomah, 1991), 189–90.

[40] Piper, 68.

[41] Again, I wish to explain that I do not think they are really consistent. By "consistent" here I only mean that they do not throw away logic and claim to believe what is absurd, which is what some Calvinists such as Edwin Palmer do.

[42] Piper, *Pleasures of God*, 175.

In a sense, the Calvinist doctrine of election is already predetermined by its doctrine of meticulous providence. However, one thing must be made clear, and that is that classical Calvinism does *not* include *universal salvation*. Some revisionist Reformed theologians have moved to universalism to get God "off the hook," as it were, for predestining people to hell. But the classical Calvinist doctrine, beginning really with Augustine, includes *double predestination*, which includes belief that some people, created in the image and likeness of God and loved by God, are predestined to spend eternity in hell for the greater glory of God.

Again, as with my exposition of the Calvinist doctrine of providence, I begin with Augustine. In his *Faith, Hope, and Charity*, the North African church father explicitly affirmed double predestination: "As the sovereign Good He [God] turned to good account even what was evil, for the condemnation of those whom He has justly predestined to punishment, and for the salvation of those whom He has mercifully predestined to grace."[43] A key word here is "justly." In what sense is God just in predestining people to hell? Augustine argued that God is just because those who spend eternity in hell deserve it because they "desired what God does not want," yet he adds that God wills that they desire what God does not want.[44]

This is an Achilles' heel of Augustinian-Calvinism—that its doctrine of providence requires that even an evil will is predetermined by God to be evil, while its doctrine of election includes that some human beings (the reprobate) deserve eternal damnation because they disobey God and go against his will. This is impossible because it is illogical. Their disobedience contributes to the greater glory of God and is foreordained and rendered certain by God and yet for that they are condemned for eternity to hell.

I now turn to Edwards, perhaps the most influential Calvinist theologian after Calvin (at least for Americans). In his treatise *The Great Christian Doctrine of Original Sin*, the Puritan preacher taught that God rendered the fall of humanity into sin certain according to his eternal plan. "For God . . . to have the disposal of this affair [the fall], as to withhold those influences, without which nature will be corrupt, is not to be the *author of sin*."[45] All one can say is "It isn't?" Here's more: "The first arising or existing of that evil disposition in the heart of Adam, was by God's *permission*; who

---

[43] Augustine, *Faith, Hope, and Charity*, 95.

[44] Augustine, 95.

[45] Jonathan Edwards, "The Great Christian Doctrine of Original Sin Defended," in *The Works of Jonathan Edwards*, vol. 3, *Original Sin*, ed. Clyde A. Holbrook (New Haven, CT: Yale University Press, 1970), 383–84; emphasis original.

could have prevented it, if he had pleased, by giving such influences of his spirit, as would have been absolutely effectual to hinder it; which, it is plain fact, he did withhold."[46] In other words, according to Edwards, God did not directly cause or force Adam (and all his posterity) to sin, but he rendered it certain according to his plan and design. The fall was foreordained and rendered certain. The editor of this treatise, Clyde A. Holbrook, concluded that for Edwards, "it must be, then, that God in his wisdom counts a necessary evil nature subject to moral blame."[47]

In his treatise *Freedom of the Will*, Edwards argued that God "orders evil" and only God may do that because he is the "lord and owner of the universe."[48] And he asserted that God ordered the first man's circumstances, such that sin would infallibly follow assuming God withheld divine influence.[49] In spite of that, however, the reprobates' eternal suffering in hell is deserved because of their "evil disposition," which God rendered certain and chose not to heal. No one doubts that Edwards believed in double predestination—that God sovereignly and unconditionally selects some fallen, sinful humans to save and others not to save. In his *Dissertation Concerning the End for Which God Created the World*, Edwards left no doubt that everything happens according to God's plan and will *for his glory*—including sin, evil, and the reprobation of the wicked.[50]

Hodge also taught double predestination, including divine reprobation of some sinners to hell according to his good pleasure and not because of anything he saw in them other than their sin. Agreeing with Calvin, Hodge argued that out of the mass of sinful perdition that is humanity, God selected some to save unconditionally. He could have saved all but chose not to. The damnation of the reprobate is the "just recompense for their sins."[51] This must be received and interpreted, however, in light of Hodge's doctrine of meticulous providence, in which the fall of humanity and all its consequences are parts of God's design. "If, therefore, sin occurs, it was God's design that it should occur. If misery follows in the train of sin, such was God's purpose. If some men only are saved, while others perish, such must have entered into the all

---

[46] Edwards, 3:393; emphasis original.

[47] Clyde A. Holbrook, "Editor's Introduction" to Edwards, *Original Sin*, 3:46.

[48] Edwards, *The Works of Jonathan Edwards*, 1:411.

[49] Edwards, 1:413.

[50] Jonathan Edwards, "Two Dissertations: 1. Concerning the End for Which God Created the World," in *The Works of Jonathan Edwards*, vol. 8, *Ethical Writings*, ed. P. Ramsey (New Haven, CT: Yale University Press, 1989), 3:405–536.

[51] Hodge, *Systematic Theology*, 2:333.

comprehending purpose of God."[52] Hodge anticipated objections, especially to the doctrine of reprobation—that God purposefully passed over some sinners he could have saved and left them to their "just recompense." He used the *tu quoque* argument ("you, too"), saying that all Christians believe God permitted the fall and sin and the eternal damnation of some sinners he could have saved. "It is just as difficult to reconcile to our natural ideas of God that He, with absolute control over all creatures, should allow so many of them to perish eternally as that He should save some and not others. The difficulty is in both cases the same. God does not prevent the perdition of those who, beyond doubt, He has the power to save."[53]

What Hodge overlooked is the belief of non-Calvinists that although he is omnipotent, God *could not save unrepentant sinners* because to do so would violate the nature of love seeking communion. He also overlooked his own doctrine of providence in which sin was foreordained and rendered certain. Non-Calvinists do not believe that. We believe in God's foreknowledge but not in God's foreordination of sin and evil. If Hodge is right, the reprobate sinner was indirectly *caused by God* to sin and not repent. That sheds a terrible light on God (or would if it were true!).

Hodge's doctrine of double predestination is impossible because, by his own account of what is possible and not possible, it makes God the doer of wrong, unless, of course, whatever God does is right just because God does it, or "wrong" means something totally contrary to any intuition we have of right and wrong.

Calvin, Edwards, and Hodge agreed entirely about double predestination and that God is good even if he chooses to save some of those he determined to be sinners and leaves others to their deserved fate in hell. Hodge especially stands out as making clear that, for him, *God could have saved all people.* He means that God is omnipotent, but to fulfill his plan and purpose of leaving some sinners unsaved to suffer in the flames of hell for eternity, he could not save them. That's because, they all agree, hell is necessary for the full manifestation of God's glory. God's attribute of justice could not be manifest fully without hell as punishment for wicked disobedience to God. All of them believe that God wills to be done, and renders certain, that which he commands not be done. Again, this is strictly impossible because it contradicts the claim that God is not the author of sin and evil and the claim that God does no wrong. For all of them, God is the ultimate cause of sin and evil and eternal suffering in hell even if he only "renders them certain" according to a foreordained plan

---

[52] Hodge, 2:332.
[53] Hodge, 2:349.

that he freely designed. This behavior would never be called good and would always be called wrong—period. That these Calvinist theologians claim it is good and not wrong is a mere assertion that has no connection with anything else we know as good and wrong. Again, in this context of belief, "God is good" becomes meaningless, uninformative, impossible.

Reformed theologian Boettner repeated and went further (than his predecessors) in his strong affirmation of double predestination, which, of course, is required by his doctrine of meticulous providence expounded earlier. In *The Reformed Doctrine of Predestination*, he averred that who is saved and who is not saved is "the sovereign choice of God" that is totally independent of "creaturely will."[54] He even went so far as to claim that "it was the sovereign choice of God which brought the gospel to the people of Europe and later to America, while the people of the east, and north, and south were left in darkness."[55] God, Boettner argued, simply has the right to save some and not others.[56] "The reason God did not choose all to eternal life was not because He did not wish to save all, but that for reasons which we cannot fully explain a universal choice would have been inconsistent with His perfect righteousness."[57]

Not only is conversion "a peculiar and sovereign gift of God,"[58] but reprobation is also "of God."[59] "We believe that from all eternity God has intended to leave some of Adam's posterity in their sins, and that the decisive factor in the life of each is to be found only in God's will."[60] "This," Boettner conceded, "is admittedly an unpleasant doctrine."[61] Not only is it unpleasant, however; it is impossible. It portrays God as monstrous, as doing wrong, as being the author of sin and evil. There can be no escaping it. Boettner attempted to escape it by saying that the reprobate deserve their damnation because they "will not come to Christ; yet if they have a will to come, it is God who works the will in them."[62] So why doesn't God work that will in everyone? Finally, Boettner comes to the point: "The condemnation of the non-elect is designed primarily to furnish an eternal exhibition, before men and angels, of God's

---

[54] Boettner, *Predestination*, 87.
[55] Boettner, 87.
[56] Boettner, 95.
[57] Boettner, 97.
[58] Boettner, 102.
[59] Boettner, 104.
[60] Boettner, 104.
[61] Boettner, 108.
[62] Boettner, 115.

hatred of sin, or, in other words, it is to be an eternal manifestation of the justice of God. . . . This decree displays one of the divine attributes which apart from it could never have been adequately appreciated."[63]

A question immediately arises: Wasn't the cross of Jesus Christ a sufficient manifestation of the justice of God, of God's hatred of sin, the perfect display of God's attribute of justice? If not, why not? Doesn't Boettner's (and other Calvinists') claim about the necessity of reprobation and hell for the perfect manifestation of God's justice and righteousness diminish the cross? It does.

For Boettner, as for previous Calvinist prototypes, double predestination—including the non-election, or reprobation, of certain individuals—follows necessarily from his doctrine of providence. And yet he seemed to forget that for his doctrine of providence, it is God who designs, ordains, and renders certain absolutely everything without exception, necessarily including the thoughts and motives of each individual's mind and heart. Even if he or another Calvinist would say that sin and evil arise not from God but from human nature, the fact that God designed the fall and rendered it certain, even if only by "withholding goodness and grace," makes God the ultimate cause of sin and evil. Or would they say that the first evil inclination arose by itself independently of God? If so, that would tear a hole so large in their doctrine of meticulous providence that it would undermine it entirely.

My conversations with Calvinist theologians often lead to this "escape clause"—that God did not cause the first evil inclination in a creature, whether Satan or Adam, but simply permitted it. But is that really allowed by their doctrine of providence, which is absolute and all-encompassing? Even if it arose without divine causation, it necessarily arose as part of God's positive will; God wanted it to happen and rendered it certain by withholding the goodness and grace the creature needed not to form an evil inclination. Again, there is no human analogy in which such behavior would be excused. A person who renders another person's crime certain, however that may be done, is just as guilty, if not more guilty, than the criminal. In fact, in such a case, most juries would acquit the committer of the crime and hold the person who rendered his act responsible and guilty.

R. C. Sproul repeated Boettner's doctrine of reprobation: "Our final destination, heaven or hell, is decided by God not only before we get there, but before we are even born. [Predestination] teaches that our ultimate destiny is in the hands of God."[64]

---

[63] Boettner, 117.
[64] Sproul, *Chosen by God*, 22.

Then, however, Sproul attempted to rescue God's reputation by simply asserting that God is not the author of sin.[65] It should be noted here that Sproul strongly criticized *contradictions* in theology. "For Christians to embrace both poles of a blatant contradiction is to commit intellectual suicide and to slander the Holy Spirit. The Holy Spirit is not the author of confusion."[66] And yet he argued that God is *just* in sending people he predestined to sin and not repent to hell.[67] That, because they deserve it. He even went so far as to affirm that "at every point of choice we are free and self-determined."[68] How this is consistent with his doctrine of providence is more than a mystery; it isn't consistent. Here Sproul fell into contradiction even as he attempted to avoid it by defining "free and self-determined" as consistent with God's determination of the necessity of all things.

Finally (about Sproul), he attempted to say in what sense God is *love*: "God is 'for' his elect in a special way, displaying his love for them. He turns his face away from those wicked people who are not the objects of his special grace. Those whom he loves with his 'love of complacency' receive his mercy. Those whom he 'hates' receive his justice. No one is treated in an unjust manner."[69]

What kind of love is this that could save everyone but positively decides not to? What kind of love is consistent with selecting some people to rescue when all could be rescued? John Wesley said in his *Predestination Calmly Considered* that this is such a love as makes the blood run cold![70]

Sproul claimed that his Calvinist doctrine of predestination did not involve a contradiction. However, it did and does. That is because it contradicts his doctrine of providence, which is all-encompassing, exhaustive, and comprehensive. Everything that happens, including sin and evil, including every atom's and molecule's movement, is under the direct control of God. Carry that over to his doctrine of sin and evil and punishment in hell. All of that must also be willed and rendered certain by God. Thus, contrary to what Sproul said, God, in his doctrine of predestination, is the author of sin and evil.

What about Paul Helm? I have already described and critiqued his doctrine of providence, which is the strongest one possible. To repeat from Helm himself: "Not

---

[65] Sproul, 31.
[66] Sproul, 41.
[67] Sproul, 38.
[68] Sproul, 59.
[69] Sproul, *What Is Reformed Theology?*, 161.
[70] Wesley, *Predestination Calmly Considered*, 33 (see chap. 8, n. 33).

only is every atom and molecule, every thought and desire, kept in being by God, but every twist and turn of each of these is under the direct control of God."[71] Keep that in mind now as I exegete his doctrine of predestination. On page 119 of *Providence* the British Baptist philosopher and theologian averred that *providence includes predestination*. Of course it does; it must. Helm affirmed double predestination while falling back on the language of "permission" to express God's relationship to the reprobate. He permits them to do evil and thereby deserve hell. However, "His permission is 'willing permission'."[72] The context makes clear that by "willing permission" Helm *means* effectual permission—permission that renders evil acts and damnation certain. According to him, God "commands men and women to love their neighbors while at the same time ordaining actions which are malicious or hateful."[73] The reprobate, then, could not be otherwise than they are and cannot act otherwise than they do—given Helm's description of God's agency in *determining their evil actions* by *withholding the goodness and grace they would need not to form morally deficient motives and act accordingly.*[74]

A profound contradiction lies at the heart of Helm's doctrines of providence and predestination. It is the same one that lies at the heart of every consistent and classical Calvinist's view of these doctrines. It is that God is the all-determining reality who decides and determines everything, including the thoughts and motives and actions of every creature, and yet sin and evil cannot be attributed to him but must only be attributed to creatures. This combination of ideas is impossible, given Hodge's first principles, because they contradict each other. This combination is not merely a "mystery," as most Calvinists claim, but it is a sheer contradiction—appeals to secondary causes and "withholdings" notwithstanding.

Exactly what *kind* of contradiction is this? Perhaps not a technically logical contradiction but certainly an intuitive, experiential contradiction because we cannot think of any analogy in human experience. No human act similar to God's (in this context of evil and reprobation) would ever be called "good" by anyone not a moral imbecile. Helm anticipated this critique of his view and argued that God's goodness must bear some analogy to the highest and best ideas of goodness held by human persons. "The goodness of God must bear some positive relation to the sorts

---

71 Helm, *Providence*, 22.
72 Helm, 101.
73 Helm, 133.
74 Helm, 171.

of human actions we regard as good. Otherwise, why ascribe *goodness* to God?"[75] Exactly true! But what Helm failed to explain is *how* his view of God's relationship to evil and reprobation bears any positive relation to the sorts of human actions we regard as good. In other words, even by Helm's own admission, given God's ordaining and rendering certain evil and eternal damnation, "God is good" is uninformative, despite his denials.

Turning now to Piper, I will focus on his view of God and the reprobate, whom he preferred to call the "non-elect." In *The Pleasures of God* Piper made crystal clear his belief in double predestination. "Election is not based on what someone does after birth. It is free and unconditional."[76] Election is for the glory of God. "Israel and the church are chosen by God to make a name for him in the world."[77] "He [God] loves a worldwide reputation."[78] Everything that happens, including the death of the wicked, the non-elect, pleases God even if it also grieves him.[79] God delights in carrying out his justice even as he grieves over having to punish the guilty.[80] Here we need to stop and ask Piper why the non-elect are guilty. According to his doctrine of God's all-determining providence, they are guilty (as demonstrated earlier) because God foreordained and rendered certain their sin and rejection of his mercy.

The issue here is God's character, so my focus will be on Piper's attempted explanation of God's goodness in view of the foreordained reprobation of the non-elect. According to him, God loves the non-elect and has sincere compassion for them.[81] God, he says, has "a true compassion, which is yet restrained, in the case of the non-elect, by consistent and holy reasons, from taking the form of a volition to regenerate."[82] One has to wonder what reasons those might be. The only reasonable answer, based on what Piper says about God's motive in everything, is God's glory and reputation. But what kind of reputation does that give God? What is glorious, loving, or compassionate about denying salvation to some when God could save all? Or perhaps Piper believes God can't save all. What does that mean for God's omnipotence?

---

[75] Helm, 167.

[76] Piper, *Pleasures of God*, 132.

[77] Piper, 106.

[78] Piper, 102.

[79] Piper, 66.

[80] Piper, 66–67.

[81] Piper, 144, 148.

[82] Piper, 145. In the context, Piper quoted the Reformed theologian Robert Lewis Dabney (1820–98).

According to Piper, God has "complex feelings and motives."[83] "I affirm that God loves the world with a deep compassion that desires their salvation; yet I also affirm that he has chosen from before the foundation of the world whom he will save from sin."[84] He doesn't say "and whom he will not save from sin," but that is implied. What about God's love? "There is a general love of God that he bestows on all his creatures," but this is *not* the love God has for the elect.[85] Presumably Piper agrees with an unknown Calvinist who famously said that God loves everyone in some ways but only some in every way. Piper needs to answer what kind of love this is, that presumably could save everyone but chooses not to. The apparent answer is *love for his own glory*. According to him, God loves his own glory above all things.[86] How can God love those he fore-ordained before the foundation of the world to suffer eternally in hell for his glory? Because they deserve it? How do they deserve it if they could not do otherwise than sin?

Jonathan Edwards famously distinguished between *natural ability not to sin*, which all people have, and *moral ability not to sin*, which no one has apart from God's supernatural grace. But the question for both Edwards and Piper (Piper refers to Edwards as "the friend of my soul"[87]) is why God withholds the moral ability not to sin (or better said, to repent and believe) from anyone. The answer is, again, as always, *for his glory*. God's sole supreme goal and purpose in everything is to manifest his glory by revealing all his attributes, including justice through wrath and punishment.

One Calvinist attempt to rescue God's reputation in the face of his reprobation of the non-elect is to say, as did R. C. Sproul, that there is no "equal ultimacy" between God's decree of election and God's decree of reprobation.[88] "The Reformed view teaches that God positively or actively intervenes in the lives of the elect to insure their salvation. The rest of mankind God leaves to themselves. He does not create unbelief in their hearts. That unbelief is already there. . . . In the Calvinist view the decree of election is positive; the decree of reprobation is negative."[89]

Is this not a distinction without a difference? It is. In any human situation, a person who could save all dying persons but chooses some to save and allows others to die would be asked why. If he said that he didn't choose to let the dead die in the same way

---

[83] Piper, 146.
[84] Piper, 146.
[85] Piper, 148.
[86] Piper, 248.
[87] Piper, 175.
[88] Sproul, *Chosen by God*, 142.
[89] Sproul, 142–43.

he chose to save the ones he saved, absolutely no one would be impressed. He would universally be accused of sophistry and held responsible for not saving everyone.

Sproul admitted that for the reprobate God "negatively" chooses not to save; "unbelief is already there." But who put it there, or rendered it certain that it would be there? The general "picture" in Calvinism is that unbelief simply developed out of Adam's (and his posterity's) nature when God withheld or withdrew his preserving goodness and grace. Wasn't God's decree to withdraw or withhold his preserving goodness and grace a positive decree? And when God decrees not to give faith to some sinners, how is that not a positive decree? Calling it "negative" appears to be a ploy only, a ploy to pull the wool over the eyes of any sensitive person looking into Calvinism to make him or her think "God is good" means something true.

The plain fact of the matter is, "God is good" means nothing in classical, consistent Calvinism. It is uninformative. It is either a tautology like saying "God is God," or it means that whatever God does is good just because God does it—in which case "good" can mean anything God does. In which case it still is not informative.

I will go further and add that *if* God were to decide and behave as classical, consistent Calvinism claims, he would not be worthy of worship and would hardly be distinguishable from the devil.

When I say these things, many Calvinists think (and claim) that I am speaking blasphemy, but that is false because God is not as classical, consistent Calvinism describes him. My point is that if God were as classical, consistent Calvinism describes him, he would not be worshipful and would be hardly distinguishable from the devil. The reason I am not committing blasphemy is that God is not as classical, consistent Calvinism describes him.

I have also said that if God were as classical, consistent Calvinism describes him, I would fear him but not worship him. What makes God worshipful is his absolute, unconditional goodness, which is absolute, unconditional *love*. Despite their attempts to rescue God's loving character, classical, consistent Calvinists cannot convince me they are describing a loving God. As Paul Helm said, God's goodness cannot be entirely different from every kind of goodness known to humanity.

It is simply *impossible* that God, the source of all being and meaning, should be a cosmic narcissist who takes pleasure in the eternal torment of those he predestined to hell. It is simply *impossible* that God, the source of all being and meaning, should be a cosmic narcissist who cares more about his "glory" (whatever that even means in classical, consistent Calvinism) than about the good of every creature.

Even Jonathan Edwards seemed to realize this in his philosophical treatise on *The Nature of True Virtue* where he defined "true virtue" as "*benevolence to being in general. Or perhaps, to speak more accurately, it is that consent, propensity and union of heart to being in general, which is immediately exercised in a general good will.*"[90] It is impossible that God be the author of sin and evil, as Edwards admitted in *Freedom of the Will*, and also be truly virtuous—given his own definition of true virtue. As I have demonstrated here, every classical, consistent Calvinist implicitly makes God the author of sin and evil and cause (however indirectly) of innocent suffering. Any who argue that there is no such thing as innocent suffering cannot say such while standing at the gates of Auschwitz.[91]

God is worthy of worship because he is good; he is good because he is love (1 John 4:8) and he loves the whole world (John 3:16–17); and "world" cannot mean only some people from every tribe and nation as some Calvinists claim. That is a lame ploy that simply cannot be taken seriously, in light of verses such as 1 Tim 2:4, which says that God wants "everyone" (*hos pantas anthropos*) to be saved.

The God described by classical, consistent Calvinism is hardly distinguishable from the devil insofar as he wills many of his creatures, created in his own image and likeness, to spend eternity in hell. The devil wants all there forever; the God of Calvinism wants many to be there forever.

At this point many Calvinists react by saying, in some words, if not these very words, "Whatever God does is good just because God does it." Again, that makes "good" equivocal, meaningless, and "God is good" uninformative. It is a desperate expression of the philosophy known as *voluntarism* (John Duns, aka Duns Scotus) that makes God's character unknowable. Jesus Christ came (among other things) to reveal God's character, and Jesus wept over Jerusalem when it rejected him (Luke 19:41–44). Why would he weep if he, being God, knew that Jerusalem's rejection of him and his mission was foreordained by God for his greater glory? No doubt Piper would appeal to God's complex emotional life in which he grieves over the fulfillment of his will—when that fulfillment involves sin, evil, reprobation, and eternal damnation. But that introduces a conflict into God's own being. Why would God (in the person of Jesus and in the Old Testament story of Hosea) grieve over that which brings him glory?

---

[90] Jonathan Edwards, *The Nature of True Virtue* (Ann Arbor, MI: University of Michigan Press, 1969), 3 (emphasis added).

[91] I have many times attributed this saying to German theologian Jürgen Moltmann, and I confirmed it with him in private correspondence in 2018. However, he did not point me to the exact location where he wrote it.

A profound contradiction exists deep within classical, consistent (or trying to be consistent) Calvinism. Some years ago, a leading American Calvinist theologian wrote that a certain theological error diminished the glory of God. I asked him if he believed that God foreordained that error for his glory and, of course, he said yes. I then asked him how something that God foreordained (and rendered certain) for his glory could diminish his glory, and I did not receive a helpful answer. He simply said that had already been solved by theodicy (any defense of God in the face of evil). He was wrong; it hasn't been solved. It is an unsolvable conundrum. In fact, it is impossible. An idea cannot both diminish God's glory and also glorify God.

People often ask me whether I think Calvinists are Christians. I say that they are. That puzzles them. How can people who have such a distorted belief about God be Christians? I offer two answers. First, what they say they believe is really impossible so I can't take it seriously. The impossible cannot really be believed. So they are true Christians due to a *felicitous inconsistency*—felicitous in that one side of the inconsistency is their confession that God is good and loving and kind and compassionate. When I meet or interact with them, I take that side of their inconsistent theology seriously and bracket out and set aside the other side—so I can embrace them as fellow Christians. They really do believe that God is good, loving, kind, and compassionate. That they contradict that with their view of God's sovereignty, divine determinism, is extremely unfortunate because it makes it difficult for me to take their intellects seriously, and I worry that some of the young, impressionable minds they influence will latch on to the wrong side of their felicitous inconsistency and picture God—to themselves and to others—as not loving, kind, or compassionate.

Second, we—they and I—believe in and worship the same God, even as we have different pictures of what he is like. I compare this to a group of resistance fighters in France during World War II. Some were Communists and at least hoped that their leader-in-exile was a Communist. Others, who fought alongside them, were Republicans and Democrats who despised Communism and at least hoped that their leader-in-exile was not a Communist. The two parties looked hopefully and faithfully to the same leader-in-exile but disagreed passionately about his political and economic views. Eventually, of course, one party turned out to be right and the other party turned out to be wrong. This is what will happen when Christ returns; Calvinists will discover that their view of God's sovereignty in relation to sin and evil and innocent suffering was false. I do not hold that against them so long as they do not go so far as to say that God actually is the cause of sin and evil. What they say *implies* that, but they deny that they believe it.

12

Determinism and Human Freedom

—— John Laing ——

Freedom is a much-cherished ideal in the liberal West, so much so that it is often cited as the primary reason for insurrections and wars. Consider the American Revolution: schoolchildren are typically taught that the famous words of Patrick Henry—"Give me liberty or give me death!"—served as the battle cry for the formation of a new nation founded on the radical idea of a free people, but the notion of freedom is a tricky one. While we all seem to agree that it is somehow tied to the individual will and choice, articulating that relationship and what it really means for questions of autonomy, responsibility, capability, and the like—and more importantly, for theological beliefs regarding God, humanity, sin, and salvation—has proven exceedingly difficult (and controversial) for philosophers and theologians alike. These challenges are compounded by the mischaracterizations that pervade the literature and discussion, whether in sermons and popular theological writings or in strictly academic works on the topic.[1]

---

[1] For example, a common misconception about Calvinism is that it denies free will. See Nathan Finn, "Southern Baptist Calvinism: Setting the Record Straight," in *Southern Baptist*

In this essay, I hope to present the case for a particular understanding of freedom, known as "libertarian freedom." I will begin with some simple definitions but throughout will also note, at appropriate times, the use of terms that are misleading or that can cause confusion for readers. I will then discuss Calvinist challenges to libertarian freedom, followed by a presentation of some of the strongest arguments in its favor. I will conclude with an examination of two theological concepts that have a significant impact on the debate.

Determinism, Incompatibilism, Libertarianism, and Compatibilism

Determinism is the claim that for every event or action there are previous events, circumstances, or actions that are its sufficient conditions or causes, so that it is impossible that the event or action not occur.[2] Christians disagree over whether such a view can be reconciled with human freedom and whether it is a proper way to understand God's providential care of the universe and sovereignty over history. Those who see it as precluding human freedom are called incompatibilists, while those who believe determinism and freedom may be reconciled are called compatibilists. Incompatibilists typically hold to a view of freedom called libertarian freedom, while compatibilists hold to (the aptly named) compatibilist freedom. Most Calvinists hold to compatibilist freedom, while most non-Calvinists are indeterminists and thus hold to libertarian freedom.

Libertarian freedom is commonly thought to include two features: (1) the ability to choose among alternatives (at least two), understood in such a way that it may be properly said that the individual could have chosen otherwise; and (2) some kind of self-determination, meaning that the choice or action originates within the individual such that nothing outside of his power causes or serves to explain the choice.[3]

Dialogue, 171–92 (see intro., n. 27). An equally common misconception about Arminianism is that it makes God subservient to humans. See, for example, Robert A. Peterson and Michael D. Williams, *Why I Am Not an Arminian*, 140 (see chap. 2, n. 8).

[2] William Hasker, *Metaphysics: Constructing a World View* (Downers Grove, IL: InterVarsity, 1983), 32.

[3] Some philosophers have argued that only the latter feature is necessary for libertarian freedom to be present, but since so much of the discussion has centered around choice and ability to do otherwise, we will refrain from entering these murky waters.

Compatibilist freedom likewise is thought to include two features: (1) the ability to choose as one sees fit, understood in such a way that the individual is wholly responsible for his choice; and (2) a compatibility with determinism, meaning that those choices could not have been other than what they, indeed, were. Most commonly, the person's beliefs, desires, character, and such are thought to dictate or constrain his live options to only one. Thus, under compatibilist principles, individuals always choose in accordance with their greatest desires and *could not have chosen otherwise*, while under libertarian principles, individuals choose between competing alternatives and *could have chosen differently*.

Compatibilist Arguments Against Libertarianism

Compatibilists have lodged numerous complaints against libertarian freedom in philosophical and theological tracts. In what follows, I will examine the most popular and most substantial of these critiques. The first, and most concerning to evangelical Christians, is the claim that it conflicts with the clear teachings of the Bible. Next, I will examine the largely philosophical arguments against its coherence and logical consistency. I will then return to two important theological issues: whether it compromises divine foreknowledge and whether it may be reconciled with divine sovereignty and providence. I will conclude that none of these complaints succeed.

Compatibilist Complaint #1: Libertarianism Is Unbiblical

In his magisterial work on theology proper, Calvinist theologian John Frame offered an extended critique of libertarian freedom, based largely on Jonathan Edwards's *Freedom of the Will.* Frame began by noting that Scripture does not explicitly teach the existence of libertarianism, Scripture does not indicate that God places any value on libertarian freedom, and it is based in philosophical concepts regarding personhood and the will. He further complained that proponents of libertarianism do not try to demonstrate its truth by means of direct exegesis, but only through indirect argument from other biblical concepts such as human responsibility and "the divine commands, exhortations, and pleadings that imply human responsibility."[4] One response to this

---

[4] John Frame, *The Doctrine of God: A Theology of Lordship* (Phillipsburg, PA: P&R, 2002), 140.

line of argumentation is to simply point out that all the same objections apply to compatibilist freedom.

As a case in point, consider Calvinist theologian Bruce Ware's use of the biblical principle of dual agency to argue for compatibilist and against libertarian freedom. According to Ware, scenarios in which God takes credit for the free actions of humans require us to infer both human choice and divine determination. He therefore concluded that determinism and freedom are compatible and offers several examples as proof.

In one example, Ware drew on the Old Testament theme of God's judgment of rebellious Israel through conquest by foreign nations. Any number of examples could be given, though Ware opted for Isaiah's description of the Assyrian conquest of Israel (Isa 10:5–15).[5] Since it is God who raised up the Assyrians and judged his people through those invasions, Ware reasoned, divine determination must be inferred. Since the Assyrians did exactly as they wished and did not intend to be used for righteous purposes (Isa 10:7), they acted freely and were justly condemned. A proper response to the question of who brought destruction upon Israel must include both the Assyrians and God: "The free and responsible actions of the Assyrians . . . is fully compatible with God's determination to raise up Assyria. . . . Divine determination and human freedom, then, are compatible."[6]

In another example, Ware drew upon the Exodus narrative where the departing Israelites despoiled the Egyptians. God clearly stated that he would give the Israelites favor in the eyes of the Egyptians so they would give of their wealth (Exod 3:21–22; 11:3; 12:35–36). As Ware saw it, this is a clear case where both determinism and free will are required; God determined the events to happen, but the people freely chose to act as they did. Ware is quick to point out that God's activity with respect to the Egyptians was not mere foreknowledge, an obvious reference to accounts of providence that incorporate libertarian human freedom and suggest God uses some form of foreknowledge to guide his providential decisions: "So, it is not that God merely foreknows what the Egyptians will do, but God determines ('I will give this people favor') what the Egyptians will do."[7] Ware concluded, then, that God determined the Egyptians' actions even while they did what they most wanted to do and that a

---

[5] See Ware, *God's Greater Glory*, 83–84, 88 (see chap. 4, n. 83); "The Compatibility of Determinism and Human Freedom," in Barrett and Nettles, *Whomever He Wills*, 215–17 (see intro., n. 22).

[6] Ware, "Determinism and Human Freedom," 217.

[7] Ware, 214.

complete explanation of why the Israelites left with Egyptian wealth requires appeal to both the free choices of the Egyptian women and divine causation of their favor toward the Israelites.

One problem with Ware's argument is that he seems to confuse "divine determination" and "causal determinism," as seen in his closing statement on the Exodus encounter: "But be clear on this: the first statement is one of human freedom expressed by those Egyptian women, and the second statement is one of the determination of God to bring something to pass through these Egyptian women that he predicted he would do; hence human freedom (of the Egyptian women giving of their wealth) and divine determination (God causing them to favor the Israelites) are compatible."[8] Most incompatibilists could agree with the first part of the quote and could even speak in similar terms about the second part, so long as it were interpreted in light of the first. The shift in language of *causal determination* to that of *bringing about free actions* is precisely the kind of distinction incompatibilists have employed to hold to both robust human freedom and strong divine providence. Most proponents of libertarian freedom agree that God can bring about events he has predicted/foretold by means of the free actions of his creatures, but they do not affirm that the only way he can do so is by causally determining those free actions. Ware seems to have assumed this to be the case and slipped it (unstated) into his argument. Much of Ware's essay begs the question.

I have often used Habakkuk's prophecy about God's use of the Babylonians to judge Israel as evidence of my own view of providence, which combines meticulous divine sovereignty with libertarian human freedom. After Habakkuk complained about the sinfulness of Israel and God's seeming inactivity, God responded by telling him that he himself will do something so incredible, so unfathomable, that Habakkuk would not believe it if he had not heard it directly from God (Hab 1:5). God will raise up the Babylonians to judge Judah (1:6–11a) but will then judge them for their impetuousness (v. 6b), self-reliance (v. 7), violence (v. 9), and haughtiness (vv. 10–11). God can use the Babylonians to judge and correct his people (v. 12), but he cannot look favorably upon evil (v. 13). In all this, I am sure, Ware would agree with me, but I take God's displeasure with the Babylonians to indicate that he had nothing to do with their choices, actions, and desires. Although he knew they would attack the Israelites in the circumstances that prevailed, he did not necessarily begin a causal chain that would result in their developing so that they would act in that

---

[8] Ware, 215.

manner. Further, I hold that God may have been unable to prevent the Babylonians' actions without violating their freedom (though that was certainly his prerogative). I doubt Ware can say the same thing, since Calvinist thought characteristically sees God as the starting point for the chain of causes leading to human action, and typically affirms that God could have ensured that persons develop differently so that they would (compatibilistically) freely act differently. Of course, Ware could justifiably accuse me of begging the question of libertarian freedom in the passage, and he would be correct, but that just illustrates the point that both views are subject to at least part of Frame's critique.

Another response to Frame's charge is to admit that much of the discussion surrounding human freedom has taken place in philosophical circles and to offer something of a biblical argument supporting libertarian freedom. Admittedly, we cannot point to a proof text stating that libertarianism is the correct view of freedom, but this is not to say the Bible has nothing to say about freedom, choice, or the will. In fact, many biblical themes at least suggest libertarian creaturely freedom, and many verses, on the most natural reading, seem to teach it quite clearly. There is not sufficient space to cover them all here, but what follows is a framework and some representative passages for consideration.

Any examination of the biblical concept of free will should probably begin with humanity's first choice: whether or not to eat the forbidden fruit. The story of humanity's fall certainly seems to allow for libertarian freedom. In his initial instructions to Adam and Eve, God told them they may freely eat from any tree in the garden except the tree of the knowledge of good and evil, implying that they had the ability to choose what to eat, not only with respect to sinning or not, but also with respect to the various other fruiting trees in Eden (Gen 2:16).[9] Eve chose to eat the fruit because it was desirable (3:6), which could substantiate claims of either libertarian or compatibilist freedom. But of particular interest are the excuses both Adam and Eve proffered: Adam deflected blame to either God or Eve, or both, while Eve charged the serpent with her guilt. Both attempts to abrogate responsibility failed, as God punished both Adam (vv. 17–19) and Eve (v. 16). Eve's attempt to deny responsibility because she was tricked did not work, presumably because she knowingly and willfully violated God's command, even if the serpent deceived her regarding the

---

[9] Too much should not be made of the term "freely," sometimes included in translations, as the Hebrew term has less to do with choice or ability and more to do with permission and access to the abundance of fruit available to them in the garden.

consequences (v. 3). In Adam's punishment, the explicit charge is that Adam listened to his wife rather than obey God, which strongly implies that Adam could have chosen otherwise, exercising libertarian freedom.

Interestingly, none other than John Calvin seemed to believe Adam had libertarian freedom with respect to eating the fruit: "Adam, therefore, might have stood if he chose, since it was only by his own will that he fell . . . he had a free choice of good and evil. . . . There was soundness of mind and freedom of will to choose the good."[10] He claims that Adam had a weak and pliable will—and was thereby susceptible to temptation—but a will still strong enough to resist, if he had so chosen. Thus, no one can complain that God did not give him a fair chance, for God created him with a will able to resist evil and choose the good, and God was under no obligation to ensure that Adam would not choose to sin.[11] So Calvin saw libertarian freedom as a viable option, a legitimate type of freedom that one can possess and that is tied to moral responsibility, though he argued that Adam was a special case because the fall destroyed this very type of freedom in humanity.[12] Thus, many Calvinists agree that Adam had libertarian freedom while they deny that we do, so other passages must be considered.

At heart, the Bible is about God's plan and its realization through covenants with humanity.[13] Many of the covenants are viewed as a grant or unconditional in nature, wherein God confers a blessing upon an individual or group with no requisite obligations to him or them. There are good exegetical reasons for questioning this understanding, as faithfulness is always required of the recipients. Unfortunately, there is not space to present a detailed argument here. Suffice it to say that both the Abrahamic and Davidic covenants are offered unilaterally by God but under the conditions that God knew Abraham and David were, and would be, men of faith.[14]

---

[10] Calvin, *Institutes*, trans. Beveridge, 1:169 (1.15.8) (see chap. 2, n. 2). See also John Calvin, *The Bondage and Liberation of the Will: A Defense of the Orthodox Doctrine of Human Choice against Pighius*, ed. A. N. S. Lane, trans. G. I. Davies (Grand Rapids: Baker, 1996), 133.

[11] "For surely the Deity could not be tied down to this condition,—to make man such, that he either could not or would not sin." Calvin, *Institutes*, trans. Beveridge, 1:170 (1.15.8).

[12] Freedom of choice with respect to spiritual matters was lost because of the fall, but it was left to Jonathan Edwards to challenge the very notion of freedom of choice.

[13] There are many theories about God's purpose for creating, though the Bible does not explicitly present one. I suspect that God had multiple purposes for creating, including to bring glory to himself, to demonstrate his love, to reveal himself, and to express various aspects of his nature (e.g., creativity, aesthetics, relationality, and so forth).

[14] I have made the case for counterfactual conditional covenants (God entering into covenant relationship with persons based on God's knowledge that those persons would respond in

For a clearer presentation of libertarian freedom in Scripture, consider the jux-
taposition of blessings and curses found throughout the Mosaic covenant (e.g.,
Leviticus 26; Deuteronomy 11, 28, 30). In each case, Moses encouraged the people
to obey with promises of blessing and warned them against disobedience with threats
of punishment. For example, in Leviticus 26, God says (through Moses), "If you walk
in my statutes and keep my commandments . . . I will make my dwelling with you . . .
I will walk among you and be your God and you will be my people" (vv. 3, 11–12,
personal translation). He continues, "If you do not obey me and do not carry out my
commandments . . . I will set my face against you . . . your enemies will rule over
you. . . . I will send disease among you. . . . I will make your land desolate and scatter
you among the nations" (vv. 14, 17, 25, 32–33, personal translation).[15] The language
of Deuteronomy 30 is similarly striking. Twice God presents the people with two
options—blessing/life and curse/death—and calls the people to *choose* blessing and
life (vv. 15, 19). In both cases, Moses explicitly states that the people *can* freely choose
between these alternatives, and that it is not *too difficult* for them (v. 11).

It must be admitted there are two places that seem to indicate the Israelites are
not able to believe or choose righteousness. In the first, we are told the Lord had not
given the people hearts to know, nor eyes to see, nor ears to hear (Deut 29:4), while
in the second, Moses told the people that God will circumcise their hearts and those
of their descendants, to love the Lord with all their hearts and souls, so that they
may live (Deut 30:6). Neither suggests an inability on the part of the people. In the
first, Moses outlined the miraculous works of God revealed in the exodus and the
wilderness wandering, designed to chastise the people for their failure to trust God.
His reference to their not having hearts to know, eyes to see, or ears to hear—far

---

faith, were he to call them) in several works. See, for example, John D. Laing, *Middle Knowledge:
Human Freedom in Divine Sovereignty* (Grand Rapids: Kregel, 2018), 304–13; John D. Laing,
"Molinism: A Biblical-Theological Analysis" (plenary address, Southwest Regional Meeting
of the Evangelical Theological Society, New Orleans, LA, 2019); John D. Laing, "Middle
Knowledge, Biblical Covenants, and the Basis of Predestination/Election" (paper presented at
the National Meeting of Evangelical Theological Society, Providence, RI, 2008).

[15] Commenting on this passage, Robert Picirilli wrote, "Who will read such a passage—and
the Bible has many like it—and say that it does not clearly speak to the possibility of choice?
The obvious purpose of the passage was to put the responsibility on Israel to choose between
the alternatives God set before them, to bless them if they chose to obey and to curse them if
they chose the way of disobedience. If we do not learn this from the whole example of Israel in
the wilderness and in Canaan, what do we learn?" Picirilli, *Free Will Revisited*, 25 (see chap. 7,
n. 120).

from reducing the blame of the Israelites by placing it on God—is meant to point to their continued disobedience. It is by their refusal to acknowledge what is right before their eyes—God's loving deliverance—that they have remained outside the Promised Land. In the second passage, the reference to circumcision of the heart serves as the culmination of God's restorative work, taking place *after*, not before, the people repent and return to him (Deut 30:2). He will bring them back from captivity, grant them many descendants, and give them success in the land (vv. 3–5), and *then* he will circumcise their hearts. There is no exegetical reason to think the circumcision of their hearts preceded their restoration; rather, it was a part of their restoration. In addition, Moses clearly stated that the commandment he had given was attainable; it was already within their hearts (vv. 11–14).[16]

There are many other passages where persons are presented with two options and the expectation is that they *really can* choose between them. For example, when Joshua received the mantle of leadership from Moses and prepared the people to enter the Promised Land, he offered them a choice between serving Yahweh or the gods of Canaan (Josh 24:15). Joshua made it clear that he intended to serve Yahweh but purposely left the choice open-ended for the people. He challenged Israel to choose Yahweh and remain faithful to him, but it would make no sense if the people could not *really* choose between the two options.[17] Similarly, when Elijah challenged the prophets of Baal and Ashtoreth at Carmel, he confronted the Israelites for their spiritual adultery: "How long will you hesitate between two opinions? If Yahweh is God, follow Him. But if Baal, follow him" (1 Kgs 18:21 HCSB). Elijah seemed to believe that the people really could choose to follow either deity, even though he clearly did not mean to suggest that they were on equal footing; he did not mean for the people to take Baal seriously. His later prayer that Yahweh would answer through miraculous fire from heaven, analogous to the fiery judgment on Sodom and Gomorrah, was meant to convey Israel's sin in allowing the prophets of Baal

---

[16] Paul referenced this passage in his discussion of salvation in the Old Testament in his letter to the Romans (Rom 10:6–8). Moses, Paul noted, was offering the gospel to the Israelites, if they would respond in faith. Some may infer from this that it therefore does not suggest the Israelites could respond in faith, but Paul went on to note the ability of the one who hears the gospel to believe in his heart and confess with his mouth that Jesus is the risen Lord (vv. 9–13).

[17] Later, Joshua seemingly referenced the inability of the people to serve God (Josh 24:19), but this is properly viewed as an admonition against falling away and to faithfulness. When the people maintained that they would serve Yahweh, Joshua warned that they were now witnesses against themselves if they were not faithful to their choice/commitment, and he exhorted them to incline their hearts toward God (vv. 22–23).

and Ashtoreth to serve Ahab's court. He hoped that God would reveal himself to the people in such a stunning way that they would know he is the true God, that Elijah is his prophet (because he had staked his life on it), and that he had "turned their hearts back" (v. 37 HCSB). The reference to God turning the hearts of the people may be thought to undermine the choice referenced before—that it indicated the people could not have refused to acknowledge Yahweh—for they seem to unanimously do so at the end of the story (v. 39). However, it need not be read this way, and could just as easily be an idiomatic expression calling attention to the people's confidence in God, since they received his revelation. In other words, it is not meant to convey that God bent their hearts so that they *could* not reject him, but rather that God had revealed himself in such a spectacular way that the people *would* not reject him; they have come to *know* that Yahweh is the true God. It is also meant to undermine the suggestion that Elijah was presenting the two options—Yahweh or Baal—as if they were equally valid. Thus, Elijah called the people to choose, and he believed they could do so, but he also hoped they would choose wisely.

A constant refrain and theme in the Prophets consisted of warnings of judgment, calls to repentance, and offers of grace. The theme was often couched in terms of a conscious choice by the people, though not stated explicitly in terms of two options. The calls to return to the Lord (Jer 4:1; Lam 3:40; Hos 6:1; Joel 2:12–13; Zech 1:3; Mal 3:7), to put away foreign gods and idols (Ezek 14:6; Jer 4:1), and to seek God and live (Amos 5:6, 14) imply the ability to do so, even though the people often do not. Some of the passages present the call in terms of conscious reflection and appeal to the intellect. For example, Jeremiah called the people to examine and reflect on their misdeeds, in hopes they would return to God (Lam 3:40), and Hosea appealed to the commonsense desire for healing and restoration as justification for the call to repent (Hos 6:1). The prophetic appeal was for the hearer to make a choice, to either heed the call or turn away, and it is evident that the people had it within their power to do either.

In the New Testament, Jesus exhorted persons to follow him and to turn from their wicked ways. In each case, he implied that the individual could respond in faith and obedience or in rebellion and sin. Take the story of the rich ruler as representative. When confronted with the requirement to keep Torah, he claimed to have faithfully and completely fulfilled all the Law, so Jesus challenged him to sell all his possessions and follow him (Matt 19:21). To be sure, Jesus knew the young man would not be willing to do so—that is why he couched the call to faith in those terms—but the text makes clear that he *could* have done so. After the young man left, Jesus lamented the difficulty the rich will have in entering the kingdom of heaven. When the disciples asked how anyone can be saved, Jesus replied, "With men this is impossible, but with God all things are possible" (v. 26 HCSB). This claim means that salvation is solely a work of God and humans cannot earn salvation through works of the law.[18] Still, there are indications that free choice was still in play with the rich ruler. Even though his refusal to follow Jesus's requirement revealed that his heart was not as pure as he contended, Jesus's words of assurance to his disciples regarding their own destinies are rooted in their faithful obedience and conscious choices to follow him (vv. 27–29). The young man could have chosen to leave everything to follow Christ, just as they had, but he chose otherwise.

The apostle Paul affirmed libertarian freedom in his letters and ministry. For example, in his letter to the Philippians, Paul noted his difficulty choosing between living and serving Christ on earth, or dying and entering Christ's presence (Phil 1:21–22). His reference to choice can be understood in two ways. It could be a way of referring to his internal competing desires. When he spoke of not knowing what to choose, he only meant to communicate that he was conflicted in heart. Both departing and remaining are appealing to him, but for different reasons. In this case, "choice" has nothing to do with freedom or the will. But it could also be a reference to Paul's lack of clarity about how to proceed, given he was imprisoned, with an impending trial, and even possible execution. Paul could fight the charges and do everything in his power to secure his release, or he could resign himself to death and prepare to greet his Savior face-to-face. In this case, Paul really had a choice, and his comments indicated he believed he could do either. He could either seek release or martyrdom, even though he was convinced that release was God's will and he should therefore pursue it (vv. 24–25).

Compatibilist Complaint #2: Libertarianism Is Incoherent

Perhaps the most common complaint against libertarianism by Calvinist detractors is that it is incoherent. There are several versions of this argument, but the two most

---

[18] The story is structured to reveal the fact that we all fall short of spiritual perfection, that unregenerate persons are literally incapable of fulfilling the law in action and heart. The final commandment Jesus cited as a requirement was to "love your neighbor as yourself" (Matt 19:19) and despite his claims to the contrary, the ruler had not kept it (v. 20). His refusal to sell his possessions and give them to the poor reveals this fact.

common are that it devolves into arbitrariness and that it violates natural laws by positing uncaused events. We will examine each in turn.

The first version of the argument claims the premises that undergird libertarian freedom make free choice arbitrary. It begins with the libertarian claim that at the moment of decision, the agent can choose between alternatives. This is correctly taken to mean that, all things being exactly as they are, the agent could have chosen differently, even though part of the conditions that persist at the time of decision are the reasons the individual had for acting as she did. Critics then argue that the same reasons she had for acting in the manner she did also serve as the reasons for acting otherwise, but this means that the reasons either have no bearing at all on the decision or violate the law of noncontradiction (reasons for both A and ~A). The result is either arbitrariness or incoherence; either way, it is fatal to libertarian freedom.[19]

There are several problems with this argument. First, it confuses the libertarian claim that the individual *could* choose other, with the idea that it is *just as likely* that she would choose other. Libertarians make no such claim. There is simply no reason to think that the ability to perform any of several actions entails their being equally likely or attractive. Second, it falsely charges that libertarians must use the same reasons for both choices, but this would make the choices not merely arbitrary; they would be utterly irrational! Rather, libertarians observe that we have different reasons for our inclinations toward various options, that those reasons are weighted differently for different persons, and that they are context specific.[20] Third (and related), the argument is based on a false dichotomy: either our reasons determine our actions, or they are arbitrary, but this does not accord with what we know about human psychology or lived reality.

The primary problem here is a misunderstanding of the role that reasons play in libertarian models. Proponents of libertarianism do not discount the influence of reasons on decision-making, even in free decisions, but they do challenge the equation of reasons and causes in much compatibilist literature and thus view the reason/action relation as explanatory, not causal.[21] An example may help clarify these distinctions.

---

[19] Ware, *God's Greater Glory*, 86.

[20] Bruce R. Reichenbach, *Divine Providence: God's Love and Human Freedom* (Eugene, OR: Cascade, 2016), 17–26.

[21] Davidson denied the distinction between reasons and causes, arguing that it is precisely the perceived causal connection between the action and the desired outcome that makes the

Suppose you are in your home office preparing a Bible study, and you feel a bit chilly. Suppose further that you come to believe that by starting a fire in the fireplace, you can both warm the air in your office and create a nice atmosphere for reflection on God's Word, and that you can do so with no ill effects on the items in your home or your family members. Having thus thought it through, you open the flue and light the fireplace. The question that needs to be answered is, What is the relationship between your lighting the fire and your feelings and beliefs about the temperature in your office? Did your feeling chilly, along with your belief that lighting the fire would address your discomfort, *cause* you to light the fire, or is it more proper to simply say that the *reason* you lit the fire was your belief that doing so would rectify your problem of being cold and your choice to light the fire was the cause of your lighting the fire? Libertarians argue that your being chilly may be a reason for your action but it need not cause your action. Our reasons influence our decisions, but they are just a part of the total picture of what goes into freewill decision-making. Timothy O'Connor rightly noted that our reasons serve as a basis for our generation (which we control) of an intention to act, and we then choose to act through an exercise of will.[22] The reasons do not cause the action, but they do influence the action.[23]

The second argument claims that libertarian freedom violates the fundamental laws of nature, expressed in the laws of causation. The complaint is that according to natural laws all events must have a cause, and this includes all free actions; there can be no uncaused events (or uncaused causes), save the original Cause (God, who is in a metaphysical category of his own). Since libertarianism cannot articulate exactly

---

reasons for the action, *reasons for acting*. See Donald Davidson, *Essays on Actions and Events* (Oxford: Clarendon, 1980), 9–11.

[22] Timothy O'Connor, *Persons and Causes: The Metaphysics of Free Will* (New York: Oxford University Press, 2000). See esp. chap. 5, "Reasons and Causes," 85–107.

[23] Hasker made a similar point about motives. Compatibilists wrongly assume a causal chain for the emergence of our strongest motive without regard for the contribution the agent makes to the relative strength of her motives. As he saw it, our free choices have at least as much to do with determining our motives as our motives have in determining our choices; in fact, the relationship seems inverted from that presupposed by compatibilists. Hasker further complained that the compatibilist maxim, "We always act on our strongest motive," is vacuous and tautological, because those who accept it take it as an *a priori* truth: the strongest motive is defined as the one on which a free agent will act, and we come to know which motive is strongest by observing which led to action. This, he maintained, "reduces to the triviality that we always act on the motive we act upon!" Ultimately, libertarians see the will as more basic, while compatibilists see motive as more basic. Hasker, *Metaphysics*, 44.

what causes free choices and actions (so the argument goes), it effectively proposes that they are uncaused events/causes, which is incoherent.

In response, it should be acknowledged that we would be hard-pressed to find any Christians—Calvinist or non-Calvinist—who should want to challenge the claim that God is the only Uncaused Cause. I know of no libertarians who suggest that there can be uncaused events or uncaused causes in the way compatibilists fear, even though some have admittedly used language suggestive of this (e.g., references to humans as "unmoved movers"). Rather, libertarians question the requirement, posed by compatibilists, that the cause of human action be fully explainable by reference to a chain of causes directly traceable back to the original Cause. This is not to say that libertarians wish to dislocate human action from divine providence, but only that the actions themselves can originate in the will of the individual, created free by God.

Libertarians typically offer one of two models for explaining causation in free actions: event causation and agent causation. An event causation account sees free actions as caused by events internal to the agent, most commonly his thoughts or mental states. One caveat is needed to distinguish this from compatibilism: the events must have their origins within the agent without reference to anything (or anyone, including God) external to the agent.[24] An agent causation account sees free actions as caused by an exercise of the agent's will without appeal to anything further. As O'Connor explained:

> I contend that the commonsense view of ourselves as fundamental causal agents—which Chisholm once expressed as "unmoved movers" but which is more accurately expressed as "not wholly moved movers"—is not merely internally consistent in a narrow sense. It is theoretically understandable in precisely the way in which one may understand the concept of event causation: through a nonreductive analysis of its internal connections to other basic concepts.[25]

In essence, agent causation sees the causal relation as fundamental or primitive, akin to the basic laws of nature and in need of no further appeal. As Randolf Clarke explained, "On an agent-causal account, an agent's *control* over her behavior resides

---

[24] Some proponents have insisted that the events not be determinative for the action or choice, leading some agent causation theorists to charge that it cannot thereby serve as an adequate explanation unless it appeals further to an agent causation account. However, this simply means that event causation reduces to agent causation.

[25] O'Connor, *Persons and Causes*, 67.

fundamentally in her *causing* what she does. Her control does not reside fundamentally in her performing some special sort of action. Since causing is bringing something about, producing it, or making it happen, causing seems to be the right sort of thing on which to base an agent's control over her behavior."[26] So in agent causal accounts, it is the actor, through movement of his will, that causes the action or choice. Just as God's actions require no further explanation than appeal to an exercise of his will, so also free human actions require no further explanation than appeal to the individual human will. The important point to note is that, whether event- or agent-causation, libertarianism offers an account of causation that effectively answers the compatibilist objection. Both accounts allow for the influence of reasons and motives but insist that they cannot be causally determinative for the action or choice, as the cause originates within the free person.

Compatibilist Complaint #3: Libertarianism Conflicts with Divine Foreknowledge

The so-called problem of divine foreknowledge and human freedom has a long history in philosophy and theology and is not confined to debates between Calvinist and non-Calvinist Protestants. Such luminaries as Aristotle, Augustine, and Aquinas (among others) have all written on the subject and offered their own answers. The problem may be simply stated: if God knows today what I am going to do tomorrow, then it seems that I really cannot choose between available options, for I really only have one option: that which God already knows I will do! Orthodox Christian theologians have traditionally offered three approaches to answering the problem, though they are not necessarily mutually exclusive: the Augustinian, the Boethian (or the Eternity), and the Ockhamist solutions. Here I will only briefly summarize them, as there are more detailed treatments readily available.[27]

---

[26] Randolph Clarke, "Toward a Credible Agent-Causal Account of Free Will," in *The Philosophy of Free Will: Essential Readings from the Contemporary Debates*, ed. Paul Russell and Oisín Deery (New York: Oxford University Press, 2013), 223; emphasis original. See also Randolph Clarke, *Libertarian Accounts of Free Will* (New York: Oxford, 2003).

[27] For a relatively accessible analysis, see my chapter on "Divine Foreknowledge and Creaturely Free Will" in Laing, *Middle Knowledge*, 121–57 (chap. 4). For more technical scholarly works on the subject, see William Lane Craig, *The Problem of Divine Foreknowledge and Future Contingents from Aristotle to Suarez* (Leiden: Brill, 1988); William Lane Craig, *Divine Foreknowledge and Human Freedom* (Leiden: Brill, 1991); Linda Trinkaus Zagzebski, *The Dilemma of Freedom and Foreknowledge* (New York: Oxford University Press, 1991).

The earliest extended discussion of the problem by a Christian theologian was that of Augustine, who argued that no conflict exists because the relationship between the two is not causal. Since God's foreknowledge does not cause the future action, it can still be a free act by the individual and God can know it *as free*. Augustine's concern with the detrimental effect of a causal relationship between God's knowledge/work and creaturely freedom will be important for what follows below. The second approach—and arguably still the most popular, at least among Christians in the pews—was first presented by medieval philosopher Boethius and later used by Thomas Aquinas. They argued that God's foreknowledge does not destroy human freedom because God's existence is eternal, understood as outside of time. From that perspective, then, God sees past, present, and future together. It follows that he does not, properly speaking, have *past* knowledge of future events, and the objection loses its force.[28] The third argument, known as the Ockhamist solution, has been inspired by medieval philosopher William of Ockham, but developed in recent years by some philosophers of religion. It can quickly become complicated but draws on the rather intuitive notion that there is a fundamental difference between the past and the future. The past has already occurred and is therefore unalterable, while the future still seems open to change or development. Thus, statements about the past and future can both be true, but they are true in different ways; those about the future have a sort of tentativeness that those about the past do not. The Ockhamist solution proposes that persons have a kind of power over the past—what is known as counterfactual power over the past—which makes past propositions either true or false. Basically, it claims that we have the power to make past statements about our actions today either true or false (by acting today). For example, if I were to buy a motorcycle today, I can cause a statement made two years ago about my buying a motorcycle in 2021 to be either true or false (depending on what the statement proclaimed about my buying). It works a little differently when applied to the problem of divine foreknowledge, since God is omniscient. Ockhamism claims we can act in ways that can make God's past beliefs to have always been other than what they were. This is not to say that we have the power to change God's past beliefs or the power to make God's past beliefs wrong (as

---

[28] We might say that since God exists outside of time, his knowledge cannot be temporally located. Since the argument relies upon the necessity of the past—specifically God's past beliefs about creaturely actions—then the argument collapses on itself. Still, it must also be admitted that this answer, if accepted, only addresses the specific issue of divine foreknowledge (by denying *fore*knowledge) and does not deal with the problem of there being true propositions in the past or present about future free actions.

that would deny his omniscience) but is only to say that God's past beliefs are in some way dependent upon how persons will freely act. As noted, all three of these solutions may be employed together in a total view of divine omniscience, which allows for both divine foreknowledge and libertarian freedom.[29]

In recent years, the question of the compatibility of God's knowledge of future human choices and actions, with those choices and actions being libertarian free, has made for strange bedfellows; both Calvinists and open theists have questioned their coherence, though they came to very different conclusions. Both agree that libertarianism precludes there being truths about future free actions, but open theists conclude God cannot know the future while Calvinists conclude there can be no libertarian free actions.

Bruce Ware has argued that libertarian freedom precludes divine foreknowledge. He has repeatedly argued that for God to know the future, the circumstances in which a person finds himself must determine his actions. Commenting on middle knowledge—a theory that claims God uses his knowledge of how all possible free creatures would act in all possible circumstances in his providential work—Ware wrote, "Because there is not a necessary connection between the circumstances in which an agent was envisioned (by God) as performing a free action, and the actual free action the agent would do, God cannot know what a free agent would do simply by knowing the circumstances related to his choice."[30] In other words, if the circumstances do not dictate the actions of the individual, then there can be no truth about how he will act, and therefore, God cannot know beforehand what the individual will do. For Ware, then, compatibilist freedom is necessary to preserve divine foreknowledge: "Since [compatibilist] freedom means that we always do what we most want, and since what we 'most want' is shaped by the set of factors and circumstances that eventually give rise to one desire that stands above all others, therefore, God can

---

[29] In some ways, the Ockhamist solution just says exactly what the Boethian solution says, and both affirm the Augustinian. The Ockhamist solution claims that if we were to act otherwise, then God would always have known *that action*, because by nature, he is omniscient. The Boethian solution claims that God sees the future free actions in a timeless eternity, but this implies that the free act is something God simply sees *as a free act*. If the agent acted otherwise, God would perceive that in his eternity. The Augustinian solution claims that God's knowledge does not cause the action, but it does seem to suggest that the reverse is true; God knows what he knows about the future because it *is* that way. Note, though, that none of this means that God is merely passive regarding the future, because at least part of what he knows includes his own future actions based on his will.

[30] Ware, *God's Greater Glory*, 113.

know the circumstances giving rise to our highest desires, and by knowing these, he can know the choice that we would make, given those particular circumstances."[31]

Part of the problem is that compatibilists and incompatibilists evidently have different notions about how God knows what he knows.[32] It seems to me that Ware (and others) cannot conceive of God knowing the future without his tracing the causal chain. As Terrance Tiessen has said, "I remain unable to conceive of how God could know what an agent would choose if that choice is not predictable on the basis of the agent's reasons for the choice (together with his values, inclinations, etc.)."[33] I take this to mean God knows the future because (and only because) he can trace the causal chain of events—a chain he ensures by means of his providential will—to their ends.

While it is surely correct that God would know the future infallibly if he were to cause it or were to trace the causal chain to its origin in his decrees, it seems wrong-headed to think this is required or even true. If God is essentially omniscient (and, we may add, infinite and eternal), then it seems he should just know all truths, as that is what it means to be omniscient. Tracing a causal chain to know its outcome seems to suggest learning and discovery, and possibly ignorance. It also appears to conceive of God's way of knowing very much like our own way of knowing, but we need not think of divine omniscience in that manner.[34] An essentially omniscient being can (and I should think, *does*) know all truths immediately and eternally. Therefore, if there are truths about the future, including future free choices and actions, he should know them without having to trace the causal chain. There seems to be no good reason to

---

[31] Ware, 114–15.

[32] John D. Laing, "Middle Knowledge and the Assumption of Libertarian Freedom: A Response to Ware," in *Calvinism and Middle Knowledge: A Conversation*, ed. John D. Laing, Kirk R. MacGregor, and Greg Welty (Eugene, OR: Pickwick, 2019), 153–55.

[33] Terrance L. Tiessen, "A Response to John Laing's Criticisms of Hypothetical Knowledge Calvinism," in *Calvinism and Middle Knowledge*, 181. It is interesting that Tiessen used the term "predictable" here, as it suggests the potential for error, though I seriously doubt he meant to imply such possibility. Most libertarians would agree that free actions are *predictable* based on the agent's reasons, values, inclinations, and the like, but maintain they are not rendered *certain* by them. Therefore, knowledge of an agent's reasons, values, inclinations, and the like cannot serve as the basis for divine knowledge of free actions (which is essentially the argument open theists make against divine foreknowledge).

[34] As Cottrell put it, "By suggesting that God could not know unless He determines, it is the Calvinist who limits God's knowledge, not the Arminian. Such a view of omniscience is patterned too closely after man's powers to know." Jack Cottrell, *The Bible Versus Calvinism* (Mason, OH: Christian Restoration Association, 2018), 69.

suppose that God must know the causes first (even taken in terms of logical priority) before he can know the outcome. If it is true that in one year I will buy a new motorcycle, then God can know the proposition, "John will buy a new motorcycle in one year" without having to deduce it from the various causes or reasons for its being true and being realized in time. Our inability to conceive of how God could know this should not be problematic, for he is mysterious, transcendent, and infinite (Eccl 11:5); we should be more troubled by a God who can only think in ways we can conceive.

Ware (and others) could respond to my critique by appeal to logical order in divine thoughts; he could claim that he does not mean to imply that God learns the outcome from tracing the causal chain, as if there were a time when he did not know the end/*telos*. Rather, he only means to say that God's knowledge of the *telos* is logically dependent upon his knowledge of the causes, or put differently, his knowledge of the causes is logically before his knowledge of the *telos*, and that in eternity, all the knowledge is present and immediate for God. Such a response is what I should expect, but this raises something of a quandary for the Calvinist. On the one hand, Calvinists have a strong commitment to the aseity (i.e., independence) of God, as seen in their standard critique of libertarianism. They complain that it makes God's knowledge and providence dependent on something outside himself because God uses his eternal perception of how free creatures will act to develop and execute his plan. On the other hand, by appealing to logical dependency between God's causation and his knowledge of the *telos,* Calvinists are committing the same "error" as libertarians.[35] So the Calvinist must abandon either this critique of libertarianism or this explanation of divine knowledge. It seems the only way out is to claim that God knows the causes not because he sees them in eternity but because he is the only real cause. However, this claim seems to remove the freedom from compatibilist freedom.

Compatibilist Complaint #4: Libertarianism Compromises Divine Sovereignty and Providence

Another common critique of libertarianism by Calvinist thinkers is that it somehow detracts from God's sovereignty or displaces him from his rightful place as ruler

---

[35] In both cases, God's knowledge is dependent upon something else, though the order is reversed. In libertarian models, God's knowledge of the future (loosely speaking, as it is more properly knowledge of *possible futures*) informs his knowledge of the present, while in this model of Calvinism, God's knowledge of the present informs his knowledge of the future.

over the cosmos. Wayne Grudem seems to think that a commitment to libertarian freedom precludes one from believing in a robust view of providence. As he put it, "Scripture nowhere says that we are 'free' in the sense of being outside of God's control," and he argued that only compatibilism allows for divine providence over the details of life.[36] Similarly, Robert Peterson and Michael Williams contended that in Arminian theology, "God cannot sovereignly govern human history, events or personal destinies."[37] It is not uncommon for critics of libertarianism to take these concerns a step further and argue that libertarian creaturely freedom turns the Creator-creature relationship on its head. Since God cannot cause free human decisions, he effectively abdicates part of his sovereignty to his creatures, namely his providence over free choices and their effects. This problem is exacerbated by the large number of free choices/actions, and the frequency with which they occur, so that God is effectively rendered impotent.

Herman Bavinck argued that the net result of libertarian creaturely freedom is that God is placed in a position of virtual servitude to his creatures. In his discussion of middle knowledge, Bavinck wrote:

> God does not derive his knowledge of the free actions of human beings from his own being, his own decrees, but from the will of creatures. . . . Conversely, the creature in large part becomes independent vis-à-vis God. . . . It sovereignly makes it[s] own decisions and either accomplishes something or does not accomplish something apart from any preceding divine decree. . . . The creature is now creator, autonomous, sovereign; the entire history of the world is taken out of God's controlling hands and placed into human hands.[38]

He continued: "What are we to think, then, of a God who forever awaits all those decisions and keeps in readiness a store of all possible plans for all possibilities? What then remains of even a sketch of the world plan when left to humans to flesh out? And of what value is a government whose chief executive is the slave of his own subordinates?"[39] He assumed the answer to each of these questions is, "Not much."

---

[36] Grudem, *Systematic Theology*, 331 (see chap. 4, n. 88).
[37] Peterson and Williams, *Not an Arminian*, 138.
[38] Bavinck, *Reformed Dogmatics*, 2:201 (see chap. 3, n. 3).
[39] Bavinck, 2:201.

Multiple reasons exist for rejecting these arguments; they are full of rhetorical flourish but devoid of much substance. First, Grudem's claim that Scripture nowhere speaks of creaturely freedom being outside God's control is notoriously vague. In one sense, every orthodox Christian should heartily agree with it, for apart from process theologians, we all agree that God works all things after the counsel of his will (Eph 1:11). In another sense, however, every orthodox Christian should challenge it, for apart from theological fatalists, we all agree that God is not the direct cause of all that occurs; he exercises his sovereignty over evil, for instance, through secondary means. Disagreements between libertarians and compatibilists are rooted in their beliefs about how he uses those secondary means and the extent of his causation in those means. Libertarians do not claim that free actions are outside God's control, unless "control" is confined to direct causation. Second, Bavinck has misrepresented freewill theologies, as most libertarians believe human freedom can be grounded in God's being without rendering such freedom necessary. God creates humans after his image (see below) with free wills capable of making decisions, and while his decision to do so involves a sort of self-limitation, so also does his decision to create in general. Simply put, proponents of libertarian freedom reject the notion that God abrogates responsibility for the history of the world or becomes subservient to humans, and instead maintain that God is sovereign over the whole creation, exercising his providence over the smallest details of life, even the growth of blades of grass in the field and the lives of birds in the trees (Matt 6:25–34). Libertarians and compatibilists disagree over the details of how that providence is administered.

Arguments for Libertarian Free Will

A well-rounded case for libertarianism must move beyond response to compatibilist critics to a presentation of the value of libertarian freedom. In this section, I will explain the most notable arguments in its favor. The most basic argument for libertarian freedom is the ubiquitous nature of its acceptance; it is the most common and natural understanding of freedom. Next, I will examine claims that libertarian freedom is necessary for personhood and vital to our understanding of the image of God in humans. I will then explain how libertarian freedom is necessary for true love to prevail; and last, I will outline the value of libertarianism for answering the problem of evil and for evaluating human moral responsibility. I will conclude that each of these arguments gives good reason for accepting libertarian freedom.

Libertarian Argument #1: Libertarianism Is the Common View of Freedom

One way to determine which view of freedom is correct is to refer to our common notions of freedom. Peter van Inwagen argued that although our everyday speech is peppered with both libertarian and compatibilist overtones, we all really believe in libertarian freedom, either consciously or subconsciously.[40] Those who deny it are either dishonest (or self-deceived) or inconsistent. He based these claims on the fact that all persons spend some time deliberating when faced with a choice, even the seemingly inconsequential ones.

Van Inwagen maintained that an individual would not deliberate about a given action unless she believes it is possible to perform or refrain from performing that action. The act of deliberating belies a belief that she actually *can* choose from competing alternatives, and this applies to deliberations about both actual choices she has to make and hypothetical choices she may face. As van Inwagen pointed out, to deliberate about which of two books to buy "manifests a belief with respect to each of these books that it is possible for him to buy it just as surely as would his holding it aloft and crying, 'I can buy this book.'"[41] Similarly, a woman who deliberates about whether to marry a particular man, should he ask, believes that she actually could accept or reject his proposal were he to ask. I assume my wife thought long and hard about how she would respond if I were to ask for her hand, and although she said yes, her deliberating beforehand shows that she believed she could have said no.

An important point for van Inwagen's argument, and others like it, is that our actions are a better indication of our beliefs than our words; our actions show what we *really* believe.[42] Van Inwagen illustrates this by reference to a husband who claims

---

[40] Colloquially, we speak in both libertarian and compatibilist terms. By way of example, consider how we speak about voting in an election. Those who are passionately opposed to a candidate often couch the situation in compatibilist terms: "I simply could not vote for that candidate!" Those who are apathetic about candidate choice often sound like libertarians: "I have no good options, but I want to exercise my right to vote, so I'll just have to choose what I determine to be the lesser of two evils." Both ways of speaking suggest a view of freedom, but neither offers a reasoned, philosophical argument for or against voter ability to choose.

[41] Peter van Inwagen, *An Essay on Free Will* (Oxford, UK: Clarendon, 1983), 155.

[42] This is generally true with respect to most of our actions, as van Inwagen's example made clear, but I'm not sure we want to turn it into a law. Paul seems to suggest that we are all inconsistent in our actions and beliefs because of the sin that resides in our flesh. We can delight in God's law even while we constantly violate it (Romans 7).

to trust his wife and to believe she is 100 percent faithful to him but who also opens her mail, checks her phone messages, hires a private detective to follow her, and so forth. The man is either being dishonest when he claims to trust her, or his actions are inconsistent with his beliefs (which is problematic). Van Inwagen goes on to argue that if one accepts that his beliefs are inconsistent, then he should be uncomfortable because it means that at least one of his beliefs is false (either his tacit belief that he has free will in his acts of deliberating, or his stated belief that there is no free will). Van Inwagen sees the rejection of free will as disastrous because it condemns the objector to "a life of perpetual logical inconsistency."[43] No one lives as if there is no free will because all persons deliberate! Thus, the objector to free will should change his commitment to conform with lived reality. Whether one will do so is debatable, but the larger point is that libertarian freedom stands at the base of how most of us carry on the everyday business of life.

Libertarian Argument #2: Libertarianism Is Essential to Personhood/Personality

Some have argued that the human sense of individuality and dignity requires in- determinism (and thus, libertarian free will). If all human actions and choices are determined such that they could not have been otherwise, or if all choices are fully explainable by reference to, for instance, chemicals in the brain or brain states, then something of our uniqueness as individuals is lost. After all, anyone else with the same upbringing and constitution would perform the same actions, think the same thoughts, realize the same achievements, and so forth, and this fact seems to dis- solve any meaningful sense of personal identity and value for the individual person (or at least seriously compromises our sense of personal accomplishment or personal worth). As Kane put it, "If I am to be held responsible for my purposes and actions *because I am their ultimate source*, then I likewise want those purposes and actions to be respected *because I am their ultimate source*—and not merely because what I do is use- ful to others. In other words, I want to be treated as an end in myself (with dignity), because I acknowledge ultimate responsibility for my own ends."[44]

---

[43] van Inwagen, *Essay on Free Will*, 160.
[44] Robert Kane, *The Significance of Free Will* (New York: Oxford University Press, 1998), 87; emphasis original.

This is not to suggest that personal worth is tied to accomplishment in a way that reduces the individual to his/her actions, but rather is meant to draw upon the concept of the whole person, which sees one's actions as expressions of, and contributing to, the development of her individual personality, perspective, desires, and fears. That is, actions are not merely products of one's personality and desires but are creative of those personalities and desires. As Forlines correctly noted, what it means to be a person is inextricably tied to one's actions, will, and the image of God.[45]

Libertarian Argument #3: Libertarianism Is a Component of the Image of God in Humans

Some proponents of libertarian freedom point to the image of God as undergirding their position, though they rarely offer an argument explaining how it does so. Evangelical Christians of all persuasions agree that humans are made in the image of God, and though the image was adversely affected by the fall, it was not lost (Gen 9:6; Jas 3:9). In the creation narrative, we are told God created humanity—male and female—in his image and likeness (Gen 1:26–27). It does not explicitly define the *imago Dei*, and theologians have long debated the relationship of the Hebrew terms for "image" and "likeness" (*tselem* and *demuth*). But most now agree that the image includes multiple aspects, even if some see one as primary, and that these aspects each reflect something of God within the created order. For ease of discussion, the aspects may be defined as three: dominion, resemblance, and relationality.

The most popular view of the image in the history of the church is dominion. God's charges to Adam to rule over the other creatures and to tend the garden both indicate that the image includes service as God's representative on earth (Gen 1:26, 28; see also Ps 8:5–8). To bear the image is to participate in the royal function of judicial discernment, decision-making, and provision. In the medieval period, it was common to conceive of the image in terms of humanity's resemblance to God and uniqueness or difference from brute animals. This approach has led to a number of proposals for the image that include spiritual, creative, moral, rational, aesthetic, loving, and free. It should be clear that image can include all these traits, as they are not mutually exclusive. In more recent years, evangelical theologians have placed more emphasis upon relationality in their understanding of the *imago Dei*. This is due in part to a resurgence of interest in trinitarian theology as it developed in the

---

[45] Forlines, *Classical Arminianism*, 5–6, 20–21 (see chap. 7, n. 6).

East, where the three divine persons are constituted in their perichoretic relations (i.e., they are who they are in virtue of the inter-trinitarian relations), and in part to its exegetical basis in the Genesis account. God is a *community of being*, relational in his very nature, and has created humanity for relationship with him and each other. This relational component to the image can be seen in several features of the text, to include the more personal deliberative introductory statement to the creation of humanity (i.e., "Let us make man . . ." versus "Let there be . . ."); the gender distinction associated with the statement that humans are made in God's image (Gen 1:27); the command to increase through sexual relations (v. 28; cf. Gen 9:1, 7); and the claim, "It is not good for man to be alone" (2:18).[46]

The important point here is that in each of these cases, libertarian freedom is needed. For humans to fulfill their function of divine vice-regency, they must have the ability to evaluate, adjudicate, and decide between competing obligations, needs, and limitations. Similarly, for humans to reflect God's nature in the many and varied proposed ways they resemble God, they must have the ability to choose. For example, to display their aesthetic sense, humans must have the ability to choose their medium to express their immediate and deeply personal feelings (e.g., Jubal in Gen 4:21). Likewise, rational and moral thought seem predicated on the ability not only to weigh the relative strength of ideas and arguments but also to choose that which seems best, and to be either right or wrong, based on one's choice. If one only has one option, then he does not really have the potential to be right *or* wrong, and seems unable to truly deliberate. More important, if humans are to act with purpose, they must have the ability to reflect on the larger consequences of their actions (past, present, and future), to assess if those actions have had or will have the intended effect(s), and to evaluate the meaning and significance of those actions within the context of the broader community and human history, all with a view to making a positive contribution beyond their own personal well-being. This requires, at a minimum, freedom of choice. Last, for humans to mirror divine relationality, they must have the ability to choose to enter into personal relations with others, dissolve those relations that are unhealthy, and engage in those activities necessary for healthy relationships and refrain from those that detract from them. More will be said about love and

---

[46] The image as relationality may also be seen in the development of the idea later in Genesis, where image appears to be tied to familial and human-divine relations. Adam has a son who is after his own image and likeness (Gen 5:3), and it is this son (Seth) who perpetuates the close relationship between God and humanity.

freedom below, but it should be clear that the image of God in humans includes and is based in freedom.

Libertarian Argument #4: Libertarianism Is Essential to True Love

Many Christians have suggested that the greater good that libertarian freedom makes possible is love and that only love grounded in libertarian freedom is true love.[47] Consider the following thought from C. S. Lewis:

> God created things which had free will. That means creatures which can go either wrong or right. Some people think they can imagine a creature which was free but had no possibility of going wrong. I cannot. If a thing is free to be good it is also free to be bad. And free will is what made evil possible. Why then, did God give them free will? Because free will, though it makes evil possible, is also the only thing that makes possible any love or goodness or joy worth having. A world of automata—of creatures that worked like machines—would hardly be worth creating. The happiness which God designs for His higher creatures is the happiness of being freely, voluntarily united to Him and to each other in an ecstasy of love and delight compared with which the most rapturous love between a man and a woman on this earth is mere milk and water. And for that they must be free.[48]

While Lewis's characterization of the options being limited to libertarian free creatures or automata could be rightly questioned, the important point is that love—at least true love, or love worth desiring and love that is enjoyable—seems to require freedom. Interestingly, Lewis provided no argument for his claim but rather takes it as self-evidently true. It is a common notion, often depicted in children's stories and Hollywood movies: while coercion can force a kind of shadowy feeling of affection, only love freely given is true.

The question of why we love is a complex one. Some have contended that love is like a reasoned response to some factors (e.g., attributes, qualities, and the like) the

---

[47] See William S. Anglin, *Free Will and the Christian Faith* (New York: Oxford University Press, 1990).

[48] C. S. Lewis, *Mere Christianity* (New York: Touchstone, 1996), 52–53; see also Lewis, *The Case for Christianity* (New York: Touchstone, 1996), 41–42.

other possesses or instantiates.[49] In other words, we love others because they are lovable, at least to us, and this means love is related to our reasoning faculties and thus includes *choice*. The command to love our enemies (Matt 5:44) requires intentionality of sorts, a choice to develop a disposition toward another who has sought to harm us or positioned himself in opposition to us. There is an active, intellectual component as well as an affective component to love. Consider the command enshrined in the Shema: Love the Lord with all your heart, soul, mind, and strength (Deut 6:5; Mark 12:30). The heart speaks to feeling, the component of love we seemingly have no willful control over, but mind, soul, and strength speak to intellect and action, both of which are tied to the will. We can actively cultivate love through control of our thoughts and actions, and we can let love wither when we refrain from thinking loving thoughts and engaging in loving actions. It is analogous to growth in virtue, or sanctification. There is an interconnectivity between our choices, intentions, and actions on the one hand, and our hearts, affections, and feelings on the other. We cannot will ourselves to love others, just as we cannot, by sheer act of will, cause ourselves to grow in holiness or to believe. But we can choose to take steps to engender that love and spiritual growth. It begins with a willful decision—which we can deny or ignore—and then moves to action—which we can also refuse. But when we take these steps, we cultivate affection and desire, which over time can develop into love. This is the reason love given freely is so desirable; it takes conscious effort, hard work, and commitment. As Kane rightly noted—and this gets at the common notion undergirding the broader claim that love must be freely given—our satisfaction from some/certain kinds of loving relationships, our characteristically closest relationships, is directly tied to the love freely given in response to us as objects of love. It is the responsive component of love that is satisfying for us: "There is a kind of love we desire from others—parents, children (when they are old [emotionally mature?] enough), spouses, lovers, and friends—whose significance is diminished . . . by the thought that they are determined to love us entirely by instinct or circumstances beyond their control or not ultimately up to them. . . . To be loved by others in this desired sense requires that the ultimate source of others' love lies in their own wills."[50]

Despite the popularity of these notions, there are some obvious counterexamples of love that most persons would view as valid but do not seem to be based in a freewill

---

[49] See, for example, Troy Jollimore, *Love's Vision* (Princeton, NJ: Princeton University Press, 2011).

[50] Kane, *Significance of Free Will*, 88.

choice (of the lover) to love the beloved.[51] Consider a parent's love for a child; the parent seems to love the child because of the relationship she has with him or because he is *her child*.[52] It is in virtue of the relationship, as it is grounded in the identities of the two persons, that love persists and, hence, the love is not a free choice (at least not in the libertarian sense). In fact, Frankfurt argued that we love our children often despite the evidence and the rationality of continuing to love them.[53] Love is mysterious and cannot (should not!) be reduced to reasons and attributes. He further argued that the relationship between the love we have for them and their value to us is inverted: we do not love them because they have inherent value, but rather they have value to us precisely because we love them. He took this to mean that love is not based in the value of the beloved and is, therefore, not grounded in free will.[54] But Frankfurt seems to have missed an important point here, for the reason we love our children and not someone else's children is not only by virtue of their identities as our children but also because we place a higher value on them as our children. In other words, value cannot be divorced from love, as Frankfurt's theory requires.

Jesus also invites us to consider the love of a parent for a child to begin to grasp the love of God (Matt 7:8–11; cf. Luke 11:10–12). Jesus assumed that an earthly father will give his child good things he desires and needs and will not give him harmful things (bread, not a stone; fish, not a serpent). In the same way, the heavenly Father will give good gifts to us when we ask. So Jesus couched the love of God in terms of action. This, of course, is also the case in the cross, the greatest demonstration of love given to humanity (John 3:16, 15:13). Jesus tied love inextricably to

---

[51] For a sustained argument against the thesis that authentic love requires libertarian freedom, see Thaddeus J. Williams, *Love, Freedom and Evil* (Leiden: Brill, 2011).

[52] Kieran Setiya points out that sometimes (often!) love exists between two parties simply due to the relationship they have together; a parent loves a child simply because he is her child, and the fact that we naturally expect her to love her child, irrespective of the qualities he may possess, points to this fact. Setiya, "Love and the Value of a Life," *Philosophical Review* 112, no. 3 (2014): 135–39.

[53] He wrote, "We generally continue to love them, indeed, even when they disappoint us or when they bring us suffering. Often we go on loving them even after we have become persuaded that the love is unreasonable." Harry G. Frankfurt, *The Reasons of Love* (Princeton, NJ: Princeton University Press, 2004), 30.

[54] Harry Frankfurt wrote, "This relationship between love and the value of the beloved—namely, that love is not necessarily grounded in the value of the beloved but does necessarily make the beloved valuable to the lover—holds not only for parental love but quite generally." He continued: "It is a necessary feature of love that it is not under our direct and immediate voluntary control." Frankfurt, 40, 44.

action, and this implies conscious choice; love *just is* the self-sacrifice on behalf of the beloved. But is it correct to say that love *is* the action, and is it correct to say that Jesus's sacrifice was a free choice that could have been other?

With regard to the equation of love and action, one could argue that the action is an *expression* of love and therefore logically follows it (Rom 5:8), but the presentation in the Scripture is not always so neat (see John 15:10, where action precedes love). It is probably best, theologically, to conceive of the relationship as analogous to that of faith and works. While philosophically they are technically distinct, biblically they cannot be separated. Faith without works is nonexistent—dead—and faith is perfected in action (Jas 2:14–26). So also, love is nonexistent without expression in action. Jesus seems to clearly tie the two together in his exhortations to his disciples to love and obey his commandments (John 14:15, 21; 15:10, 14; cf. 1 John 5:2, 3); love *is* obedience, and is thereby grounded in the *choice* to act.[55]

More important, was Jesus's self-sacrifice a libertarian free choice? Could he have refused to go to the cross? There are good arguments for the affirmative and negative. On the one hand, Jesus clearly stated that he freely gave his life for the sins of humanity; no one took it from him (John 10:17–19; somewhat ironically, there was a dispute among the disciples regarding the meaning of Jesus's words here). This at least suggests that he had the ability to either lay his life down or not lay his life down. Even when praying in Gethsemane, Jesus's yielding to the will of the Father seems predicated on his choice to set aside his own will in favor of that of the Father; he could follow his own desires, but he chose to submit to the Father's will. In fact, throughout the Gospels, Jesus communicated his self-distinction from the Father as a voluntary submission to the will of the Father. Pannenberg rightly noted, this willful submission is to be contrasted with Adam's willful disobedience, and it is constitutive for the Son in his relation to the Father (cf. Gen 3:5; Rom 5:12–21; 1 Cor 15:22, 45).[56]

On the other hand, from Jesus's words and action, a good case can be made for compatibilist freedom. It is hard to imagine the Son rejecting the will of the Father,

---

[55] Frankfurt made a similar point regarding a husband's choice to save his drowning wife—whom he loves—rather than a similarly drowning stranger. The husband does not weigh the pros and cons of saving each, but just saves his wife. While his love for her stands as his reason(s) for action, he nevertheless acts unreflectively, and we would think it odd for him to spend any time *deciding* to save her. Frankfurt, 37.

[56] Wolfhart Pannenberg, *Systematic Theology*, 3 vols., trans. Geoffrey W. Bromiley (Grand Rapids: Eerdmans, 1988–93), 1:308–19.

and in each case where Jesus spoke of freely giving his life, he also referenced his own obedience to the Father, an obedience grounded in and revelatory of his love for the Father (John 14:30–31). He also said on more than one occasion that his actions are a direct reflection of the Father's will and that he can do nothing apart from the Father (5:19–20; 8:28), suggesting a consonance of will that is more consistent with compatibilist freedom; the Son wants to do the will of the Father such that he really could do no other.

It may seem we are at an impasse, analogous to contests over the peccability of Christ, wherein theologians debate whether Jesus could or could not sin.[57] However, this is not the case, for the question is not whether the Son *would* reject the will of the Father but rather if the Son *could* have done otherwise with respect to the cross. Since Jesus was innocent, undeserving of execution, he would have been fully within his rights to refuse the cross; such refusal would not be sin. To say that Jesus could have submitted or not submitted to the cross is not congruous to saying that Jesus could have sinned or not sinned. Thus, Jesus's death was a libertarian free choice of self-sacrifice, and its effectualness is rooted in its self-giving character. Even though he could turn from the way of the cross, it was certain he would not, but the certainty is rooted in his own will.

The last consideration here is God's love. If God *is* love (1 John 4:8), then it would seem love is true to his nature, that he *must* love, and he cannot refrain from loving (i.e., not love). It therefore stands to reason that since divine love is the most pure or proper form of love—what we might call true love—then love is not a choice,

---

[57] Most debates over peccability are couched in terms of whether he was able to sin but did not, was able to not-sin and did not, or not able to sin and therefore could not. Certainly, he was able to not-sin and did not, which is clear from Scripture (Isa 53:9; 2 Cor 5:21; Heb 4:15; 1 Pet 2:22; 1 John 3:5). What is in question is the Son's ability to sin, not his ability to avoid sinning, for that is clearly established in Scripture. There are some good reasons to think that Jesus had libertarian freedom with respect to sinning. The correlation the apostle Paul makes between Adam and Christ seems to suggest that he could, for it is grounded in the similarity of situations and callings, but dissimilarity in outcome. That is, if the Son could not have done otherwise and therefore had to be obedient, then the contrast between his success and Adam's failure seems vacuous. Similarly, Jesus's perfect fulfillment of the Law and his genuine temptation seems diminished if he could not have chosen to disobey. Still, his deity mitigates against the suggestion that he really could have sinned, and there is no necessary connection between temptation and ability to act (even if one is implied or suggested). At the end of the day, an important distinction needs to be made: to say that he *could* sin is not the same as to say that he *would* or even *might*. Many fear that it is a claim that Jesus really might have sinned or spurned the will of the Father, but that is another matter.

at least not in a libertarian sense. However, saying that God is loving by nature is not the same as saying that he must love particular persons or that he must love all persons, or that his actions must always appear loving. God can manifest his love within himself through the loving relations of Father, Son, and Spirit. He has no need of humanity to fully realize his love and, therefore, he does not need humanity as an object of love. That is, an argument from God's infinite, loving nature does not prove that he must love all persons.

Further, a biblical argument could be made that God does not love certain persons, so long as hate is taken to mean not love, and the references to divine hatred are interpreted literally (i.e., God's hatred of sinners, Lev 20:23; Ps 5:5; 11:5; Prov 6:16–19; Hos 9:15; Esau in Mal 1:3; Rom 9:13). But one need not argue that God is unloving in some cases to view his love as a consequence of his libertarian free choice to love. In other words, even if he loves all persons, it does not follow that he could not have done otherwise. An analogy to grace may help make the point here. God is gracious by nature, and in one sense, he has granted grace to all persons (i.e., through what is usually termed *common grace*). In another sense, though, he grants grace to whom he chooses, and, in this sense, grace is dispositional. God chooses to whom he will grant grace, he chooses the conditions under which he will grant grace, and he does so freely; similarly with his love.

One final point about divine love and creaturely freedom has to do with the implications of love on God's sovereignty. It has become commonplace for theologians of a certain stripe to argue that since love is God's primary attribute, and love cannot be coercive, an open model of providence is required.[58] We should be wary of any attempt to identify a primary attribute in God, and we should be skeptical of the Openness conclusion. But the basic point that love is neither coercive nor controlling seems sound, if taken as a general principle (not a law).[59] It certainly captures the essence of healthy relationships among humans, many of which serve as analogous to the divine/human relation (e.g., parent/child; husband/wife). The upshot of this,

---

[58] See, for example, Clark H. Pinnock, *Most Moved Mover: A Theology of God's Openness* (Grand Rapids: Baker, 2001); Thomas Jay Oord, *The Uncontrolling Love of God: An Open and Relational Account of Providence* (Downers Grove, IL: InterVarsity, 2015).

[59] We should be wary of attempts to identify a primary divine attribute, whether love, holiness, justice, mercy, graciousness, etc., because doing so almost always results in oppositional relationships among the attributes and a denial of God's inner coherence (i.e., divine simplicity). We should be skeptical of the Openness conclusion, as there are more orthodox options available and it is destructive of divine omniscience and providence.

if accepted, should be clear. If God loves us and desires a loving relationship with us (and it seems biblically obvious that he does), then he does not control us but rather allows for genuine libertarian freedom.

Libertarian Argument #5: Libertarianism Greatly Reduces the Problem of Evil

A particularly compelling argument for accepting libertarian freedom is its value in responding to challenges to traditional theism due to the presence of evil and suffering in the world. The problem of evil is a pernicious one indeed, and its popularity, despite having been answered by theologians and philosophers alike, has not waned. Since there is an entire chapter devoted to the issue in this volume, I will not expend much space on it here. However, I do feel it necessary to point out that the freewill defense against the logical problem of evil is based on a libertarian view of freedom, and freewill theodicies require libertarian freedom to be true.[60] They are all based in the idea that a world with free creatures but also evil and suffering, even the amount of suffering in this world, is better than a world with no evil and suffering but no freedom. More to the point, they all must insist that God could not have made a world with free creatures without the possibility of evil, and most take this a step further to claim that it is likely the case that he could not create a world with free creatures who never sin. And this gets to the crux of the matter, for Calvinists cannot agree with these limitations on God. By appealing to compatibilist freedom, they maintain that God could make humans in such a way that they always freely refrain from sin; thus, the strength of the freewill theodicy is lost.

But this is not to say that Calvinists can offer no theodicy, for there are many other greater-good theodicies at their disposal, the most obvious being an appeal to the revelation of God in Christ Jesus. What I have in mind is this: it is highly likely that God's purposes in creating include his desire to glorify himself by means of relationship with beings made in his image. Since humans cannot, in virtue of their finitude, fully grasp the enormity of God's greatness and love (holiness, power, goodness, and so forth), they need a revelation that communicates this to them and to which they can relate. An incarnation meets that need, but it best does so in the

---

[60] Some Calvinists have opted for a version of free will defense. See K. Scott Oliphint, *Reasons for Faith: Philosophy in the Service of Theology* (Phillipsburg, NJ: Presbyterian and Reformed, 2006).

context of self-sacrifice, for this is the greatest demonstration of love (John 15:13). For the self-sacrifice to have meaning, it must be in terms of replacement (i.e., on behalf of humanity). Thus, for God to meet his desires in creating, and to best reveal his power, holiness, justice, love, and grace to humans, God purposed to take on flesh in the person of Jesus Christ and to die on the cross to pay humanity's penalty. He further ordained that the Son should conquer and even transform death, the most destructive and fearful force imaginable, so that humans can begin to grasp how awe-inspiring he is and respond appropriately in faith, obedience, and worship. For all this to work, it was required that sin enter the creation due to the free choice of humanity. Therefore, the evil encompassed in the fall and the crucifixion of Christ was ordained by God because it leads to the greater good of God's revelation and glorification, rooted in the salvation of humanity and the cosmos. I find this approach not only appealing, but patently biblical, although my Calvinist friends and I will surely disagree over the details of how God ordained the evil encompassed in the fall and the extent to which he ordains the many specific evils that have resulted from the fall.

Calvinists believe that although God uses the compatibilistic free, sinful choices of individuals to accomplish his purposes, he nevertheless could have ensured that they not commit those sins, and this means that God's ordination of sins is selective and specific. Each and every case of sin is ultimately caused by God in his sovereign choice to create the specific persons he does with the specific desires, characters, and so forth, that they have, so that they will commit the specific sins they commit.[61] It is also the case, then, that under these Calvinist principles, each and every sin must lead to a specific greater good, though we may not know what it is.

Libertarian freedom escapes these consequences, as proponents can argue that although God accounts for the free choices of persons to sin in his providential

---

[61] For example, in commenting on God's use of the Assyrians to judge the wicked Judeans, Calvin argued that God put it in their hearts to attack. Just as the Canaanites battled against Israel because God hardened their hearts (Josh 11:20), so also God used the Assyrians. Calvin wrote, "Not that he intends to teach wicked and obstinate men to obey spontaneously, but because he bends them to execute his judgments, just as if they carried their orders engraven on their minds. . . . And hence it appears that they are impelled by the sure appointment of God" Calvin, *Institutes*, trans. Beveridge, 1:201 (1.18.2). Note the strong, active terms Calvin used to describe God's control of the desires, and thereby the actions, of humans: "bends them," "orders engraven on their minds," "impelled by . . . God." He used such strong language purposively and specifically to avoid any notions of bare permission in God's relationship to his use of evil to meet his purposes. According to Calvin, God's providence is not an unwilling permission, but is much more active and causative.

decisions, it may nevertheless be the case that some of those sins are not what he desired, even if they fit into a larger scheme that ultimately meets his purpose(s). Some sins may not directly and specifically lead to greater good but are the cost associated with the broader goals God will meet by creating the world with free creatures. The libertarian nature of human choice, then, acknowledges that sins are the sole responsibility of the human actor, and this entails the possibility of actions contrary to God's desires. This may appear undesirable at first glance, but it has the value of greatly reducing the force of atheistic complaints against Christianity, as it abrogates God of much responsibility for evil. The point I mean to make, then, is that although Calvinists can offer a plausible and biblically grounded theodicy, they are still left with fewer resources for explaining evil than the proponent of libertarianism.

Libertarian Argument #6: Libertarianism Is Necessary for Moral Responsibility

It is widely held that human freedom is necessary for moral responsibility; even some who doubt the truth of human freedom see *belief in human freedom* as necessary for morality.[62] But a significant number of philosophers have argued that for people to be morally responsible for their actions, at least morally significant actions, they must have libertarian freedom; they must have been able to choose to act or not act. The obverse—that people cannot be held responsible for their actions if determinism is true—is also widely held, and an appeal to compatibilist freedom does not seem to help. As Roderick Chisholm noted, if a man's beliefs and desires caused him to do what he did, and he is not responsible for his beliefs and desires, then he is not responsible for his actions. By contrast, if he is responsible for the beliefs and desires he has, then he must have been able to develop either those beliefs and desires or different beliefs and desires, but this, of course, is just an appeal to libertarian freedom

---

[62] For example, philosopher Stephen Cave argues that although neuroscience has demonstrated that human behavior is determined by biology and not free choice, psychology has shown that we need belief in free choice for a number of goods associated with a healthy society and citizenry. Various sociological and psychological studies seem to show that free-will skepticism leads to increases in immorality (e.g., cheating, stealing, lying, and so forth), stress, and depression, as well as drops in creativity, academic performance, and commitment to relationships. Cave, "There's No Such Thing as Free Will but We're Better Off Believing in It Anyway," *Atlantic* (June 2016), https://www.theatlantic.com/magazine/archive/2016/06/theres-no-such-thing-as-free-will/480750/.

one step removed from the action. It is simply the claim that libertarian freedom is necessary at some point in the process of personality development and hence is necessary for moral responsibility.[63] Either way, it is taken as axiomatic that one must have control over his own actions to be held morally accountable, and such control is dependent upon libertarian freedom. The argument has much to commend it: it is simple and straightforward and draws on the common notions of moral responsibility that undergird much legal theory and thought about criminal responsibility.

However, a growing number of philosophers have challenged the connection between libertarian freedom and morality. In a much-discussed set of articles, Harry Frankfurt has questioned what he calls the principle of alternate possibilities (PAP), the idea that there must be at least two options available to an actor for him to be held morally responsible for his actions. He and others have offered several thought experiments (examples) designed to show that PAP fails.[64]

In his original article, Frankfurt offered two related examples. In each, Jones has decided to do something, and subsequent to his decision but before he acts, Black took measures to ensure that Jones will perform the action (through threat of violence, hypnosis, mind-control device, and so forth). When Jones does what he originally intended to do, it is unclear if he is morally responsible, because moral responsibility correlates more closely to intentions in acting than to the number of options available. If Jones acted purely out of his own desires, without the influence of the measures Black put in place, then Jones appears morally responsible, even if he could not have done otherwise. If, however, Jones acted as a result of the measures Black used to ensure his compliance, then he is not morally responsible. Frankfurt's point is that moral responsibility is not tied to one's ability to have done otherwise, but is instead tied to one's intentions.[65]

Frankfurt-style thought experiments do seem to serve as valid counterexamples to the general philosophical claim that for one to be held morally responsible he must

---

[63] Roderick M. Chisholm, *On Metaphysics* (Minneapolis: University of Minnesota Press, 1989), 6. See also Chisholm, *Person and Object: A Metaphysical Study* (La Salle, IL: Open Court, 1976), 53–88.

[64] John Martin Fischer and Mark Ravizza, *Responsibility and Control: A Theory of Moral Responsibility* (Cambridge: Cambridge University Press, 1998).

[65] Harry Frankfurt, "Alternate Possibilities and Moral Responsibility" *Journal of Philosophy* 66, no. 23 (1964): 829–39. See also Harry Frankfurt, "Some Thoughts Concerning PAP," in *Moral Responsibility and Alternative Possibilities: Essays on the Importance of Alternative Possibilities*, ed. David Widerker and Michael McKenna (Burlington, VT: Ashgate, 2003), 339–45.

have it within his power to act otherwise (i.e., PAP). However, this is not to say that they therefore undermine the argument for libertarian freedom from moral responsibility or buttress arguments for compatibilist freedom. More important, they do not work well when applied to theological debates about freedom and responsibility for at least three reasons.

First, Frankfurt-type counterexamples to PAP do not really help most Calvinists because they still assume that persons are responsible for their actions if and only if they chose to perform those actions and were not caused to perform those actions from anything outside themselves. While many Calvinists maintain that their versions of compatibilism do not require outside causation (as the actor's decision is in accord with his own desires and character), it should be clear that the *chain of causation argument* they employ traces back to an outside cause, God. Additionally, Frankfurt-type examples often focus only on the *actions* taken or not taken and not on the *power of choice* (which would be needed to undermine libertarian freedom); in fact, they still allow for *contrary choice* (i.e., Jones can choose to not act, even though he will then be forced to act).[66] Thus, Frankfurt's arguments may be accepted by libertarians and may not be as helpful to compatibilists as often thought.

Second, Frankfurt-style thought experiments do nothing to absolve God of guilt for human sins and seem to actually exacerbate the difficulty of the problem of evil. In instances where evil acts are envisioned, the person who serves as the analogy for God is typically an evil genius, using some sort of mechanism or device to ensure the original actor performs the evil act, but this is hardly the model for God or divine action with which any Christian theologian can agree. The Bible does not depict God as flipping switches in our brains to ensure we perform sinful actions. Its description of God's providence over evil is much more nuanced.

Third, and most important, the models require either a deficient view of divine knowledge or a fatalistic view of human action. In the examples, the way human actions are guaranteed is by means of coercion (e.g., threat, potion, hypnosis, brain-state manipulation, and so forth) that can be used to override the individual's freedom if he were to choose to do something other than what the other person (i.e., Black, the evil scientist, or, in the case of theology, God) desires. Herein lies the

---

[66] David Widerker has rightly focused his critique of Frankfurt on moral responsibility and choice, rather than moral responsibility and *action alone*. See, for example, David Widerker, "Theological Fatalism and Frankfurt Counterexamples to the Principle of Alternative Possibilities," *Faith and Philosophy* 17, no. 2 (April 2000): 249–54.

problem, for the presence of such means, even if never utilized, is based on the fact the controller does not know how the person will actually act until the moment of decision/action. Black needed the coercive measures as a backup precisely because he was ignorant of Jones's true intentions until he decides to act—that is, unless Jones's actions are determined by something other than his own choice or will—but if they are determined, the mechanism would not be necessary, fatalism would follow, and Jones would not be morally responsible for his actions.[67] Thus, the analogy breaks down when applied to God's providence, at least for those who subscribe to orthodox notions of divine foreknowledge. The conclusion to all this is that our intuition that moral responsibility depends on libertarian freedom can be sustained. Frankfurt-type examples do nothing to undermine that belief, at least not in a theistic framework.

Two Final Important Theological Considerations

The ideas considered above form the bulk of the arguments for and against libertarian freedom in philosophical circles. They have generally centered around and focused on common human thought and experience, and Christian understandings of God's relationship to his creation. There are, however, two other important theological issues that can lend valuable insight into the nature of freedom itself; in fact, they are so vital that we may even say they are definitive for our thinking about free will because they are rooted in the biblical ideal rather than the experiential. The first has to do with the kind of freedom humans have in heaven, while the second has to do with that of God. In both cases, the freedom enjoyed is one unhindered by the adverse effects of the fall, unfettered from the limitations or vagaries of this age, and therefore represents an idealized form of freedom: true freedom.

The Nature of Freedom in Heaven

Some years ago, an interesting philosophical discussion arose over the implications of human freedom in heaven for the problem of evil. James Sennett pointed out that Christians have traditionally viewed heaven as necessarily pure because of the presence of God in all his glory. That is, there could be no evil (or suffering) in heaven

---

[67] David Widerker, "Libertarian Freedom and the Avoidability of Decisions," *Faith and Philosophy* 12, no. 1 (January 1995): 113–18; Widerker, "Libertarianism and Frankfurt's Attack on the Principle of Alternate Possibilities," *Philosophical Review* 104, no. 2 (1995): 247–61.

because of God's unmediated presence; this is what makes heaven, heaven! But if this is the case, something of a conundrum arises for the proponent of libertarian freedom: if humans are free in heaven, then either heavenly purity is contingent on creaturely choices because even glorified humans could sin, or a foundational tenet of the freewill defense—that God could not guarantee a sinless or suffering-free world because humans are free—is false. Sennett claimed that the first option is undoubtedly false: "If heaven is only evil-free contingent on the choices of its human occupants, then it is constantly in danger of losing its evil-free status, since it is always in the power of those occupants to introduce evil into heaven. But the idea that heaven might yet become a place of sin and rebellion is contrary to traditional theism. For heaven to be essentially pristine and free from corruption, it must necessarily be evil-free—it cannot be possible for there to be evil."[68] The second option—jettisoning the freewill defense—should be avoided if at all possible, so Sennett considered the option that there is no freedom in heaven. This, he maintains, is also undesirable for at least two reasons: (1) If we are not free in heaven, then we lose something fundamental to who we are/were on earth; and (2) freedom on earth, at least according to the freewill defense, is a good (or a constituent part of *goods*) that outweighs evil and suffering. Without freedom, heaven would lack that good/those goods, and it makes little sense for heaven to want for a significant good. Thus, there are serious theological problems whether humans are or are not libertarian free in heaven; this is what Sennett referred to as the *dilemma of heavenly freedom*. Sennett concluded that there must be freedom in heaven that cannot allow evil; that is, freedom in heaven must be of a compatibilist sort. But he still hopes to preserve libertarian freedom on earth for the sake of its utility in the freewill defense. His ingenious answer is that humans enjoy a kind of compatibilist freedom—what he refers to as proximate freedom—which cannot allow evil and is beholden to the characters we have in heaven, but which also depends on the libertarian free actions and decisions we took or made while alive to develop those heavenly characters. Thus, the compatibilist freedom we enjoy in heaven entails the libertarian freedom we enjoy on earth.

There are some worthy criticisms of Sennett's suggestion, some from compatibilists, and some from libertarians. First, Sennett has simply assumed that it is impossible for humans to sin once in the heavenly state, and while this is the majority

[68] James F. Sennett, "Is There Freedom in Heaven?," *Faith and Philosophy* 16, no. 1 (1999): 70, https://doi.org/10.5840/faithphil19991617.

view in the church, it could be questioned.[69] Second, Cowan has questioned the need for libertarian freedom on earth if it is not needed in heaven.[70] Third, Sennett's suggestion that individuals always choose the good in heaven because their characters were so formed while alive on earth seems to negate his original theological premise that it is because they are in the presence of God that they can only do good. Fourth, tying the good character of the individual in heaven to his godly libertarian choices on earth seems to diminish the transformative power of glorification, wherein the body is sown natural, perishable, and in dishonor and weakness, but is raised spiritual, imperishable, and in honor and power (1 Cor 15:42–44, 47–49). Fifth and most important for our purposes, Sennett incorrectly assumed that an inability to sin requires compatibilist freedom.

As we have already seen, a commitment to libertarian freedom does not require one to believe that no constraints may be placed on choices. Rather, all that is required for a choice to be free is that one has the ability to decide one way or the other, often between acting or not acting. So there can be libertarian freedom in heaven, even if one cannot choose to sin. As Timothy Pawl and Kevin Timpe rightly pointed out, a person in heaven can choose between equally good actions.[71] Glorified persons could engage in many different godly actions in heaven, and we may not even be required—simply by virtue of being in heaven or being in a glorified state—to do what is best, but only what is holy.

The upshot of this is that even if humans cannot sin in heaven, they may still retain libertarian freedom. It certainly does not follow from their inability to sin or fall away once in a glorified state that compatibilist freedom is true freedom while libertarian freedom is a poor substitute. Quite the contrary; glorified human inability to sin has a close analogy (but only an analogy) to divine freedom, which, as we shall see below, is properly libertarian.

---

[69] Arguments could be offered for the ability to sin in heaven, the most obvious being the ability of Satan and his angels to rebel, even while enjoying unmediated access to God.

[70] Steven B. Cowan, "Compatibilism and the Sinlessness of the Redeemed in Heaven," *Faith and Philosophy* 29, no. 4 (October 2011): 416–31. Much of Cowan's argument is a critique of Pawl and Timpe's response to Sennett. Pawl and Timpe have responded: Timothy Pawl and Kevin Timpe, "Heavenly Freedom: A Reply to Cowan," *Faith and Philosophy* 30, no. 2 (April 2013): 188–97.

[71] Timothy Pawl and Kevin Timpe, "Incompatibilism, Sin, and Free Will in Heaven," *Faith and Philosophy* 26, no. 4 (October 2009): 396–417.

The Nature of Divine Freedom

All parties agree that God is free, so it makes sense to examine the kind of freedom God enjoys to ascertain the true nature of freedom. The correct view of freedom, or at least the best kind of freedom, will accord with the kind of freedom God possesses, and there are good reasons to think that it is libertarian and not compatibilist freedom. Since compatibilist freedom is normally couched in terms of choices made consonant with one's character, disposition, or greatest desires, it posits that only one option for action is available to the persons choosing. Applied to God, then, the argument goes something like this: God is truthful, holy, loving, and unchangingly perfect in nature. Therefore, his actions must reflect his nature (which we all affirm). Since God is perfect, his actions must also be perfect, which is synonymous with "best," and therefore, in any given set of circumstances, God must do that which is best. Since there can be only one best option, God has only one option with respect to any given action or choice. According to compatibilists, this limitation does not compromise God's omnipotence because it is no detraction to be unable to choose something other than the best. Just as it is no weakness for God to be unable to act contrary to his nature or to commit evil, so also it is no weakness for his options to be constrained to that which is best, for it would make no sense for him to do anything other.[72]

While it must be admitted that this is a rather simplistic version of the argument, it still captures the basic ideas in some Calvinist claims that God's decisions and will are grounded in his nature. Consider God's decision to create and, especially, to create this specific world or set of circumstances. Calvinist Paul Helm rejects the idea that God had several options from which to choose (i.e., several equally good worlds), because he believes this devolves to the claim that God chose arbitrarily. He

---

[72] Edward Wierenga has argued that these constraints do not necessarily mean that God's freedom is compatibilist, since it is in virtue of God's own nature that he knows what is best, desires to do what is best, is able to do what is best, and does what is best. Even though God acts out of necessity, Wierenga asserted, he does so with libertarian freedom, but only because he is the Uncaused Cause; in the case of any creature, such freedom would be construed as compatibilist. See Wierenga, "The Freedom of God," *Faith and Philosophy* 19, no. 4 (October 2002): 425–36. While the creator/creature distinction is an important one, there seems little reason to accept Wierenga's appeal to it here, as it seems like an ad hoc attempt to maintain libertarian divine freedom. At heart, then, Wierenga's position is just a statement that God has compatibilist freedom. See also Timothy O'Connor, "Freedom with a Human Face," *Midwest Studies in Philosophy* 29, no. 1 (2005): 207–27.

wrote, "There seem to be two alternatives: either he chooses on the basis of some accidental feature of one alternative lacked by all the others, a feature not related to optimificity, or he chooses as a result of pure whimsy. Neither of these alternatives is very appealing."[73] Helm evidently found it more appealing to claim that God had to create this specific world because his choice was constrained by the fact that this is the best of all possible worlds and it is best for God to create rather than not create. Now, to be fair, Helm did not use the "best of all possible worlds" language, but that is what his argument amounts to, and other prominent Calvinists have made use of such language to describe their own positions, indistinguishable from Helm's.[74]

The fatalistic ramifications of such constraints on God's creative activity should be obvious.[75] If God is a necessary being, and all his actions flow necessarily from his unchanging and eternal nature, then the results of his actions are also necessary. That is, the creation is necessary, and even we are necessary, even though not in the same way that God is necessary. His necessity derives from his eternal nature, whereas our necessity derives from his necessary action. We remain contingent in a sort of way, but not in the way we normally think. When I say that I am contingent, I not only mean that my existence is dependent upon someone else (i.e., God), but I also mean that I might not have been and that there is nothing about me to suggest that I *had to be*. Following Helm's version of Calvinism, one cannot make the same claims; we are seen as necessary beings of sorts, but this is closer to pagan fatalism than biblical faith. So, it seems we must affirm that God created freely and could have refrained from creating, and while we agree that God must do that which is best, we can affirm that there are a virtually infinite number of equally good worlds God could create. If he could have either created or not created or created differently, then he has libertarian freedom, at least with respect to creating.

In addition, if God does not have libertarian freedom, then his providence over history must be as it is and could not have been otherwise. This means that history is necessary and the future is not really open or contingent, at least not with respect

---

[73] Paul Helm, *Eternal God* (New York: Oxford University Press, 1988), 180.

[74] Most notably, John Piper has made this claim many times in sermons, podcasts, and lectures.

[75] Unfortunately, the relationship to fatalism is often missed, obvious though it seems. This is due in large part to ignorance and misinformation about the nature of historic fatalism. See John D. Laing, "Calvinism, Natural Knowledge and Fatalism" (paper read at Southwest Regional Meeting of the Evangelical Theological Society, Fort Worth, TX, 2014; and Houston Baptist University Philosophy Conference, Houston, TX, 2014).

to which events will happen and which events will not happen. They are not only determined by God's free choice of will, but they are determined by his nature so that there is really only one option for the future. Even God could not alter it! To be sure, my Calvinist friends will retort that God would not want to alter it, for it is the best future possible, but the point is that these restrictions do seem to limit God's providence and detract from his glory and omnipotence in ways that simply saying he cannot do evil, for instance, do not.

More importantly, though, they also suggest that God had to save those he did, but no one wants to say that! It is a hallmark of Christian orthodoxy to claim that God freely saves those whom he chooses. In a somewhat ironic twist, it seems that Calvinist soteriology (in at least one way) fits more closely with libertarian freedom, for Calvinists emphasize that there is nothing in the elect that makes or even inclines God to choose them for salvation, while non-Calvinists often refer to something like foreseen faith in those God eventually elects.[76] Calvinists explain that God's election of particular persons is solely based in his good pleasure and loving grace. Thus, God's choice of the elect is not typically depicted as one he *had* to make (or could not have rejected), because that would suggest something unique, special, outstanding, or otherwise worthy in the individuals elected for salvation. But this just suggests that God's election is a pure libertarian choice, for any necessity in the election would seemingly undermine either God's graciousness or the sinner's unworthiness. If he could have saved or not saved particular persons, then he has libertarian freedom, at least with respect to our salvation.

Of course, if God enjoys libertarian freedom with respect to creation, providence, and salvation, then he has libertarian freedom. Interestingly, some Calvinists have recognized the fatalistic implications of applying compatibilist freedom to God, but they also cannot accept the notion of divine libertarian freedom because they think libertarianism impossible, for reasons stated above. Thus, they propose a special kind of freedom for God, a kind of freedom creatures do not/cannot enjoy. For example, John Frame wrote, "I would say that God's essential attributes and actions are necessary, but that his decrees and acts of creation, providence, and redemption are free.

---

[76] Of course, this is not to suggest that non-Calvinists deny salvation by grace through faith, or argue for a version of Pelagianism or Semi-Pelagianism (Calvinist charges notwithstanding). When most non-Calvinists suggest that God bases his election decisions on foreseen faith, they assume that those who would have faith would only do so if the Holy Spirit were to enable them. That is, God elects persons he knows will believe if they are given the requisite enabling grace by God's Spirit.

They are free, not merely in a compatibilist sense, nor at all in a libertarian sense, but in the sense that we know nothing in God's nature that constrains these acts or prevents their opposites."[77] As I have noted elsewhere, Frame's explanation of God's freedom is indistinguishable from libertarian freedom, save his insistence that they are not identical. His claim that God's acts are free and nothing prevents their opposites is just an affirmation of divine libertarian freedom.[78]

Thus, it seems that the compatibilist is faced with a choice (no pun intended): he may continue to maintain that libertarianism is logically incoherent, claim that both God and humanity enjoy compatibilist freedom, and accept the fatalistic consequences; he may accept the logical consistency of libertarianism, claim that both God and humanity enjoy libertarian freedom, and turn from his Calvinist commitments; or he may accept the logical consistency of libertarianism, claim that God enjoys libertarian freedom while humanity only enjoys compatibilist freedom, and accept the inconsistency or chalk the difference up to the Creator/creature distinction. I personally think the last option most attractive to committed Calvinists, though I think they will have a difficult time maintaining the difference once it is placed under the microscope of biblical and theological scrutiny.

In this final section of the essay, I considered two idealized loci of freedom: the freedom of the redeemed in the final state, and the freedom God enjoys in his majesty. I demonstrated that in the case of the former, libertarian freedom is not excluded, while in the case of the latter, libertarian freedom is necessary to avoid a Christianized version of Stoic fatalism. We must affirm that God has libertarian freedom. Thus, if God *must have* libertarian freedom, and the redeemed in heaven *could have* libertarian freedom, then we ought to accept libertarianism as the correct understanding of freedom.

Conclusion

In this essay, I have defined a variety of theological and philosophical terms associated with debates over the nature of freedom, both human and divine. I have considered arguments purported to show that libertarian freedom should not be accepted by Christians—from claims that it is unbiblical, to charges that it violates the fundamental laws of logic and nature, to complaints that it elevates humanity over God

---

[77] Frame, *The Doctrine of God*, 235–36.
[78] Laing, *Middle Knowledge*, 45.

or detracts from some of God's essential attributes and work. I have demonstrated that each of these supposed deficiencies or errors is without merit. I have further presented a strong case for libertarian freedom, noting its utility in theological, judicial, and philosophical thought. Libertarian freedom serves as the ground for our everyday intuitions about right and wrong, guilt and innocence, and love and hate. It is also fundamental to a biblical understanding of humanity and covenant relationship with God. I also demonstrated that there is good reason to believe the saints in heaven enjoy libertarian freedom, and to deny divine libertarian freedom is to accept fatalism. All of this should lead the biblical Christian to view freedom as libertarian, a freedom of choice grounded in the individual will.

13

Evil and God's Sovereignty

—— Bruce A. Little ——

It was a clear morning on September 11, 2001. I was straightening up my office (having moved in only a few days earlier) when a news bulletin caught my attention. My small desk TV was tuned to the *Today* show when a news flash announced that a plane had just crashed into one of the World Trade Center's twin towers. Troubling as that was, it seemed that the immediate danger or threat was limited to those in the immediate vicinity of the event. Soon, however, it became clear that this crash was not a small-scale accident but a premeditated act of terror involving much more than the World Trade Center. It would be hours before the magnitude of destruction and cost of human life bound up in this epoch-making event etched its reality upon the memory banks of American citizens as well as the watching world. On that day, thousands of lives were lost, and many thousands more would never be the same. Where was God? Or was there a God at all, at least the Christian God?

The unthinkable had happened. Staring in the face of a nation was the reality that evil exists in a concrete way. Diplomacy and technology had not banished it to faraway places. The event startled the hearts of millions with a renewed sense of human finiteness and impotency (if only for a time), resulting in an intuitive reaction to call out to God. Instinctively people prayed to and talked of God. This reality once again raised the age-old dilemma: If God is all-powerful and all-good, how could such horrific evil be permitted in a world created and maintained by this God?[1] On the one hand, there is the instinctive need for God in such times; yet, on the other hand, if God is all-powerful and all-good, how did he allow something like 9/11 to happen? That is, if God is as all Christians claim he is, why does evil exist in a world created and maintained by this sovereign God? Furthermore, this event underscores the need of the human heart to have real answers regarding the question of the relation of God to evil. This response must consistently offer an answer concerning suffering (evil) caused by moral agents (such as rape), suffering caused by natural disasters (such as tsunamis), and physical suffering (such as cancer). Any answer that fails to account for these three areas has not yet faced the scope of the question and will be found wanting. If Christianity's claim as a superior worldview is to have any intellectual currency in the marketplace of ideas, it cannot ignore the question of evil. Of course, many have attempted to answer the question of evil, and their answers have only raised other questions.

Not that Christians have not offered answers in the past; they have. This set of answers is often referred to as a theodicy.[2] In clarification, not everybody who deals with the question of evil would subscribe to the concept of theodicy. This essay, however, does not develop or defend a theodicy.[3] In particular, this essay examines answers given by those in the theological tradition called Calvinism. Intellectual integrity presses me to disclose that I do not consider myself a Calvinist, nor an Arminian, but my theological position beyond that is irrelevant to what is going on here.

Clarification on several points hopefully will eliminate misunderstandings that can be all too common to a discussion of this nature. First, not all Calvinists are in

---

[1] The word *evil* is used in a broad sense in this discussion. Its use includes moral evil, which is evil caused by a moral human (or angelic) agent, as well as natural evil and physical evil. Its use here assumes a connection between evil and suffering. I would argue that not all suffering is evil (for example, that which comes from God when he disciplines his children as in Heb 12:6–11). Nonetheless, all suffering has its roots in evil.

[2] The word theodicy (*theos* + *dikē*) signifies the justification of God. It is how one might argue for the existence of God in light of evil.

[3] This topic receives treatment elsewhere: Bruce A. Little, *A Creation-Order Theodicy: God and Gratuitous Evil* (Lanham, MD: University Press of America, 2005).

view here,[4] as I am sure there are exceptions to the rule in any theological position. Second, I do not use the term *Calvinist* in a pejorative sense; it is simply a matter of using a traditional classification regarding a theological position. Third, it is readily acknowledged that the difference between theological positions must not be portrayed as a distinction between those who love God and want to glorify him and those who do not. Each position must stand or fall on the merits or strengths of the arguments supporting the position. Unfortunately, too often important discussions of this nature degenerate into unhelpful rhetoric that unnecessarily creates division between Christian brothers and sisters. The principle of charity is important at this point. It would be silly to think that a person claims a belief he knows is biblically wrong simply because it comes with the theological system he has adopted or because he wants to be different. While theological systems play an important role in doing theology, at the end of the day, one's commitment must be to come to the truth, not simply to defend a system.

Lastly, to my knowledge, no one propositional statement in the Bible sets forth an unambiguous full-orbed answer to this question of evil. Therefore, constructing an answer involves drawing inferences from what the Bible states clearly, a procedure not foreign to the church. In drawing these inferences, the theological inference must neither deny what God affirms nor affirm what God clearly denies; it must strive for internal consistency. Any answer to the question of evil will touch many different doctrines, but however the answer is framed, it must reflect (1) consistency with one's theological system, (2) avoidance of logical fallacies or inconsistencies, and (3) a balanced application of all the acknowledged attributes of God. Method, or what is known as hermeneutics, is therefore important, as are all prior theological assumptions with which one comes to the discussion.

Although this essay begins with the event of 9/11, other events beg for an answer as well and possibly even more so. Hundreds of evil events causing great suffering occur every day around the world; however, they often receive far less publicity because they involve much smaller numbers. Many of these events are cases of horrific evil and suffering that rip families apart and wound human beings in the innermost part of their being because the principal sufferer is a child. Fyodor Dostoevsky's *The Brothers Karamazov* wrestles with this matter, as does Voltaire's *Candide*. In a natural

---

[4] Some within the Reformed tradition take sovereignty to a different level than others. See, for example, R. C. Sproul Jr.'s book, *Almighty over All: Understanding the Sovereignty of God* (Grand Rapids: Baker, 1999).

or intuitive sense, the suffering of small children offends people's moral sensibilities, no matter who they are or what their religious beliefs are. Not only are children seen as defenseless, but the Christian perspective introduces another existential difficulty. What sense is to be made of the abusive cruelty directed toward children when Jesus says they are special in God's sight?

The Gospel of Matthew records the words of Jesus regarding God's view of children: "Assuredly, I say to you, unless you are converted and become as little children, you will by no means enter the kingdom of heaven. . . . Whoever receives one little child like this in My name receives Me" (Matt 18:3, 5).[5] Later, Jesus said concerning the little children: "Take heed that you do not despise one of these little ones, for I say to you that in heaven their angels always see the face of My Father who is in heaven" (v. 10). Jesus rebuked the disciples when they attempted to prevent the little children from coming to him: "But Jesus said, 'Let the little children come to Me, and do not forbid them; for of such is the kingdom of heaven'" (19:14). At the least, these texts indicate that children are special in God's sight. Jesus, who is God, says so. Such texts do not give an answer for why children suffer; they only acknowledge that mistreating children is an offense to God. The suffering of children not only offends God; it offends the moral sensibilities of humanity almost universally. This suffering must be understood as set against the words of Jesus. Therefore, however one answers the question of evil, it must not only address the scope of evil in general, but the suffering of children in particular.

Consider the fictional case of an elementary school student we'll call Sarah Jane, whom a convicted sex offender abuses and murders. Sarah Jane is representative of the many hundreds of real little children, some just toddlers, who are subjected to horrible abuse every year. Not only did Sarah Jane suffer inhumane cruelty, but those related to or associated with her have and will suffer for years to come. Most think if there is a God, then surely he would intervene on behalf of little children; that is, if he were to intervene for any, especially in light of what Jesus says. If God is the God of the universe, why would he allow such things to happen to the innocent ones?[6] Of course, this example does not, on the face of it, serve as a sure defeater of the claim that God exists. Nonetheless, the suffering of children does present a serious

---

[5] All Scripture references in this chapter are taken from the New King James Version unless otherwise stated.

[6] When I speak of children being innocent, I am not suggesting they are not corrupted from birth. I am not using the word in its theological sense, but rather in a sense of personal moral culpability for personal actions.

challenge to those attempting to provide an answer to the question of evil. Where is God in all this?

While this discussion has mentioned the matter of children and their innocence, Calvinists such as John Piper claim that no one is innocent. Commenting on US Airways flight 1549, which on January 15, 2009, experienced an exceptional landing on the Hudson River, Piper said, "God can take down a plane any time he pleases— and if he does, he wrongs no one. Apart from Christ, none of us deserves anything from God but judgment. We have belittled him so consistently that he would be perfectly just to take any of us any time in any way he chooses."[7] This viewpoint means that when Sarah Jane was abused and murdered, God had injured no one. After all, as it is argued, Sarah Jane is a sinner and deserving of the wrath of God, so God owed Sarah Jane nothing. Of course, it is true that God owes human beings nothing and only in Christ is there security from the penalty of sin. Christ died for the sins of the world (1 John 2:1–2), and only those in Christ are delivered from the second death. However, Piper seems to confuse suffering in time with suffering in eternity. If Christ has died for the sins of the world, then the Father has been satisfied on that account. So why claim that because Sarah Jane is a sinner, God can justifiably ordain her torment? In addition, if he ordained her death the way things turned out, then in reality it is the only way it could turn out if sovereignty means anything. It is not that it just happens this way; it is ordained to be this way because God is sovereign—or at least that is how sovereignty is applied to the situation. It is more than simply saying God allowed it to happen.

According to Calvinists such as Piper, God is not blameworthy even though he ordained this atrocity. God ordains the very evil he commands humans to refrain from doing. Either God orders the world by moral principles different from those he gives humankind, or there is a contradiction in the nature of God. What logically follows if one accepts the idea that God ordained Sarah Jane's horrible end, even though the abuser bears the responsibility? Since God ordained the particular act, God also must have ordained the pedophile to act (although according to this view, the pedophile bears the full responsibility for acting the way he does). Understand the logical force of this view: there is no way for Sarah Jane to be abused except for *someone* to abuse her. If the abuse is ordained, then so is the *abuser* ordained to act.

---

[7] John Piper, "The President, the Passengers, and the Patience of God," January 21, 2009, http://www.desiringgod.org/ResourceLibrary/TasteAndSee/ByDate/2009/3520/.

Sarah Jane, however, is not alone in all this suffering; many others suffer as well. The parents, grandparents, and other relatives must live with the knowledge of the abuse as well as with the loss of a dear daughter. One can now only conclude that God also ordained this grief. But Jesus does not seem to reflect an indifferent attitude toward suffering and loss, even though he revealed the Father to humanity (John 1:18).

What about the widow of Nain? It appears that Jesus had compassion on her when he came across the funeral procession taking her only son to be buried. On that occasion, no one begged him to do something and no one prayed. According to the text, "He had compassion on her" (Luke 7:13). Jesus simply reached down, touched the coffin, and said, "Young man, I say to you, arise" (v. 14). The boy's life came into him again. The Calvinist's view of the same God ordaining the abuse and hideous death of a child like Sarah Jane and dispassionately watching her parents grieve seems curious, considering this passage. Furthermore, according to Luke, Jesus proclaims humanity is living in "the acceptable year of the LORD" (4:19) because "God was in Christ reconciling the world to Himself, not imputing their trespasses to them, and has committed to us the word of reconciliation" (2 Cor 5:19). Surely, this passage has something to say to us regarding the way God is now interacting with the world, which seems at odds with the Calvinist's view. One must agree that God, in one sense (apart from his grace), can do as he pleases with any human being. Still, it must not be ignored he has laid something on himself in these days, to be "longsuffering toward us, not willing that any should perish" (2 Pet 3:9). While it is right to affirm God can, in one sense, do as he pleases, his commitments (promises) to his creation constrain him, as does his nature, and this constraint in no way detracts from his sovereignty. Christians are commanded to do good to all people, especially those of the household of faith (Gal 6:10). Should God do less— especially the sovereign God?

The doctrine of divine sovereignty looms large in this discussion and rightly so. If Christians did not claim that God governed as the omnipotent sovereign One over his creation, the question of God and evil would assume a considerably different shape. The doctrine of God's sovereignty stands at the center of the Calvinist position on evil. However, that others may apply divine sovereignty somewhat differently is not the problem. Rather, the problem is how Calvinists understand sovereignty in relationship to the question of evil in the larger context of God's sovereign control.

The other side of the argument focuses on free will. The term *free will* is unfortunate, since it does not precisely mean what is suggested by the term; humans are not free to will anything they wish. Libertarian freedom is a much-preferred term.[8] Many of those who affirm libertarian freedom also affirm a high view of divine sovereignty. That both human free will, which is roughly interchangeable with libertarian freedom, and divine sovereignty have support in the Scriptures explains why many Christians hold to both. The controversy develops over how to understand the relationship between sovereignty and free will. How one understands the relationship goes to the heart of how the question of God and evil is answered.

With that said, the subject at hand—how Calvinists typically answer the question of evil—can move forward. Generally, many Calvinists (as well as any who reject the notion of free will),[9] in explaining evil in this world, appeal to some form of a greater good, which finds its beginnings in Augustine of Hippo. This approach argues that God allows into this world only that evil from which he can either bring about a greater good or prevent a worse evil. Whereas there is no way to know if a worse evil was preempted or not, part of the explanation can probably be dropped. Regarding Augustine's position, Richard Middleton notes, "Whereas Augustine's explicit position in *De Libero Arbitrio* is that the world is no worse for all the evil in it, due to God's providence (technically, that all evil is 'counterbalanced' by good), by the time we get to his later *Enchiridion* Augustine boldly claims that 'God judged it *better* to bring good out of evil than not to permit any evil to exist.'"[10] For Augustine, it was better for persons to have free will than not, even though free will made evil possible (not necessary) in God's creation.[11] Augustine argued that it was God's goodness that led him to create persons with free will, for he said it is better to be a moral being than a nonmoral being: "Such is the generosity of God's goodness that He has not refrained from creating even that creature which He foreknew would not only sin

---

[8] There are some slight nuances in definition among those who affirm libertarian freedom, however. Thomas P. Flint offers the following general definition: "A theory of agent causation, according to which the ultimate cause of a free action is not some set of prior conditions, but the agent herself who performs the action." *Divine Providence* (Ithaca, NY: Cornell University Press, 1995), 32. I would add that antecedent events/conditions may incline or influence a person in making the choice, but they neither determine nor cause the choice.

[9] While I use the term *Calvinist* and quote those committed to Calvinism, the critique applies to any who would answer the question of evil in the same way. I will quote from two well-recognized spokespersons for this position: John Piper and Gordon H. Clark. These Calvinists are quoted to avoid the charge of merely responding to a straw person.

[10] Richard J. Middleton, "Why the 'Greater Good' Isn't a Defense," *Koinonia* 9, no. 1 (1997): 83–84.

[11] For clarity, this is Augustine's position before AD 414.

but remain in the will to sin. As a runaway horse is better than a stone which does not run away because it lacks self-movement and sense perception, so the creature is more excellent which sins by free will than that which does not sin only because it has no free will."[12]

Augustine affirmed that sin came by human free will and that God in no way ordained or forced humans to do evil. In fact, evil was not necessary even though God knew about it. Augustine wrote, "Your [God's] foreknowledge would not be the cause of his [man's] sin, though undoubtedly he [humanity] would sin; otherwise you would not foreknow that this would happen. Therefore, these two are not contradictory, your foreknowledge and someone else's free act. So too God compels no one to sin, though He foresees those who will sin by their own will."[13]

For the early Augustine, the will is free and, therefore, persons are truly morally responsible for their acts. Furthermore, Augustine maintained that the will is culpable for its own turning or it is its own cause. He noted that the will's turn from good to evil "belongs only to the soul, and is voluntary and therefore culpable."[14] However, he believed that God, in his providence, brings good out of the evil he allowed, thus justifying the evil being allowed. Augustine had a robust view of God's providence, which understands God's work in history to bring good out of all evil; in fact, such evil is the only evil that God would allow into the world. Today, many within the Calvinist tradition argue that the greater good is the glory of God (Augustine argued for particular goods in this life) and deny the idea of free will. Furthermore, there is a subtle shift from God *allows* to God has a *purpose*.

Some claim that God has a purpose in all evil that he allows, but they give some room for human free will. Others, such as Piper, maintain that God has a purpose and actually *ordains* or wills the evil for this purpose. In the latter case the purpose of evil is to glorify God and is solidly constructed on God's sovereignty. In other words, either God controls all things in the strong sense, or he controls nothing. To be truly sovereign means that whatever happens on earth, if it is for his good purposes, is willed by God; otherwise, there could be no assurance his purpose would be accomplished. Two questions surface from this view: (1) Does divine sovereignty require

---

[12] Augustine, *The Problem of Free Choice*, trans. Dom Mark Pontifex, ed. Johannes Quasten and Joseph C. Plumpe, Ancient Christian Writers 22 (Westminster, MD: Newman Press, 1955), 155; *De Libero Arbitrio*, 3.4.15.

[13] Augustine, *Free Choice*, 150; *De Libero Arbitrio*, 3.4.10.

[14] Augustine, *Free Choice*, 141; *De Libero Arbitrio*, 3.1.2.

this strong view to maintain a biblical view of sovereignty? (2) If God ordains or wills all things, in what way do persons, not God, stand morally responsible for their acts? Greater-good approaches differ, for in Augustine's thinking, God's providence allows evil, whereas in more recent Calvinistic views, God actually ordains or wills the evil. In the case of Sarah Jane, then, according to one view, God *allowed* her to be abused to the point of death for no reason other than pure wickedness on the part of the perpetrator, and God would bring some good from it. I do not mean to say that this view does not raise other questions as well, but I am only pointing out the difference. According to the other view, God *ordained* it for the greater glory for Christ, which is his good purpose.

Those who take what might be considered a more moderate Calvinistic view (often referred to as compatibilism) rest their answer to evil on Rom 8:28. This text, however, only affirms that God works "together for good to those who love God, to those who are the called according to His purpose." A casual reading of the text reveals that this working together applies only to those who "love God," which excludes the majority of earth's population and says nothing about natural disasters. This verse, while it provides comfort for the believer, does not provide a foundational position from which to answer the question of evil. Asserting that God allows evil because he will bring about some good from it finds no support in this verse. A cursory examination of the greater-good explanation for all evil reveals serious weaknesses.[15] Because this explanation plays a part in so many Christian responses to evil, briefly considering some of those weaknesses will be helpful. The critique will also show how these weaknesses apply to the Calvinist position under consideration here.

First, it seems rather obvious (at least to me) that something happens in this world either because God has *allowed* it or *ordained* it. I envision no objection on that point except maybe from those who hold to open theism. The point of concern arises over *why* he allows it. That God allows it because his sovereign hand will bring some good (particular good things or the good of God's glory) from the evil, faces some serious challenges. This challenge does not say that God cannot bring good from evil. The challenge is whether the good obtained morally justifies God in

---

[15] The questions from evil are difficult and complex. All views have some weaknesses to them. In the end, one should go with the answer that embraces the largest amount of biblical material consistently and with the least amount of appeal to mystery.

allowing the evil. For the moment, set aside that Rom 8:28 does not explain much of the suffering in this world; it says nothing about why God *allows* suffering. It affirms that God will bring some good from certain kinds of suffering. These are two different matters—why he *allows* suffering and what he might *do* in the suffering. To suggest that one can move from what God might do with suffering to why he allowed the suffering makes one a consequentialist, in which the end justifies the means. That is, justifying the cause by looking at the effect is tantamount to allowing the end to excuse or justify the means. The text says nothing about why God allows the suffering.

Still, if God ordains or allows the evil, a few practical matters come to light. If God allows or ordains the evil to bring about the good (regardless of what the good is), what does that say about the Christian's responsibility to uphold social justice? If God allows or ordains evil to bring good, then it would seem that Christians should not be engaged in standing against social injustice (that which the Bible calls evil). Should they stop it, they would keep the good from obtaining—a good necessary to God's plan. If God is really sovereign and he ordains the evil, it would be impossible for mere humans to stop it, so standing against social injustice would be an exercise in futility. Apply this to the matter of abortion, an act that can be properly put in the category of evil (taking of life). Since abortion is presently occurring, then God either allows or ordains it for some good. Therefore, logically, to attempt to eliminate abortion would, in fact, be frustrating (or at least attempting to frustrate) God's plan to bring some good. In addition, if God allows evil, the good must be necessary, which in turn makes evil necessary.

The second concern pertains to the relationship between good and evil within the plan of God. The good (whether the good be some particular good or the glory of God) must in some way accomplish God's purposes; therefore, the good must be necessary to his purposes. If the good can only come from the evil, then the evil also must be necessary to God's plan. Avoiding this conclusion seems difficult:

> God cannot bring about certain goods without particular evils, for if any evil will do, God should pick the least of the sufferings. Also, if God can bring about the good without the evil, then he should for if He can and He does not, then He is not the good God being defended. One could argue that if God needs particular evils to bring about certain goods, then God is not omnipotent. In this case, the all-good, all-powerful God is unable to bring a good without the help of evil. Immediately one can see how theologically

convoluted this becomes. It diminishes God and makes evil a necessary part of His plan.[16]

If evil is necessary to the plan of God, then since it is God's plan, he is the one responsible for evil, which John seems to contradict clearly by claiming that "God is light and in Him is no darkness at all" (1 John 1:5b). In the case of Sarah Jane, her abuse then was necessary to some good in the overall purposes of God, regardless of whether he allowed it or ordained it.

Once the move has been made to make evil a part of God's design within his larger plan, the direct line to God as the cause of evil becomes straighter and stronger. If the sovereign God is in control of all things, then what happens on this earth must fulfill his particular purposes. Furthermore, either all things have a purpose, or all things are chaotic or left to chance. Since chaos and chance are incompatible with God's sovereignty, it supposedly follows that all things must have a purpose, and the guarantee of this purpose is God's will. There seems to be, however, a mistake of logic at this point. The suggestion cannot be sustained that if all things in life are not a part of God's purpose, then things are left to chance. This argument fails because it does not distinguish between reason and purpose.

Undoubtedly, or so it seems to me, if God is truly sovereign, then for everything that happens (at least on earth) there is a reason, not necessarily a purpose. Often, Scripture provides the record of God's reason for something happening but not necessarily his purpose. Consider God's relationship with Israel as expressed in Deuteronomy 28. God is not giving his purpose in what he says but rather expressing the reason the outcomes in Israel's life will be different depending on her choices. Giving that explanation is not, however, the same thing as saying that for everything that happens there must be a purpose. An illustration will display the difference. If, when you ask me why I did not pay my electric bill, I say because I did not have the money, then what I have given you is a reason. Should I, however, reply that I did not pay my electric bill because I am protesting the recent hike in the price of electricity, then I have given you the purpose for which I did not pay my electric bill. As the examples illustrate, the reason and the purpose for an action differ. Therefore, it is perfectly consistent to affirm that because God is sovereign, nothing happens on this earth by chance, as there is always a reason. That God has purposes regarding history cannot be denied. Some things happen because God has a purpose, such as

---

[16] Little, *Creation-Order Theodicy*, 112.

sending his Son to be the Savior of the world (John 3:16), but that explanation does not account for all events or acts.

In a larger sense is the difference between contrivance and order. One can contrive certain things to indicate purpose. Other things, however, happen by order within the universe, which supplies the reason these things occur. If people fall off a high building, it is not a matter of chance that they hurt themselves, as that is what would be predicted because of the way the world is structured. That example illustrates a reason flowing from the natural order. If, on the other hand, people jump off the building to take their own lives, they are depending on natural order to accomplish their purposes. These two events differ not in that one is chaotic and the other is not chaotic, since both are predictable. Both have a reason, but a purpose is involved only in the latter case. God surely has sufficient reasons for allowing things to happen on this planet within the established natural order of creation, but that does not require claiming that he has a purpose in all things. Sometimes things happen because of the ordering of the universe: "Whatever a man sows, that he will also reap" (Gal 6:7). Furthermore, sometimes God purposes something, and because of the human agent's disobedience, it does not reach fruition (Isa 5:4). Israel's disobedience gives the reason things turned out as they did. God's purpose is to produce fruit. When that does not happen, he judges his vineyard (vv. 5–7) so that Israel might repent. That explains the purpose of the judgment. Israel suffered, but that was not God's purpose in planting the vineyard. In the end, God's purpose for Israel and the world will come to pass despite disobedience, because of his providential hand in history. He is the sovereign One who works through his providence to bring history to its final appointed place. Therefore, it is possible to maintain a robust view of sovereignty and order in this world, while maintaining that evil in this world is not necessarily the work of God's purposes.

A second, related matter is how to understand sovereignty. The idea of sovereignty can be understood in two ways. One way to understand that God has control (sovereignty) is by thinking of a man controlling his vehicle. If he turns the steering wheel left, the car (under normal circumstances) goes left. That is, there is a direct connection between the direction of the vehicle and the will of the driver. This form of sovereignty is *strong sovereignty*. Another way to understand God's control is the man who is in control of his family. He ensures that everybody follows the established rules. This form is called *simple sovereignty* and is the one displayed in ancient Near Eastern texts referring to the suzerain and his vassal. There is more than one legitimate way to understand God as being in control (sovereign). The latter view of sovereignty is precisely how John Piper sees God's control when speaking about Satan. Piper wrote, "God has given him [Satan] astonishing latitude to work his sin and misery in the world. He is a great ruler over the world, but not the *ultimate* one. God holds the decisive sway."[17] Surely, the same sovereign God who deals with Satan also deals with human beings. In Piper's theology, God does not give humans that same latitude as he gives Satan.

John Piper's writings display the view of strong sovereignty. Piper, an evangelical leader, has brought much spiritual encouragement to the community of faith. Therefore, the following interaction with him is only to see how, as a Calvinist, he answers the question of God and evil with a strong sovereignty view. In an Internet post, Piper referred to the event others dubbed the "Miracle on the Hudson" as a parable for our nation. The event unfolded on January 15, 2009, when US Airways flight 1549, shortly after takeoff, encountered a flock of birds (geese), some of which were sucked into the plane's engines and shut them down. Captain Sullenberger, an experienced pilot, chose to land the plane on the Hudson River rather than attempt a landing at an airport several miles away. By all accounts, it was one of those events where training, outstanding judgment, and right circumstances came together, resulting in all passengers surviving. The nation rightfully celebrated Captain Sullenberger as a hero. Piper, however, had a little different take on the event. He wrote: "Two laser-guided missiles would not have been as amazingly effective as were those geese. It is incredible, statistically speaking. If God governs nature down to the fall (and the flight) of every bird, as Jesus says (Matt 10:29), then the crash of flight 1549 was designed by God."[18] He goes on to say, "If God guides geese so precisely, he also guides the captain's hand."[19] In other words, God in his sovereignty is even responsible for the movement of the pilot's hands. Furthermore, according to Piper, this entire event was "designed" by God. This assertion can only mean that God in his sovereignty designed it before the world began to fit his purposes. If that is so, God did not merely *allow* this; he designed and executed it. In his omnipotence he executed the plan by, among other things, guiding the flight of the geese and the hands of the pilot to bring about an event that will, as Piper says, give a parable of his power to the nation. There is no way for things to turn out differently. Who is responsible

---

[17] John Piper, *Spectacular Sins: And Their Global Purpose in the Glory of Christ* (Wheaton, IL: Crossway, 2008), 44.

[18] John Piper, "Patience of God."

[19] Piper, "Patience of God."

for this event? According to this view of things, God controlled all things right down to guiding the geese into the engine and guiding the hands of the pilot. God is responsible but not morally culpable. The logic of this view means that God also designed all events that preceded that event. This view includes making sure those precise geese were there at that particular moment as well as ordaining everything in Sullenberger's life so he would be on that plane on that day. Notice it is not that God providentially intervened in the moment in response to some prayer or by his own mercy. According to this view, God designed the entire scenario to serve his purposes, purportedly to show his power to a new president and to a nation.

Only a few days after "Miracle on the Hudson" happened, another airplane mishap occurred, but this time fifty people died. According to reports, "Continental Connection Flight 3407 from Newark, New Jersey, came in squarely through the roof of the house, its tail section visible through flames shooting at least 50 feet high."[20] As the Continental commuter plane was coming in for a landing, it slammed into a house in suburban Buffalo, sparking a fiery explosion that killed all forty-nine people aboard and a person in the home. Although the investigation is unfinished, the preliminary investigation concluded that "pilot commands—not a buildup of ice on the wings and tail—likely initiated the fatal dive of the twin-engine Bombardier Q400 into a neighborhood six miles short of the Buffalo, New York, airport, according to people familiar with the situation."[21]

Applying Piper's theological explanation of the Hudson episode, it logically follows that in this case God guided the pilot of flight 3407 to misjudgment in order that God "would bring the plane down," killing fifty people. It might be argued that he only guided the hand where safety resulted and that flight 3407 was just an accident. Yet, if Piper maintains that all evil occurs to give glory to Christ, then one can reasonably conclude that in both situations God was involved, bringing his design to pass, which includes this evil. Since God owes no one anything, he has not harmed the fifty people killed. In his book *Spectacular Sins,* Piper wrote in the section titled "All Things *for* Jesus—Even Evil":

[20] "Buffalo Plane Crash: Continental Connotation Flight 3407 Crashes into House, Kills 50," HuffPost, December 6, 2017. https://www.huffpost.com/entry/plane-crashes-into-house_n_166609.
[21] "Buffalo Crash May Have Been Pilot Error—Not Ice Buildup," *Larry King Live,* February 18, 2009, https://larrykinglive.blogs.cnn.com/2009/02/18/buffalo-crash-may-have-been-pilot-error-not-ice-build-up/.

This book is also meant to show that everything that exists—including evil—is ordained by an infinitely holy and all-wise God to make the glory of Christ shine more brightly. The word *ordained* is peculiar, I know. But I want to be clear what I mean by it. There is no attempt to obscure what I am saying about God's relation to evil. But there is an attempt to say carefully what the Bible says. By *ordain* I mean that God either caused something directly or *permitted* it for wise purposes. This permitting is a kind of *indirect* causing, since God knows all the factors involved and what effects they will have and he could prevent any outcome.[22]

Later Piper claims:

So when I say that everything that exists—including evil—is ordained by an infinitely holy and all-wise God to make the glory of Christ shine more brightly, I mean that, one way or the other, God sees to it that all things serve to glorify his Son. Whether he causes or permits, he does so with purpose. For an infinitely wise and all-knowing God, both causing and permitting are purposeful. They are part of the big picture of what God plans to bring to pass.[23]

Notice the words "purpose" and "purposeful." It may be simply a poor choice of words, but context implies that it is not. Piper carefully uses his words to say that in all the evil on this earth, God has a purpose: to make the glory of Christ shine brighter. If it is for the purposes of God, and purpose reflects the will of God, then the will of God is not perfect if any evil fails to materialize. Sarah Jane's torturous death is part of God's will. This position not only makes evil necessary to the purposes of God; it makes God morally responsible for the evil.

Addressing this matter, Piper agrees that God seems blameworthy, but he claims God is not. In fact, Piper argues that in all of this, God is not blameworthy; we just do not understand how it is this way, but it is. Piper explains his claim regarding the "sovereignty of God over sin" by adding a footnote to demonstrate how he squares that view with Jas 1:13–15. He wrote:

Thus it seems to me that James is saying that *God* never experiences this kind of "being dragged away" or "being lured." And he does not directly (see

---

[22] Piper, *Spectacular Sins*, 54.
[23] Piper, 56.

Chapter Four, note 1) produce that "dragging" and that "luring" toward evil in humans. In some way (that we may not be able to fully comprehend), God is able without blameworthy "tempting" to see to it that a person does what God ordains for him to do even if it involves evil.[24]

In the end, Piper concludes that though people may not understand it, God ordains evil but at the same time is not blameworthy for the evil. What does this say about the abuse of Sarah Jane and her abductor and all the events surrounding that horrible day? Could Christ's glory not shine brighter with a lot less trauma to Sarah Jane and her friends and family? So, God not only loves the glory of Christ more than he loves Sarah Jane; he is actually willing to ordain the evil that befalls her that Christ's glory might shine brighter.

The glory of the Lord is important (1 Cor 10:31), but to say that God ordains evil to magnify the glory of Christ seems to confuse the difference between good and evil. That is, God ordained Sarah Jane's suffering for the purpose of making the glory of Christ shine brighter. Yet if a righteous life glorifies God (1 Cor 6:20), how does evil also glorify God? How do the contraries, one commanded and the other forbidden, both glorify God? That Christ *will* be glorified is not debated. It is not whether Christ *will receive* glory, because it seems that in the *eschaton* he will. As Paul said, "Therefore God has highly exalted Him [Christ] and given Him the name which is above every name, that at the name of Jesus every knee should bow, of those in heaven, and of those on earth, . . . and that every tongue should confess that Jesus Christ is Lord, to the glory of the Father" (Phil 2:9–11). But Paul's statement is an affirmation of a different sort. This only tells what the end will be and is silent on the issue of necessity or causality. The statement says only that despite the evil, God has the last word, and glory will come to Christ even though at one point he was rejected. To say that all this particular evil was necessary to Christ's glory says something quite different.

The idea of God's glory in history fills the pages of Scripture. The point of concern is whether the triumph over sin makes Christ's glory shine brighter. The night of Christ's betrayal (just before going to the cross), he prayed, "And now, O Father, glorify Me together with Yourself, with the glory which I had with You before the world" was (John 17:5). The glory for which Jesus prayed is the glory he had with the Father before the world existed. Jesus is not referring to a glory that comes because

---

[24] Piper, 24.

he is about to defeat evil on the cross, but rather the glory was before creation. Undoubtedly, Christ's work on the cross demonstrates the redemption by the incarnated Son crucified for the sins of the world; that, however, does not seem to be the argument. The argument is that God ordains all individual events of evil as part of his plan so that Christ's glory might shine brighter. In the end, when the words used are understood in the common usage, sin is a part of the plan of God. It is, as Piper said, "part of the big picture of what God plans to bring to pass."[25] For the sovereign God has only one big picture.

To be clear at this point, the question is not whether God will bring glory to himself in the end. He will. The concern is that in Calvinist theology God ordains the evil along the way in order for the glory of Christ to shine brighter. But how many acts of evil does it take to show that Christ has power over them? Does each act of evil result in the glory of Christ shining brighter? If this is the case, then it seems people need the ugly to appreciate beauty. That would mean that the beauty and glory of God could not be fully appreciated until there was the ugly—evil. So Adam in the garden could not appreciate the beauty and glory of God. Does that not necessitate the fall in the garden? The necessity of the fall, which has resulted in horrible evils of human cruelty, to say nothing of thousands going to hell, is now justified on the grounds it was needed for Christ's glory to shine brighter. The logic of this argument says the more evil there is, the brighter Christ's glory will shine. The Bible, though, does not command people to order our lives in such a way; in fact, it commands just the opposite: "What shall we say then? Shall we continue in sin that grace may abound? Certainly not!" (Rom 6:1–2). Therefore, that God would order his creation this way seems curious. At the end of the day, it certainly looks as though in the Calvinist system God not only ordained evil but *needs* evil if Christ is to get the greater glory. In fact, it makes the fall in the garden necessary, which in the end means Adam had no choice. So why is God not the one morally responsible even if for a good cause—the glory of Christ?

Gordon H. Clark, arguing for what he calls the Calvinist position on God and evil, wrote, "As God cannot sin, so in the next place, God is not responsible for sin, even though he decrees it."[26] In responding to an Arminian position, he wrote, "I wish very frankly and pointedly to assert that if a man gets drunk and shoots his family, it

---

[26] Gordon H. Clark, *God and Evil: The Problem Solved* (Unicoi, TN: Trinity Foundation, 2004), 40.

was the will of God that he should do so. . . . In Eph 1:11 Paul tells us that God works all things, not some things only, after the counsel of his own will."[27] Notice here, Clark said it is God's will and earlier he said it is *decreed* by God, and yet he maintains that God is not responsible or blameworthy for causing sin or evil. Piper says evil is *ordained* by God, but God is not blameworthy. The verse Clark quotes only says what God *does* with all things; it does not say that God *wills* all things. It says that God works all things according to the counsel of his will. This verse seems to say only that the providential work of God in human history keeps the plan of God for humanity on course. Notice this verse is saying something quite different from what Clark says.

In the middle of all this discussion lies the question of moral responsibility. Those of a Calvinistic position often disavow God's moral responsibility for evil.[28] Both Clark and Piper maintain that their deterministic explanations for evil do not shift the moral responsibility to God. Instead, both claim that God is not blame-worthy and humanity is responsible. Still, apart from assigning moral responsibility, according to the Calvinist's position, the evil in this world would not be here if God had not ordained or willed it. In other words, in the final analysis, our fictional Sarah Jane (and the hundreds of real children like her) suffered her end because of God. The Holocaust, the millions slain by Stalin, Pol Pot's killing in Cambodia, every baby beaten to death, every cancer, and so forth could not be here if it were not for God willing it or ordaining it. At the end of the day, it seems hard to escape the conclusion that God is morally responsible, despite arguments to the contrary.

Gordon Clark presents one way of responding to the charge that the Calvinist position leaves God morally responsible for evil even though he ordained it. Clark seeks to smooth out the contradiction by crafting the notion of God's secret will and his revealed will. In the context of Genesis 22, Clark wrote:

> One may speak of the secret will of God, and one may speak of the revealed will of God. Those who saw self-contradiction in the previous case would no doubt argue similarly on this point too. The Arminian would say that God's will cannot contradict itself, and that therefore his secret will cannot contradict his revealed will. Now, the Calvinist would say the same thing; but he has a clearer notion of what contradiction is, and what the Scriptures say. It was God's secret will that Abraham should not sacrifice his son Isaac; but it was his

---

[27] Clark, 27.

[28] R. C. Sproul Jr. may be an exception. However, one might argue that he is the most consistent with the Calvinist position.

revealed (for a time) [will], his command, that he should do so. Superficially this seems like a contradiction. But it is not. The statement, or command, "Abraham, sacrifice Isaac," does not contradict the statement, at the moment known only to God, "I have decreed that Abraham shall not sacrifice his son." If Arminians had a keener sense of logic they would not be Arminians.[29]

For the moment the Calvinist-Arminian debate will be put aside to consider Clark's argument on its own merit. The logic of some of his argument may not be as clear as he affirms. He claims the contradiction is removed by affirming God's secret will is that Abraham must not sacrifice his son, while the revealed will is that he should sacrifice his son. Suggesting that God knows which will prevails hardly resolves the contradiction. It is difficult to see how appealing to God's knowledge solves the problem. In fact, appealing to God's knowledge seems to strengthen the problem. The conclusion is that God has two apparently incoherent wills, since he knows two contraries simultaneously. If God is sovereign, how does he have two wills (secret and revealed) regarding the same event, especially when the wills affirm contraries? Clark admits there is an apparent contradiction in the text, but he thinks he has solved it. However, I think his solution fails on logical grounds. Undoubtedly there is a solution to this apparent contradiction, but I suggest it is not Clark's solution.

Clark's explanation in Abraham's situation involving God's secret will and the revealed will must also be applied to the drunk who kills his family. It was God's secret will that the drunk not shoot his family, but it was God's revealed will that the drunk should shoot his family. Yet it is the revealed will that is actually accomplished in time and space. So, what happens in this case is just the opposite of what happens in the case of Abraham. The secret will in the case of the drunk is that he should not murder (Exod 20:13), yet when he murders, Clark says it is God's will. Is this the secret will or the revealed will? Surely Clark cannot be saying that murder is the secret will of God. The killing of the family, since Clark affirms it is God's will, must be the revealed will of God. Still, this argument puts the revealed will and the secret will of the sovereign God in conflict, so that apparently one is a sovereign will and the other is not. The command "Do not murder" appears to be the sovereign will of God. Therefore, when Clark affirms the murder of the family as God's will, it cannot be the sovereign will, which is the affirmation he seeks to argue. Accordingly, in the

---

[29] Clark, *God and Evil*, 28.

fictitious case of Sarah Jane, both her abuse and non-abuse were God's will. At the end of the day, this view can only be called incoherent. God is presented as willing what he does not will, and yet he is not guilty of contradiction, nor is he found to be blameworthy in the murder.

If God is not blameworthy, who is? Only one other agent is involved, humanity. According to Calvinism, humanity does not have free will in the libertarian sense, so how can humanity be morally responsible? Both Piper and Clark agree that God ultimately is the cause of evil—either directly (Clark) or indirectly (Piper). Piper uses the term *ordained* (direct in some cases, or in the sense of indirect causation when it comes to evil), and Clark affirms that God directly wills the evil. If God wills or ordains the evil but is not blameworthy and persons do not have free will, then who is morally responsible? Both Piper and Clark maintain that the individual bears the moral responsibility for his evil even though he cannot do otherwise. Clark attempts an answer to this question:

> Perhaps the matter can be made clearer by stating in other words precisely what the question is. The question is, Is the will free? The question is not, Is there a will? Calvinism most assuredly holds that Judas acted voluntarily. He chose to betray Christ. He did so willingly. No question is raised as to whether he had a will. What the Calvinist asks is whether that will was free. Are there factors or powers that determine a person's choice, or is the choice causeless? Could Judas have chosen otherwise? Not, could he have done otherwise, had he chosen; but, could he have chosen in opposition to God's foreordination? *Acts 4:28* indicates he could not.[30]

Clark's point is that one cannot choose other than he did although he could have done differently, but only if God had willed differently.

Clark separates the idea of "free" from the idea of will. The will is never free in the absolute sense, but for Clark, it is not free in any sense. Clark's view entails that the human will cannot choose in any meaningful sense. The human will becomes merely the channel through which what God has willed is actualized. In the case of the man who abused Sarah Jane, he could only have chosen otherwise if God had willed otherwise. Still, the abuser is responsible. Clark affirms humans have a will because of its association with human actions, not because it functions as a will in the normal sense of the word (that which freely chooses between one thing and its contrary).

---

[30] Clark, 30.

For many, including the early Augustine, the will carried within it the freedom to move itself. Augustine noted:

> So what need is there to ask the source of that movement by which the will turns from the unchangeable good to the changeable good? We agree that it belongs only to the soul, and is voluntary and therefore culpable; and the whole value of teaching in this matter consists in its power to make us censure and check this movement, and turn our wills away from temporal things below us to enjoyment of the everlasting good."[31]

Therefore, Augustine maintains that the will is at least culpable for its own turning before the fall (and for some time he also believed it was true after the fall). In fact, Richard Swinburne claims this view persisted in the church for the first four centuries. He wrote, "My assessment of the Christian theological tradition is that all Christian theologians of the first four centuries believed in human free will in the libertarian sense, as did all subsequent Eastern Orthodox theologians, and most Western Catholic theologians from Duns Scotus (in the fourteenth century) onward."[32] Most often, theologians believe that libertarian freedom is the only way humans could be morally responsible for their actions, as the Bible clearly affirms. The notion of will carries with it the idea of the ability to choose between this and that—between contraries even. To say that the will is not free is to render what is called a will to be something other than a will, at least in any common understanding of the word.

Clark anticipates another question, namely, how can something be called a choice if it is a necessity? If God wills something (actually all things), in what sense could a person be said to have a choice? Clark responds:

> Choice and necessity are therefore not incompatible. Instead of prejudging the question by confusing choice with free choice, one should give an explicit definition of choice. The adjective could be justified only afterward, if at all. Choice may be defined, at least sufficiently for the present purpose, as a mental act that consciously initiates and determines a further choice. The ability to have chosen otherwise is an irrelevant matter and has no place in the definition.[33]

---

[31] Augustine, *Free Choice*, 141; *De Libero Arbitrio*, 3.1.2.

[32] Richard G. Swinburne, *Providence and the Problem of Evil* (New York: Clarendon, 1998), 35.

[33] Clark, *God and Evil*, 32.

Clark is emphasizing that the will is only something that initiates and determines a further choice. The will is not a kind of self-determiner, as Augustine and many of the church fathers taught, but rather the will only initiates what God has willed. It is how the will of God enters into history. One is not sure which of God's two wills, the secret will or the revealed will, enters into history. Clark seems to be saying that humankind has the ability of choice but not the freedom to choose. It is curious how this comports with the idea of moral responsibility. It sounds something like, persons can have any color car they want as long as they want black. It is true they can choose to have a car or not have a car, but they cannot in any legitimate sense say that they have a choice regarding color. In the end, the will in Clark's terms is no will at all.

The logical end of the Calvinist position on the question of sovereignty leads to a strong form of determinism, which is not the necessary outcome of biblical sovereignty. In addition, moral responsibility for sin must find its final causal agent to be God. The protest against drawing this conclusion involves an argument that commits the fallacy of equivocation (particularly with the word "will") and the fallacy of explaining by naming—just saying it is so makes it so. Yet the Bible seems to say something different. In the Scriptures, humans can choose between contraries such as life and death (Deut 30:15–19; Josh 24:15; Isa 56:4). The Old Testament is a story of God's responding to the checkered history of Israel in which at one time she is acting faithfully and the next minute she is playing the part of the harlot. The book of Judges is a sad story revealing a pattern where Israel freely chooses unfaithfulness against God's command and how God intervenes. Consider the review of God's curses and blessings in Deuteronomy 28. There, if Israel obeyed, blessing (v. 1); but if Israel disobeyed, the curses would come upon Israel (v. 15). Either this account is real history, or God makes it look as though the people have real free choices when, in fact, they do not, if the Calvinists are right. If Israelite disobedience was not a free choice, then moral responsibility cannot be imputed. Whereas definite, different outcomes resulted, depending on whether the people of Israel obeyed or disobeyed, the commonsense understanding is that the people freely chose between the contraries. Otherwise, the whole episode is meaningless. In the end their choices may be worse than meaningless—more likely illusionary and deceptive as far as the record goes. To say they chose but were not free is to void the meaning of "to choose," and then language means nothing. Not only that, but it destroys the entire notion of justice. The man who abused and murdered Sarah Jane in our earlier story could not have chosen to do differently. In the plain sense of language, that choice means he should not be held accountable. On the other hand, to affirm that God ordains but is not morally responsible cannot be solved by simply appealing to mystery.

While Calvinists such as John Piper can be respected for their desire to honor the Lord, on this issue they are simply wrong, and their position is incoherent. Unfortunately, being wrong in this area has some serious implications for areas of theology that go beyond the question of evil. At the end of the day, if Calvinists wish to hold to their view of sovereignty, they should be willing to accept the logical conclusion of their position and acknowledge that God is morally responsible for evil. Then they can attempt to build a case for why that conclusion does not directly conflict with the clear teaching of Scripture. If my critique has any legitimacy, at the end of the day, the Calvinist position logically entails that God is both causally and morally responsible for 9/11, the drunk murdering his family, and the abuse and death of Sarah Jane. The news recently reported that a man brutally murdered one relative and decapitated another, both of the victims minors, before police shot him. These acts were also ordained by God if Piper and others are right. Is that what the Bible teaches?

Some understandably disagree with the conclusion that the Calvinist position as outlined in this chapter is incoherent. In a kind critique of my position on libertarian freedom as it appeared in the first edition of *Whosoever Will,* Tom Nettles rightly concluded that the issue of freedom in relation to moral cause is at the bottom of my position. In the end, however, he claims that "the only way out for Little seems to be open theism."[34] I think that conclusion is more than a little premature. For example, Alvin Plantinga, who is clearly not an open theist, claims:

> What is relevant to the Free Will Defense is the idea of being free with respect to an action. If a person is free with respect to a given action, then he is free to perform that action and free to refrain from performing it; no antecedent conditions and/or causal laws determine that he will perform the action, or that he won't. It is within his power, at the time in question, to take or perform the action and within his power to refrain from it.[35]

So, it seems one can hold to the sovereignty of God and libertarian freedom without being incoherent or an open theist.

---

[34] Tom J. Nettles, "Review of *Whosoever Will: A Biblical-Theological Critique of Five-Point Calvinism,*" *Founders Journal* 82 (Fall 2010): 44; https://founders.org/reviews/whosoever -will-a-biblical-theological-critique-of-five-point-calvinism/.

[35] Alvin C. Plantinga, *God, Freedom, and Evil* (Grand Rapids: Eerdmans, 1977), 29.

Stephen Wellum has also severely critiqued my chapter by stating that libertarian freedom is not taught in the Bible.[36] However, he does not actually add anything new to the discussion, nor does he mount any kind of argument against the charge of inconsistency. He simply repeats the same compatibilistic refrain: "Human actions are causally determined, but free."[37] I agree with many of Wellum's theological claims but fail to see how he has rebutted the claim of inconsistency with respect to the problem of evil. What is offered instead of argument is the accusation that I have not wrestled with the biblical data. He wrote: "What Little must first wrestle with is the biblical data in regard to the divine-human freedom relationship. . . . Otherwise, Scripture is not functioning as an authority for him."[38] So if I believe in libertarian freedom, the best response against that position is that I do not have Scripture as my authority. One ought to be skeptical of a position (the Calvinist one) whose best response to a competing position is a clear *ad hominem*. This accusation is more than a little off-putting, especially since he knows nothing of my theological wrestling, whether little or great. Furthermore, in saying this he is claiming the work of the first four hundred years of church theologians was theologizing without Scripture as their authority. As Swinburne points out: "My assessment of the Christian theological tradition is that all Christian theologians of the first four centuries believed in human free will in the libertarian sense."[39] This conclusion can be established by independent research, namely, by simply reading the writings of the early church fathers, all of which exist in the public domain.

The response to my chapter from the other side of this issue is that I must be an open theist, or I do not have the Bible as my authority; therefore, I must be wrong. I find such responses not only logically invalid but simply an attempt to dismiss my position by applying the old fallacy of guilt by association without ever establishing that such an association squares with the facts. However, if there are stronger arguments to be made against the idea of libertarian freedom, I would surely give them an honest hearing in the interest of truth.

---

[36] Stephen J. Wellum, "God's Sovereignty over Evil," in Barrett and Nettles, *Whomever* He *Wills*, 231–68 (see intro., n. 22).

[37] Wellum, 236.

[38] Wellum, 237n13.

[39] Swinburne, *Problem of Evil*, 35.

14

The Public Invitation and Altar Call

—— Mark Tolbert ——

I am concerned about a dear friend. God has greatly used this friend not only in my life but also in the lives of countless others. This seasoned ally has been an incredible blessing and vehicle for multitudes to experience comfort, freedom, forgiveness, and untold joy. Although once a very familiar mainstay in evangelical circles, over time this friend has become the victim of misunderstanding, abuse, neglect, ridicule, scorn, slander, and now, near abandonment. This familiar friend is at risk of being portrayed at the least as a marginalized relic or at the worst a dangerous charlatan. I am concerned about the current state of the public invitation.

Integrity is crucial. To have your integrity questioned is far more serious than having your competency or skills questioned. The very integrity of the public invitation is under challenge. I would have to agree with those who would charge that the public invitation sometimes has been abused or mishandled. Most preachers would support a move to ensure that invitations are better prepared and extended with more clarity and integrity. This chapter addresses a more serious issue—the very integrity of the public invitation as well as the integrity of those who would extend such, in any form whatsoever, is at stake. This issue is one we need to examine.

I came to know Jesus Christ as Savior and Lord in response to a public evangelistic invitation. At the age of sixteen, I attended a Billy Graham movie at a local theatre on a date with my girlfriend. For me, it was just another Friday night at the movies. A person unknown to me placed a poster up in my high school promoting a movie. At the bottom of the movie poster I read these words: "This movie could change your life." When my date and I settled into our seats and the movie began, I did not realize we were attending a religious film or I probably would not have attended. That movie exposed me to the awareness that although I was a church member, I did not have a relationship with Christ. I was deeply moved and convicted of my sin and need for forgiveness. The Holy Spirit convicted me that I needed Christ's forgiveness and salvation. Sitting in my seat, watching the final scenes of the film, I purposed that I would commit my life to Christ someday. I distinctly remember thinking, "I really need to do this. I want to remember this and make sure that I surrender my life to Christ someday." I was a senior in high school with lots of plans for what I wanted to do: go to college, join a fraternity, build a career, and make a lot of money. But I seriously determined that I would trust Christ one day.

At the conclusion of that movie, a man gave an appeal for those who wished to make a commitment to Christ to come to the front of the theater and speak with a commitment counselor. Before that night, I was unaware of a need to make such a commitment. I had not gone to the movie with any intention of coming to Christ. No Christians had been talking with me about my need for Christ. I had never been exposed to the message of the gospel. I had never been part of hearing a public evangelistic invitation. A man quoted a scriptural invitation that night as he paraphrased an Old Testament reference (1 Kgs 18:21) that asked, "How long will you waver between two opinions? If the Lord is God, follow him." He closed by saying, "In a moment you will make a decision to say yes to Jesus or to say no to Jesus. Don't say no to Jesus; say yes." I am confident I could have said no to lots of things that night: to the church, to religion, to rules and regulations. But as I was gripped with what Christ did for me on the cross, I could not bring myself to say no to him. As the challenge was given, I realized my need to respond to the invitation and to make a commitment to Christ. I went to the front of the theater to talk with someone. Once down front, I did not see anyone available to talk with me. Others had come forward and had been joined by decision counselors, but there was no one left to assist me. Disappointed, I turned to return to my seat. From out of nowhere came a college student who asked if I needed to talk. "I sure do," I replied. He sat down with me and shared a simple gospel message with me. He encouraged me in repenting of my sin and surrendering to Christ. The gospel was made clear. I freely acknowledged my need for Christ, and God wondrously saved me. Wow! How grateful I was that an invitation was offered for me to trust Christ, not someday, but today. How grateful I was that people were prepared and available to share the gospel with me. How grateful I was that God had arranged for the movie to be scheduled in my neighborhood, for someone to place a poster in my school, for me to view the film that night, for the Holy Spirit to bring me under conviction of sin, for a gospel invitation to be extended, and for a gospel witness to be trained and skilled in presenting the gospel to me. From personal experience, I bear witness of the legitimate place of extending public evangelistic invitations. I was saved as a direct result of exposure to the gospel message along with an immediate on-the-spot challenge to say yes to Christ.

Tragically, the public invitation is in trouble. No longer is the invitation an almost universal part of evangelical worship. What once was a tool that was implemented for the evangelization of the masses is now a mere shadow of the past. Even churches that continue the practice of extending public invitations often do so with little precision or purpose. How could the once mighty and respected practice have drifted so far?

Criticisms of the public invitation move along several levels. Some charge that the public invitation is without scriptural warrant. Others allege that the public invitation is a modern invention. Some contend that the call for a public response adds human efforts to salvation, which comes solely by the grace of God. Still others have eliminated the public proclamation of the gospel with a public invitation in favor of exclusive activity in personal, relational evangelism.

Although I value the public evangelistic invitation, I have also experienced tragic abuse of the practice. Years ago, while attending the Southern Baptist Pastor's Conference, I sat through an invitation that was thoroughly manipulative and coercive. The preacher brazenly applied emotional and shameful tactics to attempt to raise doubts about one's salvation and to elicit a response at any cost. I was outraged at the entire spectacle.

Abuse of the invitation has found its way into local church ministries. I know of a young staff member who was put under enormous pressure by the senior pastor to produce invitation results. Each Friday in church staff meeting, the pastor asked the young minister, "Who do you have lined up for Sunday?" In other words, "Who will be walking the aisle during the invitation this Sunday?" The pastor expected, actually demanded, that people be primed, regardless of the means, to walk forward and make decisions in the worship service. This produced overwhelming pressure and stress on the minister to produce results at any cost. Visible results to the invitation were seen as the evidence of a successful church experience. The invitation must produce a visible response or the service was seen as a failure, and the church staff member was required to ensure visible and tangible results every week.

A seminary classmate had a similar experience. He went on staff at a large church as an evangelism intern. His job was to "produce two baptisms each week." In other words, he was to ensure that two people every week would walk forward to request baptism. Since he was an eager and gifted evangelist, he naïvely agreed to the requirement. Things went smoothly for a few weeks, as those he had evangelized walked the aisle on Sunday morning. After about a month, things went badly. No one walked the aisle for baptism. The pastor called the intern into his office and severely chastised him and threatened termination if he failed again to produce the required baptisms. Leaving the office, he was pulled aside by a senior staff member. The man explained that the pastor demanded the required baptisms to impress new families into joining the church, under the assumption that the church must be healthy and dynamic if people were walking the aisle each week. He also shared a secret to ensure success: go to the bus station early each Sunday morning and promise a free meal to anyone willing to walk the aisle that morning. The young evangelist resigned in disgust over the charade being played out, refusing to succumb to such tactics.

The other extreme is when the invitation is marginalized, at best, or abandoned at worst. Martin Lloyd-Jones, author of *Preaching and Preachers*, is a well-known critic of the practice of the public evangelistic invitation, particularly the altar call. Other well-known preachers with a Calvinist theology produce a deafening silence on the practice. In his comprehensive volume on preaching, *Rediscovering Expository Preaching*, John MacArthur included a chapter on "Conclusions" but totally omitted any comments that address the subject of the invitation. In one church where I served as interim pastor, a disciplined personal evangelist intentionally excluded any appeal or call for response to the gospel, based on the idea that all such drawing to Christ should be left entirely to the Holy Spirit without any human means.

In their current form, evangelistic invitations are of relatively recent origin, but the spirit and principle of the public evangelistic invitation is evident in the Bible. We see examples in the Old Testament. When Moses came down from Mount Sinai, he discovered the people giving themselves over to idolatry and worshipping the golden calf, and he confronted them: "Moses stood at the camp's entrance and said, 'Whoever is for the Lord, come to me.' And all the Levites gathered around him" (Exod 32:26). That was a clear call to the people to make a public declaration and take a public stand for the Lord. After Moses's death, Joshua was commanded to lead the nation of Israel. The people lapsed into idolatry. Toward the end of Joshua's life, he called all the tribes together and said, "Choose for yourselves today: Which will you worship—the gods your ancestors worshiped beyond the Euphrates River or the gods of the Amorites in whose land you are living? As for me and my family, we will worship the LORD" (Josh 24:15). That, too, was a call for a public commitment of loyalty to God.

Centuries later, idolatry again was the issue. This time Elijah was God's chosen instrument. The king summoned all the Israelites to meet Elijah at Mount Carmel. "Then Elijah approached all the people and said, 'How long will you waver between two opinions? If the LORD is God, follow him. But if Baal, follow him'" (1 Kgs 18:21). This was a clear and powerful call to public commitment and identification as a follower of God. In Ezra 10:5, the great scribe Ezra called on his contemporaries to swear publicly that they would carry out the principles of his reform. Nehemiah's book also indicates that the Jewish leaders were required to commit themselves to a covenant of loyalty to the Lord after their revival (Neh 9:38). Hosea urged the people to return to the Lord and receive his forgiveness (Hos 14:2). Throughout the Old Testament, one sees a clear picture of the man of God publicly calling people to make a public commitment to the Lord.

The New Testament records disciples urging people to decide publicly for Christ. The apostle Paul announced to the church at Corinth that Christians have been given the ministry of reconciliation (2 Cor 5:18–20). This ministry charges the believer with the task of seeking to join together sinful people and a holy God. Further, this ministry compels the Christian to urge the hearer to decide for Christ. The gospel is not to be presented in a casual, perfunctory manner, but with a sense of urgency, appeal, and persuasion (2 Cor 5:11), even as Paul did when he reasoned and persuaded the people of Ephesus to whom he preached (Acts 19:8), and as Jesus charged his disciples to do (Luke 14:23). This urging from the human instrument is to be done while relying on the Spirit of God. The evangelist must do his best to urge people to come to Christ, but there also must be a dependence on the Holy Spirit to convict and draw people (John 16:8).

Jesus made numerous appeals for people to decide publicly for him. Even early in his ministry, Jesus included public proclamation of the gospel and public calls to repentance (Matt 4:17). When he called Andrew and John, his first disciples, he extended a public appeal to follow him (v. 19), as he did with the woman of Sychar (John 4:4–42), Philip (John 1:43), Matthew (Luke 5:27), the rich young ruler

(Luke 18:18–34), and Zacchaeus (Luke 19:1–10). Additionally, Jesus made general appeals in group settings (Matt 11:28–29; John 7:37–38). Jesus insisted that a genuine confession of faith must not be secretive or private, but should be shared publicly: "Whosoever therefore shall confess me *before men*, him will I confess also before my Father which is in heaven. But whosoever shall deny me *before men*, him will I also deny before my Father which is in heaven" (Matt 10:32–33 KJV; emphasis added). Note that the believer's confession is to be made *in public*, "before men." The Lord Jesus Christ gave us his personal example in his extension of public invitations to people to follow him as Lord and Savior.

The New Testament provides other examples of preachers who called for a public decision. Aside from Jesus, the most outstanding example is John the Baptist. John came preaching a message of repentance (Luke 3:2–3), but the chief characteristic of his ministry was baptizing the people who responded to his message (John 1:28). His ministry, preaching, and appeal were public, and those who responded to his appeal did so publicly.

The followers of Jesus also extended public invitations. Andrew sought out his brother, Peter, and brought him to Jesus (John 1:42). After he went on to become a powerful spokesman for our Lord, Peter called for an immediate, public commitment to Christ, as in his sermon on the day of Pentecost (Acts 2:39–40), and in his preaching to the household of Cornelius (10:28–48). Philip preached to the Ethiopian eunuch and those in his caravan as they traveled along a desert road (8:26–38). The public proclamation of the gospel was basic to the ministry of the apostle Paul (1 Cor 15:1–11; 1 Thess 1:5–11). His preaching and appeals for Christ were often in a public arena, usually in the setting of the Jewish synagogues. This was his practice in Pisidian Antioch (Acts 13:14–48), in Iconium (14:1–7), in Thessalonica (17:1–4), in Berea (17:10–12), in Corinth (18:1–4), and in Ephesus (19:1–10). Paul and Silas challenged the jailer at Philippi to place his faith in Christ amid the public spectacle of a crowded jail cell (16:25–31). The Bible concludes with an invitation to come to Christ (Rev 22:17). Throughout the New Testament we discover ample evidence for the practice of public proclamation of the gospel, with an appeal for a public declaration of repentance and faith in Christ.

From an examination of Scripture, one discovers a clear and compelling biblical basis for public evangelistic invitations. When the preacher of the gospel makes an appeal for people to decide openly for Christ, he is on solid biblical ground. As the minister of the gospel applies biblical principles of public evangelistic invitations, he can do so with the blessing of heaven.

Critics of the public invitation often make the claim that the practice started with Charles G. Finney (1792–1875). Although Finney's "New Measures" popularized the practice, public evangelistic invitations can be traced back centuries before Finney. The preachers of the first century called on people to offer themselves as candidates for repentance, faith, and baptism. These invitations continued until AD 324, when the Emperor Constantine declared Christianity the state religion of the Roman Empire. In one sudden move, all citizens of Rome, whether believers or not, were swept into the church, and were proclaimed to be Christians. Adults and infants alike were baptized as they became members of the church. As these infants grew, the need for adult baptism diminished, and the practice of the public invitation declined.

Among Christians who continued to issue a public invitation were the Anabaptists. They opposed the Roman Catholic Church on several issues, including infant baptism. They were faithful in calling for repentance of sins, faith in Christ, and the outward sign of believer's baptism.

The Anabaptists were opposed by both Catholics and Protestants. This opposition came because the Reformers, while proclaiming the message of salvation by grace through faith and believing in the final authority of Scripture, opposed the public invitation, believing it to be an addition to faith and therefore unbiblical.

Founded by Thomas Helwys, in 1609, the Separatists broke away from the Church of England. They believed that people must repent and believe on Christ to be saved. They invited people to confess Christ publicly through believer's baptism. Famous Separatists included John Bunyan, author of *Pilgrim's Progress*. He advocated a call for a public profession of faith in Christ. One Separatist congregation was the company of Pilgrims on board the Mayflower who came to America in 1620, seeking religious and political liberty.

The eighteenth century saw unusually gifted and anointed preachers who employed a variety of public invitations for people to come to Christ. Jonathan Edwards and George Whitefield would conclude their sermons with an appeal for seekers to meet with them following the service to seek private spiritual guidance. This was the standard invitational model of the eighteenth century. Another of their contemporaries, John Wesley, would also invite seekers to come forward and sit at the "anxious seat" where they would receive spiritual counsel. This occurred some fifty years before Finney, who is often cited as the inventor of the modern altar call for the invitation. Noted historian Leon McBeth, quoting Steve O'Kelly, observed that Separate Baptists in the southern United States were known to have extended invitations for people to come to the front of the service with the singing of a hymn to make immediate commitments to Christ as early as 1758.[1] In 1799 at a Methodist camp meeting in Red River, Kentucky, a physical altar was erected in front of the pulpit where seekers might come for prayer and instruction. So popular was it that altars became permanent fixtures in many Methodist churches.[2] This is the first record of an "altar call" as a form of the public invitation.

The nineteenth century saw the ministry of Charles G. Finney popularize the modern pattern of coming to the front of the service at the time of invitation to commit to Christ. Charles Haddon Spurgeon employed a type of invitation similar to the eighteenth-century model, due in part to the physical limitations of the Metropolitan Tabernacle.[3] Although Finney certainly is credited with the paradigm with which we are now familiar, the spirit and practice of public invitations is well documented in church history.

What about the charge that calling for a response in a public invitation is adding human means to the grace of God? Some take sides along theological lines on extending the invitation. It seems there is a tendency to conclude that those who have a high view of the sovereignty of God and his supreme role in bringing about salvation tend to move away from extending a public evangelistic invitation. If such is the case, then the obvious conclusion is that those who do continue to extend an invitation have a lower view of God's sovereign work of grace. Is this the necessary case? I would argue otherwise.

Those who call for a return to the validity of the invitation come from across the soteriological spectrum. In analyzing the practice of Southern Baptists, Dr. Chuck Kelley, retired president of New Orleans Baptist Theological Seminary, observed:

> From the beginning, Southern Baptists were taught to link biblical proclamation with rhetorical intent. Preachers must proclaim the Word of God with a view to persuading men and women to respond to God's call for repentance, faith, and obedience. Giving hearers the immediate opportunity to respond,

---

[1] H. Leon McBeth, *The Baptist Heritage, Four Centuries of Baptist Witness*, 231 (see chap. 7, n. 34).

[2] Henry B. McLendon, "The Mourner's Bench" (ThD diss., Southern Baptist Theological Seminary, 1902), 10.

[3] R. Alan Streett, *The Effective Invitation* (Old Tappan, NJ: Fleming H. Revell, 1984), 97.

which is the purpose of the invitation, is a logical sequence of the historic emphasis on persuasion found in Southern Baptist homiletical theory.[4]

Dr. Danny Akin, president of Southeastern Baptist Theological Seminary, wrote: "We acknowledge that the public invitation, like many spiritual and religious practices, is open to abuse and manipulation. However, the solution is not to kill it but to redeem it. We need to extend it in a manner that is biblical, authentic, and Christ honoring, all to the glory of God."[5]

John Piper, pastor and author, wrote:

> Pleading with our listeners to make a response to our preaching is not at odds with a high doctrine of the sovereignty of God. . . . When we preach, to be sure, it is *God* who effects the results for which we long. But that does not rule out earnest appeals for our people to respond. . . . So it seems that God has been pleased to give awakening power to preaching that does not shrink back from the loving threatenings of the Lord, and that lavishes the saints with incomparable promises of grace, and that pleads passionately and lovingly that no one hear the Word of God in vain. It is a tragedy to see pastors state the facts and sit down. Good preaching pleads with people to respond to the Word of God.[6]

In extending a public invitation, the preacher should make every effort to separate the need for an inner decision from the call for an external expression. A person is justified solely by the grace of God and apart from human effort (Rom 4:1–5). The apostle Paul argued to the Romans that we are right with God based on the inward condition of our heart (2:29). And yet, the one who has a genuine inner relationship of the heart will validate it in an external expression. After Peter's sermon at Pentecost, the people asked, "'Brothers, what shall we do?' Peter replied, 'Repent and be baptized, every one of you, in the name of Jesus Christ for the forgiveness of your sins'" (Acts 2:38–39 NIV). In the tenth chapter of his letter to the Romans,

---

[4] Charles S. Kelley Jr., *Fuel the Fire: Lessons from the History of Southern Baptist Evangelism* (Nashville: B&H, 2018), 57.

[5] Daniel L. Akin, Bill Curtis, and Stephen Rummage, *Engaging Exposition* (Nashville: B&H, 2011), 215.

[6] John Piper, *The Supremacy of God in Preaching* (Grand Rapids: Baker, 2004), 95–96; emphasis in original.

Paul described the link between inner decision and external expression: "If you confess with your mouth, 'Jesus is Lord,' and believe in your heart that God raised him from the dead, you will be saved. One believes with the heart, resulting in righteousness, and one confesses with the mouth, resulting in salvation" (vv. 9–10). Outward expression is to be evidence of inner grace. To claim inner grace without external expression is to cheapen the gospel of grace. The charge of cheap grace or "easy believism" is often made by some who are of the Reformed position. One is saved not by walking an aisle, raising a hand, or praying a prayer. One is saved by repentance and faith; salvation comes when we repent and turn from sin and trust fully in the death and resurrection of the Lord Jesus Christ. This internal work of God's grace brings outward transformation. Scripture makes abundantly clear that inward grace will produce outward fruit. The public invitation provides an initial means of external expression and can serve as a legitimate and biblical means of external evidence of one who has been saved by God's grace.

The invitation provides an opportunity to respond to the proclamation of the gospel. Biblical proclamation is not intended merely to inform the mind; it is intended to spark a transformation inwardly that bears fruit outwardly. In other words, preaching is to be purposeful, and that purpose is to be more than cognitive in nature; it is to impact the affective and psychomotor domains of learning and understanding. The thrust of one's preaching should be to proclaim and expound the clear message of Scripture. God has not promised to bless one's charming personality or forceful delivery; God has promised to bless his Word. "For just as rain and snow fall from heaven and do not return there without saturating the earth and making it germinate and sprout, and providing seed to sow and food to eat, so my word that comes from my mouth will not return to me empty, but it will accomplish what I please and will prosper in what I send it to do" (Isa 55:10–11).

Since God has promised to bless and fulfill the purpose of his Word, what is that purpose? Two foundational Scriptures are informative in answering that question. Paul gave us insight into the purpose of God's Word and its proclamation in his second letter to Timothy. We read in 2 Tim 3:16–17 concerning the nature and purpose of the Scriptures: "All Scripture is inspired by God and is profitable for teaching, for rebuking, for correcting, for training in righteousness, so that the man of God may be complete, equipped for every good work." In 2 Tim 4:2 we understand the command and desired result of preaching: "Preach the word; be ready in season and out of season; correct, rebuke, and encourage with great patience and teaching." The end results of both Scripture itself and its proclamation is transformational response.

After a biblical passage has been expounded, application for the hearers and the invitation by the preacher should be extended on that foundation. Each passage of Scripture contains components, such as a doctrine to be believed, a sin to be forsaken, a promise to be claimed, or a command to be obeyed. The preacher has fulfilled only part of his task if he stops with the exposition of the text. Exposition is to be the heart of the message, but exposition is not the sum total of the sermon. As seen in the above noted texts (2 Tim 3:16; 4:1–2), explanation is to lead to application. Upon proper exposition and clear application, the invitation should follow.

The proclamation of a biblical sermon is to inform, inspire, and incline a response by the hearers. To that end, an often overlooked and minimalized component of preaching is the element of persuasion. An old adage of preaching is to "tell them what you are going to tell them, then tell them, then, tell them what you told them." This is completely inadequate. Preaching must *urge* the hearers to act on what they have heard. As we have already observed, manipulation and coercion are illegitimate and dangerous tactics in preaching. In contrast, persuasion is a legitimate and essential component of biblical proclamation. Numerous examples of the use of persuasion are found throughout Scripture.

What is persuasion? Several different definitions of persuasion exist with varying nuances; however, the key element in most definitions maintains the same emphasis. As R. Larry Overstreet, in his book *Persuasive Preaching*, suggested, "Persuasion aims at change. It may be change of attitude, or change of behavior, but change is the goal."[7] What role should persuasion play in preaching? Overstreet suggested a comprehensive helpful definition of the role of persuasion in preaching: "Persuasive Preaching contains the following elements: (1) the process of preparing biblical, expository messages using a persuasive pattern, and (2) presenting them through verbal and nonverbal communication means (3) to autonomous individuals who can be convinced and/or taught by God's Holy Spirit, (4) in order to alter or strengthen (5) their attitudes and beliefs toward God, His Word, and other individuals, (6) resulting in their lives being transformed into the image of Christ."[8]

Consider the emphasis in Scripture on the means of persuasion in preaching. A foundational passage that informs our preaching is 2 Tim 4:1–2: "I solemnly charge you before God and Christ Jesus, who is going to judge the living and the dead,

---

[7] R. Larry Overstreet, *Persuasive Preaching: A Biblical and Practical Guide to the Effective Use of Persuasion* (Wooster, OH: Weaver Book, 2014), 11.

[8] Overstreet, 14.

and because of his appearing and his kingdom: Preach the word; be ready in season and out of season; correct, rebuke, and encourage with great patience and teaching." The apostle Paul, in his apostolic authority, used strong persuasion to press upon preachers their responsibility in preaching. He "charges" the preacher; the word is "*diamartyromai*—to charge, to solemnly charge."[9] It is a word of persuasion. However, to strengthen the persuasion, Paul clarified that his charge is being put forth in the presence of God the Father and Christ Jesus who will judge the living and the dead. The unmistakable reminder is one of absolute accountability before God for the stewardship of preaching. Then he issued a command: "Preach the word." To preach is *kerysso*.[10] This is a divine imperative, the strongest expression of persuasion to obedience. Included in the command to preach are several functions: to correct, to rebuke, and to encourage, all of which are divine imperatives for the preacher. The point should be obvious: God, through the apostle Paul, is using strong terms and vivid language to seek to convince the preacher in his calling and task of persuasive proclamation.

We see persuasion at work in many of the sermons recorded in the book of Acts. The first of these, Peter's sermon on the day of Pentecost, is an example. He prefaced the sermon by calling on the hearers to "pay attention to my words" (2:14). This evinces the use of persuasion concerning what he was about to say. The main persuasive thrust of the sermon concerning the death of Jesus is that they (the Jews) were complicit in the conspiracy to kill Jesus and bore corporate guilt in his death (vv. 23, 36). So persuasive was his argument that they were convicted and desirous of knowing what they should do (v. 37). After answering their question, "repent and be baptized" (v. 38), Peter continued to persuade them: "With many other words he testified and strongly urged them, saying, 'Be saved from this corrupt generation!'" (v. 40). "To strongly urge" is "*parakaleo*—to urge, persuade, implore, plead."[11] Peter prefaced his sermon with persuasion; he preached with persuasion and continued to persuade in the conclusion/invitation phase of his famous sermon.

Throughout the book of Acts, we see frequent examples of persuasion. In Acts 9, Saul debated with the Jews (v. 29). "To debate" is "*synezetei*—to debate, dispute, argue."[12] Saul was using persuasive arguments in his preaching. At Iconium, Paul

---

[9] James Strong, *Strong's Exhaustive Concordance of the Bible* (Nashville: Holman Bible Publishers, 1940), s.v. "Logos."

[10] Strong.

[11] Strong.

[12] Strong.

and Barnabas "spoke in such a way that a great number of both Jews and Greeks believed" (14:1). Although some were unbelieving (v. 2), the message and the manner of their preaching compelled some to believe. In Thessalonica, Paul and Silas "reasoned [*dielexate*: "to dispute, reason, argue"[13]] with them from the Scriptures, explaining and proving that it was necessary for the Messiah to suffer and rise from the dead: 'This Jesus I am proclaiming to you is the Messiah.' Some of them were persuaded [*epeisthesan*—"persuaded, convinced"[14]] and joined Paul and Silas" (17:2–4). In Athens, Paul "reasoned in the synagogue with the Jews and with those who worshiped God, as well as in the marketplace every day with those who happened to be there" (v. 17). At the Areopagus in Athens, Paul proclaimed: "The times of ignorance God overlooked, but now he commands all people everywhere to repent" (v. 30 ESV). Notice, although it is Paul's voice they hear, Paul pointed out to them that it was not merely his command for them to repent, but God's. That is very persuasive. After leaving Athens, Paul arrived in Corinth where "he reasoned in the synagogue every Sabbath, and tried to persuade Jews and Greeks (18:4 ESV). After Corinth, Paul preached in Ephesus. "And he entered the synagogue and for three months spoke boldly, reasoning and persuading them about the kingdom of God. But when some became stubborn and continued in unbelief, speaking evil of the Way before the congregation, he withdrew from them and took the disciples with him, reasoning daily in the hall of Tyrannus" (19:8–9 ESV). Even Paul's critics recognized how God used him to persuade people to abandon their idols and follow Christ. Demetrius, a crafter of idols, observed, "You see and hear that not only in Ephesus, but in almost all of Asia, this man Paul has persuaded and misled a considerable number of people by saying that gods made by hand are not gods" (v. 26). Here, a critic of the apostle Paul, Demetrius, a silversmith who made figures for the worship of Artemis, gathered together other crafters of idols to speak against what Paul was doing. This critic saw that Paul was seeking to persuade people to turn to Christ. He also was alarmed that, due in part to Paul's persuasion, he had caused a considerable number of people throughout almost all of Asia to turn to Christ. Their response resulted in turning away from their worship of false gods to turn to worship the true God. What a picture of this wonderful response to Spirit-powered preaching by the testimony of a critic and an opponent!

Thus, we see that the use of persuasion in Acts was so frequent one may well conclude that in apostolic preaching the use of persuasion was not the exception but

---

[13] Strong.
[14] Strong.

the norm. The gospel was preached, the Scriptures exposed, and Jesus was presented. The message carried with it an apostolic authority, Spirit-fueled power, and persuasive argumentation.

We should note that in Ephesus, as was the case in Thessalonica and Corinth, although Paul was using the element of persuasion, some were persuaded and some were not. Thus, one may conclude that persuasion differs from coercion or manipulation. Coercion and manipulation may seek to elicit consent at any cost using any means necessary, no matter how misleading or illegitimate. Persuasion, on the other hand, employs genuine passion, while relying on the Holy Spirit to convict of sin and draw people to Christ (John 16:8–11).

Persuasion throughout the sermon as well as in the invitation can be driven by both positive as well as negative factors. In his book *Persuasive Preaching Today*, Ralph L. Lewis identified two clusters of appeals in preaching that reflect two strong human feelings—faith and fear.[15] Lewis suggested that preaching may appeal through Faith-Promises or through Fear-Threats. Faith-Promises are based on faith, promised reward, are positive in orientation, and promise benefit.[16] In contrast, Fear-Threats are based upon fear, threaten judgment, are negative in orientation, and threaten loss.[17]

Persuasion in the Bible is represented by both Faith-Promises and Fear-Threats. In the parable of the great banquet, as recorded in Luke 14, Jesus described a scene where a wonderful and elegant banquet was prepared. Servants were instructed to invite many people. Those invited, however, made excuses and declined the invitation. As a result, "the master told the servant, 'Go out into the highways and hedges and make them come in, so that my house may be filled'" (v. 23). The instruction to "make them come in" is also rendered "compel" (ESV, NASB, RSV, KJV, NKJV) and is the term *anankason*: "force, compel, make."[18] The term is used elsewhere in Acts when Paul described his arrest and subsequent decision to appeal to Caesar: "But when the Jews objected, I was forced to appeal to Caesar" (28:19 NASB). Paul acted in accord with his own free will. He could have chosen not to invoke his right as a Roman citizen, yet he chose to do so. Like the servant in the parable, we are not to coerce or manipulate people in our invitation. We should not force them against their will. Yet our invitation is to be so persuasive and compelling that people will

---

[15] Ralph L. Lewis, *Persuasive Preaching Today* (Wilmore, KY: Asbury Theological Seminary, 1979), 118.

[16] Lewis, 119.

[17] Lewis, 119.

[18] Lewis, 119.

see the positive Faith-Promise of the gospel and choose Christ. As we present the gospel in a persuasive manner and pray for the Holy Spirit to draw people, we are not in reality forcing their will. Our persuasion and presentation are focusing their will on the positive Faith-Promise of the gospel. As we pray for the Holy Spirit to convict (John 16:8) and for the Father to draw (John 6:44), we are not forcing people's will; we are freeing their will to trust Christ. Make no mistake about it: God the Father draws, God the Holy Spirit convicts, and God the Son sends; Jesus sends us out as his servants to invite people to the banquet, with the instruction to invite in a compelling way.

Persuasion in the Bible also has the element of Fear-Threat. The apostle Paul described this element of appropriate fear as a reason to employ persuasion in 2 Cor 5:10–11: "For we must all appear before the judgment seat of Christ, so that each may be repaid for what he has done in the body, whether good or evil. Therefore, since we know the fear of the Lord, we try to persuade [*peithomen*] people. What we are is plain to God, and I hope it is also plain to your consciences." Paul, describing the sober reality of the judgment seat of Christ, before which all must appear, stated emphatically that we are to try to persuade people to repent of sin and come to Christ. The motivation is clear: "since we know the fear of the Lord." The "we" here is referring to those who know Christ. Notice the distinction: Paul said we all will appear before the judgment seat of Christ. However, he did not say that everyone knows the fear of the Lord. Those outside of Christ and apart from the illuminating work of the Holy Spirit do not know the fear of the Lord. However, we—that is, believers—do know the fear of the Lord. Therefore, we try to persuade people to come to Christ. The motivation is the fear of the Lord and the sober anticipation of all of us appearing before his judgment seat. This is a Fear-Threat that should fuel our witness and our urgency to share the good news of the gospel with a view of persuading people to embrace Christ.

The task of the preacher is to preach the Word, proclaim the gospel, present the Lord Jesus Christ in the power of the Holy Spirit, and trust God with the results. One must resist pride as well as a sense of failure when it comes to the response to the message. It is not our responsibility to produce a decision. We must do our part and pray and trust the moving of the Spirit to bring conviction of sin and surrender to Christ.

I remember when I had the opportunity to teach my first seminary course. I was eager to do a good job and teach the content in an excellent manner. I do remember, however, being somewhat naïve about my role. I said to my wife, "I want to do such a good job that all of my students make an A." At the end of the course, when it was time to post final grades, one or two students, who submitted assignments past the deadline, received the grades they deserved, which were not As. I accepted the fact that it was not entirely up to me. In evangelism, the final result is not entirely up to us.

The witness must faithfully present the gospel; God, the Holy Spirit, brings illumination and conviction, and the sinner must choose to repent and trust Christ. Of course, this raises the issue of the will. Scripture indicates a tension between the election and calling of God and the moral responsibility of the lost to choose Christ. The purpose of this chapter is not to resolve that tension; other chapters have focused on that tension. Although I do not pretend to resolve the tension, I do purport that Scripture indicates that a refusal to believe is an obstacle to faith. In John 5, Jesus Christ was addressing the plight of unbelieving Jews toward faith in him. He identified several evidences for faith, including the testimony of John, the miracles he performed, and the witness of Scripture. He then charged in verse 40, "But you are not willing to come to me so that you may have life." The phrase "not willing" (*thelete*) means to refuse or to be unwilling. John MacArthur said they were "clinging to their superficial system of self-righteousness by works, in their stubborn unbelief."[19] Other scholars observe, "Ye will not (οὐ θέλετε), indicating stubborn determination."[20] Matthew Henry's *Commentary* suggested: "Their estrangement from Christ was the fault not so much of their understandings as of their wills. This is expressed as a complaint; Christ offered life, and it was not accepted. The only reason sinners die is because they will not come to Christ for life and happiness; it is not because they cannot, but because they will not."[21] "You are not willing to come to me" stresses the activity of the will; the Jews set themselves against Jesus. This passage is not unlike Luke 13:34: "Jerusalem, Jerusalem, you who kill the prophets and stone those sent to you, how often I have longed to gather your children together, as a hen gathers her chicks under her wings, and you were not willing" (NIV). Leon Morris said, "There is the same thought of a tender eagerness to save, met by a stubborn refusal to be

---

[19] John F. MacArthur Jr., *John 1-11*, MacArthur New Testament Commentary (Chicago: Moody Press, 2006), 213.

[20] Marvin R. Vincent, *Word Studies in the New Testament*, 4 vols. (New York: Charles Scribner's Sons, 1887), 2:140.

[21] Matthew Henry, *Matthew Henry's Commentary on the Whole Bible: Complete and Unabridged in One Volume* (Peabody, MA: Hendrickson, 1994), 1948.

saved."[22] "The real meaning is: in your hardness of heart you have basely *rejected* the Son of God."[23] Unbelief is the sin of rejecting the truth of God in Jesus Christ.

The invitation is our responsibility regardless of our understanding of the place of the human will in salvation. Some who avoid or despise extending an invitation do so because of their view of total depravity as it relates to the inability of the will. To such people I would point out this challenge from John Piper, an outspoken champion for the classical Reformed position:

> Can a Calvinist like Edwards really plead with people to flee hell and cherish heaven? Do not total depravity and unconditional election and irresistible grace make such pleading inconsistent? Edwards learned his Calvinism from the Bible and therefore was spared many errors in his preaching. He did not infer that unconditional election or irresistible grace or supernatural regeneration or the inability of the natural man led to the conclusion that the use of pleading was inappropriate. He said, Sinners . . . should be earnestly invited to come and accept of a Savior, and yield their hearts unto him, with all the winning, encouraging arguments for them . . . that the Gospel affords.[24]

I would argue, then, that pleading and using appropriate persuasion in presenting the gospel and extending the invitation is needful for our gospel witness, regardless of our view concerning the tension between sovereignty and free will.

Having seen the value of a proper evangelistic invitation, let us consider the form one may adopt in extending an invitation. A public evangelistic invitation may follow various formats. The traditional invitation to invite people to walk to the front of the room remains a common and effective form. Other forms are also available that may serve as alternatives. Some settings would suggest using an alternative format for the invitation. Presentations to children, youth, and specialty groups may include inviting people to raise their hands or make eye contact with the preacher during a closing prayer. One can meet privately with those who responded. It is essential that interested people may easily locate the minister and visit in an uninterrupted setting. Providing a response card for people to complete and request later follow-up and

---

[22] Leon Morris, *The Gospel According to John*, NICNT (Grand Rapids: Eerdmans, 1995), 293.

[23] Hendriksen and Kistemaker, *Exposition of the Gospel According to John*, 210; emphasis original (see chap. 1, n. 41).

[24] Piper, *The Supremacy of God in Preaching*, 94.

conversation has been used with success. Do not make the common mistake of equating a "come forward" approach with an evangelistic invitation. Other approaches can and perhaps should be used as the context demands.

Making a clear invitation is essential. Do not assume that people understand the "language of Zion." Telling people to "make a profession of faith, to come to the altar (when you may not actually have an altar), to get right with God, to walk the sawdust trail" (really?) are expressions that are meaningless and perhaps ridiculed by those unfamiliar with church culture. Be crystal clear in your invitation. Make certain that you communicate in clear and simple language what you are calling for and how people are to respond. Do not make it difficult for someone to respond; make it clear and plain.

An analogy may prove helpful. How would you invite guests to your home for dinner with you and your family? Would you assume that they knew they were welcome and, therefore, no invitation is necessary? Of course not. Would you make a vague, meaningless statement, such as "You come see us sometime"? Would you not ensure they knew the details of how to locate your house, the agreed upon date, and the time they would be expected? You might even suggest the dress code for the evening and whether they were expected to bring a side dish. Such details are not considered intrusive or manipulative; rather they are seen as helpful, courteous, and appreciated when a heartfelt and genuine dinner invitation is extended. Why would we not extend the same courtesies when issuing an invitation to attend, someday, the marriage supper of the Lamb?

Others have abandoned the practice of extending a public invitation in favor of relational evangelism. The preference for relational witness has become an exclusive preference: relational evangelism as the only means of proper witness. Adherents to this position do not merely prefer relational evangelism; they see it as the only legitimate way to evangelize. They do more than merely minimize the legitimacy of the public invitation; they question its very integrity. This view would disparage those who would extend the public invitation as well as those who would practice direct conversational evangelism with a casual acquaintance or a stranger. Although personal relationships can be a valid and perhaps even the preferred means of presenting the gospel, should it be the exclusive approach? It was not the exclusive approach of Jesus Christ, who witnessed to individuals after a brief introduction (John 3:1–21; 4:1–26) as well as to the masses (7:37–38).

An informative passage that links public proclamation with personal witness is Matt 9:35–38:

Jesus continued going around to all the towns and villages, teaching in their synagogues, preaching the good news of the kingdom, and healing every disease and every sickness. When he saw the crowds, he felt compassion for them, because they were distressed and dejected, like sheep without a shepherd. Then he said to his disciples, "The harvest is abundant, but the workers are few. Therefore, pray to the Lord of the harvest to send out workers into his harvest."

This narrative reveals a glimpse into the common practice of Jesus Christ. We read that Jesus went into all the towns and villages, something not possible in a single day. Therefore, this passage described the regular evangelistic practice of Jesus as twofold. First, he preached the gospel of the kingdom. This is public proclamation as his normal, common practice. The passage also revealed his strategy of praying to the Lord of the harvest for workers to go into his harvest. He commanded the disciples to pray for this opportunity. Next, Jesus summoned and authorized the twelve apostles and sent them out to proclaim that the kingdom of heaven is at hand (Matt 10:1–7). Here we see the practice of our Lord as well as the strategy he gave to us: public preaching and personal proclamation.

In five decades of following Jesus, I have discovered a sobering reality in my journey—I do not drift toward evangelism; I drift away from evangelism. I do not mean to do so; it is not a decision I make. It is not that I determine never again to speak of Jesus; I just drift.

We drift from evangelism despite our joy in seeing people come to Christ. We drift despite our desire to be obedient to Christ's command to proclaim the gospel. We drift despite the promise that Jesus gave to his first followers, saying, "Follow me, and I will make you fishers of men" (Matt 4:19 KJV). What prevents us from experiencing this reality in our walk with Jesus? Why do we not naturally fish for people? Why do we drift away from evangelism, and what can we do to change this?

We drift from evangelism because of internal and external forces. Internally, the fear of other people and the weakness of our flesh work against us. Even the apostle Paul experienced these obstacles. To the church at Corinth, he wrote, "I was with you in weakness and in fear and in much trembling, and my message and my preaching were not in persuasive words of wisdom, but in demonstration of the Spirit and of power, so that your faith would not rest on the wisdom of men, but on the power of God" (1 Cor 2:3–5 NASB1995).

Externally, we are engaged in spiritual warfare when we attempt to witness for Christ. Satan will seek to discourage the witness (1 Thess 2:18) as well as blind the eyes of the unbeliever (2 Cor 4:4). He will also seduce us into being a silent witness, convincing us that words are unnecessary. Although we witness by our life, we must witness by a combination of our life and our lips. The "witness" who witnesses only by his life witnesses only of himself. Jesus said, "You shall be witnesses to me" (Acts 1:8 NKJV). Romans 10:14 asks: "How then will they call on Him in whom they have not believed? How will they believe in Him whom they have not heard? And how will they hear without a preacher?" (NASB1995).

How do we counterbalance these forces? How do we overcome the internal and external forces that war against us? Several measures will enable a Christian to resist the drift. A simple tool can allow us to be consistent in our witness.

We must be intentional in our witness for Christ. How can we be intentional? A simple yet profound technique is what I call the "Monday Morning Prayer." Although not a scripted, literal prayer, what I am suggesting is a moment at the beginning of every week, Monday morning, when you ask the Lord to present you with the opportunity to share the gospel during the week. Let Monday morning be a trigger for you to begin to be intentional about seeking a divine appointment to have a gospel conversation with at least one person during that week. You are serious about asking God to place a person in your path, to lay someone upon your heart, to guide you into an opportunity (divine appointment) when you seek to talk with an individual whom God has prepared to hear the message of the gospel.

The Monday Morning Prayer is about intentionality. We do not drift toward evangelism; we drift away. We do not drift back. If we practice personal evangelism, it is because we are intentional.

The Monday Morning Prayer is also about spirituality. We do not just begin talking to people; we pray. We ask the Lord of the harvest to send us into his harvest field. We ask the Lord to convict people of sin and draw them to himself (John 16:8). Although we can proclaim truth, only the Spirit of God can impart truth and transform lives.

Scripture highlights the strategic value of prayer in evangelism. "Then he said to his disciples, 'The harvest is abundant, but the workers are few. Therefore, pray to the Lord of the harvest to send out workers into his harvest'" (Matt 9:37–38). The apostle Paul said, "Brothers and sisters, my heart's desire and prayer to God concerning them is for their salvation" (Rom 10:1). The Bible urges us to pray for those to whom God intends for us to witness. It has been said, before we talk to people about

God, we would do well to talk to God about people! This scriptural mandate is at the heart of the "Monday Morning Prayer."

The Monday Morning Prayer is about focus, focusing on the harvest and the Lord of the harvest. This helps to prevent the drift we all have experienced. It serves as a reminder every week to be about the Father's business.

Once God has placed a prepared heart in our path, we must be prepared and available to invite a person to come to Christ. Listen to the plea of one being drawn to Christ in the book of Acts. Acts 8 provides the narrative of Philip's encounter with the Ethiopian eunuch. The royal officer was returning from Jerusalem where he had been to worship. As Philip encountered the eunuch's chariot and caravan, he heard the government official reading from Isa 53:7–8, which says, "Like a lamb led to the slaughter and like a sheep silent before her shearers, he did not open his mouth. He was taken away because of oppression and judgment, and who considered his fate? For he was cut off from the land of the living." Upon hearing this, Philip asked the man if he understood what he was reading. Acts 8:31 records his response: "'How can I,' he said, 'unless someone guides me?'" This is the silent cry of many: "How can I unless someone guides me?" Here is an individual whom God seems to have been drawing to himself. The eunuch had been to Jerusalem to worship. He was reading a passage of Scripture that seemed to point to a sacrificial lamb. When God sent a surrendered servant named Philip, the eunuch needed only that God-sent messenger to guide him to Jesus. Today, as on that day, people whom God is drawing need someone to guide them to Jesus.

Whether in public preaching or personal witness, consider using a model for your evangelistic invitation. I developed a model for the public invitation as a doctoral student at Southwestern Baptist Theological Seminary. The model can be adapted to various contexts and appeals. This particular model has four components: a transitional statement, an internal decision, an external expression, and a concluding challenge. Many have found this type of model helpful in extending an invitation.

Use a transitional statement to begin your invitation. This statement enables the speaker to cross a threshold from message to invitation. Having difficulty making the transition into the invitation is common. Craft a one-sentence statement with which you are comfortable to facilitate this transition. The statement may be a propositional "if/then" statement, with phrasing such as, "If this is what you intend to do, here is what you do." Make it clear and personal to help you as well as the hearer move into the decision encounter.

Follow your transition with a call for an internal decision. This is literally the heart of the invitation and is the inner, spiritual response to the working of the Holy

Spirit. This should be tied directly or indirectly to the sermon or message that one has presented. Craft this part of the invitation as an appeal to make a response to the inner conviction of the Holy Spirit. This is the part of the invitation that is the most crucial and transformational. I am aware that critics of the invitation often accuse an invitational model of placing too much emphasis on outer form, such as walking an aisle or praying a prayer. I agree that simply walking an aisle or praying a prayer may be empty and meaningless without an inner decision and surrender. Call for a sincere inner surrender to the voice of God. Clearly call for repentance from sin and to faith as well as the need to trust in the death, burial, and resurrection of Jesus Christ alone. Stress this aspect of your invitation above all other components. Use appropriate, Spirit-directed persuasion to urge a sincere surrender of heart and life.

Then, extend an opportunity for an outward expression of one's decision. As previously observed, an inner change should produce outward evidence. Proof of the new birth is new life! James raised serious suspicions about someone who professes to have inner faith without the outward evidence of good works (Jas 2:14–26). An early confessional formula is recorded in Rom 10:8–10. This passage makes clear that heart belief and outward confession are inseparably linked together. Once an inner decision has been settled, an outward expression of the commitment is appropriate and biblical. This outward expression may take one of various forms. At this point, make clear the outward response being offered. There should be no confusion or ambiguity.

Finally, close your invitation with a clear and compelling statement. The preacher will be clear and confident if he uses similar and proven language each time the invitation is given. Give the invitation as an imperative, not a mere suggestion. Make it a real appeal and call for decision. Do not suggest that they might come someday; urge them to do so today, now, in this moment.

Using the suggested model could enable one to deliver both personal as well as public invitations in a clear and confident manner. The four-step formula has proven to be an enormous help in my evangelistic witness. I discovered that having some "tracks to run on" gave me more assurance of what to say in inviting someone to respond to the gospel. I would offer this model for anyone wishing to improve the delivery of an evangelistic invitation. Do not succumb to the trap of evaluating your invitation by the response of the person. Evaluate it by whether it is clear, compelling, and presented in the power of the Holy Spirit.

I am passionate about the public invitation. God used it the night I came to faith in Christ. I am also passionate in my desire to see it implemented with clarity and integrity. To extend the invitation in an attempt to manipulate or coerce is shameful. I resent coercion and manipulation in any context; I detest it in the setting of a public invitation. At the other extreme is the practice of extending the invitation in a passionless and perfunctory manner. To extend an invitation in a casual, unprepared, and careless manner is another type of abusing the invitation. An invitation to Christ should be made with urgency, passion, and even persuasion. Paul told the Corinthians:

> Therefore, since we know the fear of the Lord, we try to persuade people. . . . For the love of Christ compels us. . . . Therefore, if anyone is in Christ, he is a new creation; the old has passed away, and see, the new has come! Everything is from God, who has reconciled us to himself through Christ and has given us the ministry of reconciliation. That is, in Christ, God was reconciling the world to himself, not counting their trespasses against them, and he has committed the message of reconciliation to us.
>
> Therefore, we are ambassadors for Christ, since God is making his appeal through us. We plead on Christ's behalf, "Be reconciled to God." (2 Cor 5:11, 14, 17–20)

The church needs a revitalized view and practice of the public evangelistic invitation. We do not need to implement a practice that is dishonoring to God. Nor do we need our implementation or methodology to dishonor the Lord. My contention is that we need to recognize that the public evangelistic invitation is a tool of great integrity, both biblically and historically. Further, when implemented properly, its integrity is maintained through the character and methodology of the minister.

May the critics refine our methods and our motives! May God revitalize our passion and our practice! May we stand to proclaim the gospel as God's gracious gift of redemption and salvation, and may God entreat people through us, as we beg the multitudes to be reconciled to God!

EPILOGUE

Calvinists and Non-Calvinists Together for the Gospel

—— Trevin Wax ——

The title of this chapter, "Calvinists and Non-Calvinists Together for the Gospel," assumes that being *together* is a worthy aim and also assumes among Calvinists and non-Calvinists an agreement on what the *gospel* is. If *together* means worshipping the same Lord as members of a congregation, contributing with like-minded churches to the missionary task of reaching the world for Christ, pooling resources to fund theological education, and committing to the spiritual health of one another as brothers and sisters in Christ, then yes, Calvinists and non-Calvinists can be *together*. Furthermore, since we agree on the basics of the gospel message—the royal announcement of Jesus Christ, the Son of God, who died and rose again and now calls for repentance from sin and faith alone in him for salvation—we can partner together in spreading this good news to the ends of the earth.

In this chapter, my goal is to begin with a brief overview of my own theological journey, and then offer five suggestions for how we can maintain and enhance unity among believers who come to different conclusions on what the Bible teaches regarding the *ordo salutis* (order of salvation). First, we must not confuse the debate over Calvinism with the definition of the gospel itself. Second, we should avoid arguments that rely primarily on the possibility of a dangerous trajectory instead of dealing with someone's stated theological position. Third, we should recognize the reality of a spectrum when it comes to Calvinism, rather than two clearly defined sides. Fourth, we should ensure that our debates over soteriology remain connected to our fulfillment of the Great Commission. Finally, we should not police each other's language in such a way that would make our systematic theology a muzzle that keeps us from sounding like the Bible.

A Theological Journey

My earliest years were spent in an independent Baptist church that was revivalist in its culture and theology. My grandfather was at one time the printer for *The Sword of the Lord,* a fundamentalist, decidedly non-Calvinist newspaper whose editors included sermons old and new (and often featured Charles Spurgeon with his Calvinistic commentary conspicuously edited!). The church of my childhood was highly evangelistic, featuring door-to-door "soul-winning" every week, a bus ministry for bringing in children from all over town, and a public invitation with the sinner's prayer and an altar call every Sunday. It was there I first came to understand and love the Scriptures, to believe the gospel, and to follow King Jesus through the waters of baptism.

When I was in fourth grade, our family transferred our membership to a recently launched Southern Baptist church plant that would soon become one of the larger churches in town. There, our pastor preached expository sermons usually focused on one passage, as he carefully worked through entire books of the Bible. During the most formative years of my adolescence, I was blessed to hear more than a thousand sermons from a pastor who clearly loved the Word and the God who inspired it. He pointed us to Christ every week, passionately explained the text, and then led us to worship and praise the Author.

At the age of fifteen, I joined my father and my pastor on a mission trip to Romania, setting off a course of events that would eventually lead to five years of theological education and missions experience there, and to meeting my wife and starting a family. On that first trip as a sophomore in high school, I remember a conversation in the guest room of a large Baptist church (the church where just a few years later I would be married). Somehow my pastor and I had begun discussing theology, and I was passionately protesting the idea of predestination because it ran afoul of my sensibilities. My pastor did not try to convince me of his perspective on the matter. Instead, he pointed me to a couple of passages (one of them was Ephesians 1) and said, "After you've studied these, let's talk." In other words, *Pipe down, young man, and get your nose in this Book before you tell me what you will or will not believe!* Pointing to the Bible as the final authority, the one place I needed to find truth, was more influential than if he had tried to convince me of his own viewpoint. At the end of the day, he showed me that *whatever I may think* is secondary; what matters most is *what God says.*

Later, I discovered that my pastor was more on the Reformed side of the spectrum, but his soteriology never led to a de-emphasis on evangelism or a suppression of passion in the pulpit. In fact, his theological convictions fueled his ministry methodology. He gave a public invitation every week. He pleaded with people to repent and believe. In his sermons, he sounded like the Bible: in places where the text emphasized God's sovereignty, so did he, and the same was the case in places where the text emphasized human responsibility.

As a student in Romania, I devoured Millard Erickson's *Christian Theology*, one of the few systematic theologies available in both English and Romanian. Years later at seminary in the United States, we were given the choice of either Wayne Grudem or Millard Erickson's textbooks for class, and after spending time with both, I stuck with Erickson. I was impressed not only by the carefulness of his philosophical prolegomena but also with how much his soteriological stance made sense to me of the biblical witness.

Where does this put me on the spectrum when it comes to Calvinism and Arminianism? If I were to adopt Calvinist categories, my agreement with Erickson would make me a modified four-pointer (no limited atonement) who, over against most Calvinists, believes faith precedes regeneration, since faith is the instrument that unites us to Christ who is the source of the new birth. (That faith, however, remains a gift of God and springs from the effectual call.) I resonated with Erickson, and still do, because of how his position corresponds and remains consistent with what I find when I read the Scriptures. I realize that my particular place on this spectrum (which, incidentally, is where the renowned Southern Baptist pastor W. A. Criswell stood) means that some Calvinists look at me warily (*He's not really one of us!*) while some non-Calvinists believe this position is still too Reformed-leaning (*He's really just a Calvinist in disguise!*). Let the chips fall where they may. This is where I stand.

Over the years, I have sought to read from scholars who hold various positions on Calvinism, Arminianism, and everything in between (as well as some scholars who don't fit those categories at all). The meditations and sermons from church fathers like John Chrysostom and Augustine of Hippo have deepened my faith and ignited a greater passion for knowing God. The Puritans have ministered to my soul, just as John Wesley has. My favorite author is not a theologian in the classical sense of the word. He wrote essays mainly, and detective stories, and works of apologetics and plays and novels and poetry. I'm referring, of course, to the inimitable G. K. Chesterton, whose largeness of spirit (and body) did not extend into warm feelings toward Calvinism, which he conflated with the materialistic determinism prevalent among atheists in his day. Although he often misunderstood the Puritans, Chesterton did understand some of the excesses I saw in a few of my Puritan-influenced friends, for whom Chesterton's description of "the bottomless pit of predestination"[1] was apt, seeing as it led to endless speculation and despair that one was not part of the elect rather than to a never-ending fountain of assurance and comfort (which is the healthier response to unconditional election).

I commend a wide range of reading for people involved in debates over Calvinism for several reasons. First, it helps to receive spiritual nourishment from people outside of your particular tribe. It reminds you of the vastness of God's mercy and the evidences of God's grace that show up among pastors and theologians who may be in error in one area and yet spot on in another.[2] Second, it helps to put the debate over Calvinism in wider context, so that the discussions and debates that loom large in the dorm rooms of college students wrestling for the first time with free will and predestination get demoted to their proper place. This is just one debate of many, and wider context helps us maintain a balanced perspective.

Five Suggestions for Calvinists and Non-Calvinists

I have benefited from partnership and fellowship with people from across the spectrum when it comes to soteriology. These relationships have strengthened me and my ministry. My prayer is that Calvinists and non-Calvinists will continue to partner

---

[1] G. K. Chesterton, *Orthodoxy* (New York: John Lane Company, 1908), 186.

[2] Rhyne Putman recommends reading deeply and widely in the broader Christian tradition to see that even as we are "both aware of our interpretive fallibility and committed to the truthfulness of God's word, we should at least contemplate why other Bible-believing Christians throughout history have come to opinions contrary to our own." Putman, *When Doctrine Divides the People of God: An Evangelical Approach to Theological Diversity* (Wheaton, IL: Crossway, 2020), 167.

well together in getting the gospel to the nations. With that goal in mind, I offer five suggestions for Calvinists and non-Calvinists alike.

1. Do not put the debate over Calvinism on par with disagreement over the gospel itself.

It is impossible for Calvinists and non-Calvinists to be in any sense "together" for the "gospel" if there is no agreement on the gospel itself. If the gospel is at stake, then we are better off sounding like the apostle Paul in Galatians 1, who called down a curse on anyone who would preach a different gospel than the one we received from Christ himself.

What Is the Gospel?

What is the gospel we believe? We can sum up the New Testament teachings this way: the gospel is the royal announcement that Jesus Christ, the Son of God, lived a perfect life in our place, died a substitutionary death on the cross for the sins of the world, rose triumphantly from the grave to launch God's new creation, and is now exalted as King of the world. This announcement calls for a response: repentance (mourning over and turning from our sin, trading our agendas for the kingdom agenda of Jesus Christ) and faith (trusting in Christ alone for salvation).

Some might quibble with aspects of that definition (what do we mean by "the sins of the world"?) or wonder about other elements we could include (does the triumphant rise of Jesus also imply the conquering of sin, Satan, and the forces of evil?). We could widen the scope to capture the grand narrative of Scripture, which takes us from creation to new creation and even includes the second coming of Jesus in judgment (as Paul implies in Rom 2:16). But I believe this broad outline of the main announcement of the New Testament is general enough to build on when it comes to the unity of the body.[3]

Theological Triage

What often keeps Calvinists and non-Calvinists from being "together" for the gospel is when we elevate a particular soteriological position to such a high level of

---

[3] The New Testament itself includes a number of brief "mini-definitions" of the gospel, which build upon Isaiah 52:7 and involve the coming of the kingdom and the saving work of the King: Mark 1:14–15; Rom 1:3–4; 1 Cor 15:3–5; and 2 Tim 2:8.

importance that any disagreement means *the gospel itself is at stake.* Once disagreements are raised to this level, the debates grow understandably more heated because resolving the issues has become a gospel priority.

How can we avoid the tendency to elevate soteriological distinctions to such a high level of importance? One proposal is to exercise a kind of "theological triage" as a system of prioritization. The analogy comes from R. Albert Mohler Jr., who points out how doctors, when encountering multiple people with health challenges, must develop a process to determine which injuries need the most urgent attention.[4] Building on this concept, Gavin Ortlund makes the case that "doctrines have different kinds of importance,"[5] which he categorizes in this way:

- First-rank doctrines are *essential* to the gospel itself.
- Second-rank doctrines are *urgent* for the health and practice of the church such that they frequently cause Christians to separate at the level of local church, denomination, and/or ministry.
- Third-rank doctrines are *important* to Christian theology, but not enough to justify separation or division among Christians.
- Fourth-rank doctrines are *unimportant* to our gospel witness and ministry collaboration.[6]

Ortlund offers the Trinity as an example of a first-rank doctrine, baptism as a second-rank doctrine, and the timing of the events surrounding the return of Christ as a third-rank doctrine. In personal correspondence with Gavin, I asked about Calvinism (a doctrinal divide not addressed in his book), and he and I agreed that Calvinism and Arminianism would be a third-rank doctrine when the debate remains focused on the narrow soteriological distinctions. This means people could have multiple views even within the same congregation or among the church leadership. In some cases, however, the focus may widen into a range of cultural and practical issues

---

[4] Albert Mohler's "theological triage" is a recent analogy for an ancient concept. Doctrinal taxonomies or dogmative ranks have long been part of the Reformation tradition, in which "foundational doctrines are given greater weight and authority in a theological system, while other doctrines take a place of secondary or tertiary importance." R. Albert Mohler Jr., "A Call for Theological Triage and Christian Maturity," May 20, 2004, https://albertmohler.com/2004/05/20/a-call-for-theological-triage-and-christian-maturity-2/. For more on this history, see Putman, *When Doctrine Divides*, 203–40.

[5] Gavin Ortlund, *Finding the Right Hills to Die On: The Case for Theological Triage* (Wheaton, IL: Crossway, 2020), 17.

[6] Ortlund, 19; emphasis in original.

that flow from Reformed theology or revivalist impulses, and thus cause the debate to drift toward the second-rank category. This explains why some denominations have grown up around different soteriological positions and the cultural and ecclesial practices that follow from them. In either case, though, the debate over Calvinism is not a first-rank issue worthy of mutual anathemas and excommunications.

Some have pushed back on the idea of theological triage, which, like all analogies, breaks down at certain points. Why should we assume that we are the doctors treating doctrinal error? Aren't we all likely to be "infected" with some level of theological error of which we remain unaware? Do we dare rank the commands of Jesus to us, as if some are more important than others? Might this become a clever way of excusing or justifying wrong belief or behavior? Critics of theological triage make salient points, and the analogy is not without its problems. Still, the fact that the apostle Paul speaks of the gospel as being "of first importance" (1 Cor 15:3 NASB) while giving freedom for Christians to agree to disagree on other topics (Rom 14:1; Phil 3:15) shows that at some level he understood that some doctrinal disputes matter more than others. Theological triage is an analogy that, while not perfect, helps us guard the unity of the church while we passionately "contend for the faith" (Jude 3)—a faith, we should remember, that includes the importance of church unity. Our Lord prayed for unity and his apostles pursued it. We must not sacrifice the pursuit of unity for a pursuit of purity when it comes to third-rank doctrines.

Avoiding Confusion

Where do we see this confusion of Calvinism with the nature of the gospel itself? On different sides of the debate, unfortunately. Non-Calvinists sometimes assume that certain methods of ministry are so tightly connected to the experience of evangelism that any deviation calls into question one's commitment to the gospel or evangelism. For example, the lack of a public invitation, usually expressed through an "altar call" or through repeating the "sinner's prayer," is assumed to indicate theological and methodological compromise. Over the years, I've seen gospel-preaching, gospel-sharing pastors on the Calvinist side of the spectrum unfairly castigated due to caricatures that were dishonest. *He quotes from John Piper, so he must be a Calvinist, and that means he believes God casts people into hell without any say in the matter. He can't really believe in John 3:16, because the god of Calvinism he believes in is a monster. He must believe that babies who die all go to hell!* The suspicion swirls around the pastor's theological soundness until he is rendered ineffective as a leader, not only because his Calvinist convictions have been misrepresented, but also because these doctrinal distinctives have been elevated to the point that theological disagreement equals theological disaster. Resisting Calvinism becomes the way you remain faithful to the gospel itself.

Meanwhile, Calvinists often speak as if any deviation from the Synod of Dort means a lesser, incomplete expression of the gospel. After all, didn't Charles Spurgeon claim that Calvinism is the gospel? Yes, he did, but as Michael Horton points out, Spurgeon's sectarian-sounding statement cannot mean that "only Calvinists believe and proclaim the gospel," since he often "expressed respect for evangelical Arminians like John Wesley. His point was that the doctrines of grace, which for better or worse are nicknamed 'Calvinism,' are not really Calvin's, but the teaching of the Scriptures, Augustine, and a trail of preachers, reformers, missionaries, and evangelists ever since."[7] Horton may be right about the meaning of Spurgeon's controversial statement, but I still believe it is problematic to describe the doctrines of grace as "the gospel," because the New Testament does not present the gospel as a systematized look at soteriology but as the announcement of events that display the identity of Jesus the Messiah. We must not confuse our systematic presentations of soteriology with the gospel itself. Such confusion sends young Calvinists back to their churches, thinking that if their pastors haven't parsed the petals of TULIP, they aren't really gospel preachers.

Furthermore, we should avoid speaking of doctrinal development in terms that sound like a second conversion, as if we were "getting saved all over again."[8] The underlying impression in these stories is: "God saved me, praise the Lord! But I was still missing something. I needed something more." Malcolm Yarnell, a non-Calvinist scholar, was asked once by a young man, when he had "converted to the doctrines of grace." Yarnell wisely responded: "Friend, Christians convert to Christ His person, not to Calvin his doctrine."[9] (Ironically, when Calvinists speak of being "baptized into Calvinism" or being "born again again," they resemble Wesleyans— the Methodists with their "second blessing" of perfection after conversion or the Pentecostals who emphasize the post-conversion experience of speaking in tongues!)

Not Essential, but Still Important

In urging brothers and sisters to not confuse the debate over Calvinism with the gospel itself, I do not want to imply that soteriological discussions are somehow

---

[7] Michael S. Horton, *For Calvinism* (Grand Rapids: Zondervan Academic, 2011), 19.

[8] One of the chapters in Hansen's *Young, Restless, and Reformed* is titled "Born Again Again."

[9] Malcolm B. Yarnell III, "Calvinism: Cause for Rejoicing, Cause for Concern," in *Calvinism: A Southern Baptist Dialogue*, ed. E. Ray Clendenen and Brad J. Waggoner (Nashville: B&H, 2008), 93.

unimportant. Important doctrines that do not belong to the first rank are still vital in helping us preserve the gospel. Second and third-rank doctrines still matter.

Ortlund points out how some doctrines *picture* the gospel, such as the connection between the marriage relationship and Christ's relationship with the church. Some doctrines *protect* the gospel, such as promoting a high view of the inspiration and authority of Scripture. And some doctrines *pertain* to the gospel in some other way. "Rare is a doctrine that can be hermetically sealed off from the rest of the Christian faith," he wrote. "Thus, downplaying secondary doctrines can leave the primary ones blander, quieter, and more vulnerable."[10]

As we will see below, the answer to the Calvinism debate is not doctrinal minimalism. We should not downplay debates over Calvinism. But neither should we exaggerate these distinctions to the point our unity in the gospel is threatened. I long for vibrant, energetic, convictional conversations and debates on these matters. Arguments are good, as long as they rely on logical and biblical *argumentation* and do not descend into petty quarrels that rely on caricature and animosity. We can (and must) discuss third-rank and second-rank doctrines because we are people of the Book. We love and cherish the Scriptures and want to examine them closely to be faithful in our obedience. That said, the more we read the Scriptures, the more we will see that God has revealed his passion for the unity of his people, and his heart should always guide our debates.

2. Avoid making arguments based not on your opponent's beliefs but on the potential trajectory of those beliefs.

A second way Calvinists and non-Calvinists can be together for the gospel is to avoid charging your theological opponent with positions that *might* result from a logical progression or potential trajectory. It's one thing to point out the path from one position to a more problematic position, but it's another thing entirely to claim that the current position necessarily entails the more problematic position or inexorably leads to the problematic person. When we do the latter, we find a person who holds position 1 guilty (or least suspect) of holding position 2.

Do Not Bear False Witness

In his introduction to Roger Olson's *Against Calvinism*, Michael Horton explains the difference in where the two scholars believe their positions naturally lead:

---

[10] Ortlund, *Finding the Right Hills*, 57–58.

On the one hand, Roger thinks that *if* I followed Calvinism to its logical conclusions, I *should* concede that the Holocaust and natural disasters are caused
directly by God and that those condemned on the last day could justly blame
God rather than themselves. In his view, the serious error of hyper-Calvinism
is actually the position that follows most logically from Calvinism itself. In
my view, it is not at all surprising that some Arminians have abandoned the
classical Christian consensus concerning some divine attributes and original sin and have adopted moralistic theories of Christ's person and work
as well as justification. On the other hand, I think that *if* Roger followed
Arminianism to its logical conclusion, he *should* go on to deny that salvation is entirely of God's grace; that Arminianism leads inevitably to human-
centered rather than God-centered convictions if followed consistently.[11]

Although Horton and Olson recognize the complexity of logical progression, they
wisely step back and, instead of charging each other with positions neither holds, seek
to point out what they believe to be inconsistencies in each other's perspectives. "At
the end of the day," Horton writes, "Roger suspects that monergism (e.g., God alone
working) undermines God's goodness and love (as well as human agency), and I cannot see how synergism can be reconciled with *sola gratia* (grace alone)."[12]

Calvinists and non-Calvinists must take care in debate to not ascribe something
to their opponent falsely. Point out inconsistencies, yes, but do not misrepresent your
brother or sister. Do not claim that Calvinists make God out to be the author of
evil when you know that Calvinism rejects such an idea. Likewise, do not claim that
Arminians (or non-Calvinists who reject the Arminian label as quickly as they reject
the Calvinist one) are really just Pelagian or semi-Pelagian, when you know that
non-Calvinists insist on important distinctions that separate their view from heresy.

The Charge of Hyper-Calvinism

In theological debate it is proper to press on your opponent's inconsistencies, but
it is wrong to attribute to them beliefs they flatly deny. I see this happen regularly
among non-Calvinists who conflate "high Calvinism" or "five-point Calvinism" with
hyper-Calvinism. Anyone who is a Calvinist is, by default, suspected of being a
hyper-Calvinist. *If they believe this, they must believe that,* goes the logic. But there are

---

[11] Michael Horton, foreword to *Against Calvinism* by Roger E. Olson, 10 (see chap. 4, n. 28).
[12] Horton, 10.

real and enduring distinctions between Calvinism and hyper-Calvinism. Timothy George points out five:

1. Hyper-Calvinists affirm eternal justification, which downplays the need for individual conversion.
2. They deny the free moral agency and responsibility for unbelievers to repent and believe, which turns divine providence into fatalism.
3. They restrict the gospel invitation to the elect, which denies the free offer of the gospel to all people.
4. Hyper-Calvinists teach that non-Christians must be convinced they are among the elect before they have a "warrant" to believe, which undermines salvation by grace through faith.
5. Most importantly, hyper-Calvinists deny the universal love of God to all people, arguing that God loves only the elect and hates the non-elect.[13]

All hyper-Calvinists may also be five-point Calvinists, but all five-point Calvinists are not hyper-Calvinists. In fact, many of the fiercest opponents of hyper-Calvinism have been Calvinists themselves, men like Spurgeon, who was attacked for calling sinners to repentance. Iain Murray describes the hyper-Calvinists of Spurgeon's day as believing that "saving faith in Christ cannot be the duty of sinners, for if we exhort the dead in trespasses and sins to trust in Christ we are attributing a power to them which they do not have."[14]

But doesn't Calvinism lead to hyper-Calvinism? Sometimes, yes. There is good historical evidence to back up that claim. The second and third generations following fervent Calvinist preachers sometimes hardened into hyper-Calvinists who opposed men like William Carey and Andrew Fuller, or blasted preachers like Spurgeon for their evangelistic pleas. Still, it is unfair to argue against Calvinism because of a slide that *might* take place toward hyper-Calvinism. Calvinism itself does not necessitate that kind of move.

The Charge of Man-Centered Liberalism

Something similar happens frequently among Calvinists as well, except in this case, rejecting Calvinism means sliding into liberalism. Tom Nettles believes the bulwark

---

[13] Nathan A. Finn, "Southern Baptist Calvinism: Setting the Record Straight" in Clendenen and Waggoner, *Southern Baptist Dialogue*, 181 (see intro., n. 27).

[14] Iain H. Murray, *Spurgeon v. Hyper-Calvinism: The Battle for Gospel Preaching* (Carlisle, PA: Banner of Truth Trust, 1995), 58.

against theological liberalism is a robust Calvinism. He writes, "Calvinism should still occupy the place of universal adherence in Baptist life. To reject it is not theological progress, but decline; not theological wisdom, but folly; not theological erudition, but fragmentation."[15]

Diminishing God's sovereignty by moving away from five-point Calvinism and in the direction of human freedom means taking "a path that will ultimately shatter all meaning and justice and leave us not only with no god but with no humanity. When this happens, there is also no gospel, no true Christian mission, no holiness to pursue, no standard to which we are to be conformed."[16] Pastor Jeff Noblitt makes a similar case—that Calvinism is the "key to stemming the tide" of "covert liberalism" that masquerades in man-centered methods and church growth pragmatism.[17]

Is it true that movement away from Calvinism can lead to a more man-centered view of salvation and open the door to liberalism? Sometimes, yes. When Baptist professors in the early twentieth century (such as W. O. Carver) moved the SBC away from five-point Calvinism, students who followed in their wake (such as Dale Moody) challenged the truthfulness of the Bible and the doctrine that Jesus is the only way to God. A soft inclusivism was the result.

Still, it is unfair for Calvinists to argue against non-Calvinism because of a slide that *might* take place. A move away from Calvinism does not necessarily entail a move toward theological liberalism. Just as it is unfair to smear Calvinists today with the slippery slope argument of hyper-Calvinism, it is also unfair for scholars to claim that any move away from Calvinism necessitates the journey toward theological liberalism and inclusivism. This idea overlooks the degeneration of once-robustly Calvinist denominations such as the Presbyterian Church (U.S.A.) as well as the leap of some Calvinists to universalism. It also overlooks the fact that non-Calvinist leaders were the ones who led the charge in bringing the SBC back from the brink of liberalism (with the collaboration, of course, of Calvinists who held a high view of Scripture).

Let us take care not to make a case either for or against Calvinism based on what may happen in the future. We can point out inconsistencies and trajectories, yes. But to charge our brothers and sisters with beliefs they reject, or to assume

---

[15] Thomas Nettles, "The Resurgence of Calvinism," in *Readings in Baptist History: Four Centuries of Selected Documents*, ed. Joseph Early Jr. (Nashville: B&H Academic, 2008), 192.

[16] Nettles, 190.

[17] Jeff Noblitt, "The Rise of Calvinism in the Southern Baptist Convention: Reason for Rejoicing," in Clendenen and Waggoner, *Southern Baptist Dialogue*, 104.

a trajectory is inevitable, makes it harder for Calvinists and non-Calvinists to be together for the gospel.

3. Recognize a spectrum exists and not two sides.

The Southern Baptist river is made up of two streams from Baptist history in the South, often called the Charleston Tradition and the Sandy Creek tradition. The Charleston stream is characterized by confessional theology (usually more Reformed) and an emphasis on education, while the Sandy Creek stream is known more for its revivalism. The two streams bring different cultural sensibilities and soteriological perspectives into the Southern Baptist river.[18]

Which stream is more vital? Which one is older? Which stream is more necessary? Baptists today debate these questions, some pointing us to the Charleston (more cerebral and Calvinist) stream while others look back to Sandy Creek (more passionate and revivalist). Some trace our lineage back to the Reformation, particularly the Particular Baptists. Others see a direct line to the Anabaptists.

Being forced to decide which stream I belong to—Charleston or Sandy Creek—is like someone asking me to take sides in a feud between Grandpa and Grandma. I am an intellectually inclined, high-church guy who loves aspects of Grandpa Charles, but I have been nurtured by Grandma Sandy's distinct version of piety too. I love them both, and I want them to stay married. Keeping them together makes for a stronger Southern Baptist family. And one of the best ways to ensure that Calvinists and non-Calvinists stay together within the Southern Baptist Convention is to remember we have a *spectrum* of soteriological views and not two distinct, political *sides*.

The Spectrum and SBC History

The soteriological spectrum not only exists today; it has been present throughout our history. For this reason, we shouldn't be surprised when it's not always easy to peg someone (myself included) as being on one "side" or another. This has been the case for more than a century.

A good example is E. Y. Mullins. Non-Calvinists today often set Mullins next to Herschel Hobbs and Adrian Rogers as the theological trifecta for "traditionalism"

---

[18] David S. Dockery, "Southern Baptists and Calvinism: A Historical Look," in Clendenen and Waggoner, *Southern Baptist Dialogue*, 35.

in the SBC today. But Mullins, Hobbs, and Rogers were not all of one mind when it comes to the points of Calvinism.

Mullins remains an enigma for many people from all sides of the theological controversy who claim him as their own. He often tried to mediate the crosswinds of cultural and theological change by charting a middle course. He was a confession-alist who opposed creeds. He grounded theological knowledge in personal experience and championed the concept of "soul competency," but he also emphasized the importance of scriptural revelation, contributed to *The Fundamentals,* and in his last book, *Christianity in the Crossroads*, decried the doctrinal drift of his era. Interestingly, during the Scopes trial in Dayton, Tennessee, Mullins was invited to counsel both William Jennings Bryan and Clarence Darrow!

Mullins sought to maintain some of the core tenets of Calvinism, such as un-conditional election (which puts him at odds with Hobbs and Rogers), but he revised some of the other doctrines and held free will in high regard. Mullins was Calvinistic in his affirmation of God's initiative through the Spirit in the work of regeneration. "The Spirit of God must enter and change the sinner's heart before the slumbering possibilities can be brought forth," he wrote.[19] But he also insisted not merely on the truth of human responsibility but human freedom: "God made human beings free and leaves them free. God never overrides the will of humanity. In God's action upon human will God always respects that will."[20]

Mullins sought to combine the truth of God's sovereignty with human freedom in a way that emphasized the personal, not mechanical, work of the Spirit.

> Most of the difficulties about God's grace and human freedom are due to the prevalent way of thinking about grace and its action upon us. Grace comes from without, but it acts within us. It flows in, as it were, and works itself out through our minds, consciences, and wills. It moves us freely. It inclines us to act voluntarily as God wills. It is not like a crowbar resting on a fulcrum by means of which a stone is moved. It is rather like water in a millrace, filling the receptacles on the rim and turning the wheel.[21]

---

[19] E. Y. Mullins, *Baptist Beliefs* (Valley Forge, PA: Judson Press,1991), 22.

[20] Mullins, 22. "Free-will in humanity is as fundamental a truth as any other in the gospel and must never be canceled in our doctrinal statements" (Mullins, 27).

[21] Mullins, 21.

In seeking to safeguard the personal nature of grace as opposed to what he called "hardshellism" (or hyper-Calvinism), Mullins emphasized the persuasive power of grace as a personal force:[22] "Grace always persuades and convinces and makes us willing to come, however mysterious and mighty it may be in its actions upon our hearts."[23]

On the one hand, Mullins insisted on the reality of "two choices necessary in a person's salvation: God's choice of the person and the person's choice of God." On the other hand, he argued that God's choice must come first. Otherwise, God would make "the success of the divine kingdom dependent on the contingent choices of people." So, according to Mullins, "God does not fling out the possibility of salvation among human beings, say, like a golden apple, and leave it for people to use or not use as they will. God's own hands are kept on the reins of the divine government. Yet in doing so, God must needs observe the law of freedom as written by God in humanity's moral constitution."[24]

Another example is Mullins's combination of God's preservation of the believer with the necessity of the believer persevering to the end: "God preserves us by inclining us to persevere."[25] Is this "once-saved, always-saved" or "easy-believism"? No. But neither is it the classically Reformed articulation of the fifth point of the Calvinist TULIP. All throughout Mullins's work, we see his grappling with the tension of holding together Calvinists and non-Calvinists in a way that will lead to greater missionary activity.

So, was Mullins a Calvinist? Was he the forerunner for today's traditionalist? It depends on how we define our terms. There's a considerable gap between Mullins and the teacher to whom he dedicated his volume of systematic theology, Southern Seminary's founder James P. Boyce. Yet there is also a considerable gap between him and some of the people today who would claim him as a non-Calvinist hero of Southern Baptist history.

The answers are never as simple as some would like them to be, especially among those who have a vested interest in claiming people for their "side." It is better to acknowledge these doctrinal complexities and nuances that do not easily fall into one category or another, so that we recognize the existence of a spectrum on Calvinism throughout Baptist history.

---

[22] Mullins, 23.
[23] Mullins, 23.
[24] Mullins, 26.
[25] Mullins, 54.

The Spectrum Today

Even today, there are not two "sides" on soteriology in the SBC; instead, there is a spectrum. According to Lifeway Research, most Southern Baptists today do not fit neatly into categories of "non-Calvinist" or "Calvinist."[26] Our convention is not monolithic on soteriology.

Furthermore, the most recent Baptist Faith and Message (BFM) *clearly* and *deliberately* gives voice to this spectrum. The BFM reflects a robust, biblical soteriology intended to satisfy both Calvinists and non-Calvinists. For example, article 4 includes human responsibility to believe the gospel ("there is no salvation apart from personal faith in Jesus Christ as Lord"), which is "offered freely to all who accept Jesus Christ." Article 4, section A on "regeneration," upholds the view that the work of the Spirit precedes the actions of the believer toward God. Repentance and faith are responses to "the change of heart wrought by the Holy Spirit," indicating that regeneration is necessary before a person can believe. At the same time, the section states that "the new birth is a work of God's grace whereby *believers* become new creatures in Christ Jesus," indicating that faith precedes regeneration. The article is both general and specific enough to satisfy Baptists who hold diverging points of view. Likewise, article 5 declares that election is "the gracious purpose of God, according to which He regenerates, justifies, sanctifies, and glorifies sinners," and that it is "the glorious display of God's sovereign goodness, and is infinitely wise, holy, and unchangeable." The article also says that God's elective grace is "consistent with the free agency of man, and comprehends all the means in connection with the end." In addition, article 5 states clearly that believers persevere to the end, and at the same time, they are "kept by the power of God through faith unto salvation."

Does the BFM clearly define the doctrine of salvation the way I would? No. But that's the point. A general confessional statement is not meant to give voice to an individual position or one soteriological perspective. In this case, its authors meant to provide a general statement of belief for people *on a spectrum* when it comes to soteriology. Confessions, rightly understood, give us boundaries and guidelines without overly confining or overly freeing people who subscribe to them. As Daniel Akin has

---

[26] "SBC Pastors Polled on Calvinism and Its Effect," June 19, 2012, https://lifewayresearch.com/2012/06/19/sbc-pastors-polled-on-calvinism-and-its-effect/.

written, "We need a sound theology, not a soft theology or a straitjacket theology."[27] A straitjacket theology would lead us to overly narrow the bounds of our cooperation, while a soft theology would dismiss the need for a confession altogether, using arguments for individual freedom to avoid confessional accountability.

"Two Sides" and Politics

When soteriological disagreements and debates arise, and when differences on a spectrum then push people into opposing "sides," we run the risk of making everything relate to Calvinism and whatever "side" you're on. At this point, the discussions become political, not merely theological. Eventually, everything gets run through the grid of where someone stands on the five points of Calvinism.

In this chapter, I have been forthright about where I stand on these issues, but the reality is, for many of us, any debate over the specifics of Calvinism has been a minor part of our overall teaching and preaching ministry over the years. It would be an unfortunate reductionism and narrowing of one's ministry to make everything someone has taught or written about boiling down to their place on one side or the other when it comes to Calvinism. Similarly, it would be a misrepresentation to read everything about someone's ministry through the lens of their view of the end times.[28] All these doctrines are important, but for many of us, they do not stand at the center of our life and teaching. Unfortunately, there are some who, because they interpret everything through the Calvinist/non-Calvinist debate, can hardly receive even faithful biblical teaching from a Calvinist teacher, and vice versa. I believe we impoverish ourselves when we limit the blessing God may have for us from people who stand at different points on the soteriological spectrum. When we remove the spectrum and read everything through the two sides, we reduce and narrow the ministries of faithful pastors unfairly, and we lose the opportunity to benefit from others.

---

[27] Daniel L. Akin, "Answering the Call to a Great Commission Resurgence," in Clendenen and Waggoner, *Southern Baptist Dialogue*, 252–53.

[28] Furthermore, we should give people space who have not come to a firm conclusion on these matters. Not all pastors on the spectrum have spent adequate time assessing the disputed topics, and they should not be forced into sides prematurely. Withholding judgment on a topic may be wiser than rushing to a conclusion. Putman, *When Doctrine Divides*, 198–99.

Should We Tolerate a Spectrum?

Before we move on, we should engage the legitimacy of the spectrum itself. Is it *good* that a spectrum exists? Some wish there were no spectrum at all, only their side. Tom Nettles, in appealing to the Calvinism of many early Southern Baptists, believes we have only three options: (1) We can agree completely with our forefathers and build on their foundation. (2) We can reject their teaching, expose their errors, and build a different foundation. (3) Or we can conclude that "there is no such thing as truth and error exists in theological categories."[29] To put it another way, we must accept Calvinism the way many Southern Baptist forefathers did, or we must repent of it and reject it, or we must make the case that there is no objective truth in the matter.

But is there not a fourth option? A fourth option would reject the relativism of saying that there is no truth and error in this discussion, but would recognize that the spectrum exists (and has always existed), because faithful, Bible-believing Christians have *long* debated the relationship between divine sovereignty and human freedom. Most Christians at different points on the spectrum recognize that these well-defined theological positions contain conundrums. Olson writes, "One way to look at the choice between competing theologies (when Scripture is not absolutely clear) is to decide on the basis of which conundrums one can live with."[30] To deny that there are conundrums in one's theological system is to oversimplify one's theological viewpoint while exalting one's own understanding, something that—if we truly believe our minds have been affected by the fall—we should resist.

When I speak about the spectrum rather than sides, I am not advocating a doctrinal minimalism that says, "Well, Calvinists have 'their verses,' and non-Calvinists have 'their verses,' so I guess we'll never know who's right." If we believe God has revealed himself in his Word, we must listen to his voice, hear, and respond with faith and obedience, whether or not we come across something that makes our adherence to a systematic theology easier or more difficult.

Doctrinal minimalism is not the answer, even though we see it in Southern Baptist life whenever people want to shut down any debate over Calvinism because it is "divisive" or only a "distraction." These debates *can* be divisive, and they *can* be a distraction, yes, but we should not minimize the issues at stake. Ortlund writes about those who say we should just love Jesus and that's enough: "As much as we may

---

[29] Thomas Nettles, "Resurgence of Calvinism," 190–91.
[30] Olson, *Against Calvinism*, 179.

appreciate the intention, carrying out this statement is not so simple. For instance, to 'stop dividing and just love Jesus,' we must define 'Jesus.' When we do that, doctrinal division is unavoidable. In fact, we actually benefit from divisions that have already taken place and, in many cases have not been resolved."[31]

I have more fruitful conversations with a dogmatic Calvinist or a dogmatic non-Calvinist than I do with people on either side who tell me these debates don't really matter. We are all pursuing truth, seeking understanding, to be faithful to our King. What we need is wisdom and grace so that we put these debates—even heated discussions—in their proper place. There *is* a place for theological debate, but let's make clear that Calvinism and non-Calvinism disagreements do not rise to the level of importance of, say, debating a Jehovah's Witness about the deity of Christ, or convincing someone that good works are not what make you a Christian.

Shouldn't our faith in the sovereignty of God give us more confidence that God may use the differences we have with brothers and sisters on this issue for our overall health? I know some will disagree with the idea that these differences could play a positive role. Some Calvinists believe the SBC would be stronger if everyone shared their soteriological views, and other Southern Baptists believe the SBC would be stronger if there were no Calvinists at all. But what if, in God's sovereignty, he might use this spectrum for the good of his people? Is it possible though to believe that God could use *error* for our good? Yes. One of my favorite Puritan writers, Thomas Watson, made the case that God brings good even out of *heresy*—error in the first-rank doctrines:

> Be not sinfully discontented, for God can make the errors of the church advantageous to truth. Thus the truths of God have come to be more beaten out and confirmed; as it is in the law, one man laying a false title to a piece of land, the true title hath by this means been the more searched into and ratified; some had never so studied to defend the truth of scripture, if others had not endeavoured to overthrow it by sophistry; all the mists and fogs of error that have risen out of the bottomless pit, have made the glorious sun of truth to shine so much the brighter. Had not Arius and Sabellius broached their damnable errors, the truth of those questions about the blessed Trinity, had never been so discussed and defended by Athanasius, Augustine, and others; had not the devil brought in so much of his princely darkness, the champions for truth had never run so fast to scripture to light their lamps.

---

[31] Ortlund, *Finding the Right Hills*, 46.

So that God, with a wheel within a wheel, overrules these things wisely, and turns them to the best. Truth is a heavenly plant, that fettles by shaking. God raiseth the price of his truth the more; the very shreds and filings of truth are venerable. When there is much counterfeit metal abroad, we prize the true gold the more; pure wine of truth is never more precious, than when unfound doctrines are broached and vented.[32]

No doctrinal minimalism here! Watson knows there is a difference between truth and error, orthodoxy and heresy. But if Watson is right, and if his view of divine sovereignty extends even to God doing something good for his people who confront the errors of *heretics,* how much more might God use lesser errors on second- and third-rank doctrines to bring about good for those in these theological conversations? What if, in God's good providence, he uses our debates and discussions as the means by which he keeps us on mission for his kingdom? What if the way God keeps our Calvinist brothers and sisters from hardening into the evangelistic apathy of hyper-Calvinism is through ongoing conversations with those who disagree with their soteriological position? What if the way God keeps our non-Calvinist brothers and sisters from softening into the inclusivism that dilutes our evangelistic passion is through tough conversations with the more Reformed?

Perhaps God makes the SBC stronger through these discussions and debates. Perhaps God gives us an opportunity to love and cherish brothers and sisters—yes, even those we believe to be in error and totally *wrong* on these issues, as a way of making us more into the image of Jesus Christ. Let us reject the doctrinal minimalism that would claim an artificial harmony where we say the differences don't matter and also reject a doctrinal maximalism that would chase out brothers and sisters who are not of the same theological persuasion.

4. Keep discussions about soteriology connected to missions.

Several years ago, I was asked to participate in a panel discussion on Calvinism. At first I was hesitant about both the topic and my involvement. My concern was that the panel would draw a crowd but would not be beneficial to people in attendance if the focus was primarily about two sides scoring points. Eventually, I agreed

---

[32] Thomas Watson, *The Art of Divine Contentment*, ed. Terry Kulakowski (Hollis, NH: Puritan Press, 2015), 49.

because the organizers decided that if we tackled such a controversial subject, the discussion would need to be connected to mission at every point.

I'm not interested in people theologizing for theology's sake. Theology matters because theology is about God, and our view of God impacts our involvement in missions. If we want to keep Calvinists and non-Calvinists together, then our debates over the finer points of soteriology and the *ordo salutis* need to be always connected to bigger questions about missions and evangelism.

Let's be clear: There is no true gospel-centeredness that does not lead to missions, because the gospel is the story of a God with a missionary heart, a Father who desires that all come to repentance, a Shepherd who seeks and saves the one lost sheep. The purpose of God's Word is to reveal God and his plan to us, so that we might then be empowered to fulfill his Great Commission. God's plan is that people from every tongue, tribe, and nation would bring glory to him. When we study the Bible, when we engage in theological debate, we ought to see everything in light of this purpose—to equip us to be God's missionaries in our communities and around the world.

The more we grow in our faith and become like Jesus, the more the heart of Jesus should be evident in our own lives. What greater evidence is there of a Christlike heart than passion for God's mission? What greater evidence is there that the truth of the gospel has soaked into someone's life than seeing passion for the lost overflow through our witness? The gospel-centered believer will take on the role of a servant, just as Jesus served us through his life, death, and resurrection. We serve our neighbors out of love, doing good to those around us, showing the love of Christ, and sharing the good news of salvation.

Whether you're a Calvinist or a non-Calvinist, your mission mirrors God. We show others who God is and what he is like by the way we live. It's not enough to talk about the gospel in our groups, or to debate the finer points of theology. We need to recognize that the Bible intends to reorient our lives around God's mission and equip us to join him in the work he is doing. When properly understood, the gospel is the motivation for mission. We celebrate the gospel as people consumed by the gospel. The goal is that our celebration of the gospel will result in greater and wider circles of people who hear the good news and join the mission.

My hope is that conversations about Calvinism will bring glory to God by causing us to dig deeper into the Scriptures, by teaching us how to love people with whom we have substantive disagreements, and by leading us to greater engagement in God's mission. We must not only be those who are consumed with getting the gospel *right*;

we must be driven by passion to get the gospel *out*. God forbid that Calvinism becomes a debate we enjoy engaging in more than we long for unsaved neighbors to know Jesus.

5. Don't be afraid to sound like the Bible.

Here is one more suggestion I believe will help Calvinists and non-Calvinists remain together for the gospel: don't police each other's language and don't be afraid to sound like the Bible sounds. A few years ago, a non-Calvinist expressed consternation when I used the phrase "the grand narrative of God's great plan to save his people." This person was convinced that my choice of "his people" was code for limited atonement (which, ironically, is one of the points of Calvinism I do not subscribe to!). Why didn't I say *all* people or *the world*? I replied that I hadn't given much thought to the way I said it because the Bible sometimes speaks of God's love for *the world*, and sometimes talks about his love for *his people*. Sometimes I'll sound one way, and other times another, but in the end, I just want to talk like the Bible talks. If I say, "Repent and be baptized for the forgiveness of sins," I sound like Peter on the day of Pentecost. I'm not making a case for the Church of Christ position on baptism. If I warn against falling away, I sound like the author of Hebrews. I'm not making a case for Arminianism. We need to be okay with sounding like the Bible and not policing each other's language to maintain "purity" of one side or consistency with our favored systematic theologians.

I have noticed a tendency in some Reformed circles for Calvinists to bristle at the mention of Jesus dying for the sins of the world or at an evangelist's call to "choose" Christ or to "decide" to follow Jesus. After all, they might say, doesn't this type of language mislead people into thinking they can decide for Christ apart from the Holy Spirit?

I recommend that Calvinists and non-Calvinists alike follow the example of John Calvin, Charles Spurgeon, and others in not refraining from using biblical language when speaking of these matters. Yes, people are dead in their sins. But the truth is, telling people to repent and believe, or to choose Christ and live, or to follow Jesus and not the world—these types of exhortations do not shoot an arrow through God's sovereignty. The Bible itself speaks in these ways.

Calvinists and non-Calvinists alike believe that the lost sinner, under the convicting power of the Holy Spirit, does "make a decision" at the point of conversion. We do indeed respond to the preaching of the gospel. Therefore, we should not refrain from using the language of "following Jesus" or "choosing Christ."

Likewise, saying that Christ has died for the sins of the world is not necessarily a denial of limited atonement. Neither is saying Christ died for "his people" a way of secretly spreading limited atonement. These are the ways the Bible speaks of redemption. While we should interpret those verses in accordance with our soteriological perspective, we should not be afraid to speak the way the Bible speaks. Let's not put a straitjacket on our theological vocabulary.

Conclusion

I hope this epilogue has offered some helpful suggestions that will guide debates over Calvinism into a state of health and harmony for the Southern Baptist Convention. There are major points of agreement on which we can unite. David Dockery lays out several reasons we can work together:

> We can seek to stress common areas of agreement from which we can develop a shared consensus. We can agree that God is the author and the finisher of our salvation. We can all affirm that we love Him because He first loved us; and like the model of Wesley and Whitefield before us who worked together with great appreciation, we need a new respect for one another while having different perspectives on this matter. We likewise can acknowledge our differences without breaking fellowship, while recommitting to our collaborative efforts for the cause of the gospel.[33]

There is one last word I would like to offer, and it has less to do with the positions we hold in regard to Calvinism and more about the posture we have. *Humility matters.* When doctrinal concerns arise, as they inevitably will, handling them with an attitude of humility goes further than anything else. Humility doesn't mean we have a lack of conviction; it means we sincerely desire to understand where someone else is coming from.

When it comes to Calvinists and non-Calvinists doing ministry together, humility often matters more than the actual position under discussion. Criticizing and censuring people who come to different conclusions on particular points of Calvinism with a proud and arrogant spirit—no matter what side you fall on—is sinful, even if you may be right about the theological position you hold. Pride, arrogance, a smug sense of superiority—these attitudes do more damage sometimes than the errors you

---

[33] Dockery, "Southern Baptists and Calvinism," 42.

may want to confront. A haughty spirit stirs up conflict, and that sinful tendency isn't contained to only one side of the soteriological spectrum.

May God give us grace to care more about winning souls than winning arguments! May we truly experience and deepen our understanding of his great love and our great salvation. May we seek to persuade people to our point of view so they may taste the goodness of what we see in the text itself, not merely because we want to keep score or maintain a tradition. May we always remember that this debate matters, because through a greater understanding of God's Word, we want to know and love God more and then reach out to the lost he came to seek and save.

APPENDIX

Semi-Pelagianism:
The Theological Catchall

What is the heresy of Pelagianism? Simply put, it is the belief that individuals can take the initial steps toward salvation by their own efforts, apart from divine grace.[1] Pelagians and semi-Pelagians affirm that natural human beings can initiate or respond to God completely independent of God's grace. Pelagianism denies original sin and asserts wrongly that human nature is essentially unimpaired by the fall.

Many labor under the mistaken notion that the term "semi-Pelagianism" originated from the debates during and after Augustine and Pelagius in the fifth century AD. This is inaccurate. Theodore Beza invented the term in 1566 and applied it to the Roman Catholic view of grace and human will.[2] According to Beza, the central tenet of semi-Pelagianism is that it attributes salvation partly to God's grace and

---

[1] Cross and Livingstone, *Oxford Dictionary of the Christian Church*, 3rd ed., rev., s.v. "Pelagianism," 1248 (see chap. 1, n. 113).

[2] Irena Backus and Aza Gourdriaan, "'Semipelagianism': The Origins of the Term and its Passage into the History of Heresy," *Journal of Ecclesiastical History* 65, no. 1 (January 2014), 35. Beza used the term by way of analogy with "Pelagianism" to denote the Catholic conception of original sin, which, after baptism, leaves only an inclination to sin. He considered the Catholic

partly to what he described as human effort. Faith is viewed both as a gift of God and a choice of the human will.

In 1571 Nicholas Sanders, a Roman Catholic, began to use the term "semi-Pelagianism" with a shift in meaning, applying it for the first time to the fifth-century Massilians. The Massilian view is more fittingly called "semi-Augustinianism" than "semi-Pelagianism." The Massilians considered Pelagius a heretic and sided with Augustine on the priority of divine grace before human response, but they also differed with Augustine because they believed the human will acts freely in appropriating saving grace. The Massilians affirmed original sin, the necessity of divine grace for salvation, sought a balance between grace and human freedom, and "doubted whether a just predestination could avoid being based on foreknowledge."[3] The *New Catholic Encyclopedia* likewise concurs that applying "semi-Pelagianism" to those who affirm God's initiative of grace in salvation is a misnomer.[4]

"Semi-Pelagianism" came to be used for a variety of post-Reformation positions that postulated a greater or lesser degree of human free will in the process of salvation. By the 1680s the term had become common currency while its original sixteenth-century meanings and usages were virtually forgotten. Interestingly, early Catholic catalogues of heresies of the Reformation period make no mention of semi-Pelagianism.[5]

There was no theological position identified by the term "semi-Pelagianism" in the fifth and six centuries. This is not to say that the idea of semi-Pelagianism did not exist in the fifth and sixth centuries. The Council of Orange (529) condemned the theological position which was later identified with semi-Pelagianism.

Note the elasticity of the term and its usage from the sixteenth century until today. Semi-Pelagianism means different things to different people. The historical-theological context of the fifth-century debates between Augustine and Pelagius and their surrogates really have little or no correlation to current conversation between Calvinists and non-Calvinists over the nature of human sinfulness. According to

---

teaching to be somewhat different, though not fundamentally so, from the Pelagian conception of original sin as not transferrable to Adam's descendants.

[3] D. F. Wright, *New Dictionary of Theology: Historical and Systematic*, 2nd ed., ed. Martin Davie et al. (Downers Grove, IL: InterVarsity, 2016), s.v. "Semi-Pelagianism," 833–34.

[4] S. J. McKenna, *New Catholic Encyclopedia*, vol. 12, 2nd ed., ed. Bernard Marthaler et al., (Washington: Catholic University of America, 2003), s.v. "Semi-Pelagianism," 899–901.

[5] See Backus and Gourdriaan, "'Semipelagianism'" 25–46; and Rebecca Harden Weaver, *Divine Grace and Human Agency* (see intro., n. 5).

The Oxford Dictionary of the Christian Church, the semi-Pelagianism of the fourth and fifth centuries "maintained that the first steps toward the Christian life were ordinarily taken by the human will and that Grace supervened only later."[6] As recent scholars have noted, this definition needs to be refined, considering the historical evidence. But setting that aside, let's go with this definition for a moment, since this is, generally speaking, the way the term is used by many today.

All writers in this volume affirm the priority of divine grace in salvation. Sinners are saved through a faith response to the Holy Spirit's drawing through the gospel before the response of the sinner. We do not prioritize the human will over the grace of God. The free response of any sinner is not possible without God's initiation.

Some Calvinist critics seem to assume or believe that anything that is not Calvinism is, by entailment, semi-Pelagianism. Since non-Calvinists deny such things as regeneration preceding faith, total depravity entails total inability, and that faith is a special grace gift given only to the elect, some Calvinists wrongly infer that we deny prior divine initiative in salvation, and thus they conclude our position is semi-Pelagian. This is a misunderstanding and a misuse of the term—and a serious mistake. Calvinists may read semi-Pelagianism into our view, but they will not find it there. Semi-Pelagianism does not argue for the priority of grace in the matter of salvation. We do.

---

[6] Cross and Livingstone, *Oxford Dictionary of the Christian Church*, 3rd ed. rev., s.v. "Semipelagianism," 1481.

NAME INDEX

SUBJECT INDEX

A

Ad Simplicianum (Augustine), 215, 222
Against All Heresies (Irenaeus), 220
Against Calvinism (Olson), 489–90, 498
altar call. *See chapter 14, "The Public Invitation and Altar Call,"* 457–79
American Revolution, 252, 389
amillennialism, 7
Anabaptists, 463, 493
"And Can It Be" (Wesley), 292
apostasy, 2, 188–89, 196–210, 241, 244–46, 255, 274, 300
Arminian Remonstrants, 2–5, 8–9, 196–97
Assurance and Warning (Borchert), 201
atonement, 296–302
    defined, 72
    efficacy of, 101–2, 117, 119, 125, 297
    intent, extent, and application of, 77–80
    "Lombardian formula" of, 117
    sufficiency of, 116–19. *See also* limited atonement; universal atonement; unlimited atonement
Augustine's Calvinism (McMahon), 214
Augustinian-Calvinists, 225
Augustinianism, 7
Axioms of Religion, The (Mullins), 279

B

baptism
    of infants, 7, 21, 23–27, 222–23, 228, 230
    water, 21, 23, 25, 27, 222–23, 228, 230, 482

Baptist Church Manual, The (Brown), 262, 273
Baptist Faith and Message (BFM), 37–38, 273, 277, 279–80, 496
Baptists, 4–7
    in the American colonies, 247–52
    in the American North, 258–63
    in the American South, 264–74
    Arminian, 242–55
    British, 255–58
    Calvinistic, 6
    in Canada, 263–64
    Charleston, 269, 281, 493
    critique of Calvinism, 239–82
    evangelical, 276–77
    Free Will, 47, 240, 247–53, 274–76, 282
    General, 5, 36, 130, 239–59, 265, 275–76, 278, 282
    Independent, 257, 278, 281
    Landmark, 273
    non-Calvinism among, 274–81
    Northern, 240–41, 252, 260, 263, 274, 276, 281
    Particular, 5–6, 36, 130, 239–41, 250, 255–74, 278, 493
    Regular, 241, 263–64, 266–70
    Sandy Creek, 266–67, 269, 493
    Separate, 241, 262–63, 266–70, 463–64.
        See also Southern Baptists
believers, 481, 496
    biblical offers of security and assurance to, 186–87

Protestants, 22, 25, 34, 76, 233, 264, 292–93,
    299, 301, 403, 463
Providence (Helm), 374–75
Puritans
    on salvation assurance, 192–96

Q

Quest for Truth, The (Forlines), 275

R

Race Set before Us, The (Schreiner and
    Caneday), 201–7
Randall movement, 252, 274
realism, 18–19
redemption, general, 239–40, 250, 258
Rediscovering Expository Preaching
    (MacArthur), 460
reductionism, 96, 497
Reformation, 74, 191, 205, 214, 293–94, 493,
    506
Reformed Doctrine of Predestination, The
    (Boettner), 373, 380
Reformed theology
    doctrinal differences of Calvinism with,
        4–7
    on salvation assurance, 190–92
regeneration, 7
Remonstrants, 2, 4, 9, 129–34, 138, 180. *See*
    Arminian Remonstrants
repentance
    biblical theology of, 43
    total depravity and, 40–43
resistible grace, 136–50, 148, 240, 242–45, 282
responsibility
    Libertarianism and, 422–25
righteousness
    imputed, 291–93
"Rock of Ages" (Toplady), 283
Roman Catholics, 22, 190, 232, 233, 463,
    505–6
    on salvation assurance, 190–91
Roman Empire, 463

S

sacraments
    as means of grace, 7
salvation, 291–93

assurance of, 9, 186–87, 190–96, 208–9
    biblical offers of, 119–24, 186–96
    conditional, 59–60, 253
    doctrine of, 39, 50, 143, 302, 376, 496
    God's will for, 343–44, 357–58, 366
    individual, 105, 293
    means of, 46, 142, 189, 196, 200–207, 326,
        329–33
    once saved, always saved, 196, 198–99,
        202–3, 208, 495
    requirements for, 159–63, 168
    rewards of, 208–10
    security of, 186–87, 196–210
    test of genuineness, 190, 196, 198–99, 202,
        205, 208
    See also perseverance of the saints
SBC. *See* Southern Baptist Convention (SBC)
Scopes trial, 494
semi-Pelagianism, 3–4, 7, 505–7
Separatists, 463
Sermon on the Mount, 146, 294, 295
sexuality, 22–25, 27–28, 31, 366, 413
sin
    biblical concept of, 15–17
    consequences of, 16
    doctrine of, 17
    hereditary, 18–19, 22, 28
    imputation of, 19, 72, 92, 126. *See also*
        guilt: imputation of
    original, 7. *See* original sin
    problem of and solution for, 16–17
    universal, 16
Six Principles of the Christian Religion,
    247–48
Southern Baptist Convention (SBC), 241,
    273, 277–78, 281–82, 492–94, 499, 500,
    503
    history of, 493–95
Southern Baptists, 8, 264, 277–81, 464
    Calminian, 8–9
    soteriological spectrum among, 493–504
    See also Baptists
South Kentucky Association, 266, 269
Sovereign Grace Ministries, 1
Spectacular Sins (Piper), 446–48
spiritual death, 45, 107, 163–64, 225–27
    biblical theology of, 45–47

SCRIPTURE INDEX

Romans